FROM DICKENS TO HARDY

THE EDITOR

Boris Ford is the General Editor of the *New Pelican Guide to English Literature* (in 11 vols) which in its original form was launched in 1954. At the time it was being planned he was Chief Editor and later Director of the Bureau of Current Affairs. After a spell on the Secretariat of the United Nations in New York and Geneva, he became Editor of the *Journal of Education* and also first Head of Schools Broadcasting with Independent Television.

Following a period as Education Secretary at the Cambridge University Press, Boris Ford, until he retired in 1982, was Professor of Education at the universities of Sheffield, Bristol and Sussex – where he was also Dean of the School of Cultural and Community Studies. He edited *Universities Quarterly* from 1955 until 1986. He is General Editor of *The Cambridge Guide to the Arts in Britain* (in 9 vols, 1988–91), and of a forthcoming series of 9 volumes on the arts and civilization of the Western world.

From Dickens to Hardy

VOLUME

6

OF THE NEW PELICAN GUIDE TO
ENGLISH LITERATURE

EDITED BY BORIS FORD

PENGUIN BOOKS

PENGUIN BOOKS

Published by the Penguin Group
Penguin Books Ltd, 27 Wrights Lane, London w8 5tz, England
Penguin Books USA Inc. 375 Hudson Street, New York, New York 10014, USA
Penguin Books Australia Ltd, Ringwood, Victoria, Australia
Penguin Books Canada Ltd, 10 Alcorn Avenue, Toronto, Ontario, Canada m4v 3b2
Penguin Books (NZ) Ltd, 182–190 Wairau Road, Auckland 10, New Zealand

Penguin Books Ltd, Registered Offices: Harmondsworth, Middlesex, England

First published in *The Pelican Guide to English Literature* 1958
This revised and expanded edition published 1982
Reprinted in Penguin Books 1990
3 5 7 9 10 8 6 4 2

Copyright © Boris Ford, 1982
All rights reserved

Printed in England by Clays Ltd, St Ives plc
Filmset in Monophoto Bembo

CONTENTS

5

CONTENTS

PART IV

GENERAL INTRODUCTION

The publication of this *New Pelican Guide to English Literature* in many volumes might seem an odd phenomenon at a time when, in the words of the novelist L. H. Myers, a 'deep-seated spiritual vulgarity . . . lies at the heart of our civilization', a time more typically characterized by the Headline and the Digest, by the Magazine and the Tabloid, by Pulp Literature and the Month's Masterpiece. Yet the continuing success of the *Guide* seems to confirm that literature – both yesterday's literature and today's – has a real and not merely a nominal existence among a large number of people; and its main aim has been to help validate as firmly as possible this feeling for a living literature and for the values it embodies.

The *Guide* is partly designed for the committed student of literature. But it has also been written for those many readers who accept with genuine respect what is known as 'our literary heritage', but for whom this often amounts, in memory, to an unattractive amalgam of set texts and school prizes; as a result they may have come to read only today's books – fiction and biography and travel. Though they are probably familiar with such names as Pope, George Eliot, Langland, Marvell, Yeats, Dr Johnson, Hopkins, the Brontës, they might hesitate to describe their work intimately or to fit them into any larger pattern of growth and achievement. If this account is a fair one, it seems probable that very many people would be glad of guidance that would help them respond to what is living and contemporary in literature, for, like the other arts, it has the power to enrich the imagination and to clarify thought and feeling.

The *Guide* does not set out to compete with the standard Histories of Literature, which inevitably tend to have a lofty, take-it-or-leave-it attitude about them. This is not a Bradshaw or a *Whitaker's Almanack* of English literature. Nor is it a digest or potted version, nor again a portrait gallery of the great. Works such as these already

abound and there is no need to add to their number. What it sets out to offer, by contrast, is a guide to the history and traditions of English literature, a contour map of the literary scene. It attempts, that is, to draw up an ordered account of literature as a direct encouragement to people to read widely in an informed way and with enjoyment. In this respect the *Guide* acknowledges a considerable debt to those twentieth-century writers and critics who have made a determined effort to elicit from literature what is of living value to us today: to establish a sense of literary tradition and to define the standards that this tradition embodies.

The *New Pelican Guide to English Literature* consists of eleven volumes:

1, Part One.   *Medieval Literature: Chaucer and the Alliterative Tradition* (with an anthology)
1, Part Two.   *Medieval Literature: The European Inheritance* (with an anthology)
2.   *The Age of Shakespeare*
3.   *From Donne to Marvell*
4.   *From Dryden to Johnson*
5.   *From Blake to Byron*
6.   *From Dickens to Hardy*
7.   *From James to Eliot*
8.   *The Present*
9.   *American Literature*
    A Guide for Readers

Most of the volumes have been named after those writers who dominate or stand conveniently at either end of the period, and who also indicate between them the strength of the age in literature. Of course the boundaries between these separate volumes cannot be sharply drawn.

Though the *Guide* has been designed as a single work, in the sense that it attempts to provide a coherent and developing account of the tradition of English literature, each volume exists in its own right and sets out to provide the reader with four kinds of related material:

(i) *A survey of the social context of literature* in each period, providing an account of contemporary society at its points of contact with literature.

(ii) *A literary survey* of the period, describing the general character-

istics of the period's literature in such a way as to enable the reader to trace its growth and to keep his or her bearings. The aim of this section is to answer such questions as 'What *kind* of literature was written in this period?', 'Which authors matter most?', 'Where does the strength of the period lie?'.

(iii) *Detailed studies* of some of the chief writers and works in the period. Coming after the two general surveys, the aim of this section is to convey a sense of what it means to read closely and with perception; and also to suggest how the literature of a given period is most profitably read, i.e. with what assumptions and with what kind of attention. This section also includes a chapter on one of the other arts at the time, as perhaps throwing a helpful if indirect light on the literature itself. In this Victorian volume, there are two chapters on architecture.

(iv) *An appendix of essential facts for reference purposes*, such as authors' biographies (in miniature), bibliographies, books for further study, and so on.

Thus each volume of the *Guide* has been planned as a whole, and the contributors' approach to literature is based on broadly common assumptions; for it was essential that the *Guide* should have cohesion and should reveal some collaborative agreements (though inevitably, and quite rightly, it reveals disagreements as well). They agree on the need for rigorous standards and have felt it essential not to take reputations for granted, but rather to examine once again, and often in close detail, the strengths and weaknesses of our literary heritage.

BORIS FORD

PART I

PART 1

NOTES ON THE VICTORIAN SCENE

G. D. KLINGOPULOS

The centuries of history do not appear all equally relevant to us, and the impression of relevance itself tends to change. Since the end of the war and the withdrawal from India, since the creation of the Welfare State and the depreciation of sterling, a change has taken place in our attitude to the Victorians. In part this is only the turn of fashion. The word goes round that such and such a writer needs to be better known or rediscovered, and soon a flow of rather indiscriminate revivals has begun. But, in the main, the sharpening of interest in the Victorians is not artificially created. The Victorians do seem much more our contemporaries in many ways. The kinds of problem which confronted them – political, educational, religious, cultural – bear a strong resemblance to, and are often continuous with, the problems which confront us at the present time. The ironic view of the Victorians to be found in, for example, Lytton Strachey or in G. K. Chesterton now seems even more inadequate than before; there is even a danger that we may now become too respectful and find everything 'interesting', and consequently fail to see aspects of the 'Great Victorians' which Strachey and others justifiably thought ludicrous. We are impressed by the massiveness of Victorian people and of Victorian energy and success; but is there not a certain infla- tion, grossness, and insecurity, something short-lived and almost accidental, in much of their achievement? We may be inclined to over-estimate the intrinsic quality of Victorian life simply because our interest is sharper than it was. Even G. M. Young's masterly *Portrait of an Age* now seems faintly Stracheyan in attitude and seems to deal with the nineteenth century as an enjoyable and admirable panorama from which the historian is comparatively detached. He gives no sign that he thinks something 'really matters' more than anything else. When he writes, 'of all decades in our history, a wise man would choose the eighteen-fifties to be young in', we are not

at all sure that the remark expresses anything more than the light-heartedness of an enthusiastic specialist.

Though the social history of the period is to be found in the works of Halévy, Clapham, the Hammonds, L. H. Jenks, and others, the student of literature will not find an abundance of historical writing that helps him to keep in view the quality of Victorian life at different levels, or that helps him to answer the question, 'How seriously should one take the pessimism about society of a Carlyle, a Ruskin, or a Newman?' He finds, too, that the gap between one historian's view of the nineteenth century and another's is often very great. There are, of course, criteria common to historians and to students of literature which should enable them to choose between the exponents of a Whig interpretation of history, who are always in a majority, and the less optimistic writers. We find Trollope writing in his *Autobiography* (1883):

> Whether the world does or does not become more wicked as years go on is a question which probably has disturbed the minds of thinkers since the world began to think. That men have become less cruel, less violent, less selfish, less brutal, there can be no doubt; – but have they become less honest? If so, can a world, retrograding from day to day in honesty, be considered to be in a state of progress? We know the opinion on this subject of our philosopher Mr Carlyle. If he be right, we are all going straight away to darkness and the dogs. But then we do not put very much faith in Mr Carlyle – nor in Mr Ruskin and his followers. The loudness and extravagance of their lamentations, the wailing and gnashing of teeth which comes from them, over a world which is supposed to have gone altogether shoddy-wards, are so contrary to the convictions of men who cannot but see how comfort has been increased, how health has been improved, and education extended – that the general effect of their teaching is the opposite of what they have intended. It is regarded simply as Carlylism to say that the English-speaking world is growing worse from day to day. And it is Carlylism to opine that the general grand result of increased intelligence is a tendency to deterioration.

The weight we give to comment of this kind is only partly dependent on our awareness of nineteenth-century history; more important is our immediate sense, manifest in the use of language, of the quality of the mind which offers these criticisms of 'Carlylism'. The same criteria enable us to offer appropriate resistance to the more absolute Macaulay, the great trumpeter of Victorian progress. That mechanical, scientific, medical, and other kinds of 'progress' on a quite unprecedented scale did take place no one should feel

impelled to deny, though one should not concede too much to the phrase 'a higher standard of living'. The difficulty lies in holding simultaneously in our minds both the unambiguousness of such advance and the objectivity of many hostile critics of the Victorian ethos. Of Carlyle we can say that, although he had little understanding of poetry and is frequently unreadable, his experience of life did have affinities with the experience of a Blake, a Wordsworth, or a Coleridge; it is in that tradition of minority experience that comes down to Lawrence, to Yeats, and to *The Waste Land*, a poem which is still too often described as merely subjective in inspiration and content.

One could not say as much of Trollope, delightful as he is in some of his novels. When Trollope, in his turn, came to write a work of social criticism, *The Way We Live Now*, he could only indulge in crude, slightly anti-semitic, melodrama, in which the heart of the matter is never reached. Carlyle would have understood at once L. H. Myers's reference to 'the deep-seated spiritual vulgarity that lies at the heart of our civilization'; Trollope's very interesting *Autobiography* reveals as ingenuous an attitude to worldly accumulation and success as Arnold Bennett's fascinating *Journals*. It is to the protests against the drift of nineteenth-century life that we must look for that tradition of delicacy, honest feeling, and unworldliness, of 'scepticism and uncynical disillusion', out of which any art worth having must grow. Much of the opposition came from the poets and artists themselves. Their protests could be summed up in the inescapable word 'materialism'. We are all necessarily 'materialists' in very many ways. But the domination of material ends and of unenlightened, scrambling self-interest, the blindness to squalor, involved the loss of sensitiveness and a death of the spirit. At the beginning of the nineteenth-century process, Wordsworth wrote of 'a multitude of causes, unknown to former times, now acting with a combined force to blunt the discriminating powers of the mind, and, unfitting it for all voluntary exertion, to reduce it to a state of almost savage torpor'. Here is a comment from the other end of the century:

Now although perhaps nobody knew it, it was ugliness which really betrayed the spirit of man in the nineteenth century. The great crime which the moneyed classes and promoters of industry committed in the palmy

Victorian days was the condemning of the workers to ugliness, ugliness, ugliness: meanness and formless and ugly surroundings, ugly ideals, ugly religion, ugly hope, ugly love, ugly clothes, ugly furniture, ugly houses, ugly relationship between workers and employers. The human soul needs actual beauty even more than bread.

This is, of course, D. H. Lawrence, and no doubt he simplifies in seeming to blame a particular class of people for processes as uncontrollable as those which overwhelmed the older patterns of life in the late eighteenth and nineteenth centuries. But one should keep Lawrence in mind because, when one turns to social historians for amplification or confirmation of his remarks, one often finds the issues blurred by a restriction of attention to economic or other considerations. Economists do well to be non-committal if their statistics permit no interpretation either way, but the values which Lawrence and the nineteenth-century critics were concerned with lie outside the scope of economics, though perhaps they should not. Both Carlyle and Ruskin turned to criticism of the 'dismal science' of political economy and the statistical fiction of 'economic man'. As an economic historian has well written:

> The main problems of writing modern economic history lie in its inter-pretation. It is within the last twenty years, for example, that the work of economists and statisticians has begun to put within our reach a new view of the Victorian age. The difficulties of interpretation are not wholly intellec-tual; they are also moral. For when the evidence that remains has been sifted and the skein of events unravelled as far as is possible, men will still differ fundamentally in the values which they put upon the men and the deeds, the thoughts and the passions of the past.
>
> (W. H. B. Court, *A Concise Economic History of Britain*)

There is much in nineteenth-century history that seems to diminish the stature of man in comparison with impersonal processes over which he had little control; but Victorian England also supplies many reassuring examples of man's ability to organize some sort of social orderliness out of apparently inevitable chaos. It is true that the orderliness which the twentieth century has inherited is a minimal one, relating only to the externals of human relationships. The suburbs are healthier and tidier than the deserted towns, but they are still more like barracks than communities. There remains an emptiness within.

> Consume my heart away; sick with desire
> And fastened to a dying animal
> It knows not what it is.

Yet the nineteenth century abounded in sages prepared, like Bitzer defining a horse, to tell the heart 'what it is' and in what it should find its happiness.

The Democratic Experiment

A good deal of nineteenth-century writing is concerned with the refutation of inadequate notions of man and of society. As we should expect at such a time of upheaval and reorganization, there is a good deal of discussion of democracy and individualism, of nationalism and liberalism, of the growth of population and the need for controls or for emigration. Education becomes a general concern, and the place of religious teaching in a national system of education is bitterly debated. The dominant temper of the early and middle Victorian periods was intensely moralistic, heavy with responsibility and anxiety. The peaceful evolution of democratic forms of government could not be ascribed to any two or three factors, but amongst the numerous explanations of the non-fulfilment of Marx's prophecies must be counted the very real fear that the contagion of revolution might spread from the Continent; and also the sheer momentum of social change. Religion, of course, of a rather self-saving kind, counted for a great deal, as did the natural 'deference' of an insular people involved in a successful enterprise. Though the century produced a large number of theories of society, of party, and of government, the peacefulness of social evolution must also be ascribed to the empirical, unideological, tradesmanlike qualities of the rising middle class. Bagehot, surveying constitutional progress up to 1867, wrote:

The brief description of the characteristic merit of the English Constitution is, that its dignified parts are very complicated and somewhat imposing, very old and rather vulnerable; while its efficient part, at least when in great and critical action, is decidedly simple and rather modern. We have made, or rather stumbled on, a constitution which, though full of every species of incidental defect, though of the worst *workmanship* in all out-of-the-way matters of any constitution in the world – yet has two capital merits: it contains a simple efficient part which, on occasion, and when wanted, *can*

work more simply and easily, and better, than any instrument of government that has yet been tried; and it contains likewise historical, complex, august, theatrical parts, which it has inherited from a long past – which *take* the multitude – which guide by an insensible but an omnipotent influence the associations of its subjects. Its essence is strong with the strength of modern simplicity; its exterior is august with the Gothic grandeur of a more imposing age ... England is the type of deferential countries, and the manner in which it is so, and has become so, is extremely curious. The middle classes – the ordinary majority of educated men – are in the present day the despotic power in England ... The English constitution in its palpable form is this – the mass of the people yield obedience to a select few; and when you see this select few, you perceive that though not of the lowest class, nor of an unrespectable class, they are yet of a heavy sensible class – the last people in the world to whom, if they are drawn up in a row, an immense nation would ever give an exclusive preference. In fact, the mass of the English people yield a deference rather to something else than to their rulers. They defer to what we may call the *theatrical show* of society ... The apparent rulers of the English nation are like the most imposing personages of a splendid procession; it is by them the mob are influenced; it is they whom the spectators cheer. The real rulers are secreted in second-rate carriages; no one cares for them or asks about them, but they are obeyed implicitly and unconsciously by reason of the splendour of those who eclipsed and preceded them.   (Walter Bagehot, *The English Constitution*, 1867)

This is of course only a part of the truth about Victorian political life. Like Burke and Coleridge, Bagehot is inclined to stress what appeared to be stable elements in social life. But there is a vast difference between a conservatism based on land which implies, as Cobbett insisted, a social responsibility of a sort and a conservatism based on money, 'the cash-nexus' as Carlyle called it, which need imply no moral relationship or duty whatsoever. Agriculture itself had become thoroughly dominated by a business spirit. Though some politicians, such as the adroit Disraeli, were from the first in favour of combinations of workmen, the trade unions had to struggle throughout the century for a tolerable bargaining relationship with 'money', so that nowadays trade unions can be described by a Tory prime minister as 'an estate of the realm'. In their turn trade unions run the risk of being static and illiberal. This possibility was foreseen by de Tocqueville, by John Stuart Mill, and by all those constitutionally minded men who, accepting the need for democratic development, were deeply concerned about the ancient risk of tyranny latent in the word 'democracy':

I perceive mighty dangers which it is possible to ward off – mighty evils which may be avoided or alleviated; and I cling with a firmer hold to the belief, that for democratic nations to be virtuous and prosperous they require but to will it. It is true that around every man a fatal circle is traced, beyond which he cannot pass; but within the wide verge of that circle he is powerful and free: as it is with men, so with communities. The nations of our time cannot prevent the conditions of men from becoming equal; but it depends upon themselves whether the principle of equality is to lead them to servitude or to freedom, to knowledge or barbarism, to prosperity or to wretchedness.

(De Tocqueville, *Democracy in America*, Part II, 1840)

On the whole, these fears proved excessive and liberals can still give two cheers for democracy.

Part of the drama of nineteenth-century history lies in the struggle of the ascendant middle class to shape the turbulent lower levels of society in its own image, by example, by preaching, and by propaganda, little of which was as obvious as Harriet Martineau's. Well might Bagehot write, 'The use of the Queen is incalculable'. The moralizing, self-satisfied tone of much Victorian writing needs no other explanation. We should not, however, regard this self-conscious respectability, this moralizing attitude of mind, as characteristic of the middle class only in Victorian times. We can detect the beginnings of something like Victorianism as far back as Queen Anne's time in, for example, the essays of Addison, the novels of Richardson, or in the popular play by George Lillo, *The London Merchant* (1731), in which we find the following passages of dialogue:

As the name of merchant never degrades the gentleman, so by no means does it exclude him.

I have observed those countries, where trade is promoted and encouraged, do not make discoveries to destroy, but to improve mankind by love and friendship; to tame the fierce and polish the most savage; to teach them the advantages of honest traffic, by taking from them, with their own consent, their useless superfluities, and giving them, in return, what, from their ignorance in manual arts, their situation, or some other accident, they stand in need of.

It is the industrious merchant's business to collect the various blessings of each soil and climate, and, with the product of the whole, to enrich his native country.

These are on the way to becoming Victorian sentiments. They reveal that characteristic tendency to mingle business with moralism that can make 'good' intentions seem hypocritical or brutal; they

bring to mind the career of Cecil Rhodes. In their various ways Dickens, Carlyle, Ruskin, Arnold, and others attempted to mitigate, by description and irony, the complacencies and self-righteousness of an age which tended to mistake solemnity for seriousness, social respectability for goodness, and which, despite its abundance of sects and chapels, was becoming hard, gross, and impervious to criticism. Their refusal to join unreservedly in the celebration of things as they were, to surrender to the typical, seemed churlish to their contemporaries. The critics themselves were often divided and uncertain in their own minds. Tennyson's poetry and Dickens's novels are full of such vacillation, which Chesterton called a 'splitting headache'. Yet we can see that the critics were all, in various degrees, concerned with keeping the sympathies of men open, with encouraging self-critical attitudes, and with preventing that mere surrender to commercial success and to mechanical processes about which Carlyle, like Gabriel Marcel and Nicolai Berdyaev in our own time, wrote forebodingly in *Signs of the Times* (1829), long before the machine age had fully arrived:

> Were we required to characterize this age of ours by any single epithet, we should be tempted to call it, not an Heroical, Devotional, Philosophical, or Moral Age, but, above all others, the Mechanical Age. It is the Age of Machinery, in every outward and inward sense of that word; the age which, with its whole undivided might, forwards, teaches, and practises the great art of adapting means to ends. Nothing is now done directly, or by hand; all is by rule and calculated contrivance. On every hand, the living artisan is driven from his workshop to make room for a speedier, inanimate one ... What wonderful accessions have thus been made, and are still making, to the physical power of mankind; how much better fed, clothed, lodged, and, in all outward respects, accommodated men now are, or might be, by a given quantity of labour, is a grateful reflection which forces itself on everyone ... But leaving these matters for the present, let us observe how the mechanical genius of our time has diffused itself into quite other provinces. Not the external and physical alone is now managed by machinery, but the spiritual also ... These things which we state lightly enough here, are yet of deep import, and indicate a mighty change in our whole manner of existence. For the same habit regulates not our modes of action alone, but our modes of thought and feeling. Men are grown mechanical in head and heart, as well as in hand.

This is quite as relevant to our own times, when education (and the modern child is more dependent on schools for its 'education' than in the past) is necessarily becoming more and more techno-

logical and universities become even less distinguishable than they were from technical colleges, as to the early Victorian period. Industrial societies run the risk of being caged in mechanisms and the 'way of life' imposed by machines, of becoming merely the sum of their mechanical processes; and human beings of becoming docile, anxious, semi-militarized mechanics, gadgeteers and civil servants, conditioned to ask only the 'answerable' questions, not the 'why', only the 'how', car-owning or bus-catching, camping in suburbs, their morale kept up by ubiquitous entertainment machines and newspapers. 'The true Church of England,' wrote Carlyle in 1829, 'at this moment, lies in the Editors of its Newspapers.' He feared the potentialities of a Press which had not yet begun to have its full scope.

Expansion and its Consequences

As the nineteenth century proceeded and social conditions gradually improved, as the country became more and more urban and the population more mobile, as the lower classes began to have a small share in the prosperity of the higher and to imitate their habits, as the tone of self-righteousness at home developed into imperialism abroad, social questions, which for decades had been more or less directly the concern of novelists and poets, giving to their work an importance of a sort, became less and less apt for literary treatment. At the end of the century, Henry James, writing of 'the great grabbed-up British Empire', fears that he is 'too lost in the mere spectacle for any decent morality'. Henry James's feelings were shared by many at the time, but it needed the personal qualities of E. M. Forster to bring them to literary expression.

The closing quarter of the nineteenth century opened symbolically with the proclamation of Queen Victoria as Empress of India (1876) and ended with the South African War. Between 1875 and 1900 the total area of the British Empire was increased by not far short of 5,000,000 square miles, containing a population of at least 90,000,000. In other words, in the space of twenty-five years the British governing class added to the Empire territories forty times as large as Great Britain, and with a population more than twice as large. In all, by 1900 Great Britain was the centre of an Empire ruling over 13,000,000 square miles of subject territory, inhabited by nearly 370,000,000 persons, of whom nearly 300,000,000 were to be found in India alone.

(Cole and Postgate, *The Common People, 1746–1938*)

The impulse to withdraw from an inhospitable scene and to confine themselves to the expression of private moods had always been latent in the poets of the century, though dissatisfaction with the writer's self and with society had never taken that intense and absolute form to be found in Baudelaire or Rimbaud. In its last decades the impulse became irresistible and is to be discerned in all writers except the most obtuse or buoyant. It was not until the First World War that poets found themselves once more on common ground with 'their public'. Both sides needed to be shocked into communication, the rediscovery of their common human plight. But it is a reflection on modern society that it should seem to need the disaster of war to break down the dykes which separate man from man.

None of the various 'revolutions' taking place in nineteenth-century England could be described without reference to the extra-ordinary growth in population. This was a world-wide phenomenon, tentatively explained as the result of improved medical knowledge and hygiene. More people survived infancy and people lived longer. The population of Great Britain at the time of the first census in 1801 was about ten and a half millions; by the time of the 1901 census it had more than tripled to reach thirty-seven millions. In itself this natural phenomenon goes some way towards explaining the squalor in housing and in factories described by novelists, by witnesses before Royal Commissions, by Mayhew and Booth, and by the authors of *The Age of the Chartists*. Humanitarian sentiment had first to bring 'the condition of England' to public notice and initiate reforms; once the first crisis had been met, writers could face the permanent and irremediable consequences both of the condition and its cure. The ugly combination of slate and red brick, which became the standard materials for the new working-class houses, was the cheapest available in quantity. 'Cheap and Nasty', Carlyle was obliged to comment as he surveyed the London scene at the time of the second Reform Bill:

Universal *shoddy* and Devil's dust cunningly varnished over; that is what you will find presented you in all places, as ware invitingly cheap, if your experience is like mine ... Take one small example only. London bricks are reduced to dry clay again in the course of sixty years or sooner ... There lies in it not the Physical mischief only, but the Moral too, which is far

more. I have often sadly thought of this. That a fresh human soul should be born in such a place; born in the midst of a concrete mendacity.

(*Shooting Niagara: and After?*, 1867)

Carlyle's moral here seems as antique as Cobbett's denunciations of paper money, but it is not irrelevant. One wonders what he would have said of modern building, with its precarious joists, gaping floorboards, and disintegrating brickwork. The worst aspect of town development immediately after the Napoleonic Wars and in early Victorian times was the overcrowding, especially in back-to-back terraces, which yielded a higher return in rents to the landlord. Not till the second half of the century was legislation passed to impose tolerable standards in structure and in sanitation, but the absence of any sort of town-planning has left permanent evils. The blackened chapels have become what they always looked like, warehouses; and suburbia is endless.

The Englishman still likes to think of himself as a cottager – my home, my garden. But it is puerile. Even the farm-labourer today is psychologically a town-bird. The English are town-birds through and through, today, as the inevitable result of their complete industrialization. Yet they don't know how to build a city, how to think of one, or how to live in one. They are all suburban, pseudo-cottagy, and not one of them knows how to be truly urban. (D. H. Lawrence, *Nottingham and the Mining Countryside*)

It is of course true that Victorian middle-class houses, even when terraced, beknobbed and urn-crowned, now often seem spacious, solid, and immensely dignified, though their cellars and staircases needed armies of unemancipated maidservants and their single, damp-courseless walls needed abundant supplies of hard-won coal. One notices that middle-class houses were usually over-built, with stone gateposts which, broken up, could face a modern bungalow, and timbers that could support towers. Timber was expensive and had to be imported, but the pound was strong as wages were low, and England was completely autarkic in finished articles which she exported on an ever-increasing scale; first the smaller articles, then the larger, then the trains and ships that carried them, and finally the basic plant out of which the machines themselves had come. The industrial revolution created within Great Britain opportunities usually associated with the opening up of a new colonial territory, and released energies in the middle and artisan classes which could

turn impartially to the diligent prosecution of trade, to experimentation with machines, to the study of nature, to the compilation
of monumental works of real or nugatory scholarship, or to the
dissemination of opinions.

Self-help

What seems miraculous is the multiplicity of talents which suddenly seemed to find their occasion and opportunity. It was a comparatively peaceful reign when Englishmen, secure in their island
base, could complete the transformation of all aspects of their industrial, commercial, and social life without any of those risks of
violent interruption that gave quite a different quality to the history
of Continental nations. It was inevitable that religion, too, should, in
this period, become even more strongly explicit on the advantages of
insularity, and that the great headmaster Dr Arnold should, following
Coleridge, elaborate a highly ornamental theory of the Church and
the State. Kipling's *Recessional* (1897) is only a late example, and by
no means the most absurd, of attitudes present throughout the
Victorian period. As early as 1839 Dickens put into the mouth of
the politician Mr Gregsbury this broad satiric comment:

> Whether I look at home or abroad: whether I behold the peaceful industrious
> communities of our island home – her rivers covered with steamboats, her
> roads with locomotives, her streets with cabs, her skies with balloons of a
> power and magnitude hitherto unknown in the history of aeronautics in this
> or any other nation – I say, whether I look merely at home, or, stretching my
> eyes farther, contemplate the boundless prospect of conquest and possession
> – achieved by British perseverance and British valour – which is outspread
> before me, I clasp my hands, and turning my eyes to the broad expanse
> above my head, exclaim, 'Thank Heaven, I am a Briton'.
>
> (*Nicholas Nickleby*, 1839)

Though he was usually a little behind the times, Dickens could also
be prophetic.

Victorian families at all social levels were of colonial size, a fact
which made it possible that, as interest in the second British Empire
grew in the course of the century, the United Kingdom could supply
increasing numbers of colonizers for New Zealand, Australia,
Canada, South Africa, and also, of course, for America. The writings
of Samuel Smiles, celebrating the new aristocracy of great doers and

the value of self-help and thrift, expressed, about the middle of the century, the expansiveness and the sense of opportunity of more than the middle classes of society. The fall of the Railway King, George Hudson, M.P., the linen draper from York, is typical of many casualties in the race for self-advancement, and it is given a colonial significance in this contemporary comment:

The truth is that Mr Hudson is neither better nor worse than the morality of 1845. He rose to wealth and importance at an immoral period; he was the creature of an immoral system; he was wafted into fortune upon the wave of a popular mania; he was elevated into the Dictatorship of Railway Speculation in an unwholesome ferment of popular cupidity pervading all ranks and conditions of men; and, whatever be the hue of the error he may have committed, it is rather too much to expect of him that he should be purer than his time or his associates. The commercial code of 1845 was, as far as Railways were concerned, framed upon anything but moral principles ... Men who would have scorned to do a dishonest act towards any other real tangible living man, did not scruple to do acts towards the great abstraction, the public, which no morality could justify.

(*The Illustrated London News*, 1849)

But there was a great deal to be done which had nothing to do with speculation, and of this kind of self-help Mr Thornton, the Lancashire industrialist who is the hero of Mrs Gaskell's *North and South* (1855), might be taken as an example, or Mr Rouncewell, the ironmaster in *Bleak House* (1852–3). Dickens's attitude to the successful ironmaster – 'a responsible-looking gentleman dressed in black, portly enough but strong and active. Has a perfectly natural and easy air, and is not in the least embarrassed by the great presence into which he comes' – is sympathetic, the more so as Rouncewell, representing social regrouping, is shown in contrast to Sir Leicester Dedlock.

'And it is a remarkable example of the confusion into which the present age has fallen; of the obliteration of landmarks, the opening of floodgates, and the uprooting of distinctions,' says Sir Leicester, with stately gloom, 'that I have been informed by Mr Tulkinghorn, that Mrs Rouncewell's son has been invited to go into Parliament.'
Miss Volumnia utters a little sharp scream.
'Yes, indeed,' repeats Sir Leicester, 'into Parliament.'
'I never heard of such a thing! Good gracious, what is the man?' exclaimed Volumnia.
'He is called, I believe – an – Ironmaster.' Sir Leicester says it slowly, and

with gravity and doubt, as not being sure but that he is called a Lead-mistress; or that the right word may be some other word expressive of some other relationship to some other metal.

Dickens's sympathy for Mr Rouncewell, like that of Henry James for some of his successful Americans, is not unreserved. Self-help involved a good deal of stiffening of sinews and a hard-favoured concentration of interests. At all social levels there were men with a grievance. At a lower level than that of the Rouncewells, the struggle for literacy as the key to betterment often took an embittered form.

> The sinewy artisan, – the weaver lean, –
> The shrunken stockinger, – the miner swarth, –
> Read, think, and feel; and in their eyes the sheen
> Of burning thought betokens thy young birth
> Within their souls, blythe Liberty! ...
>
> Aye, they are thinking, – at the frame, and loom,
> At bench, and forge, and in the bowelled mine; –
> And when the scanty hour of rest is come,
> Again they read, – to think and to divine
> How it hath come to pass that Toil must pine
> While sloth doth revel; – how the game of blood
> Hath served their tyrants; – how the scheme malign
> Of priests hath crushed them; and resolve doth bud
> To band, – and to bring back the primal Brotherhood.

Thomas Cooper's *The Purgatory of Suicides* (1845), from which these lines are taken, is dedicated to Carlyle, but it is clear that a dedication to the memory of Shelley would have been more appro-priate. Cooper offers a good example of that mixture of motives which responded to the creation, under Radical initiative, of Mechanics' Institutes out of which most of the new universities evolved. Looking back, in 1870, to the events of the forties, Cooper was obliged to remark that the interval had not been one of continual progress in the condition of the working class.

In our old Chartist time, it is true, Lancashire working men were in rags by the thousands; and many of them often lacked food. But their intelligence was demonstrated wherever you went. You would see them in groups discussing the great doctrine of political justice ... or they were in earnest dispute respecting the teachings of Socialism. Now, you will see no such groups in Lancashire. But you will hear well-dressed working men talking,

as they walk with their hands in their pockets, of 'Co-ops' [Co-operative Stores] and their shares in them, or in building societies. And you will see others, like idiots, leading small greyhound dogs, covered with cloth, in a string! ... I found the towns vying with each other in the erection of new town-halls, and in their superior style of erecting houses of business; and I also found working men had bettered their physical conditions considerably. But I confess, with pain, that I saw they had gone back, intellectually and morally.   (*The Life of Thomas Cooper written by himself*, 1872)

There is a sergeant-majorly touch about the phrase 'with their hands in their pockets'; it is the sort of contrast which struck James Austen-Leigh when he looked back, in his *Memoir* (1869), to the more formal, abstemious, and unupholstered society in which Jane Austen lived. A certain eighteenth-century, Methody starch and simplicity survived amongst the respectable poor well into the nineteenth century. It gives to the autobiographies of such men as Cooper, Samuel Bamford, William Lovett, and others an astringent, unself-pitying distinction.

Carlyle and Dickens dominate the first half of Victoria's reign, and their work helps one to discern the centres of interaction between 'literature' and 'society' in the period. One chief concern in their work is the description and analysis of 'the condition of England'. Another is the examination of prevailing economic doctrines concerning poverty, population, and the scope of public responsibility. A third is the attempt to suggest more handsome and humanitarian alternatives to those doctrines, a work in which they had the assistance of all those who were influenced by the aspirations of the earlier Romantics, especially of Coleridge, and by the revival of religious feeling and speculation about a more Christian order of society.

In the later Victorian period questions of education, the debate about the content of English culture which, after 1870, was painfully dependent on the effects of a system of minimal state education, and the inculcation of habits of resistance to the standardizing effects of machines, predominate over all other considerations. After the second Reform Bill of 1867, which enfranchised the working classes in the towns, thus shifting the centre of political power, and the Trade Union Act of 1871, which gave recognition to the unions as part of the mechanism of modern life, workmen were no longer dependent on humanitarian sentiment. They were now 'the masters'. Could they be 'educated'? Gradually the working classes and former

Chartists developed, with help from outside their class, their own kind of Socialist idealism and carried out their own practical experiments, such as that of the Rochdale pioneers, so detaching themselves alike from the popular Toryism or British Israelitism invented by the model Anglican Disraeli, and from the high-toned, nationalistic, rather anti-democratic Christian Socialism of F. D. Maurice and Charles Kingsley. Probably the sentiments voiced by Ruskin in *The Crown of Wild Olive* (1865) were as close as any to the thoughts of the workmen towards whom so much propaganda was being directed:

That is a grand old proverb of Sancho Panza's, 'Fine words butter no parsnips'; and I can tell you that, all over England just now, you workmen are buying a great deal too much butter at that dairy. Rough work, honourable or not, takes the life out of us; and the man who has been heaving clay out of a ditch all day, or driving an express train against the north wind all night, or holding a collier's helm in a gale on a lee shore, or whirling white-hot iron at a furnace mouth, that man is not the same at the end of his day, or night, as one who has been sitting in a quiet room, with everything comfortable about him, reading books, or classing butterflies, or painting pictures. If it is any comfort to you to be told that the rough work is the more honourable of the two, I should be sorry to take that much of consolation from you.

Underlying passages of this sort, which abound in writing about society in this period, is an awareness of an Owenite, as well as Marxist, 'labour theory of value', the theory that 'labour is the source of wealth' (Wm Lovett's *Life and Struggles*, Ch. IV).

Certain matters of historical 'background' are more likely than others to engage the attention of students of literature. No reader of the Victorians could fail for long to notice, for example, frequent references to 'political economy' and 'utilitarianism', to different sorts of religious revivalism, to a renewal of the debate between Catholic and Protestant, and to Agnosticism. A certain knowledgeableness about ecclesiastical politics was part of the equipment of novelists and conversationalists throughout the century. What George Eliot had to say in an early letter about one such novelist, the Rev. William Gresley, is applicable also to the tendency in our own day for religion to become a debating topic for undergraduate societies and the Sunday papers. Gresley's novels were

sure to have a powerful influence on the minds of small readers and shallow thinkers, as, from the simplicity and clearness with which the author, by his *beau idéal* characters, enunciates his sentiments, they furnish a magazine of easily wielded weapons for *morning calling* and *evening party* controversialists, as well as that really honest minds will be inclined to think they have found a resting-place amid the foot-balling of religious parties.

Some notes on these more obtrusive matters of background may therefore be in place in a survey of this kind.

Utilitarianism: the Meaning of Plugson, Gradgrind, Bounderby & Bulstrode

Never on this Earth, was the relation of man to man long carried on by Cash-Payment alone ... The indomitable Plugson too, of the respected Firm of Plugson, Hunks and Company, in St Dolly Undershot, is invited to reflect on this.   (*Past and Present*, 1843)

Mr Gradgrind sat writing in the room with the deadly statistical clock, proving something no doubt – probably, in the main, that the Good Samaritan was a Bad Economist.

Adam Smith and Malthus, two younger Gradgrinds, were out at lecture in custody.

You saw nothing in Coketown but what was severely workful. If the members of a religious persuasion built a chapel there – as the members of eighteen religious persuasions had done – they made it a pious warehouse of red brick ... the perplexing mystery of the place was, Who belonged to the eighteen denominations?

Why, Mr Bounderby was as near being Mr Gradgrind's bosom friend, as a man perfectly devoid of sentiment can approach that spiritual relationship towards another man perfectly devoid of sentiment ... He was a rich man: banker, merchant, manufacturer, and what not. A man who was the Bully of humility.   (*Hard Times*, 1854)

It was a principle with Mr Bulstrode to gain as much power as possible, that he might use it for the glory of God. He went through a great deal of spiritual conflict and inward argument in order to adjust his motives, and make clear to himself what God's glory required ... Profitable investments in trades where the power of the prince of this world showed its most active devices, became sanctified by a right application of the profits in the hands of God's servant. This implicit reasoning is essentially no more peculiar to evangelical belief than the use of wide phrases for narrow motives is peculiar

to Englishmen. There is no general doctrine which is not capable of eating out our morality if unchecked by the deep-seated habit of direct fellow-feeling with individual fellow-men.   (*Middlemarch*, 1872)

These quotations, whilst marking a continuity of moral view, should also suggest the living complexity of the phenomenon known as 'utilitarianism'. Only a small number of Victorian men and women could be described as utilitarians or philosophical radicals in the sense of subscribing to certain views concerning the nature of man, the grounds of morality, the scope of government, the meaning of freedom, and so on. The vast majority of those who talked the language of *laissez-faire* and individual self-interest were merely rationalizing their own habits and prejudices. A good example of this unphilosophical utilitarianism is the series of statements made by Macaulay, who considered himself a Whig and an opponent of utilitarianism, at the end of his essay on Southey in the *Edinburgh Review* (1930):

On what principle is it that, where we see nothing but improvement behind us, we are to expect nothing but deterioration before us? It is not by the intermeddling of Mr Southey's idol, the omniscient and omnipotent State, but by the prudence and energy of the people, that England has hitherto been carried forward in civilization; and it is to the same prudence and the same energy that we now look with comfort and good hope. Our rulers will best promote the improvement of the nation by strictly confining themselves to their own legitimate duties, by leaving capital to find its most lucrative course, commodities their fair price, industry and intelligence their natural reward, idleness and folly their natural punishment, by maintaining peace, by defending property, by diminishing the price of law, and by observing strict economy in every department of the state.

Here there is implied a resentment of government interference with trade, and an interpretation of 'duties', 'natural reward', and 'strict economy' that agree very well with utilitarian doctrines. Macaulay is also interesting for our purposes in that he was the son of an original member of the 'Clapham Sect' of Evangelicals. It has often been pointed out, by Tawney, Halévy, and others, that the stress on self-interest of utilitarian political economy was reinforced by the Calvinist-Evangelical emphasis on personal salvation and on the conviction that poverty was ordained. Trollope's Mr Slope and Dickens's Chadband certainly answered to a social reality. That Evangelicals such as Shaftesbury did, nevertheless, have a great share

in the improvement of social conditions is an example not only of a common paradox in human behaviour but also of the strength of a diffused humanitarian sentiment which tended to make collaborators of men holding the most diverse principles. Utilitarianism itself was full of paradoxes. Though based, like so many eighteenth-century theories, upon a minimal view of human nature, 'economic man', it was nevertheless the inspiration of many of the most important reforms of the day in parliamentary and local government, in the working of the law, in standards of sanitation and in education. Though it theoretically favoured *laissez-faire* it, nevertheless, came to stand for efficient centralized administration and a strong civil service. Though in some matters, such as the agitation for cheap bread, the utilitarians were friends of the working man, in others, such as the regulation of conditions in factories, they were his enemies. Though utilitarian reformism should have appealed to Dickens, it incurred, amongst other examples of his hostility, the satire of the Circumlocution Office and of the wonderful opening of *Oliver Twist*.

The contradictions in utilitarian theory were partly the result of changing circumstances as the pure doctrine of the original utilitarian society and of the *Westminster Review* were taken over by the Anti-Corn Law League and the school of Manchester free-traders primarily interested in freeing commerce of all trammels; partly the result of internal development in the theory; and there were also contradictions in the original theories themselves. The average reader is likely to be most conscious of the difficulty of reconciling a belief in efficient democratic government, the reform of legal procedure and of education, with *laissez-faire*. On the one hand, the Benthamite legislator artificially harmonizes interests in order to ensure the greatest happiness of the greatest number; on the other, economic interests would seem to be, as Adam Smith believed, self-harmonizing, and to require as little intervention from the legislator as possible. Halévy writes:

Bentham incorporated Adam Smith's economic philosophy with his Utilitarianism. Later, in the time of Ricardo and James Mill, under the double influence of the surroundings and of the moment, the political economy of Adam Smith and his successors played a preponderating part in Bentham's system. In fact, Benthamism was the work of a jurist who was

by accident an economist ... Now, the two principles on which the juristic and the economic philosophy of the Benthamites respectively rested are two contradictory principles: the contradiction was continually breaking out in the current formulae of Benthamism. According to Bentham, the philosopher of law, the idea of 'liberty' is a generalization without scientific precision: social science is the science of restraints as it is the science of laws. The respect for liberty and the suppression of all restraints is, on the other hand, the first and last word of the wisdom of the economists.[1]

(*The Growth of Philosophic Radicalism*, English translation, 1928)

Dickens, in one of the quotations at the head of this section, coupled the names of Adam Smith and Malthus. It was the banker David Ricardo who produced the economic textbook of the 'dismal science' by applying Malthus's theories on population to the economic theories of Adam Smith. Malthus, in his *Essay on the Principle of Population* (1798), had argued that population tended to increase by geometrical progression but supplies of food only by arithmetical progression. Wars and pestilences were the main natural controls which prevented universal famine. But men could help by not marrying and by not having children.

I see no way by which men can escape from the weight of this law which pervades all animated nature. No fancied equality, no agrarian regulations, in their utmost extent, could remove the pressure of it even for a single century. And it appears, therefore, to be decisive against the possible existence of a society all the members of which should live in ease, happiness and comparative leisure.

In addition to the many miseries and vices which check the growth of population, 'famine seems to be the last, the most dreadful resource of nature'.

Malthus recommends a fatalistic resignation to this 'law':

The view of human life, which results from the contemplation of the constant pressure of distress on man from the difficulty of subsistence, by showing the little expectation that he can reasonably entertain of perfectibility on earth, seems strongly to point his hopes to the future.

This gloomy conclusion would at least have been consistent. But he goes on sanctimoniously to see earthly life not as a 'state of trial' but 'as the mighty process of God, not for the trial, but for the creation and formation of mind: a process necessary, to awaken inert chaotic matter, into spirit; to sublimate the dust of the earth into soul; to elicit an aetherial spark from the clod of clay'. After Malthus

it seems odd that people should have been shocked by Darwin's theory of natural selection.

Ricardo developed Malthus's 'law' into his iron law of wages. There was a fixed 'wages fund' to be divided amongst the workers. An increase in population would send down wages.

The natural price of labour is that price which is necessary to enable the labourers, one with another, to subsist and to perpetuate their race, without either increase or diminution.

In old countries with little fertile land,

the population increases faster than the funds required for its support. Every exertion of industry, unless accompanied by a diminished rate of increase in the population, will add to the evil, for production cannot keep pace with it ... In the natural advance of society, the wages of labour will have a tendency to fall as far as they are regulated by supply and demand; for the supply of labourers will continue to increase at the same rate, whilst the demand for them will increase at a slower rate ... These then are the laws by which wages are regulated, and by which the happiness of far the greatest part of every community is governed. Like all other contracts, wages should be left to the fair and free competition of the market, and should never be controlled by the interference of the legislature ... The clear and direct tendency of the poor laws is in direct opposition to these obvious principles. It is a truth which admits not a doubt, that the comforts and well-being of the poor cannot be permanently secured without some regard on their part, or some effort on the part of the legislature, to regulate the increase of their numbers and to render less frequent among them early and improvident marriages. The operation of the system of poor laws has been directly contrary to this. They have rendered restraint superfluous, and have invited imprudence, by offering it a portion of the wages of prudence and industry.

(*The Principles of Political Economy and Taxation*, 1817)

It was partly because they were supported by arguments of this sort that the reform of the poor laws and advocacy of birth control aroused so much opposition. Yet the practice of birth control was to prove as great and beneficent a revolution as any in the nineteenth century.

The doctrine of economic *laissez-faire* was, then, one which made a natural law of the manufacturer's untrammelled pursuit of profit and, on scientific grounds, recommended abstention from all attempts to improve the lot of the workers. Their lot could only be improved by the restriction of their numbers, thus preventing too great a drain on the wages fund. This was dismal enough; and the determinism

in such 'science' gave to the first half of the century an oppressiveness which only gradually wore off as the era of mid-Victorian prosperity set in and as the possibilities of colonial emigration were realized. But determinism of one sort or another, economic, evolutionary, Malthusian, and Darwinian, oppressed nineteenth-century minds, much as different forms of economic or historic fatalism disquiet us at the present time.

Dickens attacked the utilitarians in many places. But when he wrote his most inclusive satire in *Hard Times*, he set the opening chapters in a schoolroom and entitled the chapter 'Murdering the Innocents'. In this way he could go beyond matters of economic theory to strike at those psychological and educational ideas which formed the 'philosophical' part of utilitarianism. Bentham was only one of a number of Englishmen, in the empirical tradition, who had attempted to supply comprehensive explanations of human nature and experience. The vaguely democratic principle of 'the greatest happiness of the greatest number' was supported by a whole structure of borrowed 'explanations' and assumptions about the human mind and human nature. Equipped with these 'explanations' the utilitarians could afford to dismiss as superfluous fictions such terms as conscience, moral sense, love, right, in fact all the terms which formed the moral vocabulary of the rest of mankind. This is a kind of razor operation quite common in philosophy, and occasionally salutary when it leads to a greater care and astringency in the use of words. More frequently such an attitude to what appear to be superfluous abstractions is the sign of confident blindness and an impatient desire for simplification; the result is often stultifying rather than simplifying. This is what Susan Stebbing appears to have meant when she wrote at the end of her life:

I have no doubt that many of those with whose philosophical outlook I am in the main in agreement would not at all agree with me in holding that the specifically human excellences are rightly to be called *spiritual* excellences. They dislike the *word*. I understand the reasons for their dislike, but I should not be willing to dispense with the word; to do so is to make oneself more inarticulate than is necessary.   (*Ideals and Illusions*, 1941)

Bentham was a thorough-going simplifier. In place of 'fictions' and 'vague generalities' he would establish a moral arithmetic, a 'felicific calculus' by means of which the greatest happiness of the

greatest number might be calculated, thus making traditional ethics superfluous. John Stuart Mill testified to the dazzling persuasiveness of 'the Benthamic standard of "the greatest happiness"' as he read Dumont's version of Bentham.

> In the first pages of Bentham it burst upon me with all the force of novelty. What thus impressed me was the chapter in which Bentham passed judgement on the common modes of reasoning in morals and legislation, deduced from phrases like 'law of nature', 'right reason', 'the moral sense', 'natural rectitude', and the like, and characterized them as dogmatism in disguise, imposing its sentiments upon others under the cover of sounding expressions which convey no reason for the sentiment, but set up the sentiment as its own reason. It had not struck me before, that Bentham's principle put an end to all this. The feeling rushed upon me, that all previous moralists were superseded, and that here indeed was the commencement of a new era in thought. (*Autobiography*, 1873)

This passage is interesting not only as giving the contemporary reaction to Bentham, but also because the phrase 'no reason for the sentiment' suggests the intellectual cage which J. S. Mill had to destroy in order to live.

The children in *Hard Times* were 'little vessels' and 'little pitchers' for 'facts'. Dickens's seemingly broad comic effects are more subtle in their allusiveness than they at first appear. The word 'vessel' not only suggests the passive receptiveness which the utilitarians expected from the minds of children, but also the confidence of the utilitarians that they knew just what the contents of 'little vessels' should be.

> Mr Gradgrind walked homeward from the school, in a state of considerable satisfaction. It was his school, and he intended it to be a model. He intended every child in it to be a model – just as the young Gradgrinds were all models. There were five young Gradgrinds, and they were models every one. They had been lectured at from their tenderest years; coursed like little hares. Almost as soon as they could run alone, they had been made to run to the lecture-room. The first object with which they had an association, or of which they had a remembrance, was a large blackboard with a dry Ogre chalking ghastly white figures on it.

The word 'association' in the last sentence refers us back to the associationist psychology or science of the mind derived from David Hartley and from Locke, which Jeremy Bentham and James Mill incorporated into their scheme of man and of society. The mind was made up of an increasing complexity of associations originating in sensations. As Hartley wrote:

Any sensations A, B, C, etc., by being associated with one another a sufficient Number of Times, get such a power over the corresponding Ideas a, b, c, etc., that any one of the sensations A, when impressed alone, shall be able to excite in the Mind b, c, etc., the Ideas of the rest.

Some sensations were pleasurable and therefore the objects of desire, others were painful and therefore the objects of aversion. Men were so constituted as to seek to increase their pleasures which become synonymous with good or happiness, and to avoid what is painful or bad. There is no room in this determinism of self-interest for the growth of conscience, but this kind of theory was made the substratum of utilitarian political thought and was an essential part of the theoretical justification for the reform of the law, and for majority government.

Nature has placed man under the governance of two sovereign masters, *pain* and *pleasure*. It is for them alone to point out what we ought to do, as well as to determine what we shall do. On the one hand the standard of right and wrong, on the other the chain of causes and effects, are fastened to their throne. They govern us in all we say, in all we think: every effort we make to throw off our subjection will serve but to demonstrate and confirm it ... The *principle of utility* recognizes this subjection and assumes it for the foundation of that system, the object of which is to rear the fabric of felicity by the hands of reason and of law. Systems which attempt to question it, deal in sounds instead of sense, in caprice instead of reason ... By the principle of utility is meant that principle which approves or disapproves of every action whatsoever, according to the tendency which it appears to have to augment or diminish the happiness of the party whose interest is in question: or, what is the same thing in other words, to promote or to oppose that happiness. I say of every action whatsoever; and therefore not only of every action of a private individual but of every measure of government. (Bentham, *Introduction to the Principles of Morals and Legislation*, 1789)

This kind of 'rationalism' posits a dreary model of the individual mind, and also a rather negative, atomistic, or Hobbist view of society. As with many such rationalizations, there is frequently a certain appropriateness in the utilitarian view that societies are held together by selfishness and are merely, from some points of view, aggregates of individuals. But it is the partial view or simplification which, say, a student of the law might have, or an economist looking for economic laws, or a quartermaster distributing emergency

rations. It is not the whole truth about societies and the love, altruism, and piety rooted in them.

The terms 'pain', 'pleasure', and 'happiness' are, of course, much more vague than most of the ethical terms which Bentham sought to render obsolete. Bentham imagined that his magnanimous arithmetic had banished vagueness by assuming that pleasure and pain were quantitatively measurable and that problems of right and wrong might resolve themselves into a weighing of the quantities of pleasure against the quantities of pain resulting from an act or omission. Utilitarianism therefore claimed to be *scientific* and to have superseded old-fashioned moral casuistry. In fact, it had only given a superficial cogency to a collection of moral-sounding slogans which were of immense service in the achievement of legal, administrative, parliamentary, and social reforms, but were too crude to be relevant to the moral experience of individual men and women. Though utilitarians were committed to the extension of education and of the franchise, their educational aims, as exemplified in the Society for the Diffusion of Useful Knowledge founded by Brougham in 1827, were minimal and seemed designed to create a population entirely submissive to factories and machines. Andrew Ure's *The Philosophy of Manufactures* (1835) regards such a result as desirable and as an advance in civilization. 'The factory system' was 'the great minister of civilization'. J. S. Mill wrote of Bentham:

He had a phrase, expressive of the view he took of all moral speculations to which his method had not been applied or not founded on a recognition of utility as the moral standard: this phrase was 'vague generalities'. He did not heed, or rather the nature of his mind prevented it from occurring to him, that these generalities contained the whole unanalysed experience of the human race ... Without imagination nobody knows even his own nature further than circumstances have actually tried it and called it out; nor the nature of his fellow creatures, beyond such generalizations as he may have been enabled to make from his observation of their outward conduct. By these limits Bentham's knowledge of human nature is bounded. It is wholly empirical; and the empiricism of one who has had little experience ... He never felt life a sore and a weary burthen. He was a boy to the last ... How much of human nature slumbered in him he knew not ... Other ages and other nations were a blank to him for purposes of instruction. He measured them but by one standard; their knowledge of facts and their capability to take correct views of utility, and merge all other objects in it.

(Essay on 'Bentham', 1838)

Ruskin greatly admired *Hard Times* and urged that the novels of Dickens, 'but especially *Hard Times*, should be studied with close and earnest care by persons interested in social questions' (*Unto This Last*). Dickens mobilizes resentment against the utilitarians with a dazzling creative zest, and he is not to be dismissed, as some would do, as a 'bad economist'. We do not go to Dickens for a careful appraisal of the influence and achievements of the utilitarians, but to make connection with the living spirit. What else *can* we do?

Utilitarianism was primarily the creed of the rising middle class. '*La morale des utilitaires, c'est leur psychologie économique mise à l'impératif*' (Halévy, *La Formation du radicalisme philosophique*). Beatrice Webb has given this account of her mother:

An ardent student of Adam Smith, Malthus, and particularly of Nassau Senior, she had been brought up in the strictest sect of Utilitarian economists ... And my mother practised what she preached. Tested by economy in money and time she was an admirable expenditor of the family income: she never visited the servants' quarters and seldom spoke to any servant other than her own maid. She acted by deputy, training each daughter to carry out a carefully-thought-out plan of the most economical supply of the best-regulated demand. Her intellect told her that to pay more than the market rate, to exact fewer than the customary hours or insist on less than the usual strain – even if it could be proved that these conditions were injurious to the health and happiness of the persons concerned – was an act of self-indulgence, a defiance of nature's laws which would bring disaster on the individual and the community. Similarly, it was the bounden duty of every citizen to better his social status; to ignore those beneath him, and to aim steadily at the top rung of the social ladder. Only by this persistent pursuit by each individual of his own and his family's interest would the highest general level of civilization be attained. It was on this issue that she and Herbert Spencer found themselves in happy accord. No one of the present generation realizes with what sincerity and fervour these doctrines were held by the representative men and women of the mid-Victorian middle class.

(*My Apprenticeship*, 1926)

Utilitarianism had little to offer to the landed gentry on the one hand, and on the other it seemed to offer only Malthusian negatives to the artisans. The latter, when, after 1832, they found that their middle-class allies were not interested in further extension of the parliamentary franchise, began to discover meanings of their own in the deterministic class war expounded by Ricardo. The Chartist tailor Crossthwaite in Kingsley's *Alton Locke* (1849) says:

'Didn't they tell us, before the Reform Bill, that extension of the suffrage was to cure everything? And how can you have too much of a good thing? It was but the other day I got hold of some Tory paper that talked about the English constitution, and the balance of queen, lords, and commons, as the "Talismanic Palladium" of the country. 'Gad, we'll see if a move onwards in the same line won't better the matter. If the balance of classes is such a blessed thing, the sooner we get the balance equal the better ... We'll try – we'll see whether the talisman they talk of has lost its power all of a sudden since '32 – whether we can't rub the magic ring a little for ourselves, and call up genii to help us out of the mire, as the shopkeepers and the gentlemen have done.'

But there were many influences at work tending to soften animosities, and the slow growth of trade unions itself created responsibilities and a sense of what was possible.

The Ferment of Social Ideals

There was a tradition of thought going back to Burke and deriving from the stream of Anglican apologetics since the time of Hooker which formed the natural opposite of utilitarian atomism. It was not simply a Tory tradition, for the mere Tory-minded could find much that was congenial in the fatalistic language of Malthus and Ricardo. It was a tradition which had received an immense boost from the first Romantics, and especially from Burke, Coleridge, and from Scott. Against utilitarian doctrine it stressed history, tradition, and altruism; instead of the land-owning, the profit-making, and wage-earning contraries of the political economists, it emphasized common pieties and interests; against self-seeking atomism it insisted on an organic conception of society. Much of this idealist tradition was far too good to be quite true. Coleridge's theories of Church and State resemble Aristotle's *Politics* slightly tinged with religion – one should read them, and Burke's *Reflections*, as amateur anthropology. It was perhaps only just that, in our period, Gladstone and Disraeli should separately appropriate Coleridge's nationalism touched with emotion as obviously useful in politics. Of his early Tory phase Gladstone, whose first book *The Church in its Relations with the State* (1838) was an imitation of Coleridge, says: 'I cast over that party a prophetic mantle and assigned to it a mission distinctly religious.' Disraeli had shrewdly seen that an alliance between gentry and working class was perfectly possible in the

conditions of his time, for the lower orders hated the new poor law and the emphasis on economy and efficiency. His novels gave to the Young England programme a mystique of righteous Israelitism always congenial to different levels of society.

Sovereignty has been the title of something that has had no dominion, while absolute power has been wielded by those who profess themselves the servants of the People. In the selfish strife of factions, two great existences have been blotted out of the history of England – the Monarch and the Multitude; as the power of the Crown has diminished, the privileges of the People have disappeared; till at length the sceptre has become a pageant, and its subject has degenerated again into a self ... But Time, that brings all things, has brought also to the mind of England some suspicion that the idols they have so long worshipped, and the oracles that have so long deluded them, are not the true ones. There is a whisper rising in this country that loyalty is not a phrase, Faith not a delusion, and Popular Liberty something more diffusive and substantial than the profane exercise of the sacred rights of sovereignty by political classes.   (*Sybil*, 1845)

This is almost as good as Burke, and there is a tradition of such thought which comes down in our own day, to T. E. Hulme and T. S. Eliot among many others. T. H. Green and F. H. Bradley, the disciples of Hegel, are in this tradition, the fluctuations of which at Oxford are described in a passage of Mark Pattison's *Memoirs* (1885):

Ever since 1830, at least, there had been among us an ebb and flow; one while of nominalistic, another while of *a priori* logic. What is the curious part of the history is, that these oscillations coincide with the strength for the time being of the clerical party. In the thirties, when the revolutionary enthusiasm rose to a height, which for a few years enabled the Government to defy the Church, to suppress her bishoprics, and plunder the cathedrals – in these years Whateley's logic, or some form of nominalism, predominated in the schools. When Tractarianism had made the clergy aware of their own strength, and high sacerdotal doctrines were openly proclaimed, we fell off from Whateley, and vague, indefinite, realistic [in the strict philosophic sense] views under the influence of Coleridge and Sir William Hamilton slowly occupied the schools. They established themselves there in a more explicit form when Mansel, a Tory leader and arch-jobber, became the logical legislator of the school, and first introduced Kant into Oxford. But the High Church party received in Newman's secession a blow which for the moment seemed fatal to their cause. Coincident with this was the appearance of Mill's great work, and Oxford repudiated at once sacerdotal principles and Kantian logic. There was, in the language of the clerical platform, an outbreak of infidelity. For more than a quarter of this century Mill and nominalistic

views reigned in the schools. But gradually the clerical party rallied their forces, and since the Franco-German War have been advancing upon us with rapid strides. This fresh invasion of sacerdotalism has been accompanied by a renewed attempt to accredit an *a priori* logic, though in a less cumbrous form than the Kantian ... what is curious is that this new *a priori* metaphysic, whoever gave it shape in Germany, was imported into Oxford by a staunch liberal, the late Professor Green. This anomaly can only be accounted for by a certain puzzle-headedness on the part of the Professor, who was removed from the scene before he had time to see how eagerly the Tories began to carry off his honey to their hive.

The Christian Socialists, with F. D. Maurice as their chief thinker, also belong to the Anglican reaction against depersonalizing forces in Victorian society. Charles Kingsley, though, like many others, inclined to be jealous of Disraeli's ability to strike the right Anglican note, does at times impress us by the un-Disraelian quality of the Christian Socialist response to the Utilitarian challenge. When Alton Locke becomes a reluctant Chartist he explains his lack of conviction in a way that suggests clearly enough the kind of wrongness which the Christian Socialists especially deplored:

And so I began to look on man ... as a creature and puppet of circumstance – of the particular outward system, social or political, in which he happens to find himself. An abominable heresy, no doubt; but, somehow, it appears to me just the same as Benthamites, and economists, and highchurchmen, too, for that matter, have been preaching for the last twenty years with great applause from their respective parties. One set informs the world that it is to be regenerated by cheap bread, free trade, and that peculiar form of the 'freedom of industry' which, in plain language, signifies 'the despotism of capital'; and which, whatever it means, is merely some outward system, circumstance, or 'dodge' *about* man, and not *in* him. Another party's nostrum is more churches, more schools, more clergymen – excellent things in their way ... But the party of whom I am speaking seem to us workmen to consider the quality quite a secondary consideration compared with the quantity. They expect the world to be regenerated, not by becoming more a Church – none would gladlier help them in bringing that about than the Chartists themselves, paradoxical as it may seem – but by being dosed somewhat more with a certain 'Church system', circumstance, or 'dodge'.

There is, of course, a good deal of sentimentality in the 'honest artisan' heroes of Victorian fiction. All the moralists and novelists who might be described as critics of utilitarianism tend to become emotional as they delineate the Ideal Working Man who would atone for the gross materialism of the times by accepting a feudal

role in a very unfeudal epoch. Dickens's Stephen Blackpool represents a pervasive weakness in mid-Victorian social thought before the Marxist phase which began in the eighties. Carlyle was no Coleridgean and had no time for 'dead Churches, this dead English Church especially', yet he, too, was inclined to remain content with scriptural adjurations to the working man:

> For us was thy back so bent, for us thy straight limbs and fingers so deformed; thou wert our conscript on whom the lot fell ... Yet toil on, toil on: *thou* art in thy duty, be out of it who may. (*Sartor Resartus*, 1838)

Carlyle's influence in awakening the conscience of the middle class was great, but it was this emotionalism and vagueness about the working man which, though it explains Carlyle's popularity, betrayed him into admiration of prussianism. Ruskin, too, who saw that Stephen Blackpool was 'a dramatic perfection instead of a characteristic example of an honest workman', concluded one of his best pieces of social criticism, *Unto This Last* (1860), publication of which in the *Cornhill Magazine* was stopped by Thackeray following vigorous protests from the middle-class readers, with an all-too-common surrender of the main point at issue between capital and labour. 'Note, finally, that all effectual advancement towards this true felicity of the human race must be by individual, not public effort.' Ruskin should have seen that it is exactly the conventionality of Dickens's attitude to trade unions ('The United Aggregate Tribunal') which makes Stephen Blackpool such an imbecile and detracts so much from the force of the best chapters in *Hard Times*. It might be urged that Dickens was making his vision of hard times consistent in seeing in trade unionism merely another sign of the obliteration of individual character. But it was a mechanical sort of consistency. Dickens made a serious mistake in merely caricaturing the attempts of labour to reduce industrial insecurity and arbitrariness. There was a very hard road to be travelled before Labour members could at last take their place in Parliament. The great need of the age, as J. S. Mill and Matthew Arnold realized, was the mitigation of brutalizing social conditions and a missionary faith in education and gradualism. The attempt to achieve these aims produced over the years a working-class conscientiousness and responsibleness which have become strong and wholesome elements in English public life.

Not being a Broad Church Anglican of the Coleridge–Thomas Arnold–Kingsley tradition, nor a lapsed Calvinist from Ecclefechan, Mill could not unreservedly approve of the 'idealist' reactions against utilitarianism. Mill wrote memorable essays urging Radicals to learn from the conservative Coleridge as well as from Bentham, but he did not go on to make that synthesis of these diametrically opposed thinkers which the age so much required. Instead, he tried to broaden or liberalize the utilitarianism to which he had been trained, and by admitting the importance of qualitative non-measurable differences in 'pleasures' he entirely destroyed, though without appearing to realize it, the claims of utilitarianism to be a *science* of government, legislation, and morals. 'Better to be Socrates dissatisfied than a fool satisfied.' (Lawrence's account of Skrebensky in *The Rainbow* is relevant here.) Alarmed by the authoritarian or paternalist tendencies of Carlyle and Ruskin, and also by the illiberalism which majority government could bring about, he chose the task of formulating and defending the cause of individual liberty.

Liberty, Anarchy and Culture

De Tocqueville had brilliantly analysed, in the local example of the United States, the tendencies and risks of modern nations:

> It is in vain to summon a people, which has been rendered so dependent on the central power, to choose from time to time the representatives of that power; this rare and brief exercise of their free choice, however important it may be, will not prevent them from gradually losing the faculties of thinking, feeling, and acting for themselves, and thus gradually falling below the level of humanity ... I believe that it is easier to establish an absolute and despotic government among a people in which the conditions of society are equal than among any other ... Thus the question is not how to reconstruct aristocratic society, but how to make liberty proceed out of that democratic state of society in which God has placed us. (*Democracy in America*, 1840)

This was the theme of Mill's *On Liberty* (1859), as it was essentially the theme of Arnold's *Culture and Anarchy* (1869), which is much the livelier book and in some ways an answer to Mill's reasoning. Mill was more like Arnold than he was like Bright or Frederick Harrison, and he would have echoed Arnold's words: 'I am a Liberal, yet I am a Liberal tempered by experience, reflection, and renouncement'; and he might have gone on to the end of Arnold's sentence, 'and I

am, above all, a believer in culture'. But the great difference between the two men was that Matthew Arnold belonged to the Broad Church tradition, whilst Mill was, in his own words, 'one of the very few examples, in this country, of one who has not thrown off religious belief but never had it; I grew up in a negative state with regard to it'. Mill's conception of the 'individual', of the 'state', and indeed of 'liberty' and 'truth' themselves, seem abstract and limited and to belong to the eighteenth rather than to the nineteenth century. Amongst many things one could question in the essay is Mill's attitude to Christianity.

> Its ideal is negative rather than positive; passive rather than active; Innocence rather than Nobleness; Abstinence from Evil rather than the energetic Pursuit of Good; in its precepts (as has been well said) 'thou shalt not' predominates unduly over 'thou shalt'. In its horror of sensuality, it made an idol of asceticism, which has been gradually compromised away into one of legality.

This reads like a caricature of the nineteenth-century Rationalist attitude to Christianity. It is true that charity had long displaced love (*agape*) and had thus facilitated the descent to mere legality, but Mill seems to be making guesses about something entirely outside his experience, or generalizing on the basis of acquaintance with some strange sect or from information given him by Mrs Taylor. Mill's real, important, and noble concern is that 'the tendency of all the changes taking place in the world is to strengthen society and diminish the power of the individual'. This leads him to defend liberty on the ground that 'truth' only results from the clash of opposite views. 'The peculiar evil of silencing the expression of an opinion is that it is robbing the human race.' This is as if we were to justify exemption of individuals from military service, not on grounds of humanity and compassion towards mental suffering, but on the grounds that the objector might be 'right'. Mill is very much a utilitarian in his conception of freedom. 'The only freedom which deserves the name is that of pursuing our own good in our own way, so long as we do not attempt to deprive others of theirs or impede their efforts to obtain it.' It is this arithmetical or atomistic view of society which, in great part, justifies Matthew Arnold's propaganda on behalf of 'culture'. Mill was probably nearer to envisaging the problems of 'freedom' and 'democracy', and closer

to Arnold, when he wrote the chapter 'On the Probable Futurity of the Labouring Classes' in *Principles of Political Economy* (1848). He considers contemporary concern 'respecting the social position desirable for manual labourers', and discusses the attractions of paternalism:

As the idea is essentially repulsive of a society only held together by bought services, and by the relations and feelings arising out of pecuniary interests, so there is something naturally attractive in a form of society abounding in strong personal attachments and disinterested self-devotion. Of such feelings it must be admitted that the relation of protector and protected has hitherto been the richest source ... The arrangements of society are now such that no man or woman who either possesses or is able to earn a livelihood requires any other protection than that of the law. Of the working classes of Western Europe at least it may be pronounced certain, that the patriarchal or paternal system of government is one to which they will not again be subject. That question has been several times decided. It was decided when they were taught to read, and allowed access to newspapers and political tracts. It was decided when dissenting preachers were suffered to go among them ... It was decided when they were brought together in numbers, to work socially under the same roof. It was decided when railways enabled them to shift from place to place ... The working classes have taken their interests into their own hands, and are perpetually showing that they think the interests of their employers not identical with their own but opposite to them. Some among the higher classes flatter themselves that these tendencies may be counteracted by moral and religious education; but they have let the time go by for giving an education which can serve their purpose. The principles of the Reformation have reached as low down as reading and writing, and the poor will no longer accept morals and religion of other people's prescribing. I speak more particularly of our own country, especially the town population, and the districts of the most scientific agriculture and highest wages, Scotland and the north of England.

But Mill does not quite reach that full recognition of ambiguity in his own phrases 'pursuing our own good' and 'doing as we like' which preoccupied Arnold and many others. Arnold's *Culture and Anarchy* was also, in its way, about 'liberty'. And Bagehot also had envisaged the consequences of the dying out of 'the old bodily enjoyments' in industrialized societies. 'We are thrown back upon the mind, and the mind is a barren thing. It can spin little from itself.' Bagehot foresees an increasing exploitation of sensationalism in literature:

Exaggerated emotions, violent incidents, monstrous characters, crowd our canvas; they are the resource of a weakness which would obtain the fame

of strength. Reading is about to become a series of collisions against
aggravated breakers, of beatings with imaginary surf.

(Essay on 'Mr Macaulay', 1856)

When, after 1870, the mere ability to read became common,
enormous new markets for cheap reading matter were created. It is
in this context that Arnold's work, his emphasis on 'sweetness and
light', on standards to which all men would respond and on which
they could agree whatever their ideological differences, has its
permanent importance. Such a conception of culture has no necessary
connection with the theories of State, race, or nation which occur
in Arnold as in Carlyle. And it is important to remember that when
it came to such tests of judgement as the trial of Governor Eyre or
the Second Reform Bill, Arnold's answers agreed with those of the
Saint of Rationalism rather than with Carlyle's.

Religion and the Challenge of Expansion

From some points of view, in contrast especially with the eighteenth century, the Victorian age might be regarded as an age of
religion, an age in which Evangelicalism, the religion of the middle
class, set the tone of manners, dress, and taste which the lower orders
adopted in their struggle towards respectability, an age in which
prime ministers raised echoes of a submerged religious vocabulary
in their speeches or novels, and historical boundaries moved, the
landmarks became less clear, the near became unreal, the past seemed
present. Yet it might also be regarded as an age of religious decay and
uncontrolled sectarianism. From Elizabeth's time, Nonconformity
had always had a class basis. Partly because religious association was
one of the few means of showing group solidarity open to the non-
enfranchised, religion came more and more to reflect the interests
of social classes, with Methodism as the more recent kind of Nonconformity at the bottom of the structure of Dissent.

Many of the 'religious difficulties' about which we hear so much
in this period were not clearly religious in character; they were often
the expression of pain at social displacement as men outgrew some
of the bleaker cults in which they were reared and found themselves
no longer at home in the local tabernacles and chapels. Religious
vagrancy became and has remained a permanent and distressing

46

feature of English life. It was for such vagrants that various substitute religions of science such as Scientific Paternalism or Positivism ('Catholicism plus Science') and Spencerian Evolutionism ('Always towards perfection is the mighty movement') had their attractions. A good deal of dissenting seriousness and zeal found an outlet in science, and simultaneously, of course, found new roads to 'respectability'. Gissing's novel *Born in Exile* (1891) is an interesting though late study of careerism in a student of science (the poor man's religion) and careerism in an adherent of the national and broad Church. 'What we have to do is to reconstruct a spiritual edifice on the basis of scientific revelation', declares the Rev. Bruno Chilvers. 'The results of science are the divine message of our age ... less of St Paul and more of Darwin! Less of Luther and more of Herbert Spencer!' Protestantism, basing its justification on the all-sufficiency of Scripture, found itself more and more powerless against the new Biblical criticism. From being an open book to every Protestant, the Bible became a collection of traps for the uninitiated in the keeping of an oligarchy of 'Biblical scholars'. For all its insistence on the Word, Protestantism retained less and less of its spirit. D. H. Lawrence, who had a novelist's interest in the sociology of class and chapel, gives this symbolical background to the action in a part of *Lady Chatterley*:

... the new big Primitive chapel, primitive enough in its stark brick and big panes of greenish and raspberry glass in the windows. The Wesleyan chapel, higher up, was of blackened brick ... The Congregational chapel, which thought itself superior, was built of rusticated sandstone.

Both Methodism and Evangelicalism had been reactions against the deficiencies of the high and dry Anglicanism of the eighteenth century. The Evangelicals remaining within the Anglican fold, like the Christian Socialists later, strove to make the national Church something more than 'the Tory Party at prayer', or than 'an appendage to the Barbarians ... an institution devoted above all to the landed gentry, but also to the propertied and satisfied classes generally; favouring immobility, preaching submission, and reserving transformation in general for the other side of the grave', as Matthew Arnold half-seriously described it in *Last Essays on Church and Religion*. Anglican sentiment was entirely alien in many parts even of England, and north of the Trent had become 'missionary country'. Even now,

after more than a century of teaching, few Anglicans have heard of the *via media*, or understand why there should still be so much anxious insistence on the word 'Catholic' for so long dormant in the creed. It was a debate recommenced by Coleridge after an interval of two centuries since the time of Hooker and Laud, and given practical importance by the Catholic Emancipation Act of 1829 and by the first Reform Bill, which made Anglicans more than ever aware of the dangerous subjection of their Church to the State. The Oxford Movement was only one sign of a general reconsideration of the relation of Anglican Protestantism to the rest of Christendom and the rest of history, and it involved attempts to mitigate the 'liberalism' or individualism in religious matters to which Protestantism gave a licence, and to stress historic continuities at a time when the appeal to Scripture was losing a good deal of its force. Newman came to feel that the *via media* of High Church Anglicanism 'has never been more than a paper system' (*Apologia*, 1864), and Matthew Arnold to conclude:

... that unless one chooses to fight about words, and fancifully to put into the word *Catholic* some occult quality, one must allow that the changes made in the Church of England at the Reformation impaired its Catholicity ... Something precious was no doubt lost in losing this common profession and worship; but the loss was, as Protestants maintain, incurred for the sake of something yet more precious still – the purity of that moral practice which was the very cause for which the common profession and worship existed. Now, it seems captious to incur voluntarily a loss for a great and worthy object, and at the same time, by a conjuring with words, to try to make it appear that we have not suffered the loss at all. So on the word *Catholic* we will not insist too jealously.　　　　(*St Paul and Protestantism*, 1870)

The debate continues, though with less and less attention from an increasingly indifferent populace; but occasionally forcing itself into prominence as in the insistence, by some denominations, on the inclusion of the incongruous word Protestant in the distinctly Byzantine ceremonial of the coronation service, or again, in such touches of harmless punctiliousness as Fowler's note:

Catholic. It is open to Roman-Catholics to use C. by itself in a sense that excludes all but themselves; but it is not open to a Protestant to use it instead of *Roman-Catholic* without implying that his own Church has no right to the name of C. Neither the desire of brevity nor the instinct of courtesy should induce anyone who is not Roman-C. to omit the *Roman*.
　　　　(*Modern English Usage*)

What are the roots that clutch, what branches grow
Out of this stony rubbish?

Pater was not entirely unjustified in seeing a connection between his own rather stagnant spirituality and what we have in Coleridge, who, says Pater, 'represents that inexhaustible discontent, languor and home-sickness, that endless regret, the chords of which ring all through our modern literature' (*Appreciations*). Such velleity forms the weaker side of many Victorians. When Arnold wrote of 'the Eternal not ourselves that makes for righteousness', he must have known that he risked being told that

he resorted once more, with his usual hardened indifference to the meaning of words and the principles of true literature, to that practice of debasing the coinage of religious language, and using great sayings in a new and washed-out sense of his own.

(R. H. Hutton, *Aspects of Religious and Scientific Thought*)

Reactions against Liberalism in Religion

Arnold reveals in an interesting way a subtle division of loyalties which is a guiding thread in the study of the nineteenth century. After dismissing the dogma of the Roman Church he, the Broad Churchman, goes on to write:

Its real superiority is in its charm for the imagination – its poetry. I persist in thinking that Catholicism has, from this superiority, a great future before it; that it will endure while all the Protestant sects (in which I do not include the Church of England) dissolve and perish. I persist in thinking that the prevailing form for the Christianity of the future will be the form of Catholicism; but a Catholicism purged, opening itself to the light and air, having the consciousness of its own poetry, freed from its sacerdotal despotism and freed from its pseudo-scientific apparatus of supernatural dogma. Its forms will be retained, as symbolizing with the force and charm of poetry, a few cardinal facts and ideas, simple indeed, but indispensable and inexhaustible, and on which our race could lay hold only by materializing them.

(*Mixed Essays*, 1874)

This is a fair example of the kind of 'liberalism' against which, in the thirties and forties, the leaders of the Oxford Movement directed their teaching and tracts. Theirs was an attempt to reconcentrate and recover, under Coleridge's influence, that Anglican spirit which hardly survived the seventeenth century. To Newman the

Anglican claim to represent a middle way between extreme Calvin-
ism and Papalism came to seem untenable. Newman's secession,
given his temperament and yearning for absoluteness, now seems
perfectly intelligible, though at the time it was a great shock
to English opinion, a shock from which Anglicanism has never
recovered. Mark Pattison wrote:

> I have spoken of the sudden lull which fell upon Oxford, and, indeed,
> upon all clerical circles throughout England, the moment the secessions to
> Rome were announced. The sensation to us was as of a sudden end of all
> things, and without a new beginning. We felt that old things had passed
> away, but by no means that all things had become new. Common con-
> versation seemed to have collapsed, to have died out for want of topic. The
> railway mania of 1847 and King Hudson was the first material that rushed
> in to fill up the vacuum ... Then came the railway crash, a new and still
> greater interest, as many fellows of colleges lost their savings in it. Finally
> in 1848, the universal outburst of revolution in every part of the continent.
> It seemed incredible, in the presence of such an upheaval, that we had been
> spending years in debating any matter so flimsy as whether England was in
> a state of schism or no.   (*Memoirs*, 1885)

Pattison himself, after being on the point of following Newman
to Rome, gradually settled into agnosticism. But the intellectual and
emotional tensions we find in his autobiography are an undercurrent
in much nineteenth-century thought. No abstract formula, theory,
or 'position' would satisfy Newman and the many who followed
him. Newman wished to escape from 'that imbecile inconsistent
thing called Protestantism' by resting his scepticism in history,
tradition, and ritual to which he could give 'assent'. He put into
circulation a term and a mode of reasoning from 'cumulative prob-
abilities', of which many others have since availed themselves. In a
letter to Mrs Humphry Ward we find Pater, for example, writing:

> To my mind, the beliefs and the function in the world of the historic
> Church form just one of those obscure but all-important possibilities which
> the human mind is powerless effectively to dismiss from itself, and might
> wisely accept, in the first place, as a workable hypothesis. The supposed facts
> on which Christianity rests, utterly incapable as they have become of any
> ordinary test, seem to me matters of very much the same sort of assent as
> we give to any assumptions, in the strict and ultimate sense, moral.
> (Mrs Humphry Ward, *A Writer's Recollections*, 1918)

Much of the distress of Anglicans in a history-conscious age arose
from an awareness of shallowness, contrivance, and impervious

moralism in English religious tradition with its pagan Christmas, its muted Easter; the chasm dividing Canterbury and the old Christian centres seemed infinitely wide. In its later phase the Oxford Movement found expression in the elaboration of ritual, which was not of course merely an aesthetic aim but an attempt to rediscover an authentic liturgy. One course adopted to lessen the isolation of Catholic-minded Anglicans was the incorporation into church services of translations of Greek Christian prayers and hymns such as those of J. M. Neale (1818–66); thus stress was laid on another layer of tradition and on that meaning of the Greek word Catholic antecedent to Papalism. But the Greek Church proved no more able than the Latin to recognize the validity of Anglican orders and, as Dean Stanley reported, even considered the Pope as 'the first Protestant'. Dean Stanley's intentions in stressing that 'the Greek Church is the mother and Rome the daughter' now seem primarily tactical, to 'keep up the equipoise of Christendom', and he appears not to have seen how a mother-daughter relationship differed from a Protestant 'position'. But there were other less superficial attempts at communication. 'I do so wish', says Lady Ambrose in W. H. Mallock's *The New Republic* (1877), 'that some union could be brought about. For the Greek Church, you know, certainly have the Apostolical Succession; and then if we were only joined with them, the Roman Catholics could never deny our orders – not', she added with a most cordial smile, 'that I don't myself believe implicitly in them, as it is!' Mallock, who had turned his back on Jowett and Balliol and the ethos of *Essays and Reviews* (1860) and had inclined towards Rome, was a little uncharitable, but he was justified in pointing to the attempt to have it both ways, to a latent Toryism, as an unimpressive characteristic of Anglicanism.

There was real pain and suspense in the Anglican compromise, of which Arnold, for all his reading of Coleridge, was as conscious as Newman. The Victorians seem at times to be engaged in a quarrel with their inheritance, with a negation in Protestantism which condemned them, in a world-spanning phase of their history, to a provinciality which no amount of 'Medievalism' could dispel. There was always, too, the sense that there was no choice which could be simply 'right', that history could not be undone, that there would always be symbols 'on which our race could lay hold only by

materializing them'. Arnold made his daily readings in his Greek Testament and transcribed his Greek quotations as if Christianity were really native only in that language. Were religions as untranslatable as poems? And yet, 'the thing itself is neither Greek nor Latin, which Greeks and Latins, and men of all other tongues, long for so earnestly' (St Augustine).

Literacy and Humanism

Agnosticism had its compensations in an age of oppressive conformities and, though it entailed a puritanism of its own, it helped individuals to lead orderly lives. To Beatrice Webb, who turned away from Catholicism as 'intellectual suicide', it seemed 'impossible for a woman to live in agnosticism. That is a creed which is only the product of one side of our nature, the purely rational, and ought we persistently to refuse authority to that other faculty which George Eliot calls emotive thought?' Later she wrote: 'It was the habit of prayer which enabled me to survive and emerge relatively sound in body and sane in mind.' By prayer she meant 'communion with an all-pervading spiritual force ... For science is bankrupt in deciding the destiny of men'. It was in this late Victorian ethos that Hinduism, Buddhism, theosophy, and other cults found adherents amongst those who found the increasing secularity and commercialization of English life stifling. One need only recall the career of W. B. Yeats. This was also the period of *Robert Elsmere* (1888). The ordeal of believing scientists was described by Gosse in *Father and Son* (1907):

> My Father, after long reflection, prepared a theory of his own which, as he fondly hoped, would take the wind out of Lyell's sails, and justify geology to godly readers of Genesis ... God hid the fossils in the rocks in order to tempt geologists into infidelity.

Though moral puritanism is by no means entailed by an agnostic attitude to religion, it was the case that Victorian agnosticism developed some of the characteristic narrowness and rigidity associated with puritanism. Charles Darwin deplores the loss of the ability to enjoy poetry or painting or music:

> My mind seems to have become a kind of machine for grinding general laws out of large collections of facts, but why this should have caused the atrophy of that part of the brain alone, on which the higher tastes depend,

I cannot conceive ... The loss of these tastes is a loss of happiness, and may possibly be injurious to the intellect, and more probably to the moral character, by enfeebling the emotional part of our nature.

(*Life of Charles Darwin*, ed. Francis Darwin, 1887)

If by an agnostic we mean a person whose mind is constantly constrained, oppressed, and cramped by a negative response to Christianity – for example, 'Mark Rutherford' – or who is so nervous about his rationalism that all that side of life which is not science – the world of desire, love, hate, hope, of tragedy, comedy, and of choice – suffers paralysis, then agnostics belong to the past. Gradually in the course of the Victorian era, and almost unconsciously, there developed amongst the increasingly large number of literate men and women a humanist attitude to life which was not a matter of creeds and dogmas or their denial, but of recognition and acceptance of the human condition, of loves, loyalties, duties, respect for intelligence and feelings, which are not less relevant to religion than to art and science. The earlier Wordsworth counts for much in the development of this unassertive resolution and independence. Though it offers no transcendence except in unattended moments and no answers to ultimate questions, humanism helps to keep alive a sense of their importance and to maintain standards of sincerity, delicacy, and intellectual honesty by which religion itself must be judged. Here one should mention the services rendered to Victorian life by those large, intricately related, middle-class families – Arnolds, Macaulays, Stephens, Huxleys, Trevelyans, and others – in helping to create levels of understanding and agreements underlying differences. Humanism is necessarily incomplete though not lacking in absoluteness, and implies the acceptance of strain, a tension between our love and our absurdity, especially in societies as exposed as our own to ceaseless propaganda, and so deficient in civilizing routines; but it ought not therefore to be described as 'parasitical' or 'essentially critical'. For 'criticism is as inevitable as breathing'. Humanism works for intelligibility and fairness. It is the point at which all who would not refuse conversation must meet.

One may come to feel that a culture which lacks a firm centre of coherent life-giving wisdom, a common sensibility or *sophia* as distinct from institutions, scholasticism, and debate, is no culture at all, and that the post-Christian world is essentially cultureless; but

at this point Newman is not more useful to us than Arnold, and appears only a more sensitive and sincere Dean Stanley.

NOTE

1. Some economic historians would now stress the changes in Bentham's economic views, and would not associate him as completely as Halévy does with economic *laissez-faire*. 'But the one moral which clearly emerges from this rather confusing intellectual situation is that any attempt to pigeon-hole or classify [or "classicalize"] Bentham is bound to be particularly misleading, and any attempt at a precise and concise generalization about his views on the role of the State especially hazardous' (T. W. Hutchinson on 'Bentham as an Economist' in *The Economic Journal*, June 1956). The canonization of Bentham as a herald of the Welfare State would not, of course, diminish the force of J. S. Mill's criticisms, or of Dickens's vision of 'utilitarianism' in practice. Indeed, that force would be increased and would be more worth heeding than ever.

PART II

THE LITERARY SCENE

G. D. KLINGOPULOS

Victorian Literature

With the Victorians we reach the age of photography. That fact alone may at first suggest new possibilities of clarity, precision, and certainty in our estimates of Victorian writers. Later, the disadvantages of being close to the object, and of possessing masses of information about it, make themselves felt, especially when we attempt to review the achievements of the period summarily. Virginia Woolf, when she tried to detach the Brownings from their legend, came to the conclusion that

> they have become two of the most conspicuous figures in that bright and animated company of authors, who, thanks to our modern habit of writing memoirs and printing letters and sitting to be photographed, live in the flesh, not merely as of old in the word; are known by their hats, not merely by their poems. What damage the art of photography has inflicted upon the art of literature has yet to be reckoned.
>
> ('Aurora Leigh' in *The Common Reader*)

Nearly all Victorians wrote copiously and had little regard for eighteenth-century ideals of terseness and epigrammatic point. The mounds of unsaleable sermons and black-bound homiletic writing which, even now, make corners of second-hand bookshops look like ossuaries, remind us pungently of the special interests and demands of the expanding Victorian reading public. Both poets and prose-writers were aware of a taste for propaganda in its various forms, and this is one reason for the sheer bulk of Victorian writing and its repetitiveness. Another complication is that some Victorian novelists and thinkers are still current in a way very few earlier writers are. Family book-cases may contain their neglected rows of English classics, but Dickens, George Eliot, Trollope, and Hardy are read, and the names of Carlyle, Ruskin, and John Stuart Mill still mean something to the man-in-the-street, especially in the north.

Victorian poetry has now lost most of its popular hold. The modern reader is usually unconscious of his allusions to Tennyson, but some of Tennyson's lines and phrases are still a convenient short-hand for the attitudes, 'spectres of the mind', 'pangs of nature', 'honest doubt', and 'larger hope', of the fairly recent past. Whatever the appearances, no poet quite took Wordsworth's place in the sympathies of educated Victorians, and Arnold spoke for all when, in 1850, he thus addressed the pale ghosts of the dead in their shadowy world:

> Wordsworth has gone from us – and ye,
> Ah, may ye feel his voice as we.
> He too upon a wintry clime
> Had fallen – on this iron time
> Of doubts, disputes, distractions, fears.
> He found us when the age had bound
> Our souls in its benumbing round;
> He spoke and loos'd our heart in tears.
> He laid us as we lay at birth
> On the cool flowery lap of earth;
> Smiles broke from us and we had ease.
> The hills were round us, and the breeze
> Went o'er the sun-lit fields again:
> Our foreheads felt the wind and rain.
> Our youth return'd: for there was shed
> On spirits that had long been dead,
> Spirits dried up and closely-furl'd,
> The freshness of the early world.

Even the developments in poetry since 1918 have not entirely undermined this sort of attitude, inadequate as it is, to Wordsworth, whose verse continues to speak to us with a piercing immediacy unlike that of any other nineteenth-century poetry. The processes initiated in the Romantic Age have certainly not yet worked themselves out. It is probable that in time the titles 'Romantic' and 'Victorian' will be dropped and the whole of the nineteenth and twentieth centuries come to be described as a single epoch, manifesting one special effort and tendency.

The Victorian period now appears a time when the large middle-class public was engaged in trying to adjust itself to, and catch up with, that special 'growth of the mind' recorded by Romantic poets. It is not easy to decide how much territory was won or lost by Victorian writers. Their preoccupation with evolution and the

intense pessimism – or optimism – associated with it now seems to date and parochialize their work, whereas much Romantic poetry retains its universality undiminished. Though Wordsworth wrote well before Chambers, Lyell, and Darwin, the kind of disturbance and extreme moral effort in his poetry is a keener and more vigorous response to the modern demythologized world than what we have in any Victorian poet. The author of *The Leechgatherer* or *The Story of Margaret* is much more our contemporary, in those poems, than the authors of *In Memoriam*, of *Christmas Eve and Easter Day*, or *Empedocles on Etna*. The works of twentieth-century writers such as Conrad, Yeats, Lawrence, Forster, and Eliot have to be understood as attempts to go beyond Tennyson, or Browning, or George Eliot, and to carry a stage further the great debates about human existence initiated by the Romantic poets. Writers are worth taking seriously because, and in so far as, they collaborate in this exploration, and their work in words has an importance which the other 'arts' cannot have. Because the Victorians are so close to us in time, and because the situation which they faced is recognizably part of the modern situation, we have to make extra efforts to see them objectively.

Not so long ago, the Victorian period was considered one of literary decline, derivativeness, and disintegration, its literature was heavily penalized for its sentimentality and sanctimoniousness, it seemed a period of cultural provinciality. Now it is being acclaimed, in some quarters, as a time of great achievement in literature, even as the greatest in English literary history. This 'whirligig of taste' is very confusing even to those with leisure and inclination to work out their own judgements of value. If, however, we look carefully at the rediscoveries and reappraisals we find much with which to check the general reader's scepticism about critical objectivity. Variations of emphasis there must be so long as a literature continues to matter to a large number of people, but criticism must always work for agreements about what is fine, about those works which give substance and meaning to all the qualitative words in the language. We find some rediscoveries are of such authors as George Eliot or Disraeli or Leslie Stephen, who never before received detailed attention and who needed to be made to count more distinctly. Then there are those writers such as Tennyson, Browning, Thackeray, Meredith, Mrs Humphry Ward and others who, after much acclaim

during their lifetime, went out of favour some generations ago, and are now ready for the normal process of reconsideration. There are also the resuscitations which are the result of publishing opportunism; perhaps the lapse of copyright has something to do with these.

The thoughtful reader of Victorian literature remembers its weaknesses as well as its unusual achievements. Conspicuous amongst the weaknesses is the fact, on which critics are agreed, that the age produced no unquestionably major poet, but only a number of technically accomplished poets who look major but remain essentially minor. This is perhaps the clearest indication of some deficiency in the creative work of the period. Where so much poetry was written and read, it is puzzling that there should be so little that is comparable with Blake's *Songs of Experience*, Wordsworth's *The Prelude*, Crabbe's *Tales in Verse*, or Byron's *Vision of Judgement.* It is as if the act of composition in Victorian poetry did not take place as a result of pressures within the minds of individual poets, but had its origin in more general impressions and aims. To turn to the Victorians after studying the great Romantics is to experience a lessening of tension, a blurring of focus. We are rarely in doubt as to the particular distress or joy which inspires Romantic poetry; much Victorian poetry depends for its effect on impressiveness of manner and tone, and expresses a melancholy which appears endemic rather than personal. The tone and manner are often those of the pulpit. It is as well to stress these differences as it is possible to describe the whole of the nineteenth century in terms of Romanticism. The later poets, it is true, derive from the earlier, but after the first Reform Bill changes took place which subtly altered the creative situation and ethos. The middle classes came under the rugged tutorship of Carlyle: moral sternness, in the Age of the Chartists, became more important than moral speculation, clarity, or absoluteness. The ground was being prepared for Bagehot and the Age of Compromise.

When we stress 'derivativeness' in poetry, we do not imply that it is therefore without distinction and interest, but we certainly imply a limitation. Arnold's *The Scholar Gipsy* is a delightful and memorable work, but it is disturbing to notice how much the poem depends on the stronger movement of Keats's Odes, especially of the *Ode to Autumn*.

For most, I know, thou lov'st retired ground.
Thee, at the ferry, Oxford riders blithe,
Returning home on summer nights, have met
Crossing the stripling Thames at Bab-lock-hithe,
Trailing in the cool stream thy fingers wet,
   As the slow punt swings round:
And leaning backwards in a pensive dream,
And fostering in thy lap a heap of flowers
Pluck'd in shy fields and distant Wychwood bowers,
And thine eyes resting on the moonlit stream.

This is an unconscious dependence of one poet on the voice of another, and it draws attention also to the less vivid, rather faded language of Arnold's poem in comparison with Keats's. We are justified in describing this verse as 'derivative'. Little Victorian poetry is free from this sort of indebtedness – to the movement, the vocabulary, the excitement and the attitudes of Romantic poetry. For reasons ultimately moral, Victorian poets tended to avoid the directness of the greatest Romantic poetry, its effort to achieve a fresh perception of the world and of the powers of the mind, and to awaken wonder. They were attracted to its pastoral and less serious qualities. Words-worth's 'power' is acknowledged, diminished however, to the quality of feeling in the lines:

He laid us as we lay at birth
On the cool flowery lap of earth.

That Victorian poetry should have assimilated the Romantics, excluding the indigestibly satirical Byron, to a convention of Victorian pastoralism, must be ascribed to the influence of Tennyson and the tastes of the middle-class public, though these two influences would be hard to separate. At first, the association of this rather decorative, second-hand, 'romantic' vocabulary with the lofty, earnest, weighty themes of much Victorian poetry appears incongruous. But once we have understood the Victorian middle class, with its liking for sermons, its suspicion of wit and of all but the broadest humour, its tendency to mistake sententiousness for seriousness, then the oddity becomes intelligible, like Victorian Gothic, though it does not disappear. The total impression is of the prevalence of restricted notions of the function of poetry, and indeed of language. Arnold's distinction between the poetry of Dryden and Pope and

'genuine poetry' – 'their poetry is conceived and composed in their wits, genuine poetry is conceived and composed in the soul' – neatly exemplifies the kind of theoretical and moral limitation which explains, at least in part, the deficiencies of Victorian poetry. That a critic as gifted as Arnold should have been content to make this witless 'soul' the well-spring of poetry, suggests a general contemporary inadequacy in manners and poetic theory. We have to do, in fact, with a Romanticism not only derivative but popularized and conventionalized. Where the 'wits' or intelligence were felt to be hostile to poetry, the range of permissible moods and subjects was sharply curtailed, whilst vague emotionalism and impressiveness could enjoy the prestige of significant and profound experience.

Though critical opinion of Victorian poetry has not changed much, it would be true to say that the period, despite its cultural dislocation, is no longer considered simply one of cultural mediocrity and impoverishment. How could a period which, in addition to its scientific advances, produced, for example, Grote's *History of Greece*, J. S. Mill's *Logic*, Darwin's *The Origin of Species*, F. H. Bradley's *Ethical Studies* and *Appearance and Reality*, Frazer's *The Golden Bough*, be described as obviously provincial? Yet provinciality and decline are certainly part of our impression of the age, and it is only when we look beyond literature, which is all we can survey in these pages, at the large amount of historic, scientific, and philosophic work accomplished in the period, that we realize how much larger the field of cultural activity had become and how much new ground was cultivated by the Victorians. Even so, the account does not add up to a great literary period. More appropriate is the sort of assessment which Arnold implied in 'The Function of Criticism at the Present Time' (1865) where he distinguished between 'epochs of concentration' such as the age of Burke and 'epochs of expansion':

But epochs of concentration cannot well endure for ever; epochs of expansion, in the due course of things, follow them. Such an epoch of expansion seems to be opening in this country. In the first place all danger of a hostile forcible pressure of foreign ideas upon our practice has long disappeared; like the traveller in the fable, therefore, we begin to wear our cloak a little more loosely. Then, with a long peace, the ideas of Europe steal gradually and amicably in, and mingle, though in infinitesimally small quantities at a time, with our notions. Then, too, in spite of all that is said about the

absorbing and brutalizing influence of our passionate material progress, it seems to me indisputable that this progress is likely, though not certain, to lead in the end to an apparition of intellectual life ... I grant it is mainly the privilege of faith, at present, to discern this end to our railways, our business, and our fortune-making; but we shall see if, here as elsewhere, faith is not in the end the true prophet.

It is this predominant impression of 'expansion' which accounts for much of the loose talk of 'greatness'. The number of really fine poems, novels, and plays is small, whether we judge by the standard of achievement in earlier centuries or whether we bring to mind the scope of poetry and prose in France during the same period. What we are coming more and more to realize is the very large amount of interesting, miscellaneous reading-matter that was produced by the Victorians, in the form of biography and autobiography, history, criticism, books of travel and for children, and periodical journalism. If it is not great, it is often distinguished, useful, or entertaining, and justifies a good deal of the enthusiasm and partiality nowadays shown to things Victorian. But our partiality cannot alter the unsatisfactory and nugatory quality of so much Victorian poetry, its lack of variety and power. It cannot disguise the absolute decline of the drama, or the moral confusion of writers in the period known as 'the Nineties'. The early Victorians derived a sense of purpose from their communal attempt to improve 'the condition of England', or to face the challenge of science, or to mitigate fanaticism. By the end of the century writers felt that the middle-class values which they had helped to establish were intolerably 'Philistine', complacent, and inimical to 'Art'. There was scope here for the serious satirist, but apart from Samuel Butler, who has his limitations, little important satiric writing was produced. Instead we find various kinds of anti-Victorianism, some of it intelligent, much of it only wittily impudent or shocking. Walter Pater exemplifies both the intelligence and the muddle of anti-Victorian aestheticism.

Perhaps the readiest way to distinguish the peculiar bewilderment of writers at that time is to turn to Oscar Wilde's novel *The Picture of Dorian Gray* (1891). The story is a morality depicting the corruption of a beautiful young man by friends and doctrines recommending the importance of 'aesthetic' experience as an end in itself; the

term 'aesthetic' is here given its vulgarest meaning of sensual indulgence and moral indifference.

The worship of the senses has often, and with much justice, been decried, men feeling a natural instinct of terror about passions and sensations that seem stronger than themselves, and that they are conscious of sharing with the less highly organized forms of existence. But it appeared to Dorian Gray that the true nature of the senses had never been understood, and that they had remained savage and animal merely because the world had sought to starve them into submission or to kill them by pain, instead of aiming at making them elements of a new spirituality, of which a fine instinct for beauty was to be the dominant characteristic. As he looked back upon men moving through History, he was haunted by a feeling of loss. So much had been surrendered! and to such little purpose! There had been mad wilful rejections, monstrous forms of self-torture and self-denial, whose origin was fear, and whose result was a degradation infinitely more terrible than that fancied degradation from which, in their ignorance, they had sought to escape. Nature, in her wonderful irony, driving out the anchorite to feed with the wild animals of the desert and giving the hermit the beasts of the field as his companions. Yes: there was to be a new Hedonism that was to recreate life, and to save it from that harsh, uncomely puritanism that is having, in our own day, its curious revival ... Its aim, indeed, was to be experience itself, and not the fruits of experience, sweet or bitter as they might be. Of the asceticism that deadens the senses, as of the vulgar profligacy that dulls them, it was to know nothing. But it was to teach man to concentrate himself upon the moments of a life that is itself but a moment.

This was an obvious reference to the conclusion of Pater's *The Renaissance* (1873):

'Not the fruit of experience, but experience itself, is the end. A counted number of pulses only is given to us of a variegated, dramatic life. How may we see in them all that is to be seen in them by the finest senses? ... To burn always with this hard, gemlike flame, to maintain this ecstasy, is success in life.'

Pater's attempt to follow the French Parnassians would not appear so mistaken had he written as a poet, not as a critic and an Oxford don. But he deserved better than to be used in this way by his former pupil Wilde, whose book, for all its characteristic readableness and wit, is an example of how to make the most of both worlds. Like any Victorian melodramatist, he loads Dorian Gray with crimes, and, borrowing the shrill cry of 'Hedonist!' from the Philistine pulpit, he draws the moral of the dangers of living for 'pleasure'

very luridly indeed. Lionel Johnson's thrilled acclamation of the
book was expressed in medieval Latin:

> Hic sunt poma Sodomorum;
> Hic sunt corda vitiorum;
> > Et peccata dulcia.
> In excelsis et infernis,
> Tibi sit, qui tanta cernis,
> > Gloriarum gloria.

Wilde's anti-Victorianism is in fact only Philistinism turned inside
out; it retains the same primitive dualism. No deeper understanding
of the scope and function of the arts is implied, none of the moral
working of the imagination. His novels, like his equally witty plays,
assume the attention of a watchful, shockable middle class. He has
left a permanent confusion about 'art for art's sake'. Certainly the
'aestheticism' of Wilde, Lionel Johnson, and Ernest Dowson exemplifies decadence, but the morals to be drawn are not as simple as may
at first appear. One can sympathize with the poets of the nineties
for wanting to make a gesture of independence from, and resistance
to, the pressures of the age. But they were confused by their own
anti-Victorianism, and suffered from a disabling misunderstanding
of apparently similar, though essentially very different, literary
movements in France. Their inability to supply the sort of verse
which 'the age demanded', and which W. E. Henley and Kipling
could produce to order, appears rather creditable. It is not clear,
however, that the heroics of

> Last night, ah yesternight, betwixt her lips and mine
> There fell thy shadow, Cynara! thy breath was shed
> Upon my soul between the kisses and the wine;
> And I was desolate and sick of an old passion,
> > Yea, I was desolate and bowed my head:
> I have been faithful to thee Cynara! in my fashion.
> > (Ernest Dowson)

are at all preferable to those of

> They call you proud and hard,
> > England, my England:
> You with worlds to watch and ward,
> > England, my own!
> You whose mail'd hand keeps the keys

Of such teeming destinies,
You could know nor dread nor ease
Were the Song on your bugles blown,
  England,
Round the Pit on your bugles blown!
(W. E. Henley)

The nineties were not, as they are sometimes made to appear, a discrete phenomenon in an age of cultural greatness. Through Swinburne there runs a palpable connection with the Pre-Raphaelites, especially D. G. Rossetti. A Rossetti altar-piece, with its staring, thick-necked women and its thick-lipped men and garish colours, involuntarily brings to mind that enormously influential analysis of aesthetic religiosity, Pater's *Marius the Epicurean* (1885), which Yeats thought 'the only great prose in modern English'. We cannot separate completely those elements in the Victorian period known as the Oxford Movement, Pre-Raphaelitism, the Ritualist Movement, and the nineties. They stand for something unsatisfactory about the inner life of the period. Yeats wrote: '"Life", said Lionel Johnson, "must be a ritual" ... Some turned Catholic – that too was a tradition.' In poetry and in painting, Pre-Raphaelitism was differently interpreted by each member of the changing Pre-Raphaelite group, but Rossetti's heightening of the more static, sensual, and colourful elements of Keats's medievalism lingers like a transfiguring vapour in the literary atmosphere of the second half of the century.

One of the influences which was implicitly repudiated in poetry and in painting by the 'classicism' of the nineteen-twenties, was the ethos which had its origin in *The Blessed Damozel*, first published in *The Germ* in 1850 and later revised. The modern reaction was rather over-equipped with ideology. Much of the pontificating about tradition, politics, dogma, and the number of children a woman should be allowed to bear now seems gratuitous, though some of it may have been necessary in order to clear away the last vapours of Aestheticism and give definition to living. Thomas Hardy succeeded in writing a number of fine poems without needing to erect any theoretical scaffolding. He evolved a sensitive verse style by sheer genuineness of character, a native incorruptibility. This is not of course to see Hardy as the contemporary or equal of Yeats, Lawrence, and Eliot; his success suggests that the weakness of

Victorian poetry was not the want of authority and dogma but the lack of defining experience. Hardy, G. M. Hopkins, Emily Brontë, and, perhaps, Christina Rossetti are the poets who consistently find their inspiration, not in 'the spirit of the age' but in the stress of personal experience. In Yeats we can follow the entire process of self-extrication from Aestheticism and 'Celtic Twilight' to defining experience, and the main reason for his development was that Yeats began to have strong convictions and real experiences, and was determined to make poetry out of them.

The Victorians, especially the men, tended to be overburdened with opinions and ideas – about revelation, evolution, determinism, nature, and other large public themes. Mill's *Autobiography* records one form of this mental imprisonment. Clough's early poetry records another:

> How often sit I, poring o'er
>   My strange distorted youth
> Seeking in vain, in all my store
>   One feeling based on truth; ...
> Excitements come, and act and speech
>   Flow freely forth; – but no
> Nor they nor aught beside can reach
>   The buried world below.

And Arnold fears the effect of modern life on the Scholar Gipsy:

> But fly our paths, our feverish contact fly!
>   For strong the infection of our mental strife,
>   Which, though it gives no bliss, yet spoils for rest;
>   And we should win thee from thy own fair life,
>   Like us distracted and like us unblest.
>   Soon, soon thy cheer would die,
>   Thy hopes grow timorous, and unfix'd thy powers,
>   And thy clear aims be cross and shifting made:
>   And then thy glad perennial youth would fade,
>   Fade, and grow old at last, and die like ours.

Even when they analysed their consciousness fairly thoroughly, as Tennyson, Arnold, and Clough appear to have done, the result was the same – the predominance of a contagious discomfort of opinions and general ideas. T. S. Eliot once wrote of the late Victorian Henry James: 'James's critical genius comes out most tellingly in his mastery over, his baffling escape from, Ideas, a mastery and an escape which

are perhaps the last test of a superior intelligence.' Few Victorian writers reveal this kind of mastery.

The novelists were more free, mainly because their aims were more limited and allowed a pragmatic approach. They did not need to feel that they had to solve the mystery of life or come to terms with history before they could put pen to paper. There was an obvious demand for their work, for entertainment and edification. There were tasks to be done, causes to be championed. 'In all my writings,' Dickens wrote in the preface to *Martin Chuzzlewit*, 'I hope I have taken every available opportunity of showing the want of sanitary improvements in the neglected dwellings of the poor.' The age demanded reassuring patriarchs and matriarchs, and writers vied with preachers and statesmen in providing this reassurance. Women novelists, who had played a considerable part in the evolution of the eighteenth-century novel, now found more abundant opportunities. We must be grateful that a succession of women novelists, beginning with Fanny Burney and Jane Austen, recorded their deep feminine acceptance of, and involvement in, life, before its special social conditions disappeared in the changes and emancipations of the latter part of the century. The novelists of the nineteenth century, by multiplying the number of objects to be enjoyed and appreciated by the imagination, immeasurably strengthened the Victorians' hold on life. In the province of the novel, though there are discriminations to be made, one may justifiably speak of major achievements and of a creative period. The novel, like the Elizabethan drama, served a popular need; in this case, for influences which would soften and make intelligible the harsh conditions of Victorian life. George Eliot's testimony is representative:

> The only effect I ardently long to produce by my writings is that those who read them should be better able to imagine and to feel the pains and the joys of those who differ from themselves in everything but the broad fact of being struggling, erring human creatures ... My artistic bent is directed not at all to the presentation of eminently irreproachable characters, but to the presentation of mixed human beings in such a way as to call forth tolerant judgement, pity and sympathy.

Only the influence of Dickens is comparable with that of the women novelists in deciding the special qualities of the English novel.

They helped to give it a bias away from the intellectual comedy of moral paradox which we find in Fielding, and towards a more profound portrayal of the variety and pathos of common experience. By the end of the eighteenth century the novel had begun to be a considerable influence on the moral perceptiveness of the reading public, exemplifying, as no ethical treatise could do and as no other form of literature since the Elizabethan drama had done, the reality of the feelings and moral issues involved in given situations.

Not that we are to imagine any antagonism between what we have in George Eliot and what we have in Fielding. When she writes in *The Mill on the Floss*, 'The man of maxims is the popular representative of the minds that are guided in their moral judgements solely by general rules', George Eliot expresses a sentiment very dear to the author of *Tom Jones*. But the mid-Victorian ethos is worlds away from the mid-Augustan. Though Fielding had a virile directness in his dealings with 'low life', he was not much interested in common people *as persons*. He could not have written: 'Moral judgements must remain false and hollow, unless they are checked and enlightened by a perpetual reference to the special circumstances that mark the individual lot' (*Mill on the Floss*) – still less could he have acted on that declaration. Between Fielding and George Eliot came Methodism, Evangelicalism, and Wordsworth, after whom everything was different. 'He spoke and loos'd our heart in tears.' The Victorian novel helped to people the imagination, to exercise the moral sympathies and strengthen the feeling of human solidarity at a time of disruptive social change. The growth of a considerate, unhysterical, liberal, and responsible humanism in the course of the century was certainly helped by the work of the novelists. At its best the novel presented, with wonderful inwardness, different kinds of moral possibility and the actuality of choice; it formed an extension of consciousness, and gave life to life.

More precise explanations of the disparity of achievement between the novel and poetry cannot be given beyond those already suggested. In the thirties all explanations used to be more or less Marxist. Victorian poetry was said to have remained minor because it ignored 'society'. But Tennyson, Browning, and Arnold were only too conscious of social demands and opinions, and Yeats carries conviction when, in his tentative apology for Aestheticism, he writes:

The revolt against Victorianism meant to the young poet a revolt against irrelevant descriptions of nature, the scientific and moral discursiveness of *In Memoriam* – 'When he should have been broken-hearted,' said Verlaine, 'he had many reminiscences' – the political eloquence of Swinburne, the psychological curiosity of Browning, and the poetical diction of everybody.

The literary changes about the time of the First World War were not the result of a changed relation between poets and society, but of a sudden focusing and concentration of experience in a number of poets. This concentration was partly a reaction to the war itself and to tensions in Ireland. But it was also a crisis in *American* experience, a crisis of personal alienation so absolute that it summed up all the vague discontent of the Victorians, and distanced it. If we set aside the Americans and Yeats, or try to scale these poets down to some narrowly preconceived 'English' tradition, as some anthologists do, then what remains is a rather minor sort of poetry.

This fact lends itself to different interpretations, which will only be resolved by the next major poetry to be written in English. Summarily it can be said that the status of the English language changed in the course of the nineteenth century. And this was a rather unexpected result of Arnold's 'age of expansion'.

The Poetry

The transition from Romanticism to Victorianism was not an elusive process. Keats died, Shelley died, Byron died, and they had no successors able or willing to sustain the high Romantic view of the function of poetry, none with a comparable force of convictions and prejudices. Wordsworth lived on, but his poetry had changed so much in aim and quality, that it exemplifies all the stages of the poetic transition. There are many different ways of describing this qualitative change in Wordsworth. Though there were intervals of deeper inspiration, his later work is much more public and rhetorical than his earlier poetry. It is addressed to 'others' and *assumes* a right to be heard. Yeats's remark, 'We make out of the quarrel with others, rhetoric, but of the quarrel with ourselves, poetry', applies to the difference between the later and the earlier poetry of Wordsworth. In his more rhetorical sonnets and odes, Wordsworth falls back into that lower class of literary activity, the conventional. He ends his *Ode to Enterprise* (1822) with the lines:

But thou, O Goddess! in thy favourite Isle
(Freedom's impregnable redoubt,
The wide earth's storehouse fenced about
With breakers roaring to the gales
That stretch a thousand thousand sails)
Quicken the slothful, and exalt the vile! –
Thy impulse is the life of Fame;
Glad Hope would almost cease to be
If torn from thy society;
And Love, when worthiest of his name,
Is proud to walk the earth with thee!

This sort of verse, already Victorian, is by no means more interesting than what we have in such contemporaries of the transition as Darley or Beddoes. The stanza quoted is still largely made up of eighteenth-century apparatus, the invocations, the personifications, the rather haggard Pindaric manner, the echoes of Milton and Shakespeare. It is extremely poetic, in a professional sort of way, which Wordsworth never is when his mind is deeply engaged. For many readers, the intrinsic interest of this kind of verse is absolutely nil, and there is a great deal of it not only in the secondary writers but in the main poets of the nineteenth century. It is true, of course, that 'what can be said as well in prose can be said better in prose'; it is part of the singularity of the Victorians that they had an unusual tolerance in this matter. The public, bardic manner of the Wordsworth stanza survives in many later poets, though some, like Browning, Christina Rossetti, and Hopkins, endeavour to escape it. Eliot had this manner in mind when he wrote that Ezra Pound's epigrams and translations

represent a rebellion against the romantic tradition which insists that a poet should be continuously inspired, which allows the poet to present bad verse as poetry, but denies him the right to make good verse unless it can also pass as great poetry.

This grand manner was a hindrance to minor talent, and an example of bad convention, which the later Wordsworth helped to prolong.

Literary history concentrates on the major poets, rightly of course, for other muses and the masterpieces of other tongues also have their claims upon us. Actually poetry develops on two levels, the level of major creation and the level of conventional, sociable verse-making. Critics would be much more generous to Tennyson, and would give

more ungrudging praise to his fluency and dignity, if they could see him, not as a failed Romantic, but as a diffident poet who, by technical conscientiousness, raised what was essentially matter for conventional or minor verse to the level of important creation. As a public or social poet, Tennyson is much more impressive than Wordsworth, who aimed chiefly for volume in his rhetorical poems, whereas Tennyson tried hard to satisfy the average Victorian taste for polished verbal programme music. This attention to technical effects has given some grounds for considering him an anti-Romantic or 'classical' writer, but there is more to classicism than polish. Tennyson's verse may have some qualities in common with *Alexander's Feast* or *Windsor Forest*; it has none with *Absalom and Achitophel* and the *Moral Epistles*. The implication, too, that the Romantic poets were not interested in 'technique' is obviously absurd.

Interesting claims have been made at various times in favour of Darley's lyric gifts, of Beddoes's treatment of the theme of Death in blank verse which recalls the later Elizabethan drama, and of Hood's serious and comic verse. Hood had a talent for vigorous versification, which served him well when he was writing his popular ballad, *The Dream of Eugene Aram*, or his powerful lament for the sweated labour of the shirtmakers, but in his more 'serious' verse he is rarely able to free himself from general reminiscences of the Romantics. His sonnet *Silence*, which is considered one of his best pieces, is no exception. It begins:

> There is a silence where hath been no sound,
> There is a silence where no sound may be,
> In the cold grave – under the deep, deep sea,
> Or in wide desert where no life is found,
> Which hath been mute, and still must sleep profound.

This brings echoes of Childe Harold's wish 'that the desert were my dwelling-place', which continues:

> There is a pleasure in the pathless woods,
> There is a rapture on the lonely shore,
> There is society, where none intrudes
> By the deep Sea, and music in its roar.

Compared with Hood, Byron appears original, but even he is half-remembering better lines by Wordsworth. Neither Darley's *Nepenthe*

nor Beddoes's *Death's Jest Book* offers a strong contrast to this general second-handness. It is refreshing to turn to John Clare (1793–1864), the Northamptonshire peasant, in whose work originality of observation and description are helped by an essentially eighteenth-century background of reading. He is of his time and not, like Crabbe, of whom he reminds us, a late Augustan. There are only two or three poets in the nineteenth century who express their delight in things seen with so little distortion and so much trust in the poetic effectiveness of visual impressions. One of his *Summer Images* is of a frog:

> I love at early morn, from new-mown swath,
>   To see the startled frog his route pursue,
> To mark while, leaping o'er the dripping path,
>   His bright sides scatter dew.

He watches the nesting thrush:

> I watched her secret toils from day to day –
> How true she warped the moss to form a nest,
> And modelled it within with wood and clay;
> And by and by, like heath-bells gilt with dew,
> There lay her shining eggs, as bright as flowers,
> Ink-spotted-over, shells of greeny blue.

There is a more sombre level of experience in Clare's poetry, which is well represented by the poem *I Am*. Clare is one of the poets whose status has been greatly improved by recent criticism, and he compares favourably with his better-known contemporaries. He remains, however, a minor poet, and his case is one of only partial victory over circumstances.

Tennyson's first verses appeared several years before the beginning of Victoria's reign, and some of his most characteristic poems are in these early volumes of 1830 and 1833. In the first volume the poem *Mariana* is strongly indebted to earlier writers, especially to Keats; it illustrates perfectly Tennyson's affinities with minor derivative verse and his immense superiority to it – to what we have in Hood, for example. If his inspiration is often literary it is nevertheless the literary experience of a man very sensitive to language and to the need for unity and completeness of impression. In the *Supposed Confessions of a Second-Rate Sensitive Mind Not in Unity with Itself* from the same volume, Tennyson is already working at that theme of inner division which is central to all his later poetry:

How sweet to have a common faith!
To hold a common scorn of death!
And at a burial to hear
The creaking cords which wound and eat
Into my human heart, whene'er
Earth goes to earth, with grief, not fear,
With hopeful grief, were passing sweet!

The realistic force of the fourth line breaks up and complicates the impression of self-pitying conventionality. This happens frequently in Tennyson, most impressively in *In Memoriam* (1850):

He is not here; but far away
The noise of life begins again,
And ghastly thro' the drizzling rain
On the bald street breaks the blank day.

To read *In Memoriam* is still a moving experience. Though the hundred and thirty sections do not make a satisfactory long poem, they maintain a consistent interest which at times rises into poignancy. The particular death is the beginning of a series of meditations on mortality, the pessimistic implications of evolutionary theories, and ways of escaping from that pessimism. If there had been even a touch of Platonism in Tennyson's outlook, he would not have written quite so gloomily, and his cheerfulness might have been less like his gloom. The poem is not at all metaphysical in quality. It is an unconscious tribute to the predominance of natural science over poetry in the nineteenth century. Tennyson's meditations lead him to hopes for the evolution of a higher mankind, 'a closer link betwixt us and the crowning race'.

No longer half-akin to brute,
For all we thought and loved and did,
And hoped and suffer'd, is but seed
Of what in them is flower and fruit;

Whereof the man, that with me trod
This planet, was a noble type
Appearing ere the times were ripe,
That friend of mine who lives in God,

That God, which ever lives and loves,
One God, one law, one element,
And one far-off divine event,
To which the whole creation moves.

This is quite the opposite of what we have in, say, *The Winter's Tale*, *The Vanity of Human Wishes*, *Tintern Abbey*, or *Four Quartets*, all of which very different poems hint at the possibility of transcending the human condition by accepting and understanding its limitations more completely. Tennyson appears a diffident, pious Utopian, even, in some of his poems such as *Locksley Hall*, a forerunner of H. G. Wells. The great beauty of much of *In Memoriam* cannot disguise the triteness of its argument, in relation to which both its pessimism and its optimism appear excessive. Basil Willey has made an interesting claim that *In Memoriam* implies 'a recognition that faith is not a matter of rational demonstration ... and that its acceptance means an act of the will: a plunge, a venture, or what is now sometimes called "an existential choice"'. It could hardly be claimed, however, that the choice takes place in the poetry. To many admirers of *In Memoriam*, the poem is no more 'existential' that *Onward, Christian soldiers*.

Tennyson is at his best when his technical delicacy, his descriptive power and his intense feelings of regret, failure, and frustration can all play their part; such poems are *Ulysses*, *The Lotos Eaters*, *Morte d'Arthur*, *Break, Break, Break*, and *Tears, Idle Tears*. The story of Tithonus, to whom the gods granted immortality but not eternal youth, is dramatized in a monologue of slow power and beauty, which transforms the ageing lover into a symbol applicable not only to Tennyson but to poets generally in the history-conscious Victorian age.

> The woods decay, the woods decay and fall,
> The vapours weep their burthen to the ground,
> Man comes and tills the field and lies beneath,
> And after many a summer dies the swan.
> Me only cruel immortality
> Consumes: I wither slowly in thine arms,
> Here at the quiet limit of the world,
> A white-hair'd shadow roaming like a dream.

By his ability to sound and intensify these stately chords, Tennyson will keep his place in the affection of readers. These lines are not like Elizabethan or Miltonic blank verse, but a highly personal stylization in which the astringency of Virgil and the later Keats hold in check Tennyson's habitual descriptive diffuseness. Tennyson achieves large effects without the strenuousness of Dryden, with

whom he is sometimes compared. His sadness and noble resignation corresponded with a social reality, the intense frustration which underlay Victorian accumulation and power. Frequently the reader is aware of a certain meagreness and repetitive immobility in Tennyson's words and images, but he submits to the poet's manner and rhythmic insistence as to a familiar hymn or anthem, and there is no room for irony.

Tennyson, like Wordsworth, had a great following, not only as a poet but as a philosopher and teacher. Robert Browning (1812–89) aimed much more openly to appeal to the contemporary taste for moral casuistry, which was of course also one aim of the novel. This is quite a good reason for writing verse, as any seventeenth-century anthology would show. But for seventeenth-century poets the task was easier and more definite. The 'soul' was still a distinct theological term, and not a mere synonym for feeling. It is because the task of writing 'religious' poetry in an unmetaphysical age is so difficult that the *Four Quartets* is the sort of poem that it is, scarcely risking any assertion of dogma or doctrine, but making clearer an attitude of mind and direction of will, with more consciousness of years of failure than of moments of 'happiness' or 'meaning'. Tennyson, Arnold, and Clough seem to have been aware of what was lacking, but they could not go beyond regret and wistfulness, and perhaps they were too close to Wordsworth. Nor was anyone, poet or critic, at all clear about the sort of intellectual resistance a modern 'religious poem' would have to overcome until the *Four Quartets* had been written. That is possibly why it has been said of this poem that 'It seems to be the equivalent in poetry of a philosophical work – to do by strictly poetical means the business of an epistemological and metaphysical inquiry' (F. R. Leavis). Perhaps even Gerard Manley Hopkins, finely gifted and dedicated as he was, only shelved the difficulty when he went to school to Duns Scotus. This may be what T. S. Eliot had in mind when he described Hopkins, at first sight rather surprisingly, as 'a nature poet' and as 'not a religious poet in the more important sense'. But this judgement has only become entirely intelligible since the *Four Quartets* were written. Hopkins is certainly not a twentieth-century poet, though he has had a twentieth-century influence.

Browning, though he claimed to be mainly interested in 'the

incidents in the development of a soul', never came near to envisaging difficulties and lack of qualifications. He is too often content with a verse equivalent of the modern newspaper 'profile'. This has been the crux of discussion of him since his own day. Writing in 1864, Bagehot reduced Browning's psychological investigations to 'a suspicion of beauty and a taste for ugly reality', and he made Browning the occasion for reflections on living in a 'realm of the *half* educated. A dressy literature, an exaggerated literature seem to be fated to us.' In what is still a standard work, *Browning as a Philosopher and a Religious Teacher* (1891), Sir Henry Jones wrote that after his analysis, Browning's 'optimism was found to have no better foundation than personal conviction, which anyone was free to deny, and which the poet could in no wise prove'. This is not, however, a critical objection. The philosophic 'proof' in Wordsworth is only loosely connected with the essential poetry; the poetry is what it is. If there is to be a significant optimism in poetry, it should convince the reader that it has been paid for. There are few poems – *Two in the Campagna* is an example – which diminish the arbitrariness of the relation between Browning and the reader by establishing a ground of respect. He is usually in disguise. His manner and idiom are colloquial, after Bagehot we might say grotesquely colloquial, and we rarely catch the poet's ordinary speaking voice.

Browning is enjoyable, with fewest reservations, when he is not making claims as a psychologist or teacher. The lines everyone knows, *Home Thoughts from Abroad*, are obviously the work of a strong original talent, and remain thrilling despite their familiarity. Browning is almost alone amongst Victorian poets in his ability to express such immediate happiness and simple passion. With his positive nature, high spirits, and instinctive rejection of contagious pessimism and literary half-lights, Browning should have written poetry which altered and improved the literary climate. Instead he prematurely levelled off the explorations begun in *Pauline* and *Paracelsus*, and specialized in the ventriloquism of dramatic monologue which appealed to average tastes or, as Bagehot suggested, to 'the realm of the half-educated'. He is a kind of Victorian Hemingway. Once, as he lay in the sea – he tells us in *Amphibian* (1872) – he saw above him a marvellously delicate butterfly, 'like soul and nought beside', and he asked:

What if a certain soul
   Which early slipped its sheath,
And has for its home the whole
   Of heaven, thus look beneath,

Thus watch one who, in the world,
   Both lives and likes life's way,
Nor wishes the wings unfurled
   That sleep in the worm, they say?

But sometimes when the weather
   Is blue, and warm waves tempt
To free oneself of tether,
   And try a life exempt

From worldly noise and dust,
   In the sphere which overbrims
With passion and thought – why, just
   Unable to fly, one swims!

Emancipate through passion
   And thought, with sea for sky,
We substitute, in a fashion,
   For heaven – poetry:

Which sea, to all intent,
   Gives flesh such noon-disport
As a finer element
   Affords the spirit-sort.

Whatever they are, we seem:
   Imagine the thing they know;
All deeds they do, we dream:
   Can heaven be else but so?

This is charming but entirely self-satisfied. Browning has few doubts
about the sea of 'passion' and 'thought' in his monologues and
dramas. If one can accept the implicit ventriloquial complacency,
and the ambiguity – the wrong kind – arising from the absence of
any internal evaluation, then one should derive pleasure from Bishop
Blougram. But the metaphysical poems such as *Rabbi ben Ezra*, *Abt
Vogler*, and *The Grammarian's Funeral* tend nowadays to be valued
only as inspissated Victorianism – one can cut them with a knife.
Of Browning's love poems, one of the finest is *Two in the Campagna*,

which records, very delicately, a dissatisfaction in loving. This is the
Browning that Thomas Hardy, and other poets, could learn from.

> The champaign with its endless fleece
>   Of feathery grasses everywhere!
> Silence and passion, joy and peace,
>   An everlasting wash of air —
> Rome's ghost since her decease.
>
> Such life here, through such length of hours,
>   Such miracles performed in play,
> Such primal naked forms of flowers,
>   Such letting nature have her way
> While heaven looks from its towers!
>
> I would I could adopt your will,
>   See with your eyes, and set my heart
> Beating to yours, and drink my fill
>   At your soul's springs, — your part my part
> In life, for good or ill.
>
> No. I yearn upward, touch you close,
>   Then stand away. I kiss your cheek,
> Catch your soul's warmth, — I pluck the rose
>   And love it more than tongue can speak —
> Then the good minute goes.
>
> Just when I seemed about to learn!
>   Where is the thread now? Off again!
> The old trick! Only I discern —
>   Infinite passion, and the pain
> Of finite hearts that yearn.

Mrs Browning's novel in verse, *Aurora Leigh* (1856), which was
once popular despite its length, is no longer read, but her *Sonnets
from the Portuguese* (1847–50) are still esteemed by anthologists. They
are indeed album verses, and reveal here and there, despite the
Shakespearian verbiage, a little of her warm, playful nature. Her
translations and introductions in 'The Greek Christian Poets' were a
labour of love. Translation, when it aims at more than literalness,
requires a combination of learning and inspiration, the original must
strike some vein in the translator so that he experiences some of the
satisfaction of original creation. This happened in Fitzgerald's version

79

of *The Rubáiyát of Omar Khayyám* (1859–68), which reads like the testament of a mid-Victorian Persian.

> Ah Love! could thou and I with Fate conspire
> To grasp this sorry Scheme of Things entire,
>   Would we not shatter it to bits – and then,
> Re-mould it nearer to the Heart's Desire!

Browning's was one kind of anti-Victorianism, Fitzgerald's pleasantly desperate hedonism was another, Pre-Raphaelitism was a third, Aestheticism was a fourth. There were others.

The two important new voices of the eighteen-fifties were those of Arnold (1822–88) and Clough (1819–61), and to these one could perhaps add in a brief survey those of Coventry Patmore (1823–96) and William Barnes (1801–86). Arnold is the most distinguished of these poets, though his own conviction that his poetry possessed intellectual qualities that would lead later generations to prefer it to Tennyson's and Browning's now appears too sanguine. Arnold's is a companionable poetry, especially for rather lonely natures, and his charm never offends even when he allows himself a series of vocatives and expletives. Arnold expresses, more acceptably than any other poet, the half-humorous, half-apologetic stoicism of an academic type of mind in the period. His was very much a literary sensibility, which never gives us the flash and surprise of lines of Wordsworth or Keats or Browning, but in him, as in Thomas Gray, there is always just enough thought and feeling to transform commonplaces into poetry. He is never grim for long, and that, one feels, is rather to his credit. At the end of World War II several books about him were published and he became suddenly topical. His *Dover Beach* seemed to express the predetermined divisions and disillusionment of the peace, which only enhanced the reality of love and faithfulness. Arnold is a spectator in his poetry, though very much a participant in his prose.

Clough's poetry has the same sort of appeal as Arnold's, as was to be expected from the similarity of their careers at Rugby and Oxford. He too might have exclaimed:

> For rigorous teachers seized my youth
> And purged its faith and trimm'd its fire.

Clough has never had Arnold's popularity, except in *Say not the struggle nought availeth* – a favourite bit of mock-heroic, last-ditch rhetoric with dons and statesmen – and *The Latest Decalogue*; perhaps because, as Arnold implies in *Thyrsis*, there was some wilfulness in his unhappiness. He was inclined to blame Carlyle, and told Emerson in 1848, 'Carlyle led us out into the desert and he has left us there'. Clough brings to mind Stendhal's delightful reply to the charge of flippancy made against him by the *Edinburgh Review* which Stendhal so much admired. 'I have frequently broken a lance for the English. Yet I continue to find in all the English I have met a secret *principle of unhappiness* . . . The English are made unhappy by small misfortunes . . . What is the reason for this? A great problem. Religion, perhaps.' Clough's work is not by any means entirely sombre: much is humorous and faintly satirical. This is the case with the *Amours de Voyage* (1858) which, when one has become used to the imitation hexameters, proves to be an amusing series of love-letters recounting an English love-story in an Italian setting. Claude, the lover, half-hearted about love as about the struggles of the Italian patriots and about religion, is fated to bring about an unhappy ending. He is a precursor of Prufrock and Mr Silvero. Even when we take *Dipsychus* (1862) and *The Bothie* (1848) into account, Clough appears a less considerable poet than Arnold.

One of the characteristics of nineteenth-century poetry is a fondness for highly personal philosophizing in monologue. Presumably Wordsworth's influence had something to do with it – *The Prelude* appeared at last in 1850. Patmore's verse, lacking narrative interest and variety, typifies this philosophizing bent. Meredith has the same purpose in view in his quite large poetic output, and there were comparable transcendentalist manifestations in America. Robert Bridges's *The Testament of Beauty* (1929) is a late example. Such philosophizing verse led to a certain amount of experimentation with irregular lengths of line and distribution of stresses, but, like the novels in verse, these philosophizing poems are not thought nowadays the most compelling of reading-matter.

However, larger claims have been made for Patmore as a Catholic poet and interpreter of married love. This higher estimate co-exists with the earlier one, according to which Patmore was a poet who once enjoyed enormous popularity with his long-winded

celebrations of happy domesticity, who reveals a vaguely 'mystical' attitude to his wives and who married three times. The opinion of G. M. Hopkins has something to do with this improvement in Patmore's standing: 'Your poems are a good deed done for the Catholic Church and another for England, for the British Empire, which now trembles in the balance held in the hand of unwisdom'. Of the two long poems which are the basis of Patmore's reputation, *The Angel in the House* (1854–6) and *The Unknown Eros* (1877), the first is more readily enjoyed, despite its frequent reminiscences of the style of Martin Tupper's *Proverbial Philosophy* (1838). It celebrates Patmore's first courtship and marriage in octosyllabic quatrains in stanzas of irregular length. At its best the verse, which has little pressure behind it, pleases by its clarity of phrasing which reminds one now of Clare, now of Herrick; also by its occasional clumsiness which, like the clumsiness in Barnes or Hardy, seems a guarantee of integrity. Patmore was a mixture of innocence and sophistication. The second poem is much more ambitious. It is a series of forty-two irregular Odes which amplify the attitude expressed in some lines of the twelfth Canto of the earlier poem, about the 'married lover':

> Why, having won her, do I woo?
>   Because her spirit's vestal grace
> Provokes me always to pursue,
>   But, spirit-like, eludes embrace.

Patmore's attitude to the body and to love has prompted comparisons between him and 'the metaphysicals'. He is certainly sincere in his exalted and ideal uxoriousness, and his attitude of mind is not a literary pose. Some of the odes have a thin, eloquent beauty, but there are many passages of laboured argument, political bombast, and faded symbolism. Strangely, Hopkins appears to have approved of Patmore's rather unintelligent politics. Patmore scorns the mob who

> Brag of their full-blown rights and liberties,
> Nor once surmise
> When each man gets his due the Nation dies,

and he regrets the country's past:

> When, strong and single, in thy sovereign heart,
> The thrones of thinking, hearing, sight,

> The cunning hand, the knotted thew,
> Of lesser powers that heave and hew,
> And each the smallest beneficial part,
> And merest pore of breathing, beat,
> Full and complete,
> The great pulse of thy generous might,
> Equal in inequality.

This 'nostalgic' attitude to the past was the main inspiration of a contemporary much admired by Patmore, the Dorset poet William Barnes (1801–86), and it played a considerable part in the work of Thomas Hardy, another of Barnes's admirers. Barnes, the son of a Dorset farmer, went to Cambridge at the age of thirty-six, and became a village schoolmaster and later a clergyman. His *Poems of Rural Life in the Dorset Dialect* (1844), *Hwomely Rhymes* (1859), and *Poems of Rural Life in Common English* (1868), reveal, in their carefully reproduced 'dialect', all the passion of the genuine folklorist, and at their best they have the anonymous poignancy of ballads or of some of Hardy's verses. Sometimes we are not quite certain whether the effect is intrinsic to the poems or whether it is the charm of any rustic burr. Some of the effectiveness disappears when the spelling is normalized, but by no means all of it. Here is a stanza from a distinctly successful poem, entitled *Tokens*:

> Green mwold on zummer bars do show
> That they've a-dripp'd in winter wet;
> The hoof-worn ring o' groun' below
> The tree, do tell o' storms or het;
> The trees in rank along a ledge
> Do show where woonce did bloom a hedge;
> An' where the vurrow-marks do stripe
> The down, the wheat woonce rustled ripe.
> Each mark ov things a-gone vrom view –
> To eyezight's woone, to soulzight two.

The borrowed hedonism of Fitzgerald, the mystical love-making of Patmore, the lush idealism of Rossetti's paintings and of much of his poetry, the verbal eroticism of Swinburne and of the writers of the Yellow Book period, these are all, in their different ways, the reverse side of Victorian 'puritanism' and strictness. What the age lacked and the modern world, though thoroughly emancipated, lacks also, was an inclusive convention and symbolism which would

give the unhouseled human body some kind of status, something better than hostility, secrecy, and fear, or than clinical and hedonist 'functionalism'. The lack touches the very centre of morals in ways that were explored by D. H. Lawrence. But the Victorian poets could not get beyond a rather stereotyped dualism of Nature versus Morality, taking sides in affirming or denying life.

The contrast in much Victorian poetry between the importance of the ostensible subject and the picturesqueness of the intrinsic treatment was mentioned earlier. Pre-Raphaelitism, which is a much more important movement in painting than in literature, did not prove to be an exception. It began as an attempt by artists to break with the classical tradition of Reynolds and 'feeble reminiscences of old masters' (F. G. Stephens in *The Germ*, 1850), and to give art a social purpose by close observation of nature, 'by a firm attachment to truth in every point of representation', and by producing the visual equivalents of parables. 'The earlier painters came nearer to fact.' The movement was deeply influenced in all its phases by Ruskin's intensely moral interpretation of nature and of art, by his conviction of the close dependence of the condition of art on the condition of society, and by his idealization, following Carlyle, of the Middle Ages as a time when, through the craft guilds, the moral influence of art was at its strongest. This ideological medievalism made Keats a primary source of inspiration to the Pre-Raphaelites when they wrote poetry, whilst Tennyson, Malory, Chaucer, and Dante were secondary sources. Pre-Raphaelitism is closely associated with the Oxford Movement – were not the Gothic cathedrals, with their stained-glass windows, the work of pious craftsmen? Coleridge and Scott were other influences and helped to give the movement a slightly atavistic or even nationalist tendency, which is certainly implicit in Gothic architecture. In short, Pre-Raphaelitism was a complex moral phenomenon and not simply a coterie activity. But the importance of Pre-Raphaelitism, even when Yeats's claim that it was the equivalent of French Symbolism is considered, is not predominantly literary. Morris (1834–96) survives more in his prose than in his long narrative poems, though *The Haystack in the Floods* from the volume *The Defence of Guinevere* (1858) has a certain power, and the stories of *The Earthly Paradise* (1868–70) are very readable. He appears to have approached the task of composing verses in the

same craftsmanlike frame of mind that he brought to his other activities, but in his 'Apology' to *The Earthly Paradise* he described himself as 'The idle singer of an empty day', and he does not entirely disarm criticism when he frankly writes:

> Dreamer of dreams, born out of my due time,
> Why should I strive to set the crooked straight?
> Let it suffice me that my murmuring rhyme
> Beats with light wing against the ivory gate,
> Telling a tale not too importunate
> To those who in the sleepy region stay,
> Lulled by the singer of an empty day.

D. G. Rossetti (1828–82) survives by the distinctive atmosphere of a handful of poems and sonnets which remain in the memory long after Morris's long poems have been forgotten, but Christina Rossetti (1830–94) is in some ways a more interesting and considerable poet than either. Christina continues to attract the modern reader by the general simplicity and delicacy of her language, rather than by her Pre-Raphaelitism which in her is chiefly a matter of Keatsian and Italian influences. She is one of the few minor poets of the period who avoid the grand manner. Both by her simplicity and by the circumstances of her life she bears a resemblance to her American contemporary Emily Dickinson (1830–86), and there is a similarity, too, in the narrowly missed failure or success of many of her poems. But her modest attempts to write, not like Shakespeare but like the seventeenth-century Anglican poet George Herbert, reveal deficiencies, especially of 'wit', commonly found in modern imitators of that poet. Herbert could assume in his readers a lively interest in doctrine and an unconscious Christian 'sensibility'. Doctrine and sensibility in the nineteenth century were a very different matter. Christina achieved her most popular success in imitations of ballads with a suggestion of allegory, such as *Goblin Market* and *The Prince's Progress*, which began as a dirge 'Too late for love, too late for joy'. Some of her poems of religious acceptance can be read as bitterly ironic comments on life – for example, *Uphill*. This ambiguousness of effect disturbs but also rather oddly deepens her work. Her *Poems for Children* contain too much talk of death and transience to be useful in the nursery. But a poem like *Spring Quiet*, which is one of her *Juvenilia*, appeals to the child as

to the adult. The introductory note to the sonnet sequence *Monna Innominata* invites a contrast between the sadness of that work and the happiness of *Sonnets from the Portuguese*. A more interesting experience informs Christina's poems, though the interest may again be that of ambiguity:

> Time flies, hope flags, life plies a wearied wing;
> Death following hard on life gains ground apace;
> Faith runs with each and rears an eager face,
> Outruns the rest, makes light of everything,
> Spurns earth, and still finds breath to pray and sing;
> While love ahead of all uplifts his praise,
> Still asks for grace and still gives thanks for grace,
> Content with all day brings and night will bring.
> Life wanes; and when love folds his wings above
> Tired hope, and less we feel his conscious pulse,
> Let us go fall asleep, dear friend, in peace:
> A little while, and age and sorrow cease;
> A little while, and life reborn annuls
> Loss and decay and death, and all is love.
>
> (*Monna Innominata*, 10)

The last three words cannot transform the pessimistic resignation of the rest of the poem, which gives them a sardonic rather than the intended affirmative force. One of her finest poems is *The Three Stages* (1848–54). It is too explicit, but it is very distinguished, especially the first section:

> Alas, thou foolish one! alike unfit
>   For healthy joy and salutary pain:
> Thou knowest the chase useless, and again
>   Turnest to follow it.

Though Pater (1839–94) was, in the main, inventing when he compared the 'ideal' effect of D. G. Rossetti's 'material imagery' with that of Dante's descriptions, his comments are of use in understanding Rossetti and the real philosophic gifts and unchecked dilettantism of Pater. 'And yet, again as with Dante,' Pater writes in *Appreciations* (1889),

to speak of his ideal type of beauty as material is partly misleading. Spirit and matter, indeed, have been for the most part opposed, with a false contrast or antagonism by schoolmen, whose artificial creation those abstractions really are. In our actual concrete experience the two strains of phenomena which the words *matter* and *spirit* do but roughly distinguish play inextricably

86

into each other. Practically, the Church of the Middle Ages, by its aesthetic worship, its sacramentalism, its real faith in the resurrection of the flesh, had set itself against that Manichean opposition of spirit and matter and its results in men's way of taking life.

This shows historical insight and philosophical suppleness. Yet Pater's perceptiveness about 'matter' and 'spirit' did not heighten his feeling for the real, the 'concrete experience', but only intensified his withdrawal, his self-regarding ideality which made him read so much into Rossetti's 'pious sensuality', as the *Quarterly Review* described it. In fairness to Pater, one must add that when one looks for writers in the Victorian period or in the twentieth century who have produced work which powerfully attempts to resolve or transcend Pater's intellectual hesitations, themselves representative of so much in Victorian and modern literature, one can be sure only of D. H. Lawrence. Lawrence's novels actually show how 'matter' and 'spirit', 'nature' and 'morality', 'play inextricably into each other', with the overwhelming effect of redeeming life. Yeats does not get beyond a recognition of the difficulty. Eliot has consistently taken such a poor view of physical life that it is difficult to see what remains to be sanctified and enhanced by religion. His crucial and very moving lines in the *Dry Salvages* reduce the Incarnation to something faintly Wordsworthian.

One other important writer, Swinburne (1837–1909), is normally associated with Pre-Raphaelite influence, though he makes it still more difficult to point to anything in the writings of the Pre-Raphaelites which is as distinctive in style as the paintings of Ford Madox Brown or William Holman Hunt. From the first, in poetry and in painting, the Keatsean medievalism and idealization of Rossetti tended to clash with the emphasis on 'nature' and 'truth' as understood by other Pre-Raphaelites. In time this divergence in Rossetti favoured an attitude of withdrawal from the world, of art for art's sake. In Rossetti himself this tendency is unavowed and unconscious as it is in other Victorians, but Swinburne makes it part of an attitude to life.

> I am tired of tears and laughter,
>   And men that laugh and weep;
> Of what may come hereafter
>   For men that sow to reap:

> I am weary of days and hours,
> Blown buds of barren flowers,
> Desires and dreams and powers
> And everything but sleep.

This is not, however, a dream-like stanza, nor is *The Garden of Proserpine* as sleep-inducing as much other Victorian poetry. There is some vitality in its impudent rejection, and the dance of the heavy stresses keeps attention awake. It is effective verse, but the effect is not one of sincerity, for sincerity would have imposed a much closer relationship between 'sense' and movement, as in *Tears, idle tears*. Swinburne's outlook resembles that of immaturity which is not sure how seriously it means what it says. But neither insincerity nor immaturity is a satisfactory description. T. S. Eliot suggests 'morbidity of language', which sounds more analytic but is no more exact. It has been shown that Swinburne used a greater variety of metres and stanzas than any other poet of the nineteenth century; yet the experience of reading many of Swinburne's poems in many different stanzas and metres is strangely repetitive.

As a rule one can assume, though not without caution, that a modern writer's admiration of Greek and Latin poets would have an astringent or 'classical' effect on his own poetry, even if the astringency should be as superficial as in much academic verse. Swinburne's love of Sophocles, Aristophanes, and Catullus only increased his Romantic diffuseness and seemed to give him a repertory of metrical variations much beyond his command of experience. Pindar had had the same kind of effect on some earlier English poets, and the untranslatable choruses of Greek drama fascinated Swinburne. He is also extremely unlike Baudelaire, whose *Les Fleurs du Mal* he admired, and whose death, though the news was false, he lamented prematurely in *Ave atque Vale* (1867). Baudelaire's sonnet *La Géante*, whatever its private background, is a strongly evocative and humorous fancy. Swinburne reduces it to something very personal to himself in the sixth stanza of his elegy, which is impressive in Swinburne's fluent way.

> Now all strange hours and all strange loves are over,
> Dreams and desires and sombre songs and sweet,
> Hast thou found place at the great knees and feet
> Of some pale Titan-woman like a lover,

Such as thy vision here solicited,
Under the shadow of her fair vast head,
The deep division of prodigious breasts,
The solemn slope of mighty limbs asleep;
The weight of awful tresses that still keep
The savour and shade of old-world pine-forests
Where the wet hill-winds weep?

Swinburne reduces all his admirations, of classical writers, of Villon and Hugo and Gautier and Baudelaire, of Elizabethan dramatists and Milton and Shelley, to the essentially minor mode of post-Tennysonian poetry. To blame Baudelaire or even the Marquis de Sade, as Theodore Watts-Dunton, his guardian after 1879, might have done, would be pointless. His weaknesses were a matter of pathology, and at the same time inseparable from other characteristics of Victorian poetry. There was nothing in Swinburne's own life or in the ethos of mid-Victorian poetry to counteract or turn to profit the influences of other literature. What was there in Tennyson, Browning, Rossetti, Fitzgerald, Arnold, Clough, or Morris to work a radical change in Swinburne's verse or to suggest the possibility of different aims for poetry? Some remarks by Lawrence, 'if we have tact and can use them', about puritanism and the arts are more useful in discussing Swinburne than some accounts which see in him only a stage in an inevitable 'failure of Romanticism':

To the Restoration dramatists sex is, on the whole, a dirty business, but they more or less glory in the dirt. Fielding tries in vain to defend the Old Adam. Richardson with his calico purity and his underclothing excitements sweeps all before him. Swift goes mad with sex and excrement revulsion. Sterne flings a bit of the same excrement humorously around. And physical consciousness gives a last song in Burns, then is dead. Wordsworth, Keats, Shelley, the Brontës, all are post-mortem poets. The essential instinctive-intuitive body is dead, and worshipped in death – all very unhealthy. Till Swinburne and Oscar Wilde :ry to start a revival from the mental field. Swinburne's 'white thighs' are purely mental.

(*The Paintings of D. H. Lawrence*, 1929)

Since that was written the pathological quality of Swinburne's eroticism and love of pain has become even clearer, but Lawrence's comments remain more helpful and rational than critical attempts to present Swinburne and Wilde as the foredoomed result of a century of 'Romantic Individualism'. The analysis should go deeper. Though Victorian poetry appears static and repetitive after the

break-through of the first Romantics, we can see in its conventionality and anti-conventionality, its religiosity and irreligiosity, its responsibility and irresponsibility, its prudery and anti-prudery, the process of adaptation and intellectual suspense, of an important stage of English life. Swinburne was not the poet to break new ground, whatever the fervour he may have put into his love of liberty, his 'paganism', and his childish blasphemy. 'Glory to Man in the highest! for Man is the master of things.' Even so one can still enjoy the metrical virtuosity and generalized emotion of *Atalanta in Calydon* or *Hertha*; or the faint, delicate descriptiveness and regret of *A Forsaken Garden*, *A Vision of Spring in Winter*, *A Ballad of Dreamland*, *The Triumph of Time*, and other poems. Technically Swinburne's verse was a storehouse which supplied the poetasters of the generations down to the nineteen-twenties.

It was George Meredith (1828–1909) who discovered in Swinburne's verse the lack of 'an internal centre'. Meredith's own 'centre' represents one of the miscellaneous yea-saying attitudes in Victorian poetry. In him the affirmativeness is mainly rhetorical. These lines from *Ode to the Spirit of Earth in Autumn* (1862) are a fair example:

> Great Mother Nature! teach me, like thee,
> To kiss the season and shun regrets
>
> . . .
>
> In life, O keep me warm!
> For, what is human grief?
> And what do men desire?
> Teach me to feel myself the tree
>   And not the withered leaf.
> Fixed am I and await the dark to-be.
>   And O, green bounteous Earth!
> Bacchante Mother! stern to those
> Who live not in thy heart of mirth;
> Death shall I shrink from, loving thee?
> Into the breast that gives the rose
>   Shall I with shuddering fall?

This is a fairly simple type of cheerfulness dependent on a personification and the pathetic fallacy. The drawback of this kind of assertiveness is that it slights and throws away major areas of ordinary experience. It is no comfort to us to be told by Meredith, a few lines later:

Earth knows no desolation.
She smells regeneration
In the moist breath of decay.

The long series of sixteen-line sonnets, *Modern Love* (1862), used to be very popular, and advanced thinkers of an earlier day long preserved some of the excitement which the poem once aroused. It is a narrative, not at all easy to follow, of the breakdown of a marriage, and ends with the suicide of the wife. To the modern reader the poem appears neither subtle nor especially vivid, but as a story in verse it is at least shorter than some. A few lines from the sonnet *Sense and Spirit* may throw light on Meredith's standing as a philosophic poet. He maintained that the answer to man's loneliness is to think of the Earth as a considerate mother, much as Swinburne personified liberty as Mater Triumphalis:

> Till we conceive her living we go distraught,
> At best but circle-windsails of a mill.
> Seeing she lives, and of her joy of life
> Creatively has given us blood and breath
> For endless war and never wound unhealed,
> The gloomy Wherefore of our battlefield
> Solves in the Spirit, wrought of her through strife
> To read her own and trust her down to death.

This is interesting, not as poetry but as a typical example of the kind of debate which served as subject-matter for so much Victorian verse. Modern poets have learnt not to expect as many metaphysical supports as their predecessors, and they are usually more fastidious in their assertions or assumptions about the 'meaning' or 'meaninglessness' of 'nature' or 'the universe'. This makes a more favourable climate for poetry than the Victorian because astringency of thought is inseparable from astringency of language, and encourages implicitness rather than mere assertion.

If we place beside Meredith's some lines to *Mother Earth* written by Emily Brontë from her vantage point amongst the Haworth tombstones, we can feel the difference between her spontaneous, clearsighted personification and his philosophizing.

> Indeed no dazzling land above
> Can cheat thee of thy children's love.

We all in life's departing shine
Our last dear longings blend with thine;
And struggle still, and strive to trace
With clouded gaze, thy darling face,
We would not leave our native home
For *any* world beyond the tomb.
No – rather on thy kindly breast
Let us be laid in lasting rest,
Or waken but to share with thee
A mutual immortality.

Emily Brontë wrote some things which set her quite above the range of other Victorian poets. In one dramatic poem (*Stars*) she shrinks from the sun which drives away the stars and interrupts her dream.

Blood-red he rose, and arrow-straight
   His fierce beams struck my brow:
The soul of Nature sprang elate,
   But mine sank sad and low!

My lids closed down – yet through their veil
   I saw him blazing still;
And bathe in gold the misty dale
   And flash upon the hill.

I turned me to the pillow then
   To call back Night, and see
Your worlds of solemn light again
   Throb with my heart and me!

It would not do – the pillow glowed
   And glowed both roof and floor,
And birds sang loudly in the wood,
   And fresh winds shook the door.

Now that Robert Bridges's elaborate warnings against his modernity have ceased to matter, Hopkins (1844–89) is beginning to appear more of a Victorian. Still, it is difficult to see why Eliot should have stressed his similarity to Meredith. Even to eyes which find in Hopkins only a nature poet, the delicacy and power of his work, with everywhere the sign of sincere experience, should have presented a contrast to the more contrived lyricism of Meredith. Such poems as *Binsey Poplars*, *Felix Randal*, *The Caged Skylark* give the effect of speech with a sensitiveness which can scarcely be equalled

in Victorian poetry. The little homilies which are read into the 'inscape' are fairly simple, but the value is in the whole poem and implicitly in the 'instress' of the intensely vivid description. Occasionally, as in *The Windhover*, the poet appears to have had difficulty in drawing significance out of the marvellous opening description, and seems to stretch the meaning to a rhetorical pattern which has raised difficulties of interpretation. His religious poetry reveals an urgent personal distress which has led some critics to question the distinctly religious quality of the underlying experience. But from any point of view the last sonnets are impressive records of conflict and despair which exceed the narrow limits implied by 'nature poetry'.

After so much debate about 'beliefs' in Victorian verse it is refreshing to turn to this poet, who is not conscious of a middle-class audience and who uses poetry to define his own experience. We should have liked, it is true, more poetry occupying the middle ground between *The Wreck of the Deutschland* and *Carrion Comfort*. As it is, Hopkins's poetry gives an impression of fragmentariness and unresolved strain, as if important areas of experience and thought had been left out. He himself wrote, rather sardonically, after sending Bridges his fine sonnet lamenting his feelings of utter sterility:

> Sweet fire the sire of muse, my soul needs this;
> I want the one rapture of an inspiration.
> O then if in my lagging lines you miss
> The roll, the rise, the carol, the creation,
> My winter world, that scarcely breathes that bliss
> Now, yields you, with some sighs, our explanation.

There remains, however, a radical difference between these concentrated personal experiences and the generalized gloom of such a typically Victorian poem as *The City of Dreadful Night* (1880) of James Thomson (1834–82). This poem deserves its considerable fame, even perhaps the tribute paid to it by Edmund Blunden as 'the most anticipative poem of his [Thomson's] time'. One of the epigraphs to the poem is from the *Inferno*, but there the resemblance to the *Waste Land* ends. Early in the poem Thomson proclaims his unmitigated pessimism:

> If any cares for the weak words here written,
> It must be some one desolate, Fate-smitten,
> Whose faith and hope are dead, and who would die.

93

Despite this, there are some powerful, though lurid, Byronic stanzas in the poem, especially the description of melancholia with which the poem ends, and he achieves the same oppressive force in *To Our Ladies of Death* and *Insomnia*.

The most considerable poet between the time of Hopkins and the First World War is Hardy (1840–1928).* But in that time Yeats, compelled by the fascination of what is difficult, had been moving slowly towards 'the truth' of his later poetry.

> Through all the lying days of my youth
> I swayed my leaves and flowers in the sun;
> Now I may wither into the truth.
> (*The Coming of Wisdom with Time*)

To add the names here of poets such as Francis Thompson, Housman, and many others would be to imply an unintended and unattainable inclusiveness. Nor would their inclusion alter in any significant way the estimate of the scope and shape of Victorian poetic development which has been outlined.

The Novel

In 1873 an article in the *Quarterly Review* contrasted the state of English poetry at that time with the real moral and political commitment of Romantic poetry, and went on to ask the sort of question about the novel which was discussed in the introductory section of this survey:

But in the present day, when the foreign politics of England are expressed in the doctrine of non-intervention, when at home society itself acknowledges no standard but that of competition, it is hard for the individual to recognize any interests which are higher and wider than his own. In such a community the eager and imaginative mind is inclined to take refuge in its own ideas, and hence, perhaps, that ominous abstention from politics which is beginning to mark the professors of modern 'Culture' ... But the historian will understand the progress of events better than ourselves. He will have to determine why the most unromantic society that ever existed pleases itself with likening its own feelings to those of a Knight-errant ... Instead of the enthusiastic rhapsodies of Shelley, we have the splendid but meaningless music of Mr Swinburne, with his Herthas, his Hymns, his Litanies, and his Lamentations ... The authors of *Adam Bede* and *Martin Chuzzlewit* have not found the present a barren age.

* The poetry of Hardy and of Yeats is treated in the next volume of the *Guide*, *From James to Eliot*.

This lively article goes on to urge, with betraying emotion, the fertility of Victorian England in themes for great poetry, thus over-simplifying the relation between writers and society in a way now-adays associated with Marxism. The implicit assumption that the view of society to be found in Dickens and George Eliot was evidence of that society's cultural vitality was also unjustified. Though the novel was its dominant form of entertainment, the Victorian world did not produce a surfeit of masterpieces. In fact, when we look more closely at the works of the 'great novelists' and try to decide with what degree of consistency they maintain the high standards which they themselves set in their best writing, substantial qualifica-tions have to be made. Instead of a roomful of masterpieces, we are left with scarcely a shelf-full. No one need be surprised at this, for even Shakespeare has to be read selectively. If we keep in mind the standard which Jane Austen affirms – and there is no other – when she refers, in the famous passage in *Northanger Abbey*, to the novels of Fanny Burney and Maria Edgeworth as 'work in which the greatest powers of the mind are displayed, in which the most thorough knowledge of human nature, the happiest delineations of its varieties, the liveliest effusions of human wit and humour, are conveyed to the world in the best chosen language'; the same standard which the novelists George Gissing and E. M. Forster apply when they describe radical limitations as well as great powers in the work of Dickens; the standard which the novelist Henry James clarifies in his critical work, by far the most valuable criticism of the novel that has yet been written; the standard which the novelists D. H. Lawrence and Virginia Woolf maintain when they wittily 'place' the work of their contemporaries, H. G. Wells, Galsworthy, and Arnold Bennett; the standard which the conscientious reviewer of fiction in the more responsible Press tries desperately not to lose sight of as he distributes his praise or disparaise to each week's load of new novels – then, with this standard, affirmed by novelists themselves, in mind, we find that our first impression of an age of novelist giants has to be modified, and that we are brought to a clearer view of the special excellence of a few works by the great creative writers.

T. S. Eliot once wrote: 'But after all, how little, how very little, good poetry there is anyway.' Real greatness is not more common

amongst novelists, whatever the impression given by literary encyclopaedias. When we go beyond the handful of novelists who, whether 'great' or not, are obviously men and women of some genius who contribute something to the scope of the novel – Dickens, Thackeray, Charlotte and Emily Brontë, Mrs Gaskell, George Eliot, Trollope, Wilkie Collins, Meredith, and Hardy – we come to an array of novelists who are still readable and still read, who exhibit distinction and talent, and who have a claim to inclusion in full-scale histories of literature. Such writers are Bulwer-Lytton, Disraeli, Surtees, Charles Kingsley, George Gissing, Robert Louis Stevenson, 'Mark Rutherford', George Moore, Mary Ward – the list could be extended indefinitely, until we reach what might be called the sociological stratum, the material which is grist for the mill of the social historian, such as the best-selling novels of 'Ouida' and Marie Corelli. In short, to maintain the firm distinction between the handful of 'great' novels and the mounds of the talented, readable, amusing or historically interesting ones is the only means of ensuring that the 'powers of the mind' exhibited in them, in page after page, in chapter after chapter, and sometimes in volume after volume, are recognized for the fine things they are. Only the masterpieces really justify the amount of time spent in literary studies. The great Victorian critic, Leslie Stephen, wrote: 'I often think that the value of second-rate literature is not small, but simply zero.'

The later chapters in this volume offer the more detailed commentary which is the only means of establishing judgements of relative value. Here we can only point to some of the main developments in fiction during the period.

The main development was that described by Henry James in the eighties. He wrote:

Only a short time ago it might have been supposed that the English novel was not what the French call *discutable*. It had no air of having a theory, a conviction, a consciousness of itself behind it – of being the expression of an artistic faith, the result of choice and comparison. I do not say it was necessarily the worse for that: it would take more courage than I possess to intimate that the form of the novel, as Dickens and Thackeray (for instance) saw it, had any taint of incompleteness. It was, however, naïf ... During the period I have alluded to there was a comfortable, good-humoured feeling abroad that a novel was a novel, as a pudding is a pudding, and that this was the end of it. But within a year or two, for some reason or other, there

have been signs of returning animation – the era of discussion would appear to have been to a certain extent opened. (*Partial Portraits*, 1888)

James here feigns timidity regarding the novels of Dickens and Thackeray, but he is quite explicit in an uncollected piece of his, a review of *Middlemarch*, where he contrasts the popular English novel as 'a mere chain of episodes, broken into accidental lengths and unconscious of the influence of a plan' with the gradual development of the novel into 'an organized, moulded, balanced composition, gratifying the reader with a sense of design and construction'. He concludes this superb review by expressing his conviction that *Middlemarch* (1871–2) 'sets a limit we think to the old-fashioned English novel'.

What was gradually achieved in the nineteenth-century novel is analogous with what happened in the gradual evolution of Elizabethan drama, most conspicuously in Shakespeare's and Ben Jonson's work. A loose assemblage of episodes, lacking any strongly focused intention, gradually gave place to those powerful visions of human life which we have in, for example, *Macbeth* and *Volpone*. The most impressive Victorian example of such a continuous internal development is that of Dickens who began with episodic work, the *Sketches by Boz* and *The Pickwick Papers*, which were originally intended as mere supporting matter for a series of sporting illustrations to rival *Jorrock's Jaunts and Jollities* (1838), and achieved work, such as *Bleak House*, *Little Dorrit*, and *Hard Times*, much more concentrated in its aim and therefore much more intensely imagined and carried out – though perhaps never completely imagined and carried out. Whatever the reservations they make about Dickens, all critics agree that he had real experiences and extraordinary virtuosity of imagination which would have put a strain on any powers of organization.

This process of development towards novels requiring a total response and a complete moral resolution of imagined situations – comparable with what we have in *Coriolanus* or *King Lear* – was not confined to the nineteenth century. The rivalry between Richardson and Fielding in the previous century had been, amongst other things, a sign of the interaction of different types of moral and literary outlook, the one 'prudential' and 'sentimental', aiming at edification through literature by a strong appeal to feelings, especially of pathos;

the other more individualist and sophisticated, wittily using fiction as an intellectual exercise to demonstrate the superiority of healthy good nature over prudential theories and strict principles. The indirect influence of these two novelists, representing different layers of English culture, on the course of the English novel was great but incalculable, and it can be easily exaggerated. There were so many other agencies at work early in the nineteenth century. The work of the women novelists tended to bring sentiment and wit closer to each other, whilst the religious and secular idealism of the time favoured equally the expression of feeling and a freer play of intelligence, both sensibility and sense. What gave the Regency period and the two succeeding decades their peculiar quality of instability was the strength of these co-existing drives, one expressing a need for feeling, the other a need for its rational analysis and control. Its best-known manifestation is Byronism, and there is something similar in Scott, 'a contradiction between his romantic sympathies and sober judgement' (Herbert Grierson). Much of the interest of Lytton and Disraeli lies in this peculiar mixture of manners and the sense of a dissolving and uncertain social code. The Victorian emphasis on conformity and respectability suppressed without deeply reconciling these dual tendencies. Only in the best work of the Victorian novelists, where feeling and intelligence are equally engaged in an adequate subject-matter, is reconciliation achieved; elsewhere feeling tends frequently to be in excess of the presented occasion and to have an independent vitality. This happens at times in Charlotte Brontë, in George Eliot, and notoriously in Dickens, though the latter must often be assumed to have written with conscious exaggeration and virtuosity, like the actor he was.

Apart from the negative pressure of Victorian prudery about which Dickens, Thackeray, and, at a later date, Hardy complained, there was no social code with which the novelist's imagination could interact; the lapse of that eighteenth-century social code which was still valid in Crabbe and Jane Austen accounts in part for the impression of diffuseness and lack of tautness given by later literature. One result of the extension of the reading public by serial publication was to throw on to the novelist the entire responsibility for creating an appropriate writer-reader relationship. This was generally a disadvantage, but one could argue that, had a strong code of manners

existed, we should not have had *Wuthering Heights*, and Dickens would have been very different, lacking his magnificently unself-conscious mimicry, exaggeration, luridness, and melodrama, his unsophisticated mixture of laughter and tears. Scott's immense industry had come very near to mere exploitation of his popularity with the higher middle class, though he kept his formality even when he was pouring out such low-grade stuff as *Ivanhoe*; Dickens had even greater opportunities at a lower social level, and he exhausted himself in living up to his own popular legend. He had other powerful examples in the versatility of Bulwer-Lytton (1803–73), whose career as novelist and politician closely resembles Disraeli's, and in the sheer productivity of Scott's chief imitators, G. P. R. James (1799–1860) and W. H. Ainsworth (1805–82). Lytton has no claim to distinction beyond having written one of the best-selling historical novels of the century, *The Last Days of Pompeii* (1834), but the change in manner between his early, discursive novel of fashion, *Pelham or the Adventures of a Gentleman* (1828), and the domestic novel, *The Caxtons – A Family Picture* (1848), is tangible evidence of social change. His Advertisement to the 1848 edition of *Pelham* looks back, with characteristic rhetoric, at the intervening years:

> There is a far greater earnestness of purpose, a higher culture, more generous and genial views, amongst the young men of the rising generation than were common in the last ... Rank is more sensible of its responsibility, Property of its duties. Amongst the clergy of all sects the improvement in zeal, in education, in active care of their flocks, is strikingly noticeable: the middle class have become more instructed and refined ... Cheap books have come in vogue as a fashion during the last twenty years – books addressed, not as cheap books were once, to the passions, but to the understanding and the taste ... Mr Pelham studying Mills [*sic*] on Government and the Political Economists, was thought by some an incongruity in character at the day in which Mr Pelham first appeared – the truth of that conception is apparent now, at least to the observant.

Disraeli's novels are raised above Lytton's, not only by the interest of their social and political commentary, but by their constant surprises of irony and wit. As an extraordinary combination of romantic posturing and shrewdness, Disraeli (1804–81) deserves to rank with Byron. His unguarded racialism and myth-making must have been largely compulsive. Sidonia's grandiose Zionism now seems an unconscious and fascinating parody of the Coleridgeans, and as such

has its value. His novels exemplify the tendency of Victorians to use the novel to expound social theories and criticisms of society, though in the greater novelists the results amount to something more than is implied by the description 'novels of social criticism'; Dickens's *Little Dorrit* (1855-7) belongs to quite a different order of creation from Charles Reade's exposure of the prison system, *It is Never Too Late to Mend* (1856).

Like the Elizabethan drama, the Victorian novel could be sub-divided into novels about history, novels about crime (also known as 'sensation novels' and later as detective novels), novels of mystery of which Wilkie Collins is still the inimitable master, domestic novels, and one or two other categories. We have in fact all the variety of a popularly based genre – and all its possibilities as a field for mere commercial exploitation. Whereas the novel-reading public remained fairly homogeneous in taste and reading-power down to the time of George Eliot and Trollope (say, 1855-75), so that Dickens could show himself a keen admirer of George Eliot and she could return the compliment by trying to learn from him, thereafter a split into low, middle, and high-brow publics began to develop and has since widened. This stratification of the reading public had many causes, among them the increase in semi-literacy, which made it profitable to cater exclusively for the tastes of the minimally educated; the standardization of a middle-class type of mentality which is in many ways more of a cultural incubus than semi-literacy or only a disguised form of it – the Forsytes of Galsworthy and the Wilcoxes of Forster are examples; and the novelists' increasing awareness of the shortcomings of the English novel and their desire to make it a more thoroughly enjoyable, a more deeply exciting, serious, and significant form of art. When Henry James tried to express his sense of George Eliot's greatness, he declared that she even surpassed Fielding because 'Fielding was didactic – the author of *Middlemarch* is genuinely philosophic'. The development of the novel was towards a more inward or more 'philosophic' analysis of the implications of a situation and a more careful and 'poetic' rendering of experience. Henry James, Meredith, and Hardy represent this phase, which was also a time when novelists were conscious of Continental aims and standards in the novel. The

naturalist phase inspired by Zola is represented by George Moore, but more adequately by Arnold Bennett's best work.

It is true, of course, when we come to the question of seriousness in art, that Dickens took some pains to plan his instalments, to follow up hints for subjects contained in *The Times* leaders, that he worried a good deal about charges of exaggeration and formlessness, and that there is much evidence of his assiduousness in these matters. But extraneous information cannot affect the critical estimate of his work. There is a real difficulty in writing critically about Dickens. For all his ebullience, G. K. Chesterton, in his suggestive study of the novelist, is no less uneasy than the un-Dickensian E. M. Forster. Middleton Murry, in humorous vein, put his sense of the difficulty in this way:

Dickens is a baffling figure. There are moments when it seems that his chief purpose in writing was to put a spoke in the wheel of our literary aesthetics. We manage to include everybody but him ... Simple people ask why the books of a man who was not an artist should have this curious trick of immortality ... So we are beginning to discover that Dickens *was* an artist, but, of course, only in parts. When we have discovered which are the parts we shall breathe again.

There is no single study of Dickens which does the whole of this work of discrimination for the reader – it would need to be a very large book indeed. But it is no longer necessary to play at being baffled by Dickens, or to apologize for deciding that he is a genius without a masterpiece. His work deepened, he gained in power and concentration, especially from *Bleak House* to the unfinished *Mystery of Edwin Drood* (1852–70). There will always be readers who prefer their Dickens unconcentrated and stick to *Pickwick*. Today it is possible to say, without exaggeration or partiality, that in his best work Dickens comes close to Shakespeare and Ben Jonson.

Thackeray (1811–63) is in some ways better understood in relation to Lytton and Disraeli, both of whom he satirized, than to Dickens, for he had none of the latter's force of genius, and constantly aimed to suggest a man of the world's outlook and sophistication, to catch the tone of an observant amateur. He preferred to write, for a decade, under various *noms de plume* until his powers were concentrated in *Vanity Fair* (1847–8), in which he achieved an effect of social and

historical movement and panorama which are impressive despite some heavy moralizing and humour. The lively opening of the novel, and the title, promise a satire, but the pace is too leisurely for that. It is surprising how loose the texture of Thackeray's writing, the mental activity represented by his prose, usually is. He could be incisive, especially when he was drawing on his experience of rather rootless ex-nabobs and rather tawdry military and theatrical society. Indirectly, *Vanity Fair* gives an impression of the sprawling commercial and military involvements of Britain and of the dissolution of class structure. But his moral reference is scarcely that of a great novelist, and he is content with the task of demonstrating the comprehensiveness of a rather limited kind of worldly wisdom. His characteristic tone comes out strongly when he describes the reunion of Dobbin and Amelia:

> The bird has come in at last. There it is with its head on his shoulder, billing and cooing close up to his heart, with soft outstretched fluttering wings. This is what he has asked for every day and hour for eighteen years. This is what he pined for. Here it is – the summit, the end – the last page of the third volume. Good-bye, Colonel – God bless you, honest William! – Farewell, dear Amelia – Grow green again, tender little parasite, round the rugged old oak to which you cling!

Becky is so memorable because she completely suggests this dominant part of Thackeray's outlook. The character of Beatrix in *Henry Esmond* (1852) has some of the same vitality; she represents the type of woman who knows that her ambitions can only be satisfied by taking advantage of her beauty. The eighteenth-century social background has a certain interest, but the novel – which Trollope considered 'the greatest novel in the English language' – is not an exception to the general rule that historical novels reproduce the atmosphere of a museum. When the large amount of miscellaneous journalism is added to the four or five main novels, Thackeray appears a substantial writer, but he is decidedly not of the same order of genius as Fielding, Jane Austen, Scott, or Dickens.

If Thackeray is often given a higher place than he can fittingly occupy, Elizabeth Gaskell (1810–65) was until recently rather underrated, being regarded merely as a writer of social criticism in novel form, or at best as the author of *Cranford*. In fact, her career divides into two halves, one propagandist, the other more freely inventive.

In *Sylvia's Lovers* (1863), *Cousin Phillis* (1865), and *Wives and Daughters* (1866) she is able to use parts of her experience for which there had been little room in the Manchester novels. The latter have their interest and value, but one has only to set them beside *Oliver Twist* to feel at once the difference between Mrs Gaskell's vaguely 'philanthropic' – to use her own word – social propaganda and Dickens's fierce moral comedy. She is at her best in *Wives and Daughters*, which is one of the finest novels of the nineteenth century. It is true that the book reveals neither the confident intellectual range of *Middlemarch* (1871–2) nor quite the provincial richness of *The Mill on the Floss* (1860) or *The Scenes from Clerical Life* (1857). Nevertheless, it is a work of some size, written with great charm and completely free from those stylistic smirks and other symptoms of pretentiousness and uncertainty to be found in some of her contemporaries. Her Knutsford background had connected her with a social pattern in which Jane Austen's world survived. The story is essentially a contrast between different kinds of parental relationship and different kinds of child, and it is real enough to remind us in places of Henry James's *Washington Square* (1881) and of the unhappy marriage of Rosamund Vincy and Lydgate in *Middlemarch*. The book is more than a Thackerayan collection of characters; the consistent differentiation between examples of feminine mentality, especially in Molly Gibson, Mrs Gibson, and her daughter by her first marriage, Cynthia, becomes a varied and powerful moral analysis. The social and provincial setting is idealized without being faked, as it usually is in Dickens, Thackeray, and Meredith.

The work of the women novelists, Elizabeth Gaskell, Charlotte and Emily Brontë, and George Eliot, represents a considerable social deepening of the novel as a portrayal of English life, an increase in its capacity to analyse moral and emotional nuances; it also marks a closer relationship between the activity of novel-writing and the most serious and sincere convictions of writers. The novel in the hands of these four comes close, at times, to the subtle operation and power of poetry. This is most apparent in *Wuthering Heights* (1847) which, though it is not, perhaps, quite a mature work, involves the reader in a total response like that of poetic drama. In George Eliot (1819–80) there is a greater range of effect than in any of her contemporaries except Dickens.

In her childish days Maggie held this place, called the Red Deeps, in very great awe ... But now it had the charm for her which any broken ground, any mimic rock and ravine, have for eyes that rest habitually on the level – especially in summer, when she could sit on a grassy hollow under the shadow of a branching ash, stooping aslant from the steep above her, and listen to the hum of insects, like tiniest bells on the garment of Silence, or see the sunlight piercing the distant boughs, as if to chase and drive home the truant heavenly blue of the wild hyacinths.

This, which is so like Emily Brontë, is of course from *The Mill on the Floss*. Implicit in the description is a quality of feeling, of youth and freshness, which *gives* us the girl's experience where earlier novelists would only have told us about it or not attempted to present it at all. This delicacy of control over language is, of course, but another aspect of the strong intelligence, the large, sane, adventurous consciousness apparent in all George Eliot's work. She was in touch with the intellectual life of her time as no other novelist was. This makes her a profoundly representative figure, like Wordsworth of his period, and Milton of his.

The main inheritors from George Eliot were Thomas Hardy (1840–1928) and Henry James (1843–1916), both of whom began in the seventies. James was much the more apt pupil who could, with ease, assimilate what seem the most incompatible influences, from Jane Austen and Dickens to Flaubert, Turgenev, Balzac, and Hawthorne. He watched George Eliot's development with a clear, full awareness of her significance and superiority. Though James will be more fully discussed in Volume 7 of this *Guide*, it is important that he should be seen as belonging to the third quarter of the nineteenth century, and as deeply indebted to, if not rooted in, the English novel. It is true that he needs a larger context of history, as Conrad does but Hardy does not, and he will not fit into a narrow view of English tradition and experience. But after Lawrence and E. M. Forster there is no need to take a narrow view, for these writers are certainly not provincial in relation to James, or Conrad, or Joyce. They are all writing about different aspects of a recognizable 'modern situation' and cannot be explained in terms of insular or Victorian preoccupations and attitudes. Moreover, an adequate account of George Eliot would not leave the final emphasis on her 'provinciality'.

The extraordinarily even temper of Trollope's (1815–82) novels, which made them such companionable volumes during the war, also accounts for their steady popularity. They are exactly the sort of novel one would expect to find after reading his admirable *Autobiography*. There were events in Trollope's life which might easily have turned another man into a rebel. At Harrow the headmaster 'was in the habit of flogging me constantly'. At Winchester, his elder brother Adolphus, 'as a part of his daily exercise, thrashed me with a big stick'. Trollope was convinced that he had been 'flogged oftener than any human being alive'. He describes the poorly paid drudgery of his wonderful mother Frances Trollope, who began writing at fifty and in the next twenty-six years produced a hundred and fourteen volumes. 'She was at her table at four in the morning, and had finished her work before the world had begun to be aroused ... Of all people I have known she was the most joyous, or, at any rate, the most capable of joy.' From his mother he derived his journeyman's view of the novelist's task. Henry James, in what is still the most generous and most balanced of estimates, wrote: 'As an artist he never took himself seriously.' The Barsetshire novels are the most fertile and enjoyable of his books, though high but not very persuasive claims have been made for some of the others, notably *The Way We Live Now* (1875). Trollope, who described himself as 'an advanced conservative liberal', had unexciting political views resembling those of Bagehot but not nearly as wittily expressed. On the other hand, his understanding of the old High and Dry Anglican tradition represented by Archdeacon Grantly, and of the new clerical type Mr Slope, is lively and historically important. The Barsetshire series retain their popularity partly because the social pattern they reveal has by no means entirely disappeared.

Meredith (1828–1900) never had the broad-based popularity of Trollope, and there are too many objections to his mannerism, his style, his poetic descriptions, his anti-sentimentalism, and his philosophy for his novels to become very acceptable again, even to the restricted public that once idolized him. The radical criticism which a rehabilitation of Meredith would have to answer is the one of 'unconscious insincerity' made by his friend Henry James in conversation with Edith Wharton:

Meredith was a sentimental rhetorician, whose natural indolence or con-
genital insufficiency, or both, made him, in life as in his art, shirk every
climax, dodge around it, and veil its absence in a fog of eloquence. Of course,
neither I nor any other reader could make out what Meredith's tales were
about; and not only what they were about, but even in what country and
what century they were situated, all these prosaic details being hopelessly
befogged by the famous poetic imagery.   (*A Backward Glance*, 1934)

Meredith's philosophic evolutionism now appears as a stage in late-
Victorian 'emancipation' and 'progress'. He would have been pleased,
and would probably have felt no uneasiness, to be described as a
'highbrow'. He writes in *Diana of the Crossways* (1885): 'Be wary
of the disrelish of brainstuff', to justify both his style and his suspicion
of the 'unfailing aboriginal democratic old monster that waits to
pull us down'. Of all his books, *The Egoist* (1879) appears to have
the best chance of survival, if not as a classic, at least as a development
in the novel. It has a promising theme, the gradual education of an
egoist and a study of his relationships with other people. Whether
the intention was completely carried out may be disputed, but the
novel gives an impression of psychological subtlety and verbal
brilliance. Complexity of style ought to be the sign of complexity
of meaning and significance; the belief that style is an end in itself
soon leads to boredom, as anything does that lacks moral spontaneity.
One reads Meredith for the recurrent passages of directness and
descriptive evocativeness, which deserve study – for example, the
scene in *Evan Harrington* (1860) in which Evan finds that he lacks
the money to pay for the coach taking him to his father's funeral.
The embarrassment of the young man, and the surly, changeable
temper of the coachman are very well drawn. But in this novel,
too, the crises are only pointed at or evaded. It is hardly necessary
to compare Meredith with James in order to reveal the limitations
of his work. His best novels appear less substantial than, for example,
George Gissing's *New Grub Street* (1891) or Samuel Butler's *The Way
of All Flesh* (1903), both of which have the force of personal
experience and moral indignation behind them. Meredith's poetic
descriptions achieve a certain impressionist effectiveness; they seem,
however, contrived or artificial in comparison with the unforced
richness of Richard Jefferies's *Amaryllis at the Fair* (1887).

Jefferies (1848–87) sometimes brings Cobbett's vigour to mind,

as in his descriptions of Jearje, the labourer, at his meals; sometimes Lawrence, as in the description of the young squire Raleigh Pamment who,

in spite of indulgence, kept a good, healthy, country colour. His neck was very thick, tree-like ... The Pamments were simply Englishmen, and liable to be born big, with broad faces, thick necks, and ultimate livers. It was no disgrace to Raleigh, that jolly neck of his.

And occasionally the prose suggests the unstrained, implicit symbolism of T. F. Powys, as in the description of Miss Iden's lavender, which gave a little sweetness to the poverty-stricken farm.

There is nothing else that smells so sweet and clean and dry. You cannot imagine a damp sheet smelling of lavender. Iden liked Mrs Iden to like lavender because his mother had been so fond of it, and all the sixteen carved oak-presses which had been so familiar to him in boyhood were full of a thick atmosphere of the plant. Long since, while yet the honeymoon bouquet remained in the wine of life, Iden had set a hedge of lavender to please his wife. It was so carefully chosen and set, and watched, that it grew to be the finest lavender in all the country. People used to come for it from round about, quite certain of a favourable reception, for there was nothing so sure to bring peace at Coombe Oaks as a mention of lavender.

The prose could not be closer to speech, yet it takes us along with it like poetry. The linguistic purity and cultural preoccupations revealed in this and other novels of Jefferies, *Greene Ferne Farm* (1880), *The Dewy Morn* (1884), and *After London, or Wild England* (1885), as well as in his fine essays on country life, offer a direct contrast to the self-conscious stylishness and philosophizing of Meredith and to Victorian pastoralism generally. His work represents a fruitful interaction between literature and the unwritten expressiveness of the countryman's speech, such as we find in some of Scott, George Eliot, Emily Brontë, and Hardy. This interaction, which is certainly part of our impression of the social deepening of the novel, enriched the cultural soil by bringing evidence, more cogent than so much 'medievalism', of the moral importance of the underlying, ageless, agricultural pattern which had permeated culture before the impermeable machine age. The interaction is at once a source of vitality and the root of much intense moral preoccupation. As the vitality faded – 'the farm-labourer today is psychologically a townbird' – the preoccupation tended to become more anguished and

diagnostic. It is a central theme in modern European literature, taking many different forms, and it is far removed from mere nostalgia.

Other Prose

The Victorian novel is more successful than the poetry in establishing connection with some of the intellectual and practical interests of the age. A strong impression of that vitality and those interests is given by the very large amount of prose other than fiction produced in the period. Whatever the reservations we may make about their writings as literature, the Victorian moralists and critics, some of whom are the subject of separate studies or have been, all too briefly, mentioned elsewhere in this volume, continue to win our respect by their unremitting conscientiousness, their exemplary industry, their breadth of interests. John Stuart Mill and Carlyle, Newman and Arnold, Ruskin, Bagehot, Herbert Spencer, Leslie Stephen, John Morley, and scores of other writers reveal a distinctively Victorian willingness to engage in moral and intellectual debate, none with more passion and sense of responsibility than John Stuart Mill.

The militancy of Rationalists such as John Morley and Frederick Harrison has now become 'dated', but we should not underestimate its uses in its time. It was on the continuance of such debate, in and out of Parliament, that the success of the Victorian compromise, its experiment in Liberalism, and avoidance of civil dislocation largely depended. Mill's essays on Bentham and Coleridge indicate roughly the two poles of rationalism (or 'empiricism') and idealism (or 'intuition') between which moved the thinkers, critics, and historians of the period, in ways suggested by one of the quotations from Mark Pattison's *Memoirs* in the social survey (cf. p. 40), and foreshadowed by Hazlitt in *The Spirit of the Age*. A popular exposition of the two kinds of outlook is Macaulay's famous and characteristic essay on Bacon (1837). John Stuart Mill wrote:

> The difference between these two schools of Philosophy, that of Intuition, and that of Experience and Association, is not a mere matter of abstract speculation; it is full of practical consequences, and lies at the foundation of all the greatest differences of practical opinion in an age of progress.
>
> (*Autobiography*)

Some such distinction is to be observed in the attitude of the

important historians to their tasks. On the one hand we have, for example, Grote, Finlay, J. B. Bury, and Freeman, who try to make their work as empirical or 'scientific' as possible; on the other hand are Macaulay, Carlyle, and Froude, who wrote impressionistically and moralistically – though moralism is the great temptation of all these writers. Both kinds of historian shared in the establishment of more reliable, organic notions of historic development, of which the reader may find an account in G. P. Gooch's *History and Historians in the Nineteenth Century* (2nd edition, 1952).

The Victorians produced a large number of engrossing biographies, a mode of composition which gave to very different talents unusual opportunities for concentrating their powers and expressing their reverence for genius and greatness. The indispensable *Dictionary of National Biography* was begun by Stephen in 1882. Many writers seem to have put their best work into their biographies; according to some critics, even Mrs Gaskell is only to be remembered for her *Life of Charlotte Brontë*. At the end of his attractive *Life of Sterling*, Carlyle asks his readers to understand Sterling's life as 'an emblem, unusually significant, of the world's own during those years of his ... "Why write the life of Sterling?" I imagine I had a commission higher than the world's, the dictate of Nature herself, to do what is now done.' These remarks, though a little high-pitched, are typical of the motives of Forster in his lives of Dickens and Landor, of Morley in his *Gladstone*, of Stanley in his *Dr Arnold*, of Lockhart in his *Scott*, of Maitland in his *Leslie Stephen*, and of Froude in his *Carlyle*. Victorian regard for 'noble' qualities and extreme reticence were bound to produce a reaction at a later date, but these biographies by contemporaries, with all their faults and distortions, are irreplaceable. Indeed, they share many of the original qualities to be found in the numerous autobiographies of the period. Books of travel, such as those of George Borrow, Kinglake, Doughty, Burton, and W. H. Mallock, might indeed be regarded as varieties of autobiography. A confessional attitude, rarely entirely absent in autobiography, is especially strong in some of the finest Victorian examples, and, though it is by no means indispensable to the genre, it gives them a special authenticity, some of that representative quality which Romantic poets had claimed for their own experience. Gosse's *Father and Son* (1907) and Mill's *Autobiography* (1873) are more than

works of literature – they are concrete, historical facts. So, too, are the *Praeterita* of Ruskin (1886), Carlyle's *Sartor Resartus* (1836), and Newman's *Apologia* (1873). But the status of autobiographical writing, the importance which the different authors give it, varies as widely as the content of letters, and it is impossible to give a summary impression of works as varied as those by Leigh Hunt, Mark Pattison, Trollope, Richard Jefferies, and Harriet Martineau.

The scope of Victorian achievement in literary criticism has not yet been delineated with complete precision. A good deal of the evidence lies buried in the reviews. When it has been sifted it may prove to have forestalled much twentieth-century opinion about Victorian writers. There is not likely to be a great change in the view that the number of critics who are still of practical importance is relatively small. Only two Victorian critics, Arnold and Stephen, are really living influences – alive in the way that Dickens and George Eliot are alive, as constituent elements in modern culture. Important criticism requires, in addition to delicacy, insight, reading, and disinterestedness, a certain moral rootedness, an intelligently positive direction of mind, qualities which are very rarely found together. Some distance after Arnold and Stephen come Swinburne, Bagehot, Pater, Morley, and R. H. Hutton. The academic critics such as Saintsbury, Gosse, and Dowden do not count in the same way, though they have their uses.

One of the results of nineteenth-century sociological and historical studies was a deeper understanding of the organic nature of culture, of which linguistic clarity and literary vitality are crucial components. This understanding, as we find it in Macaulay, Arnold, Stephen, Bagehot, and others, was a great improvement on the mere listing of writers or the study of each in isolation. But this ability to think organically about literature, and to handle it as a living organism, tended in time to be reduced to a mere accumulation of what was hopefully called 'background'. There is, of course, all the difference in the world. 'They want to prove,' a distinguished critic remarked recently, alluding to Ben Jonson's famous line, 'that Shakespeare was not "for all time", but "of an age".' There is no limit to background material and only the feeling for life – which Arnold succinctly called 'tact' – can decide what historical information is

relevant and ensure that literature matters in the way it should. Good criticism is as rare as any other kind of literary excellence and, as Arnold wrote, 'at some epochs no other creation is possible'. Of the late-Victorian 'aesthetic' critics after Swinburne and Pater, perhaps the most interesting were 'Vernon Lee' (Violet Paget), though her most valuable critical work, *The Handling of Words*, did not appear till 1923; and Arthur Symons, who edited *The Savoy* (1896), wrote *The Symbolist Movement in Literature* (1899), and was W. B. Yeats's tutor in the aims of Mallarmé's poetry. On the merits and demerits of aesthetic criticism, Eliot made some interesting comments in the opening pages of *The Sacred Wood*.

The Drama

We were passing by the door of the Victorian Theatre; it was just half-price time – and the beggary and rascality of London were pouring in to their low amusement, from the neighbouring gin palaces and thieves' cellars.

(*Alton Locke*, 1850)

'There is no precedent for a nation having two great periods of drama.' 'We are not going to be deterred by a fatalistic philosophy of history from wanting a poetic drama.' (*A Dialogue of Dramatic Poetry*, T. S. Eliot)

We do not think that a play can be worth acting and not worth reading.

(W. B. Yeats)

'Do you understand French?'
'Perfectly well.'
'Very good,' said the manager, opening the table-drawer, and giving a roll of paper from it to Nicholas. 'There! Just turn that into English and put your name on the title-page.' (*Nicholas Nickleby*, 1838)

The vicissitudes of the drama show more clearly than any other literary history the difficulty or impossibility of planning a cultural revival. Poets, for example Tennyson, Browning, Swinburne, continued to write dramas, but none has the interest of their non-dramatic work. Perhaps there is a certain determinism in the flowering of the different genres. Drama, it seems, must come at a time when the dramatic occasion is one of the chief, if not the chief, means of concentrating and vigorously expressing profound social agreements and disagreements. There is therefore a certain understanding between audiences and authors, something more, at any

rate, than the price of a ticket and a willingness to be amused. The Elizabethans were fortunate in the wealth of their unconscious traditions and assumptions which helped the dramatists at all levels. Possibly as a result of the limitation of the number of serious theatres to two for more than a century, as a result of the popularity of the novel with the theatre-shy middle class, and of the predominance of great actors and mere spectacle, the Victorian theatre occupied no such central position. As *Nicholas Nickleby* and *Pendennis* suggest, the theatrical world was rather a shabby one, dependent largely on poor and economical translations of bad plays. There was no tradition of writing in which a Browning might have learnt how to progress beyond static monologue.

A better phase, more realistic and topical, is usually considered to have begun with T. W. Robertson's *Caste* (1867) and continued in the work of Henry Arthur Jones and Pinero, but no one would claim that these writers belong to literature. Reasons for this are perhaps best represented by W. B. Yeats's remarks in *Controversies*:

I saw *Caste*, the earliest play of the modern school, a few days ago, and found there more obviously than I expected, for I am not much of a theatre-goer, the English half of the mischief. Two of the minor persons had a certain amount of superficial characterization, as if out of the halfpenny comic papers; but the central persons, the men and the women that created the dramatic excitement, such as it was, had not characters of any kind, being vague ideals, perfection as it is imagined by a commonplace mind. The audience could give them its sympathy without the labour that comes from awakening knowledge.

Only with the discovery of anti-Victorian zest by Oscar Wilde and by Shaw, under the influence of Butler and a partially understood Ibsen, does the drama recover a measure of linguistic vitality and social function. About the same time a very different but comparable concentration of interests, passions, and ideals brought about an awakening of genuine dramatic life at the Abbey Theatre in Dublin. The plays of Synge are the most substantial product of that time; but the whole story of the collaboration between Synge, Yeats, and Lady Gregory, with their prose writings, is one of the most instructive events in recent literary history. If we are more aware of the difficulties of planning a literary renaissance and of the organic complexity of a flourishing dramatic tradition, the credit belongs

entirely to Synge and to Yeats. Their dislike of simplification and their insistence – whilst holding firmly to the view that 'every healthy mind is more interested in *Tit-Bits* than in *Idylls of the King*' – on aims different from Shaw's, is permanently inspiring.

PART III

PART TWO

THE GENIUS OF CHARLES DICKENS

R. C. CHURCHILL

The first thing that anyone would naturally observe about Dickens (1812–70) is that he is an immensely popular writer. With the possible exceptions of Bunyan and Scott, he has been, and is likely to remain, our most widely read author of great powers and permanent interest, the 'classic' in all English literature who is most acceptable to readers of all ages and of widely differing mental capacities. It is still quite common to find people who have never seen or read a play by Shakespeare, and to whom poetry is a closed book, who have not only read the majority of Dickens's novels but who are in the habit of re-reading them at regular intervals.

This wide and deserved popularity of Dickens, this almost unanimous opinion that he is an immensely enjoyable author, is both an advantage and a disadvantage when you come to discuss him. The chief advantage, and it is an enormous one, is that every reader knows what you are talking about; the writings you intend to consider are familiar in men's mouths as household words; the preliminary labour has already been done.

And here, of course, the chief advantage leads into the chief disadvantage. Familiarity breeds contempt – not of the novels themselves but of all attempts to discuss them. To criticize Dickens in any way is regarded by some of his more devout English readers as almost on a par with criticizing the Royal Family. Now I believe that in some respects Dickens is the greatest genius in English literature; but I also believe that no writer of any distinction at all has ever produced so much rubbish. And unfortunately the genius and the rubbish exist side by side in the same novels.

I believe that in this respect Dickens is unique. Shakespeare himself wrote some rubbish – unless such early plays as *Titus* and *The Comedy of Errors* are to be dignified by a milder term or are considered to be mostly the work of inferior hands. But this comparative rubbish

was produced at the very start of Shakespeare's career, when he was either feeling his own way or was engaged upon the doctoring of other men's scripts; there is no rubbish, no weakness of any kind, in plays like *Lear* or *Antony*. These are works of dramatic art from which the most rigorous critic would be reluctant to subtract a single line.

Contrast Dickens in this respect. I believe, for instance, that *Martin Chuzzlewit* is not only Dickens's best comic novel but the greatest work of comic genius in the whole of English literature. In the field of comedy I put Dickens above Shakespeare, Ben Jonson, Fielding, and Smollett, though recognizing, as he did himself, that he owed much to them. *Chuzzlewit*, with its immense variety of humour – consider the different ways in which the comedy is enriched by the introduction of Mrs Gamp and Young Bailey and the American scenes into the main theme of Mr Pecksniff[1] – is surely Dickens's greatest comic achievement. George Gissing said that in it 'every quality of Dickens is seen at its best'; and that, apparently, was Dickens's own opinion when he began to write: he had 'never had so much confidence in his powers'.

Yet this comic masterpiece is disfigured by some of the most ridiculous sentimentality even Dickens ever wrote. It might be said that it is easy enough to skip those parts, but nevertheless they are there in *Chuzzlewit*, as much a part of the novel as Mr Pecksniff and Mrs Gamp, and there is no evidence that Dickens admired his sentimental scenes any less than his comic. It is almost as if Shakespeare, in the midst of *Lear* or *Antony*, had introduced the crude melodrama of *Titus*. *Titus*, it is true, leads up to *Lear*, in the sense that in *Lear* the crude melodrama is transmuted into tragedy, but the point to observe is that they do not co-exist in the same play. In *Chuzzlewit* some of Dickens's most intelligent writing does co-exist with some of his most unintelligent, and apparently he was equally satisfied with each. In their reluctance to admit the need for any criticism, the more devout of Dickens's readers have on their side no less a person than the author himself.[2]

Chuzzlewit being a study in selfishness and hypocrisy, it was imperative for Dickens to have a few characters, such as the Pinches and Mark Tapley, to typify the opposite qualities. Tapley is the sort of faithful, almost feudal, retainer previously characterized in Sam

Weller, and Tom Pinch is nearly as simple-minded as Mr Pickwick. But there is not much sentimentality in *Pickwick*, whereas in the greater comic novel the sentimentality is sometimes carried to ridiculous lengths. I am not thinking only of the tendency in this novel for Dickens to cry out at frequent intervals: 'Blessings on thy simple heart, Tom Pinch!' – or ejaculations of a similar species. He did not think it necessary to call down blessings on the even simpler heart of Mr Pickwick. But there is much more to it than that. Consider, if you can bear to read them, the laboured archness of the chapters containing the courtship of Ruth Pinch and John Westlock: 'Oh, foolish, panting, timid little heart, why did she feign to be unconscious of his coming?' – and a good deal more in the same vein. This sort of thing is too often dismissed as 'typical' Victorian sentimentality, put in, we are to presume, for the benefits of the Young Person – and in a hurry, perhaps, to catch the next instalment. It will not be denied that Dickens owed part of his taste for sentimentality to the general Victorian partiality for using pocket-handkerchiefs to wipe away tears; G. H. Lewes and George Eliot, two of the most intelligent people of their time, were fond of crying together over their reading. The Dickens who satirized Young Persons, and Podsnappery in general, in *Our Mutual Friend* ('will it bring a blush into the cheek of the young person?'), was the same man who wrote passages of sentiment – some of them in *Our Mutual Friend* itself – on such a low level that no writer could possibly go any lower. To call such sentimentality 'typical' is therefore to insult our great-grandparents. Only Thackeray and Charles Reade, among Victorian novelists of any stature at all, go as low as Dickens, and less frequently; Charlotte Yonge, if memory serves, is comparatively masculine.

Or perhaps it would be fairer to say: comparatively feminine. For the lowest sentimentality among the Victorians was not usually produced by women but by men writing about women. The novelists most free of the general dampness of the age are Emily Brontë and George Eliot. It is true that George Eliot's first stories were sentimental, but it is equally true that the public thought they were written by a clergyman. Dickens spotted the woman's hand in *Scenes of Clerical Life*, and it was not by a consideration of the more sentimental parts that he judged the author to be feminine.

There is no doubt that he approved of sentimentality, both in himself and others; he laughed and cried as he wrote. Though we still laugh, most of us today find it difficult to share the tears.

The main flood of this sentimentality occurred between the years 1837 and 1850, in the novels and stories that succeeded *Pickwick*:* that is to say, in *Oliver Twist*, *Nicholas Nickleby*, *The Old Curiosity Shop*, *Barnaby Rudge*, *Martin Chuzzlewit*, the Christmas stories, *Dombey and Son*, and *David Copperfield*. It would be untrue to say that sentimentality never occurs in the later novels, though on the whole it is greatly modified. It is present in some chapters of *Our Mutual Friend*, and the ending of *Great Expectations* is to some extent spoiled by it. In the latter instance, however, Dickens is believed to have altered his original ending, which was in accordance with the general tone of the book, at the earnest request of Bulwer-Lytton.[3] So it is perhaps to Lytton rather than to Dickens that we owe the disfigurement of *Great Expectations*, though nobody was responsible but Dickens himself for the disfigurement of *Martin Chuzzlewit*; the word is not, I believe, too strong a one, when we consider what heights of comedy Dickens reaches in this novel – greater heights probably than he was ever to reach again.

One of the strangest paradoxes in the artistry of Dickens is that this most abundant of novelists was also a master – perhaps the greatest master in English – of the pithy, illuminating phrase. Dickens, says Eliot,

can with a phrase make a character as real as flesh and blood – *'What a life young Bailey's was!'* – like Farinata

> *Chi fur gli maggior tui?*

or like Cleopatra,

> *I saw her once*
> *Hop forty paces through the public street.*[4]

He can give us a couple of lines that say as much about the ruling vice of Mr Pecksniff as the rest of the hypocrite's adventures put together. I am thinking of chapter III, when Mr Pecksniff is having

---

* All Dickens's novels appeared first in monthly or weekly parts or as serials in monthly or weekly publications. For ten months in 1837 *Pickwick* and *Oliver* were running side by side. Throughout this essay, the dates of publication refer to the *parts*; the publication in volume form was immediately after the last instalment.

that conversation with Mrs Lupin at the Blue Dragon. He pulls off his gloves to warm his hands before the fire – warming them, says Dickens, 'as benevolently as if they were somebody else's, not his', and his back 'as if it were a widow's back, or an orphan's back, or an enemy's back, or a back that any less excellent man would have suffered to be cold'. It is, of course, details like this which are missing from even the most subtle portrayals of Dickens's characters on the stage or screen, but it is precisely by such details that the character is gradually built up in our reading of the novel. Dickens – by another paradox – is the most 'dramatic' of our novelists, and yet he is the novelist who probably loses most by any stage or screen adaptation.

The criticism he met with in his own time stressed the melodramatic rather than the dramatic nature of his genius; the admiring Ruskin regretted that he 'chooses to speak in a circle of stage-fire'. It would be idle to pretend that the melodramatic side of Dickens is not very obvious, though it could vary from the crudeness of *Nickleby* to the comparative delicacy of *Barnaby Rudge*, *A Tale of Two Cities*, *Bleak House*, and *Edwin Drood*. Dickens did not progress in his art in quite the straightforward way of Shakespeare and many lesser writers. His great things are scattered throughout his work, and he has no masterpiece without serious weaknesses. The apparent exception to this general rule, *Hard Times*, is, I believe, a masterpiece of a minor order – a novel of the stature of *Silas Marner* rather than of *Middlemarch*.

Dickens's first publication was in the *Monthly Magazine* as early as 1833. His pseudonym of 'Boz' is known today, not only because of the collected *Sketches by 'Boz'*, but by his keeping-up in the letters the legend of the 'Inimitable Boz', often familiarly shortened to the 'Inimitable'. But he had another pseudonym, less famous, at this early stage of his career. *Sunday Under Three Heads: As it is; as Sabbath Bills would make it; as it might be made* was published the same year as the collected *Sketches* (1836), under the name of 'Timothy Sparks'. And this essay is interesting, because it proves how early Dickens attained some of his leading ideas. He always felt deeply the melancholy of the 'Victorian' Sunday, and this essay, published in fact a year before the Queen succeeded, can be compared

with the chapter in *Little Dorrit*, written in the fifties, where Clennam, returned from China, wanders about the streets of London, wrapped in Sunday gloom:

> It was a Sunday evening in London, gloomy, close, and stale. Maddening church bells of all degrees of dissonance, sharp and flat, cracked and clear, fast and slow, made the brick-and-mortar echoes hideous ... In every thoroughfare, up almost every alley, and down almost every turning, some doleful bell was throbbing, jerking, tolling, as if the Plague were in the city and the dead-carts were going round. Everything was bolted and barred that could by possibility furnish relief to an overworked people ... Nothing to see but streets, streets, streets ... Nothing to change the brooding mind, or raise it up. Nothing for the spent toiler to do but to compare the monotony of his seventh day with the monotony of his six days ... What secular want could the million or so of human beings ... possibly have upon their seventh day? Clearly they could want nothing but a stringent policeman.

In the comparable part of his early *Sunday Under Three Heads*, as in his later, mature novel, we find Dickens criticizing in his most passionate, but at the same time his most realistic vein.

The *Pickwick Papers* (1836-7) was his first great success, but it could so easily have been his biggest failure. It was originally commissioned as the text to a series of sporting illustrations, and the feature of Victorian life Dickens knew least about was sport. 'One side of nineteenth-century life', says Orwell – 'the boxing, racing, cock-fighting, badger-digging, poaching, rat-catching side of life, so wonderfully embalmed in Leech's illustrations to Surtees – is outside his scope.'[5] *Pickwick* hung fire, in fact, until Dickens invented Sam Weller, from which time onward it was a huge success.

The term 'Dickensian' thus rests partly on an illusion. In so far as it refers to Christmas, with reference to the festivities at Mr Wardle's in *Pickwick* and Bob Cratchit's in *A Christmas Carol*, it is true enough; so, obviously, with regard to the general charity and largeness of mind in Dickens as a whole. But his connection with stage-coaches and with country life, which the term vaguely denotes, was actually rather slender. He knew little about the country, but his knowledge of London, like Sam Weller's, was extensive and peculiar. The stage-coach, with which his name is still popularly associated, was in fact in the process of being superseded at the time *Pickwick* was being written, and *Nickleby* was the contemporary of the first edition of *Bradshaw's Railway Time-table*. G. M. Trevelyan

puts the first period of railway investment as during 1836–7. 'Not only the canals but the stage-coaches were doomed; Mr Weller senior's occupation was gone.'[6] And he had only just been born!

Pickwick always makes highly enjoyable reading, but its comedy does not penetrate very deeply into the mysteries of the human soul. Compared with the subtle social criticism of *Oliver Twist*, to say nothing of the great comic achievement of *Chuzzlewit*, the comedy of *Pickwick* seems mostly of an obvious kind, resting genially on the surfaces of life. It maintains a constant level, however, and is not disfigured by the gross sentimentality of so many of the novels that followed it. The famous Trial Scene is often adapted for theatrical production, and probably *Pickwick* as a whole is the Dickens novel which loses least by being transferred to the stage or screen.[7]

It ran for ten months, as has been observed, side by side with *Oliver Twist*, completed in 1838. This concurrence is really extra-ordinary, considering the almost absolute difference between the two novels. The contrast between the light-heartedness of the one and the grim melodrama of the other has often been noticed; more important to observe perhaps is the contrast between the two kinds of comedy.

If we use the term 'comedy' in its very widest sense, covering such examples as *Volpone* and *Measure for Measure* as well as *Tom Jones* and *She Stoops to Conquer*, then we can truly say that almost all Dickens's work is in this field. Comedy can be a very serious thing and have a very serious purpose behind it. The first few chapters of *Oliver Twist*, the workhouse chapters, are among the best things that Dickens ever wrote.

That they are not generally considered to be so is due mainly to the fact that Oliver escapes from the workhouse, not to the world outside, but to the 'world' as depicted on the Victorian melodramatic stage. This is not to deny that the prototypes of Fagin and Bill Sikes and Nancy really existed, but they were a part of Victorian life of which Dickens had had little personal experience and most of his readers even less. Pictured in terms of conventional melodrama, their appeal to the contemporary public was in direct proportion to their distance from reality. If the workhouse chapters had been written in a similar melodramatic vein, Bumble would shrink from a figure of universal significance into a mere caricature of Victorian beadledom.

Dickens held strong views on the reformed workhouses, and they went clean against the views expressed by the enlightened opinion of his day. That enlightened opinion was, in fact, the main cause of the misery of those people unfortunate enough to be separated from their families under the new rule. In *The Age of the Chartists*, Dr and Mrs Hammond thus describe the system: 'They kept the mixed workhouse, but they *classified the inmates* [my italics], forbidding any communication between the different classes. In this way, husbands and wives, parents and children, were kept rigorously apart.'

Classifying the inmates! That, of course, was what Dickens pounced on. It was his particular genius that he could always put his finger on the social evil which hurt the sufferer the most. He saw the Workhouse Board, not as an institution but as so many individuals anxious to assert their authority at someone else's expense, and he was aware of the fact that this petty regulation was not only the one which hurt the pauper most keenly but the one which the Board got the most pleasure out of inflicting. That, I believe, can be inferred from the early chapters of *Oliver*, as Dickens's awareness of the sadistic sexual element in flogging can be inferred from the early chapters of *Copperfield* and *Nickleby*.[8]

The first part of *Oliver* has therefore a double interest for us today. Dickens, nearly always, is at his best as a social critic when he is displaying his greatest genius as a novelist: the two aspects of his writing become fused into one. *Oliver* takes precedence over *The Uncommercial Traveller* in the sense that Fielding's *Joseph Andrews* does over his *Proposal for the Poor*.

When his emotions were stirred only on the surface, Dickens was in constant danger of calling down blessings on the hearts of his unoffending characters. When he felt deeply his tone was rather different. 'The Board established the rule', he tells us coolly, 'that all the poor people should have the alternative of being starved by a gradual process in the house or by a quick one out of it.' They (and it is always a 'they' with Dickens) also

undertook to divorce poor married people, in consequence of the great expense of a suit in Doctor's Commons, and instead of compelling a man to support his family, as they had theretofore done, took his family away from him and made him a bachelor! There is no saying how many applicants

for relief, under these last two heads, might have started up in all classes of society … but the Board were long-headed men, and had provided for this difficulty. The relief was inseparable from the workhouse and the gruel, and that frightened people.

The 'gruel' is what everyone remembers about *Oliver Twist*, that and the murder of Nancy and the last night of Fagin in the condemned cell. But Bumble is not merely the person to whom Oliver's request for more is in the nature of a blasphemy against the Powers-That-Be; his is a subtler portrait than we commonly remember. I am thinking of passages like the one where the undertaker Mr Sowerberry is admiring the button on Bumble's coat. 'Dear me, what a very elegant button this is, Mr Bumble. I never noticed it before':

'Yes, I think it is rather pretty' [replies Bumble]. 'The die is the same as the parochial seal – the Good Samaritan healing the sick and bruised man. The Board presented it to me on New Year's morning, Mr Sowerberry; I put it on, I remember, for the first time, to attend the inquest on that reduced tradesman, who died in a doorway at midnight.'

It is the carelessness here – and later on, when Bumble refers to 'two Irish labourers and a coalheaver' as to so much cattle – that gives the irony its force. It is not only the character of Bumble which is shown up by these remarks, it is the habit of mind of the institution he represents – the refusal to take into account the needs of the individual. Chesterton observed very truly that Dickens was not so much against any institution as such as against 'an expression on the human face'.

And, of course, similar institutions, similar expressions and tones of voice, are still very much with us. There is no occasion to specify. What is important to realize here is the superiority of these early chapters of *Oliver* to the rest of the novel, which is mostly given over to melodrama and sentiment of varying degrees of absurdity. The reformed workhouses are as dead as the reformers, but there remains the universal significance of the relation between Bumble's sort, personifying Authority, and the 'two Irish labourers and a coalheaver', personifying Dependence. This, it will be agreed, is one of the fundamental themes of literature – 'the insolence of office', Shakespeare called it – and it has never been better developed than in the novels of Fielding and Dickens. That off-handed reference of Bumble's to the 'reduced tradesman, who died in a doorway at

midnight', can be compared with the celebrated parenthesis in *Joseph Andrews* on the kind-hearted postilion who lends the naked hero his coat: 'A lad', adds Fielding, 'who hath since been transported for robbing a hen-roost.'

The novels that come between *Oliver Twist* and *Martin Chuzzlewit* have never lacked admirers, but I cannot say that any of them has ever been among my own favourites or has ever seemed to me to be among Dickens's finest achievements. It is best in these matters to adopt the purely personal approach, for the work of Dickens is so vast in extent and raises so many questions of interpretation that an essay of this length can only hope to make clearer several of the main points, the argument resting inevitably on what appear to the critic to be the most important novels.

Inevitably, too, some of the other novels will be considered mainly for their incidental deficiencies. *Nicholas Nickleby* (1838–9) was the novel that immediately followed *Oliver*, and it has always seemed to me to contain – fortunately among much else – the very crudest melodrama that Dickens ever wrote. The scenes at Dotheboys Hall are truly memorable, but they end with a speech by Nicholas, when he is defending Smike from the cane of Squeers, which in its language could have come out of any of the melodramas Dickens was to satirize in the theatrical scenes of the same novel: 'Touch him at your peril! I will not stand by and see it done. My blood is up, and I have the strength of ten such men as you. Look to yourself, for by heaven I will not spare you if you drive me on!'

There are similar passages at the end of the novel, couched in language reminiscent at first glance of Victorian stage melodrama; but Dickens was evidently trying for an 'Elizabethan' effect that was beyond his powers. Ralph Nickleby dies like this, crying to the church bell:

'Lie on, with your iron tongue! Ring merrily for births that make expectants writhe, and for marriages that are made in hell, and toll ruefully for the dead whose shoes are worn already! Call men to prayers who are godly because not found out, and ring chimes for the coming-in of every year that brings this cursed world nearer to its end. No bell or book for me! Throw me on a dunghill, and let me rot there, to infect the air!'

This is surely Crummles diction, a part to make all split. It is astonish-

ing that the same man who could enjoy the posturings of Crummles and Mantalini – and of Mr Wopsle in *Great Expectations* – could write stuff like this quite seriously. And it does not stand alone in these final chapters of *Nickleby*; it goes along with such things as the triumphant cry of Nicholas: 'You are caught, villains, in your own toils!'; and Ralph's stagey hiss: 'My curse, my bitter, deadly curse, upon you, boy!' The unmasking of Pecksniff in *Chuzzlewit* ('Hear me, rascal!') is comparatively credible, and by the time we get to *Copperfield* it is significant that the exposure of the villain is performed by a *comic* character, Micawber: 'You Heep of infamy!'

The Old Curiosity Shop and *Barnaby Rudge* are the only memorable parts of a short-lived periodical, *Master Humphrey's Clock*, which Dickens started in 1840 and was glad enough to bring to a close before departing for America two years later. *The Old Curiosity Shop* ran in the *Clock* during 1840–1, and after Dickens had committed the crime – as it almost seemed to him – of killing the heroine, *Barnaby Rudge* followed to the end of the latter year. Because of the tears shed both by the author and by his readers over the death of Little Nell, *The Old Curiosity Shop* is often considered the most sentimental of all Dickens's novels. It is hardly that; indeed, Nell and the Marchioness hold as honourable a place among Dickens's studies of childhood as Quilp and Sampson Brass among his gallery of grotesques. It is more accurately described, along with *Barnaby* and *A Tale of Two Cities*, as his most *romantic* work. The wanderings of Nell and her grandfather have a mysterious, romantic quality associated in my mind with the two historical novels.

The visit to the United States produced *American Notes* (1842) and *Martin Chuzzlewit* (1843–4). The *Notes* are a more realistic and more kindly version of the severe criticism implied in the outrageously comic American scenes in the novel. This was the United States, we must remember, at the most vulnerable moment in her history: the Land of Liberty on the one hand, a slave-owning community on the other. Dickens went full of hope, and returned almost completely disillusioned.

One of the common traits of comic genius is a fascination with jargon. We find the results in *The Alchemist*, in *Tom Jones*, in *Peregrine Pickle*, in *Tristram Shandy*, in some of the novels of Scott. I have referred to the comic variety of *Chuzzlewit*, and it is in great part

a variety of language. Mrs Gamp's jargon is peculiar to herself, though we may indeed recognize in her any garrulous old woman in our own experience; while Young Bailey, 'an abstract of all the stable-knowledge of the time', is also an abstract of all the stable-language. The rhetoric of the Columbians came as an absolute gift to a novelist of Dickens's powers in what may be called the Higher Impersonation. It must be remembered that at that time few people in England knew anything at all about the United States.[9] The peculiarities of the American accent and idiom must have struck Dickens with the force of a revelation. Not Jonson when he discovered the jargon of the alchemists, nor Scott when he met with the prototypes of Mause Headrigg and Jenny Dennison, can have been more delighted than Dickens was when he first pondered the infinite comic possibilities of this strange new language.

Being a Cockney, he had always had a soft spot for that precociousness which is seen at its best in the youngsters of the London streets and which he immortalized in Young Bailey.[10] Judge his delight, therefore, when he found America full of Young Baileys, of a precocity which the most mature of Cockney immaturity could not hope to rival. When Martin and Mark Tapley arrive in America, they are met by Colonel Diver, the editor of the *New York Rowdy Journal*, who takes them to his office:

Behind a mangy old writing-table in this apartment sat a figure with a stump of a pen in its mouth and a great pair of scissors in its right hand, clipping and slicing at a file of Rowdy Journals ... a small young gentleman of very juvenile appearance, and unwholesomely pale in the face ... [Martin] had begun to say that he presumed this was the colonel's little boy, and that it was very pleasant to see him playing at Editor in all the guilelessness of childhood, when the colonel proudly interposed and said:
'My War Correspondent, sir. Mr Jefferson Brick!'

In a later chapter, Martin and Mark Tapley are privileged to be in the company of the Honourable Elijah Pogram when he is met by a deputation 'consisting of six gentlemen boarders and a very shrill boy'. The shrill boy turns out to be Dr Ginery Dunkle, 'a gentleman of great poetical elements':

The introductions being completed, the spokesman resumed.
'Sir!'
'Mr Pogram!' cried the shrill boy.

'Perhaps', said the spokesman, with a hopeless look, 'you will be so good, Dr Ginery Dunkle, as to charge yourself with the execution of our little office, sir?'

As there was nothing the shrill boy desired more, he immediately stepped forward.

'Mr Pogram! Sir! A handful Of your fellow-citizens, sir, hearing Of your arrival at the National Hotel, and feeling the patriotic character Of your public services, wish, sir, to have the gratification Of beholding you, and mixing with you, sir; and unbending with you, sir, in those moments which –'

'Air,' suggested Buffum.

'Which air so peculiarly the lot, sir, Of our great and happy country.'*

It has often been observed that the last thing that anybody ever remembers about a Dickens novel is its story, and yet it is to the melodramatic machinery of *Chuzzlewit* that we owe the variety of humour which gives the novel its supremacy among Dickens's comic achievements. But for the intricacies of the plot, we should never have had some of the ripest pieces of Mrs Gamp only a few pages away from some of the most humorous passages in Martin's American adventures; and would Tigg ever have blossomed into Tigg Montague, Esquire, of the Anglo-Bengalee, had not Dickens been forced to find some way of getting rid of the villain Jonas? In his later novels he was to make his plots more realistic.

He once remarked that 'every word said by his characters was distinctly *heard* by him'. The essentially dramatic nature of his comic genius is seen everywhere in *Chuzzlewit*: in the Young Columbian defying the British Lion – 'Bring forth that Lion! Alone, I dare him! I taunt that Lion! I tell that Lion, that Freedom's hand once twisted in his mane, he rolls a corse before me!'; in Mrs Gamp repudiating Betsy Prig – 'the words she spoke of Mrs Harris, lambs could not forgive. No ... nor worms forget!'; in Mr Moddle observing with a hollow laugh that 'there are some men who can't get run over ... Coal wagons recoil from them, and even cabs refuse to run them down'. It is an almost incredible variety of humorous invention, and Dickens was never again to reach such comic heights.

---

* In this passage, as in most of the passages of Columbian rhetoric, Dickens uses words with initial capital letters instead of italics, to denote emphasis. He had observed that an American 'emphasized all the small words and syllables in his discourse, and left the others to take care of themselves'.

David Copperfield (1849–50) is probably the most popular of all the novels,[11] and it is certainly the most autobiographical. Because of this, David is among the most credible of Dickens's heroes, and if some of us find Dora not so credible, we have the author himself in our company. It is known that Dora was based on Dickens's idealistic memories of his first love, Maria Beadnell; when he met her again after the publication of *Copperfield*, he suffered a disillusionment so strong that she became the original of Flora Finching in *Little Dorrit*:

> Most men will be found sufficiently true to themselves to be true to an old idea. It is no proof of an inconstant mind, but exactly the opposite, when the idea will not bear close comparison with the reality, and the contrast is a fatal shock to it. Such was Clennam's case. In his youth he had ardently loved this woman, and had heaped upon her all the locked-up wealth of his affection and imagination ... And now ... Flora, who had seemed enchanting in all she said and thought, was diffuse and silly ... Flora, who had been spoiled and artless long ago, was determined to be spoiled and artless now. That was a fatal blow.

A cruel thing, perhaps, to turn a Dora into a Flora, but a consolation to those who find the main strength of *Copperfield*, not in the more sentimental or melodramatic parts, highly enjoyable as these generally are, but in the early chapters up to the first meeting with Mr Micawber and afterwards in Micawber himself. Another relation between the two novels is, of course, that the debtors' prison which casts its shade temporarily over Micawber becomes one of the main scenes, indeed one of the central images, in *Little Dorrit*. It is easy to criticize *David Copperfield*, but almost impossible not to enjoy it; like *A Christmas Carol* and *A Tale of Two Cities*, it is one of those books which gains in appeal and yet which subsequently suffers in critical esteem through being first read in childhood.

The other novels which Dickens wrote in the late forties and fifties are not normally read in childhood at all (though some of them are now frequently read in school as set-texts for O and A levels); only a modern Young Bailey, an abstract of all the literary reviewing of our time, could hope to make much of them at such a tender age. Their common feature is a criticism of Victorian society which, like that in the workhouse chapters of *Oliver Twist*, goes deep enough to be a universal criticism of human nature. Like *Oliver*, they thus have for us today a twofold interest: they can be interpreted

historically, or as examples of Dickens's mature art. For though his development as a literary artist was very uneven it would be idle to deny that in these novels of the fifties – *Bleak House* (1852–3), *Hard Times* (1854), and *Little Dorrit* (1855–7) – he reached at once his most penetrating criticism of his age and his most assured grasp of his material. The novel which immediately preceded *Copperfield* – *Dombey and Son* (1846–8) – is in the same category as these three, but here Dickens's grasp was much less sure. There are some fine things in *Dombey*, but in general the novel leaves an impression of sentimentality which the author possibly never intended. In comparison with *Bleak House* and *Little Dorrit*, its criticism of Victorian life – money is the chief character – seems altogether too obvious to be convincing, though Kathleen Tillotson and F. R. Leavis have certainly found the novel powerfully successful. I see in *Dombey*, on the whole, a brave attempt at what Dickens more successfully achieved in the later novels.

Chesterton thought *Bleak House* the best of Dickens, and it must be added that it is, at any rate, among the best by reason of some most un-Chestertonian qualities. In general, Chesterton was an early-Dickensian, a critic who found Dickens's greatest genius in the more exuberant early novels, in particular in *Pickwick*. Not that *Bleak House* is gloomy; its strength lies in its combination of diverse qualities, which are all given to us in the first twenty chapters, the first third of the novel. Never before had Dickens commanded so surely such a wide range: the comedy of *Bleak House* is only inferior to that of *Chuzzlewit*, and its social criticism strikes a good deal deeper; its sentiment and its melodrama are so under control that they cease to become weaknesses of any serious order; and its symbolism is of a subtlety never before attempted.

The book opens with fog, both actual in the London streets and symbolic in the Court of Chancery. Before long we meet Krook, 'called among the neighbours the Lord Chancellor', and his junkshop symbolizes the Court. The drama of Chesney Wold is connected with the criticism of fashionable society – not so well done as in *Little Dorrit* and *Our Mutual Friend*, but of an edge sufficiently cutting to save the drama from being merely melodramatic. The first-person narration of Esther Summerson is a remarkable *tour de force* for a male novelist, and its sentiment, compared with that of most of the

early novels, is severely under control. The comedy of Guppy and Snagsby and Mr Chadband is very well done; and Mrs Jellyby with her 'telescopic philanthropy', and even more Mr Skimpole, are examples of selfish behaviour of a subtlety quite beyond that of *Chuzzlewit*.

The portrait of Skimpole is one of the best things in Dickens. The eloquence of such characters as Chadband had been given us before; but Skimpole strikes a new note, a note to be struck again in Little Dorrit's father. Chapter VI, where Skimpole is arrested for debt and has 'the epicure-like feeling' that he 'would prefer a novelty in help . . . develop generosity in a new soil', is comedy on its highest level. His treatment of the man who comes to arrest him is too long to quote in full, but here is the gist:

'Keep your temper, my good fellow, keep your temper!' Mr Skimpole gently reasoned with him, as he made a little drawing of his head on the fly-leaf of a book. 'Don't be ruffled by your occupation. We can separate you from your office . . . We are not so prejudiced as to suppose that in private life you are otherwise than a very estimable man, with a great deal of poetry in your nature, of which you may not be conscious . . .

'But when you came down here . . . it was a fine day. The sun was shining, the wind was blowing, the lights and shadows were passing across the fields, the birds were singing.'

'Nobody said they warn't, in *my* hearing . . .'

'. . . you didn't think . . . to this effect. "Harold Skimpole loves to see the sun shine, loves to hear the wind blow; loves to watch the changing lights and shadows; loves to hear the birds, those choristers in Nature's great cathedral. And does it seem to me that I am about to deprive Harold Skimpole of his share in such possessions, which are his only birthright!" You thought nothing to that effect?'

'I – certainly – did – NOT,' said Coavinses . . . utterly renouncing the idea . . .

'Very odd and very curious, the mental process is, in you men of business!' said Mr Skimpole thoughtfully.

To deceive others most successfully, it is first of all necessary to deceive oneself. Dickens had been aware of this when he created Pecksniff, but Skimpole is a more subtle instance, and when we reach the next novel, *Hard Times*, we find the faculty displayed to perfection in Gradgrind and Bounderby. The latter rests his bombast on the conviction that he is a self-made man, sprung from the gutter, when in reality his mother slaved to give him his start in life; the former condemns his children and other children to a diet of hard

facts, in the honest conviction that he is thereby providing them with the most enlightened form of education. Here again, as in *Oliver*, Dickens had the perception denied to some of the more 'progressive' elements of his age.[12]

Although it was once issued in the *Readers' Library* at sixpence, *Hard Times* has never been among the most popular of Dickens's works. It has been fairly widely read, I should imagine, but it has never received the acclamation bestowed on a good many of the other novels. Criticism till recently has concerned itself with the historical side of the novel while neglecting the artistic. There have been some good discussions of its significance in the social history of the Victorian age – by such critics as Ruskin, Shaw, Chesterton, Orwell, Jackson, Lindsay – but not until F. R. Leavis wrote his celebrated essay[13] was the extent of the novel's artistic achievement fully appreciated. With his essay on *Hard Times* a critic at long last measured up to the full stature of Dickens's achievement here. What Dr Leavis says of Dickens's language in this novel is as memorable as it is deserved; I would personally think the compliment applicable to most of the other novels as well: 'The final stress may fall on Dickens's command of word, phrase, rhythm, and image: in ease and range there is surely no greater master of English except Shakespeare.'

I have called *Hard Times* a masterpiece of a minor order, because it seems to me that the things which make Dickens great are mostly to be found elsewhere. It is, of course, superb comedy – if we use the term in the sense we did in considering the early chapters of *Oliver Twist*. The early chapters of *Hard Times* are, in fact, in very much the same style:

Let us strike the key-note, Coketown, before pursuing our tune. It was a town of red brick, or of brick that would have been red if the smoke and ashes had allowed it ... It was a town of machinery and tall chimneys, out of which interminable serpents of smoke trailed themselves for ever, and never got uncoiled ... It contained several large streets all very like one another, and many small streets still more like one another ... You saw nothing in Coketown but what was severely workful ... the jail might have been the infirmary, the infirmary might have been the jail, the town-hall might have been either.

Gradgrind and Bounderby are more credible figures than Bumble (or Mr Murdstone), as Sissy Jupe is more human than Oliver (or Little Nell). There is Dickensian comedy in the relations between

Bounderby and Mrs Sparsit (whose husband was a Powler) and between Gradgrind and the circus people; there is no melodrama at all; and the sentimentality is even more severely controlled than in *Bleak House*. These are impressive excellences. On the other side, we have the relative failure of Stephen Blackpool, bound up to some extent, we must presume, with Dickens's comparative ignorance of the North. He knew London through and through, and no novel shows this more than *Bleak House*; *Hard Times* was written after a single visit to Preston, and with all Dickens's genius for perceiving the fundamental beneath the particular, one hurried visit was hardly enough. By ordinary standards, Stephen and Rachel and Slackbridge are well observed; by the standards of Dickens at his best they constitute the one obvious weakness of the novel. The seeming other weakness – that the Dickensian comedy, though there, is comparatively slight – comes as a refreshing change in Dickens; for once, he was not to be deflected from his main theme.

Little Dorrit, the last of the four 'social novels', bears a relation also to the two novels of the sixties: *Great Expectations* and *Our Mutual Friend*. *A Tale of Two Cities* (1859) came in between, and *The Mystery of Edwin Drood* (1870) was left unfinished at Dickens's death.

I do not believe it was altogether his increasing years, nor his visits abroad, nor the time taken up by his public readings that led to a comparative slackening of the pace in which the novels were produced from about the middle fifties. I believe the primary cause was the increasing care with which Dickens had come to write. He had always taken himself very seriously, both as a literary artist and as a social critic, but in his early and middle years he could combine this serious purpose with a seemingly incredible rate of production. For months *Pickwick* and *Oliver* ran side by side, and no sooner was *Oliver* finished than *Nickleby* was begun. He wrote *A Christmas Carol* while he was engaged on *Chuzzlewit*, and *A Child's History of England* – in three volumes – while he was engaged on *Bleak House*. From *Little Dorrit* onwards the pace slackens; and in this novel, in *Great Expectations* (1860–1) and in *Our Mutual Friend* (1864–5), we have some of his most carefully considered writing.[14]

We have observed that he earlier developed a more realistic, if sometimes equally complicated, plot. With this he now combined

a more consistent outlook on his characters; he made them develop more, without doing violence to their nature – as he did violence when he made Micawber a magistrate in Australia and when he changed his mind about Mercy Pecksniff. Moreover, a novel like *Hard Times* was obviously planned throughout from the beginning; there is hardly a wasted word. In *Little Dorrit* and its successors Dickens adopted this method on a larger scale. The new method, of course, had its incidental disadvantages. If a Micawber was not in danger of suddenly becoming respectable, and if a Chevy Slyme was not forced to appear in a new guise so that the whole cast of *Chuzzlewit* could appear before the final curtain, equally there was no chance of Dickens suddenly producing a Sam Weller or a Mrs Gamp out of nowhere whenever the story seemed to flag. In the new-style Dickens we must not expect surprises of this sort, but the compensation is very great.

In the first place everything in these last novels is subordinated to the main theme. That was the lesson Dickens had learnt from the writing of *Hard Times*. And if we compare Little Dorrit with Little Nell and Little Dorrit's father with Little Nell's grandfather, we shall have some inkling of Dickens's progress in psychological realism. Dorrit must be one of the most perceptively drawn characters in all Dickens's work. Only Pip in *Great Expectations* and Gradgrind in *Hard Times* are drawn as true to life.

Truth to life is not, of course, what we normally expect from a Dickens novel, unless it be truth to the life of the imagination. Did this increase in realism mean a corresponding decrease in the comic fantasy that we usually associate with him? To some extent, I believe, it did mean that. There could not well be a way of combining the comic achievement of *Chuzzlewit* with the psychological realism of *Great Expectations*. *Little Dorrit* comes nearest to such an unlikely combination. When Flora Finching, describing her married life, says 'ere we had yet fully detected the housemaid in selling the feathers out of the spare bed, *Gout flying upward* soared with Mr F. to another sphere', we are once more in the world of *Chuzzlewit* and we remain there while we are in the company of Flora, Pancks, Mr F.'s Aunt, and Mrs Plornish. The world of *Chuzzlewit* is even too much with us, for a weakness of these last novels is a tendency for Dickens to repeat his effects. Dora of *Copperfield* had been successfully changed

into Flora, but what can we say of Flora's father but that he is a weak imitation of Mr Pecksniff? He is described almost in the same language:

'I heard from Flora,' said the Patriarch with his benevolent smile, 'that she was coming to call, coming to call. And being out, I thought I'd come also, thought I'd come also.'

The benign wisdom he infused into this declaration (not of itself profound), by means of his blue eyes, his shining head, and his long white hair, was most impressive. It seemed worth putting down among the noblest sentiments enunciated by the best of men ...

This sketch of a consummate hypocrite would have been all very well had not Dickens already created the perfection of the type in Pecksniff, and in much the same terms. (Compare with the quotation above, the first passage of conversation between Pecksniff and Mrs Lupin at the Blue Dragon.) Similarly, had not Dickens already created Harthouse in *Hard Times*, the 'chronic weariness' of Light-wood in *Our Mutual Friend*, and his languid murmurings: 'Equal honour – Mrs Boffin's head and heart...' etc., would have been more amusing.

The symbol of the dust-heap in this novel is as potent as the fog in *Bleak House*. The criticism of fashionable society both here and in *Little Dorrit* makes the attempt at it in some of the early novels seem perfunctory. If the comedy is on the whole inferior to the best of the early work, we should remember that such things as we admire in *Chuzzlewit* could not very well be maintained in a story and a theme both wedded to psychological realism. Sentiment still has a habit of descending into sentimentality, but the range of comic invention has had to be abandoned, along with the melodrama and the mawkishness which were its incidental weaknesses.

One of the signs of Dickens's greatness is that, having reached perfection in one field of his art, he turned to other fields and won new triumphs. There are great things in all the novels; *Chuzzlewit*, *Bleak House* and *Little Dorrit* seem to me the major achievements; a number of others seem to me masterpieces, if of a lesser order; and some of the novels in which we can most easily see weak points will probably remain among our favourite reading. In this sense, but in no other, Dickens is one of those rare writers whom criticism cannot affect.

NOTES

1. 'The notion of taking Pecksniff for a type of character', Forster tells us in his biography, 'was really the origin of the book, the design being to show, more or less by every person introduced, the number and variety of humours and vices that have their root in selfishness.' Dickens was in the habit of discussing his works with Forster, so there is no doubt that this estimate is correct – and no doubt also that Dickens's avowed object was achieved. Unfortunately, Dickens was also in the habit of writing lengthy and painfully facetious titles. The full title of *Chuzzlewit* would hardly prepare one for the contents (some of which Dickens, of course, did not know himself when he began on the first instalment): *The Life and Adventures of Martin Chuzzlewit: his relatives, friends, and enemies. Comprising all his wiles and his ways, with an historical record of what he did, and what he didn't; showing, moreover,' who inherited the family plate, who came in for the silver spoons, and who for the wooden ladles. The whole forming a complete key to the house of Chuzzlewit.*

2. 'The good opinion which he had of himself,' wrote Trollope, 'was never shaken by adverse criticism; and the criticism on the other side, by which it was exalted, came from the enumeration of the copies sold.' He was, of course, quite right not to take any notice of some of the adverse criticism he met with towards the end of his life, for the reviews in *Blackwood's*, the *Westminster Review*, and the *Saturday Review* were sometimes actuated by class prejudice and by dislike of Dickens's own social criticism. Their tone was similar to Leslie Stephen's in the *Dictionary of National Biography*: 'If literary fame could safely be measured by popularity with the half-educated, Dickens must claim the highest position among English novelists.' See Philip Collins (ed.), *Dickens: the Critical Heritage* (London, 1971) and R. L. Patten, *Charles Dickens and his Publishers* (Oxford, 1978).

3. For the influence of Bulwer-Lytton on Dickens, both personally and through his novels, see Jack Lindsay, *Charles Dickens: a biographical and critical study* (London, 1950).

4. T. S. Eliot, 'Wilkie Collins and Dickens', reprinted in *Selected Essays* (London, 1934).

5. George Orwell, 'Charles Dickens', *Critical Essays* (London, 1946), 39.

6. G. M. Trevelyan, *English Social History* (London, 1944), 531. Dickens, of course, had had personal experience of stage-coaches during his travels as reporter for the *Morning Chronicle*, 1834–6. But the bulk of his writing belongs to the railway age.

7. 'It is interesting to see how Chesterton, another Cockney, always presents Dickens as the spokesman of "the poor", without showing much awareness of who "the poor" really are. To Chesterton "the poor" means small shopkeepers and servants. Sam Weller, he says, "is the great symbol in English literature of the populace peculiar to England"; and Sam Weller is a valet!' (Orwell, 28). The general criticism is perhaps true, but on the

particular point of Weller, Chesterton was more accurate than Orwell. At the time *Pickwick* was written, and for a good many years afterwards, the servant class in England was enormous. 'In the third decade of the century the female domestic servants alone were "fifty per cent more numerous than all the men and women, boys and girls, in the cotton industry put together" ' (Trevelyan, 478, quoting Clapham).

8. For the latter point see Orwell's essay, 19. Gissing, in his introductions to the Rochester edition, collected under the title of *The Immortal Dickens*, had previously pointed out the originality of Dickens in his treatment of children.

9. Mrs Trollope had written her *Domestic Manners of the Americans* in 1832. Washington Irving and Longfellow were admired in England; Hawthorne was becoming known; Fenimore Cooper was being widely read. But compared with today, the two countries were almost strangers. Dickens was to play the greatest role in making English life familiar to Americans, a debt repaid by Hawthorne, Mark Twain, and others.

10. 'Phiz' collaborated in his usual masterly fashion. See in particular his illustration 'Mr Pecksniff on his Mission' (*Chuzzlewit*, ch. XIX), and note the expression of worldly wisdom on the faces of the urchins watching Pecksniff. And when he makes Pecksniff, struck down by old Martin, upset on the floor *Le Tartuffe* and *Paradise Lost* (*Chuzzlewit*, ch. LII), the artist certainly follows the novelist's more symbolic intention.

11. It is, of course, very difficult to judge the relative popularity of novels. In *Dickens and his Readers* (London, 1956), Prof. George H. Ford tells us that Pickwick chintzes and Weller corduroys were being sold in the 1830s, and that games of quotations which demanded an intimate knowledge of *Oliver Twist* were being played at Oxford and Cambridge in the fifties.

12. In his excellent book, *The Dickens World* (London, 1941), Humphry House came to the conclusion that Dickens could never have gained his tremendous hold on public opinion had he been more of a pioneer. 'He seemed topical to thousands: he was not too topical for them to see the point, nor too advanced to have the public conscience on his side ... He shared a great deal of common experience with his public, so that it could gratefully and proudly say "How true!"; he so exploited his knowledge that the public recognized its master in knowing ... and caught exactly the tone which clarified and reinforced the public's sense of right and wrong, and flattered its moral feelings.' There is a good deal of truth in this, but if in some matters Dickens was in advance – if that is the right word – of the most advanced opinion of the age, in others he certainly was not (cf. Philip Collins, *Dickens and Crime*, London, 1962).

13. F. R. Leavis, 'Hard Times: an Analytical Note', *The Great Tradition* (London, 1950).

14. He edited *Household Words* (1850–9); *All the Year Round* (1859 until his death). The social essays contributed to the latter were collected under the title of *The Uncommercial Traveller* (1861, 1868, 1875).

SOCIETY IN THACKERAY
AND TROLLOPE

SEYMOUR BETSKY

Thackeray's success as a novelist is inseparable from his exploration, tenacious and assured, of certain effects of England's expanding economy in the early and middle nineteenth century. He is not the first novelist of his age to fix the way in which middle-class forces translated superior animal cunning and luck in speculation into success confirmed by religion. He is not the first to describe their thrust upward as being in all its many forms gross and obsequious. But he is the first novelist who, hating rank and privilege in his bones, sinks bulldog teeth into every single abuse of rank and privilege: self-defeating miserliness in a Sir Pitt Crawley; unearned privilege stupidly and criminally abused in a Sir Francis Clavering; in Rawdon Crawley the prodigality of the bloods and dandies; the mediocrity of mind and talents that governed a great nation with a growing empire, exemplified in Mr Pitt Crawley; extreme brutality, in Lord Steyne, trading on its prerogatives.

That struggle includes not only major representatives in each class. In Thackeray's work it comprises many dependants over a large area: the Church, the army (in the unfinished *Denis Duval*, the navy), the civil service, the government, the fashionable public school, the governess and domestic class, the small tradesman, Fleet Street, and Bohemia. Thackeray's world is the world of London society – and its extension into the rural community. But the world of London spreads to the Continent and even to India, with Thackeray in pursuit.

Thackeray (1811–63) portrays the world he knows best. The evils of self-interest, of parasitism, and of snobbery release in him a detached ferocity. His best work comes alive at just those points where his savagery is held in control by a cool observer's eye and an assured dramatist's skill in capturing individualized speech rhythm and idiom. His best work is leavened with touches of good humour and of self-criticism. In his most successful characters he balances his

notation of unprincipled conduct with a certain admiration for its spiritedness or its aplomb; or with the mature reflection that the Great World of English gentility deserves the scoundrels it is encouraging and protecting in such numbers. Moreover, it appears to have been his evangelical upbringing, however much he hated its narrowness and however much he could not believe in its sanctions, that imposed on him the task of exposing the vices of his age and of supporting forms of decency. Besides, Thackeray maintains – and his best work supports, however precariously – the conviction that his weapon is satire and his end the end of satire; moral reform on however small a scale following an awareness of great clattering evils. He envisages no radical change in social, political, or religious institutions.

But it is precisely here that Thackeray's weaknesses become apparent. For he purchases concentrated strength at the expense of the kind of tough intelligence that the nineteenth century needed. First, he chooses to restrict his apparently wide range in important ways. He omits the whole world of industrial capitalism and labour, a damaging omission, for someone so absorbed by the very dynamic of social force and counterforce. Thackeray appears all too willing to ascribe the making and unmaking of fortunes to sheer chance and to speculation. And not only does he fail to perceive the connection between industrialism and the world of London finance; he fails entirely to see the major alignment of that century, the alignment (as Dickens saw in *Hard Times*) of industrialism and utilitarianism.

Again, an intelligent novelist who purports to be a critic of gentry society would achieve a balance. Admittedly a very substantial minority of that threatened gentry would, through abuse of privilege and lack of principle, give way ignominiously to the worst climbing elements of the middle class. But there would be, presumably, a much larger class that simply fails to move quickly enough with the times. Its vice, as Arnold, Trollope, and George Eliot perceived – and as Thackeray failed to perceive – is ineptness. And Thackeray omits almost entirely the better elements in the gentry that move, in an historical tradition of responsibility, towards reform.

Thus, in the world as portrayed by Thackeray there is almost no room for intelligent will and intelligent performance. Individuals appear to be swept up and carried along, the strong and the un-

principled winning through or occasionally defeated, the weaker almost ludicrously helpless, and the well-intentioned with some character rendered just as ineffectual. Thackeray's characters are incapable of getting beyond the reflection that, in a self-interested world, one must live by one's calculations; or that one must, from time to time, lash out against abuse, with little hope of initiating any successful action. To put it another way: Thackeray makes bourgeois sentiment, the bourgeois sentiment that affects the code of the gentleman, do the work of intelligence. He supports certain nineteenth-century pieties attaching to marriage, home, children, and friendship. And he offers generalized forms of honesty, innocence, manliness, tenderness, and charity instead of the rigorous clarity that the age demanded.

Thackeray's preparation for *Vanity Fair*, his one undoubted success, was a long, highly varied, and, with the exception of the anonymous *Book of Snobs* (1846–7) for *Punch*, a generally unsuccessful career in journalism. Yet it was a career distinguished for no servile puffery and no lowering of standards to satisfy public taste. He earned the right to speak honest common sense in *Pendennis*. In this period, Thackeray turned his hand to the stock-in-trade of such journalism: book reviews, art and dramatic criticism, parodies, travel sketches, poetry (mostly ballads and light poetry), political articles, and fictional sketches.

The book reviews, the fictional sketches, and, in particular, the *Book of Snobs* hold our attention today. In Thackeray's early reviews – and later in his parodies in *Punch* – of contemporary practice, we see, retrospectively, an instrument for blasting his way through to his own bedrock of style and subject-matter. Given his detestation of unearned rank and of finely graded class distinction, we are hardly surprised at the critical severities that demolish the fashionable novels of Mrs Gore and Lady Blessington. Again, Thackeray is devastating when he deals with the Newgate school – with the idealization of the criminal as hero in the novels of Bulwer and Ainsworth. At the same time, the evolution of the novelist of *Vanity Fair* is seen in both his fictional sketches and pre-eminently in the best of his early works, the *Book of Snobs*. Part of Thackeray's strength, already perceptible in his early work and unique among contemporary novelists, derives from his bold conviction that the transgressions of the English gentry

are commensurate with its position. That position allows for a margin and a pitch of abuse that other classes, with the exception of outright criminals, cannot dare to imitate. His gentry already exhibit all the qualities that *Vanity Fair* organizes successfully: brutal insolence in its money marriages; mediocrity and incompetence that, backed up by family, hold high rank in the army and important posts in the government; the capacity for living on nothing a year by criminal fleecing of tradespeople; and, of course, every single nuance of snobbery, translated into details of language, gesture, clothing, furniture, and style of life that already anticipates the Arnold of *Culture and Anarchy* with the Philistine as target. In fact, a good part of the world of *Vanity Fair* (and of the later novels) is already to be found in the *Book of Snobs*.

At the same time, we can see the gradual emergence of the author-commentator behind the scenes, moralizing, often tediously and with sentimental apostrophe, directly to his reader, though often soundly enough. He is conscious already of the vanity of most human effort as fortune changes and as age begins to tell. He approves the simple, the unaffected, the gentle, the manly, the unprotected. Finally, autobiographical proximities begin to show after the tragic madness of his wife in 1840, slightly in *A Shabby Genteel Story*, but more pronouncedly in *The Great Hoggarty Diamond*, as well as in the restless, social clubman, Mr Snob.

Thackeray's major strategy for the total organization of *Vanity Fair* (1848) is his use of Becky Sharp as the pivotal figure. His lesser strategy is one that employs Becky too; but this plan fails to ignite successive explosions along the way, and soon becomes a very prolonged and tedious fizzle. I refer, of course, to *Vanity Fair* as a study in contrasted destinies: Becky Sharp versus Amelia Sedley.

The essential felicity of Becky is a critical commonplace. But critics have failed to appreciate the degree to which Becky enables Thackeray to offer a powerful indictment of his society that is yet coolly controlled to the point, almost, of ostensible negligence. In the first place, Becky has a density that derives in large measure from the way in which Thackeray makes his full society gravitate around her tense little figure. Other characters gain vitality from Becky as her own kind of formidableness ignites a responding play of strongly defined character. Thackeray creates her cumulatively as a figure, beginning

easily with her departure from Miss Pinkerton's school. His satirical skill shows in dramatic particularity from the outset. He offers quick and vivid flashbacks to her tough preparation in the world of her Bohemian father and in the early skirmish with the Rev. Mr Crisp. Then he takes us step by step through the graded challenges of Jos. Sedley, Sir Pitt, Rawdon, and Steyne; through the different challenges of George Osborne, Miss Crawley, Mrs Bute Crawley, Mr Pitt Crawley, and the world of Pumpernickel: each with proliferating or connected social extensions.

Moreover, 'balance' in Becky saves the novel. 'Balance' in Amelia saves Thackeray only from the grosser excesses of sentimentality. Thackeray's conception of Becky carries the full weight of the theme. He employs all his technical resources in giving her joy in jostling, elbow-room in surveying and planning, zest in the social game as it is played. Becky has, also, resiliency, and she has good humour in defeat, so that something spills over by way of an exuberance in living that is quite unrelated to Thackeray's satirical purpose. She figures, therefore, as an indispensable distancing agent. Above all other characters she keeps Thackeray's cool ferocity in check.

Part of Becky's superiority over others lies in the absence of ill-humour, meanness, or savage intensity in her self-interest, an attitude urged on her by a situation in which she begins with nothing, has nothing to lose and everything to gain, positively enjoys the game of duplicity, and doesn't much mind slipping back into the dingy Bohemia of her origins. Unlike the others, Becky is at her best when she miscalculates seriously, is able to laugh at disastrous miscalculation and then bounce right back. She is able to maintain an attitude of detached relish even in the scene where Rawdon discovers her with Steyne. She carries her resilient slipperiness to Pumpernickel, so that the reader is hardly surprised at her good fortune, irony and all, at the end.

In fact, Thackeray has almost an affection for the Becky puppet. Compared with the figures he detests, Thackeray shows little animus towards her. Her sins, the most terrible sins in Thackeray's code, are that she is incapable of affection, love, or loyalty. But he does not make her suffer deeply. On the other hand, he visits old Osborne with the death of his only son, with a gloomy and joyless life, and with a gloomier and more joyless death. He pursues old Sedley and his wife step by inexorable step through a broken, ruined, and ignominious

beggary. He portrays in Sir Pitt an animality, a self-defeating miser-liness, at once dirty and malevolent. He makes him inhabit rotting, gloomy surroundings, reflecting a state of mind. And he reduces him in the end to a helpless, maniacal infant. He registers every detail of Miss Crawley's suffering from overeating. Later the family gnaws away at her inheritance. The Gaunt family is made to suffer from 'a mysterious taint of blood: the poor mother had brought it from her own ancient race'. Thackeray fills in as many precise details to this prelude to suffering, decay of powers, and madness in Steyne as is permissible to a Victorian novelist. He shows a refinement of savagery in creating Mr Pitt Crawley as a highly successful medi-ocrity, with only enough shrewdness to compromise gentry prin-ciples with middle-class ascendancy and climbing. But Becky, after a pleasurably dirty relapse into the Bohemian world, suffers no such fate:

> ... Rebecca, Lady Crawley, chiefly hangs about Bath and Cheltenham, where a very strong party of excellent people consider her to be a most injured woman. She has her enemies. Who has not? Her life is her answer to them. She busies herself in works of piety. She goes to Church, and never without a footman. Her name is in all the Charity lists.

Not only – and it is one of his finest touches – does Thackeray make Becky disinherited; he makes her a governess, with the impetus to advance herself, particularly when she is convinced early on that she is the superior of most of the aristocracy whom she encounters. At Miss Pinkerton's, Becky is able to show up the fashionable boarding-school: its parasitism on real learning, its finely discriminated adjustment to every single degree of snobbery, its calculated preparation for 'class' function, and, most of all, its educa-tional aim, one that is concerned principally with the marriage market. The collapse of John Sedley's fortune in effect collapses George Osborne's affection for Amelia, as Becky proves so easily. Becky's own marriage with Rawdon proves to be an almost success-ful calculation, and her relation with Steyne is self-interest in all its purity. Rawdon's marriage to Becky is the superlative of impru-dence, and he is punished accordingly; while the full weight of Osborne Senior's bourgeois ethic comes down inexorably on his son for a similar imprudence. Birth signifies an upbringing in an ambitious morality of pushing ahead. Children become the mere

instruments for their parents' goals, and death is the leaving or the not leaving of money and property. Fathers are despised by sons or sons by fathers as each succeeds or fails in these terms. Personal relations between man and man, man and woman, and woman and woman leave virtually no scope for disinterested friendship or love. The relations of Amelia and Dobbin, and of Dobbin and George Osborne, prove the point powerfully by pitiful exception.

Through Rawdon Crawley we witness the degree of sinecurism, incompetence, and cowardice in the army, while bravery is made as ineffectual there, and as overwhelmed, as in life. Indeed, by the time Thackeray is through with Rawdon and General Tufto (the latter already economically and effectively rendered in the *Book of Snobs*), and with Brussels as an ironic backdrop – one of the finest touches in the novel – against which the war is being fought, the reader begins to wonder what in fact motivates these men to fight at all. There is also the detail, forceful because presented so matter-of-factly, of Rawdon's sinecure appointment as governor of the fever-ridden Coventry Islands: Rawdon is an illiterate and an administrative incompetent. Politics is only an elaborate game of sinecurism. Even Smee, who later becomes an Academy painter, is made to portray the commercialization of art. Indeed, we meet with debasement in the smallest interstices of Thackerayan society.

Above all, the Churches are to be distinguished from the practice of the laity only in their greater cant. Thackeray pursues them like a moral bloodhound: Anglicans represented by Bute Crawley and his wife; Evangelicals by Mr Pitt Crawley and Lady Southdown; Dissenters by Osborne Senior and the relatives of Briggs. After the shocking affair of Becky and Steyne, even the Bishop of Ealing 'went and wrote his name down in the visiting-book of Gaunt House that very day'. *Vanity Fair* is so contrived that every professed man of religion is a dupe, or else uses that religion to palliate or to compound the evils that Thackeray sees around him. And all the people that Thackeray condemns – even Miss Crawley, with her revolutionary surfaces, even Becky – profess religion. Thackeray seems to have kept his respect for the clergy in real life, and to have used his novels to hit at abuse. At the same time, it is clear that in the age of Newman, Clough, and Arnold, Thackeray appears to have been virtually untouched by the spiritual question.

At any rate, that is the invariable pattern – a pattern that allows, of course, for considerable variety and for some subtlety. Yet after a while the comparative rigidity of the pattern begins to tell on the reader. It tells even with Becky. She is too much of the same thing. We know all her stratagems and her subterfuges early in the book. We watch them repeated in scene after scene, with only a change of opposing personality and different social setting to relieve those tricks. Soon the pattern of Victorian vanities becomes all too predictable, so that the last section, devoted to Becky at Pumpernickel – even a good part of the section in which Becky rises in Steyne's world – is very tedious indeed.

If Thackeray had not seemed to offer particular forms of personal and familial decency to stand as pinpoints of resistance against the hydra-headed evils of an acquisitive society, we might have little reason to come down heavily on *Vanity Fair*. But he is so aroused, apparently, by his sense of encompassing vanity that, to drive his intention home, he contrives to inject weaknesses into those characters of whom we are, in a general way, to approve: Amelia and Dobbin. The effect is, clearly, to betray our intelligence.

Thackeray achieves in good measure the very intention of *Vanity Fair*: that is, to make Amelia and Dobbin ineffectual creatures. No one can gainsay the deliberately inserted weaknesses of both. Amelia is a 'silly thing' who 'would cry over a dead canary bird; or over a mouse, that the cat haply had seized upon; or over the end of a novel, were it ever so stupid ...' Thackeray gives her the selfishness of a deeply rooted parasitic vine; or, in using Dobbin, the selfishness that luxuriates in admiration without the responsibility of reciprocity. Again, Amelia uses her passive helplessness as a weapon, indistinguishable, in crises, from contemptible cowardice. Nor is Amelia given any conscious, reflecting intelligence – we see this to be true of virtually all of Thackeray's 'good' women – so that she is almost entirely a passive receptacle of damaging experiences.

Dobbin is Amelia's male counterpart, except that he is made to carry more of our admiration. Dobbin's role as Victorian male forces him to judge and to act with more force. He is quicker about the character of Becky. He dissociates himself from the gambling-drinking-duelling-whoring-braggart-snob set in the army, and shows courage under fire. He earns his promotions. He is a gentleman

with a strong sense of a gentleman's word in friendship (even though that friend is the entirely despicable George Osborne), in the engagement vow (even though his meddling precipitates a disaster), and in marriage (even to so foolish a woman as Amelia).

Thackeray's best effects, then, are the effects of habit and temperament. They are not the effects of intelligence. He eliminates disciplined intelligence from the world of his novels. Such intelligence would trace motives to their sources in a way that enlightens more than excuses. It knows its own nature accurately and can assess itself realistically. Where it does not know and where it cannot assess, at least it probes. It discriminates among the values it holds. Moreover, an effective intelligence must be tough enough to combat what seeks to destroy it or to render it ineffectual. In that combat, it fixes the nature, the motives, the qualities of its own strength and weaknesses, as well as those of its opponents; it is capable of perceiving a balance, good and bad, in itself and in others. Where relationships are difficult, it moves to a clear recognition of the essential difficulty in some ethic of resolution.

But neither Thackeray nor any of the characters in his novels – in *Vanity Fair* or elsewhere – has such intelligence. What Thackeray does possess are powerful bourgeois sentiments relating to marriage, love, family, and friendship, sentiments amounting either to the sentimentalities of nineteenth-century theatre when he portrays characters in action, or to author-commentaries that are, on the whole, intolerable for the twentieth-century reader. When Rawdon Crawley, that 'heavy dragoon with strong desires and small brains, who had never controlled a passion in his life', reforms late in the novel, the responsible force, seen entirely from the outside and having no connection with any 'mind' we can discern, is the sentiment that attaches to 'child' and 'home'. Amelia in love makes no discriminations about an object as reprehensible as George Osborne, and yet the reader is to approve – to wallow in – the sentiment of 'love'. Nor does Dobbin make discriminations in his friendship with the same George – a friendship that is indistinguishable from lackeyship. Yet the reader is to approve the sentiment of 'friendship'. Thackeray subjects the deluded Sedleys to an attrition equal to their previous – even their later – vanities. Yet Amelia's sentiments about family duty, exercised on such a pair, are beyond reproach. Thackeray's corrective has shown

itself in Amelia's foolish fidelity to George's memory, and even in her helplessness in his reverses. But he offers no hint of criticism when she is reconciled to George in marriage. For, we must imagine, untouchable pieties attach to 'marriage' itself. And her farewell to George on the eve of the Battle of Waterloo, and her later mourning his death, are offered with a shaky pen by the author, tears blotting the pages. Indeed, the very worst scenes of nineteenth-century stage theatricality are devoted to Amelia: Amelia confronting the wicked Becky; Amelia struck down by her father's disaster and devoting herself to such a family; Amelia devoted to Georgey: mother-and-child are sacred; Amelia separated from her son.

With *Pendennis* (1848–50) the scale tips. The reader is now more conscious of weakness than of strength, for Thackeray has now subtly shifted his attitude to the 'world': he accommodates himself to it. That is to say, he remains on the one hand the old Thackeray whose writing hand comes alive in the exposure of the world of *Vanity Fair*, which in *Pendennis* happens to be the world of Major Pendennis, the Claverings, and Blanche Amory. But Arthur Pendennis, the protagonist of the story and, despite certain expected weaknesses of character (there are, we are given to understand, no 'heroes' or 'heroines' in Thackeray), presumably Thackeray's spokesman, is content to acquiesce in the inevitability of the ills without taking one step to track them down to their sources. Thackeray does not offer us any powerful images of representative health, or present any intelligent characters who, however minor or however outweighed, conduct a campaign that organizes some nucleus of intelligence. We have only George Warrington, a gentlemanly continuation of Dobbin, who remains, when all is said, a speechifying character. Warrington strikes out with a comfortable kind of quixotic idealism against the same world of *Vanity Fair*, but Thackeray envelops him, and so is able to dismiss him, within the melodramatized rhetoric of reform befitting an undergraduate radical. Arthur Pendennis, at first corrupted by this world but later saved by the love of a good woman, reappears in *The Newcomes* and *Philip*, submerged happily in a middle-class marriage, so dear to the hearts of Thackeray, Dickens, and their readers.

Accommodations must be made within the structure of the novel. Pen is to be a character manly, candid, generous, kindly, good-

natured, likeable. But he is weak, indulged by his mother, and in evoking his good qualities, Thackeray's imagination works largely in terms of nineteenth-century theatre – in turn sentimental or melodramatic. Once Pendennis moves away from the rural community of his mother, first to Cambridge and later to Fleet Street and London society, we watch the corruption of the 'world', exemplified in his uncle Major Pendennis, take hold. Pen becomes a snob, a dandy, a social climber, at once egotistic and vacillating, with an eye to a successful marriage and a seat in Parliament. Blanche Amory, with one strong, well-developed eye on the main chance and one weak one on affections so self-deceiving that she is incapable of knowing what she truly feels, is yet capable of attracting Pen to the very end of the novel. Thus Pen is never made to perceive the exact nature and qualities of his admirable traits. He never reflects about the intelligent operation of these qualities in personal relations. Defeat brings either cynicism or despair with the unshakeably wicked world. Temporary success means sentimental apostrophe or theatricality. Even more significantly, the reader never follows the inward impact of Pen's proliferating vices, from the crass exuberances of adolescent love, to gambling, idleness, imperiousness and conceit, dandyism, meretricious journalism, snobbery and climbing. In Thackeray's world the good and bad exist side by side: the connection is left out. And this formula applies particularly to the characters of whom the reader is to approve. Indeed, so patent is the flaw that one has to turn to biography to account for it.

None the less, the first part of the novel is quite successful, although much of it is also distasteful, particularly some of the excesses of Pen's infatuation, the sections devoted to Helen Pendennis, and those devoted to Mr Smirke and Dr Portman, Thackeray's by now predictable clergyman. The short section on Cambridge is also good, although marred both by sentimental nostalgia and the restrictions of biography. The section devoted to Fleet Street has a certain liveliness at the outset. It is a world that Thackeray has left untouched since the fine irony of the *Book of Snobs*. But even here we have the effect almost of caricature, as Thackeray chooses to reduce his literary figures almost entirely to their human vices. But once the book has fairly launched Pen in the literary world, it bogs down. The quality of Thackerayan 'vanity' has changed. The effects of time on

human values, the loss of friends and close ones, and the decay of one's powers ought to be confronted and faced with some mature impersonality. Instead they are now increasingly made the grounds for self-indulgent effects of pathos.

Henry Esmond (1852) is an historical novel, one of the earliest and the most successful attempts at historical reconstruction. It must be so judged. It possesses compression and thematic compactness, good narrative pace, and a descriptive skill that shows itself in flashes as well as in more extensive scenes. And in this novel, Thackeray undertakes perhaps his most difficult relationship to this time – that between Rachel and Henry. Yet if, as we have already seen, Thackeray in his normal novels tends to present characters from the outside, in *Henry Esmond* the sin is compounded. It is a novel that builds its effects cumulatively in scene after scene of costume-drama theatricality. While Thackeray is particularly skilful in the way in which he allows the relationship between Esmond and Rachel gradually to emerge, the reader is aware that his sense of that relationship depends on a mosaic of scenes acted out on a stage of strong lights and shadows, with the actors' voices pitched to the farthest gallery. Moreover, the telling moments of perplexity, where, for example, one cannot imagine how Rachel can feel for Esmond as both 'son' and 'lover', are moments of perplexity for Thackeray as well.

Henry Esmond becomes, as a result, a novel whose plan is considerably more interesting than its performance. Thackeray sets himself the task of describing, within an historical setting, the developing love between Esmond and Rachel, Rachel eight years older and married, at the outset, to Esmond's kinsman and benefactor, Viscount Castlewood. Esmond becomes hopelessly enamoured of Rachel's own daughter, Beatrix, so that Rachel herself must practise the self-discipline of a woman who knows Esmond's suit is hopeless, yet who must deny her own love for Esmond and encourage that suit.

But the performance is another matter. While Thackeray has the advantage, presumably, of historical distance, biographical closeness remains virtually unchanged, and produces all the ambiguities of his earlier novels. For in the most interesting character in the book, that of Rachel, we have only a more complex variation of Helen Pendennis, in whom generalized virtues and vices exist side by side. On the one hand, Rachel is tender, 'religious', saintly, quietly benevo-

lent. She lives entirely for her attachments, for husband and children, selfless and courageous in those loves. Then, Thackeray gives her somewhat more depth in unconscious evil than Helen. Her jealous possessiveness, self-righteous and unapproachable, first drives her husband to drink and mistresses; then alienates her children from their father when Castlewood ceases to love her; and finally causes those children to turn from her, Beatrix attempting an ambitious marriage, Frank leaving England permanently and marrying a Roman Catholic. When Rachel marries Esmond, that same jealousy competes with Esmond for the love of their daughter. Again, like Helen Pendennis, Rachel is prepared to allow for any vice of character in those she loves – even to encourage it.

But the character of Rachel fails. It is theatrically conceived and theatrically carried out. And it exhibits the flaw already alluded to in *Vanity Fair* and *Pendennis*: she possesses no psychological inwardness, a failure to know or to connect strength and limitation. And the same is true of Esmond, although he is much less interesting, being done in terms of generalized perfections. As for Beatrix, she is interesting, but only as a stage personality is interesting. It is impossible to describe her without resorting to the language of melodrama.

The historical reconstruction is a mixture. The whole amounts to a well-captured sense of the externals of the eighteenth century. But the deeper aspects of that century are lost. Admittedly, the imitation of a *Spectator* paper is very good. At the same time Thackeray does with Steele (he is hardly adequate on Addison himself, and much less just to Swift – how unjust is seen more clearly in his lectures on *The English Humorists of the Eighteenth Century*) what he did with members of Fleet Street in *Pendennis*: he reduces Steele to such vices as might belong to the ordinary man, hardly to an intelligent man of letters. Moreover, when one thinks that this was the age of Richardson's *Clarissa*, of Pope's *Dunciad*, and of Fielding, one feels that an outrage has been done to its intellectual tone.

With *The Newcomes* (1853–5) we return to the world of *Vanity Fair* as it has already been transmuted in *Pendennis*. It is as though Thackeray, mellowed and less concentrated in satirical purpose, has a second look at a deeply compromised gentry which bolsters rank through alliances with money, and which, in this way, affects other orders of society. Thackeray's savagery is now much more

controlled, more balanced, more accommodating. The only characters who carry something of the satirical force of *Vanity Fair* are Barnes Newcome, one of the most detestable snobs in Thackeray's extensive gallery, and Mrs Mackenzie, the old Campaigner, a harrowing, vindictive, relentless shrew of a woman, Thackeray's most successful portrait of the kind. On the other hand, Thackeray achieves somewhat more balance in *The Newcomes* than in *Vanity Fair* through the sheer number of characters who are meant to have the reader's sympathies. Among them, Colonel Newcome is a Dobbin spelled out in considerable detail. His openness, benevolence, love for his son, sense of honour, simplicity (amounting at times to simple-mindedness), combined with his military courage, stimulate an answering affection in the many characters of whom the reader is to approve – and an answering contempt on the part of those whom the reader is to reprehend. The colonel remains to the end an innocent, untouchable by the Great World, yet Thackeray manages in his case to achieve the effect of skilful sentimentality, especially in the famous death-scene. The most interesting failure in the book, however, is Ethel Newcome, an unusual heroine for Thackeray, since she possesses some intelligence, spirit, and a sense of humour. Nevertheless, she allows herself to be hopelessly managed by her grandmother, Lady Kew, and almost marries that superlative of fatuousness, Lord Farintosh. It takes the major catastrophe of Barnes Newcome's scandalous and unhappy marriage to effect a change. We are on the very border here of Trollope's better novels. Unhappily, the young lady is given no capacity either for self-examination or for incisive examination of others.

On the whole, however, the effect of *The Newcomes* remains what it is in *Vanity Fair*: decent people almost hopelessly submerged by the corrupt world they inhabit, and unable to draw upon any intelligence that might at least enable them to comprehend the terms of that plight. They escape into Thackeray's code of the bourgeois gentleman.

In the hands of Trollope (1815–82), the writing of novels becomes a quiet and workmanlike process. Plot, theme, dramatic scene, psychological notation, author-commentary, and a leisurely pace, encouraged by serial publication and the three-decker, are adjusted

to his remarkable sense of a modest and delicate, yet tough and sophisticated, English strength. He locates that strength not so much in the securely privileged gentry, as in the way in which the principles for which the English gentry stands affect its less privileged members as well as the lesser orders. But it is a gentry in the nineteenth century already deeply veined with a middle-class bourgeois ethic: both in Thackeray and Trollope the sanctity and respectability of the home become untouchable moral pivots. Trollope uses the novel to create a world, various and full, in which that gentry may see itself and its fortunes mirrored. He defines that world in part by those who oppose it, who betray it from within, or who would subvert it entirely.

Above all, Trollope learns from Thackeray to write convincingly and in detail of the world of London, encompassing nobility, gentry, and the extension of nobility and gentry in the society of the Continent; lawyers, doctors, clergymen, army and navy officers, painters, architects; civil servants as well as government officials of high rank; the publishing and political world; the world of the prosperous middle classes, in trade, in speculation, or in property; the shabby genteel; commercial travellers. But Trollope is at his best in dealing with the rural south, Barchester and elsewhere. Here he touches virtually all classes in finely graded detail, with the exception of Hardy's agricultural labourers. He deals with Australia, Ireland, and America. Indeed, Trollope appears to have omitted only the considerable world of industrial capitalism and labour, which he touches on indirectly.

A novel by Trollope is extraordinarily casual, informal, but it allows for considerable variations as the easy language of cultivated conversation adjusts itself to the significance of the theme or the intensity of the dramatic moment. In part the easy, leisurely unfolding of each novel appears to rest on Trollope's assured communion with his audience, which carries the expectation that each chapter could be read aloud in any cultivated English home. A Trollope novel answers, in part, to his conviction that a novelist ought to take his audience fully into his confidence. There are to be no mysteries about the nature or the fate of any character. In *Phineas Redux*, for example, we are told the name of the murderer even while 'all of London' tries to find him. In *Doctor Wortle's School*, Trollope

chooses to tell the reader the full history of Mr and Mrs Peacocke's bigamy before the details are known to any of the other characters. While such easy confidence figures as strength where the reader's interest is fully engaged on the theme, those novels where the reader's interest is not captured suffer precisely from lack of suspense and are prosaically dull.

Perhaps the most disfiguring effect of his audience on his novels is the implicit demand for the best-seller touch and the best-seller ending; or closely allied to best-sellerism, the avoidance of the tough intellectuality or the unmitigably tragic ending that many of his themes demand. The Barchester novels are all committed to the happy ending, but a happy ending in which Trollope allows his audience to indulge in the right number of apprehensions, the pain of the right number of temporary reverses, assured, at the same time, that all will come out comfortably in the end. Every once in a while he will defeat the expectation of the reader, and so achieve an easy reputation for depth where, in fact, no depth exists. None the less, in his typical novel, characters unfold gradually and the effects are cumulative. There is a reflectiveness on the part of his best characters, a reflectiveness that compels discriminations about character, society, and even civilization. Besides, Trollope, unlike Thackeray, makes his best characters entirely self-consistent and coherent. He makes them connect. In a novel by Trollope where, for example, a character suffers from ambiguities, like Mr Crosbie in *The Small House at Allington*, or from the cruellest uncertainties, like Louis Trevelyan in *He Knew He Was Right*, the terms of those ambiguities or uncertainties are fully enacted, often with well-controlled irony.

Trollope's characteristic mode, then, is easily distinguishable, and it comes alive with varying degrees of success as it subserves his predominant subject-matter: the changing fortunes of his pivotal gentry class. Here one must say, in anticipation, that it is at once Trollope's strength and weakness that the assumptions he shares with his audience and his acute sense of disturbances rarely have behind them something sharply defined, something held with an intensity of conviction that shapes a novel into a dramatic, organic whole. Rather, Trollope's sense of what makes for a gentleman, his religious or political convictions, his sense of what the relationships of men

and women ought to be, his feelings about the orders within the different classes, his confrontation of the claims of love as against property, his awareness of the threat to his squirearchy – all emerge in almost experimental form for each novel. He explores different kinds of landowners, members of the aristocracy, tenant farmers, young men and young women belonging to the different orders and seen in differing relationships, clergymen, lawyers, politicians, and the rest. It seems virtually impossible to trace a development, or even to say, as with Thackeray, that certain themes will stimulate Trollope to write movingly or forcefully. The reader must judge each novel in turn, sorting out strength and weakness. He knows that for virtually every novel he is to expect a basic theme – rarely a 'thesis'. When the love theme is not central, he knows that he will also get one or two love-stories that will touch on the theme, sometimes directly but very often distantly. And the reader knows that in most of Trollope's novels he will find extraneous material. In *Barchester Towers*, for example, the heart of Trollope's concern has to do with a struggle among higher clergy for political power within a cathedral town. The love-story of Eleanor Bold and the Rev. Francis Arabin, the caricatured triangle of Slope, Madame Neroni, and Eleanor Bold, and the comic efforts of Bertie's proposal to Eleanor Bold – all are tangents. The sports at Ullathorne are quite extraneous, disproportionately so.

The centre of gravity of the earlier Trollope appears to be the rural England of the south – the Trollope, that is, of the Barchester novels essentially: *The Warden* (1855), *Barchester Towers* (1857), *Doctor Thorne* (1858), *Framley Parsonage* (1861), *The Small House at Allington* (1864), and *The Last Chronicle of Barset* (1867). In all of his Barchester novels there is a continual movement from the comparative stability of a rural order – a stability that is almost idyllic – into the profoundly disturbing rhythms of the world of London; or a movement as London society impinges with disquieting effects upon the rural south. But in the Barchester novels the rural order is capable not only of absorbing and controlling that disquiet. It is also capable of convincing the reader that the economic and political strength of a nation derives in large measure from the well-being of the agricultural order in the south. By the time of the political novels centred around *Phineas Finn* (1869), as well as of *He Knew*

He Was Right (1869), the centre of gravity has moved slowly. With *The Eustace Diamonds* (1873), *Phineas Redux* (1874), and *The Way We Live Now* (1875), Trollope's rural order has lost the power that it once possessed in the Barchester series, whether he chooses to use London or not. While it is impossible to call Trollope by any means a pessimistic writer – there are assurances in every novel – and while a novel here and there (*Doctor Wortle's School*, for example, in 1881) will tend to dispel the gloom and preserve a tone befitting a profound dedication to law, order, and continuity, still Trollope's novels from about the middle 1860s do show an intensifying disquiet. And the number of characters driven either by their own obsessions or by a disturbed world increases.

Thus, the lesson of Thackeray is an invaluable one. But the form of Thackeray's influence is unexpected enough. For Trollope is a kind of Thackeray in reverse. He absorbs fully Thackeray's attack against the upper and upper-middle classes; then he uses that attack as a complex point of dramatic conflict against which the code of his gentry can assert itself in devious ways. Thanks to Thackeray, Trollope can assume at once the courage of a fairly radical criticism of gentry and nobility, particularly of all their vices as they show so signally in London society, including the Court. London is for Trollope the Scarlet City: the city of dissipation, ostentation, snobbery, gambling, drunkenness, sexual incontinence, idleness, drift. By the middle of the 1860s, the spirit of London begins to tell.

In the Barchester novels, as well as in most of the successful early ones – *Orley Farm* (1862), *Can You Forgive Her?* (1864), *The Belton Estate* (1866), *The Claverings* (1867) – Trollope's gentry is victimized in a number of ways by its position of privilege and pride in that privilege. But Trollope is able to use that victimization in a way that makes for spiritedness in the novel: Squire Dale unable to prevail upon Mrs Dale and Bell; Lady Lufton unable to shake Lucy Robarts; Doctor Thorne commanding respect from the Greshams; Nora Rowley turning down Mr Glascock; Grace Crawley resisting the Grantly family. Moreover, in these early novels Trollope tends to separate his Whigs, influenced by London and the Court, for whom land is only a species of business and who are, like as not, absentee landlords with an establishment in London – the Duke of Omnium and the whole de Courcy family – from his Tory Squires, hide-

bound or liberal, clerical or lay, whose responsibility remains in the county. Trollope's squires tend to domineer over every single grade of their social inferiors, and their domination begins in the family, where an imperious father (sometimes a mother) exerts his tyranny, often well-meaning and benevolent enough, over wife and children. One of the most engaging themes in Trollope's novels is the theme in which the powerful claims of property and rank assert themselves either against the imprudence on the part of children or against the price to be paid for love. Trollope's most convincing characters are the forceful members of a family who maintain, often sensibly enough, that children ought to marry within their class; or that the elder son must be mindful of his great responsibilities as the inheritor of property; or, where family fortunes have declined seriously, that sons and daughters must make advantageous marriages: Lady Lufton, Squire Dale, Lady and Judge Snaveley, Archdeacon Grantly, Gresham Senior, Sir Marmaduke Rowley.

In these earlier novels Trollope's young men are as convincing as his young women. They make highly realistic appraisals of their position and their place within family and society, and they show balance as they answer at once to the demands of love as against those of family, society, and, often enough, the 'world' influenced by London. Trollope's protagonists revere the pledged word, not only in marriage, but in all personal relations, down to the most minute detail. They detest any form of deceit, dishonesty, or lightness of concern – anything short, in fact, of unequivocal honesty, whatever the penalties.

While Trollope portrays as admirable the self-assurance of his gentry – the absence of self-doubt, self-questioning, and the expectation of deference – he is also aware of its stubbornness, its hard conservatism, its inability to be schooled, its unwillingness to move quickly enough with the times. His gentry shows a lack of intellectual grasp. It may respect cleverness, wit, talent, cultivation, and yet it has no deep interest in intellectual attainments, spiritual depth and fineness, or artistic capacities. It appears to have a dangerous tendency not to consider deeply enough the extent and increased mobility of social, political, and religious change. It is incapable of re-examining the grounds on which its right to govern and to rule rests. Trollope touches on these matters. But in the Barchester novels these

tendencies could be portrayed as a kind of picturesque corrective in the rural south to the rest of the nation. The essential quality is idyllic. Yet even in these earlier novels, London already casts its shadow.

Birth into privilege encourages all the vices, although in the earlier novels Trollope tones down the proclivities. Sons are often predisposed to dissipation, to boredom, to laziness when the times demand shrewdness, industriousness, and competence at least equal to these qualities in the prosperous middle classes. Inheritors of property show a tendency to driftlessness, weakness of character, or even all the vices made so familiar by Thackeray: Bernard Amedroz, Louis Trevelyan, Colonel Osborne, Colonel Marrable, Gresham Senior, Sir Hugh Clavering, the Duke of Omnium, and the whole de Courcy family might well come from the pages of Thackeray.

At the same time they are made to exhibit a highly flexible capacity for admitting all kinds and conditions into their ranks, however stubborn their resistance may be at any given point – such stubbornness makes for good drama, confident, as Trollope makes them, that in time their code and their way of life will continue undisturbed. At bottom, what is most important for Trollope is that any individual who – even with few or no prospects for money and advancement – is allowed into the gentry is the individual who accepts the code. Most often his protagonists come from good families, however impoverished. The gentry itself, secure in position, shows a tolerance often close to condescension, and a tough, urbane wit that keeps social distances alive.

Hence, it is a tribute to Trollope's characteristic strength that our sense of the gentry of which he approves, roughly the liberal Tory gentry, is one that cannot be divorced from that novelist's fully realized characters and themes where his protagonists maintain their virtues very shakily indeed, disturbed from within by their own limitations and vices, and threatened from without by forces that oppose them, compromise them, or would destroy them. The forces of responsibility, order, decency, cultivation and continuity struggle realistically to maintain themselves; the goods in life, as Trollope appears to have believed in them, all have to be paid for by difficult and uncertain exertion. And the gentry's supporters and dependants,

accepting their inferior position, income, and prospects with an equal pride, try in their way to live by the same code.

Trollope's clergymen deserve separate consideration because they figure so prominently in his successful earlier novels as extensions of his gentry world. His bishops, deans, archdeacons, and lesser clergy are either born gentlemen who exemplify the basic Christian precepts in a society that accepts rank and position in the hierarchical order; or, having achieved a little pre-eminence in the theological world much as, for Trollope, Sir Roger Scatcherd achieves pre-eminence in the engineering world, they are duly promoted. Here they accept their place much as Trollope appears to have accepted his entrance as a successful professional writer. Trollope rarely calls attention to theological matters, and he appears to have had no greater interest in, or qualification for, the deeper questions of religion than he had for those of law or politics. He appears to have taken it for granted that his form of moderate Anglican belief, translated almost exclusively into personal and social terms, had had throughout the centuries an incalculable civilizing and stabilizing effect on his gentry, their dependants, and their supporters, so that the basis of that gentry code is one rooted in moral principle and preached and practised through the ages.

As a self-conceived gentleman, complete with hunting uniform, Trollope shows a commendable if condescending balance in his attitude to the middle classes, but without underestimating their strength. Actually, by the nineteenth century middle-class virtues and middle-class attitudes had so permeated the gentry that often little separated them. Trollope's admiration for the rewards of industriousness and resourcefulness is middle class, though untouched in any way by religious sanctions. He appears to have believed that the progress of England and its standing among other nations depended on the continued commercial expansion that was the achievement of the middle classes. Even more deeply, however, his belief in the sanctity of marriage, the purity and innocence of young women, the virtues of respectability based on honesty and avoiding snobbery, his hatred for drunkenness, luxury, vulgar and ostentatious pride, gambling, idleness, dissipation – these are middle-class to the core. On the other side, he hated the vices of the ascendant middle class

almost as fiercely as Thackeray did – its restless ambitiousness, its crude and vicious snobberies, and its religious cant. He condemns its many members who make fortunes through speculation instead of honest work, who are unscrupulous in business practice, and who use legal and political trickery to enforce dishonesty.

In judging the strength and weakness in the earlier novels, however, we have to make discriminations that go far beyond Trollope's affinities and antipathies – his assurances – as described. For in his more interesting novels, a character will sometimes be unaware of the ultimate source of strength or weakness, and mistake one for the other: Mr Crawley in *The Last Chronicle of Barset*, or Alice Vavasor in *Can You Forgive Her?* Or a character will explore possibilities of dramatic experience of considerably greater subtlety than any generalized description can allow for. Yet the fact remains that our concern for the great majority of the issues that Trollope explores derives from his deep interest in the complex code by which his gentry and lesser gentry seeks to maintain itself, and in the ways in which that code expresses itself in the smallest details of living. In *The Warden*, the successful portion of the novel deals with the way in which Mr Harding maintains his dignity in the teeth of London manipulation, although it must be admitted that the character of Harding is wraith-like. *Barchester Towers* maintains our interest at those points where the struggle for political power, largely in the hands of Archdeacon Grantly, is fought out against Mrs Proudie, the Bishop, and *Jupiter*, the London newspaper, ostensibly *The Times*. In *Doctor Thorne*, the story maintains its interest in so far as Mary Thorne and Doctor Thorne assert their intelligent dignity against the Greshams, particularly as Doctor Thorne practises a highly difficult honesty; in the part devoted to Miss Dunstable before her marriage with Doctor Thorne; in the part in which the de Courcy family and the Duke of Omnium figure. Sir Roger Scatcherd, interesting in a Dickensian way, is seen too much from the outside. And the contrivance of the happy ending is not only a gross bid to make the book a best-seller; it is unpleasantly vindictive. In *Framley Parsonage*, the section devoted to Mark Robarts's weakness as he allows himself to be plunged deeply in debt by Mr Sowerby is perhaps the most successful. Unfortunately, serial-writing pressures compel Trollope to drop the story for a disproportionate length at

just the point at which it becomes most interesting. Again, the story of Lucy Robarts is most successful at the point at which she resists Lady Lufton, but her relationships with Lord Lufton suffer from the best-seller touch. The last of the Barchester novels, *The Last Chronicle of Barset*, is perhaps the best. The Rev. Crawley is one of the most successful of all of Trollope's characters. He is a complex mixture of proud and aggressive humility, in part compulsive because he is so isolated, in part dedicated in its quality of ascetic Christianity, rigid but with a certain elasticity and delicacy. The moral dignity inherent in the theme of the theft compels the reader's interest from beginning to end. And the Grace Crawley–Major Grantly theme helps to underpin the major section devoted to her father. But the London section, good though it is in itself, distracts.

Many of the non-Barchester novels also deserve to be re-read in our time, particularly those in which deepening shadows appear. In his later novels, however, there is only an increase of disquiet. In the first place, London society, and particularly the influence of that society in the rural community, plays a more significant role. Then, too, Trollope's clergymen, from whom the code of the gentry receives its moral sanction, tend to drop out of his stories and are replaced by politicians and lawyers. We now meet with themes in which there is a greater degree of bad faith in the gentry, of compromise, of admitting the necessity of treating land as a business that cannot afford the luxuries of traditional practices, of admitting defeat, and of placing gentry positions on the market for the highest bidder. *Mr Scarborough's Family* (1882), although not too successful as a novel, contains all these themes. Many of the later novels are Trollope's parliamentary novels, where the reader is so much more aware of the powerful alignments against county gentry and of a pitch of compromise not hitherto allowed. At the same time, Trollope refuses to take a stand or think through a problem. He simply poses questions and places on the reader the burden of finding answers to them. But he remains as genial as the theme allows him to be, and he almost invariably inserts a love-story in which either the gentry, or individuals who are accepted into the gentry, are made to win through. Trollope's most searching novel, *The Way We Live Now*, is his most drastic statement of the degree to which the world of commercial speculation has compromised

gentry and aristocracy, in London as well as in the rural community. The figure of Melmotte predominates, and there is hardly a figure who is not stained by his powerful dishonesty. Roger Carbury, Trollope's protagonist, is virtually as helpless as a rural Dobbin.

Trollope's weakness, as we read him today, is his resolute lack of any psychological penetration as searching as we find in Henry James or George Eliot, whom he resembles. He refuses to deal with the irrevocable tragedies of protagonists whom we deeply respect; and he refuses to take up a position where he could say clearly – and in dramatic terms – that his Victorian world suffers from a deep malaise or a profound disturbance here, here, and here. His basic subject-matter is his gentry. Yet he never translates his understanding of that gentry into terms that take into consideration past strength, present uncertainties, and future possibilities. He underestimates drastically the degree to which agriculture had become, necessarily, an industrialized business that could no longer afford the traditional niceties; the degree to which whole communities were, in consequence, disintegrating. If we simply juxtapose the novels of Hardy – the early Wessex novels overlap the later novels by Trollope – we perceive how seriously Trollope underestimates the changes, though he touches upon them in *The Way We Live Now*. Then, again, he never acknowledges the change which brings the middle classes, once and for all, into the ascendancy. The implication of the Barchester novels is that wealth will be absorbed into the gentry way of life and assimilated, in successive generations, within their code. And finally, Trollope's novels present somewhat increased mobility, increased sacrifice of principle, increased impoverishment, increased desperation. Yet he cannot bring himself to draw any conclusions. The best he can do is set up the equation and ask us in gentlemanly fashion to solve it ourselves.

In terms of the development of the novel, the weakness shows in Trollope's heroes. The hero ought to function as the judging centre of the novel. Should the gentry and its supporters cease to exist as heroes, the centre of Trollope's novels would collapse. That is why we feel that his presentation of the squirearchy in the Barchester novels is, in the last analysis, disingenuous, or desperate, or idyllic. Insensibly the squire, either as hero or as a point around which heroic forces might rally, disappears from Trollope's novels

as the scene moves to London. By the time of *The Way We Live Now* Trollope is able to present a grim picture, with Roger Carbury as displaced hero and the squirearchy as bankrupt in economics as well as in moral principle. In *The American Senator* and *Mr Scarborough's Family* the ritual picture reappears, but the drawing is now nervous, the magic propensities reiterated rather than done convincingly. Intelligence and pathos can do nothing to resolve a central ugliness.

THE EARLY VICTORIAN SOCIAL-PROBLEM NOVEL

ARNOLD KETTLE

A feeling very generally exists that the condition and disposition of the Working Classes is a rather ominous matter at present; that something ought to be said, something ought to be done, in regard to it. And surely, at an epoch of history when the 'National Petition' carts itself in wagons along the streets, and is presented 'bound with iron hoops, four men bearing it' to a Reformed House of Commons; and Chartism numbered by the million and half, taking nothing by its iron-hooped Petition, breaks out into brickbats, cheap pikes, and even into sputterings of conflagration, such very general feeling cannot be considered unnatural! To us individually this matter appears, and has for many years appeared, to be the most ominous of all practical matters whatever; a matter in regard to which if something be not done, something will *do* itself one day, and in a fashion that will please nobody. The time is verily come for acting in it, for speech and articulate inquiry about it!

The opening paragraph of Carlyle's *Chartism*, written in 1839, takes us directly into the situation and frame of mind out of which came the group of novels that are the subject of this chapter. They are sometimes referred to – the work of Disraeli, Elizabeth Gaskell, Charles Kingsley and their kind – as 'social novels'. It is a bad description, whether one uses the term strictly or loosely, for, strictly speaking, all novels are social novels; while if the word is used loosely as a rough equivalent of the twentieth-century 'socially-conscious', then the problem of what to do with Dickens immediately arises. For Dickens's novels are no less 'socially-conscious', no less 'engaged', no less insistently contemporary – morally, politically, colloquially – than those of the writers we are here concerned with.[1]

It is tempting to leave the distinction simply as a matter of quality. Dickens is an artist of genius who gets away with anything; the others, alas, less prodigally endowed. But what in fact distinguishes Dickens from the other comparable novelists is the total richness and complexity of his books, the depth of his commitment no less than his literary virtuosity. There is in the end nothing thin, nothing theoretic

or abstract about his novels. If they are about the condition of England (and there is no better general description of what his books are about), they cannot, somehow, be bounded by the heading of the opening chapter of Carlyle's *Chartism* – 'The Condition-of-England Question'; whereas Disraeli and Kingsley and Elizabeth Gaskell can. It is the note of abstraction involved in such words as Question and Problem that makes the difference. You cannot describe *Bleak House* (for all the insistent topicality which John Butt and Kathleen Tillotson have usefully emphasized[2]), or even *Oliver Twist* or *Hard Times*, as a 'social-problem novel'. But that is exactly what *Sybil* or *North and South* or *Alton Locke* is. And the distinction has something to do with the limit of involvement – emotional and artistic as well as social or political – concerned. To see a living complex of forces and people as a 'problem' necessarily implies a standpoint not merely detached in the artist's sense, but in a different way judicial, therapeutic perhaps, and all too easily self-righteous. It is not easy to define precisely the sense in which Kingsley, say, in *Alton Locke*, a propagandist, even passionately propagandist novel, is less fully *engagé*, more outside social struggle, than Dickens in *Our Mutual Friend*, which one would not describe as a propagandist novel at all. Perhaps the word 'preach' is one that should be indicated. The strain of abstraction involved in the word, the incompletely fused element of didacticism which even so thoroughly 'committed' a writer as Shelley abhorred, these edge into the most fundamental conceptions and standpoints of the social-problem novelist. Another way of putting it could be that, whereas Dickens at his finest achieved a poise which frees him from the more limiting aspects of his own class-position, the social-problem novelists are more basically class-bound in their whole stance as writers, sharing with a certain pusillanimity the fears as well as the challenges which Carlyle's own sentences express.

One must not, on the other hand, use the necessary contrast with Dickens as merely a back-handed means of derogation. When Carlyle calls for articulate inquiry into the 'Condition-of-England Question' he is not demanding from the point of view of the contemporary novelist something either ignoble or irrelevant. All but a handful of the very greatest writers have fairly rigid limitations, and while the sort of limitation involved in the social-problem novel is no more crippling than many others, the positive virtues which a responsible,

even if somewhat abstract, interest in the central human preoccupations of the time can bring are very considerable.

Carlyle's words form a useful starting-point, not only because he is himself so relevant a sage, so deep an influence on some of the writers concerned, but because of his immediate linking of the condition of England with certain specific issues, notably the growth of Chartism. The novels we are interested in here are essentially novels of a specific period. Whatever their particular year of publication they belong to the period of Chartism, the thirties and forties, decades – all are agreed – of deep economic and political crisis, appalling poverty, and the first assertion of a vast, popular, democratic social and political movement of the people based on the growth and desperation of the new industrial working class, the mine and factory workers who lived for the most part in the new hideous industrial centres of the North and the Midlands.

Apart from Elizabeth Gaskell, the novelists did not, by and large, write about the factory workers, though particular scenes in factories and mills do of course occur. More often they wrote about the poor of the rural areas or of London, where the social situation, though certainly not less intense or explosive, was somewhat different from that of the towns thrown up around heavy industry. The life of the London poor was not, of course, a new problem, and it had, moreover, the advantage, as far as a writer was concerned, of the literary tradition of Defoe and Fielding – to say nothing of Swift and Hogarth.

The social-problem novelists did not write primarily *for* the new proletariat, though no doubt they were happy enough if sections of the working class should happen to read their books. Much less than the more narrowly didactic writers of moral and political tracts and fables – the Hannah Mores of an earlier age and Harriet Martineaus of the present – did they aim at the new, increasingly literate if physically exhausted industrial workers. It was to the conscience – not to mention the downright factual ignorance – of the middle class that they addressed themselves.

In doing this they were not, so far as aim and method were concerned, breaking fresh ground. The novel with a specific moral, social, or even overtly political purpose did not begin with the publication of *Coningsby* (1844) and *Sybil* (1845). On the contrary,

the social-problem novelists of the forties were not more earnest in their aims nor half so abstract in their methods as their predecessors of half a century before. Then, under the influence of the French Revolution and eighteenth-century Enlightenment in general, and particularly that of two philosopher-novelists – Rousseau and Godwin – a whole spate of novels had appeared as uncompromising in their didacticism as they were highfalutin in their sentiment.

It is perhaps worth stressing, at this point, the importance of Godwin who, though he published his two major works, *Political Justice* and the novel *Caleb Williams*, in the seventeen-nineties, did not die until 1836, and was still writing novels in his old age. Godwin's novels are scarcely read nowadays, but his reputation as novelist as well as sage in his lifetime stood very high indeed, and critics as intelligent and unlike as Coleridge and Hazlitt spoke of him with great respect. *Caleb Williams* is, among other things, a social-problem novel, full of consciousness of class-division and its ramifications though the society it deals with is pre-Industrial Revolution. A link between Godwin and the novelists of the forties is Bulwer Lytton, who as a young man became very friendly with the elderly philosopher. Lytton's early novels, *Paul Clifford* (1830) and *Eugene Aram* (1832), are entirely Godwinian in spirit; while another of them, *Pelham* (1828), has much in common with Disraeli's early books.[3]

The Godwinian novelist was socially-conscious in the double sense of seeing personal and psychological problems as rooted in the organization of society and of wanting to change things. These novelists certainly did not regard themselves as above or outside the social struggle. Deeply influenced by Benthamite ideas, they were passionate reformers. But the weakness of their novels is that they are disastrously and often ludicrously abstract. Again and again, with Holcroft and Charlotte Smith, with Mary Hays and even Godwin himself, one has the sense that what is being written about is not life but ideas about life. Even when they become involved with a specific social situation, like the conditions in a prison in *Caleb Williams*, they manage to dehydrate the reality into an abstract generalization. Compared with their Godwinian predecessors, the social-problem novelists of the forties are remarkably concrete.

The change in tone and texture between the Godwinian social-problem novel and the books we are concerned with was due

fundamentally to changing social conditions and forces in which ideological developments played an important part. In the first place the actual size and urgency of the problem of poverty was so great and so obvious by the forties that it was almost impossible to treat it from a largely theoretical standpoint. In the second place, with the Reform Bill of 1832 and especially with the Chartist movement, political action had become more than a future possibility. Whereas Charlotte Smith had been concerned with what men and women *ought* to do, Elizabeth Gaskell was brought sharply up against what they were actually doing. Moreover, and this accentuated the shift in standpoint of the novelists from the 'philosophical' to the 'social/ evangelical' and even 'practical/political', the early years of the nineteenth century saw the appropriation of philosophic radicalism by the theorists of the new industrial capitalist class.

This last is a very important point. The Godwinian novels are written in the tradition of eighteenth-century rationalism. The struggle is always against 'prejudice' and 'superstition', the appeal to enlightened reason. Quite explicitly the typical Godwinian heroine 'as a matter of course makes it the object of her life to contribute to the improvement of individuals and thus widen the circle that will operate towards the grand end of life – general utility'. Yet within fifty years utilitarianism has become one of the main targets of socially-conscious novelists. *Hard Times* is of course the outstanding example, but it is outstanding only in the power and consistency of Dickens's vision, not in its uniqueness. The spirit of 'Manchester' is the villain of the piece for Disraeli and Kingsley, just as much as it is to be for Meredith's Everard Romfrey in *Beauchamp's Career*.

So long as Benthamite reforms were associated with the radical, democratic movement which in Britain felt itself in sympathy with the slogans of the French Revolution, utilitarianism in its various aspects had a strong appeal to contemporary writers. But once the doctrine of 'the greatest happiness of the greatest number' became primarily associated with the 'objective laws' of the classical economists and the outlook on life of the Manchester business-man, sensitive and humane artists were bound to see this sort of 'materialism' as one of their main enemies. Hence within half a century a striking change of tone in the social-problem novel; while the earlier novelists

had seen themselves as part of a movement of rational reform, their successors are more often concerned to assert a sense of humane feeling and solidarity *against* a vast structure of rationalized inhumanity. 'Speak the language of truth and reason to your child and be under no apprehension as to the result' Godwin had advised with a sublime confidence which a later generation, fed on the truth and reason of Parson Malthus and Mr Gradgrind, could scarcely be expected to share.

Disraeli's novels – especially those two or three which come within the province of this chapter – are quite unlike anyone else's, though the step from *Lothair* (1870) to George Meredith is not perhaps so great. But this uniqueness lies largely in the actual combination of ingredients, often apparently at almost fatal variance with one another, within a whole which somehow or other just succeeds in being a whole.

The trilogy – *Coningsby*, *Sybil*, and *Tancred* (1844–7) – was planned not only as a unity but with a specific political purpose. It was to illuminate and serve the cause of Tory Democracy, the Young England Movement which Disraeli (1804–81), with George Smythe and Lord John Manners, saw as the hope of post-Reform Bill Britain. It was the need for an alliance of populace and aristocracy – a reformed, not to say idealized, aristocracy of natural leaders – against the new barbarian industrialist class that Disraeli wished to emphasize. In the trilogy three aspects of the Condition-of-England Question were to be dealt with (the phrase falls all too appropriately) – the political, the social, the religious. *Coningsby* is a brilliant, informative, vivacious, and slightly absurd book. It is a political novel in the obvious sense that it is concerned almost entirely with political life – that is to say, the life of those who have made politics their career – and political ideas. It is in *Sybil* that Disraeli makes his most ambitious contribution to the imaginative consideration of the total social situation. In this crowded novel all England is represented: the aristocracy, in both its effete and responsible aspects, the industrialists, the rural poor, the proletariat of several categories.

The most famous page in *Sybil* is that moment when, during a conversation in the grounds of Marney Abbey between Egremont, the questing, enlightened member of the ruling class, and Stephen

Morley, the working-class theorist, the concept of the two worlds is enunciated:

'This is a new reign,' said Egremont, 'perhaps it is a new era.'

'I think so,' said the younger stranger.

'I hope so,' said the elder one.

'Well, society may be in its infancy,' said Egremont, slightly smiling; 'but, say what you like, our Queen reigns over the greatest nation that ever existed.'

'Which nation?' asked the younger stranger, 'for she reigns over two.'

The stranger paused; Egremont was silent, but looked inquiringly.

'Yes,' resumed the younger stranger after a moment's interval. 'Two nations; between whom there is no intercourse and no sympathy; who are as ignorant of each other's habits, thoughts, and feelings, as if they were dwellers in different zones, or inhabitants of different planets; who are formed by a different breeding, are fed by different food, are ordered by different manners, and are not governed by the same laws.'

'You speak of —' said Egremont, hesitatingly.

'THE RICH AND THE POOR.'

It is an impressive moment because the striking idea is most effectively expressed, Egremont's rather jejune patriotic commonplace successfully put in its place. But to abstract this key passage from *Sybil* gives a very misleading impression of what the novel is like. One might suppose, for instance, that it is essentially a novel of ideas in the sense of being a debate; and one would be wrong. What really gives Morley's speech its force in the book is the fact that it follows several chapters of brittle but vivid scenes of 'high society' in which the manners and tone of the rich are very surely, though not very profoundly, hit off.

Morley's speech is immediately followed by three more paragraphs.

At this moment a sudden flush of rosy light, suffusing the grey ruins, indicated that the sun had just fallen; and, through a vacant arch that overlooked them, alone in the resplendent sky, glittered the twilight star. The hour, the scene, the solemn stillness and the softening beauty, repressed controversy, induced even silence. The last words of the stranger lingered in the ear of Egremont; his musing spirit was teeming with many thoughts, many emotions; when from the Lady's chapel there rose the evening hymn to the Virgin. A single voice; but tones of almost supernatural sweetness; tender and solemn, yet flexible and thrilling.

Egremont started from his reverie. He would have spoken, but he perceived that the elder of the strangers had risen from his resting-place, and, with downcast eyes and crossed arms, was on his knees. The other remained standing in his former posture.

The divine melody ceased; the elder stranger rose; the words were on the lips of Egremont, that would have asked some explanation of this sweet and holy mystery, when, in the vacant and star-lit arch on which his glance was fixed, he beheld a female form. She was apparently in the habit of a Religious, yet scarcely could be a nun, for her veil, if indeed it were a veil, had fallen on her shoulders, and revealed her thick tresses of long fair hair. The blush of deep emotion lingered on a countenance which, though extremely young, was impressed with a character of almost divine majesty; while her dark eyes and long dark lashes, contrasting with the brightness of her complexion and the luxuriance of her radiant locks, combined to produce a beauty as rare as it is choice; and so strange, that Egremont might for a moment have been pardoned for believing her a seraph, who had lighted on this sphere, or the fair phantom of some saint haunting the sacred ruins of her desecrated fane.

The total effect is, it will be agreed, extremely odd. One recalls the resources of the modern cinema, the whole paraphernalia of glorious technicolour. Or one thinks perhaps of the sort of effect Puccini is after – and indeed gets – in *Tosca*, with its mixture of *roman policier*, cathedral background, political melodrama, and crude sex clichés.

The adjective 'operatic' recurs in the criticism of Disraeli's novels, and it is an appropriate word. For these intensely topical books, documented by contemporary social surveys and inquiries, are technically about as far from naturalistic realism as one could well go. The very quality of the most casual snippet of conversation indicates this. A realistic 'documentary' scene portraying the horrible conditions of life of an out-of-work weaver is interrupted by a knock at the door:

'Lives Philip Warner here?' inquired a clear voice of peculiar sweetness.

The status of Sybil (the working-class girl) as prima donna could hardly be better illustrated.

Yet the really odd thing about *Sybil* is not its absurdity but its ultimate measure of seriousness. Where does it come from? The ironic evocation of upper-class life, witty as Disraeli's observation often is, does not seem sufficient explanation.

'Private character is to be the basis of the new government [says Mr Tadpole]. Since the Reform Act, that is a qualification much more esteemed by the constituencies than public services. We must go with the times, my lord. A virtuous middle class shrinks with horror from French actresses; and the Wesleyans, the Wesleyans must be considered, Lord Marney.'

'I always subscribe to them,' said his lordship.

'Ah!' said Mr Tadpole mysteriously, 'I am glad to hear that. Nothing I have heard today has given me so much pleasure as those few words ...'

This is effective enough; but even when Disraeli is at his best at this sort of thing, in *Coningsby*, one feels the limitations as well as the qualities which V. S. Pritchett has admirably hinted at:[4]

When we are exhausted by visions he can soothe us with scandal. No one, said Queen Victoria with delight when she read his letters, – no one had ever told her *everything* before. The novels of Disraeli tell us everything. He not only plants the main spectacle, the house party of history; but he tells us the club gossip and the boudoir gossip – especially that – and speculates with malice on the dubious political career, on the unelevating comedies of political muddle and panic. He knows ambitious human nature. His eye is bright, his wit is continuous.

Neither this nor the conscientious use of documentary material to build up the picture of both the nations is in itself enough to guarantee the novel's status as serious writing. We know how faithfully Disraeli used his Blue Books.[5] Whole phrases from the First Report of the Children's Employment Commission (Mines) of 1842 and the Report of the Select Committee on Payment of Wages of 1843 are lifted into the text of *Sybil*. But the use of accurate documentation does not in fact bring most of Disraeli's working-class episodes to life.

What, in the end, makes *Sybil* readable is the total sense the book involves (a whole greater than the sum of the parts) of breadth of intelligence. This really is what Carlyle has asked for – articulate inquiry into the Condition-of-England Question. True the articulation has a self-consciousness, an artificiality, which is sometimes more than a little ridiculous, a glibness we are right to hold suspect; yet it is at the same time this very self-consciousness that gives Disraeli's novels their quality. It has been said often enough that his being a Jew allowed him a certain freedom of objectivity in his view of England, and there may be something in this (the creation of Sidonia in *Coningsby* indicates that Disraeli himself thought so). What is certain is that there is in his novels a quality of limited engagement very significant to the whole concept of the social-problem novel of the period. And he is, when all is said and weighed, extraordinarily intelligent, extraordinarily aware of what is going on in England;

and if it is not quite an artist's intelligence, that is not to say that we can dismiss his novels as not novels.

Elizabeth Gaskell (1810–66) is at once more and yet less 'engaged' as a novelist than Disraeli. Less, in the sense that she has no explicit political axe to grind, no partisan loyalty in the way of a Young England Movement, no ambition to be Prime Minister; more, in the sense that she is more deeply involved than he with the actual life of the people, more fundamentally partisan in her deepest feelings.

In her political and social *ideas*, it is true, she was a fence-sitter. When, in *Mary Barton* (1848), she has described with power and insight John Barton's class-conscious attitude towards the mill-owners, how the contrast between the lives of rich and poor is too great for him to avoid blaming the industrialist for the starvation and unemployment, she hastens to add:

> I know that this is not really the case; and I know what is the truth in such matters; but what I wish to impress is what the workman feels and thinks.

Consciously her aim is to bring Christian principles as a mediating force within class antagonisms. Unquestioningly she accepts the laws of the economists as the essential basis of social organization. Intellectually she is far less adventurous, far less radical than Disraeli. But she is also as a writer far less abstract, and this is important.

Ruth (1853) is only a 'social-problem novel' in the sense that it deals, in illegitimacy, with what we have come to recognize as a social problem; it is not, like *Mary Barton* and *North and South* (1855), a contribution to the Condition-of-England Question.

As an accurate and humane picture of working-class life in a large industrial town in the forties, *Mary Barton* is without rival among the novels of the time. Elizabeth Gaskell, for all the parson's wife or district visitor flavour which, naturally enough, characterizes her work, gets very deep into Manchester life. The Bartons' home and even old Alice's cellar become, what Disraeli's working-class scenes never are, more than the stage-sets for the necessary presentation of essential exhibits in the social story. She has a respect for her characters quite different from the social worker's interest or the responsible intellectual's effort of sympathy.

Mary Barton is as deeply impregnated as *Sybil* with the concept

of the two nations. In the very first chapter John Barton, Mary's father, trade unionist and Chartist, expresses the image very forcefully in argument with his friend Wilson:

'Don't think to come over me with th'old tale, that the rich know nothing of the trials of the poor; I say, if they don't know, they ought to know. We're their slaves as long as we can work; we pile up their fortunes with the sweat of our brows, and yet we are to live as separate as if we were in two worlds; ay, as separate as Dives and Lazarus, with a great gulf between us . . .'

The strength of the rather tiresome and cliché-ridden central plot of the novel – Mary's hesitation between rich Harry Carson and poor Jem Wilson, the murder of Carson and the excitement around Jem's trial – is that it does in some measure identify itself with and illuminate this underlying image. Even the story of Mrs Barton's sister Esther, who becomes a prostitute, is given more than a facile moral significance in the underlying pattern of the novel. For Esther is presented as something other than merely a bad girl; the abyss into which she falls is the same gulf which separates Dives from Lazarus.

If *Mary Barton* were merely a documentary, a fictionalized version of what Engels was to report in his *Condition of the British Working Class in 1844*, its material would certainly be impressive. But, as Kathleen Tillotson has pointed out,[6] even the most grimly documentary scene in the book – John Barton's visit to the foul cellar where the Davenport family are alleged to 'live' – is not really detachable, but 'is made an essential stage in Barton's experience, part of the warp of the novel'. Indeed, the word 'documentary' with its associations of scientific, sociological reporting is not really very helpful to an assessment of Elizabeth Gaskell's world. The strengths and the weaknesses of *Mary Barton* and *North and South* are bound up with the artistic point of view of the author.

Mary Barton is a dramatization of some of the real and fundamental problems of working-class life in the forties, written from the standpoint of a middle-class Christian of great integrity. If the essential vitality of working-class life eludes Elizabeth Gaskell, as it eludes all her contemporaries save Dickens, she yet captures a good deal else: material conditions, the grinding pressures of poverty and, above all, a sense of the dignity and decency of people. The forms of this

decency are not always, to the modern reader, readily sympathetic. The saintly Alice Wilson is presented with a sort of shallowness of approval which it is not easy for us to take now. Yet it would be wrong to consider the conception of old Alice as basically unrealistic; what is limiting is the degree of passive acceptance which the author herself exhibits in her revelation of the virtues of the long-suffering old dear. That intensity of indignation which breaks through in Dickens and adds an artistic dimension to his novels is muffled in Gaskell by her combination of Christian resignation and passive acceptance of the eternal laws of the economists.

What makes *Mary Barton*, despite its weaknesses, a distinguished and still powerful novel is, above all, the presentation of John Barton. The quality of desperation in the life of this upright and intelligent man is finely conveyed. The experiences which shape and confirm his political attitudes, the bitterness of his hatred of the owners, the courage as well as the fanaticism of his class-conscious morality, all these are given great force. Here very movingly Elizabeth Gaskell transcends the limitations of her conscious outlook, her instinct to tone down the extremities of feeling, her pious desire to mediate. Obviously she doesn't approve of John Barton, but this is not the point. She understands him and the understanding enters the texture of the novel. Apart from Heathcliff, he is the nearest approach to a tragic hero which the early Victorian novel permitted itself.

North and South, though it is also a contribution to the consideration of the Condition-of-England Question, is a very different kind of novel from *Mary Barton*, and one can understand Dickens's impatience with it when he serialized it in *Household Words*. Whereas the great achievement of the earlier book had lain in its insights into working-class life and the expression, through the character of John Barton, of a specifically working-class sensibility, the later novel presents its picture of English life entirely from a middle-class point of view. The main contrast in the book is not between rich and poor but, as implied in the title, between rural and industrial England; the two nations are not, of course, seen merely in geographical terms, but the conflict is between alternative societies and their values.

The interest, therefore, and the insights of *North and South* are of a different, though not for that reason necessarily inferior, order from

those of *Mary Barton*. This novel belongs, despite its subject-matter, to the tradition one associates with Jane Austen, rather than to that of which, say, the Brontës are a part. Take the description, for instance, of the passage of the Hale family through London, on their way from South to North. Mr Hale, the vicar of a country parish idyllically situated in the New Forest, has taken the decision because of (unspecified) 'doubts', to give up the ministry and migrate to a northern industrial town to earn his living as a tutor. With his ailing, self-pitying wife – a character whose presentation immediately establishes Elizabeth Gaskell's position in a literary line between Jane Austen and George Eliot – and his daughter Margaret, he stays the night in London in 'some quiet hotel' which they can in any case scarcely afford.

> The evening, without employment, passed in a room high up in a hotel, was long and heavy. Mr Hale went out to his bookseller's, and to call on a friend or two. Everyone they saw, either in the house or out in the streets, appeared hurrying to some appointment, expected by, or expecting somebody. They alone seemed strange and friendless, and desolate. Yet within a mile, Margaret knew of house after house, where she for her own sake, and her mother for her Aunt Shaw's, would be welcome, if they came in gladness, or even in peace of mind. If they came sorrowing, and wanting sympathy in a complicated trouble like the present, then they would be felt as a shadow in all these houses of intimate acquaintances, not friends . . .

The subject-matter is outside Jane Austen's and the uncertainty of the Hales' social future undermines the achievement of a perfect poise, a complete artistic confidence; but the tone and sensibility belong to Jane Austen's world, a world from which the Hales self-consciously feel themselves at least temporarily excluded.

Margaret Hale, the heroine of *North and South*, might also be seen in this perspective, between Jane Austen and George Eliot. She is an aspiring heroine, an ancestress of Dorothea Brooke, and she is in a sense a rebel, outraging the sensibilities of the Manchester middle class among whom she lands. The Manchester Thorntons are the epitome of the new bourgeois virtues: self-help is written all over Mrs Thornton's character, her son reminds one of Rouncewell the ironmaster in *Bleak House*. But Margaret Hale's battle with the Thorntons is something quite different from John Barton's tragic battle with the Carsons, for she is fighting on behalf of the past rather than the future, and this affects the whole texture and feeling of the

novel. Margaret's sympathy with the workers, though perfectly genuine, is essentially aristocratic or at least paternalist in quality; one can imagine her cheering on the Young England Movement. The effect of all this, in literary terms, is that the emotion generated by the conflict between Margaret and the Thorntons is kept within the bounds of compromise, a compromise confirmed by the marriage at the end of the book.

North and South is an interesting social document, but it lacks the passion which, almost willy-nilly, informs *Mary Barton*, or the intellectual grasp which with Disraeli does some kind of duty for passionate apprehension. And it is possible that at the root of the trouble may be Elizabeth Gaskell's failure to bring to bear on agricultural England the same sort of conscientious insight which she brings to her descriptions of Manchester.

What is left out of the South in *North and South* is put into *Yeast* (1848) by Charles Kingsley. The hero, Lancelot Smith, is not permitted to maintain any idealistic illusions about the state of the rural poor. Instead he is subjected by his friend Tregarva, the gamekeeper (a sort of socially-conscious Billy Budd), to a minute inspection of the miseries of the cottagers' existence, and comes to suffer personally from the evils of an inhumane society, for his wife – the divine Argemone – catches typhus through visiting the poor and dies.

Yeast combines the more naturalistic style of Elizabeth Gaskell with some of the more mystical and romantic aspects of Disraeli's, and it cannot be pretended that the union is a happy one. Argemone, like Sybil, is first seen by her lover framed in a Gothic doorway.

> With her perfect masque and queenly figure, and earnest upward gaze, she might have been the very model from which Raphael conceived his glorious St Catherine – the ideal of the highest womanly genius, softened into self-forgetfulness by girlish devotion. She was simply, almost coarsely dressed; but a glance told him that she was a lady, by the courtesy of man as well as by the will of God.

Kingsley's religious concern is, of course, far more earnest than Disraeli's, and *Yeast* is commonly docketed in a pigeon-hole marked 'religious novels'. But it was the social rather than the religious outlook implied in it that gave it its notoriety and led a number of readers of *Fraser's Magazine* to threaten to withdraw their subscriptions.

Alton Locke (1850) is, by any standards, a better novel than *Yeast*, and in some respects as impressive as any book we are concerned with. It is the story, told as an autobiography, of a working-class boy, an aspiring poet, who, apprenticed as a tailor, becomes a Chartist, achieves an education, is disillusioned by the crudity and violence of the 'mob', is converted to Christian Socialism by a middle-class woman, and – sailing away to America – dies before he gets there.

What is forceful in *Alton Locke* derives at least in part from the autobiographical method of narration, which forces on Kingsley an order of imaginative effort uncommon in this group of novels, and gives the book a certain unity of tone and sensibility. It is a sensibility not, perhaps, very easily sympathetic to many modern readers, yet firmly grounded in history, the history of Calvinist dissent, working-class aspiration, and the Victorian passion for 'improvement'. The world of Alton Locke's childhood is the world of the opening section of Mark Rutherford's *Revolution in Tanner's Lane* (a better book than Kingsley's), and Alton himself is one of a line of self-educated working-men of whom the most impressive was to be Hardy's Jude. Read with preconceptions about 'pure' literature, *Alton Locke* suffers from almost every fault in the vocabulary of literary criticism; yet its total impact continues to impress. Part of the interest is no doubt purely sociological: the descriptions of the tailors' sweat-shops, like comparable passages in a twentieth-century novel, *The Jungle*, do not depend for their effect on any special intensity of imaginative treatment, but simply on the revelation of facts which speak for themselves.

Alton Locke is, indeed, in the simplest sense of the term, a propaganda novel, a book designed to bring home to its readers the nature of a social situation and the author's remedies for it. But to say this is not to dismiss it. The effective work of propaganda becomes in the very achievement of its effect something which the term propagandist (with its suggestion of ulterior motivation) does not adequately encompass. *Alton Locke*, for all its crudities and 'dated' quality, for all its lack of the sort of art and intelligence one associates with those writers conscious of 'the novel as an art form', can still move us today. The stilted quality of Alton's own sensibility, which is never 'placed', may make the book impossible for some sophisticated readers, but

is an integral part of the total effect. And to dismiss the effect as not art is to beg half the questions of practical aesthetics.

One can see from a fairly typical passage the sort of critical problem *Alton Locke* raises. Alton and his friend Crossthwaite, a Chartist, have been sacked along with a few others for organizing the tailors in the shop where they work to resist the degradation of their economic position and very lives involved in the change from relatively humane craft conditions to the sweat-shops of mass-production. Having no job and therefore no money or future, Alton is not unnaturally down-hearted, but Crossthwaite, experienced in the ways of his world, is more philosophical.

'Katie and I can pick a crust together without snarling over it. And, thank God, I have no children, and never intend to have, if I can keep true to myself, till the good times come.'

'Oh! Crossthwaite, are not children a blessing?'

'Would they be a blessing to me now? No, my lad. Let those bring slaves into the world who will! I will never beget children to swell the numbers of those who are trampling each other down in the struggle for daily bread, to minister in ever deepening poverty and misery to the rich man's luxury – perhaps his lust.'

'Then you believe in the Malthusian doctrines?'

'I believe them to be an infernal lie, Alton Locke; though good and wise people like Miss Martineau may sometimes be deluded into preaching them. I believe there's room on English soil for twice the number there is now; and when we get the Charter we'll prove it; we'll show that God meant human heads and hands to be blessings and not curses, tools and not burdens. But in times such as these, let those who have wives be as though they had none – as St Paul said, when he told his people under the Roman Emperor to be above begetting slaves and martyrs. A man of the people should keep himself as free from encumbrances as he can just now. He will find it all the more easy to dare and suffer for the people, when their turn comes –'

This is crude enough. As speech it has neither the authentic turn of colloquial idiom nor the eloquence of well-turned argument. Kingsley is preaching, and there is a half-digested quality about the preaching too. The whole thing is cliché-infested and on a number of levels unconvincing, unabsorbed. The deficiencies cry out. And yet the passage, even perhaps out of context, has qualities which make the enumeration of its deficiencies seem not so much unfair as irrelevant. That vision of Crossthwaite and his marriage and the lights

by which he lives, the narrowness and splendour of him, are in every sense outside what is generally accepted as the superior literary tradition of the nineteenth century. But Kingsley is saying in *Alton Locke* something which had to be said and could not, I think, have been said much differently. Not only visions but revisions are implied. The truth is that the critical consideration of books like those I have been referring to leads one inevitably into the problem of evolving ways of discussing literature which are neither 'purely' literary nor yet non-literary. To conceive of literary value in autonomous or unchanging terms is to court one sort of disaster – the sort that removes the production and reading of a text out of its actual context and therefore out of its real human significance. On the other hand to ignore literary quality in favour of a non-evaluative 'sociology of literature' is likely to lead to the ignoring of the particular kind of value an individual text has and why we read it.

Evaluation of what we read is an integral part of reading it. Yet what we have to consider all the time is not just a book but the situation of which it is a part and to which it contributes. Hence the need to bring a historical as well as a literary sensibility to the reading of a text and to insist that the two are so intricately related as to defy abstraction from one another. To discuss adequately the early-Victorian social-problem novel involves an awareness of (among much else) the growth of mass literacy and education, the development of the publishing industry, and such factors as class-consciousness and the part played by religion in the period. Much useful work in these directions has been done in recent years.[7]

That *Alton Locke* should be concerned with the collapse of Chartism is more than fortuitous. The end of Chartism did not mean the end of the social-problem novel; but the peculiar set of circumstances which produced Carlyle's Condition-of-England Question and writers' attempts to cope with it altered. But they did not, of course, alter entirely or beyond recognition, and that is why these particular novels still have relevance for us, both in a general theoretical way and in their individual capacity to engage our emotions.

NOTES

1. It is partly on this problem that the standard work on the subject – Louis Cazamian's *Le Roman Social en Angleterre, 1830–50* (translated by Martin Fido, Henley, 1973) – founders. Cazamian, rightly feeling that, within his terms of reference, he cannot exclude Dickens, tries to get over the problem by dividing Dickens's work into the more and the less 'social', an undertaking doomed to failure and leading the critic incidentally to a disastrous underestimation of Dickens's later novels.

2. In *Dickens at Work* (London, 1957).

3. The links between Godwin, Bulwer Lytton, and Disraeli are interesting. Lytton even took the names of two of his heroes, Falkland and Clifford, from Godwin's novels. Like Disraeli, he entered Parliament. He is essentially a second-rate writer, without real originality or deep sincerity, but his career has enormous literary-historical interest.

4. In *The Living Novel* (London, 1946).

5. See L. Cazamian, above, and A. N. Jeffares, Introduction to *Sybil* (Nelson's Classics).

6. In *Novels of the Eighteen-Forties* (London, 1954).

7. See, in particular, Robert Altick, *The English Common Reader, 1800–1900* (1957); Margaret Dalgiel, *Popular Fiction 100 Years Ago* (1957); Louis James, *Fiction for the Working Man, 1830–50* (1963), *Print and the People* (1976); J. F. C. Harrison, *Living and Learning 1790–1960* (1961); P. J. Keating, *The Working Classes in Victorian Fiction* (1971); Ivanka Kovačević, *Fact into Fiction, 1751–1850* (1975); Martha Vicinus, *The Industrial Muse* (1974); R. K. Webb, *The British Working-Class Reader 1770–1848* (1955); Raymond Williams, *Culture and Society 1780–1950* (1958), *The Long Revolution* (1961), *The Country and the City* (1973).

THE REVIEWS AND MAGAZINES

R. G. COX

From our present vantage-point the nineteenth century begins to look like the great age of periodical literature. Certainly between 1800 and 1914 the periodical is a more important feature of the literary scene than at any previous time, and since 1914 the evidence clearly points to a decline. For its beginnings, of course, we have to go back before 1700, but although there was a steady development through the eighteenth century, the periodical did not begin to play its characteristic part until the foundation of the *Edinburgh Review* in 1802. The immediate success of the *Edinburgh* was due not only to the energy and talent of its founders, but even more to their seizing a moment at which such a venture filled an obvious gap. There was a need for vigorous critical opinion, much more independent of the publishing trade than that to be found in the existing journals, and paid for at rates which would command the highest talents. This the *Edinburgh* group provided, and it soon added the further impetus of a common political outlook and policy. When Scott, who had contributed to the early numbers, complained to Jeffrey of the *Edinburgh*'s increasing Whig partisanship, he was told that literature might be one of the two legs on which it stood, but 'its right leg is politics'. It is not surprising therefore that intelligent Tories, alarmed by the *Edinburgh*'s success, should have set up a rival organ within seven years.

The *Quarterly* was similar to the *Edinburgh* in format and general manner, in the length and weight of its articles,[1] in its high rates of pay, and in its independence and uncompromising critical severity. Both gave expression to the current tastes and standards of cultivated society which were still in many respects those of the eighteenth century: culturally, that is, they were conservative, but generally responsible and serious. Both were strictly reviews in that however much their articles might develop into original essays they were

always based on the criticism of books. Their circulation and influence were remarkable. By 1818 they were selling about 14,000 copies each, and when we remember that each copy was often handed round among several readers and that there was a steady sale of bound volumes, it is hardly an exaggeration to speak of them as dividing the reading public between them. They certainly dominated the field of periodical literature up to about 1832, when the old Lincolnshire squire told Tennyson that the *Quarterly Review* was 'the next book to God's Bible'. But one rival had appeared on the political Left, the *Westminster Review*, founded in 1823. This was explicitly Benthamite, with a ruthless party line which sometimes anticipates our own century. Where literature and the arts were concerned, it vacillated between two attitudes which were to become increasingly common later: a desire to discourage activities which seemed to be trivial and frivolous, and an indulgence towards amusements that it was not worth while to take seriously. The *Westminster*'s public, of course, was not on the scale of that of the *Edinburgh* and the *Quarterly*, but at a time when they were in full swing it managed to sell 3,000 copies.

If the *Edinburgh* and the *Quarterly* established the pattern for the general review of political and cultural interests, that for the lighter and more varied miscellany was set by *Blackwood's Edinburgh Magazine*, started in 1817. This covered an extraordinary range of material, from stories and verse to essays, political and literary articles of all degrees of seriousness, reviews, and such grotesque semi-dramatic topical dialogues as Wilson's *Noctes Ambrosianae*. As in the heavier reviews, all contributions were anonymous; but in *Blackwood's* they were often also of composite authorship, and the whole business was further complicated by the elaborate mystification of a series of interchangeable pseudonyms. In its early days the magazine was notorious for its virulent quarrels and irresponsible attacks on political and literary opponents – notably, of course, the 'Cockney' circle of Leigh Hunt. By 1830 it had become somewhat more sober and respectable, but it remained a miscellany, appealing at a number of surprisingly different levels. In 1818, 6,000 copies were printed, and by 1831 the circulation had risen to 8,000.

The most distinguished imitator of *Blackwood's* was the *London Magazine*, the first substantial periodical to be written mainly in support of the younger Romantics. Somewhat more serious and

more purely literary than *Blackwood's*, it had a brilliant few years from 1819 to 1825, and then lingered on under Benthamite editorship until 1829. Its liberal politics and Romantic sympathies brought it into sharp conflict with *Blackwood's*, and one result was the tragic duel in which the editor, John Scott, was killed in 1821. A growing rival of the *London* in the twenties was the *New Monthly Magazine and Literary Journal*, under Thomas Campbell.

Of weekly periodicals the most important was Leigh Hunt's *Examiner*, which began in 1808 and was selling over 7,000 by 1812. Radical in politics, it took up the cudgels for the younger Romantics against the *Quarterly* and *Blackwood's*, and published poems by Keats and Shelley. The *Literary Gazette* (1817) was more purely a comprehensive literary chronicle. Both these were to continue until late in the century, but for the Victorian period the two weeklies founded in 1828, the *Athenaeum* and the *Spectator*, were more important.

By about 1830, then, the main types of periodical had taken the shape they were to retain for the most part throughout the century, and the number, variety, and quality of existing periodicals was such as to make Christopher North's exuberant tribute in the forty-second of the *Noctes Ambrosianae* (*Blackwood's*, 1829) not altogether absurd: 'Our current periodical literature teems with thought and feeling ... The whole surface of society is thus irrigated by a thousand streams ...'

During the Victorian age the two great quarterlies continued to exert a high degree of authority and influence. A gradual sapping of their position by increased competition from new monthlies and weeklies made it impossible for them to retain the power of their earlier days, but it did not take decisive effect until well past the middle of the century. The *Edinburgh*[2] was edited by Jeffrey's successor, W. Macvey Napier, until 1847, and then in succession by W. Empson, Sir George Cornewall Lewis (1852), and Henry Reeve (1855–95). Under these editors there was little change of general policy, but literature came more and more to take second place to politics and affairs. Up to about 1845 the mainstay of the *Edinburgh* was undoubtedly Macaulay, many of whose essays began as nominal review articles. Carlyle contributed little after *Characteristics* (1831); other literary writers included Bulwer-Lytton, James Spedding, Abraham

Hayward, R. M. Milnes, Aubrey de Vere, Thackeray, Sir James Stephen, and G. H. Lewes, though it was characteristic of the *Edinburgh* that there was no rigid specialization: most of its lawyers, politicians, and economists wrote occasionally on literary topics.

The *Quarterly*[3] was edited from 1826 to 1853 by J. G. Lockhart – a Lockhart who had outgrown the worst extravagances of his connection with *Blackwood's* in its early years. Succeeding editors were Whitwell Elwin (1853–60), William Macpherson (1860–67), William Smith (1867–92), and R. E. Prothero (1892–9). Several of the older contributors continued writing under Lockhart – Southey, H. H. Milman, Francis Palgrave, and especially John Wilson Croker, who gave Lockhart a good deal of advice and assistance. Croker has acquired a bad reputation, but recent scholarship has shown that both as a man and as a literary critic he had more integrity and ability than he is sometimes credited with. He warned Lockhart against any decline in the review's concern with literature and science, and it is significant that he laid the basis for the edition of Pope, completed by Elwin and Courthope, which was to remain standard for sixty years. Other contributors included Abraham Hayward, who wrote about eighty articles between 1834 and 1884, Hartley Coleridge, H. N. Coleridge, John Sterling, Henry Taylor, Aubrey de Vere, A. W. Kinglake, Elizabeth Rigby (later Lady Eastlake), and Henry Reeve. Elwin added Bulwer-Lytton, John Forster, Thackeray, Harriet Martineau, and Mark Pattison. Later, the *Quarterly* published work by Matthew Arnold, Swinburne, Sir Sidney Lee, W. J. Courthope, J. Churton Collins, and J. A. Symonds. Gladstone wrote occasionally on literature as well as on ecclesiastical affairs. In politics the *Quarterly* remained Tory and spoke for the landed aristocracy and the Established Church. It will be noticed that the *Quarterly* and the *Edinburgh* tended increasingly to draw on the same contributors, but in literature the *Quarterly* maintained a more vigorous opposition to the Romantic tendencies of the age.

The *Westminster* had by the early thirties declined into a rather nondescript affair, and in 1835 the *London Review* was founded by the Mills and Sir William Molesworth in an attempt to replace it by a livelier and more truly Radical organ. After four numbers the two were amalgamated as the *London and Westminster Review*, under the editorship of John Stuart Mill, who aimed to broaden its basis and

eliminate the narrower Benthamite propaganda. In 1840 its next editor, W. E. Hickson, reverted to the original name; in 1851 it absorbed another periodical and became, under John Chapman, the *Westminster and Foreign Quarterly Review*. Under Mill and Hickson the *Westminster* was hardly a commercial success and its circulation was not large, but it published distinguished work and was recognized as representative of the best Radical and progressive opinion. Mill introduced an important innovation by breaking with the tradition of anonymity and requiring articles to carry some sort of signature: this was originally because he disagreed with the opinions of his father and other contributors over whose work he could exercise no control; but the custom was continued under Hickson, and G. H. Lewes (who had begun to contribute in 1840) made a severe attack on the practice of anonymity in an article of 1842. Mill's assistant editor was John Robertson, and in pursuance of his broadening policy he introduced such non-Utilitarian writers as Carlyle and Sterling. Harriet Martineau, Bulwer-Lytton, Thackeray, and R. M. Milnes all wrote occasionally, and Chapman brought in Froude, Mark Pattison, and George Eliot, who acted as assistant editor from 1851 to 1854. Later contributors included Frederic Harrison and Walter Pater. Towards the end of the century the *Westminster* became very largely non-literary; it was changed to a monthly and lasted in that form until 1913. For the most part the tone of the *Westminster* was earnest and rather heavy; it combined a moralizing didacticism with a self-conscious enlightenment and faith in scientific progress typical of the age of Comte and Herbert Spencer. Even more than the older quarterlies it tended increasingly to treat literature as less important than science, philosophy, and politics.

A new development of the later Victorian age was the rise of serious reviews appearing monthly. Of these the most important was *The Fortnightly Review* (despite its name, it became a monthly in its second year). Founded in 1865 by a group which included Trollope, it was an avowed imitation of the French *Revue des Deux Mondes*, and broke with tradition in having no explicit political policy and in completely abjuring anonymity. G. H. Lewes, the first editor, was followed in 1867 by John Morley, who continued until 1882. Morley's editorship was the *Fortnightly*'s most brilliant period, and he established it as a focus of Liberal–Rational and Positivist opinion. Its

contributors included Walter Bagehot, T. H. Huxley, Frederic Harrison, Leslie Stephen, George Eliot, Arnold, Saintsbury, Dowden, Gosse, Sidney Colvin, J. A. Symonds, Pater, Morris, Rossetti, Swinburne, and Meredith, who took control during Morley's visit to America. Some idea of the success achieved by Morley may be gathered from the circulation figures: 1,400 in 1867, they had reached 25,000 by 1872 and were still rising. The general atmosphere of the *Fortnightly*'s work may be studied in the collected essays of Morley and Harrison. They can be seen as in some respects the legitimate heirs of Mill and his *Westminster* associates; while intelligently critical of their age they share the general faith in progress, and are inclined to take for granted current dogma concerning literary values and literary history.

The *Fortnightly* soon evoked imitators in the *Contemporary Review* (1866), the *Nineteenth Century* (1877), and the *National Review* (1883). The *Contemporary* was a mainly religious periodical founded by Alexander Strahan. It had little literary significance. During the early seventies it was edited by James Knowles, architect, friend of Tennyson and founder (in 1868) of the Metaphysical Society, whose debates and discussions it reflected. In 1877 a quarrel with Strahan led Knowles to found his own periodical, the *Nineteenth Century*, taking many of his contributors with him. Beginning with a brilliant galaxy of talent and a congratulatory sonnet from Tennyson, it quickly reached a position of extraordinary influence, surpassing even that of the *Fortnightly*. The contributors included Arnold, Froude, Ruskin, Gladstone, F. W. H. Myers, Frederic Harrison, W. J. Courthope, and Henry Morley, who conducted for several years a 'Department of Recent Literature', running to about twenty pages. The *National Review* of 1883 was conservative and imperialist in politics: until 1894 it was edited by Alfred Austin. In its early days, with W. J. Courthope as assistant editor (1883–7), it contained notable criticism by Leslie Stephen and Courthope himself. It should not be confused with the earlier Unitarian *National Review*, edited by R. H. Hutton and Walter Bagehot between 1855 and 1864. This, although not primarily a literary periodical, published the greater part of Bagehot's *Literary Studies* and several essays by Arnold.

Of the magazines, *Blackwood's* continued influential and important until well past the middle of the century. In 1860 Disraeli assured John

Blackwood that he read the political article regularly. Until about 1837 the chief responsibility for the direction of the magazine rested with John Wilson ('Christopher North'), though he was never actually editor. The editorial power then passed to Robert and Alexander Blackwood, who had succeeded to the ownership on the death of their father, and so successively to other members of the family. On its literary side *Blackwood's* came to depend more and more on miscellaneous essays, short stories, and serial fiction. Novels first published in its pages included George Eliot's *Scenes of Clerical Life* and *Adam Bede*. As an influence in criticism it declined in the later years of the century.

Fraser's Magazine was founded in 1830 in close imitation of *Blackwood's*, William Maginn (the Captain Shandon of *Pendennis*) holding a corresponding position to that of Wilson. It had its fictitious editor, Oliver Yorke, its convivial debates on the lines of the *Noctes Ambrosianae*, and its noisy quarrels and scandals all in the manner of its now more sober prototype. Its politics were the same brand of hearty swashbuckling Toryism, and it drew many of its contributors from the same group, including Maginn, Lockhart, Hogg, Galt, Allan Cunningham, Dr David Moir, Robert Gleig, and R. P. Gillies. On the more serious side of the magazine there was a strong Coleridgean influence. In 1847, however, *Fraser's* was acquired by J. W. Parker, the publisher for the Broad Church movement; it became Liberal in politics and published Kingsley's *Yeast* and *Hypatia* in serial form. Earlier it had serialized *Sartor Resartus* and several of Thackeray's minor works. Under the editorship of J. A. Froude (1861–74), an attempt was made to publish Ruskin's *Munera Pulveris*, but this proved too much for the magazine's public. Leslie Stephen speaks of *Fraser's* as 'a decayed periodical' under Froude, but it lingered on until 1882, when it was superseded by *Longman's Magazine*.

The *New Monthly Magazine* continued after Campbell's editorship under Bulwer-Lytton, Theodore Hook (1836–41), P. G. Patmore (1841–52), and W. Harrison Ainsworth and his son until 1884. It gave a good deal of space to critical articles and it began to drop the practice of anonymity.

The most important magazine of the latter half of the century was undoubtedly the *Cornhill*,[4] founded in 1860 by the publisher George

Smith. Aiming to combine the critical review and the serial novel, he started with works by Thackeray and Trollope and made Thackeray the first editor. The sale of the magazine, at a shilling, exceeded all expectations, and the first number sold 110,000 copies – a degree of success staggering by present-day standards. After 1862 the editorship was in commission until Leslie Stephen took charge in 1871. Under Stephen especially, the *Cornhill* maintained a remarkable level of literary distinction. It published novels by Thackeray, Trollope, George Eliot, Mrs Gaskell, Hardy, and Henry James; as well as by Wilkie Collins, Charles Reade, James Payn, and more popular authors. Its general articles included most of Arnold's *Culture and Anarchy*, part of *Friendship's Garland*, and *Literature and Dogma*; several of Stephen's own *Hours in a Library* essays and three instalments of Ruskin's *Unto this Last* (before Thackeray had to yield to public opinion and cut the series short). Other contributors included Meredith, Swinburne, Grant Allen, Churton Collins, J. A. Symonds, and R. L. Stevenson. Stephen's own comments on his editorship (in *Some Early Impressions*) are interesting: he had a strict morality about accepting the best article offered, and not distributing charity at the cost of the magazine. He was hampered by a certain tradition of inoffensiveness which compelled him to reject *The Return of the Native* though he had published *Far from the Madding Crowd*. Arnold, we are told, finally abandoned the *Cornhill* because he 'wanted to discuss topics to which the magazine had to give a wide berth'. The circulation, of course, could hardly stay at the level of the first number. When Stephen took over it was 'not a fifth of that of the original number', and when he left in 1882 it was about 12,000 – still a respectable figure for a periodical whose 'soul' was described by Sir Edward Cook as 'the spirit of humane culture'.

A shilling magazine similar in character to the *Cornhill* and rivalling it in circulation was *Macmillan's*, founded a little earlier, in 1859 (in which year as many as one hundred and fifteen periodicals were started in London alone) with David Masson as its first editor. For a short period (1883–5) it was edited by Morley, and its contributors included Tennyson, Arnold, W. E. Forster, R. M. Milnes (Lord Houghton), F. T. Palgrave, Kingsley, R. D. Blackmore, Mrs Humphry Ward, Hardy, and Henry James. Imitators of the *Cornhill* included the *Temple Bar* (1860–1906), edited at first by G. A. Sala, and

Longman's, the successor of *Fraser's*, which was chiefly notable for its fiction.

During the Victorian age weekly periodicals came to fill a much more important place than earlier. The *Examiner* continued until 1881, and in 1845 it was selling 6,000 copies. Under Albany Fonblanque in the thirties and forties it had a reputation for steadiness and principle, but it was largely non-literary. The *Literary Gazette* remained under William Jerdan, its founder, until 1850, and from then until 1862, when it was incorporated with the *Parthenon*, it passed through a rapid succession of editors, one of whom was Morley. But the most important Early Victorian weeklies were undoubtedly the *Athenaeum* and the *Spectator*, both founded in 1828. The *Athenaeum* was at first edited by J. S. Buckingham and Henry Stebbing, and then for a time closely connected through F. D. Maurice and John Sterling with the Apostles group. It was acquired in 1830 by Keats's friend C. W. Dilke, who acted as his own editor until 1846, when he was succeeded by T. K. Hervey. Later editors were W. H. Dixon (1852–69), John Doran (1869–70), and Norman MacColl (1871–1900). Dilke made the *Athenaeum* famous for its progressive independence and critical honesty. He waged an unceasing war against puffing and the influence of publishers, and in 1831 reduced the price by half (from 8*d*., unstamped, to 4*d*.), confident that he could draw on the new reading public which supported the Mechanics' Institutes and the publications of the Society for the Diffusion of Useful Knowledge. Contrary to all expectations, the sale at once increased by six times, and four years later Dilke was able to enlarge the paper from sixteen to twenty-four pages. The circulation has been estimated at 18,000 after the reduction in price, and it continued to increase. For its contributors the *Athenaeum* drew upon a wide range of talent, including at first several of the old *London Magazine* group. Regular writers under Dilke were H. F. Chorley, W. Cooke Taylor, Sir Charles and Lady Morgan, Henry Reeve, and J. A. Heraud; later came G. H. Lewes, Henry Morley, W. M. Rossetti, David Masson, J. Westland Marston, Joseph Knight, and others too numerous to mention, including most of the familiar names of Victorian letters down to Watts-Dunton, Gosse, Henley, Lang, and Richard Garnett. Apart from its literary brilliance, the *Athenaeum* played an important part in all the progressive movements of the age. It led the agitation against

'Taxes on Knowledge' (the stamp duty on periodicals), supported all forms of popular education, and advocated prison reform, health legislation, public parks, the penny post, and many similar causes. In December 1838 the *Westminster* called it 'one of the best periodicals of its kind in Europe', and in his account of Victorian journalism E. E. Kellett has pronounced it 'in some respects the most notable achievement of the Victorian Age'.

The *Spectator* was more of a newspaper than the *Athenaeum*, and its literary matter often consisted of only one main review. But although in its early days inclined to regard all the arts as 'a sub-department of morals or utility', in criticism, as in general policy, it was independent and responsible, and its literary importance increased towards the middle of the century. Its circulation in the forties was about 3,500. Founded by R. S. Rintoul, it was edited by him until 1858, and then by Thornton Hunt (Leigh Hunt's son, who had acted as assistant editor for some time), until 1861, when it passed into the hands of Meredith Townsend and R. H. Hutton. The *Spectator* reflected Hutton's religious and philosophical interests, and Mrs Oliphant reports that it was known in the nineties as 'thoughtful and serious'. Leslie Stephen remarked that he 'always liked to be praised by it'. Its literary contributors in the later period included Swinburne, W. E. H. Lecky, H. D. Traill, Morley, Gosse, and Saintsbury.

The most brilliant weekly of the middle of the century was undoubtedly the *Saturday Review*. Founded in 1855 by A. J. B. Beresford Hope and J. D. Cook, it was understood to be mainly written by Cambridge men, and it assumed from the first a manner of almost arrogant authority. 'Few journals,' said Leslie Stephen, 'have ever had so brilliant a staff as the *Saturday Review* in its early period. When I was accepted a little later, I felt like a schoolboy promoted to the Sixth Form ...' The contributors included Fitz-James Stephen, Morley, G. S. Venables, E. A. Freeman, who aimed at raising English historical research to the German level, J. R. Green, H. J. S. Maine, Grant Duff, Mark Pattison, F. T. Palgrave, T. C. Sandars, and Leslie Stephen himself. The *Saturday*'s criticism was severe, and its writers, Leslie Stephen records, 'accepted complacently the name of Saturday "Revilers"'. He speaks of the journal's corporate tone, and concludes that it represented a real attempt to be 'an organ of what is now called culture'. The great days of the *Saturday* were those of Beresford

Hope's ownership, to 1887. Under Cook its circulation rose to probably more than 10,000. Even Arnold, whose encounters with the review were many and vigorous, could allow (in *Culture and Anarchy*) that 'within certain limits . . . my old adversary, the *Saturday Review*, may, on matters of literature and taste, be fairly enough regarded, relatively to the mass of newspapers which treat these matters, as a kind of organ of reason'.

Other weeklies included various enterprises of Leigh Hunt in the thirties and forties; G. H. Lewes's Positivist *Leader* of the fifties; the *Reader* (1863–6), which aimed at noticing all published books; the *Speaker*, which flourished in the nineties; and the *Academy*, a scholarly periodical which started in 1869 as a monthly under C. E. Appleton, became a weekly in 1874 under the same editor, modestly flourished after 1881 under J. S. Cotton, and in 1896 was given a more popular character under Lewis Hind.

In addition to the periodicals already mentioned, there were a large number designed for a particular restricted public – sectarian or specialist in various ways, and there were others aimed at a particular level of the public – especially what were often referred to as 'the new reading classes'. Some of these are discussed in another chapter.

It will be apparent even from the above brief summary that a great deal of Victorian literature, verse and general prose as well as novels, was first published in periodicals; they can be seen as forming a vast nursery for its production. Similarly the reviewing constitutes a complete and detailed record of changing taste and critical opinion. No one can go far in sampling it without perceiving the uncertainty and lack of direction of the thirties, the emergence of the major Victorian names, in verse and prose, their somewhat slow acceptance, and their final establishment as part of the orthodox picture of nineteenth-century literature. There was at one time a tendency to blame the Victorian reviewers for their tardiness in recognizing the greater writers of the age; in T. B. Lounsbury's books on Tennyson and Browning, for example, they are seen as only slightly less criminal than the Regency reviewers who attacked Wordsworth, Keats, and Shelley. A swing of critical opinion against nineteenth-century romanticism brought something of an opposite view; but the truth, as usual, is probably more complex. Not all the coolness with

which the Victorian writers were sometimes received was mere blind insensitiveness, but not all of it was unusual critical intelligence or shrewdness.

To take poetry first: at this date we can perhaps agree that the worst fault of the Regency reviewers was not so much that they were too rigidly classic and conservative in their opposition to the Romantics (this aspect of their work has been exaggerated, and it is arguable, in any case, that a firm opposition to push against has its own paradoxical value to a new movement) as that their insufficient awareness of the weaker side of the eighteenth-century tradition led them to tolerate too readily the elegant sentimentality and tawdry magniloquence of Moore, Campbell, Rogers, and the early Byron. Whatever the faults of Romantic extravagance, these were no adequate counterweight. The dangers become obvious when we find the *Edinburgh* praising Mrs Hemans, and in the thirties and forties these tendencies are carried further. Some critics show almost a kind of split personality: in 'Christopher North', Maginn, and some of their associates – even at times Thackeray – there is a curious alternation between hearty common sense of a somewhat slap-dash kind and a tear-sodden sentimentality. That something similar appears to have happened to Jeffrey at the end of his life is suggested by his maudlin letter to Dickens in praise of Little Nell.

From their predecessors, therefore, Victorian reviewers inherited both soft and tough attitudes to poetry. The former linked itself easily with sentimentality and a desire for conventional moralizing and piety, and it also fed the widespread, though half-conscious, feeling that poetry was something removed from actual life and serious adult pursuits whether practical or intellectual, demanding little in the way of concentrated attention. The latter appears at various levels of seriousness as an anti-Romantic tradition conducting a resistance campaign against most of the Victorian poets and poetic schools in turn, before, so to speak, going underground.[5] At its best this kind of criticism insists that earlier poetry had a firmer grasp of realities, a closer relation to everyday life and speech, a stronger intellectual content, a deeper humanity and a greater moral strength and profundity, and it invokes Pope and Johnson against contemporary poets. It can be found most consistently, perhaps, though not exclusively, in the *Quarterly*, and it forms a link between the eighteenth

century and Arnold. But it is always tending to lapse into less worthy forms – a simpler desire for explicit moralizing, improving and useful teaching, academic correctness, the obviously noble and pathetic. A further complicating factor was the influence of Utilitarianism in all its shades, from a systematic philosophy to a vague general cast of mind. Disapproval of literature as trivial could easily pass into a patronizing acceptance of it as a proper interest for the ladies and a pleasant holiday from the serious business of life in nineteenth-century England, so that one effect of the Utilitarian temper was paradoxically to strengthen some of the tendencies towards aesthetic withdrawal – to strengthen them directly, that is, and not merely by reaction. Thus we find that periodicals generally advanced in political and philosophical thought tend to approve of extreme romanticism and the poetry of escape; the *Fortnightly* under Morley was one of the most consistent supporters of Swinburne, Rossetti, Morris, Pater, and aestheticism generally. On the whole, the anti-Romantics fought a losing battle, except against such obviously extravagant manifestations as the 'Spasmodic' school of the mid-century: Tennyson was fairly generally accepted as a great poet and sage by the end of the fifties. Arnold's acceptance came rather later and with less unanimity, the Pre-Raphaelites and Swinburne had arrived by about the middle seventies, despite Buchanan's attack on 'The Fleshly School of Poetry' in the *Contemporary* in 1871, and the *Quarterly*'s more intelligent discussion of 'Literary Poetry' in 1872. Browning's recognition came very slowly, but he was safe by 1869 when the *Athenaeum* called *The Ring and the Book* 'the *opus magnum* of our generation'.

The reviewing of fiction in Victorian periodicals shows a good deal of uncertainty about what to expect from the novel and what standards to apply. Very often the requirements do not go much beyond those mentioned by an *Edinburgh* reviewer in 1841: 'We require from the novel that it shall be moral in its tendency, that it shall be amusing and that it shall exhibit a true and faithful delineation of the class of society which it professes to depict.' Realism must not be carried to the point of the sordid; social criticism must not become too disturbingly precise and political; and 'moral in its tendency' is often narrowed into a demand for strict poetic justice and explicit moral teaching. Nevertheless, the application of general common-sense standards of taste and morality often produced useful

comments, and accounts of fiction benefited especially from the generous allowance of reviewing space and the opportunity to quote at length. For the most part the reviewers made an effective stand against sensationalism and sentimentality of the cruder kinds, as can be seen notably in the *Quarterly*'s survey of 'Sensation Novels' in April 1863 and in George Eliot's article in the *Westminster* for October 1856 on 'Silly Novels by Lady Novelists'. Of the main figures Thackeray's reputation was secure by the fifties; he was accepted more readily than Dickens, who incurred a variety of censure for melodrama and sentimentality, for uninformed and indiscriminate criticism of public institutions, for excessive caricature, and for leaving his proper ground of broad entertainment in an attempt at greater seriousness and more carefully constructed plots. Charlotte Brontë was attacked by the *Quarterly* for bad taste and immorality, but in general she received a fair degree of recognition; Emily, on the other hand, was often ignored. Trollope was for the most part well received, and George Eliot was usually given lengthy and respectful consideration, even by those critics who found her realism excessive or her general outlook too gloomily determinist – the review of *Middlemarch* in the *Quarterly* ran to thirty-three pages. Meredith was generally allowed to be clever, and Hardy's merits had been fairly recognized before he incurred reproach on moral grounds.

Reviews of miscellaneous prose works show the same process of gradual acceptance tempered by appeals to common sense and traditional good taste, and here, of course, extra-literary opinions played an even more important part. Macaulay, Carlyle, and Ruskin all had to meet severe and often shrewd criticism before they achieved general acceptance, though naturally the *Edinburgh* reviewers were kinder to Macaulay than Croker in the *Quarterly*. Disapproval of Carlyle's style was fairly general, and his matter was not likely to commend itself to the Utilitarian temper. Ruskin furnished provocation to critics of many different persuasions, though the later tendency was to appeal back to his art criticism from his unorthodox economics. Arnold as critic and publicist met a bracing reception from such believers in progress as the *Saturday Review* and the *Fortnightly*, and indeed was stimulated by the reviewers to continual further efforts in reply.

If the criticism of the Victorian reviewers was often deflected by

various forms of evangelical morality and utilitarianism, and sometimes by political and social bias, nevertheless we can claim for it a considerable degree of seriousness and responsibility. For the most part the reviewers were conscious of performing an important cultural function, of safeguarding and preserving a living tradition. They regarded the application of severe standards as a duty to the writer as well as to the reading public. Occasionally we find hints of the notion that criticism is sterile and that new work should be met only with grateful appreciation, but this is very much the exception, at least until the end of the century, when certain rather ominous movements towards popularization began to appear. The sense of responsibility was fostered by the development in each important periodical of a kind of corporate personality which enabled writers to speak with authority for more than personal standards. This was helped, of course, by the practice of anonymity which lasted until well on in the century, when the examples of the *Westminster* and the *Fortnightly* gradually led to its disappearance. Though liable to various abuses, as Bulwer-Lytton, Lewes, and others pointed out, it had corresponding merits of which that just mentioned is probably the most important.

During the nineteenth century, then, literary periodicals performed a wide variety of functions. In the first place they expressed, made articulate, defined, and focused the ideas of the main groups of cultivated opinion, diffusing knowledge and taste and generally helping to ensure that modicum of homogeneity combined with adequate variety that constitutes a literary public. They played a large part both in creating the public and in keeping it alive, active and at once receptive and critical. To a great extent their criticism was aimed at the conscious maintenance of standards. For the reader they gave guidance and stimulus in the exploration of new work. For the author they provided a stimulus of a different kind, either acting as a healthy resistance or as a goad. At a more practical level the periodicals played an important part in furnishing an interim market for literary work. Even for established writers they provided extra opportunities, and their rates of pay were sufficiently high to make it worth while for the best authors to contribute. At the other end of the scale they constituted an important field for new aspirants to letters, helping the young writer to support himself while making a name, and furnish-

ing a training-ground in which he could practise his craft. One result was the rise of a class of high-grade literary journalists, middlemen of letters who had an important influence in the spread of ideas and the wider diffusion of taste. The periodicals, in short, ministered vitally to the maintenance of a healthy culture, and they cannot be ignored in any balanced account of Victorian literature.

NOTES

1. Each number of the *Edinburgh* or the *Quarterly* contained about ten to twelve articles, and two numbers made a substantial bound volume of 500 or 600 pages. The half-yearly volumes of the monthly magazines are rather larger, and they were often printed in double columns, so that a single monthly number was more than a third of a quarterly. Of the weeklies, the *Athenaeum* in its early days had sixteen three-columned pages of small type, of which only two or three pages were advertisements.

2. See the centenary article '*The Edinburgh Review* (1802–1902)' (*Edinburgh Review*, July 1902, CXCVI, 275).

3. See 'The Centenary of the *Quarterly Review*' (*Quarterly Review*, April 1909, CCX, 731, and July 1909, CCXI, 279).

4. See E. T. Cook: 'The Jubilee of the *Cornhill*' (*Cornhill*, January 1910, CI, 8).

5. I have discussed this in an article in *Scrutiny*: 'Victorian Criticism of Poetry: the Minority Tradition' (June 1951, XVIII).

THE VICTORIAN READING PUBLIC

R. K. WEBB

One flat generalization can be made: the reading public was never homogeneous. Charles Knight, a publisher who learned a great deal from his efforts at popular publishing, put it clearly in 1854: 'There always have been, still are, and always will be, various classes of readers and purchasers.' The lines between these classes are not always easy to discern and, of course, they could be crossed. Poor or ignorant men could be found reading good books – *Pilgrim's Progress*, *Paradise Lost*, or the best eighteenth-century novels – and James Lackington, a famous bookseller at the end of the eighteenth century, had boasted that he had been instrumental 'in diffusing that general desire for reading now so prevalent among the inferior orders of society'. But Lackington was guilty of a fallacy which Knight saw. The 'inferior orders' who desired to read good literature included few mechanics and none of the husbandry labourers, while eighteenth-century magazines rarely went beyond the gentry and superior traders. As for a 'general habit of reading through the nation', Knight said, 'there appears to have been a sort of tacit agreement amongst all who spoke of public enlightenment in the days of George III to put out of view the great body of "the nation" who paid for their bread by their weekly wages'.[1]

We can begin then in the early nineteenth century with a broad distinction between the respectable and non-respectable reading publics, which corresponds roughly to the division in society between the middle classes and the lower orders – a division very real to the Victorians, although it may defeat statistical analysis. To a tiny minority of the working classes, to men like the young Francis Place, later an important Radical politician, and William Lovett, the Chartist leader, knowledge was power. Such sober and intelligent artisans are difficult, now as then, to classify. The great majority of the lower classes at the beginning of the century were, however,

beyond the pale of respectability. Many were illiterate, and most of them entered the consciousness of the upper classes only as workers or servants, targets for abuse, or subjects for strictly limited attempts at improvement through religious or charitable activity. The respectable reading public covered a similarly wide scale. At one end there was the extended and serious reading of a small but powerful group of the well-educated and deeply concerned; at the other the frivolous reading of clerks who fancied themselves men of the world or of young girls momentarily out from under 'the careful eye' of their elders.

The modern writer, looking back at this complex situation, is likely to be misled by his own concerns and tastes. For example, our lack of enthusiasm for sermons, tracts, and devotional exercises excludes us from a real understanding of a major aspect of the nineteenth-century reading public. Of the roughly 45,000 books published in England between 1816 and 1851, well over 10,000 were religious works, far outdistancing the next largest category – history and geography – with 4,900, and fiction with 3,500.[2] There was also an immense circulation of religious periodicals and tracts. A good many middle-class readers would read nothing but devotional works; many more were deeply concerned to get religious material into the hands of the lower classes – hence the ingenious efforts at distributing tracts, from single copies tucked into baskets by benevolent ladies to distributions of over 40,000 tracts among crowds gathered at public executions.

On the other hand, with our own serious periodicals lost or in perpetual difficulties, we are likely to look back with the over-emphasis of envy to the great quarterly reviews – the *Edinburgh*, the *Quarterly*, the *Westminster* – and to the leading Victorian magazines. Their level was high and their circulations were impressive. In 1808 the *Edinburgh* was printing 9,000 copies, and, we are told, no genteel family could afford to be without it. Yet one must ask how many families took the reviews to read and how many took them as a badge of gentility – a question that must have its impact in the asking, for it can never be answered. Further, these reviews were first and foremost political organs in which partisan considerations often outweighed critical objectivity. Although they were powerful in their time and are stimulating still, modern estimation of

their impact and sometimes of their value stands higher than it should.

Of course, the middle classes read. So many of them had so much time on their hands, especially the women. One member of a family might be deputed to read while the others sewed or fussed or simply listened. In a few households there was serious discussion; in most, the matter read was not weighty enough to provoke it or to serve as much more than the pleasant background today so often provided by the radio. The intellectual attainments of most of the middle and upper classes of Victorian England were not impressive by modern standards. A very small proportion of them attended the universities and, though those institutions were better than they had been in the eighteenth century, breadth was hardly their leading characteristic. Most of the middle classes and aristocracy were abominably educated, for effective expansion and reform of the public schools came only in response to middle-class demands in mid-century. There was, to be sure, the new intellectual aristocracy about which Noel Annan has written. It was this tiny minority and tangential groups of like-minded persons who read and were disturbed by Mill, Carlyle, Tocqueville, Disraeli, and the best novelists. Because they left the most records, these impressive individuals and families tend to fore-shorten our vision. But we must not forget that Matthew Arnold divided the upper levels of English society into Barbarians and Philistines.

The great majority of the respectable reading public, then, were no better than they should have been, no better than their counter-parts today, if, in some respects, they were as good. Limited, insular, convention-bound, many of them, including some highly intelligent people, were shocked by the licence and 'crudities' of George Eliot, Meredith, and even Dickens, tending to prefer writers who today are nearly forgotten. It is often a shock to learn who the best-selling poets and novelists were and how much they could be admired by presumably discriminating minds.

For those who did not buy books there were the circulating libraries, their fees assuring the social, if not the intellectual, standing of the subscribers. The larger libraries listed serious works in their catalogues, and a firm like Mudie's, with a national circulation, took 2,400 copies of the last two volumes of Macaulay's *History*, 3,000

copies of Disraeli's *Lothair*, and ordinarily 600 copies each of the *Edinburgh* and *Quarterly*. But even Mudie's found their largest class of readers overwhelmingly devoted to the novel; while the smaller libraries were almost entirely given over to fiction, and that not of the best sort. After the Act of 1850 made public libraries possible, the lower middle classes who used them seem to have preferred light reading: the serious artisans took out the solid books.[3]

Another resource was the rapidly expanding provision of magazines, ranging from *Chambers's Journal* and *Eliza Cook's Journal* for the lower middle classes (or the servants of the rich and better educated) through Dickens's *Household Words* to the *Cornhill* and the *Saturday Review*. Most of the magazines made their concessions to fiction – 'the oratory of literature' as Bulwer-Lytton called it – and they aimed at a common denominator, relatively high perhaps, but still common. In 1833, in *England and the English*, Bulwer-Lytton used this taste for periodicals to account for the backwardness of England in speculative and scientific fields. If one diffuses knowledge, he said, one does not advance it:

> It is natural that writers should be ambitious of creating a sensation: a sensation is produced by gaining the ear, not of the few, but of the many: it is natural, therefore, that they should address the many; the style pleasing to the many becomes, of course, the style most frequently aimed at: hence the profusion of amusing, familiar, and superficial writings. People complain of it as if it were a proof of degeneracy in the knowledge of authors – it is a proof of the increased number of readers. The time is come when nobody will fit out a ship for the intellectual Columbus to discover new worlds, but when everybody will subscribe for his setting up a steamboat between Calais and Dover.

As the century moved on, this large and varied reading public underwent some significant changes. To be sure, much of it remained superficial and relatively undiscriminating, addicted to periodicals and sensational or sentimental fiction. The well-educated and the intellectual aristocracy, however, increased markedly. In an industrial and increasingly complex society there were many opportunities for the educated – witness civil service reform and the mid-century growth of new professions like engineering, architecture, or accounting. The universities turned their attention increasingly to science, and Jowett's outburst, 'How I hate learning!' became more and more anachronistic. But increasing education brought specialization.

Modern society demanded expertise; the concern with the frontiers of knowledge required concentration, a situation reflected in the notable increase in specialized journals by mid-century. And all this had its effect on reading habits. The specialist found that time available for reading declined, while what reading was done grew more and more restricted in scope. This is true of the statesman, the engineer, the physician, the scholar, and the businessman. Here, for instance, is Richard Cobden, speaking at the Manchester Athenaeum at the end of 1850:

> I take it that, as a rule, grown-up men, in these busy times, read very little else but newspapers. I think the reading of volumes is mostly the exception; and the man who habitually has between his fingers 400 or 500 newspapers in the course of the year ... and is engaged pretty entirely in business, or in political or public life – depend upon it – whatever he may say, or like to have it thought to the contrary, he reads very little else, as a rule, but the current periodical literature, and I doubt if a man with limited time could read anything else that would be more useful to him.[4]

The best newspapers, of course, were improving rapidly in quality in these mid-century years, so that Cobden's businessman was not out of touch with some important intellectual currents, but clearly a new attitude to reading was on its way to a virtually fore-ordained triumph. Reading was unquestionably useful, and it became habitual. Like walking, it was a skill to get one from one place to another; only a few used it to scale heights.

If, after the middle of the century, some persons were busier and more specialized, a great many others had more leisure, but leisure that could be used in new ways. The middle and upper classes were richer and showed it. Travelling became easier, and railway journeys required a particular kind of light reading which W. H. Smith and Son provided in the 'yellow-backs', cheap novels directed specifically at the traveller. Many of the barriers formerly raised by Evangelicalism fell: more people went to the theatre; professional sports spread rapidly; there were bicycles and lawn tennis. Other arts besides literature made their claims on time and attention. Mainzer's and Hullah's singing classes in the forties taught thousands something about music, and Novello's cheap scores helped to spread enthusiasm for local choral groups and to promote the cult of the oratorio. By the end of the century the gramophone had appeared; by 1914 there

were the first glimpses of cinema and wireless, though realization of their potentialities still lay far in the future.

Although the number of books published and the quantity of paper consumed rose impressively, reading in general and literature in particular underwent a relative decline in importance – a consequence of the changing character of a society whose dynamic was technology and whose characteristic was increasing differentiation. Comprehensive world views were going out of fashion. The 'rather wide, unspecialized and genuinely aristocratic culture'[5] of the earlier part of the century was breaking up into compartments, of which literature was only one. Where the educated man with a taste for social problems might have turned in the forties to a novel by Disraeli or an essay by Carlyle, in the nineties he probably would have read the *Fabian Essays* or Henry George – excellent in their way, but hardly literature. There were compensations, to be sure. The best writing showed a marked increase in intellectual quality, and if the serious writer found his public a smaller proportion of the whole than it had been fifty years before, he also found himself, *ipso facto*, freer to address as he wanted the specialized public that he had left to him.

These changes at the upper levels of society were relatively subtle; the spectacular developments occurred at the lower levels. In the eighteenth century there was a vast substratum of popular 'literature' – almanacs, ballads, last dying speeches, broadsides, flyers, and chapbooks. The chapbook embraced many varieties – histories, heroic tales, folk stories, accounts of crime, and very earthy humour. Some publishers in London were in the business in a big way, but more often local printers carried on a profitable sideline in compiling, pirating, and printing these tiny penny or twopenny productions sold in back-street bookshops or through hawkers and pedlars in country districts. Respectable reformers denounced the 'hawker's basket', but they made collections of chapbooks to learn how, through judicious imitation, their own more hygienic productions might be made more acceptable. A few dedicated and self-educated working men sacrificed their little luxuries to buy good books, but of the lower classes who were literate, certainly the vast majority were still drawn to these crude productions of a pre-industrial press. *The Newgate Calendar*, or *Malefactor's Bloody Register*, said Knight, was

'the glory of the number trade' from its first appearance in the 1770s: it was still going strong at mid-century.

In the nineteenth century the working-class reading public expanded and became more diversified. To begin with, there was an increase in literacy. It has often been said that the Education Act of 1870, which first set up board schools, created a new reading public. Actually the effect of these schools – two decades passed before they were both compulsory and free – was both less important and more complex than it would seem. There was a whole spectrum of schools for the working classes in the early nineteenth century. They ranged from the humble and usually contemptible dame schools to sometimes excellent private day schools run for profit, from the charity schools to the far-flung empires of the National Society of the Established Church, and the British and Foreign School Society of the Dissenters. The schools of these last two organizations were based on the monitorial system, whereby older students taught the younger children, a scheme recommended by its cheap solution for the shortage of trained teachers. From 1833 a parliamentary grant was made annually to these societies, and later to similar groups. The size of the grant was repeatedly increased. In 1839 a central office of education, with a brace of inspectors which soon grew into a corps, was set up to supervise the expenditure of these grants and to make recommendations to state-aided schools. Further, there were factory schools, workhouse schools, 'ragged schools', and a whole range of Sunday schools which taught reading, while some went on to teach writing and other secular subjects.[6]

Clearly a powerful religious impulse contributed to this widespread establishment of schools. George III had expressed a wish that he might see every child in his dominions able to read the Bible; with that hope nearly everyone would have agreed. But to educate beyond an ability to read the Bible (which oddly enough seems to have been considered a simple matter) alarmed a great many of his subjects. Hazlitt could talk about 'the march of mind' and Brougham rejoice that the schoolmaster was abroad, but reactionaries like Lord Eldon insisted that a broad education for the working classes would mean the subversion of society. They were right – and the Radicals knew it.

To the advocates of education, a literate working class seemed

essential not only for the domestic peace of England but for its progress. The new statistical societies eagerly received papers proving the direct connection between crime and ignorance. Reformers pointed to the Scots, so much better educated than the English, as an example of how education could bring about a sober, secure society. The better class of manufacturers found that their best workmen were the best educated (again the Scots could be cited) and set up factory schools which did much not only to educate but to discipline a new generation of labourers. The demands of an industrial society were pressing: an illiterate labourer, a spinner, or a weaver might remain illiterate without its adversely affecting the quality of his work; but an illiterate mechanic or engineer would be increasingly handicapped.[7] Perhaps most portentous of all, this new society grew more and more interdependent. The reading of the lower orders, which could be left out of account in the eighteenth century, could no longer be ignored. In the growing towns new (and it often seemed wrong) ideas swept through the discontented; there were novel and disturbing phenomena like trade unions, socialist societies, monster reform meetings, and radical working-class papers. A working class on the move might be explosive, but liberal doctrine preached a faith in education which could capture and direct the lower classes into right thinking. That meant schooling, not only in reading and writing but in morals, politics, and political economy.

The great majority of schools, of course, were poor enough. Although most children in England, except in some of the worst areas, must have spent some time in school, few stayed long enough to get a really solid grounding even in the rudiments. A great many learned to read. Some forgot; many more always found reading difficult. But the towns were full of ephemeral printing and advertising posters which offered encouragement and opportunity to practise simple reading. Self-education, at least for some, could supplement a poor schooling; while the distribution of literature, either through the cheap press or through the work of concerned members of the upper classes, provided a means for what might be called 'informal' education.

Degrees of literacy varied widely. The London area, the small agricultural county of Rutland, and the Northeast were high; the

Midlands, a string of counties from East Anglia through the Home Counties north of London (Bedford the worst), and the rapidly growing manufacturing towns were in a bad way, yet even there some parishes were much better off than others. As to actual ability to read, a great many surveys of varying dependability were taken. They show remarkable consistency – for instance, a continual preponderance of ability to read over ability to write of something like three to two, and some weight can be given to testimony that readers who could not write could really read. Again, literate men outnumbered literate women by a considerable margin until the coming of virtually universal literacy at the beginning of the twentieth century. There is some evidence, however, that male illiteracy remained fairly stable at around the 40 per cent mark throughout the last half of the eighteenth century, while female literacy gradually increased over the same period. After 1815, the rate of illiteracy for both sexes fell, reaching 33 per cent for men and just below 50 per cent for women in 1840; thereafter the curves plummeted to extinction at the end of the century. In so far as one dare generalize about a national average in an extraordinarily varied situation, the conclusion to be drawn from contemporary survey material suggests that two-thirds to three-quarters of the working classes were literate in the early Victorian period, a group that certainly included most of the respectable poor, who were the great political potential in English life.

More recent historical inquiries have used a different kind of evidence – the signing of marriage licenses or, after 1754, of marriage registers. Although the assumption that ability to sign one's name is a true index of literacy has been disputed, the evidence allows the tracing of long-term patterns, as the survey evidence of the early nineteenth century (itself subject to criticism) does not. The results are flattering to the accomplishments of the sixteenth and seventeenth centuries, unfavourable to the eighteenth century. For the nineteenth, though they confirm the difficulties of generalization and suggest a whole new range of causal speculation, the register evidence supports the contention that a remarkably high degree of literacy had been reached well before universal state education was available.[8] The effect of the Education Acts was to level out variations in the country, to provide longer schooling, to give more practice in and so a greater

habit of reading, and, perhaps most important, to furnish some degree of education beyond mere reading and writing.

An expanded reading public required an expanded literature, and that the mechanized press was ready to supply. In 1814 *The Times* published the first newspaper printed by steam. The original Koenig printing machine was rapidly replaced by more advanced models, with a further epoch marked by the appearance of the web press, printing from a continuous roll of paper, in the sixties. Newspapers at the beginning of the nineteenth century were limited to a maximum of five thousand copies a day, but by mid-century *The Times* could turn out forty thousand copies in under four hours from a single set of types. The appearance of practicable type-setting machines in the seventies made for even greater speed, quantity, and cheapness; and by the end of the century the figures of press output are virtually astronomical.

Parallel with this development and essential to it was the rapid improvement in and cheapening of the manufacture of paper. Domestic production stood at something over 11,000 tons in 1800 and at 100,000 tons in 1861. Chemical pulp processes developed in the sixties and seventies overcame the rag shortage, and in 1900 production was over 650,000 tons. Prices dropped in the century from 1s. 6d. a pound to three farthings, with the proportional cost of paper in publications falling from two-thirds to under one-tenth.

Other inventions had far-reaching effects. The stereotyping process allowed type to be distributed and smaller printings made at a time; that meant savings in warehousing and other expenses, greater efficiency of printing schedules, and consequent reductions in prices. Further, effective illustration became a practicable possibility. In 1827 there were twenty woodcutters in London who claimed artists' prices; by mid-century woodcutting was a manufacture. G. J. Holyoake recalled the amazement of a Derbyshire fiddler on seeing the illustrations in the *Penny Magazine*. The woodcuts in the blue-books dealing with mine labour in the forties brought home the terrible conditions underground with an impact that could not have been created otherwise. And *Punch* and the *Illustrated London News* – new and immensely influential phenomena – carried the art of wood-engraving to extraordinary heights. Photography and photo-engraving by the end of the century were to revolutionize illustration still more.

There was also a revolution in distribution. For example, the firm of W. H. Smith and Son had established itself as a distributor for newspapers in the twenties. By using fast horses to catch the morning coaches, they could assure delivery of the London papers in the provinces twenty-four hours before the night-mail coaches could bring them. When the railway appeared, the firm, of course, adopted the new mode of transport and introduced as well the railway bookstall and the railway library. Wholesaling and distribution were increasingly centralized. Simpkin, Marshall was the largest firm in the trade; and at a different level Mudie's circulating library operated on a national scale.[10]

To the people who were concerned about the direction of the expanding reading public, the mechanized press with its promise of cheapness presented a wonderful opportunity. There was a great outburst of interest in libraries – from the parish reading-rooms stocked with discards through the Mechanics' Institutions to the great public libraries after mid-century. The Society for the Diffusion of Useful Knowledge was set up in 1827, with Brougham as its chairman and Charles Knight as its principal publisher. The Chambers brothers in Edinburgh undertook a similar task, and imitators sprang up to share the market for improvement. The S.D.U.K., for a variety of reasons, failed; the Chambers firm succeeded; the fortunes of the competitors varied. But it is quite certain that the libraries and the improving works reached only a very small proportion of the working classes. The *Penny Magazine* of the S.D.U.K. reached a circulation of 200,000 for a time, thanks to its novelty and its woodcuts; *Chambers's Edinburgh Journal* reached 90,000 by mid-century, but much of this circulation was among families higher in the social scale than those aimed at.

When one asks what the lower classes read, the answer of a thousand reformers was simple – 'trash!' When the *Penny Magazine* ceased publication in 1846 and Knight blamed the cheap sensational sheets which diffused a 'moral miasma' over the land, he was echoing sentiments repeated over and over in the forties. Again some sample surveys will indicate the problem. At the end of the thirties, for instance, the following types of books were found in ten out of thirty-eight small circulating libraries in three working-class parishes in London:

	Number	Percentage
Novels by Walter Scott, and novels in imitation of him; Galt, etc.	166	7·57
Novels by Theodore Hook, Bulwer-Lytton, etc.	41	1·87
Novels by Captain Marryat, Cooper, Washington Irving, etc.	115	5·24
Voyages, travels, history and biography	136	6·21
Novels by Miss Edgeworth and moral and religious novels	49	2·27
Works of a good character, Dr Johnson, Goldsmith, etc.	27	1·23
Romances, *Castle of Otranto*, etc.	76	3·46
Fashionable novels, well known	439	20.00
Novels of the lowest character, being chiefly imitations of fashionable novels, containing no good, although probably nothing decidedly bad	1,008	46·00
Miscellaneous old books, *Newgate Calendar*, etc.	86	3·92
Lord Byron's works, Smollett's works, Fielding's works, *Gil Blas*, etc.	39	1·78
Books decidedly bad	10	0·45

Clearly the passion for fiction was endemic among the lower orders, too. Another investigator in London reported the widespread habit of owning books in working-class families, but pointed out that the Bible and religious books were the least read, while the greatest proportion of books were narrative.

In Manchester, it was reported, most of the operatives were, more or less, readers. Booksellers' shops in working-class areas were filled with a jumble of comic song-books, dream books, educational works, sectarian pamphlets, democratic essays, and 'double-columned translations from modern French novels by Eugène Sue, Dumas, Sand, and Paul Feval'. But the 'cheap and coarse penny novel, appearing in weekly parts' took the lead in popularity. Abel Heywood, the leading Manchester dealer in working-class literature, in 1849–50 sold an average of 6,000 numbers *weekly* for each of a small library of creations like *Angelina*, *Elmira's Curse*, *Claude Deval*, *Ella the Outcast*, *Gentleman Jack*, *Gambler's Wife*, and so on, but only 250 numbers *monthly* of Dickens and 200 of Bulwer-Lytton. The back-street bookshops were everywhere. Edward Lloyd and his 'Salisbury

Square School of Fiction', G. W. M. Reynolds and his wife, and a host of competitors met the demand in periodicals and in number publication. The chapbook had been modernized.[11]

The figures for periodicals give the same picture. A comparative account of circulation in the area around Manchester in the middle seventies indicates that for every three high-class political and literary magazines circulated by the principal Manchester wholesale houses (e.g. *Athenaeum*, *Saturday Review*), there were forty humorous, seventy sporting, and a hundred illustrated papers, all of a reasonably respectable character. But two wholesale houses distributed 90,000 copies of six cheap weeklies (including the *Weekly Budget*, a miscellany of tales, selections, puzzles, and so on, and the 'notorious' *Police News*) to only 22,000 for all the respectable periodicals put together.[12]

Books and periodicals could not match the popularity of the newspaper. It was a common assumption in the thirties that working men read nothing but newspapers, while the women patronized light literature. If that was true – and certainly it was very close to being so – it is the more impressive as newspapers were not easy to come by. Newspapers were subject to taxation from the beginning of the eighteenth century, and after 1815 the tax stood at fourpence gross, a deliberate attempt to keep them from circulating among the lower orders. At the beginning of our period, a daily newspaper like *The Times* cost sevenpence, far more than the ordinary working man could afford. Remarkable efforts were made to get at the news. Men clubbed together to buy single copies. Old papers circulated through entire streets. Coffee-houses and public-houses took in papers for their customers to read. The 'pothouse oracle' read aloud extracts from newspapers and commented on what he had read. And a newspaper hung up in a shop-window quickly collected a crowd eager to learn what was going on.

It was not the great London dailies, however, that formed the staple newspaper diet of the working man. There was the unstamped press: small, invariably radical papers of varying quality and success. It is often said that William Cobbett was the typical publisher of this type of paper, as he had got around the tax in 1816 by republishing his *Political Register* as an unstamped pamphlet. But Cobbett was typical of nothing: he was quite *sui generis*, a genius in his way, a

master of English prose, and the expounder of a very curious radicalism. Far more typical of the better publishers of the unstamped were
men like Henry Hetherington, Richard Carlile, and John Cleave.
Hetherington's *Poor Man's Guardian*, in particular, led the field in
the early thirties, an extraordinarily well-run paper which garnered
a circulation upwards of 20,000, a figure that must be multiplied
by as much as thirty to ascertain the number of readers. Papers of
this kind could be very profitable, but they were also subject to
prosecution which extended right down to the humblest sellers.[13]

In 1836 the Whigs reduced the newspaper stamp to a penny, and
the price of the large London dailies fell to fivepence. *The Times*,
by a combination of astute if unscrupulous journalism and an
impressive organization, held a commanding lead; other papers fell
by the wayside. But the reduction of the stamp tax virtually killed
the unstamped papers by robbing them of the margin that made it
profitable to risk prosecution, and Francis Place is authority for the
statement that this ostensibly liberal act really deprived the poorest
readers of their papers.

The great change came with the abolition of the stamp tax in
1855, the advertising duties having disappeared two years earlier;
the excise taxes on paper were removed in 1861. The first symptom
of the revolution was the appearance of the *Daily Telegraph* as a
penny paper in 1855. Further, new means of rapid communication
and the founding of common newsgathering agencies like Reuters
and the Press Association made possible a daily press in the provinces.
The commanding position of *The Times* was fatally challenged.

The Times remained, however, 'the Thunderer': as if from on
high, it spoke to those who were. It was the guide and goad for all
its competitors in creating the great age of the political press. Newspapers had, to be sure, emancipated themselves from open dependence
on the financial support of politicians and parties; the growth of
advertising allowed them the freedom that their increasingly
professional ethos demanded. But politics remained the staple of the
press, as it was the pivot of Victorian society, and the interconnection
of politicians, publishers, and editors proved only to have changed its
modes, not its substance. Where a Liberal newspaper was dominant,
Conservative well-wishers were likely to found a rival, often at the
suggestion of an ambitious newspaperman in whom private and

public interest were conveniently joined. Changes in ownership or editorship could mean political turnabouts, and political upheavals (as in 1886) could shift newspaper loyalties. But at less dramatic levels, journalists were always dependent on politicians for favours such as interviews and early hints on policy – in time they even earned titles – while politicians, at the risk of some lecturing, needed the publicity that newspapers could provide and found them useful in launching trial balloons or in creating opinion.[14]

This complex and subtle partnership continued with remarkable faithfulness to nineteenth-century forms into the twentieth century. It was, however, no more than a generation after the fifties before the supremacy of politics was seriously threatened by the 'new journalism'. The term is, nevertheless, likely to imply too much. That it meant an expansion in numbers and changes in techniques is certain; that it meant a change for the worse in the character of journalism seems untrue. The early Victorian press was a cause for alarm to many respectable people, and journalists were only beginning to admit openly to their profession. That the unstamped press, with its fire-eating radicalism and often narrow dogmatism, should be frowned on is understandable. But even the best papers of the period employed a tone of which their descendants would hardly be proud. Barnes, the editor of *The Times*, was quite frank about it.

Newspaper writing is a thing *sui generis*: it is in literature what brandy is in beverages. John Bull, whose understanding is rather sluggish – I speak of the majority of readers – requires a strong stimulus. He consumes his beef and cannot digest it without a dram; he dozes contentedly over his prejudices which his conceit calls opinions; and you must fire ten-pounders at his densely compacted intellect before you can make it comprehend your meaning or care one farthing for your efforts.

Emerson, of course, saw another aspect of *The Times*: that it detected the first signs of any impending change, taunted and obstructed the authors of every liberal measure until power was about to pass to them, when in a bold about-face it would 'strike in, with the voice of a monarch, astonish those whom they succour, as much as those whom they desert, and make victory sure'.[15] It was a combative, free-wheeling age for the press – spirited, amusing, almost heroic, but hardly edifying.

Although politics was the main concern of the intelligent artisan

class, there were newspapers to cater to other tastes as well. The Sunday press in content was very like modern Sunday papers: scandal-mongering was an important stock-in-trade, and the carryings-on in high society were not less fascinating to the less exalted classes then than they are now. Still another category of journalism growing rapidly in importance in these decades was the sporting press, helped on by the emergence of properly organized boxing and racing, the appearance of professional football in the sixties, and the larger role played by spectator sports with the increase of leisure.

Moreover, there was a wide interest in crime. To some improvers, full criminal reports seemed valuable because in pointing to the penalties of crime they contributed to the civilizing process by which the reformers set so much store; others contended that such reports pandered to depraved tastes. Both extremes of moralizing were beside the point. Reading about crime was a form of entertainment for all practical purposes morally neutral and certainly popular – witness the sale of the *Newgate Calendar* and the extraordinary vogue of the last dying speech, of which newspaper accounts are, in a way, the modern successors. Even the respectable papers carried lengthy accounts of 'horrible' and 'dreadful' occurrences brought to light in one or another police court; indeed, these accounts were much longer in proportion to the amount of news in the papers than is the case today. Only the headlines were missing – there was not enough paper to spare for big letters.

Against a background like this it is small wonder that worried observers predicted the worst from the new penny press in the fifties. They were agreeably surprised when the cheap papers displayed a remarkably high tone. As the threat of revolutions evaporated after 1848, as more people became conscious of increasing prosperity, and as the long campaigns to educate and civilize the working classes began to have their effect, many of the pressures that had produced the violence of the press in the thirties and forties disappeared. The political state of the country was dreadful, Sarah Austin wrote to Guizot in 1858, but it was saved by two things – signs of growing sense in the people and

the truly wonderful state of the lowest part of the Press, the 1*d*. and ½*d*. newspapers which *swarm* in the Metropolis, and in which nobody can find an

indecent, or blasphemous, or seditious word. We are, I think, coming to the point at which this must be our sheet-anchor. God grant it fail us not![16]

It is true that indecency, blasphemy, and sedition disappeared from the press in mid-century, or at least remained pale ghosts in suggestive accounts and essentially factual police reports in the popular papers. To that extent the press did not fail; indeed, the popular press since has been largely conservative. What did happen in the later part of the century was that the daily cheap press, with more paper and faster printing, with a huge audience and an enormous investment, increased its popularity and its income by appealing to those interests of the public that were anything but intellectual. George Newnes, one of the first rank of the new publishers, put it concisely to W. T. Stead, of the *Pall Mall Gazette* and himself an important figure in the new journalism:

> There is one kind of journalism which makes and unmakes Cabinets, upsets Governments, builds Navies and does many other great things. That is your journalism. There is another kind which has no such great ambitions. That is my journalism. A journalism that pays.[17]

Out of that attitude at the end of the century came the new papers, with enormous circulations – *Tit-bits*, *Answers*, and the *Daily Mail*, followed at its heels by the *Daily Express* and the *Daily Mirror*. Or perhaps in essence they were not so new, after all. To be sure, they used all sorts of novel circulation-building devices – contests, puzzles, bizarre advertising, sensational journalism; the cheap morning papers borrowed typographical devices from the Sunday and evening papers and learned some lessons from America. There were headlines and pictures and front pages with news instead of advertisements. But in kind they were a direct outgrowth of the earlier popular press and took over the public of the older street literature by incorporating its appeal.

George Gissing called their public quarter-educated, those who cared for no papers but the Sunday ones, who wanted only

> the lightest and frothiest of chit-chatty information – bits of stories, bits of foolery, bits of statistics, bits of jokes ... Everything must be very short, two inches at the utmost; their attention can't sustain itself beyond two inches. Even chat is too solid for them; they want chit-chat.[18]

A great many critics and moralists have spoken that way since. Yet

that same quarter-educated public – smaller to be sure – existed when Dickens was serving his apprenticeship on the *Morning Chronicle*, and the same denunciations were current. Here is a critic in 1827:

> If a daily paper is to be established, a capital of 20,000 *l.* at least must be risked. Its price, though it should sell but 100 copies per day and without a single advertisement, must be as low as that of the paper selling 10,000 copies, and making 10,000 *l.* a year by advertisements. But as, at this price, nothing short of a circulation nearly as extensive as the greatest of its contemporaries will save its capital from entire loss, the first maxim is – 'extend the circulation, *honestly if you can*; but, at any rate, extend the circulation.' . . . Accordingly, it is found that since *numbers* is the great desideratum, the tastes of *all* classes must be suited: public opinion must not be *led*, but *followed*. There must be but little of profound political discussion, and still less of refined literary criticism, because the really intellectual among mankind are so comparatively few; but there must be abundant records of crimes, in all their horrid deformities – of accidents in all their painful details – of daily brawls and nightly revels among the lowest of mankind – of sporting matches, fights, elopements, frauds – and every description of personal and private history, from the dinners and routs of the *haut ton* to the watch-house adventures of rakes and bullies, and the morbid sentimentality of debauchees and villains expiating their offences at the gallows.
>
> All this must be given, not because the Editors feel pleasure in such details, or because they conceive them to be conducive to the improvement of public morals or the welfare of their fellow-man, but because the Proprietors *must* be remunerated, and therefore ten thousand readers *must* be obtained. The very lowest appetites must therefore be pandered to – the very lowest tastes gratified: and this being done, numbers come apace.[19]

The twentieth-century echoes are deafening.

The devil theory is usually a sign of bankruptcy of historical explanation. We have already seen that the changed position of literature and general reading among the middle-class reading public was rather an inevitable corollary of an increasingly specialized and complex technological society that must be judged on different grounds from a pre-industrial society. Similarly, inescapable historical developments help to place the problem of the mass reading public in proper perspective and, incidentally, to reduce the stature of the press lords – not only by finding that their 'villainy' had good historical antecedents but by indicating that the service they performed for the public was, if not particularly admirable, in the very nature of things. Those who worry about the political impact of the popular press should remember that most of its readers are primarily

concerned with the sporting pages and the features, and read the paper for other reasons than to obtain solid information and material for careful thought and sober judgements. That pattern was established in the last half of the nineteenth century on an earlier base.

It is probably true that the fifties and sixties saw the highest level of the popular press. With relaxed tension after mid-century, with improved administration, industrial peace, and the spread of sobriety and respectability, the reforming drive among the upper classes declined. At the same time, the commitment to democracy made the old ambition of the working classes to prove their respectability and trustworthiness less important, their concern about politics less central. After 1867 working-class culture could claim the right to be judged on its own criteria, not on the very different criteria of a higher class in society. The cry of so many early Victorian working-class leaders to 'get knowledge' gave way to more concrete concerns with power that rested elsewhere than in knowledge and ideas, belief in the beneficent force of which was a legacy from the eighteenth century to the nineteenth.

When in 1863 William Chambers, the publisher, congratulated an Edinburgh audience on the disappearance of the chapbook and the improvement in tone of popular literature, Lord Neaves, the chairman of the meeting, remarked that the old chapbook had indicated a vein of human nature not to be neglected. Boston's *Fourfold State*, he recalled, was often found in cottages side by side with chapbooks, the old folks reading one, the young the other. 'No literature,' he said, 'would be popular and useful which did not look to mirthful and humorous elements in human nature.' In a slightly different vein, Charles Dickens had protested against Knight's denunciation of the publications from Salisbury Square.

> The English are, so far as I know, the hardest worked people on whom the sun shines. Be content if in their wretched intervals of leisure they read for amusement and do no worse. They are born at the oar, and they live and die at it. Good God, what would you have of them![20]

In the latter part of the century, the English working classes were, on the whole, better off, but changing demands still required the old remedy. There was more leisure, but the work was more intense and surroundings remained grim; the desire to escape was natural. Trams, the Metropolitan Railway in the sixties, and the tubes in the nineties,

must have been major if unmeasurable influences on reading habits – and travelling usually requires reading that will simply pass time, tailored to the length of a journey. The excitement of football or racing required information: to gamble one had to read. And to that formidable institution, the English Sunday, the Sunday paper provided at least some harmless relief. Dickens's expostulation, 'Good God, what would you have of them!' still applies more than a century after he made it.

The liberal Victorians had a now incredible vision: that men could reach perfection and that a perfectly functioning society could be created. To this faith the intellectuals gave their peculiar twist: Harriet Martineau thought that anyone who for one hour kept the realm of ideas closed to the working man was an agent of hell. That vision crashed before the political and social realities of democracy, technology, and power – another facet of what George Dangerfield called the strange death of liberal England. Of this new centralized and democratic society, Jeremy Bentham was the prophet. 'Prejudice apart', he said, 'the game of push-pin is of equal value with the arts and sciences of music and poetry.' However special was Bentham's meaning, however doubtful that assumption may be in individual morality, it is difficult to see how an administrator, let alone a businessman, in a democratic society can openly act on any other premise.

By 1914 push-pin had proved itself not only as good as poetry but considerably stronger. The modes and instruments of popular culture were established, one price paid for the enormous benefits that a democratic and technological society conferred throughout the community. But the threat of popular culture did not exhaust the cultural problem. To those concerned to maintain the higher, traditional culture, the future in 1914 posed two questions. One was how that culture could reconcile the unity it desired with the specialization it needed; how, in other words, communication could be restored and recognition of a wider range of cultural values expanded. The second challenge was particularly relevant to literature, as the art whose relative importance had most strikingly declined: how the claims of the cultural heritage of an elite could be re-established on the new basis of individual potentiality which constitutes the promise of democracy.

NOTES

1. Charles Knight, *The Old Printer and the Modern Press* (London, 1854), 286, 226–7.

2. Knight, 262–3.

3. Knight, 229–34. Henry Curwen, *A History of Booksellers* (London, 1873), 421–32. Hilda M. Hamlyn, 'Eighteenth-Century Circulating Libraries in England', *The Library*, 5th series, I, 197–222 (1947). National Association for the Promotion of Social Science, *Transactions*, II, 694–5.

4. *The Times*, 30 December 1850. Compare *The Times*'s own comment, 1 February 1851.

5. The phrase is Emery Neff's. *Carlyle* (New York, 1932), 102.

6. On the intense debate over whether writing could legitimately be taught in Sunday schools, see W. R. Ward, *Religion and Society in England, 1790–1850* (London, 1972), 136–40. On Sunday schools generally, Thomas Walter Laqueur, *Religion and Respectability: Sunday Schools and Working Class Culture, 1780–1850* (New Haven, 1976).

7. On the possibly inverse relationship between industrialization and literacy, see Michael Sanderson, 'Literacy and Social Mobility in the Industrial Revolution in England', *Past and Present* 56 (1972), 75–104.

8. On the contemporary surveys, see R. K. Webb, 'Working-Class Readers in Early Victorian England', *English Historical Review*, LXV, 333–51 (1950). For more recent, signature-based studies, see Lawrence Stone, 'Literacy and Education in England, 1640–1900', *Past and Present* 42 (1969), 61–139 (particularly suggestive as to causal links) and two articles by Roger Schofield, 'The Measurement of Literacy in Pre-Industrial England', in John Goody (ed.), *Literacy in Traditional Societies* (Cambridge, 1968), and 'Dimensions of Illiteracy, 1750–1850', *Explorations in Economic History*, X, 437–54 (1973). To the latter article, this survey is especially indebted for the patterns of male and female illiteracy. See also Michael Sanderson, above. For a criticism of signature evidence – and also for fascinating information on methods of teaching reading – see V. E. Neuburg, *Popular Education in Eighteenth-Century England* (London, 1971).

9. Knight, *Old Printer and Modern Press*. D. C. Coleman, *The British Paper Industry 1495–1860: A Study in Industrial Growth* (Oxford, 1958).

10. Curwen, 363–440.

11. *Journal of the Statistical Society of London*, I, 485 (1839); XI, 218 (1848). *The Cotton Metropolis*, 24–6, in *Chambers's Repository of Instructive and Amusing Tracts*, no. 1 (Edinburgh, 1852). J. L. and B. Hammond, *The Age of the Chartists* (London, 1930), 315–21. *Daily News* (London), 26 October, 2 November, 9 November 1847. On the Society for the Diffusion of Useful Knowledge, R. K. Webb, *The British Working-Class Reader 1790–1848: Literacy and Social Tension* (London, 1955) and the more favourable evaluation in Scott Bennett, 'Revolutions in Thought: Serial Publication and the Mass Market for Reading', in Joanne Shattock and Michael Wolff (eds), *The Victorian Periodical*

Press: Samplings and Soundings (Leicester, 1981). On popular literature generally, Louis James, *Fiction for the Working Man, 1830–1850: A Study of Literature Produced for the Working Classes in Early Victorian England* (London, 1963); Victor E. Neuburg, *Popular Literature: A History and Guide* (Penguin, 1977); and Martha Vicinus, *The Industrial Muse: A Study of Nineteenth-Century British Working-Class Literature* (London, 1974).

12. John H. Nodal, 'Newspapers and Periodicals: their Circulation in Manchester', *Papers of the Manchester Literary Club*, II, 33–8 (1876).

13. Patricia Hollis, *The Pauper Press: A Study in Working-Class Radicalism of the 1830s* (London, 1970); Joel H. Wiener, *The War of the Unstamped: The Movement to Repeal the British Newspaper Tax, 1830–1836* (Ithaca, NY, 1969).

14. Arthur Aspinall, *Politics and the Press, c. 1780–1850* (London, 1949); Stephen Koss, *The Rise and Fall of the Political Press in Britain: The Nineteenth Century* (London, 1981).

15. *The History of The Times* (London, 1935), I, 210–11.

16. Janet Ross, *Three Generations of Englishwomen* (London, 1893), 335–6.

17. J. W. Robertson Scott, *The Life and Death of a Newspaper* (London, 1952), 157.

18. George Gissing, *New Grub Street* (London, 1904), 419.

19. *Sphynx* (London), 8 July 1827.

20. Lord Neaves's comment is reported in *Journal of the Statistical Society of London*, XXVI, 210–11 (1863). Dickens's remark is quoted in Charles Knight, *Passages of a Working Life* (London, 1864), III, 17.

THE POETRY OF TENNYSON

ROBIN MAYHEAD

There are today few people who would feel altogether comfortable in describing Tennyson (1809–92) as an unimportant or even an uninteresting poet, though possibly just as few have been able confidently to arrive at any really satisfying conclusions as to his exact status. The reaction which followed the extravagant adulation accorded to him at the height of his fame is easy enough to understand; similarly the scant attention given to him during the 1920s and 1930s is readily explained when we remember that at that time writers and readers of serious poetry were intent upon the rediscovery of the seventeenth century and upon the analysis of its implications for the poetry of the present. Yet the year 1923 saw the publication of Harold Nicolson's study, which as a work of popularization has probably done more than any other book to fashion the shape of the present-day reader's response to Tennyson. The selection made by W. H. Auden, published in 1946, is governed by discriminations similar to those made by Nicolson. The majority of Tennyson's modern readers would no doubt be prepared to accept those discriminations, and the present account will follow them in a general manner; but many of them might well hesitate to give Tennyson quite the place indicated by Nicolson's phrase 'greatness and permanence'. Still less might they be disposed to agree with T. S. Eliot, when he asserts that Tennyson is 'a great poet' because of his 'abundance, variety, and complete competence'.[1] Even if we set aside the poetry of the seventeenth century as certainly furnishing inappropriate criteria, we have to ask how Tennyson is likely to rank in the estimation of a reader who enjoys, say, the best of Byron, Keats, Blake, Wordsworth, and Hopkins.

A good deal of what is most likely to be enjoyed in Tennyson today is to be found in the work of his early and early-middle periods; that is to say, among the volumes of 1830, 1832, and 1842, though it must

be admitted that the early period contains also some of his very worst utterances: poems in the 'Keepsake' style, with titles like *Lilian*, *Madeline*, and *Claribel*. Turning to the more congenial poems, the influence of which we are at once strongly aware is that of Keats. This assumes more than one form. In that familiar trifle, the amiably pleasant *Recollections of the Arabian Nights*, the 'vary-colour'd shells', the 'fluted vase, and brazen urn', the 'disks and tiars' of 'eastern flowers large', remind us of the sumptuous, lavishly ornate Keats of *The Eve of St Agnes*. But the sensuous in Tennyson's early work is not always so purely decorative as that. In *Mariana*, for example, the way in which language is used, the vividness with which sense-impressions are evoked, remind us at times, widely different in feeling though the two poems are, of the more 'earthy' side of Keats repre-sented by the ode *To Autumn*. This strength, a strength not habitually associated with Tennyson, comes out in the fourth stanza:

> About a stone-cast from the wall
> A sluice with blacken'd waters slept,
> And o'er it many, round and small,
> The cluster'd marish mosses crept.

Here the clustering of consonants and the heavy, clogged movement imposed on the reader who tries to articulate the words clearly aloud, play a large part in creating the total impression of thick stagnation. Tennyson did not often, unfortunately, handle language in this manner in his later work. *Mariana* is an excellent if slight piece of Romantic Tennyson, the Tennyson who is to be distinguished from the self-conscious Bard, who came to exploit poetry so often for the purposes of moral edification and the propagation of Ideas. Of a similar type are *The Kraken*, with its brief but telling vision of the 'sickly light' of eerie submarine depths, and *The Dying Swan*, which again is frankly an exercise in 'atmosphere', and whose movement and imagery, though not its feeling, somewhat recall in the final section Shelley's *The Sensitive Plant*:

> And the creeping mosses and clambering weeds,
> And the willow-branches hoar and dank,
> And the wavy swell of the soughing reeds,
> And the wave-worn horns of the echoing bank,
> And the silvery marish-flowers that throng
> The desolate creeks and pools among,
> Were flooded over with eddying song.

The authentic (though modest) success of *Mariana* and *The Dying Swan* is achieved by the same means as the success of Wordsworth's *Yew Trees*: by the manipulation of perfectly familiar natural objects to build up the impression of a unique world of the imagination. For the landscape of these poems is basically the wold and fen of Tennyson's native Lincolnshire, heightened to make a mysterious, atmospheric décor. The *Ode to Memory*, another early poem, presents this landscape explicitly. The appeal of the ode (which just escapes conventional pomposity) lies in its deft visualization of such things as

> ... the brook that loves
> To purl o'er matted cress and ribbed sand,
> Or dimple in the dark of rushy coves,

or:

> Stretch'd wide and wild the waste enormous marsh,
> Where from the frequent bridge,
> Like emblems of infinity,
> The trenched waters run from sky to sky.

The *Ode to Memory*, if we discount an element of rather artificial rhetorical gesturing ('I faint in this obscurity'), hardly reflects an unhappy state of mind. But more often, as in some of the best parts of *In Memoriam*, the grey, wide landscape is associated with a mood of loneliness, perplexity, and even fear. Nicolson is right to insist upon the strong vein of the morbid in Tennyson's sensibility. One might not, however, be prepared to go all the way with him when he identifies this trait with 'the secret of his preponderating and triumphant strength', or when he says, 'For me the essential Tennyson is a morbid and unhappy mystic'. On Nicholson's own showing, some of Tennyson's most successful poetry has nothing to do with the morbid and the melancholy. It must, nevertheless, be granted that this trait is certainly of capital importance, though it may involve the reader in some difficulty of response. The famous song, 'A spirit haunts the year's last hours', with its imagery of the sick-room and its admittedly masterly evocation of

> ... the moist rich smell of the rotting leaves
> And the breath
> Of the fading edges of box beneath,

is a case in point. Quoting the second stanza, from which those lines

come, in his discussion of the 1830 volume, Nicolson comments that he does not see 'how, for the effect desired, observation and technique could go much further'. One can agree with this, and yet at the same time feel doubts concerning the value of 'the effect desired' as a literary experience. Without venturing into the dangerous territory between literary criticism and extra-literary moral and psychological considerations, I think it is pertinent to ask whether a poet whose gifts are often, if not always, devoted to the projection of a morbid and unhealthy state of mind, may not be open to rather serious limiting judgement.

To return to the relation between Keats and Tennyson, this continues to be felt throughout the latter's career. The barely veiled eroticism of 'Now sleeps the crimson petal', from *The Princess* (1847), reminds one of numerous passages in Keats, as early as *Endymion* and as late as the sonnet 'Bright star!' But the most important Keatsian parallel is the abandoned first version of *Hyperion*, in which Milton's influence blends naturally with that of Spenser.[2] If we compare the opening of *Hyperion* with that of *Oenone* (published first in the 1832 volume but revised for the volume of 1842), we see that the resemblance depends upon more than similarity of setting (Keats begins 'Deep in the shady sadness of a vale'), and arises from a similarity in the blank-verse movement and in the whole attitude towards language:

> There lies a vale in Ida, lovelier
> Than all the valleys of Ionian hills.
> The swimming vapour slopes athwart the glen,
> Puts forth an arm, and creeps from pine to pine,
> And loiters, slowly drawn.

The slow, majestic progress of the verse, in both Keats and Tennyson, comes from Milton; and the calculated exploitation of melodious vowel-sounds (Keats's 'No stir of air was there' parallels Tennyson's 'And loiters, slowly drawn') derives from Spenser.

Tennyson, in fact, is the dominant figure in confirming this Spenserian–Miltonic tradition as the established poetic mode of the later nineteenth century. A poem like *Oenone*, successful in itself, plays its part in the process of narrowing and stultification of verbal resource that led to so much bad and lifeless poetry. Because of this, and because the interest of the present century has been diverted into

other poetic channels, the enjoyment of such poems as *Oenone*, *Tiresias*, *Tithonus*, and *Ulysses*, the effort of isolating them from the unfortunate literary situation they so much helped to create, may not be altogether easy for the modern reader. We have, I think, a useful clue to the problem of estimating Tennyson's place in the stream of English poetry if we reflect that the last three of these poems are among his most perfect achievements, that they possibly constitute his most completely unified and consistently satisfactory work, but that the whole conception of language which informs them excludes, for the purposes of verbal euphony and the Grand Manner, large areas of expressive resource. The manner of these 'dramatic monologues' is that of a lofty, solemn declamation, a declamation which does not exclude the softer tones, but which is far from the flexibility of pace and stress that we associate with such genuinely dramatic poems as Donne's *The Dream* or Eliot's *Gerontion*. Tennyson belongs representatively to an age in which the decline of drama had its effect upon verse not designed for the theatre. And to open a play like his *Becket* at any page is to realize how remote were his gifts from the dramatic virtues. The earnestly pseudo-Shakespearian verse steadfastly refuses to leave the ground, and the imagery is inept and artificial. But if the verse of *Becket* is bad Tennyson, *Ulysses* (1842) is a very decided success. The model is clearly that of the great speeches in Books I and II of *Paradise Lost*, and in this mode Tennyson moves with easy assurance. The verse has its own declamatory eloquence and naturalness:

> It little profits that an idle king,
> By this still hearth, among these barren crags,
> Match'd with an aged wife, I mete and dole
> Unequal laws unto a savage race,
> That hoard, and sleep, and feed, and know not me.

Ulysses is not a poem in which we are at all conscious of the morbid and the melancholy, though we may, if we like, see in it Tennyson's resolution to overcome the mood of despair brought on by the death of Arthur Hallam. The biographical approach, indeed, has its uses here, if only to show how admirably Tennyson has mastered his experience and turned it into the impersonal form of a work of art. *Tiresias*, like *Ulysses*, contains passages which it is difficult not to interpret as comments on existence issuing directly from the author:

> Virtue must shape itself in deed, and those
> Whom weakness or necessity have cramp'd
> Within themselves, immerging, each, his urn
> In his own well, draw solace as he may.

Yet the sentiments have the air of emerging naturally and inevitably from the situations of the imagined speakers, instead of being artificially 'plastered-on', like the more tiresome moralizing passages of *In Memoriam*. There is no hint of even indirect moralizing in the beautiful *Tithonus* (1860), where Tennyson's suavity of diction and rhythm appears at its most impressive height.

The Lotos-Eaters (1832), which, as a consummately managed verbal confection, ranks with these poems among Tennyson's most assured successes, raises a new topic. The theme of withdrawal from an uncongenial world, of escape either to death or, more often, to an ideal dream world, is an important consideration in his work, as it is in the poetry of Arnold, the Pre-Raphaelites, and the early Yeats. *The Lady of Shalott*, from the 1832 volume, is so familiar that the connections, intentional or unconscious, between the withdrawal theme and this fantasy of the Lady weaving aloof in legendary isolation and meeting death when she turns from the 'shadows of the world' in her mirror to gaze for the first time upon reality, tend to go unnoticed. The theme is explicit in *The Lotos-Eaters*. Spenser, and Keats at his most Spenserian, are triumphantly enlisted in this evocation of the dream world, the land 'In which it seemed always afternoon', where

> All round the coast the languid air did swoon,
> Breathing like one that hath a weary dream.

The atmosphere of seductive, luxurious exhaustion is pervasive. The Lotos-eaters themselves are 'pale', 'melancholy' aesthetes. In the Choric Song the Spenserian influence is not a matter of using the Spenserian stanza, but a question of direct reminiscence. Behind the whole poem one senses the presence of two lines from *The Faerie Queene*:

> ... Sleepe after toyle, port after stormie seas,
> Ease after warre, death after life, does greatly please.

Thus the mariners of Tennyson's poem crave for 'long rest or death, dark death, or dreamful ease', and having had 'enough of action, and

of motion', they welcome the sweet oblivion of 'the hollow Lotos-land':

> Surely, surely, slumber is more sweet than toil, the shore
> Than labour in the deep mid-ocean, wind and wave and oar;
> Oh rest ye, brother mariners, we will not wander more.

It must not be supposed that Tennyson officially approved of the Lotos-eating doctrine. If he was often an escapist, he made his escapes with a guilty conscience. In this connection *The Palace of Art* (1832) is a cardinal document. The poem starts from an avowedly and arrogantly hedonistic attitude towards existence; the soul will dwell 'at ease for aye' in her 'lordly pleasure-house', built upon 'a huge crag-platform' deliberately selected to exclude the world. Art takes the place of life; the soul gazes, not upon real landscapes, but upon pictorial substitutes in the form of marvellously wrought pieces of arras; the palace is ennobled with paintings of great poets and (in stained glass) great philosophers. The climax of the first part of the poem is the soul's exultant cry: 'O God-like isolation which art mine.' This mood lasts for three years. In the fourth the soul suddenly finds her isolation to be hateful and tormenting, not at all 'God-like'. Her separation from the world and humanity now seems to her a sin, bringing with it a feeling of 'sore despair' and guilt. The only cure being humility, she throws away her 'royal robes', and asks for 'a cottage in the vale . . . Where I may mourn and pray'. Tennyson does not discredit the world of art. The sin lay in cultivating art at the complete expense of life. Contact with the world of men, and the sharing of the riches of art with others, will drive out the evil:

> Yet pull not down my palace towers, that are
>   So lightly, beautifully built:
> Perchance I may return with others there,
>   When I have purged my guilt.

The Palace of Art, though an interesting poem, is not a complete success. The first part, evoking the splendours of the palace, is Tennyson at his decorative best. In the second part, where he is concerned with bringing home to us the soul's feeling of guilt and the reasons for it, the verse becomes by comparison vague and general-ized, even clumsy. It is tempting to see in this a suggestion that Tennyson's real sentiments may have been quite opposite to those he

ostensibly (and doubtless with an impression of complete sincerity) promulgated in this poem.

The Palace of Art is only one of a number of poems in which conflicts and uncertainties of one kind or another are manifest. To Tennyson, as to other sensitive Victorians, the question of religious faith was a source of anxiety. His solution to the problem was neither to ignore the evidence of science and the speculations to which it gave rise, nor to become an agnostic in the process of accepting it; but rather to effect a compromise, and this compromise has much to do with his popularity in his own age. 'In his highest mood,' observes G. M. Young, 'Tennyson sometimes speaks like an archangel assuring the universe that it will muddle through.'[3] He offered what seemed to the majority of his readers a convincing vindication of Christianity, while at the same time ministering in a comforting way to their sense that the age really was one of progress and enlightenment. The fact that this compromise settled into a smug complacency should not make us forget the genuine pain and self-questioning with which it was evolved. 'How sweet to have a common faith!' exclaims the poet in the youthful Supposed Confessions of a Second-Rate Sensitive Mind, 'To hold a common scorn of death!' And, indeed, 'Why not believe then?' But this Sensitive Mind, 'Moved from beneath with doubt and fear', is 'too forlorn, Too shaken'. The end of this poem is certainly not complacent. After reflecting that, after all, 'It is man's privilege to doubt', the speaker calls upon God:

> Let thy dove
> Shadow me over, and my sins
> Be unremembered, and Thy love
> Enlighten me.

Yet the cry, 'O damned vacillating state!', in the very last line, shows this poise to be no more than momentary and precarious. Modern readers may find the Supposed Confessions, despite some affectation, on the whole more acceptable than The Two Voices (1842). Tennyson's affirmation of the principle of Love as the answer to all ills, Divine Love reflected in the love of man and wife, with Immortality symbolized by their offspring, may awaken disappointment or even amusement.[4] Certainly the first part of The Two Voices, where the austere language and the compressed stanza perfectly convey the

sinister, plausible, undermining tones of the first voice, is much more convincing than the bland 'Be of better cheer' in the optimistic second part. Even readers perhaps disposed to share the poet's sympathies may well find the later stanzas facile and inadequate.

The problem from which *The Two Voices* begins is not so much that of belief in God (though that arises later in the poem) as belief in man. For centuries man had been regarded as obviously supreme in Creation; now science was suggesting that he was perhaps, after all, not so essentially different from other animals. The first, 'still small voice' of Tennyson's poem puts man, 'wonderfully made' though he may be, on a level with the equally wonderful dragon-fly. When the speaker objects that, among the creatures of Nature, man has 'Dominion in the head and breast', the voice replies that he is 'Self-blinded' by pride. Further, the world contains so many human beings that one more or less can make little difference:

> Tho' thou wert scatter'd to the wind,
> Yet is there plenty of the kind.

This new uncertainty about man's supremacy was responsible for an important feature of the Victorian age: its cult of the Great Man. 'No compound of this earthly ball,' says the speaker in *The Two Voices*, 'is like another, all in all.' Man's place in the scheme of things might be questioned, but at least it was plain that all men did not lie at one common level. Moreover, man had a *spirit*, and what better proof of this could be needed than the embodiment of spirit in the deeds and characters of the greatest of the species? One typical example of Victorian hero-worship is the extravagant devotion with which Tennyson himself came to be honoured. This characteristic in his own poetry is illustrated by such a piece as the *Ode on the Death of the Duke of Wellington* (1852), notably here:

> Tho' world on world in myriad myriads roll
> Round us, each with different powers,
> And other forms of life than ours,
> What know we greater than the soul?
> On God and Godlike men we build our trust.

But the *Ode* has more than a diagnostic value. It is, in fact, one of Tennyson's finest performances, and (unlike the first and better part of *The Two Voices*) it owes nothing to his predilection for the morbid.

'Performance' seems the most apt word for the *Ode*'s massive, Miltonic virtuosity, deriving its weight and sonority from the manner of *At a Solemn Musick*. Tennyson's mature mode is admirable for occasional poetry, and this category includes some of his most satisfying pieces. The *Ode sung at the Opening of the International Exhibition* (1862), for instance, though its sentiments seem sadly over-optimistic today, is recognizably and impressively a descendant of the great odes of Dryden. Discussing some of Tennyson's verse-epistles, Nicolson appropriately invokes the name of Horace. One might link them also with an English poet in the Horatian tradition – Andrew Marvell, whom, we remember, Tennyson admired. He is quite without Marvell's wit, but a poem like *To E. L. on his Travels in Greece* reminds us pleasantly of that poet's urbanity and ease:

> And trust me while I turn'd the page,
>   And track'd you still on classic ground,
>   I grew in gladness till I found
> My spirits in the golden age.

However attractive the verse-epistles may be to the modern reader, he must remember that Tennyson's popularity in his own time was founded upon the long poems, of which, apart from *In Memoriam*, the most widely admired were the *Idylls of the King* (1859–72). These make uninviting reading today. For the most part they are effectively constructed, and their language rarely falls below a certain level of accomplishment; but there is little more that can be said to give the present-day reader an appetite. Despite its assurance and for all its parade of onomatopoeia and alliteration, the verse is painfully lacking in essential vitality. *Enoch Arden* (1864) is rather more interesting, if only because its pathos, considering the nature of the theme, is surprisingly restrained. The real weakness of the poem becomes evident if one takes the hint of its Wordsworthian manner, and compares it with such tales of humble suffering as *Michael*, or, more appropriately, the story of Margaret in Book I of *The Excursion*. Wordsworth's compassionate but mature and balanced grasp of human values gives his tales a depth and 'point' inaccessible to the relatively facile morality of Tennyson's poem.

Maud (1855) is a work of quite a different order. There is real justification here for referring to Tennyson's morbid streak, for the hero of this 'monodrama' is a projection of the morbid on a grand

scale, a man ill-starred from the first, living under the shadow of his father's suspected suicide, doomed to separation from his beloved through a fatal duel with her proud brother. *Maud* presents a difficult case. One may grant that it has a more 'modern' appearance than most of Tennyson's work, and at the same time feel that this 'modernity' is not necessarily an advantage, that Tennyson is at his best a poet of a very different kind, that the calculated ruggedness of much of the verse is forced and insensitive. The undoubted originality of the poem, its abrupt changes of feeling and tone, the suppression of links in the narrative, the variety of different kinds of verse – these things are undeniably impressive. *Maud* contains much that is admirable: the section in Part II beginning 'O that 'twere possible', for instance, phrases like 'the dry-tongued laurels' pattering talk', or 'the gross mud-honey of town', not to mention the justly famous

> ... long breeze that streams to thy delicious East,
> Sighing for Lebanon,

and the really chilling and macabre end of Part II:

> I will cry to the steps above my head
> And somebody, surely, some kind heart will come
> To bury me, bury me,
> Deeper, ever so little deeper.

But the verse is extremely unequal, and often gives an effect of strain, notably in the more 'passionate' moments:

> I have led her home, my love, my only friend.
> There is none like her, none.

Or:

> She is coming, my dove, my dear;
>   She is coming, my life, my fate;

The surface excitement produced by the rhythm and the repetitions in those examples cannot make up for the essential poverty of the language. A good deal in the poem suggests the limiting word 'melodrama'. The account of the duel is decidedly 'stagey', and what are we to make of the very opening of the poem?

> I hate the dreadful hollow behind the little wood,
> Its lips in the field above are dabbled with blood-red heath,
> The red-ribb'd ledges drip with a silent horror of blood,
> And Echo there, whatever is ask'd her, answers 'Death'.

It is possible to say (as Tennyson himself said, when critics attributed to him personally the vituperation of *Maud* and the *Locksley Hall* poems) that this, and other 'strained' passages, are part of a close dramatic rendering of the hero's morbid condition of mind, and should not be taken 'seriously'. The trouble with that kind of argument is that it could easily, pressed to its logical conclusion, be made to justify writing of the very worst kind. The hero of *Maud* may be, as Bradley says, 'a poor hysterical creature',[5] but that does not necessarily mean giving him lurid and exaggerated verse. Tennyson's anxiety not to be confused with the hero of *Maud* and the speaker of the *Locksley Hall* poems is characteristic of an odd evasiveness in him. He is a representative Victorian figure in his passion for compromise, in his desire to 'get it both ways', in his vacillation between endorsement of the conventions and preoccupations of his age and outspoken criticism of them. One tends to think of him in his prosperous years as the embodiment of the respectable; yet two years after the publication of *In Memoriam* he could write contemptuously of 'our commercial mire', and 'The British Goddess, Sleek Respectability'. Disgust at 'our commercial mire' dominates the opening section of *Maud*. 'Who but a fool would have faith in a tradesman's ware or his word?' asks the hero; and he goes on:

> Is it peace or war? Civil war, as I think, and that of a kind
> The viler, as underhand, not openly bearing the sword.

We are meant to feel that the whole situation of the hero, including his morbid cast of mind, has been basically brought about by the age's materialism, its 'lust of gain', its unscrupulous commercial rivalry. These have driven his father to his death, and the opening shudder over 'the dreadful hollow behind the little wood', where the body was found, is followed by a long passage of railing against the hypocrisies and cruelties of this mercenary 'Peace':

> Peace sitting under her olive, and slurring the days gone by,
> When the poor are hovell'd and hustled together, each sex,
>   like swine.
> When only the ledger lives, and when only not all men lie;
> Peace in her vineyard – yes! – but a company forges the
>   wine.

One may respect the humanity of such a protest and admit that its

expression is not without a kind of vigour; but whether one takes it as representing Tennyson's own views or those of a purely fictitious person, the fact remains that this kind of preoccupation does violence to Tennyson's art. In his desire to be emphatic he becomes merely clumsy, as in the impossible 'and when only not all men lie'. Tennyson is infinitely less successful in this mode than in his Spenserian-Miltonic one, and there is no compensating interest, apart from scattered fragments, in extending the possibilities of poetic expression, in exploring the resources of English. Tennyson's 'social criticism' is a parallel case to that of his scientific interests. Despite numerous references to scientific ideas, despite his anxiety to keep up to date with scientific progress, science has little or nothing to do with his best and most characteristic poetry.

The question of Tennyson's 'ideas', the question of whether they are successfully digested into poetry or merely asserted with the tone and manner of the preacher, is particularly relevant in the case of *In Memoriam*. This started its existence as a collection of elegies, more or less unrelated except for their inspiration, occasioned by the death of Arthur Hallam. In the form in which it was finally published, however, in 1850, the work consists of a closely ordered sequence, the elegies being arranged to fit into a coherent philosophical scheme and architectural structure. The architectural plan is founded upon three sections, divided from one another by the Christmas odes, which mark the passing of time, and rounded-off with a Prologue and Epilogue. It is doubtful whether this scheme has anything to do with what is really valuable in the poem. *In Memoriam* began as the expression of a passionate, tormented grief. This does not mean that the verse of the elegies is necessarily vague or uncontrolled. There is admittedly something oppressive about the poem's intense subjectivity, an oppressiveness to which the unvarying stanza lends emphasis; the morbid side of Tennyson could in some ways hardly be more in evidence, yet it does not issue in the exaggerated tones of *Maud*, and the personal pathos is rarely offensive, though by the end of the poem one may have found it excessive. Probably the most impressive thing about *In Memoriam* today, in fact, is the collectedness of the way in which Tennyson analyses his sorrow. This 'calm despair' is far from the incantatory rhythm and helpless gesturing of 'Break, break, break', and is all the more effective for its sombre clarity:

What words are these have fall'n from me?
    Can calm despair and wild unrest
    Be tenants of a single breast,
Or sorrow such a changeling be?

Or doth she only seem to take
    The touch of change in calm or storm,
    But knows no more of transient form
In her deep self, than some dead lake . . .

That holds the shadow of a lark
    Hung in the shadow of a heaven?

The language often has a moving, austere precision:

But, for the unquiet heart and brain,
    A use in measured language lies;
    The sad mechanic exercise,
Like dull narcotics, numbing pain.

It is because of things like these, their 'measured language' actually intensifying rather than diminishing the poignancy of the feeling, that *In Memoriam*, though its brooding may be distasteful to some, will continue to be read. But Tennyson had ambitions to make his poem much more than the expression of merely personal feeling:

It must be remembered that this is a poem, *not* an actual biography . . . The different moods of sorrow as in a drama are dramatically given, and my conviction that fear, doubts, and suffering will find answer and relief only through Faith in a God of Love. 'I' is not always the author speaking of himself, but the voice of the human race speaking through him.[6]

Readers today are likely to feel that Tennyson is at his best in this poem precisely when he is being most personal, as in his evocations of 'this high wold' (XI), or the landscape where, in the November wind, 'The sunbeam strikes along tne world' (XV), which recall the setting of *The Dying Swan* and the *Ode to Memory*. When, on the other hand, Tennyson generalizes his feelings and takes upon himself the burden of speaking for 'the human race', the poetry is far less acceptable. Yet it was this aspect of the poem that gave it its astonishing popularity, that made it even a text for the popular preacher, that led Queen Victoria to say to Tennyson, 'Next to the Bible *In Memoriam* is my comfort.' Tennyson conceived of the scheme in its entirety as bodying forth a 'Way of the Soul', a progress from the initial stunned

grief, through gradual acquiescence, to a condition of peace and serenity in which passionate regret is replaced by 'the consciousness of union with the spirit', and in which the world now seems 'the abode of that immortal Love, at once divine and human, which includes the living and the dead'.[7] And in this Tennyson is being very consciously the Bard, the oracle:

> Our little systems have their day;
>   They have their day and cease to be;
>   They are but broken lights of thee,
> And thou, O Lord, art more than they.

The tone often has the unction of the preacher, and the weighty, explicit moralizing can prove intensely irritating to a reader for whom the experience of other poetry (including some of Tennyson's) has suggested subtler and more tactful ways of presenting moral values in literature:

> We pass; the path that each man trod
>   Is dim, or will be dim, with weeds:
>   What fame is left for human deeds
> In endless age? It rests with God.

Fortunately, despite its symmetrical outward form, *In Memoriam* is a poem whose virtues may be enjoyed without too closely consecutive reading, so that the less successful passages may be ignored.

This discussion has been a necessarily restricted one. It has not taken into account such poems as *The May Queen* or *The Charge of the Light Brigade*. Their characteristics are so obvious to anyone who has read them that such examples of Tennysonian sentimentality and Tennysonian patriotic swagger seemed to call for no special treatment. In the first Tennyson links up with the death of Little Nell and with the line of self-indulgent sorrow that produced things like Alexander Smith's *Barbara*; in the second he is part of the tradition which includes Henley and Kipling. Attention might have been given to a few more of the successful poems, but I am doubtful whether considerations of them would affect the overall picture.

We return to the question of Tennyson's status. His good poems are numerous enough to secure him a permanent place. Yet *Maud* and *In Memoriam* are both very unequal; *The Palace of Art* and *The Two Voices* are incomplete successes; the early Romantic poems are attrac-

tive, but it would be out of the question to call any one of them a great poem; the virtues of the occasional poems are considerable, but they are hardly those of greatness, with the exception of the Wellington *Ode*; the verse-epistles are delightful and surprising, certainly not great. There remain the 'Classical' poems, and it would be hard to deny greatness of a kind to the author of *Ulysses*. Yet the very nature of his achievement makes it a decidedly limited kind. If we postulate as one of the essential attributes of greatness in a poet an interest in exploiting the expressive resources of language, an interest which keeps language alive and keen, such an interest as that of Wordsworth at his best, of Byron in his satirical poems, of Keats in the Odes, of Blake and Hopkins, then Tennyson does not achieve greatness. Eliot rightly draws attention to his technical 'competence'; we have only to consider a poem like *Böadicea* to appreciate Tennyson's mastery of complex metrical effect, and *Morte d'Arthur* illustrates again and again his triumphant skill in the handling of verbal devices like ono- matopoeia. But the interest in language we associate with greatness involves more than those things. Far from opening up new possibili- ties, Tennyson helped to narrow and restrict, to establish a conven- tionally held notion of the 'poetic'. Many of his poems will always be read with enjoyment, and literature would be the poorer without them. But although he is a monumentally representative figure of his own age, he is without the qualities that would put him on a level with the great even of the nineteenth century alone.

NOTES

1. See Eliot's essay on Tennyson in *Essays Ancient and Modern* (London, 1936), and the review by F. R. Leavis in *Scrutiny*, V (1936).

2. See the essay 'Mr Eliot and Milton' in F. R. Leavis, *The Common Pursuit* (London, 1952), and the chapter on Keats in his *Revaluation* (London, 1936).

3. *Victorian England: Portrait of an Age* (Oxford, 1936), 75.

4. See Harold Nicolson, *Tennyson. Aspects of his Life, Character and Poetry* (London, 1923), 125-8; also the Tennyson chapter in *More Nineteenth-Century Studies*, by Basil Willey (London, 1956).

5. Bradley has some sensible remarks on the equivocal status of the hero of *Maud*, though his estimate of the poem is conventional. See 'The Reaction against Tennyson', in *A Miscellany* (London, 1929).

6. Quoted by A. C. Bradley in *A Commentary on Tennyson's 'In Memoriam'* (London, 1901).

7. Bradley's words; his *Commentary* is valuable both as a demonstration of what Tennyson meant by the final scheme of *In Memoriam*, and an illustration of the seriousness with which a critic nurtured by the nineteenth-century tradition could take it.

ROBERT BROWNING

LEO SALINGAR

A modern reader emerging from the formidable tracts of Browning's collected poems and plays is likely to discount the poet's early reputation for tough originality and see him rather as a typical if faintly rebellious spokesman of his age. In politics and morals he stands for the liberalism of his generation (1812–89); his religion is an undogmatic evangelical nonconformity; he is the Victorian tourist rampant in his gusto for men and cities and his patronizing connoisseurship in the art of the past; he is a representative philistine in his hearty message of progress and his shadow-boxing with Doubt. And he is typical of his age in his treatment of his verse medium, with his profuse neo-gothic ornament and his heavy-handed ingenuity in diction, rhyme, and stanza-forms. He was a poet competing with essayists and novelists; and it might have been luckier for his abounding gifts if he could have followed the tradition of Dryden and Crabbe without feeling the itch to modernize his craft or the obligation to deliver a message.

Browning himself, of course, could never have agreed with this; he was too deeply attached to the romantic conception of the poet as magician, visionary, and prophet. Shelley is the main literary inspiration behind his first poems, the half-confessional studies in 'the development of a soul' – *Pauline* (1833), *Paracelsus* (1835), and the notoriously obscure *Sordello* (1840); and to Shelley he returns, in an essay of 1851, as the type of the 'subjective' poet who finds God within himself:

> Not with the combination of humanity in action, but with the primal elements of humanity he has to do; and he digs where he stands, – preferring to seek them in his own soul as the nearest reflex of that absolute Mind, according to the intuitions of which he desires to perceive and speak.

Browning takes Shakespeare as the type of the 'objective' or dramatic writer, but it is the subjective poet, he says, who 'might seem to be

the ultimate requirement of every age'. He thus promotes Shelley to the rank of Carlyle's poet-heroes.

True, Browning had very soon begun to relinquish the ideal of pure subjectivity, to reject the anarchic and the ethereal qualities in Shelley, Keats, and Byron, and to share the desire of his own generation for a literature of 'facts' and moral usefulness, if not respectability.[1] Between 1837 and 1846 – the year of his marriage – he had written his eight plays, including *Pippa Passes*, and the two volumes of *Dramatic Lyrics* and *Dramatic Romances*, which stand as near to Scott as to Shelley. Nevertheless, his change of aim was not altogether whole-hearted. 'What I have printed gives *no* knowledge of me,' he wrote to Elizabeth Barrett in 1845; '. . . I never have begun, even, what I hope I was born to begin and end – "R. B. a poem"'; and in another letter, more regretfully:

> You speak out, *you*, – I only make men and women speak, give you truth broken into prismatic hues, and fear the pure white light, even if it is in me, *but I am going to try*.

In effect, he did not 'speak out'. On the contrary, in his essay on Shelley he tried to justify the poetry of 'prismatic hues' historically by suggesting that after the subjective prophets there must come another race of poets, 'prodigal of objects for men's outer and not inner sight', poets who 'break up' the visionary synthesis into 'parts of independent and unclassed value, careless of the unknown laws for recombining them' – though confident that progress will bring about a new synthesis in due course. This is evidently the category designed for Browning himself, and he came to resent any suggestion that he revealed his own mind in his characters. But if he put himself forward as an 'objective' poet, it was largely in spite of his own wishes. And no doubt his failure to 'speak out' must have been responsible for much of the obscurity of his verse, for its mystifying digressions, tortuous reasoning, and abnormally involved syntax. At its best his poetry has the courage of its defects. He is the poet of half-lights, of ambiguous situations, of spiritual failure.

In *Christmas Eve and Easter Day*, possibly written under his wife's influence (1850), Browning comes as near as anywhere to speaking out on religion. In the first poem he is transported, by the clumsy mechanism of a dream, from Zion Chapel, beside a dreary common

in the London slums, to St Peter's in Rome, and then to a Göttingen
lecture-hall, where a German professor expounds the Higher Criticism; his heart is with the Dissenters' form of worship, although the
congregation in Mount Zion are squalid and the preacher absurd.
Easter Day presents a more painful self-examination. The main
speaker there describes how, one Easter-night, on this same common
near Mount Zion, he had suddenly seen the whole night sky burst
into 'A fierce vindictive scribble of red Quick flame across', so that
he had known it was the Judgement Day, when he must choose
between the world and God. He clings to the beauty of the world;
whereupon the figure of Christ appears to him and condemns him to
his choice. He is forced to realize that neither nature, art, poetry, nor
love can reopen the gate of Heaven for him; all he has left is a
desperate yearning. Since he has had his chance and lost it he can really
find no comfort in the second speaker's belief that

> You must mix some uncertainty
> With faith, if you would have faith be; –

and the second speaker is Browning's normal argumentative self. At
most, the other self of *Easter Day* can hope that the vision he has seen
may be no more than a dream.

A great deal of Browning's writing is connected with the substance
of this vision. The natural world of his poems – of *Saul*, or *Caliban*,
for instance – is a solid, rough-hewn, colourful world, imbued with
an ever-changing plastic power; a world of volcanic rocks, of agitated
skies and waters, exotic stones, clustering flower-forms, and pullulat-
ing animal life; an alluring but also a menacing world for the poet's
worship.[2] It brings intense stimulus and challenge to Browning's
acquisitive men and women, his craftsmen, collectors, travellers, and
inquirers, who encounter their environment as an obstacle or a
quarry. He describes life in tangible metaphors of quest or adventure,
as a ride, a pilgrimage, a research, an ocean voyage, a task of knight-
errantry. But the goal of the adventure is not equally plain. Either
Browning makes a flourish about soul somehow sparking flesh or he
reduces his poems to bits of immediate sensation. On the whole, he
is more successful, his poetry is more consistently alive, as he leans
towards the second alternative. His inmost relationship to his world
is a state of excited, unquiet possession.

A characteristic example is the short dramatic lyric *Meeting at Night* (1845), where the lover's tingling senses acknowledge his surroundings – the 'startled little waves', the 'slushy sand', the 'sea-scented beach', the 'three fields to cross' – merely as stages on his advance to the anticipated climax of 'two hearts beating each to each'. Every detail here, including for once the syntax, contributes directly to the main impression, the sensation of pleasurable excitement – though Browning adds a tailpiece, *Parting at Morning*, to show that love is not the speaker's resting-place; he has also 'the need of a world of men'. *Meeting at Night* is one of the very few completely organized poems of Browning; another is the more sombre and impressive *Childe Roland* (1852), a poem unusual in its composition because it 'came upon' him, Browning says, 'as a kind of dream' (as a rule, he held that 'a poet never dreams'). In *Childe Roland*, too, the main effect depends on physical sensation, though in this case the sensation is heavily charged with the mood and something of the imagery of the vision in *Easter Day*. The knight, Childe Roland, has been wandering for years on a mysterious and apparently hopeless quest. He meets a repulsive cripple who points out the way. He mistrusts the cripple but obeys him, to find himself riding alone in the dusk on a ghastly plain of weeds and stunted grass where Nature seems to be waiting 'peevishly' for the fire of Judgement. He tries to cheer himself by recalling his old companions on the quest, but can only think of their disasters. He reaches a second plain, even grimmer than the first, where the ground is strangely churned by the marks of battle, and he comes upon nameless engines of torture. In the gathering dusk the plain has surrounded itself with hills: no way forward. At the same time the knight realizes that this place is, in fact, his destination:

> And just as far as ever from the end!
>   Nought in the distance but the evening, nought
>   To point my footstep further! At the thought,
> A great black bird, Apollyon's bosom-friend,
> Sailed past, nor beat his wide wing dragon-penned
>   That brushed my cap – perchance the guide I sought ...
> Burningly it came on me all at once,
>   This was the place! ...

There stands his Dark Tower; on the hills around him he perceives

'the lost adventurers [his] peers', watching and waiting. 'Dauntless',
he sets his horn to his lips and blows the signal.

Childe Roland has been compared to *The Ancient Mariner*. Browning is more self-conscious than Coleridge and more artful in manag-
ing the suspense, but then his problem is different, a problem of choice
and the will like that of the speaker in *Easter Day*. The decisive ordeal,
whatever its nature, must be faced in the present; when the knight
summons his courage the nightmare ends. But this time Browning
does not try to suggest what the ordeal means or what is its result.

There is not much room in Childe Roland's mind for reflection.
Usually, however, Browning gives his speakers more than enough
time to comment as they disclose their moment of crisis, their chance
of happiness seized or missed. They turn the action over and examine
alternatives; they stand back from their sensations, draw a moral from
them or try to, even consider what meaning they may have for
someone else:

> What? Those lesser thirds so plaintive, sixths diminished,
>   sigh on sigh,
> Told them something? Those suspensions, those solutions –
>   'Must we die?'
> Those commiserating sevenths – 'Life might last! we can
>   but try!'   (*A Toccata of Galuppi's*, 1855)

And on the basis of such speculation Browning worked out a new
conversational form of dramatic lyric, releasing an ironic interplay
between the setting, the action, and the spoken comments. The
monologue of *Two in the Campagna* (from *Men and Women*, 1855) is
a good example of his method. Two lovers are looking across the
open country that covers the ruins of ancient Rome, and the man
points out Nature's triumph over civilization:

> The champaign with its endless fleece
>   Of feathery grasses everywhere!
> Silence and passion, joy and peace,
>   An everlasting wash of air –
> Rome's ghost since her decease.
>
> Such life there, through such lengths of hours,
>   Such miracles performed in play,
> Such primal naked forms of flowers,
>   Such letting Nature have her way
> While Heaven looks from its towers!

From this reflection he draws the Shelleyan inference that they also
should love freely and naturally. But his plea marks the turning-point
of the little drama, not its climax. First Browning shows the man
groping his way towards the thought he wants; then, in the moment
of expressing it, 'the good minute goes', the ease of Nature escapes
him. The opening verses are particularly successful except for a slight
labouring of details:

> For me, I touched a thought, I know,
>   Has tantalized me many times,
> (Like turns of thread the spiders throw
>   Mocking across our path) for rhymes
> To catch at and let go.
>
> Help me to hold it: first it left
>   The yellowing fennel, run to seed
> There, branching from the brickwork's cleft,
>   Some old tomb's ruin: yonder weed
> Took up the floating weft,
>
> Where one small orange cup amassed
>   Five beetles, – blind and green they grope
> Among the honey-meal, – and last
>   Everywhere on the grassy slope
> I traced it. Hold it fast!

While Browning makes the description here move steadily forward
towards the general thought of Nature's freedom and profusion, he
makes the tempo of the speaker's mind appear slower and more
hesitant. And, together with this hesitant movement of the speaking
voice, the separate images convey a succession of gentle discords
between Nature and the mind that contemplates her. This regretful
undertone is carried on through the middle stanzas about 'Rome's
ghost', and prepares for the last stanzas where 'the good minute goes':

> Already how am I so far
>   Out of that minute? Must I go
> Still like the thistle-ball, no bar,
>   Onward, whenever light winds blow,
> Fixed by no friendly star?
>
> Just when I seemed about to learn!
>   Where is the thread now? Off again!
> The old trick! Only I discern –
>   Infinite passion and the pain
> Of finite hearts that yearn.

A poem like this recalls Browning's admiration – exceptional in his time – for Donne. But, quite apart from the difference of sentiment, a dramatic lyric by Donne has a tight, progressive logic, both on the plane of verbal reasoning and on the psychological plane, whereas Browning's poems tend to fall apart so that he has to pull them together with a resounding exclamation. The good minute goes from the poet as well as the lover.

Browning's inability to grasp a situation firmly as a whole, or, as Santayana argues, his inability to transcend 'the crude experience . . . of self-consciousness', explains 'the arrest of his dramatic art at soliloquy'. In the formal monologues in blank verse or heroic couplets for which he is famous he sets out to make a virtue of his deficiency. The earlier ones, *My Last Duchess* (1842) and *The Bishop Orders his Tomb* (1845), are striking ironic character-sketches, in a manner recalling Chaucer, but with a new wealth of sensational and circumstantial details. The later ones set out to exploit a problem; they point forward to the speeches of special pleading by the characters of Shaw. They are still dramatic in so far as they reveal character within the framework of an ironic setting, but the sense of drama in them is swamped by argument as Browning turns the monologue into a form of confidential self-justification by men called upon to defend a questionable or imperfect philosophy of life. The most notable of these apologists are Fra Lippo Lippi, Andrea del Sarto, Bishop Blougram, Karshish, and Cleon (from *Men and Women*, 1855) and Caliban and Mr Sludge, 'the Medium' (from *Dramatis Personae*, 1864). Their names alone suggest the range of Browning's human curiosity – two Renaissance artists, a semi-fictitious Victorian Catholic, an imaginary Arab physician and an imaginary Greek poet from the first century of Christianity, Shakespeare's savage (speaking as an exponent of natural religion in the light of Darwinism), and a thinly disguised American spiritualist. But they are all concerned with two allied topics – with faith and success (or self-fulfilment, or the struggle for survival). And, like the main speaker in *Easter Day*, though in varying degrees, all of them have failed or missed or evaded the test of an ultimate vision. The Arab physician and the Greek poet have brushed against the revelation they both need and have failed to grasp it. The Christian speakers are on the defensive, and their special

interest for Browning is the opportunity they afford him of putting the case for an acknowledged imperfection. In addition, their social position is ambiguous. Fra Lippo Lippi is a scapegrace monk; Andrea del Sarto has to swallow disgrace and humiliation; the great bishop and the whining medium are both in some measure charlatans:

> For Blougram, he believed, say, half he spoke . . .
> He said true things, but called them by wrong names.

The problem for the poet is where the bluffing ends and the candour begins; and this he cannot or will not resolve.[3]

The two artists are the most sympathetically drawn of these characters. Fra Lippo cannot 'paint souls', but he speaks up vigorously for Browning's naturalist aesthetic:

> . . . do you feel thankful, ay or no,
> For this fair town's face, yonder river's line,
> The mountain round it and the sky above,
> Much more the figures of man, woman, child,
> These are the frame to? What's it all about?
> To be passed o'er, despised? or dwelt upon,
> Wondered at?

And del Sarto caps the argument for his creator by minimizing the value of technical perfection:

> Ah, but a man's reach should exceed his grasp,
> Or what's a Heaven for? all is silver-grey
> Placid and perfect with my art: the worse!

But the most original conceptions are those of the Arab doctor who has examined Lazarus since his return from the dead and the Catholic bishop out-manoeuvring his guest and critic in a leisured overflow of cynical benevolence. Blougram stands at the centre of the poet's world; he makes him a fascinating and memorable figure as an epicurean prince of the Church, at once self-satisfied and earnest. Yet the irony of the portrait is self-destructive, for Browning cannot convince the reader that he knows the 'true things' in Blougram's mind from the false. Half of the bishop's argument is simply that faith pays; the other half is in effect a rejoinder to *Easter Day*. Neither total faith nor total unbelief is possible to human beings; the best that man can achieve is an unremitting suppression of doubt. The impossibility

of total submission to belief is conveyed in a few lines of violent intensity which recall the poet's own words about his fear of 'the pure white light':

> Under a vertical sun, the exposed brain
> And lidless eye and disemprisoned heart
> Less certainly would wither up at once
> Than mind, confronted with the truth of Him.

But the corollary to this, the need for intellectual struggle, is presented in terms of flimsy and desultory emotion, as in Blougram's argument against the viability of doubt:

> Just when we are safest, there's a sunset-touch,
> A fancy from a flower-bell, some one's death,
> A chorus-ending from Euripides, –
> And that's enough for fifty hopes and fears
> As old and new at once as Nature's self,
> To rap and knock and enter in our soul,
> Take hands and dance there, a fantastic ring,
> Round the ancient idol, on his base again, –
> The grand Perhaps!

The grand Perhaps may be defensible metaphysics but it produces woolly poetry.

The Ring and the Book (1868–9) is Browning's most ambitious effort to construct a whole work out of 'truth broken into prismatic hues'. Here he follows a Roman murder trial of the late seventeenth century through twelve successive monologues, containing many more than a dozen opinions of the case. As Henry James declared, *The Ring and the Book* has the elements of an excellent novel; intricate in itself, the case ramifies by way of partial evidence, pleadings, gossip and judgement, until a whole society is drawn in; there are anticipations of the method James himself was to use in the way one subjective version of the affair cancels or modifies another. And Browning is very skilful in varying the run of his blank verse to suit the speaker and the occasion. Nevertheless, the book never comes to life for long. There is no real progress from one speech to the next, no internal development, because Browning has reduced all his complex material to a simple, external contrast between chivalry and chicane; on the

one hand, he gives his people flashes of intuition, on the other, torrents of irrelevant casuistry:

> Anything, anything to let the wheels
> Of argument run glibly to their goal.

It was only a short step from *The Ring and the Book* to the tedious word-spinning of the poet's last twenty years.

Neglected while he was doing his best work, at the period of *Men and Women*, Browning was more than compensated by the reverence accorded to him as a sage after the sixties; and the reaction, as in Santayana's devastating essay on *The Poetry of Barbarism* (1900), was inevitable. Once Browning's opinions had fallen out of date, the muddle and patchwork in his art were clearly to be seen. He failed to revive the poetic drama or create a satisfying novel in verse; he failed to reach a stable compromise between the visionary and the realist. Yet much of the best of subsequent poetry, of Pound and Eliot in particular, owes a considerable debt to Browning's experiments in conversational verse and his ironic-confidential monologues; and English poetry would be much the poorer if Browning had not attempted to translate his romanticism into the language of contemporary life.

NOTES

1. See J. H. Buckley, 'The Anti-Romantics' (*The Victorian Temper*, London, 1952), and the studies of Browning by F. G. R. Duckworth, E. D. H. Johnson, and Betty Miller (see Appendix).

2. Browning's imagery: see C. H. Herford, *Robert Browning* (London, 1905), ch. IX.

3. cp. D. Smalley, *Browning's Essay on Chatterton* (Cambridge, Mass., 1948), and W. O. Raymond, 'Browning's Casuists', in *The Infinite Moment* (Toronto, 1950).

THE BRONTË SISTERS AND
WUTHERING HEIGHTS

DEREK TRAVERSI

A notable difference in imaginative quality separates the novels of Charlotte (1816–55) and Emily (1818–48) Brontë from those of the other great English novelists of the nineteenth century. The difference appears to be one of emotional intensity, the product of a unique concentration upon fundamental human passion in a state approaching essential purity. Whether this concentration is compatible with the nature of the novel as generally conceived – and there has been a tendency to regard the work of the Brontës as something of a 'sport',[1] a remarkable oddity in literary history – is no doubt open to discussion. Many of the great novelists of the period – Dickens, Thackeray, George Eliot – showed moral and social preoccupations more explicit than those revealed in *Wuthering Heights*. We may agree that the range of these writers is wider, their points of contact with the human scene more variously projected; but when this has been allowed, there remains to be taken into account an astonishing mixture of romantic commonplace and personal inspiration, primitive feeling and spiritual exaltation, which corresponds to potentialities otherwise largely concealed during this period.

This statement, true of *Wuthering Heights*, is only in part applicable to the novels of Charlotte Brontë, which reflect the workings of an acute and intensely committed mind. In her position as elder sister and, to a large extent, as substitute for a dead mother, Charlotte's contacts with the outside world were more continuous and varied than those of her sisters.[2] Her excursions into that world did not end as readily as did those of Emily in deception and retreat; and this fact is reflected in work that corresponds more closely to the habitual features of the novel form. The earlier chapters of the immensely popular *Jane Eyre* (1847) rest largely upon the author's experiences of the Clergy Daughters' School at Cowan Bridge, and her life as a governess is also reflected there; and the two periods which she spent

in Brussels at the *pensionnat* of M. and Mme Héger provided the material first for *The Professor* (1857), which remained unpublished in her lifetime, and, more forcibly, for *Villette* (1853). Finally, her father's recollections of the Luddite riots of the early years of the century, supported by her own reading in the period and her observation of the textile industry in her own time, provided in *Shirley* (1849) the background to her presentation of the relationship between the heiress, Shirley Keeldar, and the Rector's poor niece Caroline Helstone, in whom idealized pictures of Emily and herself are respectively conveyed.

Some of the best pages in these novels are those in which Charlotte recalls her experiences most vividly and in which her own intimate feelings, her lifelong need for emotional compensation, are least directly involved. The author who could write, in her preface to the second edition of *Jane Eyre*,[3] that 'Conventionality is not morality. Self-righteousness is not religion ... There is a difference; and it is a good, and not a bad action, to mark broadly and clearly the line of separation between them,' was evidently speaking from the heart and announcing a programme for her own work. She was also capable of using her firm grasp of observed detail to produce a powerful and acute picture of the aspects of life which she felt deserved her condemnation. The early chapters of the novel, in which the complacency of Mrs Reed and her children is seen through the eyes of the penniless child who has been introduced into a house where her presence is clearly unwelcome, recall similar effects in Dickens; and, in their vivid recreation of invidious social distinctions, they do not suffer in the comparison. The situations are related with a precision, an acute sense of the physical manifestations of social rank – notable for instance in Jane's account of 'the spare chamber' at Gateshead Hall, with the 'piled-up mattresses and pillows' of its bed, 'supported on massive pillars of mahogany, hung with curtains of deep red damask' and standing next to the 'ample, curtained easy chair ... looking, as I thought, like a pale throne' – which, proceeding from a vivid perception of oppressive status, reflect a penetrating and original mind.

What is true in this respect of *Jane Eyre* could equally be said of much in Charlotte's succeeding books. The earlier pages of *Shirley*, which best answer to her description of the novel as 'cool, real, and

solid, ... as unromantic as Monday morning', reflect at times the author's appreciative reading of Jane Austen and her desire to follow in the same tradition. In the opening of the first chapter the comparison can hardly be avoided:

> Of late years, an abundant shower of curates has fallen upon the north of England: they lie very thick on the hills; every parish has one or more of them; they are young enough to be very active, and ought to be doing a great deal of good.

The tone thus established is one which expands naturally into an incisive picture of human behaviour and pretension. It produces, in the novel's treatment of an important social theme, an admirably detached and understanding picture of the stresses undergone, at a critical moment of transition, by the textile districts of Yorkshire. Thorough study and intelligent reflection have gone into the making of this part of the book. The differences of class and education, the various conflicts of interest, have been picked out by a writer capable of rejecting the temptation to simplify the issues, to identify in exclusive sympathy with one or other of the contending factions.

More remarkable still, as combining acute observation with greater intensity of feeling, is the account offered in *Villette* of life in Brussels. Here, and more especially in her portrayal of M. and Mme Beck, it is obvious that Charlotte's own emotions, her feelings towards M. Héger and his wife, are deeply engaged; but, in spite of the evident temptation to offer a one-sided reading of Mme Beck's character, the impulse to belittle a person of whom she was, in real life, so gratuitously jealous, the conscience of a genuine artist imposes a salutary detachment. Her picture of 'the little Bonaparte in a mouse-coloured silk gown', of 'a figure rather short and stout yet still graceful in its own peculiar way', has about it a solidity and truth, even a kind of unwilling respect, which imposes itself as a product of true and intelligent observation. When, as is often the case in her work, she feels the need to offer an adverse judgement, she is more than likely to qualify that judgement with a recognition of the partiality which inspired it. So is it with her presentation, beyond Mme Beck, of the Belgian society which her 'English' Puritanism prompts her to reject but the virtues of which she remains capable of recognizing.

There are times, indeed, when this self-reliant integrity is in danger of being submerged by the powerful surge of less controlled feeling. With the entry of the intimate passion which, in all her work, represents at once a source of inspiration and an ever-present pitfall, a less objective note, tending obsessively to moral melodrama and answering to more unconfessed promptings of her own nature, modifies her judgement and her presentation of events. With the appearance of Mr Rochester and the exploitation of the romantic machinery of his concealed wife, *Jane Eyre* threatens to plunge dangerously into the embarrassing and the absurd. The blind Rochester is presented as a 'sightless Samson', a 'caged eagle whose gold-ringed eyes cruelty has extinguished'; and Jane, when she ventures to meet her 'master's and lover's eye', receives a smile 'such as a sultan might, in a blissful and fond moment, bestow on a slave his gold and gems had enriched'. Similarly, the idealization of M. Beck in *Villette* rises to heights of unreality at the moments of greatest emotional commitment, and Caroline in *Shirley* tells Moore that she has been allowed a glimpse of her companion's 'heart's core' and that it was 'like a shrine, for it was holy: like snow, for it was pure; like flame, for it was warm: like death, for it was strong'.

It would be wrong, however, to allow the emphasis to rest upon these potential embarrassments. Even at these moments of danger, Charlotte is struggling with her sense of a real predicament. As a woman, part of her nature moves her to present an idealized picture of the emotion which draws her female characters to their men; but, and often at the same time, another part, aware of excess and absurdity, is capable of presenting a realistic, even a disenchanted picture of the male objects of their devotion. When Rochester, striking a complacent note of masculine possessiveness, relates 'his' Jane to 'the grand Turk's seraglio: gazelle eyes, houri forms, and all!', her reaction is sharply and creditably rejecting:

'I'll not stand for you an inch in the stead of a seraglio', I said; 'so don't consider me an equivalent for one; if you have a fancy for anything in that line, away with you, sir, to the bazaars of Stamboul without delay; and lay out in extensive slave-purchases some of that spare cash you seem at a loss to spend satisfactorily here.' (ch. 24)

Once again seriousness of intent is not at this point incompatible with

a touch of comedy almost Austen-like in kind. Even beneath what may seem to be the novel's most 'romantic' excesses – as in the whole story of Rochester and his concealed mad wife – we are made aware of a woman novelist coping with very deep phobias, barely confessable fears and pressures arising out of her female condition in a society where 'ideal' fiction connected with the institution of marriage concealed disconcerting and bitter realities.

These, in turn, are extreme reflections of a finally anti-romantic truth concerning the real, as distinct from the 'ideal', relationship between men and women, of which Charlotte Brontë was well aware and to which some of her best pages give powerful expression. Typical, from *Shirley*, are Caroline's reflections upon her hopeless passion for Robert Moore which extend from the particular case to advance a disillusioned comment upon 'romantic' aspirations when required to come to terms with the bare truth of life:

> Take the matter as you find it; utter no remonstrances; it is your best wisdom. You expected bread, and you have got a stone; break your teeth on it . . . You held out your hand for an egg, and fate put into it a scorpion. Show no consternation: close your fingers firmly upon the gift; let it sting through your palm. Never mind: in time, after your hand and arm have swelled and quivered long with torture, the squeezed scorpion will die, and you will have learned the great lesson how to endure without a sob. For the whole remnant of your life, if you survive the test – some, it is said, die under it – you will be stronger, wiser, less sensitive. This you are not aware of, perhaps, at the time, and so cannot borrow courage of that hope. (ch. 7)

In this realistic vision which accepts the necessary loss of illusion in the act of turning it into a revealing and disturbing insight we are afforded access to the distillation of a highly original talent engaged in contemplating and reacting to the sobre realities of her existence.

It is possible to feel in reading Charlotte Brontë that contact with the outside world served to diversify a talent which might otherwise have tended to seek expression in a more concentrated vision. In the case of Emily, whose excursions into that world were brief and were followed invariably by a return to the true sources of her inspiration, that vision was preserved in essential purity. The poems she wrote afford a glimpse into the fiercely maintained integrity of her inner life. This is not to say that they are lacking in conventional romantic attributes. By-products in great part of the dream world in which the sisters lived, creating in close collaboration the interminable Gondal

romances of their unusually protracted adolescence, they come to life whenever Emily's own peculiar concentration of passion illuminates what would otherwise have been commonplace:

> Cheerful is the hearth, soft the matted floor;
> Not one shivering gust creeps through pane or door;
> The little lamp burns straight, its rays shoot strong and far:
> I trim it well, to be the wanderer's guiding-star.

The cheerful comforts of the home, associated no doubt with the long winter months at Howarth, become here the background for an expression of inner fortitude. The lamp, 'little' though it is, 'burns straight', its rays are 'strong and clear'; and this being so, in the last stages of the poem concentration is rewarded by true spiritual vision:

> What I love shall come like visitant of air,
> Safe in secret power from lurking human snare,
> What loves me, no word of mine shall e'er betray,
> Though for faith unstained my life must forfeit pay.

> Burn, then, little lamp; glimmer straight and clear –
> Hush! a rustling wing stirs, methinks, the air:
> He for whom I wait, thus ever comes to me;
> Strange Power! I trust thy might; trust thou my constancy.
>
> (*The Visionary*)

In verses such as these, inner seclusion of spirit, not dissipated by contact with the outer world, becomes a true source of strength. Traces of an inferior rhetoric survive, no doubt, in 'lurking human snare' and even in the 'faith unstained' opposed to it;[4] but the assertion of that faith has a force which transcends its literary origin. The visitant of the world of spirit manifests itself intimately in 'secret power', rousing a response in equally intimate dedication. That dedication, like the lamp on the hearth which serves as a focal point for affection and fellowship, burns 'straight and clear', and its felt 'might' evokes in answer a trustful 'constancy'. Here, beneath the superficial attributes of romantic sentiment, we are in touch with the sources of inner strength that determine what is most powerful in the Brontë vision.

In *Wuthering Heights* (1847) this strength finds expression in a work which, beneath the forms of a novel, has many of the qualities of a

special kind of dramatic poem. A simple account of the story of the orphan Heathcliff, his love for Catherine Earnshaw, and the revenge which he obtains through his marriage with Isabella Linton upon those who have deprived him of his proper satisfactions in life, would go far to justify a reading of the novel as one more example of a familiar 'Gothic' type: an example more coherent in design and execution than most of its kind, but still a mixture of brutal melodrama and exaggerated sentiment. To trace such a creation to its formal origins, however, is not necessarily to define its true character. In its fundamental as distinct from its accidental qualities, *Wuthering Heights* is an exploration of human passion at different levels and tending to different ends. Creative or destructive in their consequences, making for life or death, basic human emotions are presented in a state of purity and concentration; no other novel of the Victorian period has penetrated so undisguisedly into the depths of unalloyed passion, or followed with such unrelenting logic the intensity of its operations. The result is a unique imaginative creation which, largely ignoring the moral and social assumptions of contemporary fiction, aspires rather to the severe simplicity of ancient tragedy.

The presence of the distinctive power which animates *Wuthering Heights* is felt whenever the emotions of the chief characters are deeply involved. No doubt there are moments – as when Catherine is described 'dashing her head against the arm of the sofa, and grinding her teeth so that you might fancy she would crash them into splinters' – when the intended effect is compromised by the crudity of its expression; but they are hardly characteristic. The romantic melodramas with which Emily Brontë was certainly familiar are marked to a large extent by ambiguity and mistiness, lack of precision and vague suggestiveness. In *Wuthering Heights*, though the events described may strike us as incredible, they are related for the most part with remarkable clarity and precision. The qualities which distinguish the writing are apparent in the opening description of Heathcliff's house and its surroundings, as seen through the eyes of the narrator Mr Lockwood. The exposition, careful, orderly, even slightly pedantic, as befits the speaker, rises almost imperceptibly to the deeply poetic references to 'the range of gaunt thorns all stretching

their limbs one way, as if craving alms of the sun', so that this
evocation of the spirit of place does not have the effect of an intrusion.
The temptation to exploit the poetic note is equally resisted in the
description, which follows, of the interior, where firmness in the
grasp of detail and the stress laid on the normality of the setting ('The
apartment and furniture would have been nothing extraordinary as
belonging to a homely northern farmer') belong to a type of writing
diametrically opposed to romantic sensationalism.

A similar concrete foundation of imagining makes itself felt even
in Lockwood's account of his highly theatrical dream, where if
anywhere we might have expected the strained romantic note to
impose itself, but where the illusion of reality is maintained through
a sense of physical pain that borders on the intolerable: 'terror made
me cruel; and, finding it useless to attempt shaking the creature off, I
pulled its wrist on to the broken pane, and rubbed it to and fro till
the blood ran and soaked the bed-clothes'. In such a passage the
peculiar intensity of Emily Brontë's imagining achieves its effect
through a remarkable and characteristic immediacy. The capacity to
effect an intimate fusion between the thing seen, or the felt sensation,
and its emotional interpretation has enabled her to raise a melodramatic story to the level of a deeply personal creation.

Understanding of this creation requires us, then, to set aside the
machinery of 'Gothic' romance and to consider more closely the
central themes of the novel. The first of these concerns the love of
Catherine Earnshaw for Heathcliff, and of his in turn for her. The
relationship between these two is based, no doubt, on the familiar
romantic conception of irresistible passion. The expression of it is
marked, however, by an intensity which emerges powerfully in
Catherine's attempt to explain the nature of her feelings to the
sceptical Nelly Dean:

'I cannot express it; but surely you and everybody have a notion that there
is, or should be an existence of yours beyond you. What were the use of my
creation if I were entirely contained here? My great miseries in this world have
been Heathcliff's miseries, and I watched and felt each from the beginning;
my great thought in living is himself. If all else perished, and *he* remained, I
should still continue to be; and if all else remained, and he were annihilated,
the universe would turn to a mighty stranger. I should not seem a part of it.
My love for Linton is like the foliage in the woods. Time will change it, I'm
well aware, as winter changes the trees. My love for Heathcliff resembles the

eternal rocks beneath – a source of little visible delight, but necessary. Nelly, I *am* Heathcliff – he's always, always in my mind – not as a pleasure, any more than I am always a pleasure to myself – but as my own being ...' (ch. 9)

The spirit which animates this passage is unmistakably personal. It is a spirit of concentration, from which considerations of sentiment or pleasure, in the common acceptance of these terms, have been excluded; it is not an accident that some of the language in which Catherine defines her feeling has religious overtones, strikes us as an expression of what might, in another context, be immediate spiritual need. The simple affirmation 'I *am* Heathcliff' states, in the speaker's intention, a necessity based rather upon her perception of her essential nature than upon any transitory impulse of desire. False or sentimental emotions are invariably involved in verbiage to make them seem greater, more important than they really are. Here the statement of passion is presented barely, expressed with a sharp, defined clarity that guarantees its own kind of truth.

Nevertheless, powerful as it is, Catherine's passionate defiance of commonsense is not allowed to stand at its own estimate. The very structure of the novel – the initial narration by Lockwood, who in turn reports the memories and down-to-earth judgements of the prudent Nelly Dean, and even the presence of the servant Joseph, whose vernacular comments recall us to a more solid and tangible reality – is calculated to qualify these flights of passionate imagining. The resulting moral tension extends to the contrast between Heathcliff and Linton, and to Catherine's feelings as divided between them both. Linton may be held to represent the social graces of civilized life, in which Heathcliff is totally lacking. It is natural that Catherine should be attracted to him. Courtesy, charm and urbanity are qualities to be admired, and it is on this account that she is, at a certain level of her nature, moved to respond to Linton's affection; but as she herself recognizes, it is not the whole or even perhaps the deepest part of her nature which is thus involved. The conflict between the two imperatives which she senses in herself is stated in terms of a contrast between the *agreeable* and the *necessary*, between emotions which serve to adorn life and others whose absence is felt, at a level at once deeper and more dangerous, to be equivalent to the death of the spirit. The novel does not require us to coincide with her interpretation, or to neglect the element of wilful self-deception involved in it; but it

does demand of us a balanced judgement the outcome of which is likely to determine our reaction to the whole.

It is not surprising that this reaction has differed notably from reader to reader. Behind such passionate utterances there lies a conflict of a moral nature which, as the author understands it, is capable of no easy resolution. We feel the presence of this tension clearly in the process of reasoning which leads Catherine, almost in spite of herself, to abandon Heathcliff for his despised rival. Reflection, aided by Nelly, presents Heathcliff as a brutal creature whom she should certainly abandon to marry the young, rich and attractive Edgar Linton. Nelly, guided by her inherent sense of reality and by her longer if not particularly imaginative experience of life, maintains that Edgar is a good match, socially speaking acceptable and likely to bring her to normal domestic happiness, whereas devotion to Heathcliff can only end in disaster and degradation. All this is undoubtedly true, relevant to the understanding of a novel which is concerned to present the destructive consequences, not less than the transforming ecstasies of passion; but the impressive directness of Catherine's reply is sufficient evidence that it is not all the truth. 'He' [Heathcliff] 'is more myself than I am. Whatever our souls are made of, his and mine are the same, and Linton's is as different as a moonbeam from lightning, or frost from fire.' Once more, we are conscious of being transported – dangerously, even impossibly, but truly – from habitual considerations of social propriety to the world of essential passions with which, in their transforming and destructive operation, Emily Brontë is so deeply concerned.

Considered in the light of this central passion, it becomes easier to respond to the second main theme of the book, that conveyed in the contrast between the two houses that between them divide the action, Wuthering Heights and Thrushcross Grange. Wuthering Heights reflects the nature of Heathcliff, who owns it; we might, indeed, call Heathcliff its human incarnation. Severe, gloomy, and brutal in aspect and atmosphere, firmly rooted in local tradition and custom, it is an appropriate background for the life of bare and primitive passion to which its owner is dedicated. Thrushcross Grange, the home of the Lintons, is in every respect different. It reflects a conception of life at first sight altogether more agreeable, more fulfilling of human aspirations than that so uncompromisingly set against it: a

conception, indeed, not to be despised – it wins the approval of Nelly Dean's common sense – but which, when closely observed, shows signs of decadence. Like Wuthering Heights, Thrushcross Grange answers to the character of its owner. It projects refinement, kindness, the amiability which a tolerable conception of life requires; but a closer inspection reveals flaws which play a part in the development of the tragedy.

There is in the early pages of the novel a significant moment in which Thrushcross Grange and those who dwell in it are seen from the outside, by external and critical observers. Heathcliff and Catherine, still young children, and acutely conscious of themselves as intruders, climb up to look into the illuminated windows of the Linton mansion. Their first glimpse of this strange new world produces an impression of contemptuous hostility which will remain with them. They observe that the Linton children, far from feeling happy in their luxurious home, are quarrelling bitterly over a lap-dog, a symbol of pampered indulgence, which each desires to handle and pet:

'And now, guess what your good children were doing? Isabella – I believe she is eleven, a year younger than Cathy – lay screaming at the farther end of the room, shrieking as if witches were running red-hot needles into her. Edgar stood on the hearth weeping silently, and in the middle of the table sat a little dog shaking its paw and yelping, which, from their mutual accusations, we understood they had nearly pulled in two between them. The idiots! That was their pleasure! to quarrel who should hold a heap of warm hair, and each begin to cry because both, after struggling to get it, refused to take it. We laughed outright at the petted things, we did despise them!' (ch. 6)

The contempt apparent in Heathcliff's words points to a limitation in Nelly Dean's social perceptions. It represents the attitude, outside those perceptions, of a soul in which the fundamental passions are still alive for a world which it sees as claiming to be superior but which it finds trivial, selfish and empty. The emphasis laid upon the soft and clinging luxury in which the Lintons live, protected by bulldogs and obsequious servants from the intrusion of the inferior world outside, is calculated to produce an impression of excessive sweetness and decay:

'we saw – ah! it was beautiful – a splendid place carpeted with crimson, and crimson-covered chairs and tables, and a pure white ceiling bordered by gold,

a shower of glass–drops hanging in silver chains from the centre, and shimmering with little soft tapers.' (ch. 6)

The sight of so much luxury appeals to the children, strikes them from outside as 'beautiful'. It corresponds to a sense of social graciousness which the Heathcliff world is the poorer for lacking; but it also rouses in the intruders a feeling of repudiation which the behaviour of the dwellers in this 'paradise' can only intensify. The 'gold', the crimson carpets and the chair–coverings which serve to deaden, to mollify the impact of life, the slightly unreal prettiness of the 'showers of glass–drops hanging in silver chains', and the barely defined sense of exquisite decadence in the reference to the 'little soft tapers' burning in the room: all these, seen through eyes resentful of exclusion and dedicated to passionate sincerity, point to a contrast which lies at the heart of the novel.

The contrast, indeed, is carried into the main body of the story. The part of Catherine's nature which craves civilized, social fulfilment is sufficiently attracted by the agreeable aspects of life in the society of the Lintons to marry Edgar and become part of the family. She never refuses the name of 'love' for her feeling for Edgar. Yet the essential contrast remains. When Catherine brings her husband the news of Heathcliff's return and asks if she is to bring him into the parlour, the appropriate setting of gentility, he looks 'vexed' and suggests 'the kitchen as a more suitable place for him'. By so doing he conforms to the nature of his own world, which has created an elaborate system of social distinctions to deaden the impact, at once vivifying and destructive, of essential passion; but Catherine, true to the promptings of her deeper nature, replies by instructing Nelly to prepare two tables, 'one for your master and Miss Isabella being gentry; the other for Heathcliff and myself, being of the lower orders.' To the social distinctions stressed by the Lintons as human, civilizing, and repudiated as irrelevant and life-denying by Catherine, correspond a number of contrasts in the moral order which throw an adverse, or at least a qualifying light upon the Linton claim to superiority. 'Pettish', 'silly', 'whining', 'envious' are adjectives applied to Edgar by his wife; and Emily Brontë is at some pains to relate them to the world of pampered ease in which the family are represented as living. It is no accident that the man who, as a child, had been protected by bull-dogs from the intrusion of two children

calls upon his servants, after attempting to retire himself, to eject his hated rival from his house. As we come to know the Lintons better,[5] we find beneath their essentially unformed characters refinement certainly, but also selfishness, meanness, and even a cruelty which, though very different from Heathcliff's brutality, is hardly less inhuman in some of its manifestations.

Wuthering Heights represents, then, not the presentation of a 'naturalist' thesis, nor a return to primitive instinct, but a statement of clashing emotional needs presented in terms that tend to the poetic. In one of the book's finest and most representative passages Cathy, daughter of Catherine and Edgar, and thereby heiress to two conflicting outlooks, describes a discussion between herself and the sickly son of Heathcliff and Isabella:

'One time, however, we were near quarrelling. He said the pleasantest manner of spending a hot July day was lying from morning till evening on a bank of heath in the middle of the moors, with the bees humming dreamily about among the bloom and the larks singing high up over head, and the blue sky and bright sun shining steadily and cloudlessly. That was his most perfect idea of heaven's happiness – mine was rocking in a rustling green tree, with a west wind blowing, and bright, white clouds flitting rapidly above; and not only larks, but throstles, and blackbirds, and linnets, and cuckoos pouring out music on every side, and the moors seen at a distance, broken into cool dusky dells; but close by great swells of long grass undulating in waves to the breeze; and woods and sounding water, and the whole world awake and wild with joy. He wanted all to lie in an ecstacy of peace; I wanted all to sparkle, and dance in a glorious jubilee. I said his heaven would be only half alive, and he said mine would be drunk.' (ch. 24)

Here once more we may detect the operation of that peculiar emotional intensity which Emily Brontë imparted to her characters, and which is the same type as that we find in the most personal of her poems. It is characteristic that what begins as a discussion of the best way of passing a hot summer's day turns into a comparison between two contrasted ideas of celestial happiness. Whereas Linton is concerned with no more than 'the *pleasantest* manner' of passing a July day, Catherine shifts the conception of felicity to quite another order by transposing 'pleasant' into 'perfect'. The contrast is underlined by the different choice of words. For Linton the bees hum 'dreamily', the sun shines 'steadily' and 'cloudlessly' in the sky; the ideal which

attracts him, reflected in the tranquil immobility of the rhythm in the parts of Cathy's speech which refer to him, is one of stillness, passivity, peace. It is only when she sets against it her own thirst for identification with a world in which vitality finds expression in an increasing emotional tempo that the tone of the speech is transformed: she imagines herself 'rocking' at the heart of a world in motion, with the wind 'blowing' and the clouds 'flitting rapidly above', and all this leads up to an overpowering vision of the birds, not of one kind alone, like Linton's larks invisibly suspended in the heights of a uniform blue sky, but innumerable and diversified in species – 'pouring out music on every side', whilst the grass is 'undulating' to the breeze, the water 'sounding', and the 'whole world *awake* and *wild* with joy'.

At stake here, poetically conveyed in two different reactions to natural beauty, is a clash between opposed conceptions of fulfilment, each of which gives, by contrast, added meaning to its opposite. For Linton Heathcliff life tends to peace, calm passivity; for Cathy, it consists in active identification with the surrounding world. Yet the fact that Cathy's emotion is so powerful as to seem to sweep aside the impression of passivity left by Linton cannot alter the fact that both emotions formed a part of the author's intuition of life, that Catherine's identification with the forces of universal motion tended as its end towards a peace and quiescence which, if not that of Linton, is none the less powerfully present in the novel. That Emily felt the presence in herself of *both* emotions, that her creative impulse rested upon the tension set up between them, is sufficiently clear from this passage and from others which abound in the book. If her primary reaction to nature was one of eager and active acceptance, it is also true that she sought through and beyond this acceptance an intuition of permanence which was essentially contemplative in kind. The need to unite these two necessities of her nature is the ultimate source of inspiration in a novel that aspires, as consistently as any written during the time, to achieve the condition of a tragic poem.

This craving for unity is associated with the tendency to see human life and individual passion under the shadow of death.[6] The presence of death is felt intensely throughout, at times as something against which the characters react with all the force of their passionate and concentrated energies, and at others as a profoundly evocative intui-

tion of peace. Once again, we shall do well to refrain from any simple identification. The death of Mr Earnshaw and the final lingering of the narrator over the graves of the sleepers 'in that *quiet* earth' no doubt answer to that attraction for the peace of the grave which appealed so strongly to romantic sentiment and to part of Emily Brontë's own nature. They do not, however, stand unchallenged. When Nelly Dean, after Mr Earnshaw's death, hears the children comforting each other for their loss, she makes indeed her own sentimental comment – 'no person in the world ever pictured heaven so beautifully as they did in their innocent talk' – but the next sentence comes as the intrusion of a more real and more truly tragic reaction, as unexpected as it is moving in its simplicity: 'While I sobbed and listened, I could not help wishing we were all there *safe* together.' The end of Heathcliff, too, stands in the closest relation to a tragedy in which life and death, the exclusive fulfilment of passion and the self-destruction which accompanies it, are fused. If he appears at the end of his story to envision the prospect of a kind of peace, this seems to be associated less with extinction than with a mysteriously restored vision of Catherine and with his expectation of being reunited with her after his own death. One of his last phrases indicates that his was no simple slipping into unconsciousness, no surrender to the craving for fictitious repose: 'My soul's bliss kills my body, but does not satisfy itself.'

Nor, significantly, do the last words of the novel focus exclusively upon Heathcliff's end. Reconciliation of a more sane and valid kind is conveyed by the picture of the representatives of a new generation, Hareton Earnshaw and Catherine Linton, whose names correspond to the qualities of their respective houses, drawn together over the pages of their book and moving, tentatively and with an underlying gesture of reborn trust, towards mutual understanding. The exchange between them is exquisitely natural and tender in its effect, and made the more so by the contrast with the preceding savagery:

He trembled, and his face glowed – all his rudeness, and all his surly harshness had deserted him – he could not summon courage, at first, to utter a syllable, in reply to her questioning look, and her murmured petition.

'Say you forgive me, Hareton, do! You can make me so happy, by speaking that little word.'

He muttered something inaudible.

'And you'll be my friend?' added Catherine, interrogatively.

'Nay! you'll be ashamed of me every day of your life,' he answered. 'And the more, the more you know me, but I cannot bide it.'

'So, you won't be my friend?' she said, smiling as sweet as honey, and creeping close up. (ch. 32)

What we are witnessing, through the eyes of a narrator, Nelly Dean, to whom sentiment answers at this point to a recognition of natural values, is a renewal of the healing energies of life after the long process of death associated with Heathcliff's actions, and implicit in the nature of his passion, has at last worked itself out to exhaustion: a restoration through the new generation of the human dimension which the very reticence of Nelly's following comment so delicately affirms:

'I overheard no further distinguishable talk; but on looking round again, I perceived two such radiant countenances bent over the pages of the accepted book, that I did not doubt the treaty had been ratified, on both sides ...' (ch. 32)

Nelly's observation points to no facile or simple moralizing conclusion. It requires for its understanding a full exposure to the preceding tale of misspent and self-destroying passion. The process of recovery is – as such things are – gradual, tentative, and vulnerable. 'Earnshaw was not to be civilized with a wish; and my young lady was no philosopher, and no paragon of patience.' It remains true that the reconciling process has been initiated, and that we – no less than Nelly Dean, who in this respect speaks for the author's deepest understanding of the implications of her story – have been led to a recognition of the healing action of time working through the gradual processes of restored normality and pointing to a serene and humanly acceptable conclusion.

NOTES

1. F. R. Leavis used the word in *The Great Tradition* (London, 1948).

2. It will not be necessary to refer here to Anne Brontë's novel, *The Tenant of Wildfell Hall*, which was published, together with *Jane Eyre* and *Wuthering Heights*, in 1847. The novel has its powerful moments, but offers little which is not better appreciated in the two greater works.

3. The second edition of the novel appeared, after the immediate success of the first, at the end of 1847.

4. Rhetorical, too, in its effect, though clearly the work of no ordinary personality, is the greater part of the famous *No coward soul is mine*, described by Charlotte as 'the last lines my sister Emily ever wrote'.

5. When Charlotte, in her preface to the 1850 edition, singles out Edgar as 'an example of constancy and tenderness', she is surely showing something less than a complete understanding of the nature of her sister's genius.

6. The treatment of death in the work of the Brontës is the subject of interesting comment in Philippe Ariès' study *The Hour of our Death* (New York, 1981), 432–46.

GEORGE ELIOT

LAURENCE LERNER

When the youthful Dorothea Brooke – 'enamoured of intensity and greatness, and rash in embracing whatever seemed to her to have those aspects' – married Mr Casaubon, they went to Rome on their wedding journey. Up to this point, we have seen Dorothea as an enthusiastic young woman, longing for a noble task that would satisfy her 'inward fire', and accepting the middle-aged Mr Casaubon in the hope that she will be able to help him in his great work of scholarship; now, in the twentieth chapter of *Middlemarch* (1871–2), we are shown the first shock of her disillusionment:

> Two hours later, Dorothea was seated in an inner room or boudoir of a handsome apartment in the Sistina. I am sorry to add that she was sobbing bitterly, with such abandonment to this relief of an oppressed heart as a woman habitually controlled by pride on her own account and thoughtfulness for others will sometimes allow herself when she feels securely alone. And Mr Casaubon was certain to remain away for some time at the Vatican. Yet Dorothea had no distinctly shapen grievance that she could state even to herself; and in the midst of her confused thought and passion, the mental act that was struggling forth into clearness was a self-accusing cry that her feeling of desolation was the fault of her own spiritual poverty.

For what has Dorothea to complain of? She has married the man of her choice; she admires the dedication that takes him to libraries each day, while she is shown the best galleries, the grandest ruins, the most glorious churches, by an experienced courier. But this Rome which is the spiritual centre of the world means little to Dorothea. To understand why, we are invited to dwell on a contrast:

> ... the gigantic broken revelations of that Imperial and Papal city thrust abruptly on the notions of a girl who had been brought up in English and Swiss Puritanism, fed on meagre Protestant histories and on art chiefly of the hand-screen sort; a girl whose ardent nature turned all her small allowance of knowledge into principles, fusing her actions into their mould, and whose quick emotions gave the most abstract things the quality of a pleasure

or a pain; a girl who had lately become a wife, and from the enthusiastic acceptance of untried duty found herself plunged in tumultuous preoccupation with her personal lot.

It is the difficulty of coming to terms with her personal lot, as it is now turning out, that has so upset Dorothea. Not that there is anything unusual in this:

Nor can I suppose that when Mrs Casaubon is discovered in a fit of weeping six weeks after her wedding, the situation will be regarded as tragic. Some discouragement, some faintness of heart at the new real future which replaces the imaginary, is not unusual, and we do not expect people to be deeply moved by what is not unusual. That element of tragedy which lies in the very fact of frequency, has not yet wrought itself into the coarse emotion of mankind; and perhaps our frames could hardly bear much of it. If we had a keen vision and feeling of all ordinary human life, it would be like hearing the grass grow and the squirrel's heart beat, and we should die of that roar which lies on the other side of silence. As it is, the quickest of us walk about well wadded with stupidity.

The twentieth chapter of *Middlemarch* is not only one of the most brilliant and powerful which George Eliot ever wrote; it is written from so near the heart of her concerns as a novelist, and introduces so many of her central themes, that a short discussion of it may constitute the best possible introduction to her work.

First, we can notice the way in which the situation is presented. There is no dialogue: we are given a lengthy account of Dorothea's thoughts by an author who knows what her character is thinking but is also watching her from outside – the technique of using a so-called 'omniscient narrator', a narrative method that was almost universal in the nineteenth century, came in for a good deal of disapproval from some strictly formalist schools of criticism early in this century, but can now be seen as one perfectly proper way to write a novel. The first bit of dialogue in the chapter is in fact introduced as a representative sample, to illustrate a point the author has already' made in general terms:

Her husband's way of commenting on the strangely impressive objects around them had begun to affect her with a sort of mental shiver: he had perhaps the best intention of acquitting himself worthily, but only of acquitting himself. What was fresh to her mind was worn out to his; and such capacity of thought and feeling as had ever been stimulated in him by the

general life of mankind had long shrunk to a sort of dried preparation, a lifeless embalmment of knowledge.

When he said, 'Does this interest you, Dorothea? Shall we stay a little longer? I am ready to stay if you wish it,' – it seemed to her as if going or staying were alike dreary. Or, 'Should you like to go to the Farnesina, Dorothea? It contains celebrated frescoes designed or painted by Raphael, which most persons think it worth while to visit.'

'But do you care about them?' was always Dorothea's question.

'They are, I believe, highly esteemed. Some of them represent the fable of Cupid and Psyche, which is probably the romantic invention of a literary period, and cannot, I think, be reckoned as a genuine mythical product. But if you like these wall-paintings we can easily drive thither; and you will then, I think, have seen the chief works of Raphael, any of which it were a pity to omit in a visit to Rome. He is the painter who has been held to combine the most complete grace of form with sublimity of expression. Such at least I have gathered to be the opinion of conoscenti.'

This kind of answer given in a measured official tone, as of a clergyman reading according to the rubric, did not help to justify the glories of the Eternal City, or to give her the hope that if she knew more about them the world would be joyously illuminated for her. There is hardly any contact more depressing to a young ardent creature than that of a mind in which years full of knowledge seem to have issued in a blank absence of interest or sympathy.

A novelist who relies so heavily on her own explicit statements must be able to write with power when not describing action or reporting dialogue; and must, for instance, be able to produce a phrase like 'mental shiver'. Like so much of her best writing, this is perfectly poised between an image and a generalization: it conveys Dorothea's repeated disappointment as a physical experience, and at the same time indicates the nature of that disappointment and of the situation. Even more memorable is the previous paragraph quoted ('Nor can I suppose . . .'), which has become justly famous, but is always worth looking at afresh. The content of what it says is a favourite doctrine of George Eliot's, that tragedy need not reside in the exceptional, that the stuff of great literature can be found in the lives of people like ourselves; this is part in fact of a wide movement in nineteenth-century literature that sought (in the words of one of Charlotte Brontë's first reviewers) to bring romance from the palace to the cottage. Having made this point in sober prose, George Eliot turns to restating it with such sudden poetic vividness ('like hearing the grass grow . . .') that the shock is like that of a line by Keats, sensing the fearful mystery of things. And then, returning briefly to the pro-

saic, comes the final terse sentence, in which the moment of vision is offset, but in no way undercut, by the cool wit of 'wadded'.

There are at least three major concerns of George Eliot's fiction that we can read off from this chapter. First, the dialectic of culture and the personal lot. Though Rome itself looms in Dorothea's thoughts as an oppressive weight, the chapter is obviously not the work of a Philistine, indifferent to its beauty and history: in case we are in danger of suspecting this, one sentence tells us explicitly that

To those who have looked at Rome with the quickening power of a knowledge which breathes a growing soul into all historic shapes, and traces out the suppressed transitions which unite all contrasts, Rome may still be the spiritual centre and interpreter of the world.

Middlemarch is not a *Künstlerroman*, concerned with the life and creative processes of the artist, for George Eliot's concern with what is basically human draws her away from men and women of exceptional talents as her heroes; it is certainly concerned with the relation of the individual to his or her culture, but the individual who responds and appreciates, rather than the artist who contributes to the tradition. Such appreciation is always tugged in two directions, depending on whether the starting point is the subjective condition of the individual, or the objective tradition itself. If we ignore the subjective, and do not ask of the great monuments that they speak to our condition, we are in danger of ceasing to feel, and the culture will exist only as a dead hand; this is the danger into which Mr Casaubon has fallen. But if we remain locked up in our subjectivity, if the 'gigantic broken revelations' of Rome reveal nothing to us and merely bewilder, then we are in danger of never learning anything, of drawing no sustenance from what is outside us; this is the state from which Dorothea has not yet emerged. It is obvious which is the worse danger in this case; but we must not generalize too rashly.

There is a very different situation in *Daniel Deronda* which raises similar issues, Gwendolen's attempt to learn from Klesmer whether she will be able to earn her living as a singer. Here too the eager individual is crushed by the demands of art, but this time we are more conscious of the egoism of the young woman's aspirations. Dorothea's intensity is, to be sure, also deeply egoistic, but it is rescued by her ardent desire to be taught: she has the potential for learning

to respond, for 'her quick emotions gave the most abstract things the quality of a pleasure or a pain'. That phrase (which is also a perfectly apt description of the generalizing style of the author) shows that Dorothea is *alive*, that the very qualities which make her incapable of responding to Rome could lead to a truer appreciation than the scholarship which knows what 'most persons think it worth while to visit'.

Next, it is worth pointing out what sort of person George Eliot has chosen for her heroine. Dorothea Brooke is a study in what some psychologist might, by now, have labelled the Theresa-complex: a yearning to do good in the world which is so intense that it must answer to some deep emotional need in the Theresa herself. This theme is announced at the beginning of the novel, in the *Prelude* with its account of the young Theresa 'walking forth one morning hand-in-hand with her still smaller brother, to go and seek martyrdom in the country of the Moors'. Though this opening is ironic ('Out they toddled from rugged Avila'), there is nothing ironic about the central description of Theresa's flame, soaring 'after some illimitable satisfaction, some object which would never justify weariness, which would reconcile self-despair with the rapturous consciousness of life beyond self'.

The deliberate ambivalence of the *Prelude* – a clear perception of the clumsinesses, the ineffectualities, the occasional absurdities both of Theresa herself and of the 'later-born Theresas', along with an undimmed, unhesitating sympathy for the flame itself – is continued in the far more complex presentation of Dorothea herself. We see her mainly from the outside, in dialogue with her sister Celia, and in the level commentary of her unruffled author, and it is natural, therefore, that we should first be struck by the critical, ironic tone ('Riding was an indulgence which she allowed herself in spite of conscientious qualms; she felt that she enjoyed it in a pagan, sensuous way, and always looked forward to renouncing it'), by the open reference to her love of extremes, by the self-righteousness and 'Puritan toleration' which she shows to Celia during the sharing of the jewels; and it is equally natural that when the writing shifts (as it does several times) in favour of Dorothea, it should usually be by a counter-irony, at the expense of Celia, or of a general 'you' or passive voice which disconcertingly identifies the reader with the common run of Dorothea's acquain-

tances and neighbours: 'Women were expected to have weak opinions; but the great safeguard of society and of domestic life was, that opinions were not acted on.' A discriminating reading of the chapter will notice these shifts, and appreciate their delicacy, will perceive that the general impression is more critical than sympathetic, yet will reflect that none of the critical details is wholly to Dorothea's discredit. In chapter 20 we are given her first serious quarrel with her husband, caused by her over-eager urging of him to settle to writing up his notes, 'and begin to write the book which will make your vast knowledge useful to the world', followed by his irritated reproof that 'you may rely on me for knowing the times and the seasons, adapted to the different stages of a work which is not to be measured by the facile conjectures of ignorant onlookers'. In urging her husband like that, Dorothea was driven by a devotion, even an admiration, more intense than most wives feel; but it was precisely this intensity that stung Mr Casaubon, sounding to him more like rebuke than devotion. The sharp accuracy with which she wounds her husband can be seen as springing from the essential egoism of the Theresa; yet the enthusiasm she feels is one of which Casaubon is unworthy, and which he would be the better for appreciating. As in the case of her response to Rome, she is self-centred in a way that is potentially enlarging.

Dorothea is not the only intense idealist in George Eliot's fiction. Almost every novel has one – Dinah Morris, Romola, Felix Holt, Mordecai – and one at least has an emotional life that is very similar. Maggie Tulliver, in *The Mill on the Floss*, feels a compelling need to love, and longs that her life should have a wider meaning; she too goes through an intense Puritan phase, when renunciation seems to be its own reward. She differs from Dorothea in that her concern is less with her impact on the world (she designs no cottages) and more with the expression of her own emotions (she is artist *manquée* rather than saint *manquée*), but this difference is unimportant compared with the emotional resemblance.

We meet Maggie, as we do not meet Dorothea, when she is still a child. The first two books of *The Mill on the Floss* make up what may well be the finest childhood idyll in English fiction. It is right to call it an idyll because it sees childhood as laying the foundation for the positive emotions of adult life ('we could never

have loved the earth so well if we had had no childhood in it'), but in other respects it is not at all idyllic, for childhood is shown as a time of intense suffering as well as joy ('These bitter sorrows of childhood! When sorrow is all new and strange'). The actuality of the childhood episodes – Maggie forgetting to feed Tom's rabbits, cutting off her hair, pushing Lucy into the mud – is something we now take for granted in stories about children, but it is an extension of fictional subject-matter that we owe to George Eliot as much as to anyone.

Childhood is presented as a time of emotional intensity ('We learn to restrain ourselves as we get older'); the opposite to this is not the intellectual life – that too is lived more intensely by Maggie than by anyone – but the conventional. The sense in which Maggie and Dorothea do not grow up when all around them do, is that they do not fade into the light of common day, 'keep apart when they have quarrelled, express themselves in well-bred phrases'; and it is therefore especially appropriate that *The Mill on the Floss*, with its irresponsible, intensely loving heroine, should begin with childhood. We know that it is the most autobiographical of George Eliot's novels, and that Maggie and Tom are based on Mary Anne Evans and her brother Isaac; in a series of sonnets called *Brother and Sister*, written some ten years later, George Eliot gave more direct expression to this intense early relationship. They make a fascinating pendant to the novel, the conventionality of George Eliot's verse reminding us of the marvellous intellectual control in her highly emotional prose. Dorothea too has a deep autobiographical element: when *Middlemarch* was in the press, G. H. Lewes wrote to her publisher, John Blackwood, that Dorothea 'is more like her creator than anyone else, and more so than any of her other creations'. None of this should surprise us: the reader who knows nothing of the biographical background might well guess how close the author was to Maggie's need for love and to Dorothea's 'loving heart-beats and sobs after an unattained goodness'.

Is it a strength or a weakness, artistically, for a novelist to identify so closely with a character in a novel? Perhaps no general answer is possible. If there is a danger of the book being too theoretical and dry (an illustration of the author's belief in positivism, say) then such involvement may bring it to life; if on the other hand the danger is

of gush and excessive sentiment, then such emotional identification is likely to do harm, and a cooler, more detached attitude would be a gain. Critics as varied as F. R. Leavis and Lord David Cecil have objected to Dorothea and her emotional life as a 'day-dream ideal self' of the author, but a careful reading of the twentieth chapter alone should be enough to refute such a view. At no point does the deep sympathy with Dorothea lead the author to abandon her objectivity: we are offered a profound identification with her grief along with the cool ability to step back and describe her as 'a girl who had been brought up in English and Swiss Puritanism, fed on meagre Protestant histories and on art chiefly of the hand-screen sort'. A sentence not yet quoted will serve as a fuller example of this blend of identification and objectivity:

Our moods are apt to bring with them images which succeed each other like the magic-lantern pictures of a doze; and in certain states of dull forlorn-ness Dorothea all her life continued to see the vastness of St Peter's, the huge bronze canopy, the excited intention in the attitudes and garments of the prophets and evangelists in the mosaics above, and the red drapery which was being hung for Christmas spreading itself everywhere like a disease of the retina.

This has the ring of authenticity, and one suspects that an actual memory of the author's may lie behind it; and this feel of intense subjectivity is combined (in a way very characteristic of George Eliot) with an objectivity that regards Dorothea as a character to be understood: even the wording of 'in certain states of dull forlornness Dorothea all her life continued ...' suggests the objective use of sub-jective material, before we are moved along to a vividly perceived description of the church, one visual detail building on another and fixing our attention on the external scene, until the brilliant con-cluding image returns us to the subjective mood from which we began.

One final comment on this twentieth chapter, perhaps the most important of all. What is Dorothea learning during her painful sojourn in Rome? Essentially, that the outside world is not moulded to her wishes: that our intensest aspirations may clash against the brute otherness of what is. 'The large vistas and wide fresh air which she had dreamed of finding in her husband's mind were replaced by anterooms and winding passages which seemed to lead nowhither.'

The same discovery has to be made, just as painfully, by Mr Casaubon, who just before their quarrel 'had no idea of being anything else than an irreproachable husband'. The quarrel teaches them that the world, and in particular the world as very immediately represented by the other partner, is not a projection of themselves.

This is the moral dimension of George Eliot's realism. Some such discovery has to be made by every one of her characters who is capable of growth:

> Examining the world in order to find consolation is very much like looking carefully over the pages of a great book in order to find our own name, if not in the text, at least in a laudatory note: whether we find what we want or not, our preoccupation has hindered us from a true knowledge of the contents. But an attention fixed on the main theme or various matter of the book would deliver us from that slavish subjection to our own self-importance.

Thus Theophrastus Such, the persona she used in the book of essays written at the end of her life. The same thought occurs in novel after novel, most vividly perhaps in another of the famous images in *Middlemarch*: 'We are all of us born in moral stupidity, taking the world as an udder to feed our supreme selves.' If the freeing of oneself from such stupidity is the moral development of the characters, this will need conveying to the reader through an art that frees us from our own self-importance by displaying to us the pages of that great book in which our name is not written. The name of such art is realism.

For a very different example of such art, we can turn to *Adam Bede*, George Eliot's first full-length novel. This is a dignified and moving book, whose great success with contemporaries is easy to understand: 'it is a first-rate novel,' wrote *The Times*, 'and its author takes rank at once among the masters of the art.' It is carefully constructed to convey some of the author's favourite moral points (the irrevocability of evil, the liberating effect of warmth of feeling), and its picture of rural England, richly textured, is written with knowledge, love and wit. It is a representative early Victorian novel, in fact, which the modern reader might be expected to read with respect, enjoyment, even sympathy, but without his imagination

being seized – except for one episode, which stands out from the rest with compelling power: the journey of Hetty Sorrel in search of the father of her illegitimate child.

Hetty is a very different figure from Dorothea. Indeed, if we make a rough and ready division of George Eliot's female characters into two, the pretty, conventional, unimaginative egoists with whom men fall all too easily in love, and the turbulent, unstable, intensely yearning Theresas, then Hetty and Dorothea can stand contrasted as representatives of each, and the fact that they both have to learn to read 'the mighty volume of the world' shows the centrality of the theme in her fiction. The initial presentation of Hetty, locked into her 'narrow bit of an imagination', is done with a coolness (almost a cool dislike) that fixes her as a study in simple egoism; her inability to be interested in a world that does not include herself is made quite explicitly plain, sometimes in authorial commentary that now seems to us prolix, sometimes with powerful bluntness, as in the chilling sentence, 'Hetty did not understand how anybody could be very fond of middle-aged people'. But when Hetty's trouble comes upon her, and she sets out to find Arthur with only the vague information that his regiment is somewhere near Windsor, there is no moralizing, and the shock of confrontation with a world that is not interested in her is conveyed, quite simply, as shock. Two chapters (36 and 37) describe her journey to Windsor, and her journey home in despair; they are followed by her trial for child murder, and her eventual confession in prison (this last scene was the germ of the whole novel, but its execution – perhaps not surprisingly – has less originality than what leads up to it). The narrowness of Hetty's imagination is actually a help to the author's art in describing the journey: it conveys the numbing effect of her suffering in a way that is all the better for lack of commentary. When the coachman who gives her a lift teases her, with laborious archness, about her sweetheart, 'Hetty felt her face flushing and then turning pale. She thought this coachman must know something about her.' The directness of this corresponds perfectly to the naïve alarm that Hetty felt; but this was not the moment to soften the effect with an explanatory generalization ('It is difficult for country people to believe . . .') that betrays an author too anxious to tell us everything.

Hetty's limited sensibility is of course a limitation as well as a

strength. But after the baby is born the story takes on an impersonal sympathy of great power. When Hetty is brought to trial she refuses to speak; this forces the author to tell us the story through witnesses, which not only eliminates comment, but enriches the effect through the mere change of viewpoint. The effect of the witnesses announcing themselves ('My name is Sarah Stone', 'My name is John Olding. I am a labourer, and live at Tedd's Hole, two miles out of Stoniton') sends a ripple of authenticity into the narrative, and there could be no better version of the discovery of the child than John Olding's:

And just as I was stooping and laying down the stakes, I saw something odd and round and whitish lying on the ground under a nut-bush by the side of me. And I stooped down on hands and knees to pick it up. And I saw it was a little baby's hand.

When Hetty at last tells her story a new dimension of meaning is introduced but the style does not change: 'I heard the baby crying, and thought the other folks heard it too, and I went on.' There is no need to say explicitly that Hetty in her despair could not escape the clutch of compassion, and at this point George Eliot has the restraint not to say it.

E. M. Forster, in *Aspects of the Novel*, compared the climax of *Adam Bede* with Dmitri's dream in *The Brothers Karamazov*, and by contrasting the conventionally religious language of Dinah with the imaginative intensity of Dmitri's 'Why are they crying? Why are they crying?', he had no difficulty in showing that, as he put it, Dostoyevsky is a prophet, George Eliot only a preacher (he was, after all, comparing her first novel with Dostoyevsky's masterpiece). But if he had chosen to concentrate on Hetty's abandoning of the child rather than on her conversion, he would have found a less conventional, and more realistic, note, and the comparison would have been a fairer one.

These two episodes, the twentieth chapter of *Middlemarch*, and Hetty's journey in *Adam Bede*, have in common the theme of learning to come to terms with a world that is not as you wish it, but in almost every other respect – in characterization, narrative method, authorial stance and style – they are utterly different. The *Middle-*

274

march chapter is the more representative of George Eliot's genius, but it is important to realize that she can do both.

We read the fiction of the past with a double concern: to see it for what it originally was, and to relate it to the awareness of our own time. On no issue have there been more interesting developments in the last generation or so than on our understanding of the relation between society and the individual, a question that is as problematic in fiction as it is in real life. One traditional school of novel criticism has seen the art of fiction simply as the creation of essentially autonomous characters, and their social setting as the mere backdrop for the acting out of universal passions. More recent critics, sometimes (not always) Marxists, have often reversed this, denying that character can meaningfully be discussed except in relation to the particular society in which it functions. This dispute belongs to the interpretation rather than the writing of novels – the same novel could be seen either way, depending on the position of the critic; and we can therefore behave like creatures of our own time and look at the personal conflicts of George Eliot's fiction as manifestations of the social context in which they take place. We shall, after all, have her own support in this: 'there is no private life,' she wrote in *Felix Holt*, 'which has not been determined by a wider public life.'

As George Eliot's fiction developed, so did her view of society. *Adam Bede* is set in a society that is static, hierarchical and close to nature. It is a world without rebels, and aware of the rhythm of the seasons; the kind of society that in the Romantic tradition is called organic, and that the nineteenth-century sociologist Tönnies, in his famous contrast, designated as *Gemeinschaft*, not *Gesellschaft*. The rituals of that world are the young squire's coming-of-age party, which both celebrates community and reminds everyone of their dependence on authority, and the harvest supper, which is seen in pagan terms ('It was enough to make Adam feel he was in a great temple, and that the distant chant was a sacred song'); the Poyser family provide a commentary of earthy commonsense and traditional raciness; and the plot could come from folk-tale or ballad.

The contemporary readers who so loved this story must have

valued it, among other things, for its conservatism, the counter-weight it afforded to change and modernism. Today's reader is more likely to find in this implicit conservatism a reason for resisting it; and though we can now see the element of grit in that smoothly functioning world (such as the Methodism that George Eliot clearly perceives as a product of social change) it would be foolish to deny that *Adam Bede* belongs with the conservative wing of Romantic organicism.

Her next novel, *The Mill on the Floss*, offers a much less ideal picture of society:

> Good society has its claret and its velvet carpets, its dinner-engagements six weeks deep, its opera and its faery ballrooms; rides off its ennui on thoroughbred horses, lounges at the club, has to keep clear of crinoline vortices, gets its science done by Faraday and its religion by the superior clergy who are to be met in the best houses: how should it have time or need for belief and emphasis? But good society, floated on gossamer wings of light irony, is of very expensive production; requiring nothing less than a wide and arduous national life condensed in unfragrant, deafening factories, cramping itself in mines, sweating at furnaces, grinding, hammering, weaving under more or less oppression of carbonic acid – or else, spread over sheep-walks, and scattered in lonely houses and huts on the clayey or chalky cornlands, where the rainy days look dreary. (Book IV, ch. 3)

This passage is worth careful attention. The basic linguistic device in the first sentence – the series of very active verbs attached to the abstract subject – turns 'good society' into a series of people who live hard without ever quite coming to life. They are willing to improve themselves, say at a lecture, especially on something that might help to keep their factories going, but the touch of contempt they feel for those who are paid to be intelligent is present in 'gets its science done'. The second sentence has none of the wit of the first, re-placing it with a firm cumulative anger as it moves relentlessly through industrial, then rural labour. Even this very contrast is appropriate to the attitudes expressed: the willingness to fence with good society in an ironic tone it will appreciate, the simple bluntness of the glimpse of exploited labour. A good deal of social comment-ary is contained in the style.

The society here described is more representative of her last novel, *Daniel Deronda*, than of *The Mill on the Floss*, which is set in a country town, and describes a world in which the respectability of trade is

seen interacting with the more rural world of the mill and – below that – with the near-poverty of the small farmer. For the most complex social analysis in George Eliot's fiction, and the subtlest awareness of the pressure of the public on the private life, we must return to *Middlemarch*.

The novel is called 'A Study of Provincial Life'. Provincial society implies the existence of metropolitan society, towards which it will feel both superior and dependent; and in the novel we are shown a static community on which change has begun to impinge from the outside. This change is political, intellectual and economic.

First, political. The action of *Middlemarch* lasts from 1829 to 1832, the time of the passing of the Reform Act. The hectic political activity taking place in the distance, while Middlemarch pursues its traditional prejudices, is introduced into the novel in two ways: first, the continual reminders of what was happening on the national scene, which form both a chronological framework and an ironic perspective; and second, the irruption of the issues into Middlemarch politics through the decision of Mr Brooke to stand for Parliament as a Reform candidate. It is one of the richest ironies of the novel that Reform is introduced into Middlemarch by this affable incompetent who neglects his own tenants, and who finds 'that his ideas stand rather in his way when he was speaking'. The serious representative of progressive political thinking is Will Ladislaw, who is employed by Mr Brooke as a political journalist. Ladislaw, with his light-brown curls, his sketch-book and his idealism, has had a bad press from the critics, and as Dorothea's lover he is a conventional success at best; but Ladislaw the dilettante artist and political idealist is a brilliant portrait, drawn with a fine balance of sympathy and irony. He represents the sophisticated radicalism of which Middlemarch knows little and wants to know less, and an idealism which the political solidity of the provinces is inclined to look down on.

The nearest thing to Ladislaw in George Eliot's other work is the figure of Klesmer in *Daniel Deronda*, also an artist, also a political idealist. In both cases, George Eliot shows us the mingling of xenophobia with Philistinism in the stiff English suspicion with which they are regarded. The conversation in chapter 22 of *Daniel Deronda* between Klesmer and Mr Bult, the 'esteemed party man', is a masterpiece of subdued brilliance, in which a narrowness of imagina-

tion worthy of the most provincial Middlemarcher stumbles upon the world of foreign culture, unfamiliar and clearly not good at making money. It is George Eliot's equivalent to the Philistinism of Mr Podsnap, and his uproarious conversation with the foreign gentleman in *Our Mutual Friend*. Though she has none of the rich humour of Dickens, it is striking that her style (without ceasing to be her own) is here at its most Dickensian: Mr Bult 'had the general solidity and suffusive pinkness of a healthy Briton on the central table-land of life'. And there is nothing in Dickens – there never is – corresponding to George Eliot's objectivity: we can see through Mr Bult's narrowness, realize that Klesmer is a superb musician and a humane man, and yet understand perfectly why Mr Bult considers him a 'coxcomb'; just as Ladislaw's immense intellectual superiority to Mr Brooke does not prevent amusement at his gratitude for the 'chance bray of applause falling exactly in time' when he manages to elicit praise from his patron.

Ladislaw is one of the two main representatives of intellectual change as it impinges on Middlemarch society. He it is who realizes that Mr Casaubon's researches have been overtaken by German scholarship, and though his knowledge of the question is second-hand, and his motives in talking of it to Dorothea are petty, this does not prevent him from being right. The other example of new thought is Lydgate, who arrives in Middlemarch as a medical reformer, determined 'to do good small work for Middlemarch and great work for the world'. The story of Lydgate is perhaps the most universally admired in George Eliot's work, and there is no finer justification of her explicit and omniscient method than the account of his 'spots of commonness', the fact that 'that distinction of mind which belonged to his intellectual ardour did not penetrate his feeling and judgement about furniture or women, or the desirability of its being known (without his telling) that he was better born than other country surgeons.'

I will select one detail from the Lydgate story (on which there is already so much appreciative criticism), a detail that reminds us again how the private life is determined by a wider public life. Before the mid-nineteenth century, a great deal of human life did not find its way into fiction: the concentration on sexual love, marriage choice

GEORGE ELIOT

and domestic relations shut out, among other things, the problems of work. We do not think of George Eliot as an innovating novelist, but she did a great deal to extend the range of subject-matter dealt with in fiction. I have already remarked on her treatment of childhood; she was also among the earliest novelists to deal seriously with a man's career, not simply in terms of status, but by sharing with us the complex concerns of professional life. If anyone anticipated her in this it was Balzac, and even he has not the same level-headed understanding of both the emotional and intellectual issues involved. And Dickens, the English Balzac, is for all his wide-ranging curiosity never really interested in work: if we compare Mr Dombey with Bulstrode, it is striking that of these two bankers we know so much about Bulstrode's business activities, and so little about what the house of Dombey and Son actually does. The supreme example of this willingness to use the professional life as material for serious fiction is the fifteenth chapter of *Middlemarch*, with its detailed account of the awakening of Lydgate's scientific interests, and his plans for reforming the practice of medicine. This development in fiction was itself determined by a wider public life: for the rise of the professions in the nineteenth century almost seems to call into being the new profession of novelist.

To return to the society of *Middlemarch*, we can look, finally, at its treatment of economic change. Here again, change comes from outside, and the form it takes is the railway. The coming of the railway is used with some ingenuity in the unfolding of the plot; its social significance is best understood if we relate it to the figure of Caleb Garth. Caleb, who is for the railway, is in many ways a highly traditional figure – honest man and skilful artisan, he is modelled, like Adam Bede, on Robert Evans, the author's father. 'His virtual divinities were good practical schemes, accurate work, and the faithful completion of undertakings: his prince of darkness was a slack workman.' Insofar as the industrial revolution represents a new, more imaginative attitude to capital, Caleb is pre-industrial man: he is no entrepreneur and, we are told, had failed in business when he set up on his own. But insofar as industrialism represents continuity, as in the field of technology it largely does, one improvement leading to another with increasing speed, Caleb is of it. He admired deeply

that myriad-headed, myriad-handed labour by which the social body is fed, clothed and housed. It had laid hold of his imagination in boyhood. The echoes of the great hammer where roof or keel were a-making, the signal-shouts of the workmen, the roar of the furnace, the thunder and plash of the engine, were a sublime music to him.

There are passages like this in the work of most early Victorian novelists: Dickens, Elizabeth Gaskell and Disraeli all have their colourful and enthusiastic descriptions of the new technology, often presented as a modern version of the poetry of fairy-tale. The Victorian imagination accepted with delight the technological aspects of industrialism, even while protesting indignantly against its social consequences. George Eliot is less of a technocrat than the others, and this is virtually her only celebration of the 'myriad-handed labour'. She is able to warm to a description of it by attributing it to the sensibility of an essentially conservative figure like Caleb, for whom 'dust and mortar, the damp of the engine or the wet soil of woods and fields' are equally valid manifestations of 'business'. This does not mean she was unaware of, or even unsympathetic to, the radical consequences of industrialization, but it means that she preferred to understand them, as she preferred to understand everything, in terms of continuity. Caleb represents that element in the old, pre-industrial world, that is needed by the new.

To see *Middlemarch* as offering a version of English provincial society around 1830 does not, of course, deny the value of those discussions of the novel that begin from individual characters (or from its structure, or its handling of language); it is simply to follow George Eliot's own lead when she said 'it is the habit of my imagination to strive after as full a vision of the medium in which a character moves as of the character itself'.

This essay has concentrated on *Middlemarch*, which has so many claims to being the greatest English novel; so it should be said in conclusion that all George Eliot is worth reading, and much of her work shows the same blend of cool gaze and warm heart that gives *Middlemarch* its distinction. She wrote eight works of fiction in all. The earliest, *Scenes of Clerical Life* (1858), won attention because of its treatment of the secular and human problems of clergymen – the material that Trollope had already begun to put to such successful

use in the Barchester novels. Both *Amos Barton* and *Mr Gilfil's Love Story* seem very conventional to us now, but the former has at least one claim to originality. When a complimentary copy was sent to Dickens he guessed immediately that it was by a woman. We do not know why, and probably he didn't either, but the most likely explanation seems to be its willingness to take seriously the trivia of domestic life, its awareness that mending clothes and paying the butcher's bill may set limits to one's spiritual life. *Janet's Repentance* is easily the best of the *Scenes*: it may not have Trollope's technical competence, but it moves beyond his range, both in its social understanding of religious enthusiasm, and in its Feuerbachian view of religion.

Adam Bede (1859) and *The Mill on the Floss* (1860) have already been discussed. *The Mill* is probably the best of her books to read first: both the emotional life of its heroine and its description of St Oggs society plunge us into quintessential George Eliot, and prepare us for the greater maturity of *Middlemarch*. *Silas Marner* (1861) begins with a vivid portrayal of the life of a dissenting chapel, but drops its realism half-way through to turn into an almost symbolic narrative about the love of gold and golden love, to the extent that she wondered herself if it 'would have lent itself best to metrical rather than to prose fiction'. This makes it seem, despite the lively scenes at the Rainbow Inn, the most dated of her works; and the two long stories that were later bound up with it probably repay reading more today. *The Lifted Veil*, her one venture into the supernatural, is not a mere Gothic thriller but a chilling exploration into the horror of living in a world in which the consciousness of others is accessible to us; and *Brother Jacob*, which has almost all the qualities of a George Eliot novel in miniature, makes one regret she did not try that length more often.

Romola (1863), her historical novel set in fifteenth-century Florence, has had a very bad press. She poured her immense energy into the research she did for it, and then struggled conscientiously to bring the material to life: the result is Nello's barber-shop and its buzz of plausible idiom – 'Good-day, Messer Domenico ... you come as opportunely as cheese on macaroni'. That the liveliness of Mrs Poyser cannot be transposed to the fifteenth century by hard work is no doubt true, and those who have found the dialogue of

Romola dead have often included their complaint in a blanket condemnation of the historical novel as a kind of waxworks of fiction. To this indictment two replies can be made. One is that when it is not dutifully striving for liveliness the novel's reconstruction of Renaissance Italy is deeply alive: the scene in chapter 38 when the half-mad Baldassare, who had once been a scholar, finds under the sudden shock of emotion that he can read again, is a rendering of the Renaissance passion for learning as powerful as anything in Browning. The other is that the story of Tito and Romola, though firmly located in the particular setting, rehearses, often with great power, some of George Eliot's recurring concerns: the steady corruption of a nature which has no protection against egoism except in its own charm, and the contrast between the moral naivety of the once-born nature (Tessa) and the capacity for suffering of the twice-born Romola. And it has at least one statement of its author's creed as memorable as anything in her other fiction, the reflection of Romola (in chapter 36) comparing her own ruined happiness with the austere refusal of the world by her monkish brother:

> Her trust had been delusive, but she would have chosen over again to have acted on it rather than be a creature led by phantoms and disjointed whispers in a world where there was the large music of reasonable speech, and the warm grasp of living hands.

Felix Holt the Radical (1866) quite explicitly addresses itself to the interaction of the public and the private. Its political scenes are more central than those of *Middlemarch*, and are directly concerned with the question of radicalism: Felix, Harold Transome and the congregationalist minister Rufus Lyon represent the three versions of radicalism that we are invited to compare. We may not share the author's evident preference for the first, for Felix is unconvincing both as radical and as hero. His highly moral radicalism is as conservative in its implication as *Culture and Anarchy*, written three years later – though with her usual objectivity, George Eliot allows others to notice and say this. As a hero, he is the most upright and the most lifeless she created. Those critics who have felt that George Eliot idealized Ladislaw, the heroine's dream lover, because of her own emotional needs, should have paused to compare him with Felix Holt: the honest working-class hero whom she so sexlessly admires is by far the more idealized. The greatness of the novel lies in the

portrayal of the Transome family: the self-willed, ambitious Harold, with his coarse and selfish charm, and the curiously static picture of his mother sitting in dignified despair in her bedroom, more static than one would have thought acceptable in so realistic a work, but deeply moving in its slow remorseless analysis.

After *Middlemarch* (1872) there was one more novel, the extra-ordinary *Daniel Deronda* (1876), about which the main critical argument has tended to be whether it falls into two separate halves or not. The story of Gwendolen Harleth, the spoilt child, and how her gentlemanly husband succeeded in breaking her will, and the story of Mordecai, the prophetic and consumptive Jew with his vision of his people's future, are linked only by the figure of Deronda him-self, the well-bred young Englishman of mysterious birth, whose spiritual restlessness leads him to be the mentor of the one and disciple of the other. From its first publication, it was received as two novels clumsily joined together, most non-Jewish readers finding the former magnificent and the latter tedious. Attempts to defend the unity of the book have no difficulty in showing the care with which parallels are inserted, but it is always easier to describe such intentions than to convince sceptical readers that the result is an artistic success, and the novel is sure to owe its continuing fame to the story of Gwendolen and Grandcourt. This moves, after the vivid opening episode in the casino, through a long analysis of Gwendolen's character, in which George Eliot's leisurely explicitness is seen at its finest; and then shows the breaking of her will by the terrifying aristocratic calm of her husband, the one figure of impenetrable egoism in George Eliot, the one character she makes no attempt to feel sympathy for. The irruption of such a figure into her work can almost be taken as a testimony to the possibility of evil, an evil that even a writer of such wide sympathies cannot come to terms with. Yet there is nothing allegorical about him, and her realistic observation is never abandoned as we are shown this nineteenth-century gentleman spending the evening in his drawing-room 'sitting meditatively on a sofa and abstaining from literature'. The cool steady style never takes its eye from the cool steady cruelty of its subject. George Eliot's last novel is her most deeply serious without losing anything of her wit.

Is George Eliot the greatest English novelist? When she died, the

claim would have seemed bold but tenable; forty years later, it would have seemed absurd – in the surge of modernism, she had become a Victorian dodo; in the 1950s, it was almost an orthodoxy; in the 1980s she seems once more to be slipping slightly, as Marxists find her bourgeois and structuralists find her realism naïve. The assessment of past literature is perforce a dialectic between the world-view of the reader and the intrinsic qualities of the writer, and we must expect George Eliot's reputation, like anyone's, to fluctuate. What she has to offer us today will be slightly different even from what she offered a generation ago. Two things seem best worth emphasizing now: one, which I have tried to draw attention to, is her concern with the individual as a social being, with character as formed within a medium; the other is her realism, for after some of the intense post-modernist concern with literature as being about its own processes, to return to George Eliot is to discover that a great novel is not simply a game, but a view of the world.

LANGUAGE AND LITERATURE IN THE VICTORIAN PERIOD

CHRISTOPHER GILLIE

In several respects, I consider my Father as one of the most interesting men I have known. He was a man of perhaps the very largest natural endowments of any it has been my lot to converse with: none of us will forget that bold glowing style of his, flowing free from the untutored Soul; full of metaphors (though he knew not what a metaphor was), with all manner of potent words (which he appropriated and applied with surprising accuracy, you often could not guess whence); brief, energetic; and which I should say conveyed the most perfect picture, definite, clear not in ambitious *colours* but in full *white* sunlight, of all the dialects I have ever listened to. Nothing did I ever hear him undertake to render visible, which did not become almost ocularly so. Never shall we again hear such speech as that was: the whole district knew of it; and laughed joyfully over it, not knowing how otherwise to express the feeling it gave them ... I call him a natural man; singularly free from all manner of affectation: he was amongst the last of the true men, which Scotland (on the old system) produced, or can produce; a man healthy in body and mind; fearing God, and diligently working in God's Earth with contentment hope and unwearied resolution.

This is from Carlyle's *Reminiscences* published in 1881, just after his death. It commemorates a figure of the old oral culture of the rural communities: Carlyle's father was a village artisan. One cannot, of course, suppose him to have been altogether representative; on his son's showing he was an exceptional man, and there were obviously great differences among rural communities in different parts of Britain. Nevertheless Carlyle is implying changes, including changes in language, occurring between the beginning of the nineteenth century (he was born in 1795) and the later part of it. A number of Victorian writers, with origins having some resemblance to Carlyle's, interested themselves in the speech of village communities, and when we remember the immense movement into the towns in the course of the century it is not surprising that by the middle of it the interest tends to be retrospective and sometimes nostalgic. Such writers were often themselves of socially modest background:

their recovery of the environment and speech may have been a means to self-discovery. George Eliot's *Adam Bede* (1859) and *Silas Marner* (1861) are village stories set about twenty years before her own birth in 1819, and the characters in both use a half-poetic figurative idiom suggestive of the speech Carlyle describes. For instance, Mrs Poyser to her mean landlord:

'You may run away from my words, sir, and you may go spinnin' underhand ways o' doing us a mischief for you've got Old Harry to your friend, though nobody else is, but I tell you for once as we're not dumb creatures to be abused and made money on by them as ha' got the lash i' their hands, for wanting t'undo the tackle. An' if I'm th'only one as speaks my mind, there's plenty o' the same way o' thinking i'this parish and the next to't, for your name's no better than a brimstone match in everybody's nose – if it isna two-three old folks as you think o'saving your soul by giving 'em a bit o'flannel and a drop o'porridge. An'you may be right i'thinking it'll take but little to save your soul, for it'll be the smallest saving y'iver made, wi' all your scrapin'.'

Tennyson's few dialect poems – *The Grandmother*, *The Northern Farmer Old Style* and *New Style* – have a homeliness, pungency and pathos from a level of his nature quite overlaid by his usual elevated poetic style. Most of all, of course, one finds the rural idiom in Thomas Hardy, both in his poetry and in his novels. His use of rustic speech in his fiction sometimes has a poetic eloquence, without loss of simplicity, which evokes the cadences of a time when speech suffered less from social divisiveness. Thus Mother Cuxsom in *The Mayor of Casterbridge* on the dying Mrs Henchard recalls, by her mixture of pathos and comedy, Mistress Quickly on the dying Falstaff:

'And she was as white as marble-stone,' said Mrs Cuxsom. 'And likewise such a thoughtful woman, too – ah, poor soul – that a minded every little thing that wanted tending. "Yes," says she, "when I'm gone, and my last breath's blowed, look in the top drawer o'the chest in the back room by the window, and you'll find all my coffin clothes; a piece of flannel – that's to put under me, and the little piece is to put under my head; and my new stockings for my feet – they are folded alongside, and all my other things. And there's four ounce pennies, the heaviest I could find, a-tied up in bits of linen, for weights – two for my right eye and two for my left," she said. "And when you've used 'em, and my eyes don't open no more, bury the pennies, good souls, and don't ye go spending 'em, for I shouldn't like it. And open the windows as soon as I am carried out, and make it as cheerful as you can for Elizabeth-Jane."'

It seems important to recall the rural theme in Victorian writings because the period was the last to originate partly in the culture of that environment. George Sturt (pseudonym 'George Bourn') describes in his book *Change in the Village* (1912) his own experience of the self-sufficiency of the old style of community and its progressive disintegration under the influence of urban commerce in the later nineteenth century. Such self-sufficiency allowed the folk of the village or country town to share work, leisure and tradition, giving them the possibility of roundedness in their living and fulness of expression in their speech. Life in the towns was more atomistic, or it stimulated new kinds of community with differing styles of speech. The obvious source for the study of these, in the middle of the century, is Henry Mayhew's *London Labour and the London Poor* (1851).

Mayhew was a journalist who documented the ways of life of a great variety of the London populace, introducing each with a brief graphic description, and then allowing the subjects to record themselves in their own language. Often the result is authentic and vivid, as in the account by the little watercress girl, whose naivety and courage issues in her concluding words:

'I ain't a child, and I shan't be a woman till I'm twenty, but I'm past eight, I am. I don't know nothing about what I earns during the year. I only know how many pennies goes to a shilling, and two ha'pennies goes to a penny, and four fardens goes to a penny. I knows, too, how many fardens goes to tuppence – eight. That's as much as I wants to know for the Markets.'

Sometimes the very authenticity of the speech, and of the text as a social document, leaves crucial elements to the reader's guesswork. For instance the 'Returned Convict' describes his boyhood beginnings in crime with a series of bare statements each of which demands amplification or explanation:

'Money was no object in those days; it was like picking up dirt in the streets. I ran away from home. My parents were very kind to me; indeed, I think I was used too well, I was petted so, when I was between twelve and thirteen. I got acquainted with some boys at Bartlemy-fair a little before that, and saw them spending lots of money ...'

One's mind goes at once to another 'returned convict' – Abel Magwitch, describing his own beginnings in crime in chapter 42 of *Great Expectations*:

'This is the way it was, that when I was a ragged little creetur as much to be pitied as ever I see (not that I looked in the glass, for there warn't many insides of furnished houses known to me), I got the name of being hardened. "This is a terrible hardened one," they says to prison wisitors, picking out me. "May be said to live in jails, this boy." Then they looked at me, and I looked at them, and they measured my head, some on 'em – they had better a measured my stomach – and others on 'em giv me tracts what I couldn't read, and made me speeches what I couldn't unnerstand.'

Dickens gives the imagination what it needs to realize the predicament: we can see that Magwitch's career in crime was inevitable, and that it was socially initiated. The difference, of course, is that whereas Mayhew is recording a statement, Dickens is putting on a performance; he means us to hear the rhythms of his character's speech, the due emphasis of every word, just as though it was spoken aloud (as indeed it often was, whether by Dickens himself in his public readings or in reading circles, especially family ones). This is not Mayhew's purpose; he is a reporter, not an artist (though he must have edited his scripts to get coherence into them), and it is not his fault if the language of his characters does not always bring them fully into life.

The industrial working class had an imaginative literature of its own,[1] some of it political (the Chartist poets), some of it continuing a taste for ballad and song from rural traditions. The latter often depended on performance for their effect, and were sustained most vigorously by the popular Music Hall and Melodrama. It was fiction, especially that of Dickens, which contributed to the life of language most vigorously in literature and extended furthest through the layers of social class. However, the Victorian novel, as we know it, was essentially a middle-class product, and even though we bear in mind that the class covered more of the population and was vaguer in its limits than in any previous period, this implies limitations. The most notorious of these as they affected language was verbal prudery. We think of this as a particularly Victorian characteristic, but in fact the movement to purify literature began in the Regency period with Dr Bowdler's *Family Shakespeare* (1818), the purpose of which was to eliminate 'those words and expressions ... which cannot with propriety be read aloud in the family'. It was no doubt partly inspired by Evangelical reaction against the indecency of the Regency

Court, and extended by the strength of the Evangelical influence in the Victorian middle class; but probably it was the growing practice of family reading which made it expedient. Even so, the degree of severity is astonishing to a modern public which has difficulty in deciding whether any language is improper: '*leg* was too natural, and *limb* was preferred, and *nude* or *undraped* seemed less suggestive than *naked*'.[2] The most respectable novelists were obliged by their publishers to refine phrases which the primmest modern reader would not even notice: Trollope, for instance, had to alter 'fat stomach' in *Barchester Towers* to 'deep chest'. Disapproval might extend to whole episodes if they dealt with an improper topic. The pregnancy of Hetty Sorrel in *Adam Bede* is treated so reticently that the birth of her baby may strike a modern reader as quite unexpected, but the *Saturday Review* stigmatized it because it 'read like the rough notes of a man-midwife's conversation with a bride'. A serious disadvantage of this invisible censorship was that English novelists (unlike Balzac and Zola) could never deal adequately with the brutalities of urban life: *Oliver Twist* could be read as a picture of the London underworld without any recognition that Bill Sikes's Nancy is a prostitute.

However, there were also positive sides to the middle-class influence on the writers. The concern with decency arose especially from the importance of the family, which in a new way had become a fortress of moral and social security in this period of rapid change, hope and uncertainty. The children of the family needed moral as well as physical protection, but they also assumed a new importance both as a subject and as a public for literature. As a subject, childhood had of course been important since the early poetry of Wordsworth and Blake, but Victorian writers indulged themselves in the child's world as well as in the nature of childhood. Their preoccupations with childhood could indeed result in sentimentality and false idealism – the notorious death of little Nell in *The Old Curiosity Shop* – but it could also result in fresh uses of language, especially in fantasy. The opening of *Great Expectations* portrays a child authentically and timelessly because Dickens uses exactly the dreamlike, associative processes by which a child's mind works.

As I never saw my father or my mother, and never saw any likeness of either of them ... my first fancies regarding what they were like, were

unreasonably derived from their tombstones. The shape of the letters on my father's, gave me an odd idea that he was a square, stout, dark man, with curly black hair. From the character and turn of the inscription, 'Also Georgiana Wife of the Above', I drew a childish conclusion that my mother was freckled and sickly. To five little stone lozenges, each about a foot and a half long, which were arranged in a neat row beside their grave, and were sacred to the memory of five little brothers of mine ... I am indebted for a belief I religiously entertained that they had all been born with their hands in their trousers-pockets, and had never taken them out in this state of existence.

Dickens combines the child's vision ironically with the gently mocking adult style, but the writers for children, more and less successfully, often sought to use the child's own idiom. Carroll's Alice has the practical sense of a child combined with the child's openness of mind to any occurrence; after all, adult behaviour is unpredictable enough without the addition of magic. For adult readers and writers, the child's world of nonsense was not merely an agreeable release from their own perplexities and anxieties but an opportunity for mild satire of them, and, even more, to release some of the fantasy in their own subconscious. It is a mistake to suppose that Victorians were all innocent of the subconscious; one critic, E. S. Dallas,[3] even invented a suitable term for it – the 'undersoul'. They did not, of course, anticipate all that it would wreak on our twentieth-century view of experience, but they were happy to use it as comment on their unduly inhibiting codes of thought and conduct. Lear and Carroll, in particular, were happy to exploit the unconscious proclivity to invent words:

> Twas brillig, and the slithy toves
>   Did gyre and gimble in the wabe:
> All mimsy were the borogoves,
>   And the mome raths outgrabe.

These are no doubt among the most quoted lines in English verse. 'Gyre' in this extract from Carroll's Jabberwocky (in Alice through the Looking Glass) seems to be a reinvention from the Greek – though that is not how Humpty-Dumpty explains it – but 'mimsy' is original and half accepted, like Lear's 'runcible'; 'chortle' and 'galumph' from later in the poem are entirely so. But there were far more extensive sources of word innovation than nonsense verse, and one of the chief of these was slang.

Of course every period with standards of correct speech has had its slang, but in the Victorian period various influences made it much more prevalent. New urban coteries developed their own special terms for their distinct ways of life, and again Mayhew is a rich source for these, including expressions which are now so familiar that they are hardly considered slang at all. For instance, a young man, fallen in the world, meets a girl disposed to be friendly:

Having elicited what I did for a living, she popped the startling question to me, 'Where do you "hang out" in Sheffield?' I told her that I had never been in Sheffield, and did not 'hang out' my little wares, but used my persuasive art to induce the purchase of them. The lady said, 'Well, you are "green". I mean where do you *dos*?' This was no better, it seemed like Greek ... but the etymology was no relief to the perplexity. 'Where do you mean to sleep?' she inquired.

Fascination with the urban world, especially its underworld, made some novelists, particularly those stigmatized by Thackeray as the 'Newgate novelists', specialists in slang. Harrison Ainsworth and Dickens were among these, but Dickens was outstanding for his enjoyment of many kinds of speech, which he sometimes opposed in comic contrast. Thus in *Hard Times* the utilitarian Gradgrind, failing to get a definition of a horse from Sissy Jupe, who lives amongst them, succeeds in getting one from Bitzer, who doesn't:

'Quadruped. Graminivorous. Forty teeth, namely twenty-four grinders, four eye-teeth and twelve incisive ...' Thus (and much more) Bitzer.
'Now girl number twenty,' said Mr Gradgrind, 'You know what a horse is.'

This might be described as 'utilitarian' English in caricature; the facts are bled white, as, in Dickens's description of him, is Bitzer himself. The description is exact, comprehensive and concise. But a few chapters later, on visiting 'the horse-riding' where Sissy Jupe's father is employed, Gradgrind is confronted by an idiom that wastes language even less; he learns that

'Jupe has missed his tip very often, lately.'
'Has – what has he missed?' asked Mr Gradgrind glancing at the potent Bounderby for assistance.
'Missed nis tip' ...
'Didn't do what he ought to do. Was short in his leaps and bad in his tumbling,' Mr Childers interpreted.
'Oh!' said Mr Gradgrind, 'that is tip, is it?'

'In a general way that's missing his tip,' Mr E. W. B. Childers answered.

Dickens, as Eric Partridge says, 'freshened and sweetened the English novel' by his use of the idiom of ordinary folk. However, one of the contributors to his periodical *Household Words* of 24 September 1853, in an essay entitled 'Slang', expressed anxiety about its influence on the language. This was the journalist George Sala.[4] In this caustic essay, Sala interprets slang to include many kinds of borrowed and invented expressions used by all classes of society. One to which he takes special exception is the American import: inflated words divorced from their derivations and applied emptily and inappropriately, such as *monster*, *leviathan*, and *mammoth* used as adjectives to evoke a notion of vastness. Another is the jargon of trades and professions, high and low, including thieves' slang. He complains in particular of the redundancy which slang creates, when there is already a sufficiency of terms in the language:

Money – the bare, plain, simple word itself – has a sonorous significant ring in its sound, and might have sufficed, yet we substitute for it – tin, rhino, blunt, rowdy, stumpy, dibbs, browns, stuff, ready, mopusses, shiners, dust, chips, chinkers, pewter, horsenails, brads.

He also objects to terms which we have taken up and would regard as perfectly acceptable innovations for a new technology: 'We may say the same of the railway phraseology: buffers, switches, points, stokers and coal bunks – whence is their etymology, and whence their authority?' He is more justifiably critical of the gallicisms of fashionable society, pointing out that some of them would be barely intelligible to the French themselves: *thé dansant*, 'on the *tapis*', *chaperon*, *recherché* –

and Julie, my child, hand me my *vinaigrette*, and take a shilling out of my *porte monnaie*, and tell Adolfe to get some *jujubes* for Fido; and, let me see, if I go out in the pilentum to-day, or stay, the barouche (we have a char-à-banc down at our place, Doctor) . . .

Sala wanted the language purified of all 'slang', but, if this were impossible, at least that it should be systematized by a new dictionary. His main complaint was that the vocabulary was being deprived of all precision, so that 'if we persist in yoking Hamlets of adjectives to Hecubas of nouns, the noble English tongue will become, fifty

years hence, a mere dialect of colonial idioms, enervated ultra-montanisms and literate slang'.

Sala's essay is in accord with a widely supported movement to purify the language, led by the Dorsetshire poet William Barnes (*An Outline of English Speechcraft*, 1878) who wanted to substitute Anglo-Saxon compounds for words of Greek or Latin derivation, especially in science: *fireghost* for *electricity*, *forestoning* for *fossil*. The movement, however, has left little legacy. Scientists persisted in deriving their terms from Latin and Greek, and their innovations were very large. Most of these were specialist vocabulary, though a number have passed into common speech: *accumulator* (1877), *dynamo* (1882), *ozone* (1840), *chromosome* (1890), *conifer* (1851) are examples.[5] We have come to accept, even beyond the need to accept, specialist languages; Victorians like Sala, Barnes, William Morris and the historian Edward Freeman were fighting rearguard actions to keep all language in common currency.

Another kind of motive for verbal innovation was personal need. Thomas Carlyle, stubbornly persisting in his defiance of the English political and cultural establishment, kept some of his Scottish diction, conveying into English such words as *feckless*, *lilt*, and *outcome*; it is more surprising to find that *environment* and *decadent* are attributed to him by Logan Pearsall Smith in *The English Language*, although one can see how much his line of criticism would have needed them if they were not already in existence. Indeed, the most interesting verbal innovations arise when the individual invents a term to define a position in the intellectual conflicts which surround him. When George Eliot was asked whether she was an optimist or a pessimist, she replied that she was a *meliorist*, meaning that she believed in improvement by personal effort. Thomas Huxley invented *agnostic* – *agnosticism* to define the position of one who is neither a believer in orthodox religious doctrine nor an atheist. William Whewell, the philosopher and historian of science, wrote in 1840 that 'we need very much a name to describe a cultivator of science in general. I should incline to call him a scientist'.[6] He also inaugurated the term *physicist*. In doing both, he helped to distinguish the physical sciences, subject to test by experiment, from other forms of thought which are not. Such expressions contributed to clarifying issues which so much disturbed the public mind, and still do today.

These issues were as urgent for discussion as they were hard to distinguish, and they gave rise to the class of writers who have come to be known as the 'Victorian Sages'. The designation is very imprecise; there would be no agreement about which writers were or were not 'Sages'; Carlyle, J. S. Mill, Matthew Arnold, Ruskin, Disraeli, Macaulay, George Eliot, Thomas Hardy and Cardinal Newman all have been or could be included among them. They have been described by John Holloway as having in common 'interest of a general or speculative kind in what the world is like, where man stands in it, and how we should live'.[7] The description indicates the new uncertainties of an age in which scientific thought, technological advance, commercial expansion and social transformation were changing the horizons of values and beliefs as never before. Most of the 'Sages' had, in their earlier lives, suffered a crisis of doubt concerning the beliefs in which they had been nurtured, subsequently emerging into a new faith, often highly personal, which they hoped might re-establish a coherence of meaning for society. The variety of their beliefs differentiated them greatly in their styles of expression. This expression, moreover, commonly had personal peculiarities – special techniques of persuasion – because, although their public was potentially larger than it had ever been, it no longer contained a coherent nucleus. When Samuel Johnson in his life of Gray (1779) remarked that he rejoiced 'to concur with the common reader', we know that his public had an identity for him, and we can understand the assurance and precision of his prose; when Matthew Arnold in *Culture and Anarchy* (1869) divided English society into Barbarians who were indifferent to culture, Philistines who were alienated from it, and the populace whom it had never reached, we realize that he was much less certain, and can understand the frequent ironic self-deprecation in his style.

Mid-Victorian prose, in fact, achieved a greater variety of styles than that of any previous period, extending from the practical, scientific expression of the utilitarian tradition to the elevation of the most eloquent of the Sages. But the impulse for eloquence was in the spirit of the time, and even a proponent of the Laws of Political Economy – Carlyle's 'Dismal Science' – could be eloquent on occasion. The following example is from a lecture by the Oxford Professor of Modern History, Goldwin Smith, in 1859:

The laws of the production and distribution of wealth are not the laws of duty or affection. But they are the most beautiful and wonderful of the natural laws of God, and through their beauty and their wonderful wisdom they, like the other laws of nature which science explores, are not without a poetry of their own. Silently, surely, without any man's taking thought, if human folly will only refrain from hindering them, they gather, store, dispense, husband if need be, against scarcity, the wealth of the great community of nations.[8]

Ruskin, expressing an opposite view of political economy in 'The Nature of Gothic' (*The Stones of Venice* 1851–3), sounds almost drily precise in comparison:

We have much studied and perfected, of late, the great civilized invention of the division of labour; only we give it a false name. It is not, truly speaking, the labour that is divided; but the men: – Divided into mere segments of men – broken into small fragments and crumbs of life; so that all the little piece of intelligence that is left in a man is not enough to make a pin, or a nail, but exhausts itself in making the point of a pin or the head of a nail.

There is however a biblical cadence in both, like that of a preacher who has just finished reading the 'Lesson' and is proceeding to his sermon in a similar style. It is in fact worth remembering how widely, under Evangelical influence, the Bible was read in Victorian times; Evangelical societies distributed Bibles in vast quantities, and biblical studies were considered essential in education. Ruskin himself was given rigorous training in the Bible by his Evangelical mother, and instead of coming to resent this, since he became a sceptic, he describes it in *Praeterita* as 'the one essential part of my education'.

The eloquence of Victorian prose was perhaps partly compensating for what Victorian poetry was unable to do; although the poets (especially Tennyson) were popular and widely read, a note of disappointment recurs through the reign about what they actually achieved. This may be partly due to the shadow of Goethe who had died (in 1830) not long before the reign began, and whose immense scope was so much admired that no poet who did not rise to his stature seemed good enough. Sometimes the deficiency was felt to be a lack of intellectual energy. Arnold, himself one of the finest of the poets, made the point about his own poetry in a letter to Clough in 1853:

I am glad you like the Gipsy Scholar – but what does it *do* for you? Homer *animates* – Shakespeare *animates* . . . the Gipsy Scholar at best awakens a pleasing melancholy. But this is not what we want.

> The complaining millions of men
> Darken in labour and pain –

what they want is something to *animate* and *ennoble* them – not merely to add zest to their melancholy or grace their dreams.

Much Victorian prose has this animating energy. It is not what we usually understand by rhetoric, a term already in disrepute before the Victorians; De Quincey in his essay on 'Rhetoric' in 1828 had written that 'A man is held to play the rhetorician, when he treats a subject with more than usual gaiety of ornament; and perhaps we may add, as an essential element in the idea, with *conscious* ornament'. This is probably how most of us still understand the word, though De Quincey goes on to remark that it is an inadequate description since true rhetoric is the art of persuasion by argument. In that sense the Sages were indeed rhetoricians, but they were more aware of the Romantic and Evangelical reverence for true and deep feelings and the importance of arousing them; as the Evangelical Dinah Morris puts it in *Adam Bede*:

... sometimes it seemed as if speech came to me without any will of my own, and words were given to me that came out as the tears come because our hearts are full and we can't help it.

This is not to say that the best sort of Sage was just another kind of Evangelical preacher, purely emotive. He blended argument with feeling, abstraction with concrete illustration. In the words of John Holloway,

His aim is to make his readers see life and the world over again, see it with a more searching, or perhaps a more subtle and sensitive gaze. His essential equipment is some insight that is abnormally keen. He utilizes what Pater called 'the sort of philosophical expression, in which ... the language itself is inseparable from, or essentially a part of, the thought'.[9]

Pater, however, belonged to a later phase of Victorian prose,[10] refining itself away from the earnestness of the mid-Victorians into the aesthetic movement of 'art for art's sake'. Robert Louis Stevenson, with his essay on 'Style', and the critic George Saintsbury cultivated an aesthetic critique amounting to a prosody of prose style, and prose competed still more with poetry to the extent that Pater's description

of the Mona Lisa in his essay on Leonardo da Vinci was later used by W. B. Yeats as the opening 'poem' in his edition of the *Oxford Book of Modern Verse*. But aestheticism did not outlast the century, because by then other forms of coarser or more vigorous reaction to the mid-Victorians were setting in.

One of these was the final arrival of a 'popular press' for the masses. It inverted the proper sense of the term 'popular', as Raymond Williams has pointed out, for it did not, of course, rise from the people (like the street ballad and the Music Hall) but exploited the now almost universal literacy for commercial profit: journalist–businessmen like Alfred Harmsworth, George Newnes and Cyril Pearson were founding periodicals of mass entertainment such as *Tit-Bits* (1880), *Pearson's Weekly* (1890), and, in 1896, the *Daily Mail*, the first newspaper to reach a wide working-class public. Culturally the vulgar commercialism of the popular press has always been considered a very unhappy development; the critic Edward Dowden remarked in 1889 that 'Our caterers nowadays provide us with a mincemeal which requires no chewing, and the teeth of a man may in due time become as obsolete as those which can still be preserved in a foetal whale'.[11] On the other hand George Sturt noticed that the country people he knew, hitherto baffled by the commercializing disruption of their way of life, seemed to be regaining confidence by access to a press calculated to appeal to them.

Another important development in language and literature was the revival of the drama. Various changes, including the rise of literacy and the development of Trade Unions, were producing a hardening of conscious divisions in society: socialism and feminism were clarifying the frontiers of political debate and giving it salience. The Victorian period had hitherto been peculiarly empty of significant dramatic writing, and there are many possible reasons why this should be so: one that is comparatively clear is that the novel had usurped the theatre in the family circle; and another, more obscure, is that the Victorians had been interested in the processes of change and too concerned to find solutions to the complexities of their dilemmas to be capable of the confrontations which drama provides. Now that debates were more nakedly political, and that the influence of Ibsen was helping minds like Shaw's to discern how perplexities could be transfigured into the dramatic opposition of ideas, the dramatic

medium was once more feasible. Moreover it is interesting that Shaw and Wilde were both Anglo-Irish, and that all the significant dramatists of the eighteenth and nineteenth centuries had been of the same stock; it may be that the *game* of argument and debate survived better in Ireland than in England, perhaps because language there had been less subject to economic and philosophic pressures for use as an instrument of analysis and exposition. The criticism that Shaw's characters do not converse with each other but make speeches at each other is partly justifiable, but it also implies his dramatic enjoyment of rivalry in speech. The opening of *The Doctor's Dilemma* (1906) is a brief and slight example. In a doctor's consulting-room, the servant Emmy is addressing the medical student Redpenny:

EMMY (entering and immediately beginning to dust the couch): There's a lady bothering me to see the doctor.
REDPENNY (distracted by the interruption): Well, she can't see the doctor. Look here: what's the use of telling you that the doctor can't take any new patients, when the moment a knock comes to the door, in you bounce to ask whether he can see somebody?
EMMY Who asked you whether he could see somebody?
REDPENNY You did.
EMMY I said there's a lady bothering me to see the doctor. That isn't asking. It's telling.

Prose became less poetically eloquent, and, on a popular level of appeal, more practical about great issues. A new style of more straightforward language began to take hold, cultivating wit rather than eloquence. In his novel *Howards End* (1910), E. M. Forster presents a clerk in the process of self-education:

Leonard was trying to form his style on Ruskin: he understood him to be the greatest master of English Prose. He read forward steadily, occasionally making a few notes.
'Let us consider a little each of these characters in succession, and first (for of the shafts enough has been said already), what is very peculiar to this church – its luminousness.'
Was there anything to be learnt from this fine sentence? Could he adapt it to the needs of daily life? Could he introduce it, with modifications, when he next wrote a letter to his brother, the lay-reader? For example –
'Let us consider a little each of these characters in succession, and first (for of the absence of ventilation enough has been said already), what is very peculiar to this flat – its obscurity.'

Something told him that the modifications would not do; and that something, had he known it, was the spirit of English Prose. 'My flat is dark as well as stuffy.' Those were the words for him.

The late Victorians are a bridge between ourselves and the mid-Victorians in the sense that they reconciled themselves to the loss of relatively stable values which had issued from the beginnings of English literature, and which the mid-Victorians had struggled to retain or renew. If the 'spirit of English prose' is, as Forster implies, the spirit of truth, then for his clerk, Leonard Bast, it had become the spirit of bare fact. We ourselves have had to accept 'bare fact', but it is not enough for us, as it was not enough for Leonard Bast, to satisfy us that what has been lost can be renounced without the deepest misgiving.

NOTES

1. For an account, see M. J. Vicinus, *The Industrial Muse* (New York, 1974).

2. J. A. Sheard, *The Words We Use* (London, 1954).

3. E. S. Dallas, *The Gay Science* (1866).

4. Partridge, in *Slang Today and Yesterday*, attributes the essay to Dickens himself, but see the bibliography *Household Words* compiled by Anne Lohrli (Toronto, 1973).

5. T. H. Savory, *The Language of Science* (London, 1967).

6. Raymond Williams, *Key Words* (Fontana, 1979).

7. John Holloway, *The Victorian Sage* (London, 1965).

8. Christopher Harvie, George Levine and William Madden, eds, *Industrialization and Culture, 1830–1914* (1970).

9. *The Victorian Sage*, see above.

10. See Travis B. Merritt in *The Art of Victorian Prose*, eds George Levine and William Madden (New York, 1968).

11. Richard Altick, *The English Common Reader* (Chicago, 1957).

THE VOICE OF PROPHECY:
CARLYLE AND RUSKIN

E. D. MACKERNESS

'The intellect of a man who believes in the possibility of "improvement" by such a method [as parliamentary reform],' wrote Thomas Carlyle (1795–1881) in August 1867, 'is to me a finished-off and shut-up intellect, with which I would not argue . . .' This abrupt dismissal, which occurs in the third section of *Shooting Niagara: and After?* is characteristic of a man who has now moved right away from a position in which 'radical' sentiments and melioristic formulations are congenial. To Carlyle, the Reform Bill of 1867 seemed an immense national disaster; it would bring into being a 'completed Democracy' and establish a state of society in which the principle of *laissez-faire* (to say nothing of worse consequences) would prevail without any adequate safeguards. Once again, the Collective Wisdom of the Nation, as Carlyle called it in *Chartism* (1839), had failed to meet a dangerous situation; and the author of *Latter-Day Pamphlets* (1850) had now, as he thought, to witness the constitutional stupidity which prevented the giddy multitude from recognizing that at a juncture like this political power should be vested in the class obviously fitted by nature to use it wisely. 'One thing I do know,' he had written in 'The Present Time' (1850), '. . . That the few Wise will have, by one method or another, to take command of the innumerable Foolish; that they must be got to take it; – and that, in fact, since Wisdom, which means also Valour and heroic Nobleness, is alone strong in this world, and one wise man is stronger than all men unwise, they can be got.' The phrase 'by one method or another' is indicative of the serious lack of grasp which underlies so many of Carlyle's more petulant utterances. But it was by a curious irony that he saw fit in *Shooting Niagara* to round on Disraeli ('a superlative Hebrew Conjuror . . .') as being partly responsible for the coming catastrophe; for in the 1840s Disraeli's 'Young England' associates had subscribed to a view of history very similar to Carlyle's own.

And the reference to 'The end of our poor Old England (such an England as we had at last made of it) ...' takes us back beyond the *Latter-Day Pamphlets* to *Past and Present* (1843) and some of Carlyle's earlier essays.

In *Characteristics* (1831) Carlyle observed that human society resembles a living creature in the sense that it passes through periods of youth, maturity, and senescence, exhibiting from time to time phases of vigour and decrepitude. The present, as he insisted again and again, was an epoch of chronic ill-health. For, as John Morley pointed out in a trenchant essay (*Critical Miscellanies*, 1), Carlyle kept before his readers the notion that the nineteenth century was an era of crisis. And in order to give imaginative embodiment to this general truth, he worked into his prose a large number of ingenious metaphors and symbols which illustrate separate aspects of the abnormal state of affairs under consideration. The clothing figure of speech upon which *Sartor Resartus* (1831) is constructed, recurs in various forms in *Heroes and Hero-Worship* (1841) and *Past and Present* to suggest the countless ways in which basic realities have come to be obscured by the perversities of modern custom. A related conception – that of the *simulacrum* – is presented figuratively through the agency of the 'quack' or 'sham' individual who symbolizes the current anxiety to turn the 'trend of events' to advantage in the readiest way. Another frequent image is that associated with the act of varnishing, in the sense either of attempting to trick out a drab exterior or of covering up mean appearances. Stylistically, *Past and Present* is a *tour de force* because the technical devices employed to support the hypotheses advanced are held subservient to the author's main intentions and are not, as in some of the later works, allowed to get out of control. The general argument that 'things are growing disobedient to man' and thus causing a manifold disruption of society carries conviction by reason of the thoroughness with which Carlyle has developed the ramifications of his central theme.

In the second section of the book, Carlyle reconstructs a very different England from that of the Hungry Forties. We are asked to imagine the 'comparatively blessed' twelfth century, and to follow the career of Abbot Samson as set out in the chronicle of Jocelin de Brakelond, a monk of the Bury St Edmunds Convent. As yet there are no Poor Laws, no 'monster Utilitaria', no scrambling after

profits; instead – and this is evident from the quality of general social life – men are still able (and happy) to order their existence in a way that implies obedience to a power not themselves, yet making, in Arnold's phrase, for righteousness. As Carlyle claimed in *Characteristics*: 'Every Society, every Polity, has a spiritual principle; is the embodiment, tentative and more or less complete, of an Idea.' Within the framework of the medieval society evoked for us in *Past and Present*, the Religious Principle asserts itself quite naturally and gives men a purpose in life. There is thus no incentive to evade the practical duties which minister to the spiritual life. 'For it is *in* the world that a man, devout or other, has his life to lead, his work waiting to be done. The basis of Abbot Samson's ... was truly religion, after all.' The 'doctrine of work' which plays so large a part in Carlyle's writings – the reiterated insistence that idleness is a crime as well as a sin – is here tactfully educed from a discussion of far-reaching issues (among them the nature of feudal government) and not, as in a few of the later pieces, incorporated for the sake of rhetorical display.

How far Carlyle understood the real nature of medieval society is open to question; and we must remember that *Past and Present* is an essay in imaginative compilation as well as a piece of social criticism. His particular 'use' of history is suggested in 'Morrison Again' at the end of Book III: 'A Life of Antique devoutness, Antique veracity and heroism, has again become possible, is again *seen* actual there [i.e. in Jocelin's Chronicle], for the most modern man.' But it can only *be* seen if it is properly presented: and Carlyle's view was that the methods used by orthodox historians were not sufficiently ingenious to bring before the reader the essential significance of historical occurrences. His own technique – as exemplified in *The French Revolution* (1837) – relies on a seemingly casual selection of circumstantial details, supplemented by biographical sketches, the whole being arranged in such a sequence as to give the impression that each episode dealt with is in its way especially ominous. In two essays, 'On History' (1830) and 'On History Again' (1833), Carlyle has explained how he regards history as a form of 'articulate communication', reproving the present moment by a studied reference to the follies of the past. A similar importance attaches to the cognate study of biography, since any account of a man's life must necessarily be a revelation of 'social history'. To Carlyle, Boswell's *Life of Johnson* was

valuable for just that reason; but it was something much more important than a 'portrait of an age': it was a presentment not of a 'Clothes-horse and Patent Digester, but [of] a genuine Man'.

Johnson does, indeed, figure in *Heroes and Hero-Worship*. But an earlier review of Croker's *Boswell* (1832) already provides a detailed summary of the qualities which make the author of the *Lives of the Poets* a wholly admirable and honourable human being. We do not find Carlyle paying homage to all men of letters: in turn, Keats, Shelley, Byron, Scott, and Hazlitt are seen to have their short-comings (including a touch of dilettantism in some cases!). But John-son is a notable exception. Born into an age of disunity, infidelity, and political unrest (already drifting towards 'the great chaotic gulf'), Johnson knew the value of strong convictions; he was courageous enough to dismiss the 'idle jargon and hollow triviality' of useless speculation and settle down to honest literary work. 'Johnson does not whine over his existence,' Carlyle tells us, 'but manfully makes the most and best of it.' For this reason he is of much greater signifi-cance than the snivelling romancers and dandiacal Wertherites of more recent date. Yet at a deeper level than that of mere letters, Johnson can be regarded as the preserver and transmitter of whatever was genuine in the spirit of English Toryism; he has, moreover, the prophetic attributes which belong to the true literary hero.

In his two essays on Johnson, of course, Carlyle reads a good deal into his subject; and as in other biographical studies he ascribes to the man whose life he is writing qualities he believed himself to possess. He extols, among other things, Johnson's gospel of prudence; he dwells on the strength of conscience which enabled Johnson to with-stand the impertinent attentions of Lord Chesterfield; and he softens the great Cham's prejudices by linking them to particular traits of national character. *Heroes and Hero-Worship* presents other strangely assorted examples of the Noble Spiritual Man. But though humanity needs its Mohammed, its Dante, its Luther, and its Shakespeare, it also requires their counterpart, the Noble Practical Man; so Carlyle char-acterized several varieties of this species, 'guides of the dull host – which follows them by an irrevocable decree'. A particular import-ance, however, attaches to Cromwell, whose *Letters and Speeches* brought Carlyle face to face, as editor, with the problem of vindicat-ing an historical figure hitherto largely misrepresented. On 2 April

1866 Carlyle told an audience at Edinburgh University that the Protectorate was 'the most salutary thing in the modern history of England'; in *Heroes and Hero-Worship* Cromwell stands in front of Napoleon ('The Hero as King'); in *Past and Present* he is spoken of as the 'Ablest Man of England', the last individual really fit to be entrusted with the office of 'Governor' in Britain.

From the *Letters and Speeches* it is clear that Cromwell, the spiritual descendant of John Knox, also fulfils most of the conditions required of the Hero as Priest. 'Nothing that was contrary to the laws of Heaven was allowed to live by Oliver', Carlyle told his Edinburgh audience. And when in the *Letters and Speeches* he comes to the point where Cromwell's decision to join the Calvinists is to be announced, it is impossible to escape the sense of gratification with which the author of *Signs of the Times* and *Past and Present* admits the Puritan statesman to membership of a community in which the 'feeling of a Heavenly Behest, of Duty god-commanded, over-canopies all life' ('Sir Walter Scott', 1838). The influence of Calvinistic theology on Carlyle has been much discussed; if he had what can rightly be called a 'faith' it may perhaps be described as a somewhat indefinable theism without the adjunct of Christianity. In 1854 J. S. Mill wrote that Carlyle's creed consisted simply in the belief that 'everything is right and good which accords with the laws of the universe' – a position sufficiently *safe* as to be unassailable except by the most obstinately doctrinaire. But that Carlyle believed himself to have been in some way elected to call both sinners and the righteous to repentance is evident from the tone of almost everything he wrote, except, perhaps, his specifically literary essays; the glorification of brute strength and ruthless order which disfigures the *History of Friedrich II of Prussia* (1858–65) and the essays on Dr Francia, Negro Slavery, and Mirabeau is the outcome of an over-earnest Puritanism which insists that Law, Moral Duty, and the Cause of Righteousness must prevail – at the expense, if need be, of less ostentatiously heroic values.

That Carlyle should have been credited with a coherent 'philosophy' by Leslie Stephen and others may seem surprising when we consider his apparent unwillingness to engage in consecutive thinking; and the peculiar idiosyncratic style in which so much of his work is cast makes it difficult to appreciate that he was once a popular

author. Yet the fact that logical analysis, such as we find in Mill's essays, is absent from much of his work should not blind us to the imaginative qualities in Carlyle's writing. Some of these are seen very well in an essay on 'The Opera' (1852) which, in spite of its strain of philistinism, sets out some very provocative observations:

> Of the Haymarket Opera my account, in fine, is this: Lustres, candelabras, painting, gilding at discretion; a hall as of the Caliph Alraschid, or him that commanded the slaves of the Lamp; a hall as if fitted-up by the genii, regardless of expense. Upholstery, and the outlay of human capital, could do no more. Artists, too, as they are called, have been got together from the ends of the world, regardless likewise of expense, to do dancing and singing, some of them even geniuses in their craft ...

To regard the opera as 'exotick and irrational' is plainly not quite good enough for Carlyle; he obviously *does* take that view of it, but he also pursues the suggestions which come to him as a consequence of the free association of ideas, endeavouring to pose indirectly the question, Is Art and Amusement worth the price we pay for it? This is, of course, a style of composition similar to that employed in *Sartor Resartus*. But the vogue enjoyed for so long by that work can also be accounted for partly by reference to the clamorous manner in which the author enforces attention from the reader by acting as interlocutor, private counsellor, and *vates* in quick succession. We may, if we wish, regard this procedure as 'charlatanical'; all the same, *Sartor Resartus*, despite its mass of thinly disguised commonplaces, does contain a spiritual autobiography of some power. The force and originality of *The French Revolution* do not appear very extraordinary until we compare the book with the work of 'Dryasdust' himself, and also with that of more recent historiographers who have debased Carlyle's technique in order to woo a non-specialist public. Of the works written after *Past and Present* it cannot be denied that, with certain exceptions, they suffer from a defect to which all prophetic utterances are subject – they appeal to a certain strain of masochism which causes mankind to take a moderate delight in hearing themselves and others made the objects of vilification. To this extent Carlyle's later career follows a not unfamiliar pattern; his is the case of an author dominated by an exploitable mode of composition.

★

In Carlyle's works no special attention is paid to the Hero as Artist or Man of Science. Carlyle was no more than tolerant towards the 'scientific head'; and his view of the Artist, as given in several letters to John Sterling and elsewhere, is such as to suggest that he regarded the arts with disfavour. This is perhaps the most significant point of divergence between Carlyle and Ruskin (1819–1900); and it may be suggested that the catholicity of Ruskin's tastes in artistic and scientific pursuits serves to emphasize by contrast the serious limitations of Carlyle's sensibility. For Ruskin's painstaking studies of geology, botany, and meteorology reveal an acuteness of observation and depth of response to physical phenomena which find no parallel in Carlyle's experience. The conception of life as a prolonged holy war between the powers of light and darkness inhibited Carlyle from giving to external nature the kind of detailed consideration called for as of right by moral issues. Ruskin, on the other hand, was continually training himself to perceive accurately the forms and qualities of the things all around him. His life was an endless self-education within a wider field of awareness than Carlyle tried to cover. It is, of course, indisputable that Carlyle possessed literary gifts which Ruskin did not share, among them an eager ability to produce 'graphic' depictions of certain historical periods. But since Ruskin has, in *Praeterita* (1885–9) and in other books, dwelt on the fortunate circumstances of his youth, it is as well to recall that the astonishing versatility which enabled him to produce a work like *Modern Painters* at the age of twenty-four was as much the result of laborious self-discipline as of exceptional mental endowment and rigid parental care.

It seems pertinent to stress this basic dissimilarity between Ruskin and Carlyle since Ruskin acknowledges many times his admiration for the 'Solitary Teacher',[1] and makes no secret as to the nature of his discipleship. A more obvious difference lies in the fact that Ruskin commanded an incisive expository prose style which could achieve effects beyond Carlyle's reach. At his best Ruskin uses words with a precision and delicacy which few art critics of equal pretensions have since succeeded in mastering, so subtly personal is his sense of rhythm and imagery. The 'Beauties of Ruskin' are innumerable; his feeling for the *variousness* of nature may perhaps be illustrated from a passage in *Modern Painters*:

The leaves then at the extremities become as fine as dust, a mere confusion of points and lines between you and the sky, a confusion which, you might as well hope to draw sea-sand particle by particle, as to imitate leaf for leaf. This, as it comes down into the body of the tree, gets closer, but never opaque; it is always transparent with crumbling lights in it letting you through to the sky: then out of this, come, heavier and heavier, the masses of illumined foliage, all dazzling and inextricable, save here and there a single leaf on the extremities: then, under these, you get deep passages of broken irregular gloom, passing into transparent, green-lighted, misty hollows.

(Vol. I. pt. 2, sec. vi. ch. 1 §18)

The descriptions of mountains, rocks, rivers, and flowers found in the same work have a comparable acuteness. But in so voluminous a writer as Ruskin we should expect, when following his arguments from one book to another, to find contradictions, anomalies, and perversities. Ruskin realized this, and did a good deal to offset such inconsistencies by submitting himself to stringent criticism. Carlyle was not given to public self-examination; but some of the most informative parts of Ruskin's work are those in which he reviews the positions he has previously advanced and then goes on to summarize the reasoning used in reaching them. Thus in the third of his Edinburgh Lectures of 1853 (on 'Turner and his Works') he gives concisely an account of the theories upon which he had earlier claimed a pre-eminent place for Turner among European painters. Ruskin's flair for Turner, as is well known, is bound up with his conception of the art of landscape painting. In the hands of Claude and Salvator Rosa, we learn:

... painting was like a scene in a theatre, viciously and falsely painted throughout, and presenting a deceptive appearance of truth to nature; understood, as far as it went, in a moment, ... and, in all its operations on the mind, unhealthy, hopeless, and profitless.

But with Turner the arid formalism of earlier landscape artists was superseded by a careful delineation of natural objects as in themselves they were really conceived to be.[2]

The arguments which make up the main body of *Modern Painters* cannot, of course, be adequately reduced to simple headings (as the synopses suggest!); and it would not be an exaggeration to say that the work contains a complete Principles of the Human Understanding. For the moment we may perhaps discuss briefly two topics which Ruskin developed in later writings – the 'cultural' significance

of art, and the moral value of arts and crafts in general. Part of the intention of *Modern Painters* was to discredit the view that art is merely a form of innocent recreation, rather than an activity intimately associated with the major preoccupations of life. All art that aims to amuse, Ruskin tells us in *The Cestus of Aglaia* (1865–6), is inferior and *probably harmful*. This way of stressing the feeble nature of so much mid-nineteenth-century design helps us to make the transition to Ruskin's great thesis that the 'ideas' presented to us by satisfactorily accomplished works of art are essentially *moral* ideas in the sense that they enhance our faculties of perception and render us less subject to the allurements of ignoble pleasure. As he put it in *Modern Painters*: 'the sensation of beauty is not sensual on the one hand, nor is it intellectual on the other, but is dependent on a pure, right and open state of the heart.' Variations upon this notion are ubiquitous in Ruskin's work, though he was not alone in wishing to establish the view that genuine art springs from a 'right' moral state and can exert a 'right' moral effect on the percipient. Art for Art's sake was never part of his creed, as is evident from his lecture on 'The Deteriorative Power of Conventional Art over Nations' (*The Two Paths*, 1859).

Ruskin's insistence on the interconnection between art and morality obviously presents a host of difficulties. Of these he was fully aware; or at least he soon came to realize that serious reservations are called for before we can accept the proposition that a good work of art *necessarily* reflects the moral condition of its creator. In a lecture on 'The Unity of Art' in *The Two Paths* he confronts the most damaging objection to this theory, namely, that many great artists (Turner included) have not led lives of impeccable moral purity. He answers the charge that he has been trying to make art 'too moral' in a manner which implies that by 'good' and 'moral condition' as applied to the artist he means something more like 'artistic integrity' than conformity to specific moral codes. And this standpoint can be adopted without doing violence to the belief that, under normal conditions, a completed work of art does minister to the ethical state of the observer.

The general theory of the Morality of Art – set out with reference to the non-representational arts in his Rede Lecture of 1867 on 'The Relation of National Ethics to National Arts' – has made Ruskin the subject of ridicule among those who can see in it only an attempt to

render art vaguely elevating or uplifting. Yet when we reflect on the showy and *vulgar* quality of so much nineteenth-century art (inside and outside the studio), Ruskin's preoccupation with moral strength appears less incongruous than it might at first seem. His own definition of vulgarity (in an essay on 'Water-Colour Societies', *Academy Notes*, 1859) is a shrewd one: according to him vulgarity is 'the habit of mind and act resulting from the prolonged combination of insensibility with insincerity'. Ruskin goes on to record his conviction that modern vulgarity has proceeded in the first place from the withdrawing 'of all right, and therefore, all softening, or animating motive' from the work of most artists; and secondly 'from the habit of assuming, or striving by rule to express, feelings which did not, and could not, arise out of their work under such conditions'. This, again, brings us back to a section of *The Stones of Venice* which places the relationship of art to morals in a somewhat different light. While staying in Venice in 1851–2 Ruskin made an extremely detailed study of the buildings of that city. He had already compared Byzantine and Greek architecture with the Cis-Alpine Gothic styles in *The Seven Lamps of Architecture* (1849).[3] But from an exhaustive survey of the ornamentations used on the Gothic buildings of Venice, Ruskin came at length to the conclusion that the extreme variety of ornament found in Venetian Gothic indicated one inescapable fact; namely, that the workmen employed to produce it were evidently allowed a great deal of freedom to exercise their own ingenuity. Ruskin attributed this to the probability that the 'Gothic' artisans served masters who recognized 'the individual value of every soul', and did not try to restrain the worker's capacities by making him execute geometrical forms or insipid stylized patterns. This may or may not have been the case. But the manner in which the evidence presented itself to Ruskin forced him to believe that, by and large, the medieval craftsman was able to derive from his work a kind of gratification denied to latter-day monumental masons. And, moreover, as Ruskin saw it, this hypothesis was enough to account for much of the tawdriness of modern art as a whole, since the person who takes no fundamental interest in his work (whether he be a mechanic or a carefully trained draughtsman degraded by the exigencies of commercialism) will inevitably turn out productions that are carelessly designed, shabbily finished, untrue, and to that extent 'immoral'.

In the 'Nature of Gothic' chapter of *The Stones of Venice* Ruskin had worked around to a view of medieval society very similar to that outlined in Carlyle's *Past and Present*. But whereas Carlyle made the comparison with modern social tendencies in a way that was intended to stir the conscience of his readers, Ruskin spoke more temperately about the debasement of the operative into a machine. 'It is not that men are ill fed,' he declares, 'but that they have no pleasure in [their] work ... and therefore look to wealth as the only means of pleasure. It is not that men are pained by the scorn of the upper classes, but they cannot endure their own; for they feel that the kind of labour to which they are condemned is verily a degrading one, and makes them less than men.' The pleasure-in-work *motif* was taken up by writers like William Morris (see, for example, Morris's address on 'Art and its Producers', 1888), who shared Ruskin's belief that life should afford some considerable measure of enjoyment (Ruskin would not allow himself to be described as 'Puritanical'). And in the fourth of his Oxford Lectures (1870), Ruskin gave his followers further confirmation that he was still sceptical about the kind of progress represented by great exhibitions and trade fairs; for he described as the 'main nineteenth-century faith, or infidelity' the notion that it is permissible and right to substitute mechanism for skill, photography for pictures, and cast-iron for sculpture. But fallacious though his view of the essential value of craftsmanship may appear to be (he seems to have taken very little account of the hard and uncreative drudgery eliminated by the use of mechanical power), there is still a central validity in Ruskin's reasoning on this point. When discussing the present position of the artisan class Ruskin does not, like Carlyle, denigrate the intellectual capacity of the ordinary man.[4] For Ruskin, once certain conditions are granted, man need no longer be regarded as an unreclaimable, sheep-like creature; whatever his natural ability, or lack of ability, he does not deserve to be dehumanized. Ruskin could no more have written a tirade like 'Model Prisons' in the *Latter-Day Pamphlets* than Carlyle could have produced an *Ethics of the Dust*. 'Examine once more', Ruskin writes in *The Stones of Venice*, 'those ugly goblins, and formless monsters, and stern statues, anatomiless and rigid; but do not mock at them, for they are the signs of the life and liberty of every workman who struck the stone; a freedom of thought, and rank in scale of being, such as no laws, no charters, no

charities can secure; but which it must be the first aim of all Europe at this day to regain for her children.'

That Ruskin idealized the Middle Ages and made stupid statements about the Renaissance is true enough; it is also clear that in his later years he was highly imprudent in practical affairs. But those who contend that his writings on political economy represent a blundering intrusion into a field he had no right to enter would do well to reconsider the implications of 'The Nature of Gothic'. It should be plain from *Unto This Last* (1860, 1862) that the motive behind Ruskin's somewhat fussy assault on the earlier economists is a fundamentally sensible one; his aim being to bring into prominence human factors which have come to be obscured by generations of abstract discussion. Conceiving that his was a still small voice, Ruskin made the mistake of over-emphasizing what he took to be worth saying about wages, profits, supply and demand, and so forth. But he did not take the precaution of stopping to consider whether some of his contentions might not have been entertained – though in another form – by the writers he criticized. He makes great play, for example, with what he regards as the vagaries of 'Mr Mill'; yet a reading of the chapter headed 'Of The Stationary State' in Mill's *Political Economy* shows that Mill was equally sympathetic to the claims of humanity in a modern competitive society. And when, in the 'Ad Valorem' section of *Unto This Last*, Ruskin gives us his definition of 'the real science of political economy' ('... that which teaches nations to desire and labour for the things that lead to life ...' etc.), he is describing not a 'science' properly so-called, but an exalted form of 'propaganda' to which art and religion will be the principal contributors.

Books like *Time and Tide* (1867) and *Fors Clavigera* (1871–84), which have their origins in the vantage ground upon which *Unto This Last* and *Munera Pulveris* (1872) stand, still retain a high degree of interest. But they are the work of a writer who is respectfully talking down to those he believes to be his inferiors. Without much apparent faith in the efficiency of modern governments (see, for example, his censure of Modern Liberalism in Letter 14 of *Fors Clavigera*), Ruskin tells his 'working cork-cutter of Sunderland', Thomas Dixon – to whom the *Time and Tide* letters were sent – that some kind of authoritarian leadership is necessary to secure law and order in the state, though the administrators of the land are to be overseers and pastors

rather than ruthless tyrants. The government Ruskin has in mind will not rely on that 'further development of democracy' which is advocated in William Morris's four *Letters on Socialism* (1894);[5] yet the interests of the people will be well taken care of because the upper classes will observe their responsibilities to the lower, and will not only keep them in order but will also provide for such things as education and the welfare of the sick. The culminating point of *Time and Tide*, perhaps, occurs in the twenty-fifth letter, 'Hyssop', where Ruskin recalls the Parable of the Prodigal Son – 'The lost son began by claiming his rights. He is found when he resigns them. He is lost by flying from his father, when his father's authority was only paternal. He is found by returning to his father, and desiring that his authority may be absolute, as over a hired stranger.' This is merely one of countless instances in which Ruskin acts as an agency by means of which the substance of biblical narratives can be given a modern application. As in the case of Carlyle, we have some difficulty in determining the precise nature of Ruskin's religious faith;[6] yet we know from *Praeterita* and *The Bible of Amiens* (1880–85) that to him the Scriptures held within them a kind of archetypal wisdom 'transcending all thought and ordaining all conduct'.

Biblical references are quoted extensively in Ruskin's later works. But the conception of society put forward in *Time and Tide* – that of an obedient family bowing before the kindly ministrations of a benevolent father – is quite unrealistic because it takes no account of the nature of herd instincts or of the manner in which men and women of average intelligence assimilate ideas. But from *Fors Clavigera* onwards it becomes clear that the projection of fantasies in which he himself figured as the chivalrous Overlord was an indulgence Ruskin could not deny himself. With this must be associated his partiality for the company of juveniles, for whose delectation several of his books (*The Ethics of the Dust*, 1866, for instance) were specially composed. The Guild of St George project, by means of which a band of dedicated Companions was to seek emancipation from wage slavery, symbolized more than it achieved; rooted in its Master's belief that an outmoded form of social organization might be utilized to promote good labour relations, the guild principle could not survive under conditions for which the Middle Ages offered no parallel. The yearly reports which Ruskin drew up in the seventies

and eighties are as explicit as anything he ever wrote; they stand, in the thirtieth volume of his *Works*, as a suitable monument to what after all was a noble failure to implement by practical means the proposition that there is no wealth but life.

Ruskin's long discussions on the possibility of bringing about social reforms by educating the masses and inducing a desire for the moral life would perhaps be tediously naïve (parts of *Fors Clavigera* are, indeed, mawkish and patronizing) if it were not for certain qualities which give his work as a whole a more than temporary significance. His protests against muddy canvases and unsound architecture are occasionally wrong-headed and over-confident; but in general his pronouncements are characterized – even when dogmatic to the point of perversity – by a kind of intellectual honesty that is rare in any age. For he directed his mind to the study of conditions which, as we now realize, have a tendency to recur under different guises in successive epochs. He noticed, for one thing, that no society in modern times has succeeded in making full use of what it has inherited from the past; as a consequence, he experienced some anxiety about the future of a 'civilized nation' that put its trust in capitalists, gamblers, and champagne-bibbers (*Fors Clavigera*, Letter 67). His bad-tempered outbursts against mechanical contrivances make it appear that he was an unenlightened obstructionist (though he did, in fact, give a good deal of thought to the correct use and design of machines): yet his fulminations are really a way of uttering the plea that existing potentialities shall be utilized before new ones are opened up. Then again, Ruskin's advocacy of a certain measure of 'austerity' in life was a means of communicating to the well-to-do that some considerable pleasure may be derived from simplicity. And the insistence that self-cultivation is a gratifying experience – a theme that runs through all Ruskin's 'teaching' from his appearance as lecturer on art at the Working Men's College during the 1850s right up to the *Bibliotheca Pastorum* venture in the eighties and beyond – serves as a reminder that at a time when men are struggling to secure their rights they are in danger of forgetting that the claims they can make upon society are not infinite, and that in many things they must of necessity practise self-reliance and self-help.

There are, of course, dozens of particular issues which arise from an examination of Ruskin's sociological writings.[7] Towards the end

of his life he obviously composed far too much and acquired a certain facility that was unworthy of him; yet, as Derrick Leon has pointed out, he never became complacent, 'and in his deepest heart, he never forgave himself his own weaknesses'. For this and other reasons the voice of prophecy in Ruskin has an urgency that does not appear quite so consistently in Carlyle's volumes. It is no injustice to Carlyle to say that his work must be seen more narrowly within the framework of the period he belongs to; but Ruskin's major writings retain that sense of immediacy and inner power that is shared by all durable literature.

NOTES

1. See the Appendix III on 'Plagiarism' in *Modern Painters*, volume III.

2. An interesting short assessment of Ruskin's 'gigantic scheme of personal empirical observation and record' appears on p. 183 of R. H. Wilenski's *The Study of Art* (London, 1934).

3. The extent to which Ruskin's theories were anticipated by other writers is discussed by Sir Kenneth Clark in *The Gothic Revival* (London, 1928). Also relevant in this connection is ch. v ('The Ethical Fallacy') of Geoffrey Scott's *The Architecture of Humanism* (London, 1914). Mention should also be made of 'The Fine Arts in Florence' by Francis Cohen (F. T. Palgrave) in *The Quarterly Review* for September 1840.

4. The qualities which distinguish Ruskin's points of view are shown at some length in the fifth lecture of *The Two Paths* ('The Work of Iron ...', 1858).

5. The nature of Morris's dissent from Ruskin's standpoint is suggested in a letter from Morris to Robert Thompson on 24 July 1884 (*The Letters of William Morris to His Family and Friends*, ed. Philip Henderson (London, 1950), 204).

6. This aspect of Ruskin's life is treated with great understanding by Derrick Leon in his *Ruskin the Great Victorian* (London, 1949), 568–9.

7. There are some masterly discussions of advertising, 'subtopia', the monarchy, usury, republican government, and so on in *Fors Clavigera* alone.

MATTHEW ARNOLD

J. D. JUMP

As a poet, Arnold (1822–88) had no wish to write in conformity with the fashion of his time. He said as much in a letter to his favourite sister, Jane, shortly after the publication of his first collection of poems: 'More and more I feel bent against the modern English habit (too much encouraged by Wordsworth) of using poetry as a channel for thinking aloud, instead of making anything.' Four years later, in the 'Preface' to his volume of 1853, he made a more elaborate rejection of Romantic subjectivism. Appealing to the authority of the ancients, he asserted that nineteenth-century poets needed to learn three things: 'the all-importance of the choice of a subject; the necessity of accurate construction; and the subordinate character of expression'.

In accordance with this classical doctrine, he composed one tragedy, *Merope*, and two works in the epic manner, *Balder Dead* and *Sohrab and Rustum*. *Balder Dead* is tame; *Merope* is almost unreadable. Both are academic in the most damaging sense of the word. If *Sohrab and Rustum*, on the other hand, sometimes transcends academicism, this is because a pressure of personal feeling makes itself felt at certain critical points: in the description of the fight, for example. Nor is it hard to divine one source of this personal feeling. *Sohrab and Rustum* is in part an unconscious imaginative projection of the conflict, concerning which we have independent biographical evidence, between Matthew Arnold and his formidable father, Dr Arnold of Rugby, who had died more than ten years earlier.

The relative success of *Sohrab and Rustum* is symptomatic. Arnold attempted too complete an exclusion of subjective elements from *Merope* and *Balder Dead*. His verse is more interesting when he allows it to be more personal. But even then he repeatedly falls short of entire poetic success by indulging in precisely that ruminating, that 'thinking aloud, instead of making anything', which he deplored in

his contemporaries. *The Buried Life* is a favourable instance of his ruminative manner. In it he expresses himself with a quiet, grave lucidity, but without compelling us to share his state of mind. We believe what he says because we happen to know that he was a sincere man and not because he says it in such a way as to make disbelief difficult.

He is more successful when, instead of merely declaring his thoughts and feelings, he presents for our contemplation something which will immediately and powerfully suggest them to us. Such is the Berkshire countryside with which he associates his ruminations in *The Scholar-Gipsy* and *Thyrsis*; such is that setting on the shore of the English Channel with which he fuses them in his one great poem, *Dover Beach*. It is remarkable how many of Arnold's finer poems consist, like these, of elegiac broodings more or less intimately linked with symbolic landscapes.

Perhaps it seems niggardly to allow greatness only to *Dover Beach*. But Arnold himself insists that 'excellence is not common and abundant' ('Milton'); and comparison with *Dover Beach* shows up the limitations even of poems as charming and as moving as *The Scholar-Gipsy* and *Thyrsis*. These elegies express Arnold's lifelong attachment to the countryside which he had explored in his youth with Arthur Hugh Clough and other Oxford companions. They provide many vivid and attractive glimpses of the well-loved scenes: for example, of

> those wide fields of breezy grass
> Where black-wing'd swallows haunt the glittering Thames
> > (*The Scholar-Gipsy*)

and of

> the mowers, who, as the tiny swell
> Of our boat passing heaved the river-grass,
> Stood with suspended scythe to see us pass.
> > (*Thyrsis*)

The whole landscape, rendered as here with a distinctly Keatsian sensuousness and charm, suggests Arnold's own longing for a freshness and spontaneity not easily attainable by one who is committed to hard and uncongenial work for a living.

The world in which this work is to be done and in which men

are 'Light half-believers' of their 'casual creeds', the world of 'sick
hurry' and 'divided aims', of 'heads o'ertax'd' and 'palsied hearts'
(*The Scholar-Gipsy*), is contrasted with the countryside around
Oxford which offers a temporary refuge from it. But the workaday
predicament of those whose escape is necessarily so brief is not
brought home to us with any force. Its reality is blurred by the graceful, conventionally poetical language which Arnold uses. This
language, essentially that taken over by the Victorians from Keats,
is better fitted for the evocation of the idyllic landscape. So where
the Oxford elegies succeed is in enabling us to close our eyes to the
harsh requirements of life and to dream of a relaxing pastoral week-
end. In this direction their success is genuine enough. But it is not
the most important, the most challenging and disturbing, kind of
success.

Dover Beach is entirely free from such poeticality. It is a short poem,
but it embraces a great range and depth of significance. As elsewhere,
Arnold discloses his melancholy preoccupation with the thought of
the inevitable decline of religious faith; and he expresses the belief
that in a successful love-relationship he may realize values to which
'the world' is hostile. But he does not merely ruminate upon these
ideas. He conveys them to us more by the 'moon-blanch'd' landscape
which he creates than by his direct statement of them.

Moving with a steady and weighty *rallentando*, the opening lines
record a series of particular items suggestive of the serenity, poise,
and stability which Arnold desires for himself:

> The sea is calm tonight.
> The tide is full, the moon lies fair
> Upon the straits; – on the French coast the light
> Gleams, and is gone; the cliffs of England stand,
> Glimmering and vast, out in the tranquil bay.

There follows a contrasting tender appeal to the poet's companion:

> Come to the window, sweet is the night-air!

and then the noise and movement of the sea are rendered with a
wonderful richness and fullness in the lines which conclude this first
paragraph:

> Only, from the long line of spray
> Where the sea meets the moon-blanch'd land,

> Listen! you hear the grating roar
> Of pebbles which the waves draw back, and fling,
> At their return, up the high strand,
> Begin, and cease, and then again begin,
> With tremulous cadence slow, and bring
> The eternal note of sadness in.

Here, 'grating roar' admirably defines the sounds made by waves breaking on shingle; 'draw back' and 'fling ... up' are so placed that we read them with an almost physical sense of the muscular effort they suggest; a combination of metrical and syntactical means makes the ebbing and flowing of the waves vividly present to us; and the Miltonic 'tremulous cadence slow' both summarizes what has gone before and by its solemnity permits the unforced introduction of the 'eternal note of sadness'.

After a short paragraph referring to a Sophoclean use of the image of the waves, Arnold begins his commentary. He does so in a quietly explanatory tone:

> The Sea of Faith
> Was once, too, at the full, and round earth's shore
> Lay like the folds of a bright girdle furl'd.

From this he might easily have lapsed into mere 'thinking aloud'. Instead, he develops the image of the sea of faith through five haunting lines. The sequence of open vowels in the second of these, with the near-rhyme 'draw: roar', gives an eerie resonance which echoes down the remainder of the sentence. From the main verb, 'hear', introduced early, the whole sentence falls away in keeping with the ebb of the tide, and of religious faith, which it describes.

> But now I only hear
> Its melancholy, long, withdrawing roar,
> Retreating, to the breath
> Of the night-wind, down the vast edges drear
> And naked shingles of the world.

In his last paragraph, the poet again appeals to his companion. Since the loss of religious faith makes it impossible to believe that the universe is in some degree adjusted to human needs, that it is 'peopled by Gods' (*Empedocles on Etna*, II), he must seek in human love for those values which are undiscoverable elsewhere. Moreover,

the lovers must support each other if they are to live in the modern world without disaster.

> Ah, love, let us be true
> To one another! for the world, which seems
> To lie before us like a land of dreams,
> So various, so beautiful, so new,
> Hath really neither joy, nor love, nor light,
> Nor certitude, nor peace, nor help for pain;
> And we are here as on a darkling plain
> Swept with confused alarms of struggle and flight,
> Where ignorant armies clash by night

Only in the last line, which startles us by its brevity after the seven longer lines preceding it, does Arnold reveal the full strangeness and horror of his concluding analogy. Emphasized in this way, the image becomes his most memorable poetic comment on the modern world. Nothing that he says of 'this strange disease of modern life' in *The Scholar-Gipsy* approaches it in urgency and power.

Arnold wrote the greater part of his poetry before he was thirty-three and practically all of it before he was forty-five. In the main, it is conspicuously the work of a young man suffering from a painful sense of limitation, finding it difficult to adjust his longings and expectations to the despotism of fact. *The New Sirens*, the two sonnets *To a Republican Friend, 1848, Resignation*, the Marguerite poems, *Stanzas in Memory of the Author of Obermann*, and *Empedocles on Etna* alike turn very largely on this conflict between desire and necessity. But as Arnold developed he came increasingly to accept the inevitable without protest and to direct himself to purposive activity within the bounds it imposed. In two poems of the middle eighteen-sixties, *Thyrsis* and *Obermann Once More*, we find him resolving, though with some backward glances, to do just this.

Prose, however, was to be the chief literary instrument of his maturity; and from the time of his election to the Chair of Poetry at Oxford in 1857 he began to write it regularly. His first published series of lectures, *On Translating Homer* (1861), contains some of the finest of his strictly literary criticism.

In it he writes primarily for intending translators of Homer. Wishing to supply them with practical advice, he examines four widely different versions of the *Iliad* and tries to say where each is deficient. This involves him in detailed literary analysis. For example, finding

Cowper's rendering elaborately Miltonic, he has to assess the suitability of Miltonic blank verse for the purpose in hand. He does so with discrimination and point.

Homer's movement ... is a flowing, a rapid movement; Milton's, on the other hand, is a laboured, a self-retarding movement. In each case, the movement, the metrical cast, corresponds with the mode of evolution of the thought, with the syntactical cast, and is indeed determined by it. Milton charges himself so full with thought, imagination, knowledge, that his style will hardly contain them. He is too full-stored to show us in much detail one conception, one piece of knowledge; he just shows it to us in a pregnant allusive way, and then he presses on to another; and all this fullness, this pressure, this condensation, this self-constraint, enters into his movement, and makes it what it is – noble, but difficult and austere. Homer is quite different; he says a thing, and says it to the end, and then begins another, while Milton is trying to press a thousand things into one. So that whereas, in reading Milton, you never lose the sense of laborious and condensed fullness, in reading Homer you never lose the sense of flowing and abounding ease. With Milton line runs into line, and all is straitly bound together: with Homer line runs off from line, and all hurries away onward. Homer begins, Μῆνιν ἄειδε, θεά – at the second word announcing the proposed action: Milton begins:

> Of man's first disobedience, and the fruit
> Of that forbidden tree, whose mortal taste
> Brought death into the world, and all our woe,
> With loss of Eden, till one greater Man
> Restore us, and regain the blissful seat,
> Sing, heavenly muse –

so chary of a sentence is he, so resolute not to let it escape him till he has crowded into it all he can, that it is not till the thirty-ninth word in the sentence that he will give us the key to it, the word of action, the verb. Milton says:

> O for that warning voice, which he, who saw
> The Apocalypse, heard cry in heaven aloud –

he is not satisfied, unless he can tell us, all in one sentence, and without permitting himself to actually mention the name, that the man who heard the warning voice was the same man who saw the Apocalypse. Homer would have said, 'O for that warning voice, which *John* heard' – and if it had suited him to say that John also saw the Apocalypse, he would have given us that in another sentence. The effect of this allusive and compressed manner of Milton is, I need not say, often very powerful; ... but ... it is always an un-Homeric effect.   (Lecture III)

In *Last Words on Translating Homer* (1862), an additional lecture provoked by retorts to the original series, a discussion of the view that Tennysonian blank verse is plain and simple enough to serve for an English Homer leads to an equally sensitive and perceptive analysis of the Poet Laureate's style.

Arnold rarely offers us close analysis in his criticism. Perhaps the relative uniformity of literary training and experience, and consequently of reading habits, in the nineteenth century exempted him from the obligation, which the twentieth-century critic characteristically assumes, of showing in some detail how in his opinion the text should be read and apprehended. But the instances of close analysis in his Homer lectures enable us very directly to appreciate the alertness and responsiveness of his reading; and everywhere in his work we come upon particular observations which further illustrate its quality.

Moreover, these lectures contain, in hints and scattered statements, a preliminary draft of the programme for criticism which Arnold was later to draw up more fully. On the one hand, he wishes criticism to testify to the existence of true and impersonal standards of value, and in so doing to foster in his fellow-countrymen that conscience in matters of intellect and taste which they so gravely lack. On the other hand, he does not wish it to harden into summary judgements made with reference to arbitrary external rules. 'The critic of poetry should have the finest tact, the nicest moderation, the most free, flexible, and elastic spirit imaginable; he should be indeed the "ondoyant et divers", the *undulating and diverse* being of Montaigne' (*Last Words*). He should be open-minded, adaptable, and enquiring.

In short, Arnold's aim seems to be to find a middle way between the objective, judicial approach adopted by such classical critics as Johnson and the eager, responsive approach made by such Romantic critics as Hazlitt. In two more of the lectures which he delivered at Oxford, he dwells in turn on the need to acknowledge the authority of intellectual and aesthetic standards and on the need for flexibility and receptiveness. These two lectures, 'The Literary Influence of Academies' and 'The Function of Criticism at the Present Time', made their earliest appearance in book form in the first series of *Essays in Criticism* (1865).

In the former, Arnold describes and exemplifies the damage which can be done to the literary and intellectual life of a nation by the lack of any widespread belief in the validity of standards of criticism. A belief in these may find expression in an academy, 'a high court of letters', 'a recognized authority, imposing ... a high standard in matters of intellect and taste'; or it may operate less conspicuously through a fairly coherent body of educated opinion. But if such a belief does not exist in one form or another, the intellectual life of society will be free to run too easily into 'hap-hazard, crudeness, provincialism, eccentricity, violence, blundering'. This is what Arnold thinks he sees happening in the England of his own day.

In 'The Function of Criticism at the Present Time', perhaps his finest essay, he emphasizes more particularly the other half of his programme. He starts by replying to those who accuse him of over-rating criticism. He agrees that, in general, criticism must rank below creation. But, he insists, the creation of great works of art is not always equally possible. Even the leading English poets of the Romantic period were partially disabled by the absence from society generally of a vigorous intellectual life such as had sustained Sophocles, Shakespeare, and other more fortunate writers. 'This makes Byron so empty of matter, Shelley so incoherent, Wordsworth even, profound as he is, yet so wanting in completeness and variety.' Criticism can help to reinvigorate our intellectual life, and can serve future creative writers, by discharging its true function. This is 'simply to know the best that is known and thought in the world, and by in its turn making this known, to create a current of true and fresh ideas'. Doing this, it will contribute to the production in time of an intellectual and spiritual situation of which creative genius will be able profitably to avail itself.

If it is to succeed, criticism must be essentially the exercise of a freely ranging, open-minded curiosity. Moreover, it must be disinterested; it must steadily refuse to lend itself to 'ulterior, political, practical considerations'. The practical man sees an object, above all, as helping or hindering his plans; the critic must try to view it more detachedly, to see it 'as in itself it really is'.

Criticism, so conceived, is to be directed not only upon works of art but also upon life in general. Arnold himself in this essay directs it upon passages from two recent political speeches celebrating the

greatness of the English race and its achievements. He shows up what is excessive and offensive in these rhapsodies by placing beside them a brutally compact newspaper report of a squalid child-murder recently committed in the very country which they extol. This is the comparative method which we have already seen him use so skilfully in his critique of Milton's blank verse. For Arnold holds that the habit of dispassionate appraisal fostered by strictly literary criticism can be of the widest social utility.

Towards the end of the essay, he offers a few recommendations for specifically literary criticism. After saying that the English critic, in search of 'the best that is known and thought', must dwell much on foreign literature, he continues:

Again, judging is often spoken of as the critic's one business, and so in some sense it is; but the judgement which almost insensibly forms itself in a fair and clear mind, along with fresh knowledge, is the valuable one; and thus knowledge, and ever fresh knowledge, must be the critic's great concern for himself. And it is by communicating fresh knowledge, and letting his own judgement pass along with it, – but insensibly, and in the second place, not the first, as a sort of companion and clue, not as an abstract lawgiver, – that the critic will generally do most good to his readers. Sometimes, no doubt, for the sake of establishing an author's place in literature, and his relation to a central standard (and if this is not done, how are we to get at our *best in the world*?) criticism may have to deal with a subject-matter so familiar that fresh knowledge is out of the question, and then it must be all judgement; an enunciation and detailed application of principles. Here the great safeguard is never to let oneself become abstract, always to retain an intimate and lively consciousness of the truth of what one is saying, and, the moment this fails us, to be sure that something is wrong.

So Arnold wants criticism to be 'sincere, simple, flexible, ardent, ever widening its knowledge'. It is criticism of this sort that he has in mind when he describes poetry as 'a criticism of life'. A good deal of nonsense has been written about this phrase by commentators who were so impatient to reject it that they could not wait to understand it. But 'The Function of Criticism at the Present Time' makes it perfectly clear what Arnold means by criticism: a disinterested attempt to see things as they really are, in the course of which value-judgements naturally and almost insensibly form themselves. It would be difficult to find fault with this as an account of the ideal attitude of a poet, or other creative artist, towards his experience.

The phrase, 'a criticism of life', occurs in 'The Study of Poetry',

which opens Arnold's *Essays in Criticism: Second Series* (1888). The revaluation of the poetry of the English Romantics is one of his chief concerns in this collection. It was active enough in the first series of *Essays in Criticism*: the sentence on the subject already quoted from 'The Function of Criticism at the Present Time' rests upon the fuller account of the limitations of the Romantics given in 'Heinrich Heine'. But in *Essays in Criticism: Second Series* it inspires separate essays on Keats, Wordsworth, Byron, and Shelley; and it has an important place in 'The Study of Poetry'.

This essay consists mainly of a quick survey of English poetry from Chaucer to Burns. It contains much that is both revealing and just. But Arnold, as is well-known, ignores Donne, overrates Gray, and underrates Chaucer, Dryden, Pope, and Burns. The trouble seems to be that, despite his endeavours, he is no more able completely to liberate himself from romantic presuppositions in his criticism than he is able regularly to shake off romantic habits of feeling and expression in his poetry; his quick survey is distorted by the fact that he suffers from the common nineteenth-century fixation on 'elevated' poetry.

So far we have been dealing only with Arnold's literary essays. Even in these his belief that the critical attitude is valuable not only in the study but also in the outer world leads him frequently into social criticism. In the Homer lectures, for example, he remarks upon the disabling weakness of the intellectual conscience among the English; and in 'The Function of Criticism at the Present Time' he quotes specimens of the clap-trap which circulates all too easily among them in the absence of such checks as the intellectual conscience should provide.

In 1867 he finished his period of service as professor of poetry at Oxford. As the date came near, he turned decisively from literary to social criticism; and his chief work in the new field, *Culture and Anarchy*, appeared in book form early in 1869. After this, he devoted himself for some years to religious criticism, before making further important contributions to literary criticism, though not only to that, during the last eleven years of his life.

The decade of his political and religious writings, 1867–77, is described by George Saintsbury under the heading 'In the Wilderness'. Few present-day readers will see Arnold's writing of the period in

so unfavourable a light. *Culture and Anarchy*, in particular, is the wisest and wittiest of his longer prose works. His lively comic sense, wide acquaintance with English life, quick perceptions, alert intelligence, and fundamental seriousness are all evident in it; and there is no better instance of his cool, elegant, sinuous, and mischievously ironical prose.

Culture and Anarchy is a lay sermon on the disadvantages of 'doing as one likes'. The theme was no new one with Arnold. In 'The Literary Influence of Academies', as earlier in the Homer lectures, he had pointed out that, in the absence of any widespread belief in the validity of standards of criticism, English writers were too free to do as they liked and consequently slipped headlong into 'hap-hazard, crudeness, provincialism, eccentricity, violence, blundering'. Public events between 1866 and 1869 provoked a treatment of the theme with much closer reference to social and political actualities.

During these years, the Reform Bill of 1867 enfranchised the working men in the towns and almost doubled the electorate. Much mass agitation, and even a little disorder, preceded the passage of this Bill; and during the same period there were disturbances also from other causes. Some observers – Carlyle, for example – panicked. But Arnold was level-headed enough to realize that social chaos was not quite imminent. As a liberal, moreover, he was in general sympathy with the democratic movement. In any case, he recognized the inevitability of the transition to democracy, and saw the problem of his generation as that of helping it to occur without the destruction of the whole social fabric. (In his religious criticism, similarly, he recognizes the inevitability of a decline of belief in the supernatural and devotes himself to showing that what is essential in religion need not decline with it. Such are the ways in which, in his mature writings, he resolves that conflict between necessity and desire which we have identified in his poetry.)

The transition to democracy is unlikely to occur without disaster if the English persist in their belief that in all circumstances, 'it is a most happy and important thing for a man merely to be able to do as he likes' (ch. ii). For lately the Englishman has begun to assert and put in practice 'his right to march where he likes, meet where he likes, enter where he likes, hoot as he likes, threaten as he likes, smash as he likes' (ch. ii). Among other examples, Arnold refers to certain

recent riots provoked by an inflammatory anti-Catholic orator whom he handles with characteristic irony:

Mr Murphy lectures at Birmingham, and showers on the Catholic population of that town 'words', says the Home Secretary, Mr Hardy, 'only fit to be addressed to thieves or murderers'. What then? Mr Murphy has his own reasons of several kinds. He suspects the Roman Catholic Church of designs upon Mrs Murphy; and he says, if mayors and magistrates do not care for their wives and daughters, he does. But, above all, he is doing as he likes; or, in worthier language, asserting his personal liberty. 'I will carry out my lectures if they walk over my body as a dead corpse; and I say to the Mayor of Birmingham that he is my servant while I am in Birmingham, and as my servant he must do his duty and protect me.' Touching and beautiful words, which find a sympathetic chord in every British bosom! The moment it is plainly put before us that a man is asserting his personal liberty, we are half disarmed; because we are believers in freedom, and not in some dream of a right reason to which the assertion of our freedom is to be subordinated. Accordingly, the Secretary of State had to say that although the lecturer's language was 'only fit to be addressed to thieves or murderers', yet, 'I do not think he is to be deprived, I do not think that anything I have said could justify the inference that he is to be deprived, of the right of protection in a place built by him for the purpose of these lectures; because the language was not language which afforded grounds for a criminal prosecution.' No, nor to be silenced by Mayor, or Home Secretary, or any administrative authority on earth, simply on their notion of what is discreet and reasonable! This is in perfect consonance with our public opinion, and with our national love for the assertion of personal liberty.

If their individualism is not to sweep them into anarchy, says Arnold, the English must modify their attitude towards public authority; in other words, they must acquire 'the notion, so familiar on the Continent and to antiquity, of *the State* – the nation in its collective and corporate character, entrusted with stringent powers for the general advantage, and controlling individual wills in the name of an interest wider than that of individuals' (ch. ii). None of the existing social classes is fit to exercise this power. The aristocracy is impervious to ideas; the middle class is narrow and self-satisfied; the working class is rude and intemperate. So the State must represent the 'best self' or essential '*humanity*' (ch. iii) of all its citizens – just as an academy can represent their intellectual conscience.

If some such 'firm State-power' (ch. ii) is to be established and accepted, Englishmen must devote their energies less exclusively to immediate practical tasks and rather more to trying to understand

the larger issues which confront them. Culture, by fostering an understanding of these, will bring them to see the necessity for, and the possibility of, a just and impersonal State-power. In this fashion, it will help them to avoid the anarchy to which 'doing as one likes' must lead.

One task of this 'firm State-power' will be to promote a greater social equality than at present prevails in Great Britain. Ever since his long stay on the Continent on official business in 1859, Arnold's conviction had been growing that such 'signal inequality of classes and property' ('Equality') as he observed in his own country was a grave obstacle to civilization. During his last years, this conviction provided the theme of his most valuable social criticism.

'Equality', the second of his *Mixed Essays* (1879), is his classical statement of it. He argues

that the great inequality of classes and property ... which we maintain because we have the religion of inequality ... has the natural and necessary effect, under present circumstances, of materializing our upper class, vulgarizing our middle class, and brutalizing our lower class. And this is to fail in civilization.

He has even the boldness, for a man of that generation, to suggest that civilization might be well served by some tampering with the supposed rights of property!

Arnold was a great man of letters. Whatever the shortcomings of his poems, there is some justification for the claim he made when writing to his mother in 1869 that they 'represent, on the whole, the main movement of mind' of the previous quarter of a century; and their sincerity almost invariably secures our interest. In his prose, he exemplifies the value to the community of the flexible, non-specialist, critical intelligence. Writing on literature, education, politics, and religion, he tries to encourage a free play of the mind upon the material before it and so to help his readers to get rid of any stock notions and pieces of mental petrifaction which may be hampering their thought. Naturally, he is not always himself entirely free from prejudice. He is, however, remarkably fair-minded – the more so for not subjecting himself to any tyrannical system or orthodoxy. His wide experience of contemporary England and even of western Europe, his nimble intuitive intelligence, his urbane wit, and his pre-eminent sanity make him one of the most stimulating and engaging of our commentators upon literature and upon life.

NOTE

The main ideas expressed in this essay receive a fuller treatment in my *Matthew Arnold* (London, 1955). I have also made a number of verbal borrowings from the book.

GEORGE MEREDITH: NOVELIST

F. N. LEES

'That book is good in vain, which the reader throws away', wrote Dr Johnson. For no form of literature does this observation hold more warning than for the novel; and no novelist, surely, more illustrates its truth and points its moral than does George Meredith (1828–1909).

Read the account (here abridged) of the hero's climactic change of heart towards the end of Meredith's first true novel, *The Ordeal of Richard Feverel* (1859). Richard, victim of a rigorous and inflexible 'System' of upbringing devised by his embittered father, Sir Austin, defiantly marries a local farmer's niece. Under pressure of inveterate paternal opposition the marriage weakens and Richard yields to the beckonings of dissipation, in particular to the calculated advances of a certain Mrs Bella Mount. In remorse and despairing (at bottom in the grasp of a self-regarding pride), he exiles himself to the Rhineland, and it is here that he receives the news that his wife has borne him a child. The news astounds him, and with his dog he sets off walking through the forest. The moon is bright, the summer air heavy and still:

An oppressive slumber hung about the forest-branches. In the dells and on the heights was the same dead heat. Here where the brook tinkled it was no cool-lipped sound, but metallic, and without the spirit of water ... The valleys were clear ... the distances sharply distinct ... Richard beheld a roe moving across a slope of sward far out of rifle-mark ... Tongue out of mouth trotted the little dog after him; crouched panting when he stopped ... rose weariedly when he started afresh. Now and then a large white night-moth flitted through the dusk of the forest.

On a barren corner of the wooded highland looking inland stood grey topless ruins set in nettles and rank glass-blades. Richard mechanically sat down on the crumbling flints to rest, and listened to the panting of the dog. Sprinkled at his feet were emerald lights: hundreds of glow-worms studded the dark dry ground.

He sat and eyed them, thinking not at all ... He sat as a part of the ruins, and the moon turned his shadow. Westward from the South. Overhead, as she declined, long ripples of silver cloud were imperceptibly stealing toward

her. They were the van of a tempest. He did not observe them or the leaves beginning to chatter. When he again pursued his course ..., a huge mountain appeared to rise sheer over him, and he had it in mind to scale it. He got no nearer to the base of it for all his vigorous out-stepping ... Then heavy thunder-drops struck his cheek, the leaves were singing, the earth breathed, it was black before him and behind. All at once the thunder spoke. The mountain he had marked was bursting over him.

Up started the whole forest in violet fire. He saw the country at the foot of the hills to the bounding Rhine gleam, quiver, extinguished. Then there were pauses; and the lightning seemed as the eye of heaven, and the thunder as the tongue of heaven ... Lower down the lightened abysses of air rolled the wrathful crash: then white thrusts of light were darted from the sky, and great curving ferns, seen steadfast in pallor a second, were supernaturally agitated, and vanished. Then a shrill song roused in the leaves and the herbage. Prolonged and louder it sounded, as deeper and heavier the deluge pressed. A mighty force of water satisfied the desire of the earth. Even in this, drenched as he was by the first outpouring, Richard had a savage pleasure. Keeping in motion he was scarcely conscious of the wet, and the grateful breath of the weeds was refreshing ... Suddenly he stopped short ... He fancied he smelled meadowsweet. He had never seen the flower in the Rhineland ... he stooped and stretched out his hand to feel for the flower ... Groping about, his hand encountered something warm that started at his touch, and he, with the instinct we have, seized it, and lifted it ... a tiny leveret ... He put the little thing on one hand in his bosom, and stepped out rapidly as before.

The rain was now steady ... So cool and easy had his mind become that he was speculating on what kind of shelter the birds could find ... Lovingly he looked into the dripping darkness of the coverts on each side, as one of their children. He was next musing on a strange sensation ... It ran up one arm with an indescribable thrill. It was purely physical, ceased for a time, and recommenced, till he had it all through his blood, wonderfully thrilling. He grew aware that the little thing he carried in his breast was licking his hand there. The small rough tongue going over and over the palm of his hand produced the strange sensation he felt. Now that he knew the cause the marvel ended; but now that he knew the cause, his heart was touched ... The gentle scraping continued without intermission as on he walked. What did it say to him? Human tongue could not have said so much just then.

A pale grey light ... displayed the dawn. Richard was walking hurriedly ... was passing one of those little forest-chapels, hung with votive wreaths, where the peasant halts to kneel and pray ... He looked within, and saw the Virgin holding her Child. He moved by ... his strength went out of him, and he shuddered ... He was in other hands ... He felt in his heart the cry of his child, his darling's touch ... And as they led him he had a sense of purification so sweet he shuddered again and again.

When he looked out from his trance on the breathing world, the small birds hopped and chirped; warm fresh sunlight was over all the hills. He was

on the edge of the forest, entering a plain clothed with ripe corn under a spacious morning sky.

Certainly there are signs of weakness, which elsewhere flourish and proliferate; there is a tendency to the merely emphatic adjective – '*imperceptibly* stealing', '*indescribable* thrill'; there is that more obvious form of the same thing, the explicit authorial comment such as 'with the instinct we have', or 'Human tongue could not have said so much just then'; and there is the forcing of conventional grammar as in 'no *cool-lipped sound*', 'He saw the country ... gleam, quiver, *extinguished*'. But these must bow to the rich and suggestive counterpointing of symbols, which gives the piece its significance and imaginative reach. We have the progression of living creatures: the roe seen as victim for a hunter; the night-moths, ephemeral, insubstantial, and restless, fit companions for Richard in the dusk; the humble busy glow-worms, which do not register on his consciousness; and then the leveret which awakens his compassion. We move from ruined towers, crumbling remains of pride, prowess, and strife (Richard throughout thinks of himself as a knight), to the living, tended shrine of humility, submission, and love. The themes come together in the progress from frustrated physical prowess ('*out of* rifle-mark'; the impulse to scale the elusive and illusory mountain), and the 'savage pleasure' in the deluge, through the response to the homely meadow-sweet (contrasted with the nettles and rank grass), to the crucial instinctive flow of feeling towards the leveret and the decisive revelation of Madonna and Child; and they finally combine with the accompanying cycle of deadening heat, storm, and reviving rain, in the freshness, quickened life, and peaceful fruitfulness of the closing paragraph.

Whatever the critical reservations necessary in the final account (and they must be many and grave), Meredith should have his due: except in *Wuthering Heights*, this kind of imaginative technique was new in the English novel – and it has remained rare. It was to poetry that he was most drawn by nature (he returned gladly to writing it whenever he could), and it is plain that a poetic mind is at work in the passage just quoted; the poetic mind which so strongly distrusted anything like the Naturalism or 'documentary' Realism which acquired its formal would-be scientific rationale in Zola's *Le Roman Expérimental* (1880); the mind which insisted on the value of

metaphor, and which saw the novel, once 'having attained its majority', as coming to embody, to express, values – values fostered by 'Truth'. And this 'Truth' would be 'the summary of actual Life, the within and without of us' and not the partial and false 'dirty drab' accounts of 'Realists' or the equally partial and false 'rose-pink' ones of 'Sentimentalists'. 'To such an end let us bend our aim to work, knowing that every form of labour, even this flimsiest, as you esteem it, should minister to growth' (*Diana of the Crossways*, 1885).

But intentions are not results, and a respect for metaphor may become, and with Meredith did become, a weakness for it. And an insistence on the affirmation of significance can, and did, engender an element of personal assertion, often and naturally (in this case) of a lyrical emotional kind; and this not only interrupts the basically dramatic illusion but, more important, either weakens what has been successfully 'objectified' or 'realized', or damagingly diverts the author's energy from the effort to 'realize' – which is the vitalizing principle of the novelist's art. Hence such an effusion of eager fancy and feeling as that when young Richard and Lucy meet to plight their troth:

Away with Systems! Away with a corrupt World! Let us breathe the air of the Enchanted Island.

Golden lie the meadows; golden run the streams ... The sun is coming down to earth, and walks the fields and the waters.

The sun is coming down to earth, and the fields and the waters shout to him golden shouts. He comes, and his heralds run before him, and touch the leaves of oaks and planes and beeches lucid green ...

The flaming West, the crimson heights, shower their glories through voluminous leafage. But these are bowers where deep bliss dwells, imperial joy, that owes no fealty to yonder glories ... Descend, great Radiance! embrace creation with beneficent fire and pass from us! ... For this is the home of the enchantment. Here, secluded from vexed shores, the prince and princess of the island meet:* here like darkling nightingales they sit, and into eyes and ears and hands pour endless ever-fresh treasures of their souls.

Roll on, grinding wheels of the world: cries of ships going down in a calm, groans of a System which will not know its rightful hour of exultation, complain to the Universe! You are not heard here ...

'Lucy! my beloved!'

'O Richard!'

Out in the world there, on the skirts of the woodland, a sheep-boy pipes

* But it is not an island, nor are they prince and princess. This is part of the likening of them to Ferdinand and Miranda in *The Tempest*.

to meditative eve on a penny-whistle. Love's musical instrument is as old, and as poor: it has but two stops, and yet, you see, the cunning musician does thus much with it! . . .

The tide of colour has ebbed from the upper sky. In the West the sea of sunken fire draws back; and the stars leap forth, and tremble, and retire before the advancing moon, who slips the silver train of cloud from her shoulders, and, with her foot upon the pine-tops, surveys heaven.

'Lucy, did you never dream of meeting me?'

'O Richard! yes, for I remembered you.'

'Lucy! and did you pray that we might meet?'

'I did!'

Young as when she looked upon the lovers in Paradise, the fair Immortal journeys onward. Fronting her it is not night but veiled day. Full half the sky is flushed. Not darkness, not day, but the nuptials of the two . . .

A soft beam travels to the fern-covert under the pine-wood where they sit, and for answer he has her eyes . . . through her eyes her soul is naked to him.

'Lucy! my bride! my life!'

The night-jar spins his dark monotony on the branch of the pine. The soft beam travels round them, and listens to their hearts. Their lips are locked! . . .

So Love is silent! Out in the world there, on the skirts of the woodland, the self-satisfied sheepboy delivers a last complacent squint down the length of his penny-whistle, and, with a flourish correspondingly awry, he also marches into silence, hailed by supper!

The sentiment of this scene is so alien to the taste of our own time that it is difficult to accept the chapter with due passivity; and, all effort made, it ends as an instance of great poetic inventiveness in indirect symbolic expression, defeated by the promptness to personal and fanciful lyric rhapsody and overt 'philosophizing'. With much intense and suggestive scenic denotation there is, too, a good deal of mannered, part-archaic, so-called 'poetic' diction and a proportionately disturbing self-congratulatory flourish: the reminders of Carlyle and Keats may perhaps be taken as symptoms. Yet some of the high-flownness seems to be part of the intentional near-ironic, tongue-in-cheek tone which carries the foreboding of disillusionment – and also creates a suspect note of sophisticated nostalgic sentimentality. But the endeavour is a valiant one. What Meredith is seeking is a *narrated*, but 'dramatic', prose equivalent to the 'balcony scene' of *Romeo and Juliet* which will incorporate the wise, amused tolerance of, say, Chaucer to his Squire, and a judicial awareness of the fatally imperious character of Richard. A formidable problem, it should be agreed: and *Feverel* was Meredith's first novel. His originality lies in

his attempt to solve it by creating for the emotional, inarticulate state of mind of the lovers, a symbolic equivalent, an 'objective correlative' (to use T. S. Eliot's phrase[1]), which shall also place them in a scale of values, something of an immediate imaginative tangibility outside the compass of plausible prose dialogue accompanied by normal description.

Feverel has been dwelt on here, not only because it is the best introduction to Meredith, but because, though neither the maturest, the most free-flowing, the most entertaining, nor the least blemished of his works, it carries in it the seed, at least, of most of his moral preoccupations and artistic methods. There are the beginnings of his destructive analysis of egoism and sentimentalism which gains direction through *Sandra Belloni* (1864) and *Rhoda Fleming* (1865), is near to the Feverel-like hero of *Beauchamp's Career* (1876), and in *The Egoist* (1879) pounces on Sir Willoughby Patterne and reaches a clear peak of definition; and which then recurs in Alvan of *The Tragic Comedians* (1880), Ormont of *Lord Ormont and his Aminta* (1894), Victor Radnor of *One of Our Conquerors* (1891), and Lord Fleetwood of *The Amazing Marriage* (1895, but, significantly, begun in 1879) – the latter a figure much resembling Feverel and Beauchamp, and thereby witnessing to the enduring attraction for Meredith of the glamorous, impetuous young aristocrat fired by a 'knightly' honour. (It is a quality of 'heart' that distinguishes these heroes from Sir Willoughby; though one may think the scales over-loaded against him – the limitations of 'honour' in the others are acknowledged, but the glamour persists, and respect for impulsiveness of heart dazzles Meredith's judgement.) Between Bella, emancipated by her disreputability, and Lucy, the simple and pure Victorian idealized image of woman, there is in suspense the demand for an acknowledgement and nurture of the intellectual and social potentialities, the individuality and rights of women, and for the discarding of a 'double standard' of morality – demands pressed forcibly in *The Egoist* and *Diana of the Crossways*, in *Rhoda Fleming* and *One of Our Conquerors*. The educational concern expressed in the notion of the 'System' (apparently precipitated by Herbert Spencer's progressive essay on education of 1858) finds an inverse, positive expression in Lady Jocelyn of *Evan Harrington* (1860), and appears again in *Lord Ormont*.[2] And the basic pattern of the young hero's journey to maturity is the

pattern of most of Meredith's novels until *The Egoist* (1879); starting in the allegorical, *Arabian Nights*-like allegory of *Shagpat* (1855), taking a distinctly personal, almost autobiographical, form in *Evan Harrington* (1860) and (though more in the realms of fantasy) *Harry Richmond* (1871) – with the former of which two it is interesting to compare *Great Expectations* (also a study of snobbery) and (as a realistic 'socially-conscious' study) Kingsley's *Alton Locke*, while *Richmond* calls out for comparison with *David Copperfield*. And the part-Wordsworthian feeling for Nature, the belief in it as a force, not a mere background, is central in his work.

In matters of artistic method, too, *Feverel* clearly adumbrates Meredith's later progress. The effort to open the novel to a poetic, imaginative technique leads to much in *The Egoist* (more like a play in its construction than any other of his works), to its dismissal of customary demands for a detailed setting and for elaboration of incidentals, and to its advanced (though not perfected) use of symbolism – as in the part given to the richly described cherry-tree under which Vernon Whitford is found asleep, and the part played by the shattered porcelain vase (to be associated with the 'porcelain' simile used of the heroine, Clara). One can see the gravitation to symbolism, and part arrival at it, in, say, the following passage, which describes Clara's resolution to escape from her imminent marriage to Willoughby, after a night of anxiety and indecision:

> After a fall of tears ... she dressed herself, and sat by the window and watched the blackbird on the lawn ... She had gone through her crisis in the anticipation of it. That is how quick natures will often be cold and hard ... when the positive crisis arrives, and why it is that they are prepared for astonishing leaps over the gradations which should render their conduct comprehensible to us, if not excuseable. She watched the blackbird throw up his head stiff, and peck to right and left, dangling the worm each side of his orange beak. Speckle-breasted thrushes were at work, and a wagtail that ran as with Clara's own little steps. Thrush and blackbird flew to the nest. They had wings. The lovely morning breathed of sweet earth into her open window and made it painful, in the dense twitter, chirp, cheep, and song of the air, to resist the innocent intoxication. O to love! was not said by her, but if she had sung, as her nature prompted, it would have been ...

The symbolic play of the birds, so palpably rendered (the movement of the prose is vivid in 'throw up his head stiff, and peck to right and left' – as, too, in 'the dense twitter, chirp, cheep, and song of the

air'), incisively tells in relation to Clara's own drama; though the analogy is not free from blurring and there are intermittent characteristic failures to render concretely in the moral essayist's overt remarks about 'quick natures', in the over-direct exclamations, 'They had wings' and 'O to love!', which demanded too much the reader's own provision of vehemence to establish their required enunciation. It is illuminating to compare this scene with those of similar crises in George Eliot's *Middlemarch* and James's *Portrait of a Lady*, both of which are more consistent in handling: James stands out as in full technical and evaluative control; George Eliot, while consistent in her handling, is deficient in analysis and evaluation of feeling; while Meredith shows, though in imperfect form, a distinct insight and power of his own. (It is not beside the point to recall that what George Eliot's Dorothea sees when she, too, looks out of the window, is 'a man with a bundle on his back and a woman carrying her baby ... figures moving – perhaps the shepherd with his dog'; and she self-accusingly feels 'the largeness of the world and the manifold wakings of men to labour and endurance'.)

Further, in *Feverel* we have that interest in motivation and self-knowledge, that concern with the inner consciousness, that leads to the exhaustive explorations of, most signally, *The Egoist* and *One of Our Conquerors*; that concern which is customarily indicated by aligning Meredith with Browning, and whose foundations in a strenuous self-scrutiny may best be seen in the poem of his which has continued most to attract readers, *Modern Love* (1862). (The poem is itself a novelette in sonnet-sequence form; while it has a certain flavour of Browning, it more resembles, in its heavy, direct emotionalism, Tennyson's *Maud*.[3]) Matter of values though this is, in novels it appears most obviously as one of technique of presentation, and though Meredith never took a firm and unremitting grasp of the third-person mode of narrating thought and feeling which Flaubert seems to have been the first fully to excogitate, nonetheless he took it far. Though it was James who perfected this technique, Meredith has a fair claim to have been at least level with him in the advance, even the later James's brilliantly detached use of it in *In the Cage* being preceded by *One of Our Conquerors*, where the 'stream of consciousness' handling of Victor goes far in the somewhat different direction of Virginia Woolf. It is not without import that

Victor's frequent recurrence to an embarrassing and humbling fall in the street should remind one of Proust and his uneven paving-stone. Imperfect (and, for other reasons, very unfortunate) as it is in its result, *One of Our Conquerors* is a work of remarkable originality, and the inventiveness is working for truth and suggestiveness of presentation, for the author's command of his characters, of his own feelings and impulses. 'You must feed on something,' Meredith writes in the prelude to *Diana of the Crossways*; 'Matter that is not nourishing to brains can help to constitute nothing but the bodies which are pitched on rubbish-heaps. Brainstuff is not lean stuff; the brainstuff of fiction is internal history, and to suppose it dull is the profoundest of errors' – a phrase which, for all the truth of its content, shows plainly its author's chronic tendency to a rhetorical vehemence, showy and over-emphatic and not fully embodied in his language (the reader has again personally to devise the stressing for 'you *must* feed on *something*'); and is a fair example of Meredith's accompanying commentaries, of which an anthology could be compiled ample enough to make him appear, not a novelist but an essayist – author, perhaps, of something like Carlyle's *Latter-Day Pamphlets*.

Feverel has as well its share of 'the Comic Spirit' – to Meredith the saving sword of common sense (see the lecture *The Idea of Comedy*, delivered in 1877, and the Prelude to *The Egoist*). Stimulated by Peacock, responsive to the spirit of Fielding, Carlyle, and the German Richter, Meredith abounds in humorous incident and, often witty, portraiture. Here is Adrian Harley, Richard's cousin and tutor:

Adrian was an epicurean; one whom Epicurus would have scourged out of his garden, certainly: an epicurean of our modern notions. To satisfy his appetites without rashly staking his character was the wise youth's problem for life . . . He possessed peculiar attributes of a heathen God. He was a disposer of men: he was polished, luxurious, and happy – at their cost. He lived in eminent self-content, as one lying on soft cloud, lapt in sunshine. Nor Jove, nor Apollo, cast eye upon the maids of earth with cooler fire of selection, or pursued them in the covert with more sacred impunity. And he enjoyed his reputation for virtue as something additional. Stolen fruits are said to be sweet; undeserved rewards are exquisite . . . In a word, Adrian Harley had mastered his philosophy at the early age of one-and-twenty. Many would be glad to say the same at that age twice-fold: they carry in their breasts a burden with which Adrian's was not loaded. Mrs Doria was nearly right about his heart. A singular mishap (at his birth, possibly, or before it) had unseated that organ, and shaken it down to his stomach, where it was a much

lighter, nay, an inspiring weight ... Throned there it looked on little that did not arrive to gratify it.

Somewhat slack in its irony and perhaps over-tinged with enjoyment of Adrian's immoralism (and Adrian strongly brings to mind Oscar Wilde, who greatly admired Meredith); distinctly juvenile in its Dickensian part (Dickens looms large in respect of Richard's friend, Ripton, as in *Evan Harrington* and other novels, but his influence was never to be developed to the peculiar fineness to which the Dickensian heritage was cultivated by James); but not negligible in itself, and as joined with the other elements in *Feverel*, token of the ambitious aim that Meredith never fully achieved – one of combining passionate feeling and a due romantic response to life and Nature with a coolly corrective satiric humour, of amalgamating, one may say, the spirits of Emily Brontë, Charlotte Brontë, and Jane Austen – though the last of these would be less at home with the result than would Fielding or Thackeray. Most of Meredith's novels, incidentally, have tragic or near-tragic endings.

The greatest products of Meredith's feeling for the comic (in the common conception of the term) are, however, the Countess Louisa in *Evan Harrington*, who stands out in a novel whose final values are uncertain (because of the pull on Meredith of the snobbery he criticizes) and which is inconsistent in style and method, and overloaded with mere incident; and Richmond Roy in *Harry Richmond*. Both are created with complete vitality and fluency, sufficient surely, except on an excessively solemn count, to override the fact that the satisfaction they offer is largely one of fantasy – fantasy which, however, does not go uncorrected. These are, in fact, Meredith's two most 'readable' works, and the latter seems to the present writer his one thoroughly clear-running success – admittedly on a level of human exploration much below that towards which he struggled in, for example, *The Egoist* or *One of Our Conquerors*; a great achievement in the fantastic picaresque, written in decisive and clear, 'un-Meredithian' prose, and permeated by alert intelligence.

Where his aims may be considered to be of a more serious order, his achievement is always gravely marred, and not only by a wavering grasp of technique and by difficulty of style (which often merits James's pronouncement with regard to *Lord Ormont*, '... so many of the profundities and tortuosities prove when threshed out

to be only pretentious statements of the very simplest propositions'). but also by an inability (probably increased by serial publication) to avoid proliferation of incident and character (for instance, the tiresome superfluous interposition of Colney Durance, with his rather Arnoldian comments, in *One of Our Conquerors*); and, most important, by a fundamental irreconciliation between his romanticizing and his satiric questioning. *The Egoist*, unquestionably Meredith's nearest approach to a serious success, is most compactly designed as to incident and character, but it misses its full possibilities because of the degree to which Willoughby is deprived of our sympathy; and this is surely because Meredith never brought to terms his admiration for the aristocratic, (in Arnold's word) 'barbarian' virtues and his detestation of egoism. With Victor Radnor, a *nouveau riche*, he is on easier ground, and there the combination of analysis, criticism, and sympathy convinces and satisfies – in a novel which despite its frequent perversity of style (James's comment just quoted is most apt to it), has excellent things to offer – such as the illegitimate Nesta's growing sense of her own and her mother's position and of her father's weakness (ch. 30, read in its context, is a fine thing).

Finally, *Feverel* exhibits an originality and power, a serious concern with enduring issues in life, and a willingness to go deep into reality, that makes it difficult not to blame its unsympathetic contemporary readers, whose general hostility persisted through work after work of remarkable promise and, sporadically, of still enduring power, until *Diana of the Crossways*.

The topicality of many of Meredith's social and political preoccupations has now faded, his command of method is imperfect, his humour often wearisomely facetious and long-winded, and much of his prose is a peering through rippled glass; but he was a novelist of great originality, with important aims, one of insight and honesty, whose full-bloodedness and searching intimacy of feeling makes his work (differences, and important ones, notwithstanding) more akin to that of D. H. Lawrence than is that of any other English novelist.

A novel must indeed 'work' if it is to be a great one; but it is not a machine, and value can exist in one which, strictly, fails. A first-hand understanding and sympathetic appreciation of Meredith's novels seems to the present writer indispensable to any serious novel reader, in spite of E. M. Forster's dismissal of him (in *Aspects of the*

Novel) as a 'suburban roarer'.[4] James, after all, in 1912 wrote to Gosse as follows:

> Still it abides, I think, that Meredith was an admirable spirit even if not an *entire* mind ... The fantastic and the mannered in him were as nothing, I think, to the intimately sane and straight; just as the artist was nothing to the good citizen and the liberalized bourgeois.

Meredith certainly makes his work difficult to read; but it would be grievous to distort Johnson's shrewd observation of fact and warning to writers into a handy pretext for an unwillingness that our contacts with literature should entail exertion.

NOTES

1. For this term and its explanation, see 'Hamlet' in *Selected Essays*, T. S. Eliot (London, 1932), 145.

2. See J. S. Mill's *Autobiography* and Dickens's *Hard Times*, with which *Feverel* must take its place in any study of Victorian educational throes.

3. For further comment on Meredith's poetry, see the essay 'Gerard Manley Hopkins' in this present volume (pp. 381–2).

4. For another, even less approving, view of Meredith, see F. R. Leavis *The Great Tradition* (London, 1948), 23. Leavis in his dismissal of Meredith adduces the critical testimony of E. M. Forster here referred to, and quotes the comment of James on *Lord Ormont*. See, too, Jack Lindsay, *George Meredith* (London, 1956), the only substantial recent attempt to restore Meredith to esteem: an illuminating book and nearer the mark in stressing Meredith's radicalism than has been generally admitted, but marred by its strong ideological bias.

THREE AUTOBIOGRAPHICAL NOVELISTS

R. C. CHURCHILL

We have become so used, in the twentieth century, to the sort of novel which is really a disguised autobiography that we tend to forget how recent is the origin of the species. It can be admitted that the *Pilgrim's Progress* and *Gulliver* are, in their different ways, symbolic of their authors' lives, and that Fielding put part of himself into *Amelia*, as Sterne did into *Tristram Shandy*. But the novel, in general, did not become really personal till the Victorian age, with such productions as *Villette*, *Agnes Grey*, and some of the novels of Dickens and George Eliot; and even here there remained a considerable distance between the person who suffered and the mind which created. It was only in the later Victorian age that we find novels deliberately written as part of an attempt by their creators to understand their own lives, as criticism of life that was also self-criticism. It is interesting from this point of view to consider three novelists who are not among the greatest but who are of permanent and not simply historical significance: Mark Rutherford, George Gissing, Samuel Butler – three writers who are also connected with each other by reason of their isolation from the main tendencies of their age.*

William Hale White, the author of *The Autobiography of Mark Rutherford* (1881) and *Mark Rutherford's Deliverance* (1885), once spoke to Holyoake of his *alter ego* as 'a victim of the century'. It is true, that there were certain discrepancies between the actual life of Hale White and the autobiographies and novels supposedly written 'by Mark Rutherford, edited by his friend, Reuben Shapcott'. (This double concealment of identity is paralleled by Samuel Butler when he published *The Fair Haven* by 'the late John Pickard Owen, edited

---

* They were not exact contemporaries: Rutherford (1831–1913) wrote his main work in the eighties; Gissing (1857–1903) belongs mostly to the eighties and nineties; Butler (1835–1902) wrote from the seventies onwards, but his chief work – his only real novel – was not published till after his death.

with a memoir of the author by W. B. Owen'.) Shapcott dwells on the defects and limitations of his friend, on his morbidity of mind, on the painful gulf between his dreams and his capacities: 'In sleep a King, but waking no such matter.' Yet White was actually quite a successful Civil Servant at the Admiralty – rising in 1879 to become Assistant Director of Naval Contracts – besides being a valued contributor to the London and provincial Press. He wrote one of the best studies of Bunyan we have; edited Spinoza and Johnson's *Rambler*; was associated with Chapman and George Eliot in their publishing business, and turned down Chapman's offer of a partnership;[1] he wrote one of the ablest pamphlets in the movement for universal manhood suffrage: *An Argument for an Extension of the Franchise: A Letter Addressed to George Jacob Holyoake, Esquire*; and he was a competent amateur astronomer, once reading a paper before the British Astronomical Association on 'The Wilsonian Theory of Sun-spots'. We are bound to be reminded of the discrepancies between the lives of Samuel Butler and Ernest Pontifex, and between Gissing and his characters, for the legend is not quite true that Gissing 'seemed born to encounter mischances in life, and it is fitting that he became the chronicler in fiction of lives in which success had no part'.[2]

The resemblance, Irvin Stock persuades us, was inner; White's criticism of Rutherford was really self-criticism:

and, as often when a writer's self-criticism goes deep, Rutherford's limitations, failures, and suffering are at least not those of other people but of humanity ... That gulf between his dreams and his capacities – who has not known this? The man who is not aware of any Mark Rutherford inside himself, but who takes literally, so to speak, his own Assistant Directorship of Naval Contracts, is perhaps to be envied, but more for his happy temperament than for his wisdom.[3]

We still have the distance, necessary for art, between the man who suffers and the mind which creates, but combined here, as I believe it is also combined in Gissing and Butler, with a searching criticism of the novelist's life and environment. The criticism of the environment is now mainly of historical interest, but the criticism of 'life' is of permanent importance. It was not for nothing that Rutherford was first led to question the Nonconformist orthodoxy of his boyhood, not by a study of Strauss, but by a reading of the *Lyrical Ballads*, which

he likens, in its effect upon him, to the revelation which St Paul received on the road to Damascus. For 'the God of the Church', he tells us in the *Autobiography*, was substituted a 'God of the hills . . . in which literally I could live and move and have my being'. He was later to learn from Spinoza that the study of Nature is the study of God.

There is a striking difference between the current estimate of Rutherford, as being interesting only as a lonely figure on the path from Victorian Dissent to Victorian Agnosticism, as the hero of a kind of Pilgrim's Regress, and the high opinions paid to him by his successors in fiction. Rutherford has a claim to be regarded as the Novelists' Novelist. The view of D. H. Lawrence is well known: 'I *do* think he is jolly good – so thorough, so sound and so beautiful.' Arnold Bennett thought *The Revolution in Tanner's Lane* 'the finest example of modern English prose'; and André Gide wrote in his *Journals*: 'I find in *Catherine Furze* the so specifically Protestant qualities and virtues which awakened such profound echoes in me, when, for the first time, I read his two little volumes: *Autobiography* and *Deliverance*. Here honesty and integrity become poetic virtues.' Stock quotes other examples of enthusiasm from Conrad and Stephen Crane – and also from the finest critic of the Victorian age, Matthew Arnold, who told a friend never to miss anything that Rutherford wrote.

No one would claim that Rutherford is an immediately attractive writer; he is far less entertaining, for example, than E. M. Forster, who is perhaps his nearest recent parallel in style. But there is much to be said on the other side. As every sen itive reader must feel, the *Autobiography* and the *Deliverance* are not only Rutherford's story but our own – and this is true also of the effect of *Catherine Furze*, *Miriam's Schooling*, and *Clara Hopgood*, those three little novels on much the same theme which Rutherford wrote in the nineties. The 'deliverance' proposed is not such as would be acceptable to a convinced Christian, because Rutherford maintained only those parts of the Christian spirit which he considered to be capable of a life outside the orthodox forms. (Compare Butler in *The Way of All Flesh*: 'The spirit behind the Church is true, though her letter – true once – is now true no longer.') He wrote in his study of Bunyan: 'Religion is dead when the imagination deserts it. When it is alive abstractions

become visible and walk about on the roads.' He undoubtedly thought the Dissent of his own day to be lacking in the imagination which had produced the Puritan – and, by extension, the Radical – heroes of the past; that is the theme, not only of the autobiographical novels, but of *The Revolution in Tanner's Lane* (1887), probably the best of the novels proper. And yet I first read all three of these books at the earnest recommendation of a convinced and life-long Methodist. There is some quality in Mark Rutherford which appeals, not only to those who agree with him but to those who disagree, and even to those who reject both the orthodoxy of his youth and the painful deliverance of his maturity.

One of the pains suffered by Rutherford, and recorded in the *Deliverance*, concerns the weekly columns of parliamentary debates he is forced to write for provincial papers in order to eke out his meagre official income. Like Dickens, he finds the House of Commons at close quarters a disillusioning experience; but that is not the worst thing about this hateful task. His editors keep on demanding a kind of 'graphic and personal' writing, which upsets his literary conscience and which he feels to be degrading. In a few chapters of the *Deliverance*, in fact, we are in the literary world of George Gissing.

This, in common estimation, is rather a grim little world, almost the prose parallel to Thomson's *City of Dreadful Night*. But it is only possible to take such novels as *The Unclassed* or *Born in Exile* as 'typical Gissing' if we have previously made up our minds what 'typical Gissing' is. His best work – including *Isabel Clarendon* (1886), *A Life's Morning* (1888), *New Grub Street* (1892), and *The Town Traveller* (1898) – shows a power of ironic detachment that is wrongly regarded as uncharacteristic. Q. D. Leavis thought *New Grub Street* by far the best of Gissing, and if it had retained its popularity, the legend of a permanently gloomy Gissing would not have been able to gain so much ground.

With the exception of *The Private Papers of Henry Ryecroft* (1903), *New Grub Street* is the most autobiographical of Gissing's writings, and it is autobiography with a similar underlying purpose to that of Rutherford's. Like Rutherford's, it has a double interest for us today – it can be considered both historically and as a human document of perennial interest. The central character, in relation to whom

we see all the other characters, is the novelist Edwin Reardon. A self-portrait of the author we may say. Yes, and drawn warts and all. 'It would be ridiculous,' said the novelist's intimate friend Morley Roberts, 'to cover up the truth that in Edwin Reardon's portrait Gissing drew himself, not without self-pity and yet as an artist pitilessly.'[4] The same could be said of Rutherford in regard to the *Autobiography*, and there is a sense in which it is also true of that very different creation, Butler's *Way of All Flesh*.

But the scholarly novelist Reardon could no more have written *New Grub Street* than the ex-minister Mark Rutherford the *Autobiography*. There was surely far more sheer journalistic ability in both Gissing and White than they could ever bring themselves to recognize. It has been said that the tragedy of Gissing was that he tried to maintain the standards of Dr Johnson in an age when the *Daily Mail* was just around the corner. Being a 'classic' in the early Harmsworth era was, admittedly, very different from being one in a period when Greek and Latin had been thrashed into the background, as it were, of a considerable proportion of the public. But the reader of Boswell knows that, in his early life, Johnson turned his hand to anything in the journalistic line he could possibly make an honest penny by, and the 'higher journalism' that began in the eighteenth century was by no means dead in Gissing's time, though he could observe the writing on the wall. There were, in fact, more journals in Gissing's time than in Johnson's to which an intelligent man could contribute, and we know from his letters how well he could have fitted in with their point of view, which was, on most fundamental matters, his own.

Reardon, the scholar, is nicely balanced against 'Jasper of the facile pen'. Though cynical and self-seeking, Jasper is not a character to be altogether condemned, nor does Gissing so condemn him. The strong points of his nature are as well brought out as the weak ones of Reardon's. And he is sometimes made the vehicle for the author's literary comment. When he says, 'It's the easiest thing in the world to write laudation; only an inexperienced grumbler would declare it was easier to find fault', we are reminded of those book reviews which are almost indistinguishable in their literary expression – 'He has a cool, crisp style ...' – from advertisements for corn flakes.

As a kind of subordinate theme to the main contrast of Jasper

Milvain with Reardon, there is the contrast between Whelpdale and Biffen. Whelpdale, a superb Dickensian character – it is not true that Gissing was simply an admirer of Dickens who never tried his hand at the master's effects[5] – becomes an Adviser to Literary Aspirants, after much literary failure on his own account. 'A man who can't get anyone to publish his own books,' cries Milvain, 'makes a living by telling other people how to write!' Whelpdale has, however, another string to his bow; he makes an astonishing success by altering the title of the magazine *Chat* to *Chit-Chat* and having no article in it more than two inches in length: 'And every inch must be broken into at least two paragraphs.' It will be recalled that *Tit-Bits* started its long career in 1881.

Biffen labours like a lesser Flaubert at his novel *Mr Bailey, Grocer*:

'The decently ignoble – as I've so often said . . . I shall do it slowly, lovingly. One volume, of course; the length of the ordinary French novel. There's something fine in the title, don't you think? *Mr Bailey, Grocer!*'

In a cheerful moment Reardon asks him a riddle: 'Why is a London lodging-house like the human body?' The answer is: 'Because the brains are always at the top.' The joke will pass, as Biffen admits, but it is 'distinctly professional, though. The general public would fail to see the point.' *New Grub Street* as a whole is perhaps too 'professional' a novel ever to attain the widest popularity.

Half-starved geniuses in attics are, of course, the real connecting-link between Gissing's New Grub Street and the original Grub Street of the *Dunciad*, the *Epistle to Arbuthnot*, and the early Dr Johnson. There is another link of the same kind: 'Attic' in the sense of Athenian or Greek. Reardon and Biffen, 'the Attic Survivors', are the last relics of the literary genius of legend, who cannot make a decent livelihood by his pen, but can talk about the classics for hours and cap a quotation from the Greek over his bread and dripping. It is worth noticing that Gissing, whose sympathies are so obviously with Reardon and Biffen, can make Whelpdale, whose writings are trash, a man of great generosity and delicate feeling; at the close of the novel he marries Milvain's sister Dora, who does not share her brother's cynical outlook on life.

We should be grateful for Gissing's stubbornness, for his refusal to have anything to do with journalism, even in its higher forms.

For without the personal 'Attic' experience, we should not have had either the convincing quality of this novel or its classic detachment. Though some chapters must have been written in bitter remembrance, the novel as a whole gives the impression of masterly ironic power, of a field of experience covered in a satisfying work of art. One of the favourite themes of Henry James is the literary life and the changes in public taste; but not even James – in *The Lesson of the Master* and similar stories – has written more convincingly of the subject than Gissing in *New Grub Street*. But it was rather against his own theories of literature that this novel, probably his masterpiece from the artistic point of view, should also have been the first of his work 'to receive anything like popular recognition'.

There is a domestic tragedy in *New Grub Street* which the hero Reardon sees as inevitably bound up with his own literary tragedy. Forgetting Blake and many others, he comes to the despairing conclusion that a writer who lives in poverty has no right to get married. Samuel Butler would have extended the prohibition to all writers, and indeed to mankind in general if the race could be reproduced – as he thought it might – without the institution of the family. He began *The Way of All Flesh* about 1872, only ten years after Charles Reade, smiling through his tears, had ended *Hard Cash* with the hero married safely to the heroine and settling down in the same house as his parents-in-law:

> They all lived together at Albion Villa, thanks to Alfred ... Oh, you happy little villa! You were as like Paradise as any mortal dwelling can be ...

'As like Hell', Butler would have said. Ernest Pontifex reflects the mood of his creator when he exclaims to himself:

> 'There are orphanages for children who have lost their parents – oh! why, why, why are there no harbours of refuge for grown men who have not yet lost them?' And he brooded over the bliss of Melchisedech who had been born an orphan, without father, without mother, and without descent. (ch. 67)

Ernest, like Butler himself, eventually attains that haven of refuge. It is a happy ending somewhat at variance with the stock 'happy ending' of Victorian fiction, as seen, for example, in *Hard Cash* and *Nicholas Nickleby*;[6] something more after this style:

> He lived alone with his cat in his chambers in the Temple, thanks to himself and despite his parents ... Oh, you happy little bachelor chambers! You were as like Elysium as any modern dwelling could be ...

The question immediately confronts us: who was right? Granted Butler had an original mind, but was his picture of the Victorian family truer to the facts than the pictures drawn by Charles Reade and Dickens and Charlotte Yonge and *Sunday At Home*? We are sufficiently distant from the Victorian age, I believe, to understand that there was something to be said for both views. Published memoirs of the more prosperous Victorian families convince us that family life in those days was often extremely happy; and it was not less happy for being conventional; for, by a stroke of irony that might have made Butler smile on the other side of his face, Mark Rutherford's daughter has revealed how deprived and lonely she used to feel as she watched neighbouring children go off to Sunday-school.[7] Memories of one's own parents and grandparents, the usual allowances being made for distance having lent enchantment to the view, add a like conviction in regard to more ordinary folk; while even at the lowest end of the social scale, where misery might have been supposed capable of snapping the thread of family affection, we find Henry Mayhew recording impressions of family loyalty in the meanest of streets: 'She's been very good to us, has mother, and so's father'; 'No mother couldn't love a child more than mine did me' – such phrases recur throughout Mayhew's volumes.[8]

Was Butler, then, simply a cantankerous haunter of the British Museum Reading Room, a man who mistakenly supposed that his own personal crotchets were the common experience of everyone else? That was possibly one side of him, but it is not the most important. He disliked Dickens's novels,[9] not only because he was in the habit of disliking everything he considered merely conventionally esteemed, but because in them he must have seen his enemy, the Victorian Family, held most genuinely up to applause. He forgot, perhaps, that there are a fair number of Dickensian parents who are not very satisfactory as human beings: Mr Podsnap, Mrs Nickleby, Mr Dorrit, Mr Turveydrop, Mrs Jellyby spring to mind – to say nothing of Mr Murdstone, the steepest of stepfathers, whose canings are remarkably like those of Theobald in *The Way of All Flesh*. But this does not answer our question. Was Butler seriously wrong?

He was completely wrong, I believe, only in the sense that a man who mistakes the part for the whole can be said to be completely

wrong. And, of course, in this sense, Charles Reade and Dickens in their more fatuous moments were as completely wrong as Butler. Everything was not as happy in the Victorian family garden as it was commonly made out to be, and it was in being the first to point this out that Butler displayed both his originality and his courage. The book was not, of course, published in his lifetime; nor, incidentally, in the lifetime of the Queen. But that was because he was not the hard-hearted wretch his detractors have imagined; he wished to postpone the book's publication till all his relations were dead, and in fact only his two sisters were still alive when the novel was published by his literary executor in 1903.

It is, of course, an autobiographical novel; we might almost say *the* autobiographical novel. No novelist before Butler had ever been so studiously autobiographical as to use actual family letters in his fiction. And yet it is, after all, a work of art, like *New Grub Street* and the *Autobiography* and *Deliverance*, though in *The Way of All Flesh* there are two Butlers, whereas Gissing and White made do with one *alter ego* each.

The young Butler is represented, often in accurate detail, by the young Ernest Pontifex; their lives continue roughly parallel with each other till the Cambridge period, when they drift asunder. All after that in the novel (about chapter 50 or 51 to the end) is entirely imaginary, save that Ernest becomes in the closing chapters something like Butler himself, but by a path of suffering that the novelist himself did not have to tread. So we have in the end two Butlers, for the whole story is told by an imaginary friend of the family, Edward Overton, who is simply Butler without Butler's genius. It is Ernest who loves Handel to idolatry, as Butler did; it is Ernest whom we are to believe capable of writing Butler's books – his *Erewhon*, his *Life and Habit*, his *Fair Haven*, his *Evolution Old and New*. Overton is just the kindly narrator who has a sufficient income and no other encumbrances. His own writings are mostly of the burlesque kind; whereas Ernest, like Butler himself, is fundamentally a serious-minded person.

All the criticism in the novel is not directed against the parents, though they are the main figures in a comedy of Victorian manners whose originality has hardly been affected by the many imitations it gave rise to. There are few comic episodes in Victorian fiction

equal to the courtship of Theobald and Christina; I have always been particularly fond of this piece of dialogue from chapter 12:

'We, dearest Theobald,' she exclaimed, 'will be ever faithful. We will stand firm and support one another even in the hour of death itself. God in His mercy may spare us from being burned alive. He may or may not do so. O Lord' (and she turned her eyes prayerfully to Heaven), 'spare my Theobald, or grant that he may be beheaded.'

'My dearest,' said Theobald gravely, 'do not let us agitate ourselves unduly. If the hour of trial comes we shall be best prepared to meet it by having led a quiet, unobtrusive life of self-denial and devotion to God's glory. *Such a life let us pray God that it may please Him to enable us to pray that we may lead.*'

Nine-tenths of that dialogue could perhaps have been written by any Victorian novelist of similar comic powers, but the last sentence, which I have italicized, could only have been written by Butler. It has the peculiar stamp of his genius upon it. No Victorian before him had so seen the comic possibilities of clerical speech, though it is surprising that he should have disliked the novels of the creator of Mr Chadband.

Criticism, however, as I say, is not all directed at the parents of Ernest, nor at Ernest's headmaster, Dr Skinner; some of it is unmistakably directed at Ernest himself – that is to say, it is fundamentally self-criticism. We have an impression at the end, and it is surely not accidental, that Theobald and Skinner have shrunk from monsters of the deep into amiable old fellows, somewhat conceited and overbearing, but harmless enough. And the criticism implicit in the transformation is that the abnormally sensitive Ernest made heavier weather of them both than he need have done. Butler in real life was probably a child of equal sensibility; we know he was early devoted to music and painting, in both of which he became a distinguished amateur.[10] But he toughened more quickly than his *alter ego* and, instead of going through Ernest's tragi-comedy as a clergyman, gave up his vocation in 1859 and went to New Zealand to learn sheep-farming. The moral of the book is not only for the Theobalds and the Skinners but for the Ernests, too.

There is a general self-criticism in the last few paragraphs, where Overton is discussing Ernest's literary position with his publisher; both Gissing and Hale White would have smiled in sympathy:

'He is in a very solitary position, Mr Overton,' continued the publisher. 'He has formed no alliances, and has made enemies not only of the religious world but of the literary and scientific brotherhood as well. This will not do nowadays. If a man wishes to get on he must belong to a set, and Mr Pontifex belongs to no set – not even to a club.'

I replied, 'Mr Pontifex is the exact likeness of Othello, but with a difference – he hates not wisely but too well . . .'

Butler himself hated too well: it is the burden of most of the complaints made about him since his death, but it has not been noticed that he made the criticism first. He was a natural enthusiast, and thought he was doing the subjects of his enthusiasm a service by disparaging what he conceived to be their opposites. Thus his enthusiasm for Handel caused him to disparage unduly other composers generally considered equally great; and he was aware of his peculiarity in this matter, though he could have found someone more worthy than Miss Skinner to support Bach and Beethoven:

'And are you still as fond of music as ever, Mr Pontifex?' said Miss Skinner to Ernest . . .

'Of some kinds of music, yes, Miss Skinner, but you know I never did like modern music.'

'Isn't that rather dreadful? – Don't you think you rather –' she was going to have added, 'ought to?' but she left it unsaid, feeling doubtless that she had sufficiently conveyed her meaning.

'I would like modern music, if I could; I have been trying all my life to like it, but I succeed less and less the older I grow.'

'And pray, where do you consider modern music to begin?'

'With Sebastian Bach.'

'And don't you like Beethoven?'

'No; I used to think I did, when I was younger, but I know now that I never really liked him.'

His hatred of convention caused him to disparage writers whom he supposed to be admired for conventional reasons only; his admiration for Lamarck may have led him to criticize Darwin. He knew his weakness, though it was sometimes rather a self-satisfied knowledge; but he continued to indulge in it. As he might have said himself: *blessed are they who do not know their weakness but continue to indulge in it.*

NOTES

1. In the *Autobiography*, Mary Ann Evans, the future George Eliot, appears as the character Theresa (with reference to *Middlemarch*?); Rutherford falls in love with her, and in real life White once remarked to his wife of George Eliot: 'I could worship that woman.' In *Confessions of a Self-Tormentor* he says that he can never forgive the shyness that prevented him from keeping up their friendship.

2. George Sampson, *Concise Cambridge History of English Literature*, 810.

3. Stock, *William Hale White* (London, 1956), 91. The quotation shows the strength of this excellent study. Its weakness lies in the author's over-estimation of his subject – a pleasant weakness, for Mark Rutherford has commonly been under-estimated.

4. Roberts later wrote a thinly disguised biography of Gissing under the title of *The Private Papers of Henry Maitland*.

5. He wrote the first full-length criticism of Dickens: *Charles Dickens: A Critical Study* (London, 1898). See also *The Immortal Dickens* (London, 1925), a collection of his introductions to the unfinished Rochester edition.

6. For the Victorian 'happy ending', see George Orwell, 'Charles Dickens', *Critical Essays*, 41–3.

7. Stock, 63–4.

8. Henry Mayhew, *London Labour and the London Poor* (London, 1851), originally articles in the *London Chronicle*. See *The Street Trader's Lot: London 1851*, ed. Stanley Rubinstein, with introduction by Dr Dorothy George (London, 1948).

9. He refers to Ernest's reading of Kingsley's *Alton Locke*, which 'he had devoured as he had devoured Stanley's *Life of Arnold*, Dickens's novels, and whatever other literary garbage of the day was most likely to do him harm ...' (*Way of All Flesh*, ch. 53). The period is the late fifties, just after Ernest had become ordained, so the 'literary garbage' of Dickens referred to is probably mainly the novels of the fifties: that is, *Bleak House*, *Hard Times*, *Little Dorrit*, and *A Tale of Two Cities*.

10. He was occasionally hung at the Royal Academy. There is no doubt, though, that his views on art, as on music, were unacademic. He evidently speaks in Overton Senior when he replies to his son's disparagement of old John Pontifex. Overton had asked 'could he to save his life have got a picture into the Royal Academy Exhibition?' and the father replies unanswerably in the spirit of Blake: 'Could Giotto or Filippo Lippi, think you, have got a picture into the Exhibition?' (*Way of All Flesh*, ch. 1).

PRE-RAPHAELITE POETRY

W. W. ROBSON

The poets of the Victorian age were numerous, and they included some people of talent and even of genius. But the greatest imaginative writers of the period are novelists, not poets. The reasons for this decline of poetry are disputable, but the fact of the decline itself can hardly be questioned. For Victorian poetry, though it often reaches a high degree of sophistication and shows a conscious care for style and form, does not satisfactorily embody the life of the age; it is not at its best when it tries to put to poetic use a wide range of the emotional, intellectual, and moral interests of an intelligent adult. It is usually more successful when it either ignores these or transposes them, by more or less subtle means, into some mode of evasion. And this is true even of the poets who dutifully attempt to grapple with the world they lived in; who offer thought, or a moral burden for the times; since their success as poets, when they are truly poets, is significantly *like* the achievement of their avowedly un-didactic successors: in creating a dream world; in withdrawing to memories of childhood over which a glamour of ideality is thrown; or in making incantation, decoration, emotional overtones, and other incidental beauties of style, serve as beguiling substitutes for the centrality of themes, and completeness of command of them, characteristic of great poetry. This comes out clearly when we consider the nature of the contrast between the good and the bad things in Tennyson's work. But it can also be said of Matthew Arnold's: which is a striking tribute to the strength of 'tradition' in limiting 'the original talent' not robust enough to oppose it. Browning's case is rather different; but even he cannot be considered a triumphant exception.

Perhaps Arnold had this contemporary situation in mind when he made his celebrated formulation: 'Poetry is at bottom a *criticism of life*.' Certainly he was the opponent, in his critical propaganda, of a trend which he discerned in the work of the great Romantic

poets: a separation between 'poetry' and 'life'. It is these poets whose joint influence constitutes the Victorian poetic tradition. And the influence of none of them – not even Wordsworth's – was such as to counteract the trends which Arnold saw. One of them, indeed, was a chief inspiration and sanction to poets in the phase of Victorian Romanticism succeeding that of Tennyson and Ruskin; the original high priest of their Religion of Beauty was John Keats.

The Religion of Beauty is today somewhat unpopular. The work of the Pre-Raphaelites (like that of their successors in the Aesthetic Movement) is now generally judged to be not only inferior to, but in some ways deeply unlike that of Keats. Pre-Raphaelite poetry is seen to bear a derivative and subordinate relation to that of the great Romantics, and even to the contemporary poetry of Tennyson and Browning. Its relation to Tennyson I shall discuss presently; I shall merely note here that the influence of Browning on Rossetti (as in *Jenny*) has not often been emphasized; and, correlatively, there is a 'Pre-Raphaelite' element in Browning:

> Only, they see not God, I know,
> Nor all that chivalry of his,
> The soldier-saints who, row on row,
> Burn upwards each to his point of bliss.
> (*The Statue and the Bust*)

And so it is relevant to mention here a related symptom of this change of taste: the enlistment of Gerard Manley Hopkins as a 'modern' poet, alongside T. S. Eliot and the later Yeats; and the consequent exalting of him above Tennyson and Browning, the official great poets of the Victorian period. Hopkins himself remains unmistakably a Victorian – as those who read him as a living poet are the first to acknowledge; but his art, the way in which he uses the resources of the English language, has been aptly characterized (by F. R. Leavis) as 'un-Tennysonian'. Pre-Raphaelite poetry, on the other hand, though not exactly like Tennyson's, contains far less that is likely, either by its matter or its manner, to disturb the admirer of Tennyson. And so it has suffered the neglect which has befallen other Victorian poetry of which the same could be said. My purpose here is not to suggest reasons for reversing this implicit verdict; nor to discuss whether other poets – notably Hopkins, but perhaps also Beddoes, Darley, or John Davidson – have better claims to be regarded as

the true heirs of the great Romantics. I wish rather to consider what kind of interest Pre-Raphaelite poetry can be made to yield to the reader who shares, substantially, Arnold's view of the right relation between 'poetry' and 'life'.

By 'Pre-Raphaelite poetry' I mean the poetry of Dante Gabriel Rossetti (1828–82), of his sister Christina (1830–94), and of William Morris (1834–96) – though other poets, from Swinburne to Yeats, have Pre-Raphaelite connections. D. G. Rossetti, the strongest personality and effective organizer of the group, deserves the chief critical attention. But he has hardly received it: his picturesque life and habit of confession have proved a biographical lure too strong for most critics. What is now known as the 'cult of personality' existed among the Pre-Raphaelites themselves and their followers; and the flood of autobiography, memoirs, and letters has not yet subsided. I am not of course saying that Rossetti's private life is irrelevant to the study of his poetry; any more, or any less, than the relation between devoutness and morbidity in Christina Rossetti, or the activity of Morris as designer, printer, or propagandist of Socialism, is irrelevant to the study of theirs. These things have their importance even for the literary critic: but they must be recalled in their due place, as ancillaries, not as substitutes, for the study of poetry, which is the study of what poets do with words.

But at this point an obvious objection must be met. Is it proper, or useful, to discuss Pre-Raphaelite poetry without discussing Pre-Raphaelite theory and practice in painting? The term 'Pre-Raphaelite' itself, as is well known, came to be used when the young Holman Hunt and the young J. E. Millais adversely criticized Raphael's *Transfiguration*, challenged the 'classical' doctrines expounded by Sir Joshua Reynolds, and extolled the superior purity and simplicity of the Italian primitives. And the movement began, at the close of the 1840s, as an attempt to introduce into visual art, not only the qualities of medieval Italian painting, but the naturalistic accuracy of detail thought appropriate to the dawning age of science. But by the 1850s what is now associated with Pre-Raphaelite painting – the merely decorative neo-medievalism, the subjectivity, the dreaminess – had become its dominant style. Painters were turning their eyes away from a contemporary industrial and urban world which was *ipso facto* hideous and hence, on Ruskinian principles, intractable to treatment

in art. In any case, Rossetti himself – who is the literary critic's first concern – seems to have had no very intense interest in the philosophical basis of the early naturalism of Hunt and Millais. (The general lack of wide intellectual interests in the circle of Rossetti and Morris comes out clearly in contemporary accounts.) And that dogmatic concern with precision of detail, which excited the admiration of Ruskin and the scorn of Dickens, appears in Rossetti – the Rossetti of *Ecce Ancilla Domini* – only as a transient phase of style. He was always essentially a 'literary' painter, and the Pre-Raphaelite Brotherhood was fundamentally literary and preoccupied with literature. A literary approach, therefore, seems to be quite in order.

The adjective 'Pre-Raphaelite' in *literary* criticism suggests certain idiosyncrasies of style – sometimes they are hardly more than tricks – associated with the Rossettis and the early Morris. Yet many of them are to be seen in earlier poetry: in Tennyson's *Mariana* poems; in Coleridge's *Christabel* (which might be called the first Pre-Raphaelite poem); or in Keats's *The Eve of St Mark*. There is the deliberate simplicity (or *simplesse*) of manner, often found in conjunction with that curious trick of particularizing, e.g. numbers:

> She had three lilies in her hand,
> And the stars in her hair were seven.
> (Rossetti, *The Blessed Damozel*)

> There were five swans that ne'er did eat
>   The water-weeds, for ladies came
>   Each day, and young knights did the same,
> And gave them cakes and bread for meat.
> (Morris, *Golden Wings*)

There is the particularity of sensory detail, of which again the thematic relevance is not obvious; visual detail, as here:

> Without, there was a cold moon up,
>   Of winter radiance sheer and thin;
>   The hollow halo it was in
> Was like an icy crystal cup.
> (Rossetti, *My Sister's Sleep*)

Or auditory detail:

> Twelve struck. That sound, by dwindling years
>   Heard in each hour, crept off, and then
>   The ruffled silence spread again,

Like water that a pebble stirs.
Our mother rose from where she sat;
  Her needles, as she laid them down,
  Met lightly, and her silken gown
Settled: no other noise than that.
                    (*My Sister's Sleep*)

There is the archaizing and medievalizing, the cultivation of the ballad-mode and similar archaic forms, accompanied (especially in Morris) by a liking for archaic technical vocabulary:

'They hammer'd out my basnet point
  Into a round salade,' he said.
'The basnet being quite out of joint
  Natheless the salade rasps my head.'
                    (Morris, *Old Love*)

There is a characteristic Pre-Raphaelite taste in decoration, as in:

Raise me a dais of silk and down;
  Hang it with vair and purple dyes;
Carve it in doves and pomegranates,
  And peacocks with a hundred eyes;
Work it in gold and silver grapes,
  In leaves and silver fleur-de lys;
                    (Christina Rossetti, *A Birthday*)

But these are superficial traits of style. More important for the critic is the recurrence of certain habits of feeling; especially a mood associated with autumn, regarded as the season of listlessness, decay, desolation, death; never, in Pre-Raphaelite poetry, the 'close bosom-friend of the maturing sun', but Tennyson's 'spirit' that 'haunts the year's last hours, Dwelling amid these yellowing bowers'; as in

          ... the sere
Autumnal springs, from many a dying year
Born dead;
                    (Rossetti, *The Stream's Secret*)

          ... the year grown old
A-dying mid the autumn-scented haze,
That hangeth o'er the hollow in the wold,
Where the wind-bitten ancient elms enfold
Grey church, long barn, orchard, and red-roofed stead,
Wrought in dead days for men a long while dead.
                    (Morris, *The Earthly Paradise: October*)

> [Life's] very bud hangs cankered on the stalk,
>> Its very song-bird trails a broken wing,
>> Its very Spring is not indeed like Spring,
> But sighs like Autumn round an aimless walk.
>> (Christina Rossetti, *Later Life*)

Finally, there is the habit suggested by such passages as these:

> O thou who at Love's hour ecstatically
> Unto my lips dost evermore present
> The body and blood of Love in sacrament;
> Whom I have neared and felt thy breath to be
> The inmost incense of his sanctuary;
>> (Rossetti, *Love's Redemption*)

> This feast-day of the sun, his altar there
>> In the broad west has blazed for vesper-song;
>> And I have loitered in the vale too long
> And gaze now a belated worshipper.
>> (Rossetti, *The Hill Summit*)

This is religiosity: the use of religious language for evocative purposes, by a man to whom real religion means nothing. But with this example we have left the Pre-Raphaelite group as a whole and become aware of the need to make distinctions; religiosity is not a characteristic of Morris's poetry: formal religion meant little to him, and he was not tempted to exploit its language in this way; neither was Christina Rossetti – though for an opposite reason. But it is significant that the last two passages quoted from Rossetti could be endlessly paralleled in other Victorian poetry.

One feature all these examples have in common with each other, and with mid-Victorian poetry in general: their obvious literariness. In Rossetti especially, whether in his simple or his elaborate manner, one is conscious all the time of the artifice, the sophistication, of a poet using a diction and movement which he well knows to have been used before by other poets. There is little that is fresh, spontaneous, un-literary, immediate. The contrast with another poet-painter, William Blake, is illuminating. In reading Blake's successful poems (*O Rose, thou art sick*, for example) we do not merely hear words, we 'see' things, and our 'seeing' is not confined to mere visualization ('In my mind's eye, Horatio'); since Blake's own 'seeing' is an activity of the intelligence, manifesting itself in an almost clair-

voyant power of notation of mental and spiritual realities. In a Rossetti sonnet – to show the contrast with Blake at its most extreme – our response is predominantly a response to *words*, words heavily charged with literary association and reminiscence; there is nothing that is strong in imagery or concrete in evocation:

> So it happeneth
> When Work or Will awake too late, to gaze
> After their life sailed by, and hold their breath.
> Ah! who shall dare to search through what sad maze
> Thenceforth their incommunicable ways
> Follow the desultory feet of Death?
>
> (*Known in Vain*)

We have only to ponder the metaphorical value of 'sailed' or 'maze' here, or the literal meaning of 'incommunicable', to see how small a part they play in the total effect. The words seem to be 'saying' a great deal, but to be 'doing' very little; and when we look up the passage in its context, the impressiveness of this 'saying' seems to be the *raison d'être* of the whole poem.

A care for finish of style and polish of phrasing takes the place of a scrupulous effort at definition of meaning. And when we admire the phrasing and music of

> Thenceforth their incommunicable ways
> Follow the desultory feet of Death?

and try to characterize more exactly the spirit of Rossetti's manipulation of the language, it is tempting to recall his Italian origin. But this use of English is an important part of English poetic history from Spenser and Milton to Keats and Tennyson. And the reservation we have about this use of language is not only that it leaves out, or does not employ creatively, so much that is centrally characteristic of English, the language of Shakespeare: its concrete expressiveness and mimetic vigour, its colloquial force, and the much richer music that arises from the playing-off of its speaking rhythm against the patterns of formal metre. It is not merely that the 'Italianate' use of English deprives it of the typically English energy of the verbs. The great limitation of the 'music' cultivated by Tennyson and Rossetti is that it is a medium unsuited to precise expression *of any kind*. This, no doubt, could be said to some extent of its earlier phases of development,

in Spenser or in Milton. But it would be easy to find passages
from those earlier poets in which there is plenty of general mental
activity going on; whereas the Victorian development of this use of
English, even in a 'sage-poet' like Tennyson, tends towards confusion,
vagueness, and a progressive emaciation of the *content* of poetry.
Thus, while Swinburne has his own music, which is not Tennyson's
or Rossetti's, his well-known sacrifices of sense to sound, his rhythmic
self-intoxication, his hypnotic cadences, his hallucinations of meaning
dissolving inextricably into one another, may be considered as an
exotic variant of the same tradition.

What is most important, for critical purposes, in this verbal music,
appears not so much in frankly incantatory poetry like much in the
early Morris (*The Blue Closet*, for example), but in passages where the
poet is making a sustained offer of thought and 'message'. It will be
noted that the passage quoted above from Rossetti is sententious.
And though Rossetti does not come before us, as Tennyson sometimes
does, in the role of the Sage, but rather as a fellow-sufferer, his
mature poetry is quite as sententious as Tennyson's, and ostensibly
stakes quite as much on the reader's thoughtful acceptance of a message solemnly delivered. (Rossetti is never humorous or ironic in his
successful poetry – at any rate, not in the *House of Life* sequence,
where the moral–philosophical ambition is as apparent as the stylistic
virtuosity.) And the admirer of Rossetti discovers 'fundamental
brainwork' even in the more lush and mannered specimens of his
later style (*The Stream's Secret*, for example). But it seems fairest to
verify the attribution of 'fundamental brainwork' by considering
a poem in which Rossetti appears to be offering a deliberated and
credal affirmation of his religion of beauty. This is the famous sonnet
Sibylla Palmifera, from which I quote the sestet:

> This is that Lady Beauty, in whose praise
> Thy voice and hand shake still, – long known to thee
> By flying hair and fluttering hem – the beat
> Following her daily of thy heart and feet,
> How passionately and irretrievably,
> In what fond flight, how many ways and days!

Those who do not dislike this poem are not likely to be persuaded
to do so by detailed fault-finding. But such is not my intention:
I wish merely to show, by a particular inspection of the way Rossetti

uses words, that the poem does not owe what impressiveness it has to 'fundamental brainwork', to the communication of anything precisely defined or clearly imagined; it is, rather, a gesture in a *general* direction, depending for its effect on the reader's anterior readiness for vague sympathy with the attitude suggested. Poetic skill is certainly there, in the means by which the despairing yet unchecked pursuit of 'Beauty' is communicated by the delayed caesura of the fourth line, the assimilation through alliterativeness of the '*flying* hair' and '*fluttering* hem' to the poet's 'Following'; and, more subtly, by the breathlessness conveyed in the associated aspirates in 'hair' and 'hem' and 'heart and feet'. But it is a skill which does little but display itself; we are merely *told* what this ardent though desperate pursuit, of which we are given a general sense, is a pursuit *of*; 'Beauty' remains something only vaguely gestured at, as in the poem's opening:

> Under the arch of life, where love and death,
> Terror and mystery, guard her shrine, I saw
> Beauty enthroned . . .

If we dislike the poem, we will be inclined to say that 'Beauty' from beginning to end remains as much a mere word as 'life', 'love', 'death', 'terror', and 'mystery' in this poem. And if we find ourselves resisting the hierophantic manner of the opening lines, we may be provoked in reaction to a closer examination of the seeming impressiveness of phrasing, the appearance of lapidary conciseness, exemplified in the sestet – '. . . in whose praise/Thy voice and hand shake still'. If we reflect for a moment – which the lines do not encourage us to do – on the meaning of 'shake' here, it will appear that whatever propriety the verb has in regard to the 'voice' of the poet trembling in praise of 'Beauty', it cannot have in regard to the 'hand' (of the painter); the word 'shake', in fact, represents the articulation of one vague meaning with another even vaguer. There is no real gnomic or graphic precision, only an appearance of it. Similarly with '. . . the beat/Following her daily of thy heart and feet': the appearance of compression, or effective zeugma, dissolves immediately we bring the meaning of the word 'beat' here into focus. But bringing into focus is not, of course, what we are supposed to do. It is only the general effect that matters to the admirer of this poem; the predisposition to accept an attitude which is never more than suggested

by the poet. But in compensation, the tone in which the suggestion is made combines grandiloquent expansiveness with unction. And it is on this tone of voice that objections will primarily centre; even the most sympathetic reader-aloud of the sonnet will find it hard to play down its unctuous rectitude:

> The allotted bondman of her palm and wreath.

It is significant that those who dislike this poem are usually told that they have an initial prejudice against its subject ('aestheticism'). But this retort in a way itself confirms the observations made above about the character of this sonnet; what is approved, or disapproved, by one reader or another, remains something *general*, something outside the poem which the poem itself merely gestures at; what is found impressive, or unimpressive, as the case may be, is nothing more specific than a manner and a tone of voice.

Rossetti, of course, wrote much better poems than *Sibylla Palmifera*. Nor is the range of his powers best seen in things like *The Blessed Damozel*, charming as that is. His most interesting work, in my opinion, is his turbid, mannered love-poetry, with its characteristic alternation of the hectic and the languid, of overripe voluptuousness and the chill of desolation.

> Stand still, fond fettered wretch! while Memory's art
> Parades the Past before thy face, and lures
> Thy spirit to her passionate portraitures:
> Till the tempestuous tide-gates flung apart
> Flood with wild will the hollows of thy heart,
> And thy heart rends thee, and thy body endures.
> (*Parted Love*)

Over-sophisticated as this is, it has a certain power, though perhaps not of a very pleasing kind: the power of

> 'O ye, all ye that walk in Willowwood,
> That walk with hollow faces burning white;' ...
> Alas! the bitter banks in Willowwood,
> With tear-spurge wan, with blood-wort burning red.
> (*Willowwood*)

Willowwood is everywhere in this poetry: romantic idealization, and half-glimpsed behind it, its corollary of selfishness, and incapacity for a mutually respecting relation with another; ahead of it, the

nemesis of inevitable disappointment, weariness with oneself, a sense of irretrievable waste and loss. The Rossetti of *Barren Spring*, of *Lost Days*, of '*Retro Me, Sathana!*', could have echoed Baudelaire's

> Mais mon cœur, que jamais ne visite l'extase,
> Est un théâtre où l'on attend
> Toujours, toujours en vain, l'être aux ailes de gaze!

But the comparison with Baudelaire reminds us that the Rossetti of such poems is still the Rossetti of *Sibylla Palmifera*. They reveal subtler ways in which the poetry insinuates an over-valuation of the experience it presents, but their limitation is essentially the same; the temptation, yielded to by the poet, to find in spiritual sickness the occasion for suggesting a spiritual superiority. That temptation is insidious, and I do not say that Baudelaire always overcame it; but his greatness is surely that he succeeded, in his finest poems, in diagnosing his own malady, and thereby making us see his own very special case in relation to more universal feelings, principles of health, and moral judgements. If Baudelaire's weaknesses as a poet are due to his Romanticism, his strength is that he was able at times to turn it into a creative force. Rossetti's guilt, remorse, and sensation of spiritual bankruptcy remain egocentric. The result is that doom of the emotionalist: monotony; the monotony which so soon afflicts the reader of his poetry, small in bulk though it is. Worse still is the pretentiousness which commonly accompanies the over-valuing of one's experience:

> Because our talk was of the cloud-control
> And moon-track of the journeying face of Fate,
> Her tremulous kisses faltered at love's gate
> And her eyes dreamed against a distant goal:
> But soon, remembering her how brief the whole
> Of joy, which its own hours annihilate,
> Her set gaze gathered, thirstier than of late,
> And as she kissed, her mouth became her soul.
>
> (*Secret Parting*)

The relation of the highfalutin of the opening to what follows is very obvious and very distasteful; the last line of the quotation is curiously vulgar. It is clear that the Meredith of *Modern Love* had forerunners.

But that is Rossetti at his worst. And there is at least one poem in

which we glimpse a remarkable freshness and directness of perception, which suggest that Rossetti's potentialities as a poet were greater than his achievement. I am thinking of *Song IV* in the *House of Life*, the poem called *Sudden Light*, which begins:

> I have been here before,
>   But when or how I cannot tell:
> I know the grass beyond the door,
>   The sweet keen smell,
> The sighing sound, the lights around the shore.

From the first line onwards we have an unusually direct presentment of an individual's experience in a sensitively particularized situation. This particularity is very different from anything in *The Blessed Damozel*: it contributes functionally to the recreation of that peculiar state, at once one of bewilderment and of clarity ('sudden light'). We notice how it brings in a lightness, a fresh air, 'the sweet keen smell' – so un-Rossettian, un-Pre-Raphaelite, un-Tennysonian. The 'sighing' is no mere poeticality; it is precise in evocation, and the stanza as a whole, with all its rich suggestiveness, has no incantation, but rather the effect of statement.

But for critical purposes, the stanza in its context can only confirm the general judgement on Rossetti's poetry. For the poem modulates back into a familiar Pre-Raphaelite key: the static, dreamy atmosphere, which has not the transitory vividness of real dreams, but rather the insubstantiality of a waking dream or reverie:

> Shall we not lie as we have lain,
>   Thus for Love's sake,
> And sleep, and wake, yet never break the chain?

In view of Rossetti's love-poetry in general, with its ardours, hungers, opiates, and derelictions, it is interesting to note the plausibility here lent to Freud's theory that the *déjà vu* sensation is associated with the wish to return to the mother. But here we reach the frontier between criticism and psychiatry. And we may leave Rossetti to pass the final judgement on his own work in those characteristic lines:

> Look in my face: my name is Might-have-been;
> I am also called No-more, Too-late, Farewell.
>   (*A Superscription*)

Christina Rossetti's poetry has the Rossetti skill and the careful concern with form and design, and it has a Pre-Raphaelite vocabulary and colouring. But it has none of the over-sophistication and artificiality of her brother's poetry; it is never lush or mannered; nor does it succumb to the temptations, gross or subtle, which beset the poet who must seek, as becomes a devotional poet, to express an attitude of humility and self-forgetfulness. It is significant that one finds oneself appraising her work in these negative terms. For negation, denial, deprivation are the characteristic notes of Christina's religious poetry: and it must be admitted that an extensive reading of it is depressing. The sadness, often morbidity, which is felt even in her delightful poetry for children, even in *Goblin Market*, certainly in *The Prince's Progress*; the felt absence of any outlet for aggressive impulses, deepening into depression or resignation; the compensating yearning for death imagined as an anodyne, an eternal anaesthetic – these are familiar to every reader of her poetry. And it is difficult to find many poems in which she either transcends them or turns them into the conditions for major creation.

One of the rare occasions on which her religion appears in her poetry as a source of revival and refreshment is the (significantly titled) sonnet *A Pause*:

> They made the chamber sweet with flowers and leaves,
> And the bed sweet with flowers on which I lay;
> While my soul, love-bound, loitered on its way.
> I did not hear the birds about the eaves,
> Nor hear the reapers talk among the sheaves:
>   Only my soul kept watch from day to day,
>   My thirsty soul kept watch for one away:–
> Perhaps he loves, I thought, remembers, grieves.
> At length there came the step upon the stair,
>   Upon the lock the old familiar hand:
> Then first my spirit seemed to scent the air
>   Of Paradise; then first the tardy sand
> Of time ran golden; and I felt my hair
>   Put on a glory, and my soul expand.

The simplicity and naturalness of this writing, the trace of the speaking (not intoning) voice:

> Perhaps he loves, I thought, remembers, grieves . . .

the exquisite good taste and spiritual good manners (if the expression be permitted) of the way in which the two worlds are related – the religious and the everyday – are characteristic distinctions of Christina's poetry. And a comparison of her better-known *Spring Quiet* ('Gone were but the Winter') with Hopkins's early *Heaven-Haven* ('I have desired to go') brings out a certain community of temperament (though even the latter, slight as it is, has Hopkins's idiosyncrasy – 'sharp *and sided* hail'). But it reminds us also that *Heaven-Haven*, unlike *Spring Quiet*, by no means represents a high point of its author's achievement.

The distinctiveness and the limitation of Christina Rossetti's talent are alike illuminated by the parallel her sonnet 'Remember' offers to Shakespeare's 71st sonnet ('No longer mourn . . .'). Perhaps, indeed, she was remembering Shakespeare's poem when she wrote it.

> Remember me when I am gone away,
> Gone far away into the silent land;
> When you can no more hold me by the hand,
> Nor I half turn to go yet turning stay.
> Remember me when no more day by day
> You tell me of our future that you plann'd:
> Only remember me; you understand
> It will be late to counsel then or pray.
> Yet if you should forget me for a while
> And afterwards remember, do not grieve:
> For if the darkness and corruption leave
> A vestige of the thoughts that once I had,
> Better by far you should forget and smile
> Than that you should remember and be sad.

The superficial similarity of theme does not disguise the deep difference between the two poems. Shakespeare's sonnet, though not one of his greatest, is characteristic of his best work in the Sonnets, in the effect it produces of a mind intent upon its argument, charged with the determination to deliver its meaning, and taking the emotional effect of that meaning so much for granted, that the poet can afford to deploy his statement in a highly formal, 'logical' progression. For all the element of poignancy, the total effect is therefore akin to wit; the satisfactory following-through of an exaggeration, a hyperbole, to its completion. The result is that a poem which, on the face of it, expresses as much loving self-abnegation and tender

humility as Christina's, conveys at the same time a graceful compliment and a hint of rebuke. And thus the *precise* value we are to give to Shakespeare's overt humiliation of himself and his poetry has been beautifully defined, and the beauty of this defining is the beauty of the poem. Christina's poem calls for no such subtle adjustment; the shy reserve, tenderness, and wistfulness of the speaker are presented simply and truthfully, and our acceptance of her truthfulness is bound up with our recognition of her authentic speaking voice:

> Yet if you should forget me for a while,
> And afterwards remember, do not grieve . . .

But by the time we reach the closing lines, with their (hardly successful) epigrammatic turn of phrasing which sends us back to the Shakespeare sonnet, we feel a slight discomfort with the poem; its modest acceptance of very limited pretension which makes it seem, if not mawkish, a little thin:

> Better by far you should forget and smile
> Than that you should remember and be sad.

The comparison with Shakespeare's sonnet leads us to call the other sonnet, with a limiting intention, 'feminine': in the absence of the verve and chargedness there is felt to be a thinness, a lack of substance.

But what is also evident in this poem is the very welcome absence of anything like the sonorous and vatic manner, at one and the same time declamatory and embarrassingly intimate, which we associate with Mrs Browning – and, perhaps, with one or two later women poets. If we pay Christina Rossetti the archaic compliment of calling her a lady, this will be understood to have no implication of snobbery.

The deprived, depressed, monotonous quality of her poetry is to be accounted for, as we know, very largely by the circumstances of her life and her renunciation. But in one form or another this is a common feature of Victorian Romantic poetry. And if we ignore the personal accent of Christina Rossetti, and the devotional vocabulary and setting of her poems, their moods and tones are immediately recognizable as moods and tones of the period. This is certainly not because of any affectation of fashionable melancholy on Christina's part: no poet could be more touchingly sincere and disinterested. Yet we may wonder if, had she been in contact with a tradition allowing

the exercise, in serious verse, of her sharp wits and her astringency, the substance of her work might not have been more considerable and its styles more various. Certainly, after reading her poetry, we are keenly reminded of the advantages enjoyed by some seventeenth-century religious poets.

William Morris is, in my opinion, much the least interesting of the three poets considered here. What he can do best is illustrated in the early (1858) *Defence of Guinevere* volume, especially the title poem; yet we may find even that poem plaintive and picturesque, rather than rising to the tragic possibilities of its subject; and for the other poems in the volume only a limited compliment seems appropriate, such as that implied when we say they are 'charming'. Arnold, regretting Burns's background, remarked that it is a great advantage to the poet to live in a beautiful world; and so it must have seemed to the Morris of *Golden Wings*:

> Midways of a walled garden,
>   In the happy poplar land,
>   Did an ancient castle stand,
> With an old knight for a warden.
>
> Many scarlet bricks there were
>   In its walls, and old grey stone;
>   Over which red apples shone
> At the right time of the year.
>
> On the bricks the green moss grew,
>   Yellow lichen on the stone,
>   Over which red apples shone;
> Little war that castle knew.
>
> Deep green water fill'd the moat,
>   Each side had a red-brick lip,
>   Green and mossy with the drip
> Of dew and rain . . .

This is certainly charming. But the 'beautiful world', from which everything harsh or disagreeable is excluded, turns out to be day-dream world and, in no very long run, an uninteresting one. Morris, of course, has his characteristic emotional tone, his pathos, in these shorter poems, and it might well be said that even the happier ones imply the sadness from which they withdraw. But in his poetry

Morris's protest against the actual world is confined to the protest of ignoring it.

The Life and Death of Jason makes pleasant reading, but again one cannot feel that Morris has glimpsed the tragic power of the story he is telling; the sin of Jason seems to have little moral significance; the poet's activity as poet is directed, again, to charming incidentals of visual observation, of costume, colour, and landscape. In *The Earthly Paradise*, however much Morris may have felt himself the successor of Chaucer, there is none of Chaucer's vigorous interest in and command of life in so many of its forms, the sense of *nihil humanum a me alienum puto*. Morris's interest is always in the picturesque, the decorative, in the romantic 'feel' of the legends, as in the 'northernness' of *Sigurd the Volsung*. When human beings are at the ostensible centre of interest, there is a queer externality, difficult to illustrate convincingly just because it is so pervasive. Hence it would be futile to enter the controversy about *The Earthly Paradise* – is it not really poetry of escape, but a sociological sermon in the form of an allegory? Whatever Morris's deeper intention, no effective message of the kind he is credited with could be delivered in such verse.

We almost always have the sense in reading Morris's poetry – and indeed his prose romances, too – that what he is doing is quite marginal, quite apart from the main activities of his life. Outside his poetry we know Morris as an energetic, strenuous figure and strong character, the last of the great Victorian 'prophets', and more than a 'prophet' in being a man of action and a maker. But in his poetry – even after his 'Pre-Raphaelite' phase – we observe in an extreme, and a naïve form, the Pre-Raphaelite separation of 'art' from 'life'. 'Art' for Morris was essentially a relaxation, an amusement, something to do; writing poetry came easily to him, and he was not the poet to resist the temptations (of profusion and careless workmanship) inherent in being one's own publisher and printer:

> The fascination of what's difficult
> Has dried the sap out of my veins, and rent
> Spontaneous joy and natural content
> Out of my heart.

Morris the poet could not have applied to himself these words of Yeats. And it is significant that there is no parallel between *his*

development and that of Yeats – who also began as a Pre-Raphaelite, born out of due time.[1] Indeed, 'development' is not a word with any obvious application to Morris's poetry. His work as translator of epic and saga – and the greater part of his verse is translation – shows him as responding to certain 'romantic' qualities which may well be in his originals but which are not necessarily the most important there. The socialist songs have their merits, but they hardly concern the student of poetry.

It is difficult, then, to give Morris a high place purely as a writer. Even in the prose work, *News from Nowhere*, in which his dream-world is realized more interestingly than in his poetry, it is still the impulse to 'Forget six counties overhung with smoke' that predominates. His lack of human centrality, the lack of concentration and pressure in all his imaginative writing, the day-dream habit of his verse, may be mainly attributed to his having other things to do. The expression of the robuster side of his nature was to be reserved for the Anti-Scrape Society, the settlement-house, and the socialist meeting; above all, for the noble effort to fulfil (in the world of Victorian industrialism, Karl Marx, and Mr Podsnap) the prophecy of John Ruskin. But the poetic tradition which he accepted was not, anyway, calculated to encourage the expression of anything robust, and one of the most telling criticisms of it may be that it confined William Morris to minor poetry.

NOTE

1. 'The dream-world of Morris was as much the antithesis of daily life as with other men of genius, but he was never conscious of the antithesis and so knew nothing of intellectual suffering' (W. B. Yeats, *Autobiographies*, London, 1955, 175.)

GERARD MANLEY HOPKINS

F. N. LEES

The collected poetry of Hopkins was first published in 1918,[1] and by that time there had already appeared Ezra Pound's early poems, some of Yeats's maturer work, and T. S. Eliot's *Prufrock* volume. Yet Hopkins had been born in 1844 and had died in 1889, and some of the poems in the 1918 edition went back in date to 1866. By 1866 Swinburne had written *Atalanta in Calydon* and Meredith *Modern Love*, but Rossetti's *Poems* (1870), Tennyson's complete *Idylls of the King* (1872), and Patmore's *The Unknown Eros* (1877) were still to come.

The time into which Hopkins's poetry made its belated entrance was one of experiment and innovation, of poetry that was 'difficult'; but Hopkins himself had been an innovator, and as his work was consequently often 'difficult', it readily took a place with the new, the 'modern' of the post-war world. It is true that it played its part in the pushing aside of familiar, stock rhythms and vocabulary, in the furthering of attempts to attain a fresh immediacy of expression – aid which it would be wrong to obscure by excluding it from the place it has so often occupied, at the beginning, or thereabouts, of anthologies of 'modern' verse. But it is none the less important to realize that he is not in fact, in any useful sense of the word, a 'modern' poet; and to see his poetry against that of his own time rather than against that of the twentieth-century company into which it was accidentally led by Bridges's excessive, if not culpable, timidity in launching it. Much of Hopkins's significance may be blurred by the clash in subject-matter and attitude between his work and that of the Yeats, the Pound, and the Eliot of the twenties, or of Auden, say, whose early poetry nearly enough coincided with the first really popular edition of Hopkins in 1930 (the 750 copies of the first edition were not all sold until 1928); Hopkins was not working in the same materials.

In 1863 Hopkins went up to Oxford, which he left in 1867; soon to enter the novitiate of the Society of Jesus and, in his own words, to put aside the writing of poetry 'as not belonging to my profession' – a poetic silence terminated only in 1875, by *The Wreck of the Deutschland*. We have, therefore, an unusually clear division between his juvenilia and the rest of his work, and one of much significance. The early work has a streak of originality: *The Deutschland*, a poem of ambitious size and scope, shows his style in a stage of development that it is difficult not to describe as fully grown.

The early Hopkins may be seen in *A Vision of the Mermaids* (1862), the title of which alone is enough to place its author in a stream of influence, fanciful and romantic, flowing direct from Keats – though not enough to prepare one for the poem's independent power:

> Soon – as when Summer of his sister Spring
> Crushes and tears the rare enjewelling,
> And boasting 'I have fairer things than these'
> Plashes amidst the billowy apple-trees
> His lusty hands, in gusts of scented wind
> Swirling out bloom till all the air is blind
> With rosy foam and pelting blossom and ...

Heading dangerously in the direction of Swinburne, clearly – despite its striking energy and sensuous palpability. But in the poems written at Oxford this tendency is quelled. Of these, chiefly of note for their autobiographical implications (they are mostly religious in subject), two are of particular interest. The first is *Heaven-Haven: A nun takes the veil*, which, though not free of the sentimental and of a very minor scope (though it compares well with Yeats's *Innisfree*), shows none the less great sureness of touch. *The Habit of Perfection*, though less of a unity, even more shows a peculiar grasp of language:

> Be shelléd, eyes, with double dark
> And find the uncreated light:
> This ruck and reel which you remark
> Coils, keeps, and teases simple sight.
>
> Palate, the hutch of tasty lust,
> Desire not to be rinsed with wine:
> The can must be so sweet, the crust
> So fresh that come in fasts divine!

Nostrils, your careless breath that spend
Upon the stir and keep of pride,
What relish shall the censers send
Along the sanctuary side!

O feel-of-primrose hands ...

Sensory vividness (at times uncomfortably rich); keenness of intelligence (there is a flavour of 'Metaphysical' poetry here and there): the two not inseparable qualities are together, and in distinctly individual form. It is curious actually to watch the aesthetic thus seeking union with the ascetic (symbolically, Pater was Hopkins's tutor for a time, and Newman received him into the Roman Catholic Church); but it is the signs of independent power shown in both these poems that call for notice as Hopkins becomes a religious poet and enters the sphere of influence of Dante Gabriel and Christina Rossetti.

The Wreck of the Deutschland,* however, shows a development quite beyond the reach of reasonable prediction. It is a personal poem, a religious one, and it is rich in Nature-imagery: such a description would suggest nothing surprising. But read the poem itself:

> Thou mastering me
>   God! giver of breath and bread;
> World's strand, sway of the sea;
>   Lord of living and dead;
> Thou hast bound bones and veins in me, fastened me flesh,
> And after it almost unmade, what with dread,
>   Thy doing: and dost thou touch me afresh?
> Over again I feel thy finger and find thee.

>   I did say yes
>   O at lightning and lashed rod;
> Thou heardst me truer than tongue confess
>   Thy terror, O Christ, O God;
> Thou knowest the walls, altar and hour and night:
> The swoon of a heart that the sweep and the hurl of thee trod
>   Hard down with a horror of height:
> And the midriff astrain with leaning of, laced with fire of stress ...

>   I am soft sift
> In an hourglass – at the wall

---

* The *Deutschland* was wrecked in the mouth of the Thames in 1875. On board were five Franciscan nuns, exiled from Germany, who were drowned.

Fast, but mined with a motion, a drift,
　　And it crowds and it combs to the fall;
I steady as a water in a well, to a poise, to a pane,
　　But roped with, always, all the way down from the tall
　　　Fells or flanks of the voel,[a] a vein
Of the gospel proffer, a pressure, a principle, Christ's gift.

　　　I kiss my hand
　　To the stars, lovely-asunder
　　Starlight, wafting him out of it; and
　　　Glow, glory in thunder;
Kiss my hand to the dappled-with-damson west:
Since, tho' he is under the world's splendour and wonder,
　　His mystery must be instressed,[b] stressed;
For I greet him the days I meet him, and bless when I understand.

There is nothing by the Rossettis to stand up to this in immediacy, intensity, or range. Francis Thompson's *The Hound of Heaven* (1890) comes to mind, of course, as akin in content to this part of the poem, and as having grown, we must suppose, from much the same poetic stock; but in Thompson the feeling is softened, sweetened, and lingering, and excites a wish for George Herbert's seventeenth-century energy and incisiveness. In the *Deutschland* stanzas there is an expressive co-operation of metre and what is said; slow, perhaps (because of the compression of syntax), in taking shape in the reader's mind, but once shaped, penetrating in effect and communicating through the very process of emergence. This is what produces the activity, the energy, the sheer reality, which grip, and makes the poetry an experience. And this originates in an avoidance of conventional syllable-counting versification and 'poetic' locution and diction. In a general way, the aim witnessed to is that manifested in Browning's search for actuality of language – and its result too, though with a difference, is something we may call 'dramatic'; but Browning was not working at the same depth of intimate personal experience.

Yet what had happened was an action on elements of thought and feeling that in character were Pre-Raphaelite and Tractarian; but it was not the deliberately religiose, often vaguely medievalist, impulse most prominent in D. G. Rossetti's poetry that brought a religious understanding and feeling far stronger, in any case, than Christina

---

[a] Welsh word for a *bare hill*; [b] 'realized' – see note 2.

Rossetti's into this arresting form. It was a desire to capture the actuality of Nature and the truth of the thing rendered – and this had been the essential aim of Pre-Raphaelite *painting*. Hopkins's was a parallel concentration on the particular and individual rather than the general and universal, on the distinctive in things, on their 'self', their 'inship', what he called their 'inscape';[2] and it drew strength from the philosophy of Duns Scotus. His drawings[3] show a Pre-Raphaelite meticulousness; but more important are the jottings made in his Journal during his years of silence as a poet; jottings in which he struggles to record his Nature-observations exactly, in words that will arouse sensations as well as notions. In 1872, for example, at the Isle of Man, he writes:

About all the turns of the scaping from the break and flooding of the wave to its run out again I have not yet satisfied myself. The shores are swimming and the eyes have before them a region of milky surf but it is hard for them to unpack the huddling and gnarls of the water and law out the shapes and the sequence of the running: I catch however the looped or forked wisp made by every big pebble the backwater runs over ...; then I saw it run browner, the foam dwindling and twitched into long chains of suds, while the strength of the backdraught shrugged the stones together and clocked them one against another. (*Punctuation as in original*)

Such descriptions at once recall the careful verbal and pictorial de-lineations of Ruskin in *Modern Painters* (1843–60): a clear reinforce-ment of the belief that Hopkins had affinities with Pre-Raphaelitism. Hopkins's notes are, in fact, like a painter's 'studies': they are not mere attempts at picturesque writing. They are word-exercises im-pelled by the intellect, aimed at clarification of the poet's senses; and Hopkins added to them, during these 'silent' years, a careful study of prosody, undertaken chiefly for teaching purposes.

The vital technical agent in this galvanization of common materials is his principle of rhythm which he called 'Sprung Rhythm'. This he extracted for free use as a general metrical medium from earlier verse or chants, in which it had at times previously occurred. The principle is that English is a language of stress (with syllables *heavy* or *light*) and not of quantity (syllables *long* or *short*), and that therefore its verse *cannot* be strictly quantitative (as was, apparently, Latin verse), and *need not* be pseudo-quantitative, as was normal English syllabic verse. For Hopkins a single stress made a single metrical foot, and it could equally well (sense permitting) stand alone in that foot or be

accompanied by any number (at need) of light, unstressed syllables. The character of the movement of such verse is that of expressive common speech; but for it to have the benefit of rhythmic form, a line will have its pattern of a certain number of feet, though a single foot may run on into the next line – in Hopkins's own words, 'the scanning runs on without break from the beginning of, say, a stanza to the end and all the stanza is one long strain, though written in lines asunder' (Author's Preface to *Poems*). Without such a scheme his bold syntactical compression is hardly imaginable. The objective is, of course, meaningfulness and feeling – in a word, expressiveness, in preference to mere tunefulness; and in reading this poetry reaching in to the meaning is what will set going the rhythm. The opening lines of *Spring and Fall* (1880) make a good introductory illustration:

> Márgarét, are you grieving
> Over Goldengrove unleaving?
> Leáves, líke the things of man, you
> With your fresh thoughts care for, can you? ...*

The insertion of a 'poetic', conventional 'O' ('O Margaret') at the beginning would at once transform not only the first line but also the second (and thereby progressively the whole) into lilting syllabic verse, calling for more orthodox syntax, losing the realistic gradual growth of meditativeness in the third line, and diminishing the gravity and importance of the thought. The versification of *The Wreck of the Deutschland* is of the same kind.

Whitman was similarly motivated, similarly anxious for realistic expression – witness this description of a sinking ship:

> Formless stacks of bodies and bodies by themselves, dabs of
>   flesh upon the masts and spars,
> Cut of cordage, dangle of rigging, slight shock of the soothe of
>   waves,
> Black and impassive guns, litter of powder-parcels, strong scent,
> A few large stars overhead, silent and mournful shining ...
> The hiss of the surgeon's knife, the gnawing teeth of his saw,
> Wheeze, cluck, swash of falling blood, short wild scream,
>   and long, dull, tapering groan ...
>
>   (*Song of Myself*, 1855)

---

* Crucial (not all) stresses marked thus ´ by Hopkins.

There is some vividness of vocabulary here – indeed, much effectiveness; but verse has been curbed so completely as to deprive the poetry of its rights, and the piece is, strictly, vivid prose. Or another piece from the same poem:

> I understand the large hearts of heroes ...
> How the skipper saw the crowded and rudderless wreck of the
>   steamship, and Death chasing it up and down the storm,
> How he knuckled tight and gave not back an inch, and was
>   faithful of days and faithful of nights ...
> How he saved the drifting company at last,
> How the lank loose-gown'd women look'd when boated from
>   the side of their prepared graves,
> How the silent old-faced infants and the lifted sick, and the
>   sharp-lipp'd unshaven men; ...

Compare with these part of Hopkins's shipwreck scene:

> She drove in the dark to leeward,
>   She struck – not a reef or a rock
> But the combs of a smother of sand: night drew her
>   Dead to the Kentish Knock;
> And she beat the bank down with her bows and the ride of
>   her keel:
> The breakers rolled on her beam with ruinous shock;
>   And canvas and compass, the whorl and the wheel
> Idle for ever to waft her or wind her with, these she endured ...

> They fought with God's cold –
> And they could not and fell to the deck
>   (Crushed them) or water (and drowned them) or rolled
>   With the sea-romp over the wreck.
> Night roared, with the heart-break hearing a heart-broke rabble,
> The woman's wailing, the crying of child without check –
>   Till a lioness arose breasting the babble,
> A prophetess towered in the tumult, a virginal tongue told.

One might notice the effect of word-sound in producing something for which the term 'close-up' is hardly adequate; of what we may call the interchangeability of 'rabble' and 'babble'; or of the Shakespearian flow of imaginative association which causes 'told' to release its sense of both 'spoke' and 'was effective' while gathering the reverberation from 'tolled' which spreads from 'towered' (as a bell-tower); and one might note, too, a danger in the weakness of 'whorl'. But the point here is the animating rhythm and its relation

to the daring syntax. Or compare *The Leaden Echo and the Golden Echo* (1882) which, with its very irregular verse and its cumulative enumerations, might seem likely, so described, to resemble much of Whitman:

> How to keép – is there ány any, is there none such, nowhere
>   known some, bow or brooch or braid or brace, láce, latch or
>   catch or key to keep
> Back beauty, keep it, beauty, beauty, beauty, . . . from vanishing
>   away? . . .

Again it is rhythm that vitalizes.

With Swinburne, on the other hand, while there is ample rhythm and as frequent a use of alliteration as in Hopkins, the effect is mainly melodious, and the verse runs free to an extent that only a degree of meaningfulness so light as to be elusive and slippery would permit. *Atalanta in Calydon* (1865) begins with this invocation to the 'fair-faced sun':

> . . . let thine hair
> Lighten as flame above that flameless shell
> Which was the moon, and thine eye fill the world
> And thy lips kindle with swift beams; let earth
> Laugh, and the long sea fiery from thy feet
> Through all the roar and ripple of streaming springs
> And foam in reddening flakes and flying flowers
> Shaken from hands and blown from lips of nymphs
> Whose hair or breast divides the wandering wave . . .

Alliteration here is largely only effective in producing delicious sound; that of the opening stanza of *The Deutschland* (given above, p. 373), apart from giving structural strength to the unusual verse (as in, say, *Piers Plowman* – which Hopkins studied), serves to open up the meaning. 'Flesh' runs across to 'afresh' and evokes the raw tenderness of the spot touched, and thence the 'f' of 'finger' draws an active association of feeling; and 'flesh' has already acquired much of its suggestion of sensitivity from the softening sequence of related consonants in '*b*ones', '*v*eins', '*f*astened'. Or, in stanza 4 (also given above), we may notice how 'soft sift' functions in a metaphor of 'metaphysical' subtlety quite essential to the expression of a complex idea.

In the last few years of his life Hopkins wrote a number of deeply personal sonnets known frequently as the 'terrible' sonnets. Here

comparison is challenged, it will be obvious, with certain characteristic work of the Rossettis; and not only as expressing similar moods, but also as similar in form (even to the rhymes), ideas, and imagery employed. Hopkins at one time copied into his notebook Rossetti's *Lost Days*:

> The lost days of my life until today,
> What were they, could I see them on the street
> Lie as they fell? Would they be ears of wheat
> Sown once for food but trodden into clay?
> Or golden coins squandered and still to pay?
> Or drops of blood dabbling the guilty feet?
> Or such spilt water as in dreams must cheat
> The throats of men in Hell, who thirst alway?
>
> I do not see them here; but after death
> God knows I know the faces I shall see,
> Each one a murdered self, with low last breath,
> 'I am thyself, – what hast thou done to me?'
> 'And I – and I – thyself,' (lo! each one saith,)
> 'And thou thyself to all eternity!'

It is difficult not to feel that Rossetti has deliberately adopted an attitude for the sheer enjoyment of emotion with a remorseful flavour; the Biblical and Dantean elements in idea and diction remain 'literary', and the verse-movement demands a pretence of emotion in the reader. A compelling actuality, on the other hand, is what marks this sonnet by Hopkins, written probably in 1885:

> I wake and feel the fell of dark, not day.
> What hours, O what black hoürs we have spent
> This night! What sights you, heart, saw; ways you went!
> And more must, in yet longer light's delay.
> With witness I speak this. But where I say
> Hours I mean years, mean life. And my lament
> Is cries countless, cries like dead letters sent
> To dearest him that lives alas! away.
>
> I am gall, I am heartburn. God's most deep decree
> Bitter would have me taste: my taste was me;
> Bones built in me, flesh filled, blood brimmed the curse.
> Selfyeast of spirit a dull dough sours. I see
> The lost are like this, and their scourge to be
> As I am mine, their sweating selves; but worse.

The actuality is attained through a rhythm which is not aimed at a tune of a certain sentimental toning; and from the non-'literary' language (it is at times disconcertingly 'everyday') which searchingly renders the mood – a mood which by its recoil ('but worse') from imminent despair is not so much the more acceptable as the more convincing. The harrowing suggestiveness of the last line may be thrown into relief if we consider the broad asseveration into which a not unsimilar swing of mood swells in a poem by Christina Rossetti:

> If only I might love my God and die! –
> But now he bids me love him and live on,
> Now when the bloom of all my life is gone,
> The pleasant half of life has quite gone by.
> My tree of hope is lopt that spread so high;·
> And I forget how summer glowed and shone,
> While autumn grips me with its fingers wan,
> And frets me with its fitful windy sigh.
> When autumn passes then must winter numb,
> And winter may not pass a weary while.
> But when it passes spring shall flower again:
> And in that spring who weepeth now shall smile –
> Yea, they shall wax who now are on the wane,
> Yea, they shall sing for love when Christ shall come.

Certainly there is a positive impression made by the 'tree' metaphor, by the phrases 'glowed and shone', 'lopt', 'grips me with its fingers wan'; but the impression, sufficient as it is to guarantee some sincerity of response, is a shallow one, and the rather sweet sadness of the verse, the slow elaboration of the 'seasons' idea, as well as the final outburst, place the poem not far above the average level of devotional verse. One notices how differently Hopkins handles a form of the 'tree' analogy in another late sonnet:

> Thou art indeed just, Lord, if I contend
> With thee; but, sir, so what I plead is just.
> Why do sinners' ways prosper? and why must
> Disappointment all I endeavour end?
> Wert thou my enemy, O thou my friend,
> How wouldst thou worse, I wonder, than thou dost
> Defeat, thwart me? Oh, the sots and thralls of lust
> Do in spare hours more thrive than I that spend,
> Sir, life upon thy cause. See, banks and brakes
> Now, leavéd how thick! Lacéd they are again
> With fretty chervil, look, and fresh wind shakes

Them; birds build – but not I build; no, but strain,
Time's eunuch, and not breed one work that wakes.
Mine, O thou lord of life, send my roots rain.

Here, with greater activity of rhythm and language ('difficult' at first glance, but in fact the contrary of 'obscure'), there is also something other than the passive acceptance of an ever-ready, though sound, metaphor. The banks, the brakes (and birds) constitute the *scene*, and the poem is virtually a *discovery* of the relationship of Man with that natural scene. There is rendered simultaneously a glimpse of Nature's power to rebuke and to assuage, both, and a realization of the limits to the operancy of sympathy with Nature. Neither of these sonnets of Hopkins is written in Sprung Rhythm, but the effect this form of metre has had on his versification in them will be evident.

It is Meredith, however, according to T. S. Eliot (in *After Strange Gods*), with whom one should bracket Hopkins, and certainly the best of the sixteen-line 'sonnets' of *Modern Love* go some way, in their own manner, towards the dramatic immediacy of Hopkins – for instance:

> Mark where the pressing wind shoots javelin-like
> Its skeleton shadow on the broad-backed wave!
> Here is a fitting spot to dig Love's grave;
> Here where the ponderous breakers plunge and strike,
> And dart their hissing tongues high up the sand:
> In hearing of the ocean, and in sight
> Of those ribbed wind-streaks running into white.

But a true clarity in the experience offered is prevented by the insistent pressure of the author's emotion, which in fact imposes its needs on the natural scene rather than extracts a truth from it. Much of Meredith's Nature-poetry witnesses to an affinity with Hopkins in sensory response to Nature and to a like search for vivid and exact expression, but the differences in poetic embodiment are great and finally show most obviously in a difference of rhythmic character. Meredith's explorations are largely confined to words and word-order, and his ear seems to have been readily satisfied by established, mostly sweeping rhythms – on the whole inappropriate because they prevent the individuality of diction from fully registering. (The attractive and curiously 'modern' *Melampus* and *Bellerophon*, with their taut and subdued rhythm, are quite uncharacteristic.) There are,

however, deeper (though allied) differences. Briefly, while the language of Hopkins in his Nature-poetry *creates*, we may say, catches the material alive, and thereby *evokes* the significant response (though he often then states and points the thought), Meredith *urges* his thought and supports it by impassioned *reference* to the things and happenings of Nature – the beauty thereby offered depending largely on the reader's visual memory, and often being merely latent in the metaphor with which he was so prompt, and which by its insistence and the excess of it numbs rather than illuminates. For both of them Nature had a significance, but for each a different one. To Hopkins the beauty of Nature spoke of God, its Creator; it was the emergence of this belief, encouraged and authorized by Scotism,[4] that released Hopkins from his self-imposed abstention from poetry. 'Man was created to praise, reverence and serve God our Lord', wrote St Ignatius in the *Spiritual Exercises* which form the basis of meditation in the Society of Jesus; Nature speaks of God, its Creator; therefore, to celebrate Nature's beauty was proper. For Meredith, Nature was a force of which Man ('evolved', Darwinian Man) was a part; and, alien to neither its glories nor its cruelties, Man must accept and unite with it. The difference is radical, and in it is to be seen the division of the Wordsworthian re-discovery of Nature into two firmly diverging streams; the one acted upon by, bluntly, the Oxford Movement, the other by its opponent Rationalism.

Hopkins's greatest poetry, however, is not that which can be adequately described as Nature-poetry. It is to be found in the late sonnets of inner disturbance, two of which have been quoted here; in *The Windhover*[5] (1877), which perhaps more than any other shows pure Sprung Rhythm working with boldness of vocabulary and syntax, and vividness and precision of imagination, in the presentation of an experience of great spiritual intensity and complexity; in other poems which, though they have a considerable 'Nature' content, are ones of spiritual drama; in *The Wreck of the Deutschland* (despite difficulties of sentiment and symbolism for non-co-religionists); and in the apparently unfinished *On the Portrait of Two Beautiful Young People* (1886). In this last he meditates on the moral dangers that may lie ahead for even the most favoured of the young; one stanza will perhaps show that his range was not yet exhausted:

Man lives that list, that leaning in the will
No wisdom can forecast by gauge or guess,
The selfless self of self, most strange, most still,
Fast furled and all foredrawn to No or Yes.

In a mode not dramatic now, but meditative and philosophical, there is achieved a calm and a lovely music, appropriate to the kind of thought being invoked; but this is not at the expense of the subtlety of thought any more than is that of Yeats's *Among School-Children*, the true poetic music of the last stanza of which may be recalled by this of Hopkins. The effect of real speech, the pointedness in the alliteration, the manifoldness of meaning in 'list' (one thinks of three aspects of the word), and the illuminating paradoxicality of the third line – these are characteristic of Hopkins; but the total effect is new in him.

Hopkins's novelty of diction and metre was not, as it has been with much of the most original poetry of the twentieth century (and was, for the most part, with Browning), the accompaniment of novel subject-matter. It came simply from a deeper penetration into material common to his contemporaries, and was actuated by impulses that he shared with them. It is among the Victorians that he must be set if we are to grasp the full significance of his work: but his union of receptive sensibility with probing intellect, of humility with determination, ensures that his achievement is no merely comparative one. Language that quickens as well as communicates, that sensitizes as it reveals; this at the service of a scrupulous mind and spirit constitutes a poetry of inalienable importance.[6]

NOTES

1. For the history of the preservation and eventual publication of Hopkins's manuscripts by his friend and literary executor, Robert Bridges, see: *Letters of Gerard Manley Hopkins to Robert Bridges and R. W. Dixon*, 2 vols. (London, 1935), and *Further Letters of Gerard Manley Hopkins* (London, 1938; with additions, 1956), both ed. C. C. Abbott. Fresh facts have been presented in 'Bridges, Hopkins and Dr Daniel', by S. Nowell-Smith, *The Times Literary Supplement* (13 December 1957).

2. For Hopkins's ideas of 'inscape' and 'instress' in relation to his whole philosophy of perception, the reader should consult W. A. M. Peters, s.j., *Gerard Manley Hopkins* (London, 1948), a most penetrating study of Hopkins's language and mind.

3. See *The Journals and Papers of Gerard Manley Hopkins* (London, 1959), edited by Humphry House and completed by S. Storey.

4. See Note 2 above.

5. References to many of the suggested interpretations of this poem will be found in *The Victorian Poets* (London, 1956), ed. F. A. Faverty, to which John Pick contributes a survey of scholarly work on Hopkins. It seems appropriate here to mention 'The Windhover', by F. N. Lees, in *Scrutiny*, XVII, 1 (1950).

6. It would not be proper to end without mentioning the important discussion of Hopkins by F. R. Leavis in his *New Bearings in English Poetry* (London, 1932) and in his later essays in *The Common Pursuit* (London, 1952).

THE LAST PHASE

ALLAN RODWAY

It has been said that 'the nineties' was not a period but a point of view. Much that is ninetyish is to be found before 1890 and after 1900, just as much that is typically Victorian occurs before and after the reign of Victoria. Indeed, the aesthetic or decadent viewpoint that the term conjures up was probably more characteristic of the eighties. Certainly, it was not the most significant, though it may have been psychologically the most necessary manifestation of the decade 1890 to 1900. For this was the period of Shaw and the Fabians, of Wells and scientific humanism, of James and Hardy, as well as the period of such writers as Wilde, Dowson, Thompson, or the young Yeats – to say nothing of Kipling and Henley, Housman and David-son. All these figures represent different aspects of a general ferment. But not all represent the last phase of Victorianism.

In 1887, the year of the Queen's first Jubilee, both Victorianism and British power seemed to be at their height; but during the next few years, in almost symbolic fashion, Arnold, Browning, and Tennyson were to die. The death of Gordon had lowered British prestige in the East; at home, the influx of American prairie wheat was increasing agricultural distress; in the United States, production was increasing faster than in England; the Home Rule problem was becoming more acute, German competition more successful; and working-class unrest, as the Dock Strike of 1889 showed, was taking an organized form. The solid, Victorian age was coming to an end; and naturally voices were raised, like those of Wilde and Whistler, to observe that it was high time it did; or to insist, in the manner of Kipling or Henley, that it never would; or to announce a Shavian or Wellsian programme for the future.

Not all these voices are relevant to the purposes of this chapter, for some of these writers require fuller examination elsewhere. Shaw and Wells are not really the last phase of anything: they represent new

attitudes to society. Nor is Henry James particularly *characteristic* of the period. The early Yeats is, of course, but his work must obviously be considered as a whole, in the next volume of this *Guide*.

On the other hand, writers like Wilde and Dowson, though contrary in kind to writers like Kipling and Henley, do share with them the fact that they carry further tendencies already characteristic of the Victorian age. In that sense they are representative of 'the last phase', though some of their contemporaries are not. But the aesthetic members of the Rhymers' Club were *fin-de-siècle*, the jingoistic patriots were *end-of-the-century*. The former derived their inspiration and attitudes mainly from France, the latter were blatantly British – a difference that partially explains why 'the aesthetes' are usually so much the more associated with the nineties. They irritated like a foreign body lodged in the insular ethos.

The Patriots carried further a majority attitude already well established and approved (the music-hall song which brought 'jingoism' into the language being popular as early as 1878); an insular attitude unavailingly castigated by Arnold and Dickens long before. They were middlebrows writing for their like, the solid bourgeois; and the content of their work, by period standards, was healthy, while that of the aesthetes was decadent. By the standards of modern psychology this is not the case; so it would seem better – if the word must be used – to say that if the aesthetes are characterized by decadence, it is a decadence of language. In any case, decadence cannot be a definitive characteristic, since the Patriots are no less characterized by a decadence of intelligence.

The aesthetes, representing only a small sophisticated minority, seemed to be outrageous innovators. Though Beauty, as Max Beerbohm said, had existed before, it 'was Mr Oscar Wilde who managed her début'. Though Swinburne had expressed an anti-Christian, un-English, and rather perversely sensual morality, that was long ago. Since then, 'the rebel, republican, and internationalist [had] merged into the moral patriot, conservative and insular'.[1] Moreover, though aestheticism owed something to Pre-Raphaelitism, it was a development with a difference. Rossetti, Morris, and Ruskin upheld the strong moral tone of Victorian art, and believed in a medieval world (largely of their own invention) in which culture was serious, satisfying, and unified. The nineties had no belief, and

little interest, in such a world or such a culture. In painting, Whistler had come to be preferred to Rossetti ('literary' paintings giving place to 'musical' ones); in poetry, Swinburne to Morris; and in prose, Pater to Ruskin. The aesthetes had suddenly accelerated the movement begun by Swinburne, from a Ruskinesque to a Paterian position – and ended beyond it.

For the Pre-Raphaelites, influenced by Ruskin, the creation of beauty had been a duty owed to society; for the aesthetes, influenced by Pater, it was a duty owed to oneself. An idealized Renaissance supplanted an idealized Middle Ages as a source of inspiration; individualism was arrayed against conformism, sensibility against morality – or, at most, alongside morality. 'But why should we be good, Mr Pater?' an undergraduate is supposed to have asked. 'Because', he replied, 'it is so beautiful.' It was inevitable that the equation should be reversed and the beautiful be taken to be so good. Had not Pater himself written that success in life consisted in maintaining an ecstasy of the cultivated senses? Adding:

> The theory or idea or system which requires of us the sacrifice of any part of this experience, in consideration of some interest into which we cannot enter, or some abstract theory we have not identified with ourselves, or what is only conventional, has no real claim upon us.[2]

Such an outlook was not inconsistent with that of the French Symbolists, and it seemed to justify the current interest in 'black' books such as Huysman's *A Rebours*, Gautier's *Mlle de Maupin*, or Baudelaire's *Fleurs du Mal*. Pater became the chief English source of Aesthetic theory – and to a lesser extent of its style. Admiration of his style, however, was not universal. Even Wilde had reservations, though he sometimes unhappily allowed it to influence his own. All that was baleful in that influence is charmingly implied in Max Beerbohm's *Diminuendo*, wherein, recalling his desire in 1890 to attend Pater's lectures, he adds:

> Even then I was angry that he should treat English as a dead language, bored by that sedulous ritual wherewith he laid out every sentence as in a shroud – hanging, like a widower, long over its marmoreal beauty or ever he could lay it at length in his book, its sepulchre.

Pater's theory, on the other hand, gave rise to no such doubts among his followers. It tallied with Gautier's doctrine of Art-for-Art's-sake,

and with Whistler's depreciation of Nature. Above all, it was a red rag to John Bull, who believed in Wordsworth, Tennyson, and Art-for-Morality's-sake.

Such generalizations are necessary signposts in an essay of this scope; they are not destinations. However, some idea of the concrete literary realities of the period can be given by examining two major representative figures to obtain an impression of the range of attitudes within each type.

Wilde (1854–1900) and Kipling (1865–1936) obviously choose themselves as the major figures. They are not necessarily the best artists, but they are certainly the chief spokesmen of their respective groups. Moreover, they are the only two whose significant quality cannot be fairly assessed in terms of their poetry alone.

At first glance they are in every way contraries: psychologically, politically, and aesthetically. Wilde was a tolerant, Kipling an authoritarian; Wilde was a socialist (on the grounds that socialism led to individualism), Kipling was so far to the right that he thought his cousin, Stanley Baldwin, 'a Socialist at heart'; Wilde's is an art for Art's sake, Kipling's an art for Empire's sake; Wilde's humane feelings are inhibited by his intelligence, Kipling's intelligence by his aggressive feelings. Their antagonism can be clearly indicated by quotation:

> As one turns over the pages of ... *Plain Tales from the Hills*, one feels as if one were seated under a palm-tree reading life by superb flashes of vulgarity ... The mere lack of style in the story-teller gives an odd journalistic realism to what he tells us. From the point of view of literature Mr Kipling is a genius who drops his aspirates ... He is our first authority on the second-rate ...
>
> (*The Critic as Artist*)

> The things I knew was proper you wouldn't thank me to give,
> And the things I knew was rotten you said was the way to live.
> For you muddled with books & pictures, an' china, an' etchin's an' fans,
> And your rooms at college was beastly – more like a whore's than a man's.
>
> (*The Mary Gloster*)

> The English country gentleman galloping after a fox – the unspeakable in full pursuit of the uneatable.   (*A Woman of No Importance*, Act I)

> 'Believe me', Parnesius turned again to Dan, 'a boy is safe from all things that really harm when he is astride a pony or after a deer.'
>
> (*Puck of Pook's Hill*, 'On the Great Wall')

Yet, despite all this they have something in common.

After all, 'decadence' can be regarded as 'a form of imperialism of the spirit, ambitious, arrogant, aggressive, waving the flag of human power over an ever wider and wider territory'.[3] Indeed, Wilde really expresses the self-confident expansiveness of a secure age much more than does Kipling, who often reminds one of a man cheering to keep his courage up. Wilde felt that the age needed, Kipling that it could not afford, aestheticism. It is interesting to note, furthermore, that Kipling's first patriotic poem, *Ave Imperatrix* (1882), was a direct imitation of Wilde's poem of the same title, published the previous year, which celebrates Empire and 'the spears of crimson-suited war'. At this time, however, Kipling was usually 'a rebel and a progressive, which is to say – paradoxically – that he was a decadent ... his tastes were "aesthetic" '.[4] Again, one could instance the subtle emotional affinity indicated by the aesthetes' tendency to become converts to the authoritarian Roman Catholic Church and the tendency of the Patriots to make imperialism a religion. Kipling and Henley are constantly invoking the Virgin of the Sword, the Red Angel of war, the Lord God of Battles, or the Lord of our far-flung battle-line. In the early poem, *Libertatis Sacra Fames*, too, Wilde shows himself to be part of the attitude of which Kipling was to be the last phase (when Wilde had abandoned it): 'Spite of this modern fret for Liberty, better the rule of One, whom all obey.'

There is, however, a more general affinity: both Wilde and Kipling remain emotionally adolescent and are afraid to be other than superficial. Each, at heart, knows more than he says but refuses to live up to his knowledge. They are, however, superficial in different ways (and Wilde's *Ballad of Reading Gaol*, to be examined separately, is hardly superficial at all).

In *Ave Imperatrix*, Wilde writes:

> In vain the laughing girl will lean
> To greet her love with lovelit eyes:
> Down in some treacherous black ravine,
> *Clutching his flag*, the dead boy lies.[5] [my italics]

Kipling's sentimental superficiality takes a tougher form (though, on occasion he can be embarrassingly mawkish; witness his poem *Mother O' Mine*). In *The Galley Slave*, surely one of the nastiest poems

of the century, he suggests that the slaves really like the whip. The aged slave, released at last, cries – by the galls, welts, and scars – 'I am paid in full for service. Would that service still were mine.' What *is* the service? Running 'mighty merchandise of niggers in the hold'! And Kipling wholeheartedly endorses this attitude. The poem concludes:

> But today I leave the galley. Shall I curse her service then?
> God be thanked – whate'er comes after, I have lived and toiled
>   with Men![6]

In both *The Galley Slave* and Wilde's *Ave Imperatrix* the reader's imagination is being anaesthetized instead of awakened to realities, and he is being seduced into accepting attitudes from which the awakened mind would recoil.

This sort of poem, however, is not characteristic of Wilde. He is usually superficial, not from repressed aggressiveness, like Kipling, but on principle. He chooses to put beauty before meaning.

The doctrine of Art-for-Art's-sake, as Wilde expressed it, is by no means so absurd as it has been supposed to be. Among the merely provocative epigrams of *The Critic as Artist* or *The Decay of Lying* are many brilliant *aperçus*, almost as much needed today as they were in 1891. In the first essay, for instance, he emphasizes that criticism is a mode of recreation; or he writes:

> We, in our educational system, have burdened the memory with a load of unconnected facts, and laboriously striven to impart our laboriously acquired knowledge. We teach people how to remember, we never teach them how to grow. It has never occurred to us to try and develop in the mind a more subtle quality of apprehension and discernment.

Moreover, in his wonderful essay *The Soul of Man under Socialism*, stimulating, witty, well-argued, he makes a superb attempt to reintegrate art and society. Unfortunately, he also believed, rather inconsistently, that art should only be beautiful ('All art is perfectly useless'). This opinion he derived mainly from French art-criticism, which argued that tone, line, and mass were what counted in painting. But it is one thing to maintain that painting should not be literary, quite another to maintain that literature should not. To attain a pure aesthetic beauty, like that of a design unsullied by meaning, is a difficult and hardly worthwhile task for the poet. That is why Wilde's

poetry, which attempts that task, is less satisfactory than his prose, which has something to *say*. His prose – at least where it mocks philistinism or expounds a provocative theory – has life.

His poetry aspires to the condition of painting, and is languid. One gets the impression of a man sampling various synthetic moods, with no intention of buying. *Charmides*, admittedly, is a pretty piece of paganism in a somewhat sexy Swinburnian manner. Occasionally, too, a pastoral landscape is effectively peopled with pagan figures. But no use is made of them to contrast with, or comment on, current reality. And too often, in aiming for Beauty and letting the sense look after itself, Wilde falls into mere whimsy:

> ... yet here the daffodil
> That love-child of the Spring, has lingered on
> To vex the rose with jealousy ...
> (*The Garden of Eros*, stanza 2)

Why 'love-child'? Or 'jealousy'? In *The Sphinx*, the last poem before his imprisonment, Wilde does give hints of development. His fabulous, antiquarian imagery is used slightly humorously in this cat poem, as in the line 'Lift up your large black satin eyes which are like cushions where one sinks!', with its surreal synaesthesia, pivoted on the ambiguity of 'satin'. But on the whole, the most satisfying poems are those which most resemble Whistlerian paintings: *Impression du Matin*, *Les Silhouettes*, *Symphony in Yellow* (which shows its disdain for verisimilitude by describing the Thames as 'a rod of rippled jade'), or *Les Ballons* with its airy impressionistic charm:

> Against these turbid turquoise skies
> The light and luminous balloons
> Dip and drift like satin moons,
> Drift like silken butterflies.

In Kipling's case, no such distinction between poetry and prose is necessary. The same brash lowbrowism noted in *The Mary Gloster* is to be found, for instance, in his short story, *The Conversion of Aurelian MacGoggin*:

Instead of keeping to the study of the vernaculars he had read some books written by a man called Comte, I think, and a man called Spenser (You will find these books in the Library) ... There was no order against his reading them but his Mamma should have smacked him.

The same gloating enthusiasm for violence is to be found in poems like *Loot* or *The Galley Slave* as in stories like *The Bronckhorst Divorce Case* or *In the Matter of a Private*. It has been argued that in *Loot* Kipling is not to be identified with the speaker, or that, 'finding the whole system pretty good', he was carried away by 'a misplaced enthusiasm' for 'the exciting picturesqueness of some of its defects'.[7] But when all the evidence is taken into account, it is apparent that these contentions will not hold water. On the contrary, it is clear that his approval of the 'law of the Jungle' in the Mowgli stories represents a fully developed adult attitude. The gospel of duty and realism, in fact, usually turns out to be a moralized translation of the law of the jungle, and under that guise permits the expression of many unhealthy repressions. In the jungle there are different species, and the law applies to them in different ways. But even for sahibs, Kipling prefers violence to litigation:

> Biel came out of the court, and Strickland dropped a gut-trainer's whip in the verandah. Ten minutes later, Biel was cutting Bronckhorst into ribbons behind the old Court cells, quietly and without scandal. What was left of Bronckhorst was sent home in a carriage, and his wife wept over it and nursed it into a man again.
>
> (*The Bronckhorst Divorce Case*)

Furthermore, the rhythm of the chorus, and the enthusiastic hunting cries in *Loot* (bearing in mind Kipling's mystique about hunting) are alone sufficient to implicate the writer:

> Now remember when you're 'acking round a gilded Burma
>   god
>   That 'is eyes is very often precious stones;
> An' if you treat a nigger to a dose o' cleanin'-rod
>   'E's like to show you everything 'e owns . . .

> (*Chorus*)   Yes, the loot,
>   Bloomin' loot!
> In the tunic an' the mess tin an' the boot!
>   It's the same with dogs an' men,
>   If you'd make 'em come again
> Whoop 'em forward with a Loo! loo! Lulu!
>   Loot! loot! loot!
> Heeya! Sick 'im puppy! Loo! loo! Lulu!
>   Loot! loot! loot!

Such a poem stands at the centre of a complex, dangerous adolescent attitude, as evident throughout his work as it is in the notorious stories and poems of World War I. It is related not only to 'lesser
breeds without the law', but to the notion of war as a game; a notion
which also crops up both in prose and verse, and itself taps cruel
religious impulses. One quotation will suffice:

> But each man born in the Island broke to the matter of war.
> Soberly and by custom taken and trained for the same,
> Each man born in the Island entered at youth to the game –
> As it were almost cricket, not to be mastered in haste,
> But after trial and labour, by temperance, living chaste . . .
> Weighed and pondered and worshipped . . .
>
> (*The Islanders*)

Shanks, an admirer of Kipling, argues plausibly that he was at
heart a Mithraist. Certainly that militaristic religion, with something
of the character of a secret society about it, was congenial to Kipling,
but there is no evidence in his work of any such thought-out position.
He simply seems to have dignified an irrational fascination with
violence and action (perhaps the result of his being a small, short-
sighted man, who had never been able to play games) by adopting a
religiose tone and rhythm – often quite regardless of sense. His *Song
of the Sons* – to take one instance out of many – begins:

> One from the ends of the earth – gifts at an open door –
> Treason has much, but we, Mother, thy sons, have more! . . .
> Count, are we feeble or few? Hear, is our speech so rude?
> Look, are we poor in the land? Judge, are we men of The
>   Blood?
> Those that stayed at thy knees, Mother, go call them in –
> We that were bred overseas wait and would speak with our
>   kin.

A typical specimen of vague uplift – or, rather, downlift – faintly
tinged with an air of bluff common sense: smoky glass masquerading
as rough diamond. What is the grammar of the first sentence? What
is the subject of 'gifts'? Does 'One' mean one song, son, or family?
And 'much' what? Then, why should those that stayed be called in
(save that something has to rhyme with 'kin')? If they stayed at her
knees they are presumably already in. Anyway, it seems odd to
exhort Mother England to go away from the brood at her knees, and
then call them, instead of staying where she is and telling them!

In prose, Kipling is never quite so incoherent; rather, he tends to introduce an air of unreality by emotional intrusion. This is characteristic even of his best stories.[8] *The Man Who Was*, for example, contains not merely a good deal of weak facetiousness but also sentences like this:

> That Sacrament of the Mess ['drinking the Queen'] never grows old, and never ceases to bring a lump into the throat of the listener wherever he be by sea or by land.

Note the pompous rhythm of the last phrase, as if it were about to break into Kiplingesque verse:

> Wherever he be, by land or by sea,
> That Sacrament never grows old,
> Never ceases to bring, when Mess glasses ring,
> A lump to the throat of the Bold.

Sometimes, he is more subtly unsatisfactory. What *is* wrong with the last clause of this sentence, one wonders?

> [He] began to understand that he was not alone in the world, and also that he was afraid for the sake of another, – which is the most soul-satisfying fear known to man.   (*Without Benefit of Clergy*)

Is it merely a grammatical queasiness about the 'which'? Or is it that he turns a vice (smugness) into a virtue (big-heartedness)? Or that by emphasizing the man's psychological compensation he implies that the woman's physical danger is somehow made worth while? Or is it mainly the fact that the author is rudely intruding, the moral comment being gratuitous as well as unctuous?

Again, it is perhaps some time before one realizes why his referring to the admired natives of *The Tomb of his Ancestors* as 'the wild Bhil' is so irritating – it suggests that he subconsciously regards them not as a tribe but a *species*.

At this point, however, it is obviously necessary to pass to a consideration of style, for it is in this field that Kipling's achievement lay. Occasionally – on the rare occasions when he felt no impulse to domineer or pulpiteer – it is an undeniable linguistic achievement, both in prose and verse. His story *At the End of the Passage* well conveys the horror and heat, the boredom and irritation, of men isolated in the plains during the hot season, though it is slightly marred by

the journalistic twist in the tail. Similarly, in *William the Conqueror* Kipling is most effective in conveying the facts of famine-administration. One may feel revulsion at the worship of his masculine woman, William, who 'enjoyed seeing justice administered, with a long stick, in the open under trees' – especially if one recalls Orwell's *Shooting an Elephant*; one may feel that there is an unintentional give-away in his uncritical approval of Jim who 'beamed on the company. Things were going well with his world. Three of his more grossly incompetent men had died, and their places had been filled by their betters'; but these are defects of sense and sensibility. The style is competent enough. Certainly it avoids the Olde-Tea-Shoppe manner that bedevils it when he intends to be uplifting. On the whole, he is at his best in children's books, where his ingrained obsessions have less play and subtlety of mind would be inappropriate.

If the handful of his best verse is compared with Wilde's lyrics, this competence assumes larger proportions. Where Wilde refines Tennyson or Rossetti almost to nothing, Kipling makes of Browning something genuinely original. *The Sergeant's Wedding*, for instance, is an excellent ballad in the broadside vein, a sort of poor man's 'Soliloquy in a Spanish Cloister', salted with a vigorous singable chorus:

> Cheer for the Sergeant's weddin' –
> Give 'em one cheer more!
> Grey gun-'orses in the lando,
> An' a rogue is married to, etc.

Cleared is good invective, and in *Stellenbosch* popular idiom is used in a lively symbolic way more reminiscent of eighteenth-century street-ballads than the degenerate music-hall songs or popular hymns that Kipling usually modelled himself on:

> And it all goes into the laundry,
> But it never comes out in the wash
> 'Ow we're sugared about by the old men ...

Similarly, *The Three-Decker* neatly mingles a colloquial tone with a hackneyed diction to make an ingenious critique of the three-volume romance, imagined as a sailing vessel superseded by steam. Its crew are missing heirs who 'shipped as Able Bastards till the Wicked Nurse confessed/And they worked the old three-decker to

the Islands of the Blest'. It is, however, spoilt by a moralistic ending which implicitly contradicts both the satire of the remainder and Kipling's own enthusiasm for mechanical progress. Why did he do this? It is difficult not to conclude that he simply wrote without thinking – save at the most superficial level – for journalistic effect. *M'Andrew's Hymn*, however, is a fully unified creation. The Browningesque characterization of his Scots engineer is appropriate for the setting and theme, the linking of the ship's machinery with Calvinist predestination is, as Professor Pinto has put it, 'one of Kipling's few memorable poetic images ... embodying a profound historical truth',[9] and, for once, the mechanical rhythm is right for the subject. To ask that it should embody a less simple attitude would be to ask for a different poem – and perhaps a different poet. None the less, it is simpler than certain comparable poems. The following lines, for instance, are reminiscent of Burns's *Holy Willie*, but they lack Burns's irony and are thus comparatively naïve:

> Years when I raked the Ports wi' pride to fill my cup o'
>   wrong –
> Judge not, O Lord, my steps aside at Gay Street in Hong Kong!
> An' waur than all – my crownin' sin – rank blasphemy an'
>   wild.
> I was not four and twenty then – Ye wadna judge a child?

Generally, Kipling's rhythm is significant only in its irrelevance, which confirms the suspicion engendered so often by his tone (the tone of a man writing to rouse a mob) that he is not even attempting to 'develop in the mind a more subtle quality of apprehension and discernment'. *Fuzzy-Wuzzy* gives fair play to the natives – but how crude and inadequate it is as a comment on a war of spears versus maxim-guns:

> So 'ere's *to* you, Fuzzy-Wuzzy, at your 'ome in the Sudan;
> You're a poor benighted 'eathen but a first-class fightin' man;
> We gives you your certificate, an' if you want it signed
> We'll come an' 'ave a romp with you whenever you're inclined.
>
> (*1st Chorus*)

One could make various points by analysis of such words as 'romp' and 'but'. (Why shouldn't heathens be first-class fighting men? And why *should* Christians?) But the rhythm alone indicates the uselessness of analysing the sense. This meaningless jog-trot simply shakes

the sense into a batter. Thus the poem purports to be enlightened, but in fact avoids reality. 'Like the typical "man of action" of his period, he loved facts but hated and feared reality'[9] – a superficiality far worse than Wilde's.

Kipling's main achievement was to introduce into poetry a diction more living than that of the aesthetes and potentially more fruitful than that of Hopkins, which is so often muscle-bound and obscure. But he made little worthwhile use of it.

Strangely enough, it is to Wilde that one has to turn for the one great poem of a popular kind in 'the last phase'. Admittedly, *The Ballad of Reading Gaol* is sometimes melodramatic, its diction arty (the ghostly dancers of section 3 – shades of *The Ancient Mariner* – are particularly out of place), but these are minor blemishes in a magnificent and unpretentious whole. Without making the mistake of pretending to be an illiterate convict, Wilde uses whatever diction is most effective for conveying his meaning. It is a ballad of feeling – for the two-year torment, which broke his spirit and health, also broke his polished protective shell – but not now of feeling only. Behind the feeling is the hard thought which had gone towards *The Soul of Man Under Socialism*. Consequently, this long poem very rarely degenerates into sentimentality, despite the slightness of the narrative element. That is countered by an intelligent use of binding repetition, and a subtle variation of tone. Thus, the same plain diction can convey nauseated horror ('The hangman with his gardener's gloves'), or grim humour full of implications:

> The Governor was strong upon
>   The Regulations Act:
> The Doctor said that Death was but
>   A scientific fact:
> And twice a day the Chaplain called,
>   And left a little tract.

Or sardonic observation:

> The warders strutted up and down
>   And watched their herd of brutes,
> Their uniforms were spick and span,
>   And they wore their Sunday suits,
> But we knew the work they had been at,
>   By the quicklime on their boots.

Moreover, Wilde is technically efficient in making the most of what drama the 'story' does permit (for example, it is not till the sixth stanza that the reader learns why 'his step seemed light and gay'), and his implicit comments are highly intelligent – sufficiently so to bear some lapses in diction.

Unfortunately, the *Ballad of Reading Gaol* was unique. Contemporary aesthetes – generally better poets than Wilde – were too little concerned to put life on the page; other poets too limited to create major poetry.

Yeats recalls, of Lionel Johnson (1867–1902),

that he once said to me that Wilde's pleasure and excitement were perhaps increased by the degradation of that group of beggars and pathics, and I remember, too, his smile at my surprise, as though he spoke of psychological depths I could never enter.[10]

The comment itself is evidence of a knowledge of such depths – precisely the territory a 'decadence' worthy of the name ought to be exploring – yet nothing of this awareness escapes into Johnson's poetry, which is lucid, melodious, impeccable, and lifeless. Dowson is probably the best poet of the group but, aiming at the quintessence of a quintessence, he too often ended with the emptiness of a typical 'pure' poem – apparently made by varying to taste the standard 'Aesthetic Recipe':

Take a handful of golden hours, a lost love, two faded roses, a mute music, and a wisp of moonshine. Add one conchful of sacring oils and mix well in a vial of mercy. Season with a whiff of incense (or brimstone) and allow to stand for one seeming-eternity in a fragrant shrine. Decorate with a *verily*, an *ywis*, and a *wherewithal*, sprinkle liberally with *thees* and *thous*, guerdon with joy or sorrow (either will do), and serve piping cold in crystal stanzas.

There is little that could not have been made to order, and that little is usually found when the writer has something to say. In Dowson's case it is to be found mostly in the poetry unpublished in his lifetime, as in the attack on Lady Burton, who burnt her husband's manuscript 'To her one God – sterile Propriety', or in *Awakening*, which faces facts squarely:

> We have believed the beautiful, false stories,
> Fed on the faiths that after childhood fail.

Francis Thompson is customarily verbose, sentimental, and religiose. His rhapsodic mode of communication gives the impression of a man with more words at his command than he knows what to do with, the effect being glittering, insubstantial, and, in bulk, unreadable. The following lines (part of a sentence) are fairly representative:

> And one there stood
> Against the beamy flood
> Of sinking day, which pouring its abundance,
> Sublimed the illuminous and volatile redundance,
> Of locks that, half dissolving, floated round her face;
> As see I might
> Far off a lily-cluster poised in sun
> Dispread its gracile curls of light.
>
> (*A Child's Kiss*)

Such wordy opulence, and the emphasis on tonal effect rather than content, links him with the aesthetes, although he purported to seek a fuller life through asceticism, not sensation. He has, however, an occasional flash of brilliance, as, for instance, in the revelation and embodiment of masochism at the heart of renunciation, in his best poem, *The Hound of Heaven*:

> Naked I wait Thy love's uplifted stroke!
> My harness piece by piece Thou hast hewn from me,
> And smitten me to my knee;
> I am defenceless utterly.
> I slept, methinks, I woke,
> And, slowly gazing, find me stripped in sleep.

This revelation, however, is not intellectually 'placed'. One overhears it, so to say, as the self-communing poem rushes by.

W. E. Henley (1849–1903), in contrast, is the extrovert. He was the first editor to take Kipling's *Barrack-Room Ballads*, and was in turn admired by Kipling, not only for his writing but for his 'organic loathing of Mr Gladstone and all Liberalism'. A cripple from boyhood, he shared Kipling's love of war, and like Kipling maintained that it weeded out the weak. He is as gruesomely jingoistic as Kipling at his worst; for example, he urges *The Man in the Street* to get in and fight for 'the fun of it all', concluding:

> And if, please God, it's the Rag of Rags, that sends us
> roaring into the fight,
> O we'll go in a glory, dead certain sure that we're
> utterly bound to be right!

This is well known. Less commonly known is the fact that in his first poems, the splendid series *In Hospital*, he created work which tries not to boost morale but simply to tell the truth – to awaken one's imagination to the realities of a particular world. How different is his record of experience *Before* (the operation) and 'After':

> Face to face with chance, I shrink a little:
> My hopes are strong, my will is something weak . . .
> > *(Before)*

> I thank whatever gods may be
> > For my unconquerable soul . . .
> Under the bludgeonings of chance
> > My head is bloody but unbowed.
> > *(Out of the Night)*

Though nothing he wrote later matches the hospital poems, with their spare, iron diction, recording the poetry of drabness and pain, certain later descriptive poems, in *London Types* and elsewhere, do approach that standard. But when he leaves description, he invariably sentimentalizes or hectors – urging readers to gird their loins, arise, or light their lamps. Moreover, the wrong poems have been anthologized. Consequently his real achievement, one of diction (earlier than Kipling's), has been neglected.

Not all poets of the period, of course, can be forced into one camp or the other. Housman (1859–1936) is an exhorter, and he regards war as a game (though a love-game, not cricket). On the other hand, his rather morbid toying with death and an occasional preciosity of diction link him with the aesthetes. Furthermore, he is apt to fall into their characteristic pseudo-precision:

> Wake: the vaulted shadow shatters,
> > Trampled to the floor it spanned,
> And the tent of night in tatters
> > Straws the sky-pavilioned land.
> > *(Reveille)*

A vault can hardly be a tent, 'straw' is not appropriate for something shattered (*can* a shadow be shattered?), and the image of a tent (or is it a vault?) on the floor of a pavilion is not a happy one. However, Housman has sensibility enough to feel the injustice and hardness of life, to see the pathos of unreturning time, and he tries to avoid sentimentality in expressing his awareness:

> Some can gaze and not be sick
> But I could never learn the trick.
> There's this to say for blood and breath,
> They give a man a taste for death.
> (*Additional Poems*, XVI)

But the force of his revulsion always spends itself in a generalized tough-tenderness. Any profound criticism of life or society is still-born. So he tends to be at his best in a mode which is not character-istic of either group – in the lapidary rendering of some general human experience, with a suppressed wry humour:

> Now times are altered: if I care
> To buy a thing, I can;
> The pence are here and here's the fair,
> But where's the lost young man?
> (*Last Poems*, XXXV)

John Davidson (1857–1909) is obviously influenced by both parties, and even more obviously unassimilable to either. But unlike Hous-man, he never succeeds in creating a characteristic poetry. Tone, style, and outlook vary erratically from period to period and even from poem to poem. That this is probably the result of his having a far wider range, emotionally and intellectually, and a more daring independence, unhappily does not make him a better poet. His potentialities were greater, but so was the gap between potentiality and achievement. Davidson – a rare visitor to the Rhymers' Club – was no doubt right in saying that the Rhymers lacked 'blood and guts', but Yeats's comment on Davidson was equally valid:

I think he might have grown to be a successful man had he been enthusiastic ... about Dowson or Johnson, or Horne or Symons, for they had what I still lacked, conscious deliberate craft.[11]

Many of his poems are 'aesthetic', in a clumsy, sentimental way, both in diction and content. In others, such as the *Ballad of a Workman*, aesthetic diction is incongruous with the content and tone:

> Better a hundred times to die,
> And sink into the mould,
> Than like a stagnant puddle lie
> With arabesques of scum enscrolled.

His *Song for the Twenty-fourth of May*, on the other hand, almost outdoes Kipling or Henley in its jingoism:

Sea-room, land-room, ours, my masters, ours,
Hand in hand with destiny, and first among the Powers!
Our boasted Ocean Empire, sirs, we boast of it again,
Our Monarch, and our Rulers, and our Women, and our Men!

Thirty Bob a Week, however, uses common idiom more successfully than Kipling usually did. He manages not to sound patronizing
and not to give the impression of dropping his aitches with calculated pedantry. But the poem is marred by Davidson's queer Nietz-
schian emphasis on the will, which makes his clerk insist: 'I woke
because I thought the time had come;/Beyond my will there was no
other cause ... I was the love that chose my mother out;/I joined
two lives and from the union burst.'

In his later poetry, particularly his Fleet Street poems, Davidson
attempted to develop this 'unpoetic' idiom, but very rarely succeeded. *The Testament of Sir Simon Simplex Concerning Automobilism*,
for example, goes on as it begins:

That railways are inadequate appears
Indubitable now. For sixty years
Their comfort grew until the *train de luxe*
Arrived ...

This is not bad poetry; it is bad prose.

Yet *Crystal Palace*, in the same volume, opens excellently, in an
easy free verse, not too ostentatiously colloquial or too self-effacing
for its subject:

Contraption, – that's the bizarre, proper, slang,
Eclectic word, for this portentous toy,
The flying-machine, that gyrates stiffly, arms
A-kimbo, so to say, and baskets slung
From every elbow, skating in the air ...

Very soon, however, it passes into mannered jargon – and in this, if
nothing else, it is characteristic of the age.

If there is one thing common to all writers of the last phase, whatever their political or psychological complexion, it is the tendency
to strike a pose and adopt a manner. Occasionally, as in *The Importance of Being Earnest* or *M'Andrew's Hymn*, it produces what is at once
a technical *tour de force* and a minor masterpiece. More usually, of
course, it prevents the writer from being faithful to the complexities
of his real experience. Such mannered art can be not unpleasing in a
frivolous writer; it is ill-mannered in one who presumes to preach.

NOTES

1. William Gaunt, *The Aesthetic Adventure* (London, 1945), 210.

2. Walter Pater, Epilogue to *The Renaissance*, 1873. Removed from the edition of 1877 – lest it should harm young men – and restored after slight modification in 1888.

3. Holbrook Jackson, *The Eighteen-Nineties* (London, 1913), 63.

4. Charles Carrington, *Rudyard Kipling* (London, 1955), 40.

5. All quotations of Wilde's poetry are from *Poems* (London, 1951).

6. All quotations of Kipling's poetry are from *Rudyard Kipling's Verse*, Inclusive Edition 1885–1918, 3 vols (London, 1919).

7. Edward Shanks, *Rudyard Kipling* (London, 1940), 81.

8. All further quotations of Kipling's stories are from *A Choice of Kipling's Prose*, ed. Somerset Maugham (London, 1952).

9. V. de S. Pinto, *Crisis in English Poetry* (London, 1951), 32.

10. W. B. Yeats, *Autobiographies* (London, 1926), 382.

11. W. B. Yeats, 392.

HARDY'S TALES ANCIENT AND MODERN

G. D. KLINGOPULOS

The sense of Hardy's (1840–1928) distinction, which, while he lived, may have appeared to owe some of its strength to general esteem of his personal qualities, has not weakened in the years since his death. This is all the more impressive considering the absence of agreement about the centre of his achievement. As Edmund Blunden wrote in his attractive English Men of Letters volume: 'There is a kind of friendly contention for the ownership of Hardy's true greatness as a writer, and hitherto it has swayed one way and another with the hours and the incidents of opinion.' On the whole, Blunden favours Hardy's poetry and is content to describe the novels in general terms, with numerous irresistible illustrations of his 'inartistic knottiness', his 'remarkable spasms of contorted and straggling English'. Ideally, Hardy's work should be regarded as the indivisible expression of a poet-novelist, but there are several good reasons for discussing the fiction separately. All the novels are strictly Victorian in date, whilst the verse, though often composed earlier, was collected between 1898 and 1928, and has become an indispensable part of any account of twentieth-century poetry. From Hardy's verse some admirers would detach The Dynasts (1903–8), which others find disappointing, as being the most important of his works. 'In The Dynasts we feel the full force of Hardy's matured character and thought: by comparison, his stories, poems, and novels, even the finest of them, seem puny and somehow lacking in masculine virility.'[1] Much of the difficulty of writing critically about Hardy is acknowledged in this writer's 'somehow'. (Hardy's verse is considered in Volume 7 of the Guide.)

Although they may not represent his 'true greatness', Hardy's novels bring into literature a very rare combination of influences and gifts. In his work a more than personal richness, which might easily have gone unrecorded, found expression. None of his novels, with the possible exception of The Hand of Ethelberta, is metropolitan in its

setting; all contain evidence, implicit or explicit, of the tension in Hardy's mind between Dorset and London. There is no comparison between his Wessex and Barsetshire. His local attachment or piety had in it, no doubt, some desire for simplification; but Hardy was not self-deceived. He knew that a way of life was vanishing in his time, and on the whole, as a 'meliorist', he was on the side of the steam-engines. It was probably fortunate that Hardy did not go to a university. Academic influences would have broken that unaffected, slightly archaic, connection with his native place which his self-education and his architectural training did not destroy. He might have become like his own Mr Lackland, the returned emigrant, whose arrival is the occasion for the telling of all the stories in *A few Crusted Characters*:

> The figure of Mr Lackland was seen at the inn, and in the village street, and in the fields and lanes about Upper Longpuddle, for a few days after his arrival, and then, ghost-like, it silently disappeared. He had told some of the villagers that his immediate purpose in coming had been fulfilled by a sight of the place, and by his conversation with its inhabitants: but that his ulterior purpose – of coming to spend his latter days among them – would probably never be carried out. It is now a dozen or fifteen years since his visit was paid, and his face has not again been seen.

We are not, however, to think of Hardy as a prophet of *The Waste Land*, which was published before the end of his long lifetime. He was much preoccupied with the idea of the return of the native, but he was primarily aware of his own good luck, his rich sense of connection, though much of what he felt connected with was already a matter of antiquarian lore, or recollection in 'the Mead of Memories' where 'the sad man sighed his fantasies'.[2] When all deductions have been made, and the merely literary, faintly Shakespearian, ancestry of many of his rustic humorists has been pointed out, there remains more than enough truthfulness in Hardy's vision of Wessex to make his attitude of suspense between things ancient and modern a poignant one. Anecdotes abound of his unpretentiousness, independence, and simplicity. Edmund Blunden tells of an occasion when Lawrence of Arabia and Hardy discussed the *Iliad* and Hardy said: ' "I've always thought it was as good as *Marmion*" (quite seriously).' Hardy's much-analysed prose, which sometimes reads like the work of the local newspaper reporter on his mettle, is itself evidence of the

same personal judgement and genuineness. His notebooks include a high proportion of laboriously excogitated commonplace, but there are sudden shrewd observations like the following:

> 1891, Feb. 10. Newman and Carlyle. The former's was a feminine nature, which decides and then finds reasons for having decided. He was an enthusiast with the absurd reputation of a logician and reasoner. Carlyle was a poet with the reputation of a philosopher. Neither was truly a *thinker*.

This entry may of course owe something to Hardy's friendship with Leslie Stephen. Hardy's account of his visit to Stephen's house late one evening (23 March 1875) to witness the signature of Stephen's renunciation of holy orders seems at first a little incongruous, but the scepticism of the countryman was the complement of the intellectual's. Probably Stephen saw in Hardy the spokesman of continuities which would survive an age of change. And he may have recalled especially, from the novel which Hardy, at Stephen's invitation, had contributed to the *Cornhill Magazine* in the previous year, the description of the sheep-shearing in the ancient barn, set between medieval castle and medieval church:

> The old barn embodied practices which had suffered no mutilation at the hands of time. Here at least the spirit of the ancient builders was at one with the spirit of the modern beholder. Standing before this abraded pile, the eye regarded its present usage, the mind dwelt upon its past history, with a satisfied sense of functional continuity throughout – a feeling almost of gratitude, and quite of pride, at the permanence of the idea which had heaped it up. The fact that four centuries had neither proved it to be founded on a mistake, inspired any hatred of its purpose, nor given rise to any reaction that had battered it down, invested this simple grey effort of old minds with a repose, if not grandeur, which a too curious reflection was apt to disturb in its ecclesiastical and military compeers ... This picture of today in its frame of four hundred years ago did not produce that marked contrast between things ancient and modern which is implied by the contrast of date.
>
> *(Far from the Madding Crowd)*

Much has been written about Hardy's 'pessimism' and 'philosophy', and about the influence on him of various thinkers, notably J. S. Mill, Spencer, Stephen, and Schopenhauer. It is true that the sombre vision which underlies his comedy intensifies in the later novels except in the last, *The Well-Beloved*, which, though a revision of earlier work and not meant to be taken very seriously, reveals a

characteristic Shelleyan preoccupation with marriage in relation to an ideal. But no account of Hardy's outlook would be appropriate which did not recognize the inherited and timeless quality of his scepticism. It deepened into pessimism under the stress of personal experience and the spirit of the age. Fundamentally, his was the normal scepticism which subsists peaceably beside local pieties and traditions. It resembles the fatalism of the milkmaids in *Tess*, who 'had been reared in the lonely country nooks where fatalism is a strong sentiment'. Florence Hardy wrote in *The Later Years of Thomas Hardy 1897–1928*:

He said once – perhaps oftener – that although invidious critics had cast slurs upon him as Nonconformist, Agnostic, Atheist, Infidel, Immoralist, Heretic, Pessimist, or something else equally opprobrious in their eyes, they have never thought of calling him what they might have called him much more plausibly – churchy; not in an intellectual sense but in so far as instincts and emotions ruled. As a child, to be a parson had been his dream; moreover he had several clerical relatives who held livings, while his grandfather, father, uncle, brother, wife, cousin, and two sisters had been musicians in various churches over a period covering altogether more than a hundred years. He himself had frequently read the church lessons, and had at one time as a young man begun reading for Cambridge with a view to taking orders.

This is clearly not the outlook of a consistent thinker and it would be futile to attempt to reconcile Hardy's remarks about the Church in the passage quoted above from *Far from the Madding Crowd* with those in, say, his Apology to *Late Lyrics and Earlier*. Hardy's consistencies are based on feeling, habit, a keen sense of romance and of life's little ironies, an eye for significant detail, and on increasing personal discomfort with its tendency to return to the same themes such as marriage, or the nature of woman, or the symbolic death of village bands. Hardy never outgrew a preoccupation with class – his first novel, never published and now lost, was entitled *The Poor Man and the Lady* – and he frequently betrays a certain amount of personal involvement or self-projection in his fiction.

April 28, 1888. A short story of a young man – 'who could not go to Oxford' – his struggles and ultimate failure. Suicide. [Probably the germ of *Jude the Obscure*.] There is something [in this] the world ought to be shown, and I am the one to show it to them – though I was not altogether hindered going, at least to Cambridge, and could have gone up easily at five-and-twenty.[3]

The impression given of the author by the sum of Hardy's fiction is not of a powerful analyst of human life, but of a meditative story-teller or romancer, sharing keenly the imagined vicissitudes of his characters who move in an agricultural setting menaced by the forces of change. He had the story-teller's unselfconscious liking for his own command of dialect, which accounts for the length of some of his rustic dialogues. His short stories counterbalance the intense pessimism of a part of his fiction and help us to see the novels as the creation of a writer, not, like George Eliot, primarily interested in the processes of moral choice, frustration, and fulfilment, but rooted in place, reflective, fond of pathos, fluent, humorous rather than witty, slightly bewildered and upset by his later notoriety as the exponent of advanced moral views. Hardy could not have written anything like the sustained wit of the opening chapters of *Middlemarch*. But he had a splendid gift for the broader kinds of pastoral comedy. His short story *The Distracted Preacher* which, like much of his fiction, relies a great deal on action minutely described, is a faultless narrative of adventure and romance, enriched by Hardy's unavowed approval of the independent morality of the vanished smuggling villages. Partiality for old customs, representing unconventional moral patterns, always brings a certain warmth into Hardy's sentences, as in his references, in *The Well-Beloved*, to the islanders' way of making 'formal ratification of a betrothal, according to the precedent of their sires and grandsires'. In another mode, *The Fiddler of the Reels* delicately yet powerfully evokes the effect of music and dancing on the mind of a simple woman. No symbolism appears to be intended, and one cannot even be sure that Hardy was conscious of an implicit contrast between the ecstasy of the woman's relationship with the fiddler and her submissiveness towards her husband Ned. It is the same kind of uncertainty we experience when reading of Sergeant Troy's swordplay before the fascinated Bathsheba Everdene; Hardy's intention seems to be the limited one of exhibiting the childishness of womankind.

The modern reader, with Lawrence and Freud as part of his self-knowledge, is frequently tantalized by episodes in Hardy which seem to promise a rich development of themes but are rarely worked out or followed up. Even the throwing of the pig's genitals in *Jude the Obscure* is not really used in the delineation of the character

of the hero. To be sure, Hardy had to consider the susceptibilities of his readers, but he expected the symbolic missile to do much of his work for him. It is easy to misjudge Hardy's conscious intentions and to read too much into such pieces as *The Withered Arm* or *Barbara of the House of Grebe*, the story which Eliot thought 'had been written solely to provide a satisfaction for some morbid emotion'. There may have been a morbid element in Hardy's lifelong interest in hanging and maiming; but these tales aim, not to evoke 'a world of pure Evil', but to supply examples of life's abundant strangeness as a means of passing the time. Hardy implies as much when he arranges some of his stories as a sequence told in turn by a group of country people and explains that:

the pedigrees of our country families ... mostly appear at first sight to be as barren of any touch of nature as a table of logarithms. But given a clue – the faintest tradition of what went on behind the scenes – and this dryness as of dust may be transformed into a palpitating drama.

If the reader did not control his palpitations by recognizing the degree of seriousness, the mode of discourse, represented by each story, some of Hardy would make rather painful reading. Hardy is obviously more deeply involved in writing *Tess of the D'Urbervilles* than in writing *The Romantic Adventures of a Milkmaid*, a story easily misread. He was fond of writing about the bewitchment of his characters by the opposite sex; indeed, his view of love tends to take that form but the impression is frequently not one of 'drama' but of perfunctoriness. This is only made tolerable by Hardy's ready command of charm and pathos. Such tales as *Our Exploits at West Poley*, *Interlopers at the Knap*, and *The Three Strangers* help to give a more definite picture of Hardy's idiosyncrasy, his preoccupation with ancient things and his tendency to use them as 'symbols', his distinctive formality, and his enjoyment of a tale well-told, especially a tale of courtship with an ironical twist in it.

Hardy's true greatness, if it is to be found in his fiction, cannot be said to reside in his short stories, memorable as they often are, but must be sought in his novels, more particularly in the later novels, *The Return of the Native* (1878), *The Trumpet Major* (1880), *The Mayor of Casterbridge* (1886), *The Woodlanders* (1887), *Tess of the D'Urbervilles* (1891), and *Jude the Obscure* (1896). All these work towards a sombre dénouement and must be regarded as the practical application

of Hardy's lifelong notemaking on the subject of 'tragedy'. Though they represent a concentration of his permanent interests and attitudes, they are not by any means the only novels which have retained their popularity. *Far from the Madding Crowd* (1874), the book which established Hardy's reputation and made it possible for him to marry, is in many ways one of his most assured successes, with more of his characteristic freshness of observation in it than several of the later works. Even his failures among the novels have their interest for anyone with an affection for Hardy's singularity. For example, *The Laodicean* (1881), which was dictated during a long illness, has an architect for its hero, utilizes professional and romantic experiences in Hardy's life, including his theological reading, and deals with the recurrent theme of the impact of the railway and telegraph age on rural England. The railways are symbolized by Paula Power, daughter of the railway builder and staunch Baptist John Power, who bought the castle which forced him to make a bend in his railway line – 'a clash between ancient and modern'. Under the influence of this medieval property Paula is in danger of losing her Nonconformist outlook, refuses to be baptized in the new red-brick chapel, becomes interested in family trees, especially that of the previous owners of the castle, and develops a distaste for 'the nobility of talent and enterprise'. She is saved from the consequences of such Laodicean indifference to her own Baptist and Industrial ancestry by the nice young architect George Somerset who has 'more of the beauty – if beauty it ought to be called – of the future human type than of the past' and is free from the vices and encumbrances of aristocracy in decline. The story contains none of Hardy's special richness but it is a competently written serial which, besides adding to our knowledge of his outlook, reveals Hardy's characteristic faintheartedness in following up his themes.

Henry James's praise of a Conrad novel, that it had been 'done so as to undergo most doing', is only occasionally applicable to Hardy's work, and then to his description and dialect rather than to his main plots. And D. H. Lawrence's long 'Study', in which he seems to be on the point of re-writing Hardy's novels for him, is an impressive outburst of exasperation at his frequent preference for the obvious, his 'genius for the commonplace', and his tendency to keep to the level of romance and fantasy – of which coincidences are the instru-

ments – rather than go more thoroughly into his imagined situations and themes. This does not matter where Hardy is aiming only at a comedy of incidents as in *The Hand of Ethelberta* (1876), or where he is writing what used to be called a 'sensational' novel such as his first, *Desperate Remedies* (1871), in which an architect is again the hero. When, however, the novelist himself, in what appears only another bitter-sweet love story, imagines that he has opened up immense perspectives, some failure of communication is involved. *Two on a Tower* (1882) is the story of the love between the young wife of an absentee baronet and a poor youth with a passion for astronomy, and the far-fetched consequences of a clandestine marriage. It contains some good passages but also much melodrama and unintentional farce. Yet this was a novel which, Hardy tells us, 'was the outcome of a wish to set the emotional history of two infinitesimal lives against the stupendous background of the stellar universe'. To create this setting he labours the marvels revealed by the telescope, but the effect is trivial and his motives confused. The insistence on the 'horror' and 'nightmare' of space contrasts with the unforced delight in constellations and their names in *Far from the Madding Crowd* which is quite free from factitious attempts to achieve profundity. The strength of this novel is in the freshness and vividness of its descriptive passages such as the accounts of Gabriel's courtship, his battle with the storm, and his skilful surgery on the wind-swollen sheep. Its weakness is the common one in Hardy of unsatisfactory or sketchy moral dénouement. The ending leaves an impression of cynicism or callousness. Could anything have been worse than indefinite imprisonment for a man of Boldwood's temperament, and did Troy have to die to make room for Gabriel? Hardy always had difficulty in resolving his fictional entanglements. His Bathshebas are too fickle to be taken seriously as moral agents. Hardy's ideal of woman tended to approximate to that ascribed to young Springrove, the architect, in his first novel:

> He says she must be girlish and artless: yet he would be loth to do without a dash of womanly subtlety, 'tis so piquant. Yes, he said that must be in her; she must have womanly cleverness. 'And yet I should like her to blush if only a cock-sparrow were to look at her hard,' he said.

Nevertheless one cannot begrudge eventual success to the patient ingenious stayer Gabriel Oak, especially as Hardy later denied the

prize to his steadfast heroes as part of his tragic or ironic view of things. This is what happens to the more noble of Miller Loveday's two sons in the delightful tragi-comedy of the Napoleonic wars, *The Trumpet Major* (1879), in which Hardy succeeded in expressing some of his lifelong interest in that epic period of history without moving outside his special province. The novel was a by-product of the long process of reading and sight-seeing which preceded the writing of *The Dynasts*. Hardy rightly classed it with his *Romances and Fantasies*, for the main subject is a rustic courtship and the effect of soldiers and soldiering on the unmartial peasantry who much prefer choir practice to drilling. The heroine is once again a changeable creature, and the manner in which John the trumpet-major takes his disappointment and Bob the sailor accepts congratulations leads up to the irony and sentiment of the last paragraph.

The Return of the Native is a more ambitious work. As the title suggests, it is Hardy's attempt to write directly about some of his main interests and attitudes. The result is disappointing, a fact which is half recognized by the frequent critical assertion that the true subject of the novel is the background, Egdon Heath itself. Hardy's intentions are certainly represented in the story – by the permanence and inhospitableness of the heath, by the labour of the furze-cutters, by the Christmas mumming, and by the implied contrast between the settled and the unsettled characters. But nothing can make up for the vagueness of the main actors, especially Clym the returned native, who ought to carry much of the book's significance. The one definite action in the novel is Wildeve's leap into the weir after Eustacia. It is painful to watch Hardy, who ought to have had so much to say about Clym, scraping around to give him significance, almost as if the moralizing novelist had been defeated by his own plot. Unintentionally Clym is made to seem inadequate as the partner of Eustacia, and his blindness and reabsorption into the heath are certainly not a convincing regeneration, rather the reverse. Yet we are told that Clym represents the intellectual type of the future, as the Heath represents the scenery which best suits the 'more thinking among mankind'. The Heath is 'a near relation of night', it 'had a lovely face suggesting tragic possibilities'. After the death of Eustacia, 'Yeobright found his vocation in the career of an itinerant open-air preacher and lecturer on morally unimpeachable subjects'. Here, where one might

suspect irony, Hardy is entirely serious, but even he seems doubtful about the substance of Yeobright's lectures. As for Eustacia, in so far as she is anything more than a figure out of melodrama, she attracts too much sympathy for her boredom to fit passively into Hardy's moral scheme. Much is made of the Reddleman as an emanation of the heath, but the dominant impression is of an extraordinary resemblance between him and the heroes of cowboy stories; he is resourceful, fast-moving, handy with the dice, a good shot, a skilled eavesdropper, good at self-concealment and camouflage, with a perfect knowledge of terrain and short-cuts.

More is implied by the comparative failure of *The Return of the Native* than the limitations of Hardy's moral interest. It suggests that when attempting to write more seriously than, say, in *Far from the Madding Crowd*, about themes which might be considered to lie at the heart of the Wessex novels, Hardy is not quite sure what he means and is felt to be the victim of a slightly sentimental and over-simple attitude to his problems. It was one thing to picture, in the last quarter of the nineteenth century, a Gabriel Oak as quite at home in Weatherbury, but it was another matter to do the same for Clym Yeobright. Hardy was faced with a rather similar difficulty in portraying Angel Clare in *Tess of the D'Urbervilles* though, unlike Clym, Angel is not required to justify a novel's title. It is enough that, milking the cows, he should become 'wonderfully free from the chronic melancholy which is taking hold of the civilized races with the decline of belief in a beneficent Power'. Despite all its well-known falsities and fatalism, its insipid hero and diabolic villain, *Tess* is the most poignant of all Hardy's stories. This is not because of anything that the heroine may be thought to symbolize, or any thesis that may be implied, but because Hardy is here writing more singly than in any other work about casual wrong, the will to recover, the growth of love, faithfulness, frail happiness, and death. It is a much simpler novel than most of Hardy's, and it contains some of his best writing as well as some of his worst. Much of Tess's suffering results, of course, from Angel's obduracy which seemed unreal even to Hardy: 'With all his attempted independence of judgement this advanced and well-meaning young man, a sample product of the last five-and-twenty years, was yet the slave to custom and conventionality, when surprised back into his early teachings.'

Hardy is at pains to explain that because everything is fated, the characters can only suffer as they follow their appointed courses. Like all dogmas which oversimplify the moral texture of life, Hardy's deterministic notions, whether derived from Aeschylus or nineteenth-century science, did not help him to overcome his great weakness as a novelist, his inability to go beyond stereotypes of character and to deepen the intrinsic development of his plot. There is always a gap between Hardy's general statement of themes and the action which should embody them. As with the symbolism of Egdon Heath, the reader of *Tess* has to make what rough connection he can, in the fine threshing-machine passages, between the sooty engineman with his 'strange northern accent' and the intruding Alec Stoke-d'Urberville, the son of the northern tradesman-turned-gentleman. Here as elsewhere it is probably as well to ignore Hardy's symbolism which, when closely examined, increases the impression of melodrama and simplification. Hardy's difficulties in developing the 'interest' of his characters give ironic force to his exasperated comment on Henry James: 'James's subjects are those one could be interested in at moments when there is nothing larger to think of.'

The wood in *The Woodlanders* has the same kind of status as Egdon Heath, and there are other resemblances between the novels in the functions of characters and the underlying theme of the returning native. Though Hardy is here once more defending the countryside against the outside world, he is not deluded about the outcome and no longer tries to score fictitious triumphs. Giles Winterbourne dies, Grace returns to the townsman Fitzpiers, and only the defeated Marty is left to mourn. She appears to mourn more than the death of a man:

'Now, my own, own love,' she whispered. 'You are mine, and only mine; for she has forgot 'ee at last, although for her you died! But I – whenever I get up I'll think of 'ee, and whenever I lie down I'll think of 'ee again. Whenever I plant the young larches I'll think that none can plant as you planted: and whenever I split a gad, and whenever I turn the cider wring, I'll say none could do it like you. If ever I forget your name let me forget home and heaven!'

Hardy's resigned acceptance of the disappearance of a way of life informs many passages in this novel, especially those describing the lives of Winterbourne and Marty South. But once more the flimsy main plot, the love-affairs of Fitzpiers with Grace, Mrs Charmond,

and Suke Damson, and the incongruity of Winterbourne's martyrdom to Victorian convention prevent anything like a complete
response. Such a response, in which the reader is carried along by the
swift concentration of events, by the reality with which the town, its
business, its taverns, its river, and its people are created, is achieved
by *The Mayor of Casterbridge*. The reason for this success is that Hardy
has kept to a minimum the explicit statements of his permanent attitudes so that here there is no gap between action and symbolism.
The defeat and death of Henchard, the survival of the ingenious,
machine-minded, thrifty Scot, who is ever 'giving strong expression
to a song of his dear native country that he loved so well as never to
have revisited it', these carry Hardy's sardonic intention quite adequately without any injection of additional symbolism and commentary. There is no insistence here on tragic significance, nor does
Hardy claim more in his preface than to have written a 'story [which]
is more particularly a study of one man's deeds and character than,
perhaps, any other of those included in my Exhibition of Wessex
Life'. The effect of Henchard's downfall is impressive enough, but
one could call it tragic only in a newspaper sense, for he is plainly a
doomed puppet. The power of the novel is in the density and confidence of its localization, and the sense of historical reality which the
action derives from being put back to the years before the Repeal
of the Corn Laws (1846):

> Casterbridge was a place deposited in the block upon a cornfield. There was
> no suburb in the modern sense, or transitional intermixture of town and down.
> It stood, with regard to the wide fertile land adjoining, clean-cut and distinct,
> like a chessboard on a green tablecloth. The farmer's boy could sit under
> his barley-mow and pitch a stone into the office-window of the town-clerk;
> reapers at work among the sheaves nodded to acquaintances standing on the
> pavement-corner; . . .

Hardy was not a deliberate realist, but he could not help writing
with rich particularity about the town of Dorchester. The result is a
tale in which the typical quality of the characters is more than compensated for by the poetic clarity of the setting and episodes. The
novelist is here not as deeply committed to his theme as in some of
Tess or *The Woodlanders*, but this novel with *Far from the Madding
Crowd* will probably come to represent Hardy's powers as a novelist.
Jude the Obscure is the one novel which is frequently disliked even by

Hardy's admirers. It is in many ways a change of subject and of ground. His permanent attitude to the talented poor man, his tendency to exaggerate his own struggles for self-education, his acceptance of the decline of his own world and the emergence of a colourless modernity requiring an effort of adjustment like Jude's uprooting, all these combined with obscure bitterness, possibly influenced by Schopenhauer, about sexuality, marriage, and love to make an action which is oppressive and far from luminous. Well might Edmund Gosse exclaim in a review of the book: 'What has Providence done to Mr Hardy that he should rise up in the arable land of Wessex and shake his fist at his Creator?' Among other things Hardy here poses a problem, 'the deadly war between flesh and spirit', which is implicit in the limitations of his characterization in all his novels, in his white and black representation of Good and Bad, and his stereotypes of men and women. His lifelong attachment to Shelley suggests an affinity usually overlooked. But Shelley could only accentuate Hardy's stultifying intellectual and emotional difficulties, whereas a deeper study of George Eliot, such as Henry James gave to her work, might have helped Hardy to find a new sense of purpose as a novelist. As it is, his determination to show in *Jude* 'the contrast between the ideal life a man wished to lead and the squalid real life he was fated to lead' rigidly dominates the novel. The contrast was 'meant to run all through the book. It is, in fact, to be discovered in everybody's life, though it lies less on the surface perhaps than it does in my poor puppets.' This, from a letter, concedes much of the critical case against *Jude*, that it is too simply an illustration of Hardy's later ideas and attitudes. 'In writing *Jude* my mind was fixed on the ending.' But the ending is only lugubrious and Jude is as much of a puppet as Henchard. Nevertheless, the earlier parts contain the most careful presentation of experience in all his work.

Hardy himself always considered that his true vocation lay in poetry, and gave the impression that his novels were a means to that end. 'Now *there* is clarity,' wrote Ezra Pound, reading Hardy's *Collected Poems* in 1937. 'There *is* the harvest of having written 20 novels first.' Hardy's true genius is indeed less securely represented by his novels than by his poetry, though two or three of the novels should remain minor classics. And as a poet's record of ancient ways that were submerged by modern life, much of his fiction is poignant

and historically indispensable. If it cannot be said to represent a culmination of the powers of the Victorian novel, for it has little of the comic abundance and vitality of Dickens on the one hand, or the intellectual and moral penetration of George Eliot and Henry James on the other, it contributed to the social deepening of the novel and to the discovery of the poetry of dialect speech. Hardy is among those writers who have increased the amount of reality in the world. When his poetry and prose are considered together, he appears one of the most important mediators of continuity between the nineteenth and the twentieth centuries.

NOTES

1. Evelyn Hardy, *Thomas Hardy: A Critical Biography* (London, 1954).
2. See his poem, *The Dead Quire* (1897).
3. F. E. Hardy, *The Early Life of Thomas Hardy 1840–91* (London, 1928), 272.

THE CHANGING ENVIRONMENT:
CITY AND COUNTRYSIDE

ASA BRIGGS

The Victorians were as much preoccupied with change in their living and working environments as they were with change in their society and culture. Indeed, some of the most eloquent of them, like Ruskin and Morris, traced direct connections between the two.

To succeeding generations the preoccupations took different shapes, however. Before the advent of the railway, questions concerning town and country were raised and discussed in much the same form and manner as they had been in the late eighteenth century. There was no agreement about the answers, for some writers took pride in numbers and others feared them, and some welcomed the growth of industry and others were shocked by it. Macaulay's critique of Southey's *Colloquies* (1830) revealed the extent of the gap:

> Mr. Southey has found out a way, he tells us, in which the effects of manufactures and agriculture may be compared. And what is that way? To stand on a hill, to look at a cottage and a factory, and to see which is the prettier.[1]

The railway brought something new into the argument: Thackeray compared the state of affairs before and after the railway with the state of affairs before and after the Flood.[2] It changed the tempo of life and altered relationships between people and places as much as it transformed the physical environment both of country and of town. 'Railroads,' wrote Surtees in 1858, 'have taken the starch out of country magnificence as well as out of town.'[3] There was as much disagreement about the aesthetics of railways, however, as there had been about the aesthetics of early industrial towns. Dickens pointed out the devastation that railways could do to London. Yet the conservative Croker could write to a constituent who condemned the desecration of the countryside that when he contemplated a railroad which ran through 'the beautiful valley of the Derwent', he

concluded that 'triumph of art sets off, as well as renders more accessible, the natural beauties of the scene.'[4]

By 1870 there were 13,500 miles of railway track, a figure which increased to 18,000 in 1895. They made up what was called a 'railway system', just as the factories, main units of industrial production, by the end of the century some of them large, made up a 'factory system'. The increasing use of the word 'system' suggested industrial order rather than industrial revolution, though the term 'industrial revolution' began to be widely used only after the 1880s, when industry had come to be taken for granted, setting the framework and routines of life. Even agriculture came to be described as Britain's largest industry. Only a few people, if any, recalled that a century before the word 'industry' had denoted a desirable human quality, not a visible segment of the economy and of the landscape.

What was visible in the industrial scene was a product of a particular and now dated technology and of a particular and less dated 'economic system', memorably described by an American historian of cities, Lewis Mumford, as 'carboniferous capitalism'. The main motive power was steam, source of metaphor as well as energy, and it was steam which propelled the railway as well as drove machines. The main basic resources, employed wastefully, were coal and iron, with steel replacing iron in many uses only during the late 1850s and 1860s. The main by-product was smoke, and attempts to abate the volume of smoke by legislation provoked tough opposition. Behind the visible industrial scene was the invisible hand of the market, for it was shaped and re-shaped by market forces with only limited elements of planning. Yet there was ample evidence of a desire to plan as well as to regulate.

Descriptions of the industrial landscape include the impressionistic, the photographic, and the symbolic, although in an age when painters preferred other themes, ranging from honeysuckled cottages to lake-land peaks, they were mainly verbal. The early industrial landscape had sometimes inspired the writers both of prose and of poetry. The gorges of Coalbrookdale in Shropshire, for example, with the main sight there the first iron bridge in the world, were picturesque enough to appeal to the romantic imagination.[5] Only by night, however, could the Black Country exert a similar appeal a century later. The best-known literary response to industry of the mid-nineteenth

century, Dickens's picture of Coketown in *Hard Times* (1854), was neither romantic nor photographic but satirical. Coketown was not exciting, but monotonous. Every street was like every other street, every day like every other day. Coketown was a product of what seemed to Dickens to be a false utilitarian philosophy. Yet because it was a town of 'unnatural red and black' it presented a face 'like the painted face of a savage'.[6] Mumford was wrong to suggest that all industrial towns were like Coketown or that they were all the same place 'with different aliases',[7] for there were many differences between industrial towns, even in their appearance. He was right, however, to note the emergence of a new species of industrial town, what a writer of the time called 'a system of society organized according to entirely new principles'.[8]

By the end of the century industrial towns were taken for granted, and interest in cities had shifted from the provincial cities, which had been transformed by the industrial revolution, back to the metropolis, London, 'the world city'. Yet the critique of the new industrial environment never lost its force. D. H. Lawrence, born in a mining village in Nottinghamshire, extended William Cowper's dictum 'God made the country, man made the town' to read 'the country is so lovely: the man-made England is so vile'. For Lawrence 'the real tragedy of England' was 'the tragedy of ugliness', and it was 'ugliness which really betrayed the spirit of man in the nineteenth century'. The tragedy now lay, however, not in the fact that people were affronted by what they saw, but that they were 'beaten down' by it. They had forgotten how to look. As Lawrence wrote:

The English are town-birds through and through, today, as the inevitable result of their complete industrialization. Yet they don't know how to build a city, how to think of one, or how to live in one.[9]

Other writers saw their immediate urban or industrial surroundings in different ways from Lawrence: they might even feel the smoke to be romantic and the marble halls of the central city to be magnificent. Even the 'classic slum' – and the word, deriving from slang, seems to have been first used in the 1820s – appeared to have social, if not aesthetic, merits – an 'organic' way of life with a tangle of intimate personal relationships.[10] Where Lawrence was wrong in fact was to identify urbanization exclusively with industrialization.

Related though the two processes undoubtedly were, they were not synonymous. Some cities were not industrial in the same way that Manchester was – and even Manchester emerged in the nineteenth century as the mercantile and servicing capital of a textiles-producing region, Cottonopolis, rather than as a manufacturing centre. It was the smaller cotton towns in Lancashire which fulfilled that latter role. One other city in Lancashire, Liverpool, was port and mercantile centre also, often sharply contrasted with Manchester both by local inhabitants and by sophisticated visitors. Wherever there were large numbers of dockers, casual labourers, there was a different kind of society, but there were other differences in the social structures: there were 'gentlemen' in Liverpool, too, who felt themselves superior to self-made employers in Manchester.

Other categories of towns and cities included growing 'country towns', closely associated with their rural neighbourhoods, and holiday towns, like Brighton which grew more rapidly than any other town in England between 1821 and 1831. Its close associations were with London, and as early as 1841 it was described as 'the greatest sanitarium of the largest and wealthiest city in the world'.[11] Bath had once fulfilled this purpose, but Georgian Bath was felt to be dull to look at, and Victorian resorts like Bournemouth and Eastbourne came into their own.

London as a capital city was always *sui generis*. It had to be compared with Paris or Rome rather than with Manchester or Liverpool. Yet in a sense, *pace* Mumford, every town or city was *sui generis*. Birmingham, for example, proclaimed a civic gospel in the 1870s, which involved comparisons in its case with Florence and even Athens. Moreover, since the civic gospel was proclaimed above all others by nonconformist ministers, there was always in the background the example of the Biblical city. 'Every town,' wrote W. R. Lethaby in 1900, 'is a Zion and has had its prophets.'[12]

It was in 1851, the year of the Great Exhibition of Industry in the newly built Crystal Palace – itself dependent for its design and construction on iron – that the census revealed that fractionally more than half the total population of England and Wales were 'town birds', that is to say living in urban districts with a population of 10,000 or more. 'For the first time in modern history a body politic had got into a mainly urban condition' and 'no other country in

the world approached such a condition until after 1900.'[13] Already, indeed, nearly a quarter of the population were living in urban areas with a population of over 100,000. In 1801 there had been no cities of this size outside London: by 1851 there were 23. It was in 1851 also that the first absolute declines in county population totals were revealed, and by 1861 the position was beginning to concern contemporaries. Among the counties which lost in total numbers during that decade were Norfolk, Somerset and Suffolk. A writer on 'rural life and labour' in 1911 was still bemoaning the 'alarming and increasing depopulation of our rural districts'.[14]

As industry developed throughout the nineteenth century, the relative importance of agriculture declined: 22% of the population were engaged in it in 1851, only 8% by 1911. There was much talk in consequence not only of 'rural depopulation' but of a challenge to traditional rural ways of life, some perhaps less traditional than at first sight they seemed. In the words of Lady Bracknell, 'what between the duties expected of one during one's lifetime and the duties exacted from one after one's death, land has ceased to be either a profit or a pleasure'.[15] The experience of Edwardian England, when the country house was at the heart of society, proved that at least the second part of Lady Bracknell's firm statement was untrue, and with all the vicissitudes of agriculture there were more people living in the English countryside on the eve of the First World War in 1913 than there had been before the repeal of the corn laws in 1846.

The decennial censuses, the first of which was carried out in 1801, encouraged statistical interpretation of what was happening. Yet the interest in statistics, which had eighteenth-century, even late seventeenth-century origins, was not reserved for ten-year reviews. It was particularly strong during the 1830s and 1840s, as the Blue Books, the great official enquiries of the 1840s, testify, and it was satirized not only by Dickens in *Hard Times* but almost each week in the pages of *Punch*. Indeed, despite *Hard Times* it has been suggested that 'the rise of statistics may be an important factor in the general subsidence of satire during the nineteenth century';[16] for even Dickens wrote that his satire of statistics was concerned only with those 'who see figures and averages, and nothing else'.[17]

Statistics certainly had a moral dimension, for it was the moral as well as the physical implications of differential disease and

mortality rates which promoted 'the sanitary idea', an ideal which appealed to George Eliot as much as to Dickens. Another of its spokesmen, Charles Kingsley, was explicit:

The moral state of a city depends – how far I know not, but frightfully, to an extent as yet uncalculated, and perhaps incalculable, on the physical state of that city; on the food, water, air and lodging of its inhabitants.[18]

Between the great statistical enquiries of the 1840s and the 1890s there was one other fascinating enquiry, only in part statistical, to supplement articles in the *Journal of the Royal Statistical Society*, which celebrated its jubilee in 1885, and the *Transactions of the National Association for the Promotion of Social Science*, founded in 1857. Henry Mayhew's *London Labour and the London Poor*, the first volumes of which appeared in 1861, dealt as much with characters as with numbers, and as much with contrasts as with trends. Mayhew did not 'discover' London poverty, but he spread knowledge of it among sections of society from which it was hidden, and he did so in such a way that he caught the colour as well as the horror. His own moral stance was as explicit as Kingsley's:

My earnest hope is that the book may ... cause those who are in 'high places' ... to bestir themselves to improve the condition of a class of people whose misery, ignorance and vice, amidst all the immense knowledge of 'the first city in the world' is, to say the very least, a national disgrace to us.[19]

Later nineteenth-century statistical enquiries by private individuals shared the same exploratory quality as Mayhew, although they were less colourful (and journalistic) in their content. Charles Booth, a businessman from Liverpool, a city which demanded study as much as London, wrote in a famous passage in his *Life and Labour of the People in London*, the first volume of which appeared in 1889, that

it is not in country but in town that 'terra incognita' needs to be written on our social map. In the country the machinery of human life is plainly to be seen and easily recognized: personal relations bind the whole together. The equipoise on which existing order rests, whether satisfactory or not, is palpable and evident. It is far otherwise with cities, where as to these questions we live in darkness, with doubting hearts and ignorant unnecessary fears.[20]

Booth's London was so huge and sprawling that he had no

difficulty in convincing his readers that they really were reaching *terra incognita* and having it mapped for them, but Seebohm Rowntree showed in his *Poverty, A Study of Town Life* (1901) that there was as much darkness in the medieval city of York with a population of less than 80,000.[21]

Both Booth and Rowntree recognized – as, indeed, did Mayhew – that cities were not only problem places: they had their attractions too. This was a fact overlooked by some social historians, who compared unfavourably the nineteenth-century cities with cities of earlier periods – the Greek *polis*, for example, or the 'free' medieval city or the Italian cities of the Renaissance. Their growth depended in part, at least, on their 'pull'. 'What was it,' one of Booth's helpers asked, 'which brought so many people to London?' The answer was

the contagion of numbers, the sense of something going on, the theatres and music halls, the brightly lighted streets and the busy crowds – all in short, that makes the difference between the Mile End Fair on a Saturday night and a dark and muddy country lane, with no glimmer of gas and nothing to do.[22]

The fact that the cities had 'problems' did not necessarily repel, for one man's problem could be another man's beguilement – drink, for example, or anonymity. As far as their collective problems were concerned, by generating interest and promoting voluntary effort to change things the cities encouraged a more forceful approach to the study of social action, beginning with more informed awareness of matters relating, for example, to the problems of public health (the first national Public Health Act, which even then deliberately left out London, was not passed until 1848), to public order and to public education. Yet the problematic approach did not take over easily. It has been said that for Dickens a bad smell was a bad smell in *Pickwick Papers* whereas in *Our Mutual Friend* it was a problem.[23] In between, however, there were twenty years of incomplete civic education. The machinery in relation to public health was discarded in 1854, and it was not until 1875 that a further major Public Health Act clearly divided the country into urban and rural sanitary districts. There had been a significant time gap earlier in the century, too, between the introduction of the Metropolitan Police in 1829 and the County and Borough Police Act of 1856, and there was no national Education Act until 1870.

The attractions of cities, whatever their problems, and particularly the attractions of London, were noted by many writers at different stages of the nineteenth century from the Cockney writers during the first decades to Henry James and beyond. What could be sweeter than Charles Lamb's evocation of 'thy pleasures, O London-with-the-many-sins'? 'Streets, streets, streets, markets, theatres, churches, Coven Gardens, shops sparkling with the pretty faces of industrious milliners ... gentlemen behind counters lying, authors in the street with spectacles ... lamps lit at night ...' and so on.[24] 'So far from the smoke of London being offensive to me,' wrote Benjamin Haydon just as comprehensively in his autobiography in 1841, 'it has always been to my imagination the sublime canopy that shrouds the City of the World.'[25] James, who observed in 1881 that London was 'not a pleasant place ... not agreeable, or cheerful or easy, or exempt from reproach' added at once that it was 'the biggest aggregation of human life, the most complete compendium of the world'. 'We are far from liking London well,' he remarked in 1888, 'until we like its defects.' During the 1890s it was fashionable to place first among all its attractions 'the lamps lit at night' and to prefer London by gaslight to London in the daytime: Beardsley loved the brightly lit advertisements, Lord Alfred Douglas compared the gas lamps to pale flowers, and Richard Le Gallienne apostrophized:

> London, London our delight,
> Great flower that opens but at night,
> Great city of the midnight sun,
> Whose day begins when day is done.[26]

Of course, the London which was hymned by the aesthetes was a very different London from that which spilled out for miles through border territories which were neither urban nor rural and through single-class suburbs, where the lights came not from the streets but from the houses – detached villas with gardens, semi-detached and with gardens too, or in the working-class suburbs, houses in long rows.

The visible differences in suburbia reflected the 'social system' as much as the industrial scene reflected the 'economic system', and the two were of course interrelated. The significant occupational

shifts of the nineteenth century included not only the decline in agriculture but the growth in the 'service sector' of the economy and in the professions. Even in 1851 there were more shoemakers than coalminers, and in 1911, when no one doubted that Britain had become an 'industrial state', there were more domestic servants than coalminers, cotton workers and building operatives put together.

Without a hierarchy of domestic servants, the golden age of the country house in Edwardian England would have been impossible. But so, too, would life as it was actually lived in the small villas of suburbia. Hampstead had eighty servants for every hundred of the population; industrial Rochdale only three.

Working-class suburbs were characterized by sameness, many middle-class suburbs by differentiation of dwellings. Working-class suburbs consisted of long straight streets; middle-class suburbs could indulge in curves, crescents and *culs de sac*. In some towns, like Nottingham and Bradford, the early streets might consist of back-to-back houses. Later in the century, however, there was improvement in standards without necessarily concomitant improvement in appearance. There were municipal 'housing estates' before 1914 – following the Housing of the Working Class Act of 1890, but it was not until 1919 that local authorities were required to survey housing needs and to prepare and carry out housing schemes accordingly.[27] One new development was the creation of public parks, sometimes provided by a benefactor, sometimes by the local authority, often called 'Victoria Park': these are 'interesting for their aesthetic pretensions as well as for their social significance'.[28]

Middle-class suburbia did not need parks. Indeed, some such suburbs formed part of old landed estates, like Edgbaston in Birmingham, while others were built in attractive rural settings. Suburbia was 'neither the town built thin nor the country built close', although the garden suburb ideal, like the garden city ideal, propounded by Ebenezer Howard in his book *Tomorrow*, later called *Garden Cities of Tomorrow*, published in 1898, made much of the 'marriage' of town and country: 'all the advantages of the most energetic and active town life' could be united 'in perfect combination' with 'all the beauty and delight of the country'.[29] The 'garden cities', which developed in the twentieth century – Letchworth (1903) was the

first – never quite lived up to this ideal, but likewise the retreat to the propertied owner-occupied suburbs did not always satisfy those who wished to 'escape'. 'The more the idea caught on, the more the idyll was threatened.'[30]

There was, of course, one other element determining the appearance of suburbia, comparable to the element of technology in the industrial scene – taste in domestic buildings. The public buildings of nineteenth-century Britain had reflected cycles of taste with local variations in timing and contemporaneously in certain cases in styles. The 'rule of taste' had ceased to be universally accepted during the 1830s, and despite the efforts of tastemakers to 'educate' the public no single rule of taste was ever imposed again.

There was an emphasis on monumentalism, however, of building to last, in town halls, law courts, banks, hospitals, water works and even factories. Victorian cemeteries, too, were very different from earlier graveyards. Classical styles, which were accepted naturally in the late eighteenth century, either began to look dull or became a matter of ideological conflict during the 1830s and 1840s, although even outside London impressive classical buildings could be erected as late as the 1830s. 'Tyneside classical', for example, associated with Grainger, Dobson and Clayton, was characterized by its symmetry and its elegance, qualities which did not seem incompatible with 'the improving spirit of the age'.[31] Gothic, by contrast, was often deliberately advertised as being in direct conflict with that spirit, and A. W. Pugin's *Contrasts*, which appeared in 1836, one year before Victoria came to the throne, deliberately set the glories of the medieval city, visual, social and above all spiritual, against the confusion of the modern city. The sense of a 'revival' was explicit. A key text is Ruskin's chapter on 'The Nature of Gothic' in *The Stones of Venice* (1849–53).

Ruskin set out to be an arbiter of taste. Yet during the mid-Victorian years all kinds of architecture became acceptable in all kinds of combination, and the use of the adjectives 'free' and 'eclectic' implied praise rather than condemnation. The Renaissance served as a source of inspiration as much as the middle ages, but it was the Renaissance 'freely treated'. Diversity was the order of the day, not unity.

Many of the buildings reflected the preferences of clients. When

Ruskin addressed an audience in the Town Hall in industrial Bradford in 1864, therefore, his central theme was the relationship between aesthetics and economics. The presiding deity of the age, he maintained, was the 'goddess of getting-on', Britannia of the Market, whose devotees could produce 'railroad mounds vaster than the walls of Babylon' and 'chimneys more mighty and costly than cathedral spires', but who were incapable because of their money values of commissioning anything Ruskin thought worthwhile.

Ruskin's formidable indictment left much out and had its own weak points. First, it did not do justice to all manufacturers. Not far from Bradford, for example, Sir Titus Salt had built a new town at Saltaire, with mills, houses, nonconformist chapel, hospital, dispensary, club and institute. Opened in 1860, it was a model town, planned in a careful way and in complete contrast to unplanned Bradford. The countryside was on the doorstep too. Second, Ruskin had his own prejudices. He had an ideological objection to iron, and he did not appreciate the urge of some of his fellow countrymen to produce a new architecture for a new age. It was unfortunate perhaps that when railway stations were built they were always disguised in old styles – classical iike Euston or Gothic like St Pancras – although both these buildings and many others have had many admirers then and since. Third, in the light of twentieth-century architectural history, there has been a friendly, if sometimes undiscriminating, reappraisal of Victorian architecture as a whole and of particular buildings – Keble College, Oxford by Butterfield is a test case – which were once dismissed as summarily as the Victorians themselves dismissed Georgian buildings. Guided by John Betjeman, architects and historians alike have been willing to take a new look. The result has been a serious re-examination of the work of William Butterfield, G. E. Street, William Burges, and Alfred Waterhouse, not to speak of less well-known architects, like Cuthbert Broderick, architect not only of Leeds Town Hall but of a highly distinctive Corn Exchange. There has also been a reappraisal of the later generation of 'Queen Anne' architects. Both Norman Shaw and C. F. A. Voysey have been singled out, the former for his 'urban picturesque' style and the latter for his 'puritanical style for uncompromising country-lovers (though Shaw built many country mansions and Voysey a few town houses)'.[32] Fourth, this time

guided by Sir Nikolaus Pevsner, historians of tastes and styles have emphasized continuities linking William Morris, the 'Arts and Crafts' movement and *art-nouveau* with modernist movements of the twentieth century. Ruskin would have been surprised at such continuities, although even he has been fitted into the story line.[33] He was disturbed in his own long lifetime, of course, to note the misuse, as he saw it, of his own philosophy. 'There is scarcely a public-house near the Crystal Palace (which was moved from Hyde Park to Sydenham after the Exhibition) but sells its gin and bitters under pseudo-Venetian capitals.'[34]

Victorian public houses have been studied as carefully as Victorian country houses – and by the same writer.[35] And there has been an interest in nineteenth-century materials, including the cast iron which Ruskin deplored, terra cotta, a favourite Victorian product, which could be used cheaply for every kind of mass-produced effect in every colour, and brick, which was used by Butterfield and others in polychrome combinations. Comparing the nineteenth with the twentieth centuries there was more reliance on local materials. There was more stone in Bradford and more brick in Leeds, but brick was winning through in cheap domestic architecture almost everywhere by the 1880s and 1890s, and most of the characteristic new towns of the century, like Middlesbrough, 'the infant prodigy', Barrow in Furness, incorporated in 1867, or Crewe and Swindon, the new railway towns, were made of brick.

It is possible as a result of the boom in local history and the increasing interest of historians in 'visual history' to trace chronological patterns in relation to particular places and, to some extent, for the country as a whole. As early as 1907, Lady Bell, writing of Middlesbrough, claimed that

the genesis of an iron-making town is breathless and tumultuous ... There springs, and too rapidly, into existence a community of a preordained inevitable kind, the members of which must live near their work. They must, therefore, have their houses built as quickly as possible, the houses must be cheap, must be as big as the workman wants and no bigger; and as they are built there arise hastily created, instantly occupied, rows and rows of little brown streets. A town arising in this way cannot want to consider anything else but time and space.[36]

Yet Lady Bell would have recognized that this was only the

beginning of a building sequence. A later generation would want to build churches – or nonconformist chapels – town halls, theatres, hospitals and other public buildings too. The Victorian town and city were not 'insensate', as Mumford claimed: they were bustling with life, and noisy and messy though they were on the surface, underneath there was usually a most elaborate system of drains and sewers. Their construction was the greatest Victorian achievement in civil engineering.

By contrast, the countryside, which might look picturesque, kept its worst features out of view. The 'cottage' was frequently glamorized, particularly if it was thatched. It had historical as well as aesthetic qualities, for, unlike the American log cabin, it was a symbol of continuity. So, too, was the village itself, though there were as many variations between different villages – in form as well as in function – as there were between different towns and cities. Some villages were closely dependent on nearby market towns; others were remote and isolated. Some were badly hit by the decline in arable farming; others flourished on the basis of market gardening or dairying. Many had an industrial element in them, or in the Midlands and the north of England could be completely industrial: all above a certain size had craftsmen as well as workers on the land.

The social relations of the village depended a great deal on whether or not there was a local squire. Yet his presence or absence was not decisive, and other factors, like the religious composition of the population, could influence even the appearance of property. In any event, different squires or great landlords had different personal qualities and followed different policies, so that it is almost impossible for the historian to generalize. It is equally difficult to generalize about landscapes; they ranged from moorland and fen to highly cultivated and relatively dense settlement. The only generalization possible is that most of the landscape was the product of human activity, including speculation, rather than of undisturbed 'nature'. There are now far more detailed studies of the Victorian countryside than there were ten years ago: the urban studies boom is being followed by at least a boomlet in rural studies.[37]

Yet difficult though it is to generalize, many Victorian writers tried to do so. There was a strong rural bias in much of the literature of the 1880s and 1890s, and it influenced reviewers and even

politicians as well. Thus, when the Poet Laureate, Alfred Austin, produced his *Haunts of Ancient Peace* in 1902, the liberal *Daily News* (with which Dickens had been associated in the mid-nineteenth century) hailed it as a magical book. 'Under its spell,' the reviewer claimed, 'we lose for a time the brick-and-mortar civilization that sometimes seems all-pervading, and gladly fly with the writer ... to the green fields and lanes outside our prison.'[38] Thomas Hardy's *Far from the Madding Crowd* (1894), his most distinctively 'country book', was his most popular novel. Richard Jefferies's portrait of rural society *Hodge and his Masters* (1880) was originally called 'The Heart of England'. George Gissing, who was born in the West Riding of Yorkshire and educated in Manchester and who described London with the skills of both sociologist and novelist, makes Henry Rycroft say in *The Private Papers of Henry Rycroft* (1903), 'The last thought of my brain as I lie dying will be that of sunshine upon an English meadow'.

NOTES

1. T. B. Macaulay, *Critical and Historical Essays* (1830): 'Southey's Colloquies on Society'.

2. Quoted in K. Tillotson, *Novels of the Eighteen-Forties* (1954), 105–6.

3. Quoted in O. F. Christie, *The Transition from Aristocracy* (1927), 222.

4. Christie, *Transition from Aristocracy*.

5. See A. Briggs, *Images of Industry: From Coalbrookdale to the Crystal Palace* (1979).

6. *Hard Times* (1854), ch. V, 'The Keynote'.

7. L. Mumford, *The Culture of Cities* (1938), ch. III, 'The Insensate Industrial Town'.

8. *Bentley's Miscellany*, Vol. VII(1840).

9. D. H. Lawrence, *Selected Essays* (1950), 151.

10. O. O. Roberts, *The Classic Slum* (1900).

11. See E. E. Gilbert, *Brighton, Old Ocean's Bauble* (1954), ch. V.

12. See W. R. Lethaby, *Form in Civilization* (1900), 100.

13. G. Best, *Mid-Victorian Britain* (1971), 6.

14. F. G. Heath, *British Rural Life and Labour* (1911), V.

15. Oscar Wilde, *The Importance of Being Earnest* (1893).

16. A. Welch, *The City of Dickens* (1971), 80.

17. Quoted by G. Ford and S. Monod (eds), *Hard Times* (1966), 277.

18. C. Kingsley, 'Great Cities and their Influence for Good and Evil', quoted in *Miscellanies*, Vol. II (1859), 320–21.

19. H. Mayhew, preface to *London Labour and the London Poor* (1861).

20. C. Booth, *Life and Labour of the People of London*, 2nd series, Vol. I (1903), 18.

21. For a contemporary assessment of Rowntree's 'thunderclap', see C. F. G. Masterman, 'The Social Abyss' in the *Contemporary Review*, Vol. LXXI (1902).

22. Booth, Vol. III (1892), 75.

23. H. House, *The Dickens World* (1941), 80.

24. Quoted in R. W. King (ed.), *England from Wordsworth to Dickens* (1928), 151.

25. B. Haydon, *Autobiography* (1841), 100.

26. See A. Briggs, *Victorian Cities* (1963), ch. 8, 'London, the World City'. cf. The *New Monthly Magazine*, Part I (1841): 'To the true London man, the metropolis is all in all ... Any change of scene is a change for the worse; for what other place can, even in an indifferent degree, satisfy his wants or adapt itself to his habits?'

27. See M. Bowley, *Housing and the State* (1945). E. Gauldie, *Cruel Habitations: A History of Working-Class Housing, 1780–1918* (1974).

28. See G. F. Chadwick, *The Park and the Town* (1966).

29. See Briggs, *Victorian Cities*, 75.

30. Quoted in D. Reeder, 'Suburbanity and the Victorian City', Dyos Memorial Lecture (1980).

31. See L. Wilkes and G. Dodds, *Tyneside Classical* (1964).

32. C. Handley-Read, this volume, pp. 433–53.

33. N. Pevsner, *Pioneers of the Modern Movement from William Morris to Walter Gropius* (1936), and many later works.

34. Quoted in this volume, p. 436.

35. M. Girouard, *The Victorian Country-House* (1971) and *Victorian Pubs* (1975).

36. Lady Bell, *At the Works* (1907), 80. She went on to add of the people that many of them had as 'deeply rooted an attachment to Middlesbrough as though it were a beautiful village'. 'There are many who are nourished by human intercourse rather than by natural beauty'.

37. See R. Williams, *The Country and the City* (1973) and V. C. Knoepflmacher and G. B. Tennyson (eds), *Nature and the Victorian Imagination* (1979).

38. For the most recent collective work, see G. E. Mingay (ed.), *The Victorian Countryside*, 2 vols (1981), and A. Briggs, 'The Victorian Countryside in England and the United States', Dyos Memorial Lecture (1981).

ASPECTS OF VICTORIAN ARCHITECTURE

CHARLES HANDLEY-READ

If with an effort of the imagination we survey the heterogeneous mass of buildings which make up the Victorian architectural scene, bearing in mind particularly the thousands of representative examples never shown in the textbooks, the following observations may help to steady our approach and provide points for discussion: that the 'diversity' of the age, and the elements of paradox apparent in the literature are equally apparent in the architecture; that any attempt to condemn nineteenth-century architecture because it is dressed up in historical styles would lead to the condemnation of nearly every building the age produced – though the kind and degree of historicism can be highly revealing (cf. Pugin, Salvin, Cockerell; Street, Webb, Burges; Shaw and Bentley); that very few buildings reflect accurately the teaching of Pugin, Ruskin, or Morris – if only because few architects held strong religious or social views (exceptions are Butterfield and Street; Webb, Voysey, Ashbee, and a few others); that from the point of view of appearance and construction, very few buildings merit a place among those which in the historical development lead towards the modern movement; that when reforming zeal is translated through legislation into useful public architecture – e.g. Commissioners' churches, hospitals, sewage buildings, and schools – most of the buildings are architecturally second rate (though not on this account the less interesting); that in an age of many new needs, most buildings continue to derive from palace, temple, cathedral, or cottage prototypes, while buildings of a truly original form-language, usually the outcome of private enterprise of the first half of the century, derive from the use of iron and glass (railway sheds, markets, Bunning's Coal Exchange, the Crystal Palace). To this we may add that the best classical buildings in the British Isles were also designed in the first half of the century, and were built in stone (by, among others, Barry, C. R. Cockerell, Elmes; Philip Hardwick, Thomas

Hamilton, and W. H. Playfair); that most of the best Gothic buildings (Pugin's and Salvin's work excepted) were designed in the second half of the century by, among others, Butterfield, Street, and Brooks, as a rule in brick; by Burges, Pearson, and others, in stone; and by Waterhouse, sometimes with a facing of terra cotta; and that, finally, architects worked in isolation, apprentice-trained and often very well trained in practical building, but without attachment to any central, authoritative architectural policy or theory, the Academy being virtually ineffective (cf. the influence of the state-aided Beaux-Arts in France).

Several of these points are worth pursuing further, particularly as they may help to explain why certain buildings came to be built when they were built and where they were built, and why they looked as they did. From the point of view of the appearance of buildings, the direct and indirect influences of Pugin (1812–52), Ruskin (1819–1900), and Morris (1834–96) claim immediate attention. Nothing is more difficult, in a short essay, than to summarize their effective contributions to architecture and the applied arts. For one thing their very numerous publications, frequently re-appearing in new editions, are collectively scattered right through the reign – which makes it hard to pin down the moment of impact of a given book. Their views are often inconsistent and self-contradictory and their attitude to historicism in architecture, for example, is ambivalent – never a simple matter merely of borrowing forms and details from the past. While Pugin built something like thirty churches, Ruskin was directly associated, on the site, with only one building – the University Museum, Oxford (by Deane and Woodward, 1855–9) – and then chiefly in connection with the carved decorations; and Morris never practised as an architect. Through their passion for Gothic and the Middle Ages, Pugin and Ruskin changed the whole nature of the Gothic Revival. Ruskin and Morris also laid the foundation for the Arts and Crafts movement (with the 'Guilds') and the so-called Domestic Revival (Shaw, Webb, Voysey, Ashbee, Mackintosh); and they were the inspiration of Art Nouveau on the Continent which, because it broke with historicism, because it set great store on plant and other natural forms (as Ruskin did), and gave a new emphasis to revealed structure, in its turn leads ultimately towards modern architecture. Above all else, Pugin, Ruskin and Morris tried

to inculcate in their contemporaries a *moral* approach to architecture. Pugin broke down (though at first he seemed to continue, e.g. in his details for the Houses of Parliament) the eighteenth-century Rococo tradition in Gothic; and Ruskin, by the injection of moral overtones into architectural theory, tried to inspire in the public mind and in the minds of architects responsible and lofty aims, which for him were inextricably associated with problems both social and economic. Here Ruskin and Morris were in many ways alike.

It is permissible at this point to make use of borrowed weight. Professor Hitchcock writes[1] of Pugin's *Contrasts* (1836) that 'as much as any other single event its publication marked the end of the Georgian age in architecture'. Professor Hitchcock shows that Pugin, by a process partly of revival and partly of invention, introduces new and useful plan-types into church building, that he is archaeologically much more serious than the eighteenth century, that he uses, along with other new kinds of decoration, shapes based on plant forms (thus anticipating Ruskin) and that, also in *Contrasts*, Pugin lays down principles of which present-day architects could approve – for example, that the 'construction of old "pointed" architecture was always varied to accord with the properties of the different materials employed', and that 'pointed architecture "decorates" the useful portions of buildings instead of concealing or disguising them'. Professor Hitchcock sums up Pugin's achievement as an architect by saying that before his death 'few Victorian churches were built by others ... and none perhaps completed in Gothic ... that have stood up so well in the considered estimate of posterity'. But Professor Hitchcock also says that 'practically none of his executed works except St Augustine's, Ramsgate [which he built for himself], achieved the standards of pseudo-medieval design that he set from the first as a critic'. A study of Pugin is bound to leave the impression, among others, of a fantastic body of work accomplished in a short time, and of frustration and disillusion.

Lord Clark,[2] discussing Ruskin's *Seven Lamps* (1849), says of this book that it was 'in the history of taste perhaps the most influential ever published'. Much lies behind these words, among other things the fact that English architects lavishly and wantonly applied 'Ruskinian' details to their buildings, including of course those taken from medieval Italy. Lord Clark also shows up the irony of the

situation by quoting Ruskin's now famous remark: 'I have had indirect influence on nearly every cheap villa builder ... and there is scarcely a public-house near the Crystal Palace but sells its gin and bitters under pseudo-Venetian capitals ...' And we are shown how, through popular acceptance, Ruskin's own teaching recoiled on him – so that he is 'not only the man who made the Gothic Revival; he is the man who destroyed it'.

For a summary of the inspiration generated by Pugin, Ruskin, and Morris within the spheres of the Arts and Crafts movement in England, and Art Nouveau abroad (each with a certain significance for the Modern Movement, and ultimately for present-day architecture), we may turn to Dr Stephan Tschudi Madsen's important book, *Sources of Art Nouveau*. It is not too much to say that if reference to these three men had been withheld, the book could scarcely have been written. We are reminded that progressive men in Germany, Belgium, Holland, and France all looked back to Pugin, Ruskin, and Morris and often quoted their written and other work. Emile Gallé (a leader among Art Nouveau designers at Nancy) and Jean Lahor, whose book on William Morris was published in 1897, believed that these three men were the precursors of Art Nouveau; and since, as Dr Madsen points out, 'most of the Art Nouveau designers constantly regarded nature as their main source of inspiration and renewal', a definite link between Pugin, Ruskin, Morris, and Art Nouveau will be readily understood. Horta (an advanced Belgian architect and a prolific writer) included in a bibliography six lectures by Morris. Muthesius in 1904 said that 'the whole of our movement is based on the results in England achieved from 1860 and up to the middle of the 1890s'.

Muthesius, who published in Germany designs for houses by Baillie Scott, Voysey, and Mackintosh, was given considerable prominence by Professor Pevsner in his *Pioneers of Modern Design*,[3] and quotations from this book will help to round off the impression that must be given of the importance of the three men under discussion. For example, it was partly due to the difficulty of furnishing decently his Red House at Bexley Heath (by Webb) that in 1861 Morris founded the firm 'Morris, Marshall and Faulkner, Fine Art Work in Painting, Carving, Furniture and the Metals'. 'This event', according to Professor Pevsner, 'marks the beginning of a

new era in Western art.' And he goes on to quote Morris's now celebrated utterances: 'I don't want art for a few, any more than education for a few, or freedom for a few', and 'What business have we with art at all unless all can share it?' And indeed a study of Pugin's churches and his books, and of the writings of Ruskin and Morris, throws into very prominent relief their inspiring insistence on the moral connections between architecture and religion, or art and life. But, in the case of Ruskin and Morris particularly, two central threads in their teaching (the insistence on hand work, and the bias towards the Middle Ages) show above all a refusal to come to terms with the means of production of their age. And, it has to be added, their social teaching in a sense misfired. Professor Pevsner says of Morris that when, 'partly as a consequence of his own socialist propaganda, riots began in London . . . he recoiled and gradually withdrew back into his world of poetry and beauty'. For each of these men, in spite of monumental positive achievement, the reverse of the coin of idealism was disillusion.

In 1870 Ruskin first published those Oxford lectures[4] in which (to judge from the text) he had said with considerable emphasis: 'The art of any country *is the exponent of its social and political virtues*', and again, 'The art, or general productive and formative energy of any country, is an exact exponent of its ethical life'. In the same passage he goes on to elaborate one of his favourite themes, that you can have 'noble art only from noble persons . . .' As we have seen, Ruskin was directly concerned with only one building, and he acknowledged that his own indirect influence was as a rule disastrous. Looking about him at the time of his lecture, he must have concluded that architects were too often ignoble persons and that most of the buildings he saw reflected a total absence in the country as a whole of social and political virtue. Yet reformers there were whose work *was* translated, though often with a time-lag, into useful public architecture – Chadwick, Southwood Smith, Kay (later Kay-Shuttleworth), and Florence Nightingale or, locally, for example at Birmingham, men like Dixon, Chamberlain, and Collings. Reforming zeal, in its passage through Arnold's spheres of Barbarity and Philistinism for the benefit of the Populace, was not often matched by good architecture, judged, that is, by Ruskinian

standards, or indeed our own. But much depends on the critical approach. For architecture, as Ruskin saw, particularly public architecture, inevitably *is* a symbol in various ways of social and political states (if not of virtues); and criticism of nineteenth-century public buildings will only be comprehensive if it discusses the buildings fully and in their true context – as it were, by reversing Ruskin and taking into account the social and political background out of which they arose. From the point of view particularly of nineteenth-century public building, studies have yet to be made which balance the intricate connections between the work of individual reformers on one hand, parliamentary and local government legislation on the other, and at the same time the special local problems confronting the architect – factors all having their effect on the actual designs. Studies of the kind here suggested would combine architectural analyses like those of Professor Hitchcock with social and economic analyses of the type collected together in, for example, *A Century of Municipal Progress, 1835–1935;*[5] and these studies would indeed be 'thick'. But they would form part of a social and economic history of Victorian architecture and would help to provide a full and rounded assessment of some of the work.

It is worth remembering here, what seems to be true, that legislation for certain public buildings was often a panic measure, and to some extent this fact helps to explain both where they were built and several of their visual characteristics. In the case of the Commissioners' Churches (Act of 1818), it was fear of revolution, ungodliness, and Dissent. Six hundred and fifteen churches were built by 1857, chiefly in the London suburbs, in the industrial North, and in the Midland towns. The problem was to build, quickly and cheaply, large numbers of new churches for populations which were now pouring into the towns and which had increased enormously since the last wave of church building after 1711. Many of these churches were shoddy – box-like aisled halls, with galleries – and Pugin, in *Contrasts*, was quick to pillory the element of 'sham'. In them can be studied the significant transition from the application in the twenties, thirties, and earlier forties of the 'styles' (Greek, Romanesque, and Gothic) to the gradual adoption, at least from 1849 onwards, of 'ecclesiological' principles and, archaeologically speaking, a much more serious attitude to church building. Built

of brick, Butterfield's All Saints' Church in Margaret Street, London (completed in 1859 from designs begun ten years earlier), exhibited these principles and, as is well known, was a mid-century example of 'constructional polychromy'. Butterfield did not 'apply' the Gothic style: from the point of view of the construction and appearance of this church he re-created it. In the case of buildings connected with the very important problems of sewage and drainage, legislation was tardily motivated out of fear of disease, notably cholera; and a typical building connected with sewage will be discussed presently. In the case of schools, the Education Act ultimately went through in 1870, but it is probably too simple to say that the Act was motivated by fear of widespread illiteracy; the effects had been noted of compulsory education on the Continent, particularly in Prussia, and employers were beginning to realize that poor returns might be due to inefficient, i.e. uneducated, workers. These 'Board Schools'[6] are often to be seen in groups in the London suburbs, and because expenses had to be kept down, because also they were built in densely populated districts, they sometimes rise in three or even four storeys, so that at least a small area of the available site could provide a playground. They are in marked contrast to the single- or two-storey schools of today. Behind the architecture of Museums (Act of 1845), Libraries (Act of 1850), Assize Courts, Town Halls (before and after the Municipal Corporations Act of 1882), and many other types of building, there is a basis of moral and legislative thought and work, often revealing tensions between private enterprise and public works. Since the significance of buildings of this type lies to a great extent in social history, it can seem inadequate to approach them primarily in terms of architects and styles. One advantage of taking these background factors fully into account might be to bring Victorian architecture to the notice of those whose interest is not captured by its architectural merits.

Public architecture often exhibits what was weak and what was strong during the reign, but it is easier to note what in our estimation appear to be the weaknesses than to understand what to the Victorians were the real merits. During the middle and later years of the century Western European countries developed a new kind of urban civilization on a scale which had no precedent since the Roman Empire. This remains true even while we remember what was built under

the Medici princes, in seventeenth-century Rome, or under Napoleon. This urban development is very well represented in English cities by the town halls, assize courts, museums, concert halls, etc., which, seen as an expression of confidence, the will towards 'Improvement', and a real belief in the benefits of material progress, together constitute one of the most impressive groups of buildings from a single epoch since classical times. Here we may remember particularly St George's Hall, Liverpool (designed by H. L. Elmes, 1839–40; built and decorated 1841–54 chiefly under C. R. Cockerell), Leeds Town Hall (Cuthbert Brodrick, 1855–9), Manchester Town Hall (Alfred Waterhouse, begun 1869), the New Law Courts (G. E. Street; competition 1866, begun 1874, completed 1882), and the Imperial Institute (Thomas Collcutt, 1887–93). Monumental architecture of this kind was the *panache* to the general run of Victorian building. To us these buildings usually seem over-dressed or inappropriately dressed for their role as a symbol of civic grandeur, and in many of them the superb confidence which lies behind the unsparing effects of display seems to have over-reached itself. Netley Hospital, another example, was presumably designed to look like an eighteenth-century palace and as a result its endlessly long corridors were extremely inconvenient; our museums, above and below ground, are nearly full; many churches are now used for purposes for which they were not intended; the public halls which perfectly catered for the mammoth performances of the *Messiah* are sometimes difficult to fill; and certain buildings as different as the Imperial Institute, St Thomas's Hospital, the Southern Outfall station at Crossness, the Columbia Market, and Kensington Barracks are all due (1960) for demolition – either because they are no longer efficient in their present form and need to be rebuilt, or because they no longer serve a useful purpose commensurate with the valuable sites they occupy.* But if machine sheds or hospitals sometimes have to be rebuilt, it must be stressed that as a rule the inadequacy of Victorian buildings in meeting our needs and fashions must be discussed in their context, from the point of view of their function in their own day. It can be said that the Victorians failed in foresight; but we do not criticize the Parthenon adversely because pagan rites are no longer practised; and twentieth-century arenas, cinemas, etc., are already being closed down.

* See Notes.

Among the real weaknesses of Victorian architecture is the inability to plan towns or districts intelligently;[7] and very often (a similar point) there is a lack of sensitivity in the way single buildings are related to a site. The classic case of calculated yet utterly pointless district planning occurs with that very important group of buildings of 'popular improvement' between (and including) the Albert Hall and the Natural History Museum; each one of these symmetrical buildings is regimented into position on the same axial line, but the intended effect can only be appreciated from the air, never from ground level. Not infrequently Victorian thoroughfares show ugly proportions between house height and street width, and a lack of light is the result; defence of this practice would have been based on the high price of land. While the enormous length of Netley Hospital can at least be taken in from Southampton Water, it is impossible in the relatively narrow areas in front of them to get a full façadal view of, say, the Natural History Museum or the Imperial Institute. But even here the designers might have pointed in their defence to a characteristic of design which today is some-times criticized; in the case of the Imperial Institute, the long façade is subdivided into small units which are most readily taken in at close range and from oblique angles – the views the observer sees as he passes by.

Some of the strangest buildings arising from reforming legislation are those connected with London's main drainage.[8] The series of cholera epidemics of 1831/2, 1848/9, and 1853/4 were due to the fact that during the first half of the nineteenth century London's sewage was discharged into the Thames and its tributaries and, in-credible though it may now seem, it was from the same sources that during this period most of London's drinking water was drawn. Several public bodies attempted to deal with the problem of sanita-tion and met fierce opposition based on libertarian principles and, more understandably, on the probable cost of improvements. But in 1854 Dr John Snow discovered that cholera was caused by drinking contaminated water, and in 1855 the Metropolitan Board of Works was set up, charged 'to prevent sewage from entering the Thames within the London area'. An Act of 1858 left the Board free to carry out a vast sewage scheme devised by Joseph Bazalgette (1819–91), who was ultimately knighted. Broadly, he aimed to divert con-

1. *Abbey Mills Pumping Station, Barking (one of the buildings in Sir Joseph Bazalgette's scheme for London's sewage disposal, 1856–c.1876). Opened 1868. Polychrome brickwork, white stone trim and slates.*

taminating matter from the Thames by means of intercepting sewers and to discharge the flow into the Thames at Barking and Crossness (i.e. outside the County). His system involved over a hundred miles of large-diameter sewers, and a series of interesting buildings, notably the Outfall and Pumping Stations (the pumps raised the sewage, where necessary, so that flow to the Outfalls could continue by gravity). The North and South Outfall Stations were completed by 1864 and 1865 respectively, the latter being opened by the Prince of Wales, on which occasion 'fairy' lights decorated the subterranean reservoir.[9]

The Outfall at Crossness is due (1960) for demolition, so attention is claimed by Abbey Mills. It was in the main engine-house of this pumping station that Bazalgette and his assistants let themselves go; for here he evidently intended to signify to the public, through un-

necessary display, the importance of the underground work which was not normally seen. The plan of this building is cruciform, each arm of the cross originally housing two of the great beam-engines (now replaced) and the corresponding fly-wheels. From the exterior, apart from out-buildings (the chimney stack has gone) we now see a two-storey building with a slate-covered mansard roof. Very well built in brick (as at Crossness), and with coloured bricks in the pointed arches above the round-headed windows, white stone trim is here used lavishly – in the plinth, the heavy porches, the keystones, cornice, dormers, and extraordinary angle-turrets; also in the thick but plain course between the storeys and in the richly floriated courses and capitals which in each storey mark the springing line of the window-arches. Among other interesting details are the rainwater pipes and stone corner-shafts, each resembling the celebrated Venetian 'rope' moulding. The most opulent feature is the high octagonal lantern which crowns the building – a projection of the control tower beneath it (cf. Crossness where, however, no feature appeared externally). Inside the building the lantern is particularly well-proportioned; partly lined with plates of metal, it is clean, crisp, and elegant. As at Crossness the interior columns, capitals, grilles, brackets, and railings, all in cast-iron, are extremely rich (though not inappropriately heavy); and the small concave stars on many of the flat areas of metal, a motif uncommon in the sixties, are details reminiscent of the Regency.

What can one say of the building as a whole? Seen from a little distance the roof looks French, the stone and coloured brick details are debased Ruskinian, and the lantern, turrets, and porches suggest that this might be some kind of religious building, conceivably a Greek Orthodox church. In 1894 – after Bazalgette's death – a notice appeared in *London* (24 May) which said that by comparison to the 'miserable overcrowding of our County Hall at Spring Gardens', this pumping station was 'like a palace'. There are 'few samples of better brick work in London', the 'solidarity of the building was necessary for the machinery it contains'. And after acknowledging the temptation to 'condemn as extravagant some of the ornate work', the explanation is given: 'There is an excuse for this ornamentation: the engineer [Bazalgette] pleaded that, as the public saw nothing of the great underground works continually in operation

for the safety of their health, not to say the convenience of their entire existence in London ... a little extra and apparently unnecessary ornamentation might safely be permitted in a building which would stand above ground.'

Because terra cotta was very widely used in the later nineteenth century, especially in towns, and because the reasons for its popularity throw light on Victorian taste and architectural procedure, it is worthy of a paragraph here. Artificial stone, chiefly 'Coade' stone, appeared in later Georgian architecture and, following the collapse of the Coade stone factory (c. 1840), terra cotta gradually became the Victorian equivalent. It is nearly always recognized on sight but it eludes neat definition. It is enough to say here that terra cotta is a clay body pressed by hand into absorbent moulds and subsequently fired. The finished blocks, usually small and hollow, and as a rule filled with concrete, are sometimes glazed and the material is then called 'faience'. Late Victorian delight in terra cotta will be understood if we remember that it was made out of a basically cheap substance from which very elaborate detail could be mass-produced; from one good model endless copies could be cast, and to some extent this overcame the problem caused by the absence of good carvers in stone. Terra cotta was at the same time an enduring material, virtually indestructible, highly resistant to the acid-laden atmosphere of towns, light by comparison to stone and easily handled in other ways; bricklayers could be trusted with it, thus saving the employment of the more skilled and more expensive stone-masons – the masons' strike of 1877 led, perhaps through Waterhouse, to a boom in its use. Furthermore terra cotta could be produced in a variety of colours, glazed or unglazed and, what may have increased its appeal in the last thirty years of the reign, the sheer industry and ingenuity behind its production (for there was a Victorian love of technique for its own sake) could be read off those encrusted façades as from a book: the hard work over details at the drawing-board stage, the adaptations from sketch-books[10] and pattern books, the mechanical problems overcome with staggering efficiency during modelling, mould-making, casting, and above all in firing the hollow blocks, were all more or less self-evident. It was the perfect medium in which to reproduce quasi-historical detail, and for certain Victorian

architects it had everything to recommend it. A lavish display of terra cotta, sometimes controlled and scholarly, sometimes merely pretty, sometimes indescribably hideous, made available to the middle classes a richness of detail which in the past only the patrons of Wren, say, or the Adam brothers could have commanded. Snug in the heart of the bourgeoisie, the late-Victorian patron could indulge, with a 'varnish' of terra cotta, his taste for conspicuous consumption.

Several threads in this essay meet in the Birmingham Assize Courts, by Aston Webb and Ingress Bell (Fig. 2, p. 447). As early as 1864 an application was made for a grant of Assizes, but the Home Secretary raised objections and it was not until 1883 that negotiations were successful. By 1886 one hundred and thirty competition designs had come in, and Waterhouse praised the winning entry (from Webb and Bell) for its 'mastery of details ... and its general picturesqueness'. He added that the terra cotta and brick, proposed by the architects, were 'undoubtedly ... the best materials for Birmingham'. The plan is simple: the main hall, lit by five large windows, stands between two smaller blocks of unequal projection at each end, and at right angles to it. A low corridor, with the entrance porch, runs across the central block connecting up the three units. Two rhetorical towers (favourite apostrophe of Victorian architecture) mask what would otherwise be an ugly juxtaposition of heights and angles. Completely dazzling, within and without, is the display of terra cotta. Technically superb, and detailed as though it were jewellery, the smooth and enriched decorations are nicely contrasted.

The student who seeks to account for the historical sources from which the designers derived some of the details of this building is faced with a complex task. Aside from the figure sculpture modelled by William Aumonier, the external and internal decorations show plainly a knowledge and admiration of certain types of Northern European architecture dating from the first half of the sixteenth century. Examples at the Assize Courts of precisely copied historical detail seem to be rare (as they were rare at this date generally) but the designers were probably familiar with buildings as different as King's College Chapel at Cambridge, Layer Marney Towers in Essex, and the church of St Pierre at Caen: also with some of the interiors

for Francis I in the Loire Valley. Precisely how Ingress Bell and Aston Webb divided the work of design between themselves may never be known. But the architectural character of the Assize Courts is in many ways dissimilar to Aston Webb's later work produced on his own (the main façades of the Victoria and Albert Museum, and Buckingham Palace); and it is probably safe to assume that the design of the Birmingham building, with its strong but imprecise flavours, reflects in large measure the taste of Ingress Bell. Our understanding of this building may therefore be advanced if we turn to some of his remarks about architectural design. Between 1879 and 1886 he published five articles in the *Magazine of Art* ('On some Pictorial Elements in English Secular Architecture') the last two of which – of 1880 and 1886 – seem especially relevant here.

In the article of 1880 he begins by saying that 'the eighteenth century may be ... called the dark ages of domestic architecture as in *art*': for him much eighteenth-century architecture was 'simply insipid', its faults lay in an 'over refinement of detail and a kind of simpering grace'. But he praises Kent's Horse Guards – although he compares it with Chambers's Somerset House, of which he says that no one would 'think of taking that dreary pile [the river front] as a subject for his pencil' (he has already reminded us that Kent was 'more of a painter than an architect').

In the article of 1886 the pictorial attitude towards architecture is sustained and amplified. He says 'it is difficult to account for the passion for employing one particular period of Gothic for an entire building' (as in some of the work of G. E. Street or J. L. Pearson); and on the subject of Salisbury Cathedral – substantially completed in one generation – he doubts whether 'for pictorial and artistic effect it is not inferior ... to buildings which exhibit the whole range of our native architecture from early Norman to Tudor'. He admires the pictures of David Roberts who 'with a painter's true instinct ... selects for his subjects precisely those works where the divergence of style is most marked' – where the 'vaulting of the thirteenth century is "set off" by the elaborate Cinquecento stalls of the choir'. He admires also buildings where the 'artistic or pictorial charm' results even from 'an incongruous juxtaposition of elements'. And in this article (with the sub-title 'Archaeology *v.* Art') he says of

2. *The 'Victoria' Assize Courts, Birmingham. 1886–91. Terra cotta. Aston Webb and Ingress Bell, architects.*

the architects of the remoter past: 'they were the original authors; we are at best but skilful adapters. We have the whole of their work before us, and see, or think we see, that a great part of its charm, pictorially – and that is mainly how we are affected by it – is due to the fact that it is made up of many and various styles.'

The views expressed in these two articles, separated by six years, are remarkably consistent; and the Assize Courts, with its broken skyline, its unequal projections on plan and its richly textured cladding of varied details executed in terra cotta, seems to reflect very accurately Ingress Bell's admiration for pictorial values. It is true that from the point of view of the date of the sources, the building shows a certain stylistic consistency, even if the sources were to be found on both sides of the channel; and perhaps Aston Webb exercised a restraining hand to prevent the inclusion of a wider 'range' of styles and of 'incongruous juxtapositions' generally. But the designers were nothing if not 'skilful adapters' – as the student soon discovers when trying to trace the source of the motifs; and the presence everywhere of these free adaptations (cf. the term 'Free Renaissance' style), rarely if ever exactly similar to the historical examples from which they seem to derive, is once again what we should expect to find after reading Bell's articles.[11] But above all, perhaps, the building represents a protest, more than usually vigorous even in the later nineteenth century, against the urbane and dapper street-architecture of the Georgian Tradition – architecture of a type which to many Victorians besides Ingress Bell seemed monotonous, 'insipid' (to use Bell's own word), and dull.

It is not surprising that Goodhart-Rendel, who discussed this building with calculated brevity,[12] included it among the 'bric-à-brac'; yet from it much could be learned (in an extended study) about the incorporation of modelled sculpture in architecture of this type – Aumonier was well-known and respected in his day; about the problems of design and construction in terra cotta, and particularly about one current of late Victorian architectural taste (the building was contemporary with the very different achievements in the sphere of the Arts and Crafts Movement). It should be added that the Assize Courts cost nearly £150,000 and became the 'chief permanent memorial in Birmingham of the first Jubilee celebrations'. Queen Victoria herself laid the foundation-stone (in 1887 – hence

'Victoria' Courts), and the opening ceremony was performed (in 1891) by the Prince and Princess of Wales.

Domestic architecture now claims attention. Private houses built between *c.* 1830 and *c.* 1860 show that the 'Castellated' and Classical Italianate styles are the leading favourites at the extremes of taste (Anthony Salvin, Edward Blore, P. C. Hardwick, Pugin himself;

3. House and studio for the painter Luke Fildes, Melbury Road, Kensington. 1877. Bricks and tiles. Norman Shaw, architect.

Sir Charles Barry, Lewis Vulliamy); but buildings by two other men, John Shaw and the novelist Thackeray, must be mentioned here. John Shaw, unrelated to Norman Shaw, built the Royal Naval College, New Cross (now the Goldsmiths' College) in the early 1840s. This building is described by Professor Pevsner as of a 'chaste Italian style',[13] though in appearance it is quite unlike the Italian of Charles Barry; while Shaw's better-known Wellington College (begun 1856) is described in the same article as built in 'a style developed from two sources equally remarkable in the 1850s, Wren's Hampton Court and the French Dix-huitième'. The significance of

derivations from Wren at this date (i.e. before Norman Shaw and Nesfield) cannot be discussed here, but these two buildings may yet prove to be more important landmarks than is usually conceded, especially as they show French influence. In 1859, as we know, came the very important Red House by Webb for Morris; and a year or two later (1860 or 1861) Thackeray designed No. 2 Palace Gardens (Kensington) for himself and his daughters. Red House is discussed in a dozen books; Thackeray's house is not.[14] Professor Pevsner says that it is 'neo-Georgian ... although Thackeray designed it when no one was dreaming of a Georgian revival'.[15] The neo-Georgian elements are again significant because they appear before the time of Shaw and Nesfield. A description of it here is impossible for reasons of space but Thackeray, we must remember, had learnt to draw in Paris and had lectured in America on the Four Georges; with these signs of his interests, the small *Dix-huitième* windows in the roof of his house, the odd details of the entrance door and porch, and the overall Georgian look need cause no surprise. The house was noted by that very interesting architect-critic, Paul Sédille, in his *L'Architecture moderne en Angleterre* (Paris, 1890). After saying that Thackeray built his house in the style of the Queen Anne epoch, and that it has a 'certain classic savour', Sédille states emphatically that it is 'without doubt the first [house] built in London in the style that will soon dominate everywhere' (translation). It may be added that Sédille then goes on to discuss Red House and No. 1, Palace Green (both by Webb); Nesfield's celebrated Lodge in Regent's Park; the use by Shaw of the Sparrowe House windows (there are several good pages on Shaw); the popularization of the so-called Queen Anne style by Robson and Stevenson in the Board Schools, and a number of other significant buildings and details. In other words, Sédille, by 1890, has put his finger on many of the buildings today regarded as occupying key positions among those displaying innovations of style. The Queen Anne style, it should be explained, is taken to involve the use of tall, segment-headed windows, thick glazing bars, white painted woodwork and, very often, contrasting (smooth and semi-smooth) red bricks and tiles, and an irregular skyline.

Born a generation apart, Shaw perfects an urban-picturesque type of house, while Voysey eventually builds in a puritanical style for

4. *Broadleys, Lake Windermere. 1898. Rough cast and slate.*
C. F. A. Voysey, architect.

uncompromising country-lovers (though Shaw built many country mansions and Voysey a few town houses). Shaw is the subject of a full-dress biography (by Blomfield), Voysey of a few articles and a short (but invaluable) 'outline'.[16] Shaw's work, in its diversity, must surprise if not delight the least informed observer; Voysey's might easily appear monotonous except to the specialist. Shaw's buildings are robust, richly textured, and immensely varied in their different units and by comparison to each other. He borrows details freely, some of them from abroad. It is highly significant of the character of his work that he built six or seven large houses for successful artists (see Fig. 3). Voysey was proudly insular and he never used foreign motifs. He deeply admired Pugin and believed (in accordance with one of Pugin's chief tenets) that function and construction were the basis of all good design. His houses are long, low, and Quakerly (see Fig. 4) and of a neutral tone and texture ('whitened rough cast' and slate); they at once suggest high-thinking and austere patrons. Shaw uses the roof – dormers, chimney-stacks, lantern, etc.; the upper third or less of his tall London houses – to provide the picturesque outline, and for the servants' bedrooms. In houses by Voysey the roof-to-wall proportion is often half and half, and this alone gives them an earthbound look. Where Shaw loves

a broken pattern in his windows, and especially the generous vertical spread of a window taken up through two floors, Voysey is proto-contemporary in his use of the long horizontal window-line emphasized, very often, by the roof which sweeps down to a gable running along immediately above the windows. Shaw and Voysey resemble each other in providing, in their different ways, spacious and very agreeable interiors (tall, formal and complex; long, low and simple) and in relating their buildings to the site with great feeling. Shaw's houses represent what may be called the artistic materialism of the eighties and nineties; while Voysey's monster cottages reflect the intellectual, almost aristocratic restraint which at the end of the century opposes middle-class indulgence and display.

Sheer ground-consuming size, and the superb confidence of the architects who sought to build (like the Egyptians) 'for eternity', render many seemingly indestructible Victorian monuments un-economic to maintain, inelastic to convert and, therefore, vulnerable. Only public opinion, backed by numbers and capable of expressing a balanced judgement (where indiscriminate enthusiasm could prove fatal), will in the end prevent the destruction, almost before their interest and significance have been absorbed, of many fine buildings. The future is always liable to make a mockery of the present. The likely charge against the later twentieth century of irresponsible demolition could, however, be avoided.

NOTES

The drawings in this chapter
are by Albany Wiseman

Editor's Note: It has not been possible to update this article due to the author's death in 1971. Of the buildings mentioned on p. 440 as being due for demolition in 1960, the decision was reversed on two of them – the Outfall station at Crossness and most of St Thomas's Hospital.

1. In *Early Victorian Architecture in Britain*, 2 vols (London, 1954).
2. In *The Gothic Revival* (London, 1928, 1950).
3. Subtitle: 'From William Morris to Walter Gropius', (3rd edn, Penguin, 1960).
4. *Lectures on Art* (5th edn, London, 1890).
5. Edited by Harold J. Laski, W. Ivor Jennings, and William A. Robson (London, 1935).

6. See *School Architecture* by E. R. Robson (London, 1874); also 'Towers of Learning' by D. Gregory-Jones, *Architectural Review*, CXXIII, 737, June 1958.

7. Garden cities from *c.* 1875 onwards excepted.

8. See the brochure produced by the L.C.C.: *Centenary of London's Main Drainage, 1855–1955.*

9. See *The Illustrated London News*, 1864, 1865. I am indebted to Miss Felicity Burden for information about Bazalgette and his work.

10. See *English Architecture Since the Regency*, by H. S. Goodhart-Rendel (London, 1953), p. 167: 'Ernest George ... early casting off his allegiance to Street, spent a large part of his professional career making very soft and pretty drawings of elaborate Anglo-Dutch architecture and getting them carried out in terra cotta that is very hard and ugly.' Goodhart-Rendel no doubt wrote sincerely; but there is both truth and phrase-making in this sentence. The drawings are not all 'soft and pretty', nor is all the architecture 'hard and ugly', cf. Note 11.

11. See *The Picturesque* by Christopher Hussey (London, 1927), p. 229: 'Not the least cause of much vile architecture of last century is the inaccuracy of borrowed features'. Mr Hussey believed that inaccuracies occurred because the architects merely sketched the features and details concerned instead of making measured drawings. This interpretation suggests that the adaptations were due to slovenly draughtsmanship. My own belief is that variations were usually deliberate. Many architects could sketch with astonishing accuracy and it was probably in varying a feature that they saw a chance to be 'original' while preserving a stylistic 'flavour'. It must be added that to quote Mr Hussey's words is not necessarily to agree that the examples he had in mind were 'vile', or that the presence in them of adaptations (whether deliberate or brought about by careless sketching) contributed to the alleged vileness.

12. *English Architecture Since the Regency*, p. 176.

13. In *The Architectural Review*, III, 661, June 1952.

14. It is mentioned by Goodhart-Rendel, p. 163.

15. In *The Buildings of England, London, except the Cities of London and Westminster* (Penguin, 1952), p. 261.

16. See 'C. F. A. Voyse' by John Brandon-Jones in *Architectural Association Journal*, May 1957.

Price, R. G. G. *The History of 'Punch'*, 1957

Robertson Scott, J. W. *The Story of the 'Pall Mall Gazette'*, 1950

Roll-Hansen, D. *The Academy 1869–79: Victorian Intellectuals in Revolt*, 1957

Saintsbury, G. *A History of English Prose Rhythm*, 1912

Shattock, J. *Politics and Reviewers: The 'Edinburgh' and the 'Quarterly' in the Early Victorian Age*, 1989

Sutherland, J. A. *Victorian Novelists and Publishers*, 1976

Thayer, W. R. 'Biography in the Nineteenth Century' in *North American Review* CCXI, 1920

Thomas, Sir William Beach, *The Story of the 'Spectator'*, 1928

Thrall, M. *Revellious Fraser's: Nol Yorke's Magazine in the Days of Maginn, Thackeray and Carlyle*, 1934

Victorian Periodicals Newsletter, 1968 – in progress

Welcome, H. S. *The Evolution of Journalism*, 1909

Woodward, E. L. *British Historians*, 1943

Worcester, D. *The Art of Satire*, 1943

Buckley, Vincent *Poetry and Morality*, 1959

Church, A. J. 'Criticism as a Trade' in *Nineteenth Century* XXVI, 1889 (reply by W. Knight in same issue)

Dallas, E. S. *The Gay Science*, 2 vols., 1866

Dingle, H. *Science and Literary Criticism*, 1949

Eigner, E. M. and Worth, G. J. (eds.) *Victorian Critics of the Novel*, 1985

Lester, J. A. *Transformations in British Literary Culture 1880–1914*, 1968

Levin, H. (ed.) *Perspectives of Criticism*, 1950

Martin, R. B. *The Triumph of Wit: A Study of Victorian Comic Theory*, 1974

Orel, H. *Victorian Literary Critics*, 1984

Peters, R. L. *The Crowns of Apollo: Victorian Criticism and Aesthetics*, 1965

Saintsbury, G. *A History of English Criticism*, 1911

Tillotson, G. *Essays in Criticism and Research*, 1942

Tillotson, G. *Criticism and the Nineteenth Century*, 1951; rev. edn 1967

Wellek, R. *A History of Modern Criticism:* Vols II–III, 1955–66

Wellek, R. *The Rise of English Literary History*, 1941

Wimsatt, W. K., and Brooks, C. *Literary Criticism: A Short History*, 1957

APPENDIX

VOLUME 6

COMPILED BY NORMAN VANCE

PART FOUR

List of Abbreviations

E. & S.	Essays and Studies by Members of the English Association
E.L.	Everyman's Library edition
M.L.N.	*Modern Language Notes*
M.L.R.	*Modern Language Review*
M.P.	*Modern Philology*
N.C.B.E.L.	*The New Cambridge Bibliography of English Literature*
O.E.N.	Oxford English Novels
P.C.	Penguin Classics
P.M.L.A.	*Publications of the Modern Language Association of America*
P.Q.	*Philological Quarterly*
R.E.S.	*Review of English Studies*
W.C.	World's Classics edition
abr.	abridged
b.	born
c.	circa
ch.	chapter
d.	died
ed.	edited, editor
edn	edition
pt.	part
repr.	reprinted
rev.	revised
trans.	translated
vol.	volume

Under each author there appears first a short biography, second the standard edition(s), and third a selection of books and articles for further study.

FOR FURTHER READING
AND REFERENCE

The Social and Intellectual Setting

I. HISTORIES: GENERAL AND POLITICAL

Best, G. F. A. *Temporal Pillars*, 1964
    Mid-Victorian Britain, 1851–75, 1971; new edn 1979
Briggs, A. *The Age of Improvement*, 1961
    (ed.) *Chartist Studies*, 1959
Brinton, C. *English Political Thought in the Nineteenth Century*, 1933
Bury, J. P. T. (ed.) *The New Cambridge Modern History*, Vol. 10, 1960
Butler, J. R. M. *The Passing of the Great Reform Bill*, 1914
Chambers, J. D. *The Workshop of the World*, 1960
Clark, G. K. *The Expanding Society: Britain 1830–1900*, 1967
Davis, H. W. C. *The Age of Grey and Peel*, 1929
Ensor, R. C. K. *England 1870–1914*, 1935
Faber, R. *The Vision and the Need: Late Victorian Imperialist Aims*, 1966
Hanham, H. J. *Elections and Party Management in the Time of Disraeli and Gladstone*, 1960
Harrison, J. F. C. *Early Victorian Britain 1832–51*, 1971; new edn 1979
Hobsbawm, E. J. *The Age of Revolution*, 1962
Keir, D. L. *Constitutional History of Modern Britain 1485–1937*, 1938
McCord, N. *The Anti-Corn Law League*, 1958
Newton, A. P. *A Hundred Years of British Empire*, 1940
Shannon, R. T. *The Crisis of Imperialism, 1865–1915*, 1974; new edn 1976
Smellie, K. B. *A Hundred Years of English Government*, rev. edn 1951

Feiling, K. G. *The Second Tory Party 1714–1832*, 1938
Feuchtwanger, E. J. *Disraeli, Democracy and the Tory Party*, 1968
Fraser, D. *Urban Politics in Victorian England*, 1976
Gash, N. *Politics in the Age of Peel*, 1953; new edn 1977
Hammond, J. L. *Gladstone and the Irish Nation*, 1938
Hammond, J. L. and Foot, M. R. D. *Gladstone and Liberalism*, 1952
Harrison, R. *Before the Socialists*, 1965
Maccoby, S. *English Radicalism 1832–1914*, 3 vols., 1935–53
Moore, D. C. *The Politics of Deference*, 1977
Pelling, H. *Popular Politics and Society in Late Victorian Britain*, 1968; rev. edn 1979

PART FOUR

Semmel, Bernard *The Governor Eyre Controversy*, 1962
Thomas, J. A. *The House of Commons 1832–1901*, 1939
Tyler, J. E. *The Struggle for Imperial Unity 1868–95*, 1938
Woodward, E. L. *The Age of Reform 1815–1870*, 1936

II. THE SOCIAL AND ECONOMIC BACKGROUND

Ashworth, W. *English Economic History, 1800–1870*, 1960
Booth, C. *Life and Labour of the People in London*, 17 vols., 1902–3; Selections, ed. H. W. Peautz, 1968
Briggs, A. *Victorian People*, 1954
　　Victorian Cities, 1963
　　Victorian Things, 1988, new edn. 1990
Brodie, B. *Sea Power in the Machine Age*, 1944
Burn, D. L. *The Economic History of Steel Making 1876–1939*, 1940
Burn, W. L. *The Age of Equipoise*, 1964
Butterfield, H. *History and Human Relations*, 1951
Cannadine, D. *The Decline and Fall of the British Aristocracy*, 1990
Chesney, K. *The Victorian Underworld*, 1970
Clapham, J. H. *The Bank of England*, 2 vols., 1945
　　An Economic History of Modern Britain, 3 vols., 1930–38
Cohen, E. W. *The Growth of the British Civil Service 1780–1939*, 1941
Cole, G. D. H. *A Short History of the British Working Class Movement*, rev. edn 1948
Dyos, H. J., and Wolff, M. Y. (eds.) *The Victorian City: Images and Realities*, 1972
Fay, C. R. *Palace of Industry, 1851*, 1951
Finer, S. E. *The Life and Times of Sir Edwin Chadwick*, 1952
Fisher, John (ed.) *Eye Witness*, 1960
Frazer, W. M. *A History of English Public Health 1834–1939*, 1950
Gayer, A. D. et al. *The Growth and Fluctuation of British Economy 1790–1850*, 2 vols., 1953
Halévy, E. *A History of the English People 1815–1915*, 4 vols., rev. edn 1951
Hinde, R. S. E. *The British Penal System 1773–1950*, 1951
Horn, P. *Labouring Life in the Victorian Countryside*, 1971
Jefferys, J. B. *The Story of the Engineers 1800–1945*, 1946
Kitson Clark, G. *The Making of Victorian England*, 1962
Marcus, S. *The Other Victorians*, 1966
Mathias, P. *The First Industrial Nation*, 1969
Mayhew, H. *London Labour and the London Poor*, 1862; repr., 4 vols., 1968; Selections, ed. S. Rubinstein, 1947; ed. V. E. Neuburg, 1985
　　The Unknown Mayhew ed. E. P. Thompson and Eileen Yeo, 1971
Mingay, G. E. (ed.) *The Victorian Countryside*, 2 vols., 1981
Petrie, Charles *The Victorians*, 1960
Phelps-Brown, E. H. *The Growth of British Industrial Relations*, 1959
Pike, E. R. *Human Documents of the Industrial Revolution*, 1966

Pike, E. R. *Human Documents of the Victorian Golden Age*, 1967

Poovey, M. *Uneven Development: The Ideological Work of Gender in Mid-Victorian England*, 1989

Quennell, M. and C. H. B. *A History of Everyday Things in England*, 1933

Redford, A. *Labour Migration in England 1800–1850*, 1964

Robinson, R., and Gallagher, J. *Africa and the Victorians*, 1961

Rostow, W. W. *British Economy of the Nineteenth Century*, 1948

Royle, E. *Modern Britain. A Social History 1750–1985*, 1987

Smith, K. *The Malthusian Controversy*, 1951

Spring, D. *The English Landed Estate, its Administration*, 1963

Taylor, B. *Eve and the New Jerusalem*, 1983

Thompson, E. P. *The Making of the English Working Class*, 1963

Thompson, F. M. L. *The English Landed Classes in the Nineteenth Century*, 1963
 The Rise of Respectable Society: A Social History of Victorian Britain 1830–1900, 1988
 (ed.) *The Cambridge Social History of Britain, 1750–1950*, 3 vols., 1990

Vicinus, M. (ed.) *Suffer and be Still: Women in the Victorian Age*, 1972
 A Widening Sphere, 1977

Webb, S. and B. *English Local Government*, 8 vols., 1904–29
 History of Trade Unionism, 1907, new edn 1950
 Industrial Democracy, 1907

Wrigley, E. A. *Continuity, Chance and Change: the Character of the Industrial Revolution in England*, 1988

Young, G. M. *Victorian England*, annotated edn 1977
 (ed.) *Early Victorian England*, 2 vols., 1934

Altick, Richard D. *The English Common Reader 1800–1900*, 1957

Aspinall, Arthur *Politics and the Press c. 1780–1850*, 1949

Boyce, G., Curran, J., and Wingate, P. (eds.) *Newspaper History from the Seventeenth Century to the Present Day*, 1978

Brown, L. *Victorian News and Newspapers*, 1985

Chapman, R. *The Victorian Debate: English Literature and Society, 1832–1901*, 1968

Curwen, H. *A History of Booksellers*, 1873

Graff, H. J. *The Literacy Myth*, 1979

Harrison, J. F. C. *Learning and Living, 1790–1960: A Study in the History of the English Adult Education Movement*, 1961

The History of 'The Times', 4 vols., 1935–52

Hoggart, R. *The Uses of Literacy*, 1957

James, Louis *Fiction for the Working Man, 1830–1850*, 1963
 Print and the People 1819–51, 1977

Knight, Charles *The Old Printer and the Modern Press*, 1854
 Passages of a Working Life through Half a Century, 3 vols., 1864

Koss, S. *The Rise and Fall of the Political Press in Britain: The Nineteenth Century*, 1981

Leavis, Q. D. *Fiction and the Reading Public*, 1932

Neuburg, V. E. *Popular Literature: A History and Guide*, 1977

Read, Donald *Press and People, 1790–1850: Opinion in Three English Cities*, 1961

Shattock, J., and Wolff, M. *The Victorian Periodical Press: Samplings and Soundings*, 1981

Wadsworth, A. P. *Newspaper Circulations, 1800–1954*, 1955

Webb, R. K. *The British Working Class Reader 1790–1848*, 1955

Williams, Raymond, *The Country and the City*, 1973
> *Culture and Society 1760–1950*, 1958
> *The Long Revolution*, 1961

III. DIARIES, LETTERS, MEMOIRS, REMINISCENCES

See under *Authors*: Arnold, Browning, Butler, Carlyle, Carroll, Clough, Darwin, Dickens, Disraeli, Eliot, Fitzgerald, Gissing, Hopkins, Kipling, Meredith, Morris, Pater, Patmore, Rossetti, Stevenson, Swinburne, Thackeray, Trollope.

Albert, Prince *Letters 1831–1861*, ed. K. Jagow, 1938

Allingham, William *Diary 1824–1889*, ed. J. J. Norwich, 1985

The Amberley Papers, ed. B. and P. Russell, 2 vols., 1937

Arnold, J. B. *Giants in Dressing Gowns*, 1942

Aspinall, A. (ed.) *Three Early Nineteenth Century Diaries: D. la Marchant (1795–1874); E. J. Littleton (1791–1863); Lord Ellenborough (1790–1871)*, 1952

Bamford, S. *Autobiography* (2 vols). 1844–59

Brooke, Margaret *My Life in Sarawak*, 1987

Brown, Ford Madox *Diary*, ed. V. Surtees, 1981

Brunton, John *John Brunton's Book: Memoirs of an Engineer*, 1939

Chamberlain, J. *A Political Memoir 1880–92*, ed. C. H. D. Howard, 1953

Christian, G. (ed.) *A Victorian Poacher: James Hawker's Journal*, 1976

Collier, Mary *A Victorian Diarist: Extracts from the Journals 1873–95*, ed. E. F. C. Collier, 1944
> *Later Extracts*, ed. E. F. C. Collier, 1946

Cooper, T. *Autobiography*, 1871; new edn 1967

Croker, John Wilson *The Croker Papers*, ed. E. L. Jennings, 3 vols., 1884

Dowson, Ernest *Letters*, ed. D. Flower and H. Maas, 1968

Emerson, R. W. *English Traits* ed. H. Mumford-Jones, 1966

Fontané, Theodor *Journeys to England in Victoria's Early Days*, ed. D. Harrison, 1939

Fox, Elizabeth *Elizabeth, Lady Holland, to her Son: Letters 1821–45*, ed. Earl of Ilchester, 1946

Franklin, Lady Jane *Life, Diaries and Correspondence*, ed. W. F. Rawnsley, 1923

Gladstone, Mary *Diaries and Letters*, ed. L. Masterman, 1930

Gladstone, W. E. *Gladstone to his Wife*, ed. A. T. Bassett, 1936

The Gladstone Diaries, ed. M. R. D. Foot, 10 vols., 1969–

Green, John Richard *Letters*, ed. L. Stephen, 1901

Green, V (ed.) *Love in a Cool Climate: the Letters of Mark Pattison and Meta Bradley 1879–1884*, 1986

Greville, Charles Cavendish Fulke *The Greville Memoirs: A Journal of the Reign of Queen Victoria, 1837–1852; 1852–1860*, 3 vols. 1885; 2 vols., 1887

Guest, Lady Charlotte *Extracts from the Journal 1833–52* ed. Earl of Bessborough, 1950

The Haldane Papers ed. S. M. Ellis, 1930

Holyoake, G. J. *Sixty Years of an Agitator's Life*, 1892

Hughes, M. V. *A London Family 1870–1900*, 1946; new edn 1981

Kellett, E. E. *As I Remember*, 1936

Lovett, W. *The Life and Struggles of William Lovett in his Pursuit of Bread, Knowledge and Freedom*, 1876; ed. R. H. Tawney, 2 vols., 1920; new edn, 1 vol., 1967

Lucas, William *A Quaker Journal (1804–61)* ed. G. E. Bryant and G. P. Baker, 2 vols., 1934

Macready, William Charles *Diaries* ed. W. Toynbee, 2 vols., 1912

Martineau, H. *Selected Letters*, ed. V. Sanders, 1990

Mozley, Thomas *Reminiscences*, 2 vols., 1882–5

Newman, Francis William *Memoir and Letters* ed. I. G. Sieveking, 1909

Northcote, Stafford *Life, Letters and Diaries* ed. A. Lang, 2 vols., 1890

Oman, Charles *Memories of Victorian Oxford*, 1941

Plomer, W. (ed.) *Kilvert's Diary*, 3 vols., 1938–40; new edn 1977°

Richmond, E. (ed.) *The Earlier Letters of Gertrude Bell*, 1937

Schreiber, Lady Charlotte *Extracts from the Journal 1853–91* ed. Earl of Bessborough, 1952

Sitwell, O. (ed.) *Two Generations*, 1940

Skelton, J. *The Table Talk of Shirley*, 2 vols., 1895

Somerville, Alexander *The Autobiography of a Working Man*, 1848; new ed., intro. J. Carswell, 1951

Stanley, Lady Maria Josepha *The Ladies of Alderley* (letters 1841–50) ed. N. Mitford, 1938

    The Stanleys of Alderley (letters 1851–65) ed. N. Mitford, 1939

Taine, H. *Notes on England* tr. Edward Hyams, 1957

Terry, Ellen *Memoirs* ed. Edith Craig and Christopher St John, 1933

Ticknor, G. *Life, Letters and Journals*, 2 vols., 1876

Victoria, Queen *Leaves from a Journal of our Life in the Highlands*, 2 vols., 1868–83; ed. D. Duff, 1 vol., 1968; new edn 1977

    Letters ed. A. C. Benson *et al.*, 9 vols., 1907–32

Webb, B. *Diary*, ed. N. and J. MacKenzie, 4 vols., 1982–5

    My Apprenticeship, 1926; new edn 1979

    Our Partnership ed. B. Drake and M. Cole, 1948; new edn 1975

Webb, S. and B. *Letters* ed. N. MacKenzie, 3 vols., 1978

PART FOUR

IV. PHILOSOPHY, RELIGION AND EDUCATION

See under *Authors*: Arnold, Carlyle, Hopkins, Hutton, Huxley, Kingsley, Lewes, Mill, Newman, Pattison, Ruskin, Spencer

Benn, A. W. *The History of English Rationalism in the Nineteenth Century*, 2 vols., 1906

Brose, O. *Church and Parliament*, 1959

Budd. S. *Varieties of Unbelief*, 1977

Burrow, J. W. *Evolution and Society*, 1966

Chadwick, O. *The Secularization of the European Mind in the Nineteenth Century*, 1977

Gilbert, A. D. *Religion and Society in Industrial England*, 1976

Halévy, E. *The Growth of Philosophic Radicalism*, rev. edn 1949

Houghton, W. E. *The Victorian Frame of Mind 1830–1870*, 1957

Hutton, R. H. *Contemporary Thought and Thinkers*, 2 vols., 1894

Inglis, K. S. *The Churches and the Working Classes*, 1963

Jones, P. D'A. *The Christian Socialist Revival 1877–1914*, 1968

Mead, G. H. *Movements of Thought in the Nineteenth Century*, 1936

Metz, R. *A Hundred Years of British Philosophy*, 1938

Muirhead, J. H. *et al. Contemporary British Philosophy*, 2 vols., 1924–5

Robertson, J. M. *A Short History of Free Thought*, 1906

Sorley, W. R. *A History of English Philosophy*, 1920

Stephen, L. *The English Utilitarians*, 1900

Thomas, W. *The Philosophic Radicals*, 1979

Willey, B. *Nineteenth Century Studies: Coleridge to Matthew Arnold*, 1949
      More Nineteenth Century Studies: a Group of Honest Doubters, 1956

Wright, T. *The Religion of Humanity: The Impact of Comtean Positivism on Victorian Britain*, 1986

Binfield, C. *So Down to Prayers: Studies in English Nonconformity 1780–1927*, 1977

Bradley, I. *The Call to Seriousness*, 1976

Chadwick, O. *The Victorian Church*, 2 vols., 1966–70; new edn 1971–2

Church, R. W. *The Oxford Movement*, 1891; new edn 1970

Dawson, C. *The Spirit of the Oxford Movement*, 1933

Elliott-Binns, L. E. *The Development of English Theology in the later Nineteenth Century*, 1952
      English Thought 1860–1900: The Theological Aspect, 1956

Faber, G. *Oxford Apostles*, 1933; rev. edn 1936

Gillispie, C. C. *Genesis and Geology*, 1951

Hilton, B. *The Age of Atonement: The Influence of Evangelicalism on Social and Economic Thought 1795–1865*, 1987

Jay, E. *Faith and Doubt in Victorian Britain*, 1986

Newsome, D. *The Parting of Friends*, 1966

Overton, J. H. *The English Church in the Nineteenth Century*, 1894

Prickett, S. *Romanticism and Religion: The Tradition of Coleridge and Wordsworth in the Victorian Church*, 1976

Reardon, B. M. G. *Religious Thought in the Victorian Age*, rev. edn 1980

Robertson, J. M. *A Short History of Free Thought*, 1906

Sandall, R. *The History of the Salvation Army*, 3 vols., 1947–55

Sanders, C. R. *Coleridge and the Broad Church Movement*, 1942

Sellers, I. *Nineteenth-Century Nonconformity*, 1977

Storr, V. F. *The Development of English Theology in the Nineteenth Century 1800–60*, 1913

   Freedom and Tradition: A Study of Liberal Evangelicalism, 1940

Tulloch, J. *Movements of Religious Thought in Britain during the Nineteenth Century*, 1885

Valenze, D. M. *Prophetic Sons and Daughters: Female Preaching and Popular Religion in Industrial England*, 1985

Vance, N. *The Sinews of the Spirit: The Ideal of Christian Manliness in Victorian Literature and Religious Thought*, 1985

Vidler, A. R. *The Church in an Age of Revolution*, rev. edn 1971

Ward, Wilfrid *William George Ward and the Oxford Movement*, 1889; repr. 1968

Wheeler, M. *Death and the Future Life in Victorian Literature and Theology*, 1990

Adamson, J. W. *English Education 1789–1902*, 1930

Armytage, W. H. G. *Civic Universities*, 1955

Barnard, H. C. *A Short History of English Education*, rev. edn 1952

Birchenough, C. *History of Elementary Education in England and Wales from 1800*, rev. edn 1938

Boas, L. S. *Women's Education Begins: the Rise of the Women's Colleges*, 1938

Bradley, I., and Simon, B. (eds.) *The Victorian Public School*, 1975

Engel, A. J. *From Clergyman to Don: The Rise of the Academic Profession in Nineteenth-Century Oxford*, 1983

Honey, J. R. de S. *Tom Brown's Universe*, 1977

Hunt, F. (ed.) *Lessons for Life: The Schooling of Girls and Women 1850–1950*, 1987

Hurt, J. *Education in Evolution*, 1971

Laqueur, T. W. *Religion and Respectability: Schools and Working Class Culture 1780–1850*, 1977

Peterson, A. D. C. *A Hundred Years of Education*, 1952

Rothblatt, S. *The Revolution of the Dons: Cambridge and Society in Victorian England*, 1968

Rowntree, J. W., and Binns, H. B. *A History of the Adult School Movement*, 1903

Simon, B. *Studies in the History of Education 1780–1870*, 1960

Smith, J. W. A. *The Birth of Modern Education*, 1954

Ward, W. R. *Victorian Oxford*, 1966

Wood, E. M. *The Polytechnic of Quintin Hogg*, 1932

V. ART, ARCHITECTURE AND MUSIC

See under *Authors*: Butler, du Maurier, Lear, Morris, Rossetti, Ruskin

Ford, B. (ed.) *The Cambridge Guide to the Arts in Britain, 6. Romantics to Early Victorians*, 1990; 7. *The Later Victorian Age*, 1989

Bell, Q. *Victorian Artists*, 1968
     A New and Noble School: The Pre-Raphaelites, 1982
Bendiner, K. *An Introduction to Victorian Painting*, 1985
Boase, T. S. R. *English Art, 1800–1870*, 1959
Chesneau, Ernest *English School of Painting*, 1891
Farr, D. *English Art 1870–1940*, 1978
Gaunt, William *The Aesthetic Adventure*, 1945
     The Pre-Raphaelite Dream, 1943
Harvey, J. R. *Victorian Novelists and their Illustrators*, 1970
Honour, H. *Romanticism*, 1979
Hubbard, H. *A Hundred Years of British Painting 1851–1951*, 1951
Hunt, J. D. *The Pre-Raphaelite Imagination: 1848–1900*, 1968
Hunt, W. H. *Pre-Raphaelitism and the Pre-Raphaelite Brotherhood* 2 vols.,
     1905
Hutchinson, S. C. *The History of the Royal Academy 1768–1986*, 1986
Maas, J. *Victorian Painters*, rev. edn 1978
MacColl, D. S. *Nineteenth Century Art*, 1902
Pointon, M. (ed.) *Pre-Raphaelites Re-Viewed*, 1989
Newall, C. *Victorian Watercolours*, 1987
Rossetti, W. M. *Pre-Raphaelite Diaries and Letters*, 1900
Ruskin, John *Modern Painters*, 5 vols., 1843–60
     Pre-Raphaelitism, 1851
     Art in England, 1884
Strong, R. *And When Did You Last See Your Father?*, 1978
Sussman, H. L. *Fact into Figure*, 1979
Symons, Arthur (ed.) *The Savoy*, 1896; repr. 5 vols., 1968
Treuherz, J. (ed.) *Hard Times: Social Realism in Victorian Art*, 1987
Welland, D. S. R. *The Pre-Raphaelites in Literature and Art*, 1953
Wolff, J. and Seed, J. (eds.) *The Culture of Capital: Art, Power and the
     Nineteenth Century Middle Class*, 1987

Bøe, A. *From Gothic Revival to Functional Form*, 1957
Casson, Hugh *An Introduction to Victorian Architecture*, 1948
Clark, K. *The Gothic Revival*, new edn 1962
Clarke, Basil F. L. *Church Builders of the Nineteenth Century*, 1938
Eastlake, C. L. *History of the Gothic Revival*, 1872
Edwards, R., and Ramsey, L. G. G. (eds.) *The Early Victorian Period 1830–
     60*, 1958
Girouard, M. *The Victorian Country House*, rev. edn 1979
Goodhart-Rendel, H. S. *English Architecture since the Regency*, 1953
Hitchcock, H.-R. *Early Victorian Architecture in Britain*, 2 vols., 1954
     Architecture: Nineteenth and Twentieth Centuries, 1958
Hubbard, Hesketh *Some Victorian Draughtsmen*, 1944
Meeks, Carroll L. V. *The Railway Station: An Architectural History*, 1957
Muthesius, S. *The High Victorian Moment in Architecture 1850–1870*, 1972
Pevsner, N. (ed.) *Seven Victorian Architects*, 1977

Smith, W. H. *Architecture in English Fiction*, 1934
Summerson, John *Heavenly Mansions and Other Essays on Architecture*, 1949
Turnor, R. *Nineteenth Century Architecture in Britain*, 1951

Ames, W. *Prince Albert and Victorian Taste*, 1968
Cooper, N. *The Opulent Eye: Late Victorian and Edwardian Taste in Interior Design*, 1977
Eastlake, C. L. *Hints on Household Tastes in Furniture*, 1868
Gibbs-Smith, C. H. *The Great Exhibition of 1851*, 1950
Klingender, Francis D. *Art and the Industrial Revolution*, 1947; rev. Arthur Elton, 1968
Madsen, S. T. *Sources of Art Nouveau*, 1956
Pevsner, N. *High Victorian Design*, 1951
    Pioneers of Modern Design, 3rd edn, 1960
    Studies in Art, Architecture and Design, Vol. II; *Victorian and After*, 1968
Steegman, John *Victorian Taste*, new edn 1970

Brooke, Iris, and Laver, James *English Costume in the Nineteenth Century*, 1947
Hansen, H. H. *Costume Cavalcade*, 1956

Disher, M. W. *Victorian Song*, 1955
Maitland, J. A. Fuller *English Music in the Nineteenth Century*, 1902; repr. 1976
Mellers, Wilfrid *Romanticism and the Twentieth Century*, 1957
Pearsall, R. *Victorian Popular Music*, 1973
Russell, D. *Popular Music in England 1840–1914*, 1987
Temperley, N. (ed.) *The Athlone History of Music in Britain*, Vol. 5: *The Romantic Age 1800–1914*, 1981
    The Lost Chord: Essays on Victorian Music, 1989

VI. SCIENCE

See under *Authors*: Darwin, Huxley
Bernal, J. D. *Science and Industry in the Nineteenth Century*, 1953
Bowler, P. J. *Fossils and Progress*, 1976
Bush, D. *Science and English Poetry*, 1950
Chapple, J. A. V. *Science and Literature in the Nineteenth Century*, 1988
Christie, J., and Shuttleworth, S. (eds.) *Nature Transfigured: Science and Literature, 1700–1900*, 1989
Dingle, H. (ed.) *A Century of Science 1851–1951*, 1951
    Science and Literary Criticism, 1949
Eiseley, Loren *Darwin's Century*, 1959
Evans, B. I. *Literature and Science*, 1954
Howarth, O. J. R. The *British Association for the Advancement of Science: A Retrospect 1831–1921*, 1922
Hull, D. L. *Darwin and his Critics*, 1973

Irvine, William *Apes, Angels and Victorians*, 1955
Merz, J. T. *History of European Thought in the Nineteenth Century*, 4 vols., 1896–1914
Moore, J. R. *The Post-Darwinian Controversies*, 1979
Rayleigh, Lord *Scientific Papers*, 1900; repr., 3 vols., 1966
Rupke, N. A. *The Great Chain of History: William Buckland and the English School of Geology 1814–1849*, 1983
Sherwood Taylor, F. *The Century of Science*, 1941
Singer, C. *A Short History of Science in the Nineteenth Century*, 1941
Stimson, D. *Scientists and Amateurs: A History of the Royal Society*, 1949
Stocking, G. *Victorian Anthropology*, 1987
Tolstoy, Ivan *James Clark Maxwell, A Biography*, 1981
Whitehead, A. N. *Science and the Modern World*, 1926

The Literature

VII. BIBLIOGRAPHIES

Bateson, F. W. *A Guide to English Literature*, 1965; rev. edn 1976
Bennett, S. *et al. Victorian Periodicals: A Guide to Research*, 1978
DeLaura, D. J. *Victorian Prose: A Guide to Research*, 1973
Faverty, F. E. *et al. The Victorian Poets: A Guide to Research*, 1956; rev. edn 1968
Ford, G. H. *Victorian Fiction: A Second Guide to Research*, 1978
Houghton, W. E. (ed.) *The Wellesley Index to Victorian Periodicals 1824–1900*, 5 vols., 1966–89
Sadleir, Michael *Nineteenth Century Fiction: A Biobliographical Record*, 2 vols., 1951
Templeman, W. D. *Bibliographies of Studies in Victorian Literature 1932–44*, 1945 – collected from M.P. xxx–xlii, 1933–45: this series is continued annually; *1945–54* ed. A. Wright, 1956
Watson, G. (ed.) N.C.B.E.L. III, 1969
The Year's Work in English Studies, annually since 1919

VIII. GENERAL STUDIES

Altholz, J. (ed.) *The Mind and Art of Victorian England*, 1976
Altick, R. D. *Painting from Books: Art and Literature in Britain 1760–1900*, 1986
Auerbach, N. *Woman and the Demon: The Life of a Victorian Myth*, 1982
Avery, G. *Nineteenth Century Children: Heroes and Heroines in English Children's Stories 1780–1900*, 1965
Bagehot, W. *Literary Studies*, 2 vols., 1879
Batho, E., and Dobrée, B. *The Victorians and After 1830–1914*, 1938; rev. edn 1950
Baugh, A. C. *A History of the English Language*, 1935

Brantlinger, P. *Rule of Darkness: British Literature and Imperialism, 1830–1914*, 1988; new edn 1991

Brightfield, M. F. *John Wilson Croker*, 1940

Buckley, J. H. *The Triumph of Time*, 1967
    The Victorian Temper: A Study in Literary Culture, 1952

Chandler, A. *A Dream of Order: The Medieval Ideal in Nineteenth Century English Literature*, 1971

Chesterton, G. K. *The Victorian Age in Literature*, 1913; new edn 1966

Cooke, J. D., and Stevenson, L. *English Literature of the Victorian Period*, 1949

Culler, A. D. *The Victorian Mirror of History*, 1986

Fraser, H. *Beauty and Belief: Aestheticism and Religion in Victorian Literature*, 1986

Goodwin, Michael (ed.) *Nineteenth Century Opinion*, 1951

Gosse, E. *A Short History of Modern English Literature*, 1897; rev. edn 1924

Gross, J. *The Rise and Fall of the Man of Letters*, 1969

Harrison, F. *Studies in Early Victorian Literature*, 1895

Harvey Darton, F. J. *Children's Books in England*, 1958

Henkle, R. B. *Comedy and Culture: England 1820–1900*, 1980

Horne, R. H. *A New Spirit of the Age*, 1844; w. c., 1907

Hough, Graham *Image and Experience*, 1960

Ideas and Beliefs of the Victorians (B.B.C. Talks), 1949

Jackson, H. *The Eighteen Nineties*, 1913

Landow, G. *Victorian Types, Victorian Shadows*, 1980

Leavis, Q. D. *Fiction and the Reading Public*, 1932

Lerner, L. D. (ed.) *The Victorians*, 1979

Magowan, J. P. *Representation and Revelation: Victorian Realism from Carlyle to Yeats*, 1986

Mix, K. L. *A Study in Yellow*, 1960

Moers, E. *Literary Women*, 1976; repr. 1980

Muir, P. *English Children's Books*, 1954

Phillips, K. C. *Language and Class in Victorian England*, 1984

Pollard, A. (ed.) *The Victorians*, 1970

Prickett, S. *Victorian Fantasy*, 1979

Saintsbury, G. *A History of Nineteenth Century Literature (1780–1895)*, 1896; rev. edn 1901

Spiers, J. *Poetry Towards Novel*, 1971

Starkie, Enid *From Gautier to Eliot: The Influence of France on English Literature, 1851–1939*, 1960

Stephen, L. *Hours in a Library*, 3 ser., London, 1874–9; repr. 1968
    Some Early Impressions, 1924
    Studies of a Biographer, 4 vols., 1898–1902

Stewart, J. I. M. *Eight Modern Writers* (includes Hardy and Kipling) (*Oxford History of Eng. Lit.*, Vol. XII, 1963)

Thomson, P. *The Victorian Heroine*, 1956; repr. 1978

Tillotson, G. *A View of Victorian Literature*, 1978

Tillotson, G. and K. *Mid-Victorian Studies*, 1966

Tinker, C. B. *Essays in Retrospect*, 1948

Vance, N. *The Sinews of the Spirit: The Ideal of Christian Manliness in Victorian Literature and Religious Thought*, 1985

Vicinus, M. *The Industrial Muse*, 1974

Victorian Studies, 1957 – in progress

Vincent, D. *Literacy and Popular Culture: England 1750–1914*, 1989

Ward, A. W., and Waller, A. R. eds. *The Cambridge History of English Literature* XIII and XIV, 1915; new edn 1932

Wiener, M. J. *English Culture and the Decline of the Industrial Spirit 1850–1950*, 1981

Willey, B. *More Nineteenth Century Studies*, 1956

Williams, A. S. *The Rich Man and the Diseased Poor in Early Victorian Literature*, 1986

Wright, A. (ed.) *Victorian Literature*, 1961

Wyld, H. C. *A History of Modern Colloquial English*, 3rd edn 1936
   A Short History of English, 3rd edn 1927

IX. POETRY

Anderson, H. *The Colonial Minstrel*, 1960

Armstrong, I. *Language and Living Form in Nineteenth-Century Poetry*, 1982

Austin, A. *The Poetry of the Period*, 1870

Ball, P. M. *The Heart's Events: Victorian Poetry of Relationships*, 1976

Bateson, F. W. *English Poetry and the English Language*, 1934; 3rd edn 1973

Beach, J. W. *The Concept of Nature in Nineteenth Century English Poetry*, 1936

Braybrooke, P. *Some Victorian and Georgian Catholics: Their Art and Outlook*, 1932

Bristow, J. (ed.) *The Victorian Poet: Poetics and Persona*, 1987

Bush, D. *Science and English Poetry*, 1950

Davie, D. *Purity of Diction in English Verse*, 1952

Evans, B. I. *English Poetry in the later Nineteenth Century*, 1933; rev. edn 1966

Fairchild, H. N. *Religious Trends in English Poetry*, IV, 1957

Foakes, R. A. *The Romantic Assertion*, 1958

Grierson, H. J. C. *Lyrical Poetry from Blake to Hardy*, 1928

Grigson, G. *The Harp of Aeolus*, 1948

Heath-Stubbs, J. *The Darkling Plain*, 1950

Hough, G. *The Last Romantics*, 1949

Hunt, W. J. *Pre-Raphaelitism and the Pre-Raphaelite Brotherhood*, 2 vols., 1905

Johnson, E. D. H. *The Alien Vision of Victorian Poetry*, 1952

Leavis, F. R. *New Bearings in English Poetry*, 1932; rev. 1950

Lucas, F. L. *Ten Victorian Poets*, 1940; repr. 1968

Pinto, V. de S. *Crisis in English Poetry 1880–1940*, rev. edn 1968

Praz, M. *The Romantic Agony*, 1933

Price J. B. 'Parody and Humour' in *Contemporary Review* CLXXX, 1951

Richards, B. *English Poetry of the Victorian Period 1830–1890*, 1988

Roppen, Georg *Evolution and Poetic Belief*, 1956

Ruskin, J. *Pre-Raphaelitism*, 1851

Saintsbury, G. *A History of English Prosody*, 1910

Shaw, W. D. *The Lucid Veil: Poetic Truth in the Victorian Age*, 1987

Sinfield, A. *The Dramatic Monologue*, 1977

Stevenson, L. *Darwin among the Poets*, 1932

Stratford-upon-Avon Studies no. 15: Victorian Poetry, 1972

Symons, A. *The Symbolist Movement in Literature*, 1899

Tennyson, G. B. *Victorian Devotional Poetry*, 1981

Tinker, C. B. *Essays in Retrospect*, 1948

    Victorian Poetry, 1963 – in progress

Warren, A. H. *English Poetic Theory 1825–65*, 1950

Weinstein, M. *W. E. Aytoun and the Spasmodic Controversy*, 1968

Wellend, D. S. R. *The Pre-Raphaelites in Literature and Art*, 1953

X. THE NOVEL

Allen, W. *The English Novel*, 1954

Allott, Miriam *Novelists on the Novel*, 1959

Baker, J. E. *The Novel and the Oxford Movement*, 1932

    The Re-interpretation of Victorian Literature, 1950

Beer, G. *Darwin's Plots: Evolutionary Narrative in Darwin, George Eliot and Nineteenth-Century Fiction*, 1983

Cazamian, L. *Le Roman Social en Angleterre*, 1903; tr. 1973

Cunningham, G. *The New Woman and the Victorian Novel*, 1978

Cunningham, V. *Everywhere Spoken Against: Dissent in the Victorian Novel*, 1976

Dalziel, M. *Popular Fiction a Hundred Years Ago*, 1957

Devonshire, M. G. *The English Novel in France 1830–70*, 1929

Drummond, A. L. *The Churches in English Fiction*, 1950

Ellis, S. M. *Wilkie Collins, Le Fanu and Others*, 1931

Elwin, M. *Old Gods Falling*, 1939

Foster, S. *Victorian Women's Fiction*, 1985

Gallagher, C. *The Industrial Reformation of English Fiction*, 1985

Gilmour, R. *The Novel in the Victorian Age: A Modern Introduction*, 1986

Graham, K. *English Criticism of the Novel, 1865–1900*, 1965

Hardy, B. *Forms of Feeling in Victorian Fiction*, 1986

Harrison, F. *Studies in Early Victorian Literature*, 1895

Hawthorn, J. (ed.) *The Nineteenth-Century British Novel*, 1986

Haycroft, H. *Murder for Pleasure: The Life and Times of the Detective Story*, 1942

Henkin, L. J. *Darwinism in the English Novel, 1860–1910*, 1940; repr. 1968

Horsman, A. *The Victorian Novel*, 1990

Hunter, S. *Victorian Idyllic Fiction: Pastoral Strategies*, 1984

Jay, E. *The Religion of the Heart: Anglican Evangelicalism and the Nineteenth Century Novel*, 1979

Johnson, R. B. *Women Novelists*, 1918

Keating, P. J. *The Working Classes in Victorian Fiction*, 1971

Kettle, A. *Introduction to the English Novel*, 2 vols. 1951–3; rev. edn 1959

Kovačević, I. *Fact into Fiction, 1751–1850*, 1975

Leavis, F. R. *The Great Tradition*, 1948; 1967

Lilly, W. S. *Four English Humorists of the Nineteenth Century*, 1895

Lucas, J. *The Literature of Change: Studies in the Nineteenth Century Provincial Novel*, 1977

Maison, M. M. *Search Your Soul, Eustace: A Survey of the Religious Novel in the Victorian Age*, 1962

Marriott, J. *English History in English Fiction*, 1940

Nestor, P. *Female Friendships and Communities: Charlotte Brontë, George Eliot, Elizabeth Gaskell*, 1985

    Nineteenth-Century Fiction, 1945 – in progress

Phillips, W. C. *Dickens, Reade and Collins; Sensation Novelists*, 1919

Praz, M. *The Hero in Eclipse in Victorian Fiction* tr. A. Davidson, 1956

Priestley, J. B. *The English Novel*, 1927

Pritchett, V. S. *The Living Novel*, 1946

Qualls, B. *The Secular Pilgrims of Victorian Fiction*, 1982

Quiller-Couch, A. T. *Charles Dickens and other Victorians*, 1925; repr. 1968

Sadleir, M. *Things Past*, 1944

Sandison, A. *The Wheel of Empire: The Imperial Idea in Fiction*, 1967

Smith, S. *The Other Nation: The Poor in English Novels of the 1840s and 1850s*, 1980

Speirs, J. *Poetry towards Novel*, 1971

Stang, Richard *The Theory of the Novel in England*, 1959

Stubbs, P. *Women and Fiction*, 1979

Sutherland, J. *The Longman Companion to Victorian Fiction*, 1990

Tillotson, K. *Novels of the Eighteen-Forties*, 1954; rev. edn 1956

Van Ghent, D. *The English Novel: Form and Function*, 1953

Wheeler, M. *English Fiction of the Victorian Period 1830–1890*, 1985

White, A. *The Uses of Obscurity*, 1981

Williams, R. *The English Novel: From Dickens to Lawrence*, 1970

Wilson, E. *The Wound and the Bow*, 1941; rev. edn 1952

Wolff, R. L. *Gains and Losses: Novels of Faith and Doubt in Victorian England*, 1977

XI. DRAMA

Archer, W. *Masks or Faces*, 1888; ed. Lee Strasberg, 1957

    The Old Drama and the New, 1923

Booth, M. R. *The Revels History of Drama in English* Vol. 6, 1975

Cunliffe, J. W. *Modern English Playwrights: A Short History of English Drama from 1825*, 1927

Disher, M. W. *Blood and Thunder: Mid-Victorian Melodrama and its Origins*, 1949

Frank, M. A. *Ibsen in England*, 1919

Hudson, L. *The English Stage 1850–1950*, 1951

Lewes, G. H. *On Actors and the Art of Acting*, 1875

Morley, H. *The Journal of a London Playgoer 1851–66*, 1866

Nicoll, A. *A History of Early Nineteenth Century Drama 1800–1850* 2 vols., 1930; repr., 1 vol., 1955

Nicoll, A. *A History of Late Nineteenth Century Drama 1850–1900* 2 vols., 1946; repr., 1 vol., 1959

Reynolds, E. *Early Victorian Drama 1830–1870*, 1936

Rowell, G. *Theatre in the Age of Irving*, 1981
  The Victorian Theatre 1792–1914, 1956; rev. edn 1978

Scott, H. *The Early Doors: Origins of the Music Hall*, 1946

Shaw, G. B. *Our Theatres in the Nineties*, 3 vols., 1932

Smith, J. L. *Melodrama*, 1973

Stephens, J. R. *The Censorship of English Drama 1824–1901*, 1980

Tolles, W. *Taylor and the Victorian Drama*, 1940

Trewin, J. C. *The Pomping Folk in the Nineteenth Century*, 1968

XII. PROSE AND CRITICISM

Adrian, A. A. *Mark Lemon: First Editor of 'Punch'*, 1966

Barnes, H. E. *A History of Historical Writing*, 1937

Bevington, M. M. *The Saturday Review 1855–68*, 1941

Bourne, H. R. F. *English Newspapers*, 2 vols., 1887

Brownell, W. C. *Victorian Prose Masters*, 1901

Burrow, J. W. *A Liberal Descent: Victorian Historians and the English Past*, 1981

Casford, E. L. *The Magazines of the 1890s*, 1929

Cockshut, A. O. J. *Truth to Life: The Art of Biography in the Nineteenth Century*, 1974

Cox, R. G. 'The Great Reviews' in *Scrutiny* VI, 1937

Everett, E. M. *The Party of Humanity: The 'Fortnightly Review' and its Contributors 1865–74*, 1939

Graham, W. *English Literary Periodicals*, 1930
  Tory Criticism in the 'Quarterly Review', 1921

Holloway, J. *The Victorian Sage: Studies in Argument*, 1953

Johnson, E. *One Mighty Torrent: The Drama of Biography*, 1937

Kellett, E. E. 'The Press 1830–65' in *Early Victorian England* ed. G. M. Young, 1934

Kitchin, G. *A Survey of Burlesque and Parody in English*, 1931

Marchand, L. A. *The Athenaeum: A Mirror of Victorian Culture*, 1940

Morison, S. *The English Newspaper 1622–1932*, 1932

Neff, E. *The Poetry of History: The Contribution of Literature and Literary Scholarship to the Writing of History since Voltaire*, 1947

Nesbit, G. L. *Benthamite Reviewing*, 1934

Nowell-Smith, S. (ed.) *Letters to Macmillan*, 1967

Oliphant, Margaret, and Porter, M. *Annals of a Publishing House: William Blackwood and his Sons*, 1897

Price, R. G. G. *The History of 'Punch'*, 1957

Robertson Scott, J. W. *The Story of the 'Pall Mall Gazette'*, 1950

Roll-Hansen, D. *The Academy 1869–79: Victorian Intellectuals in Revolt*, 1957

Saintsbury, G. *A History of English Prose Rhythm*, 1912

Shattock, J. *Politics and Reviewers: The 'Edinburgh' and the 'Quarterly' in the Early Victorian Age*, 1989

Sutherland, J. A. *Victorian Novelists and Publishers*, 1976

Thayer, W. R. 'Biography in the Nineteenth Century' in *North American Review* CCXI, 1920

Thomas, Sir William Beach, *The Story of the 'Spectator'*, 1928

Thrall, M. *Revellious Fraser's: Nol Yorke's Magazine in the Days of Maginn, Thackeray and Carlyle*, 1934

Victorian Periodicals Newsletter, 1968 – in progress

Welcome, H. S. *The Evolution of Journalism*, 1909

Woodward, E. L. *British Historians*, 1943

Worcester, D. *The Art of Satire*, 1943

Buckley, Vincent *Poetry and Morality*, 1959

Church, A. J. 'Criticism as a Trade' in *Nineteenth Century* XXVI, 1889 (reply by W. Knight in same issue)

Dallas, E. S. *The Gay Science*, 2 vols., 1866

Dingle, H. *Science and Literary Criticism*, 1949

Eigner, E. M. and Worth, G. J. (eds.) *Victorian Critics of the Novel*, 1985

Lester, J. A. *Transformations in British Literary Culture 1880–1914*, 1968

Levin, H. (ed.) *Perspectives of Criticism*, 1950

Martin, R. B. *The Triumph of Wit: A Study of Victorian Comic Theory*, 1974

Orel, H. *Victorian Literary Critics*, 1984

Peters, R. L. *The Crowns of Apollo: Victorian Criticism and Aesthetics*, 1965

Saintsbury, G. *A History of English Criticism*, 1911

Tillotson, G. *Essays in Criticism and Research*, 1942

Tillotson, G. *Criticism and the Nineteenth Century*, 1951; rev. edn 1967

Wellek, R. *A History of Modern Criticism: Vols* II–III, 1955–66

Wellek, R. *The Rise of English Literary History*, 1941.

Wimsatt, W. K., and Brooks, C. *Literary Criticism: A Short History*, 1957

AUTHORS AND WORKS

Collections and Anthologies

Barton, M., and Sitwell, O. (eds.) *Victoriana*, 1931
Bloom, H., and Trilling, L. (eds.) *Victorian Prose and Poetry*, 1973
Bowyer, J. W., and Brooks, J. L. (eds.) *The Victorian Age: Prose, Poetry and Drama*, 1938
Grigson, G. (ed.) *The Victorians*, 1950
Routh, H. V. (ed.) *England under Victoria*, 1930
Secker, M. (ed.) *The Eighteen Nineties*, 1948

Auden, W. H. (ed.) *Nineteenth Century Minor Poets*, 1967
Buckley, J. H., and Woods, G. B. (eds.) *Poetry of the Victorian Age*, 3rd edn 1965
Hayward, J. (ed.) *Oxford Book of Nineteenth Century Verse*, 1964
Heath-Stubbs, J., and Wright, D. (eds.) *The Forsaken Garden: An Anthology of Poetry 1824–1909*, 1950
Henderson, W. (ed.) *Victorian Street Ballads*, 1937
Jerrold, W., and Leonard, R. M. (eds.) *A Century of Parody and Imitation*, 1913
MacBeth, G. (ed.) *The Penguin Book of Victorian Verse*, 1969
Messenger, N. P., and Watson, J. R. eds. *Victorian Poetry: The City of Dreadful Night and Other Poems*, 1974
Miles, A. H. *et al.* (eds.) *The Poets and Poetry of the Nineteenth Century*, 12 vols., 1905–7; repr. 1968
Parrott, T. M., and Thorp, W. (eds.) *Poetry of the Transition 1850–1914*, 1932
Quiller-Couch, A. T. (ed.) *The Oxford Book of Victorian Verse*, 1912
Richards, B. (ed.) *English Verse 1830–1890*, 1979
Ricks, C. (ed.) *The New Oxford Book of Victorian Verse*, 1987
Rossetti, W. M. (ed.) *The Germ*, 1850
Scott, P. G. (ed.) *Victorian Poetry, 1830–1870*, 1971
Sitwell, E. (ed.) *The Pleasures of Poetry: The Victorian Age*, 1932
Stephens, J. *et al.* (eds.) *Victorian and Later English Poets*, 1934–7
Thornton, R. K. R. (ed.) *Poetry of the Nineties*, 1970
Williams, C. (ed.) *A Book of Victorian Narrative Verse*, 1927

Aldington, R. (ed.) *The Religion of Beauty: Selections from the Aesthetes*, 1950
Allott, K. (ed.) *Pelican Book of English Prose: v*, 1956
Armstrong, I. (ed.) *Victorian Scrutinies: Reviews of Poetry 1830–70*, 1972

Booth, B. A. (ed.) *A Cabinet of Gems: Short Stories from the English Annuals*, 1938

Cockshut, A. O. J. (ed.) *Religious Controversies of the Nineteenth Century: Selected Documents*, 1966

Cofer, B. D. (ed.) *Nineteenth Century Essays from Coleridge to Pater*, 1929

Cosslett, T. (ed.) *Science and Religion in the Nineteenth Century*, 1984

Davies, H. S. (ed.) *Poets and their Critics: Vol. II Blake to Browning*, 1962

Fletcher, I. (ed.) *British Poetry and Prose 1870–1905*, The Oxford Authors, 1987

Harland, H. (ed.) *The Yellow Book*, 13 vols., 1894–7

Harrold, C. F., and Templeman, W. D. (eds.) *English Prose of the Victorian Era*, 1938

Hayward, J. (ed.) *Silver Tongues: Famous Speeches from Burke to Baldwin*, 1937

Jay, E. (ed.) *The Evangelical and Oxford Movements*, 1983

Jay, E. and R. (eds.) *Critics of Capitalism: Victorian Reactions to 'Political Economy'*, 1986

Johnson, R. B. (ed.) *Famous Reviews*, 1914

Jones, Edmund (ed.) *English Critical Essays (Nineteenth Century)*, 1916; new edn, 1970

Levine, G., and Madden, W. A. (eds.) *The Art of Victorian Prose*, 1968

Mayer, F. P. (ed.) *Victorian Prose*, 1935

Nye, R. (ed.) *The English Sermon 1750–1850*, 1976

Reardon, B. M. G. (ed.) *Religious Thought in the Nineteenth Century*, 1966; rev. edn 1978

Reynolds, R. (ed.) *British Pamphleteers*: Vol. II, 1951

Sampson, G. (ed.) *Nineteenth Century Essays*, 1929

Small, I. *The Aesthetes: A Sourcebook*, 1979

Smith, J. H., and Parks, E. W. (eds.) *The Great Critics*, 1932

Strong, L. A. G. (ed.) *English Domestic Life During the Past 200 Years: An Anthology Selected from the Novelists*, 1942

Walbank, F. A. (ed.) *England Yesterday and Today in the Works of the Novelists 1837–1938*, 1949

Booth, M. (ed.) *English Plays of the Nineteenth Century* 5 vols., 1969–76
    Hiss the Villain: Six English and American Melodramas, 1964

Krause, D. (ed.) *The Dolmen Boucicault*, 1965

Moses, M. J. (ed.) *Representative British Dramas: Victorian and Modern*, 1918

Rowell, G. (ed.) *Nineteenth Century Plays*, 1972
    Late Victorian Plays, 1972

Slater, M. (ed.) *Barnstormer Plays*, n.d.

Authors and Works *

AINSWORTH, WILLIAM HARRISON (1805–82): Novelist; b. Manchester; educated for the law, but transferred to publishing after marrying the

---

* Under each author there appears first a short biography, second the standard edition(s), and third a selection of books and articles for further study.

daughter of the publisher John Ebers, 1926; *Sir John Chiverton* (1826) written in collaboration with J. P. Aston won praise of Sir Walter Scott; general success with *Rookwood*, 1834; other novels include *Jack Sheppard* (1839), *The Tower of London* (1840), *Old St Paul's* (1841), and *Windsor Castle* (1843); proprietor of *Ainsworth's Magazine* from 1842–53; and of *New Monthly Magazine* from 1853.

Collected Works, 16 vols., 1875; 31 vols., 1878–80; 12 vols., 1923
See:
S. M. Ellis, *William Harrison Ainsworth and his Friends*, 2 vols., 1911
K. Hollingsworth, *The Newgate Novel 1830–47; Bulwer, Ainsworth, Dickens and Thackeray*, 1963
G. J. Worth, *William Harrison Ainsworth*, 1972

ARNOLD, MATTHEW (1822–88): Poet, critic, and Inspector of Schools; b. Laleham, nr. Staines; son of Dr Thomas Arnold, Headmaster of Rugby; educated at Winchester, Rugby, and Balliol College, Oxford; fellow of Oriel College and colleague of A. H. Clough (q.v.); private secretary to Lord Lansdowne, 1847–51; *The Strayed Reveller*, 1849; appointed Inspector of Schools, 1851; married Frances Lucy Wightman, 1851; *Empedocles on Etna*, 1852; Professor of Poetry at Oxford, 1857–67; lectures subsequently published as *On Translating Homer* (1861–2), *Essays in Criticism* (1865), *On the Study of Celtic Literature* (1867); *New Poems* (1867); travelled widely in Europe to study educational systems; *Culture and Anarchy*, 1869; *Literature and Dogma*, 1873; died suddenly at Liverpool.

Life by C. W. Stanley, 1938; E. K. Chambers, 1947; repr. 1968; P. Honan, 1981
Collected Works, 15 vols., 1903–4
Complete Poems ed. H. S. Milford, rev. edn 1950
Complete Poems in E.L.
Poems ed. K. Allott, 1965; rev. edn, ed. M. Allott, 1979
Complete Prose Works ed. R. H. Super 11 vols., 1960–77
Essays in Criticism and *On the Study of Celtic Literature* in E.L., 2 vols.
The Portable Matthew Arnold ed. L. Trilling, 1949
Selections (The Oxford Authors series) ed. M. Allott and R. H. Super, 1986
Letters ed. G. W. E. Russell, 2 vols., 1901
Letters to Arthur Hugh Clough ed. H. F. Lowry, 1932; repr. 1968
A Matthew Arnold Prose Selection ed. J. D. Jump, 1965
See:
K. Allott (ed.) *Matthew Arnold*, 1976
W. D. Anderson, *Arnold and the Classical Tradition*, 1965
V. Buckley, *Poetry and Morality*, 1959
D. Bush, *Matthew Arnold*, 1971
S. Collini, *Matthew Arnold*, 1988

W. F. Connell, *The Educational Thought and Influence of Matthew Arnold*,
1950

A. D. Culler, *Imaginative Reason: The Poetry of Matthew Arnold*, 1966

C. Dawson (ed.) *Arnold: The Poetry: The Critical Heritage*, 1973

C. Dawson and J. Pfordsheimer (eds.) *Arnold: Prose Writings: The Critical
Heritage*, 1979

D. J. DeLaura in *Hebrew and Hellene*, 1969

T. S. Eliot, 'Arnold and Pater' in *Selected Essays*, 1932
    The Use of Poetry and the Use of Criticism, 1933

D. G. James, *Matthew Arnold and the Decline of English Romanticism*, 1961

J. D. Jump, *Matthew Arnold*, 1955

A. P. Kelso, *Matthew Arnold on Continental Life and Literature*, 1914

F. R. Leavis, 'Arnold as Critic' in *Scrutiny*, VII, 1938

W. A. Madden, *Matthew Arnold: A Study of the Aesthetic Temperament in
Victorian England*, 1967

W. Robbins, *The Ethical Idealism of Matthew Arnold*, 1959

Leslie Stephen, *Studies of a Biographer*, 1898

G. Tillotson in *Criticism and the Nineteenth Century*, 1951

C. B. Tinker and H. F. Lowry, *The Poetry of Matthew Arnold: A Commentary*,
1940

L. Trilling, *Matthew Arnold*, rev. 3rd edn 1963

BAGEHOT, WALTER (1826–77): Economist, social and literary critic; b.
Langport, Somerset; son of a banker; called to the Bar, 1852; subsequently
joined his father in the West of England banking business; marriage to Eliza
Wilson, daughter of the Secretary of the Treasury, gave him inside view of
political life of time; editor of *The Economist* from 1860; best miscellaneous
prose appears in *The English Constitution* (1867), *Physics and Politics* (1869),
and *Literary Studies* (1879).

Life by E. I. Barrington, Vol. x of *Collected Works*, 1915; W. Irvine, 1939;
A. Buchan, 1959

Collected Works ed. F. Morgan, 5 vols., 1889; ed. E. I. Barrington, 10 vols.,
1915; ed. N. St. John-Stevas, 15 vols., 1966–86

The English Constitution in W.C.

See:

The Economist 1843–1943: A Centenary Volume, 1943

H. Orel in *Victorian Literary Critics*, 1984

Herbert Read, 'Bagehot' in *The Sense of Glory*, 1929

Norman St. John-Stevas, *Walter Bagehot: A Study of his Life and Thought*,
1960

C. H. Sisson, *The Case of Walter Bagehot*, 1970

G. M. Young, 'The Greatest Victorian' in *Today and Yesterday*, 1948

BARNES, WILLIAM (1801–86): Poet; b. Blackmoor Vale, Dorset, son of a
farmer; educated at St John's College, Cambridge, entering in 1838; took

orders and became rector of Came, 1862; wrote many poems in the Dorset dialect, published as *Poems of Rural Life*, three series, 1844, 1859, and 1863.

Life by his daughter, L. Baxter, 1887
Poems ed. B. Jones, 2 vols., 1962
Selected Poems ed. T. Hardy, 1908; ed. G. Grigson, 1950; ed. R. Nye, 1972
See:
G. Dugdale, *William Barnes of Dorset*, 1953
G. Grigson in *The Harp of Aeolus*, 1948
W. D. Jacobs, *William Barnes, Linguist*, 1952
W. T. Levy, *William Barnes: The Man and the Poems*, 1961
V. de S. Pinto, 'William Barnes: an Appreciation' in *Wessex*, June 1930

BORROW, GEORGE (1803–81): Novelist, traveller, and linguist; b. East Dereham in Norfolk of middle-class Cornish family, educated Norwich grammar school; articled to a firm of Norwich solicitors but neglected law to study languages; moved to London, 1824; *Romantic Ballads* (translation from Danish), 1826; left London to tramp round England; agent for Bible society in St Petersburg, 1833–5; visited Spain, Portugal, and Morocco (1835–40) as correspondent to the *Morning Herald*; great success with *The Bible in Spain*, 1843; *Lavengro*, 1851; *The Romany Rye*, 1857; *Wild Wales*, 1862; died at Oulton.

Life by M. D. Armstrong, 1950; W. I. Knapp, 2 vols., 1899; H. Jenkins, 1912; C. Shorter, 1913
Collected Works, 16 vols., 1924
Lavengro, *Romany Rye*, and *The Bible in Spain* in E.L.
See:
E. Bigland, *In the Steps of George Borrow*, 1951
R. Fréchet, *George Borrow: Vagabond, polyglote, agent biblique, écrivain*, 1956
R. R. Meyers, *George Borrow*, 1966
J. E. Tilford, 'Contemporary Criticism of *Lavengro*: a Re-examination' in *Studies in Philology* XLI, 1944.
    'The Critical Approach to *Lavengro-Romany Rye*' in *Studies in Philology* XLVI, 1949
    'The Formal Artistry of *Lavengro-Romany Rye*' in P.M.L.A. LXIV, 1949
R. A. J. Walling, *George Borrow: The Man and his Work*, 1908

BRIDGES, ROBERT (1844–1930): Poet and essayist; b. Walmer; educated at Eton and Corpus Christi College, Oxford; studied medicine and became consulting physician at Great Ormond Street Children's Hospital; abandoned medicine for poetry, 1882; eight plays published between 1885–94 won him a reputation among classical scholars; *Shorter Poems*, 1890; appointed Poet Laureate, 1913; *The Spirit of Man*, 1916; *New Verse*, 1925; *The Testament of Beauty*, 1929.

Life by E. Thompson, 1944; G. S. Gordon, 1946
Collected Works, 6 vols., rev. edn 1936
Poetical Works, 2nd edn, 1953
Poetry and Prose ed. J. Sparrow, 1955
See:
G. S. Gordon, *Robert Bridges*, 1932
A. Guerard, *Bridges: A Study of Traditionalism in Poetry*, 1942
J.-G. Ritz, *Robert Bridges and Gerard Hopkins*, 1960
H. V. Routh, *English Literature and Ideas in the Twentieth Century*, 1948
N. C. Smith, *Notes on the Testament of Beauty*, rev. edn 1940
W. B. Yeats in *The Bookman*, London, June 1897; repr. in *Correspondence of Robert Bridges and W. B. Yeats*, 1977
F. E. B. Young, *Robert Bridges: A Critical Study*, 1914

THE BRONTËS:

CHARLOTTE (1816–55): Novelist; eldest daughter of Patrick Brontë, Rector of Haworth; little formal education but for one year at Cowan's Bridge, a dismal establishment later described as 'Lowood' in *Jane Eyre*; moved to Miss Wooler's School at Dewsbury, 1831; after one year returned to instruct Emily and Anne; governess at Miss Wooler's, 1835; MSS criticized by Southey, 1838; went with Emily to learn French at Pensionnat Héger in Brussels, 1842; returned as instructress to Brussels, 1843; brother Branwell became drunkard, 1844; poems (with those of Emily and Anne) published under pseudonym Currer Bell, 1846; *Jane Eyre* (1847) immediately successful; death of Branwell and of Emily, 1848; death of Anne, 1849; *Shirley*, 1849; *Villette*, 1853; married Arthur Bell Nicholls, curate of Haworth, 1854; died of illness following childbirth.

EMILY JANE (1818–48); Novelist and poet; sister of Charlotte; educated at home but for brief stay at Miss Wooler's where Charlotte was governess, 1835; accompanied Charlotte to Brussels, 1842; poems published under pseudonym Ellis Bell, 1846; *Wuthering Heights* (1847) completely overshadowed by success of Charlotte's *Jane Eyre*.

ANNE (1820–49); Novelist and poet; youngest of the Brontë sisters; educated at home; poems published with her sisters' under pseudonym Acton Bell, 1846; *Agnes Grey*, 1847; *The Tenant of Wildfell Hall*, 1848.

Life and Letters ed. T. J. Wise and J. A. Symington, 4 vols., 1932
Collected Works, 20 vols., 1938
The Clarendon Brontë ed. J. Jack *et al.*, 1968 – in progress
Novels and *Poems* in E.L. and W.C.
Jane Eyre in O.E.N.; *Jane Eyre*, *Shirley* and *Wuthering Heights* in P.C.
The Complete Poems of Emily Jane Brontë ed. C. W. Hatfield, 1941; ed. P. Henderson, 1951

See:

Transactions of the Brontë Society, since 1895

C. Alexander, *The Early Writings of Charlotte Brontë*, 1983

M. Allott (ed.) *Charlotte Brontë: The Critical Heritage*, 1974

W. A. Craik, *The Brontë Novels*, 1968

E. Duthie, *The Foreign Vision of Charlotte Brontë*, 1975

T. Eagleton, *Myths of Power*, 1975

B. Ford, 'Wuthering Heights' in *Scrutiny*, VII, 1939

E. C. Gaskell, *The Life of Charlotte Brontë*, rev. edn 1908

W. Gérin, *Anne Brontë*, 1959
  Branwell Brontë, 1961
  Charlotte Brontë, 1967
  Emily Brontë, 1971

W. T. Hale, *Anne Brontë*, 1929

L. and E. M. Hanson, *The Four Brontës*, 1949; new edn 1967

J. Kavanagh, *Emily Brontë*, 1985

G. D. Klingopulos, 'Wuthering Heights' in *Scrutiny* XIV, 1947

Q. D. Leavis, intro. *Jane Eyre*, P.C. 1966

R. B. Martin, *The Accents of Persuasion: Charlotte Brontë's Novels*, 1966

J. Maynard, *Charlotte Brontë and Sexuality*, 1984; new edn 1987

J. P. Petit (ed.) *Emily Brontë*, 1973

F. Ratchford, *The Brontës' Web of Childhood*, 1941; rev. edn 1964

C. P. Sanger, *The Structure of Wuthering Heights*, 1926

C. B. Tinker, 'The Poetry of the Brontës' in *Essays in Retrospect*, 1948

V. Woolf, '*Jane Eyre* and *Wuthering Heights*' in *The Common Reader*, 1925

BROWNING, ELIZABETH BARRETT (1806–61); Poet; b. Durham; eldest daughter of Edward Moulton Barrett; brought up at Hope End in Herefordshire; moved to London, 1833; poems in Lord Lytton's *New Monthly Magazine*, 1836; met Wordsworth, 1837; delicate health aggravated by broken blood vessel, became invalid in 1838; shattered by deaths of two of her brothers (1840); remained seriously ill for five years; corresponded with Robert Browning (q.v.), whose poetry she admired, from 1844; married him against her father's wishes, 1846; subsequently lived mostly in Italy; *Sonnets from the Portuguese*, 1847; only child, Robert, b. 1849; *Casa Guidi Windows*, 1851; *Aurora Leigh*, 1856; ardent supporter of Napoleon III during the Italian War; died in Florence.

Life by I. C. Willis, 1928; D. Hewlett, 1952; G. B. Taplin, 1957; M. Forster, 1988

Poetical Works ed. F. G. Kenyon, 1897

Complete Poems, 1904

Letters ed. F. G. Kenyon, 2 vols., 1897

Letters of Robert Browning and Elizabeth Barrett, 2 vols., 1899

Elizabeth Barrett to Miss Mitford ed. B. Miller, 1954

Letters to Mrs Ogilvy, 1975

Diary 1831–2, 1969
See:
A. Hayter, *Mrs Browning*, 1962
A. Leighton, *Elizabeth Barrett Browning*, 1986
D. Mermin, *Elizabeth Barrett Browning: The Origins of a New Poetry*, 1989
D. Rosenblum, 'Face to Face: Elizabeth Barrett Browning's *Aurora Leigh* and Nineteenth-Century Poetry' in *Victorian Studies* XXVI, 1983
P. Turner, 'Aurora versus the Angel' in R.E.S. XXIV, 1948

BROWNING, ROBERT (1812–89): Poet; b. London, educated at home and locally; encouraged by father to write; *Pauline* published anonymously, 1833; this, with *Paracelsus* (1835) and *Sordello* (1840), won him reputation for obscurity; met Macready (1835) and wrote play *Strafford* for him; success established with *Bells and Pomegranates*, a series of pamphlets, 1841–6; corresponded with Elizabeth Barrett (q.v.) from 1844; married her secretly, 1846; subsequently lived in Italy; *Christmas Eve and Easter Day*, 1850; *Men and Women*, 1855; returned to London after wife's death, 1861; *Dramatis Personae*, 1864; *The Ring and the Book*, 1868. Browning Society founded 1881.

Life by W. H. Griffin and H. C. Minchin, 1910; rev. edn 1938; G. K. Chesterton, 1903; W. Irvine and P. Honan, 1975; J. Maynard, 1977
Works ed. F. G. Kenyon, 10 vols., 1912; ed. R. A. King *et al.*, 13 vols., 1969 – in progress
Poems ed. J. Pettigrew and T. J. Collins, 2 vols., 1981
Poetical Works 1833–64 ed. I. Jack, 1970
Poetical Works 1833–64 ed. I. Jack and M. Smith, 1983 – in progress
The Ring and the Book ed. R. D. Altick, 1971
Letters of Robert Browning and Elizabeth Barrett, 2 vols., 1899
Letters ed. T. L. Hood, 1933
The Brownings' Correspondence ed. P. Kelley and R. Hudson, 1984 – in progress
Browning to his American Friends ed. G. R. Hudson, 1965
Poetry and Prose (selected) ed. S. Nowell-Smith, 1950
A Choice of Browning's Verse ed. E. Lucie-Smith, 1967
See:
R. D. Altick and J. Lorcks, *Browning's Roman Murder Story*, 1968
I. Armstrong (ed.) *Robert Browning: Writers and their Background*, 1974
H. Bloom and A. Munich (eds.) *Robert Browning: A Collection of Critical Essays*, 1979
N. B. Crowell, *The Convex Glass*, 1968
P. Drew, *The Poetry of Browning*, 1970
I. Jack, *Browning's Major Poetry*, 1973
E. D. H. Johnson, *The Alien Vision in Victorian Poetry*, 1952
R. Langbaum, *The Poetry of Experience*, 1957
B. Melchiori, *Browning's Poetry of Reticence*, 1968

J. H. Miller in *The Disappearance of God*, 1963
W. O. Raymond, *The Infinite Moment and other Essays on Robert Browning*, 1950
G. Santayana, 'The Poetry of Barbarism' in *Interpretations of Poetry and Religion*, 1900; included in *Robert Browning: A Collection of Critical Essays*, ed. P. Drew, 1966
W. D. Shaw, *The Dialectical Temper: The Rhetorical Art of Robert Browning*, 1968
D. Smalley and B. Litzinger, *Browning: The Critical Heritage*, 1970

BURTON, RICHARD FRANCIS (1821–90): Explorer, diplomat, orientalist, and eccentric; b. Torquay; travelled widely in Europe; entered Trinity College, Oxford (1840), but sent down, apparently for eccentricity; joined Bombay Native Infantry, 1842; wrote several books on Indian customs that attracted little attention; became famous for pilgrimage to Mecca, 1853; explored interior of Somaliland for Indian Government, 1854; discovered Lake Tanganyika, 1858; married Isabel Arundell and entered Foreign Office, 1861; wrote many travel books without much success; translated *The Thousand Nights and a Night*, 1885–8; Knighted 1886.

Life by his wife, 1893; F. M. Brodie, 1968; M. Hastings, 1977
Pilgrimage to El-Medinah and Mecca ed. Lady Burton and S. Lane Poole, 2 vols., 1906
First Footsteps in East Africa ed. G. Waterfield, 1966

BUTLER, SAMUEL (1835–1902): Satirist and painter; grandson of Samuel Butler, Bishop of Lichfield; educated at Shrewsbury and St John's College, Cambridge; emigrated to New Zealand, 1859; became interested in Darwin's theory of the origin of species and published several articles on it; returned to England, 1864; regularly exhibited paintings at the Royal Academy; *Erewhon*, 1872; *The Fair Haven*, 1873; disagreed finally with Darwin and expounded his own biological theories in *Life and Habit* (1877), *Evolution Old and New* (1879), *Unconscious Memory* (1880), and *Luck or Cunning?* (1886); developed new theories about the authorship of the *Iliad* and *Odyssey*; *The Life and Letters of Samuel Butler*, 1890; *Erewhon Revisited*, 1901; *The Way of all Flesh*, written between 1873 and 1875, published posthumously in 1903.

Life by J. F. Harris, 1916; H. F. Jones, 2 vols., 1919; P. Raby, 1991
Works, The Shrewsbury Edition ed. H. F. Jones and A. T. Bartholomew, 20 vols., 1923–6
The Way of all Flesh, Erewhon and *Erewhon Revisited* in E.L., 8 vols.
Erewhon and *The Way of All Flesh* in P.C.
A First Year in Canterbury Settlement ed. A. C. Brassington and P. B. Maling, 1964
The Fair Haven, intro. Gerald Bullett, 1938
The Note Books of Samuel Butler ed. H. F. Jones, 1912; ed. G. Keynes and B. Hill, 1951

The Family Letters of Samuel Butler, ed. A. Silver, 1962
See:
C. Bissell, 'A Study of *The Way of all Flesh*' in *Nineteenth-Century Studies*, 1940
G. D. H. Cole, *Butler and 'The Way of all Flesh'*, 1947
P. N. Furbank, *Samuel Butler*, 1948
L. E. Holt, *Samuel Butler*, 1964
U. C. Knoepflmacher in *Religious Humanism in the Victorian Novel*, 1965
P. J. de Lange, *Samuel Butler: Critic and Philosopher*, 1925
M. Muggeridge, *Earnest Atheist*, 1936
V. S. Pritchett, 'A Victorian Son' in *The Living Novel*, 1946
R. H. Streatfield, *Samuel Butler: A Critical Study*, 1902
B. Willey, *Darwin and Butler: Two Versions of Evolution*, 1960

CARLYLE, THOMAS (1795–1881): Essayist, historian, and philosopher; b. Ecclefechan, eldest son of Calvinist mason and small farmer; educated at Annan grammar school and Edinburgh University; mathematics master at Annan, 1814; moved to Kirkcaldy where he met Edward Irving, 1816; ceased to believe in Christianity and left teaching to study law, 1818; deeply influenced by Goethe, with whom he corresponded; married Jane Welsh, 1826; *Sartor Resartus* published in instalments in *Fraser's Magazine*; moved to London, 1834; became friendly with J. S. Mill and Ralph Waldo Emerson; *French Revolution* (1837) established him among chief writers of the day; *Chartism*, 1839; *Past and Present*, 1843; quarrelled with Mill over political issues; *Life and Letters of Oliver Cromwell*, 1845; *Life of Sterling*, 1851; great success with *Frederick the Great*, 1858–65; elected Rector of Edinburgh University, 1865; death of Jane Carlyle, 1866; worked until his own death on *Reminiscences* and annotating Jane's letters, subsequently published (1883) as *Letters and Memorials*; by his own wish buried in Annandale.

Life by J. A. Froude 4 vols., 1882–4; B. W. Metz, 1902; D. A. Wilson, 6
  vols., 1923–34; J. Symons, 1952; I, Campbell, 1974
Collected Works, Centenary Edition ed. H. D. Traill, 30 vols., 1896–1901
Selected Writings in P.C.
Selected Works ed. G. M. Trevelyan, 1953; ed. J. Symons, 1955
Past and Present, Essays, Reminiscences, Sartor Resartus, and *The French
  Revolution* in E.L., 7 vols.
On Heroes and Hero-Worship in W.C.
Letters ed. C. E. Norton, 4 vols., 1886–8
Letters to his wife ed. T. Bliss, 1953
Collected Letters of Thomas and Jane Carlyle, 40 vols., 1969 – in progress
Correspondence between Goethe and Carlyle ed. C. E. Norton, 1887
Correspondence of Emerson and Carlyle ed. J. Slater, 1965
See:
O. Burdett, *The Two Carlyles*, 1930
J. Clubbe (ed.) *Carlyle and his Contemporaries*, 1976
K. J. Fielding and R. L. Tarr (eds.) *Carlyle Past and Present*, 1976

C. F. Harrold, *Carlyle and German Thought*, 1934
A. J. LaValley, *Carlyle and the Idea of the Modern*, 1968
C. Moore, 'Sartor Resartus and the Problem of Carlyle's "Conversion"' in
    P.M.L.A. LXX, 1955
F. W. Roe, *Social Philosophy of Carlyle and Ruskin*, 1921
J. D. Rosenberg, *Carlyle and the Burden of History*, 1985
J. P. Siegel (ed.) *Carlyle: The Critical Heritage*, 1972
G. B. Tennyson, *Sartor Called Resartus*, 1965
R. Wellek in *Confrontations*, 1965
L. M. Young, *Carlyle and the Art of History*, 1939

CARROLL, LEWIS – Charles Lutwidge Dodgson – (1832–98): writer of
children's stories and mathematician; b. Daresbury, Cheshire; son of a
clergyman; educated at Rugby and Christ Church; lecturer in mathematics
at Christ Church 1855–81; *Alice's Adventures in Wonderland*, 1865; *Phantasmagoria*, 1869; *Through the Looking Glass*, 1871; *The Hunting of the Snark*,
1876; *Rhyme and Reason*, 1883; *A Tangled Tale*, 1885; *Sylvie and Bruno*,
1889–93.

Life by S. D. Collingwood, 1898; F. B. Lennon, *Victoria through the Looking
    Glass: The Life of Lewis Carroll*, 1945
Complete Works ed. A. Woolcott, 1939; new edn 1949
Alice in Wonderland, Through the Looking Glass, The Hunting of the Snark,
    etc. in E.L. (1 vol.), *Alice* and *Looking Glass* in O.E.N. (1 vol.)
Diaries ed. R. L. Green, 2 vols., 1954
Lewis Carrol and the House of Macmillan (letters) ed. M. N. Cohen and A.
    Gandolfo, 1987
See:
H. M. Ayres, *Carroll's Alice*, 1936
W. Empson in *Some Versions of Pastoral*, 1935
M. Gardner, *The Annotated Alice*, 1960; rev. edn 1970
D. Hudson, *Lewis Carroll*, 1958; rev. edn 1977
F. Huxley, *The Raven and the Writing Desk*, 1977
Walter de la Mare, *Lewis Carroll*, 1932
S. Prickett in *Victorian Fantasy*, 1979
E. Sewell, *The Field of Nonsense*, 1952
R. D. Sutherland, *Language and Lewis Carroll*, 1967
V. Woolf in *The Monument and other Essays*, 1948

CLOUGH, ARTHUR HUGH (1819–61): Poet; b. Liverpool, son of a cotton
merchant; family moved to Charleston, U.S.A., 1822; sent home to be
educated at Rugby and Balliol College, Oxford; fellow of Oriel College
and contemporary with Matthew Arnold (q.v.); appointed Principal of
University Hall at University College, London, 1849; friend of Carlyle and
Emerson; short early poems published jointly with Thomas Burbridge in
Ambarvalia, 1949; *Amours de Voyage*, novel in verse written in Rome, 1894;

Dipsychus, 1850; pursued steady official career until failing health compelled him to travel, 1860; *Mari Magno or Tales on Board*, 1861; died in Florence.

Life by J. I. Osborne, 1920; G. Levy, 1938; M. Timko, 1966
Collected Poems ed. C. Whibley, 1913; ed. H. F. Lowry *et al.*, 1951
Poems and Selected Letters, ed. by his wife, 2 vols., 1869
Poems ed. A. L. P. Norrington, 1968; new edn 1986
Selected Prose Works ed. B. B. Trawick, 1964
Selected Poems ed. H. S. Milford, 1910
Letters ed. F. Mulhauser, 1957
Oxford Diaries ed. A. Kenny, 1990
See:
W. Bagehot, 'Mr Clough's Poems' in *Literary Studies*, 1879
R. K. Biswas, *Arthur Hugh Clough*, 1972
K. Chorley, *Arthur Hugh Clough: The Uncommitted Mind*, 1962
H. W. Garrod, 'Clough' in *Poetry and the Criticism of Life*, 1931
W. E. Houghton, *The Poetry of Clough*, 1963
J. D. Jump, 'Clough's *Amours de Voyage*' in *English* IX, 1953
A. Kenny, *God and Two Poets: Arthur Hugh Clough and Gerard Manley Hopkins*, 1988
F. W. Palmer, 'The Bearing of Science on the Thought of Clough' in P.M.L.A. LIX, 1944
M. Thorpe (ed.) *Clough: The Critical Heritage*, 1972
A. M. Turner, 'A Study of Clough's *Mari Magno*' in P.M.L.A. XLIV, 1929

COLLINS, WILLIAM WILKIE (1824–89): Novelist; b. London, elder son of William Collins the painter; educated locally; family lived Italy, 1836–9; articled to a firm in the tea-trade, 1839; decided to study law, called to the Bar, 1849; first book a biography of his father, 1848; *Antonina*, 1850; *Basil*, 1852; *Hide and Seek*, 1854; friendly with Charles Dickens and a regular contributor to *Household Words*; among his most successful later works are *The Woman in White* (1860) and *The Moonstone* (1868), two of the earliest examples of detective fiction.

Life by K. Robinson, 1951; rev. edn 1974; N. P. Davis, 1956; W. M. Clarke, 1988
The Woman in White and *The Moonstone* in E.L. and P.C.
The Moonstone, No Name and *The Woman in White* in W.C.; *The Woman in White* in O.E.N.
See:
R. P. Ashley, 'Wilkie Collins and the Detective Story' in *Nineteenth-Century Fiction* VI, 1951
B. A. Booth, 'Collins and the Art of Fiction' in *Nineteenth-Century Fiction* VI, 1951
T. S. Eliot, Introduction to *The Moonstone* in W.C.
A. Hayter in *Opium and the Romantic Imagination*, 1968
C. K. Hyder, 'Collins and *The Woman in White*' in P.M.L.A. LIV, 1939

N. Page (ed.) *Wilkie Collins: The Critical Heritage*, 1974
J. B. Taylor, *In the Secret Theatre of Home: Wilkie Collins, Sensation Narrative and Nineteenth-Century Psychology*, 1988

DARWIN, CHARLES ROBERT (1809–82): Naturalist; b. Shrewsbury, grandson of Dr Erasmus Darwin; educated at Shrewsbury School, Edinburgh University, and Christ's College, Cambridge; naturalist for a surveying expedition on H.M.S. *Beagle*, 1831–6; secretary of the Geological Society, 1838–41; married Emma Wedgwood, 1839; settled at Down and worked on his theories of natural selection; *The Origin of Species* (1859) aroused intense opposition, but supported by Huxley, Lyell, and Hooker; *The Variation of Animals and Plants under Domestication*, 1868; *Descent of Man and Selection in Relation to Sex*, 1871.

Life of his son F. Darwin, 1902; G. A. Adlerz, 1909; P. Brent, 1981
Autobiography ed. N. Barlow, 1958
Autobiographies of Darwin and Huxley ed. Sir Gavin de Beer, 1974
The Origin of Species and *The Voyage of the 'Beagle'* in E.L.
The Origin of Species ed. J. W. Burrow, 1982
Letters ed. F. Darwin, 3 vols., 1887; 2 more vols., 1903
Correspondence between Wallace and Darwin 1857–81, 1910
Collected Papers ed. P. H. Barrett, 2 vols., 1977
See:
J. Howard, *Darwin*, 1982
L. Huxley, *Charles Darwin*, 1921
D. Kohn (ed.) *The Darwinian Heritage*, 1985
B. J. Loewenberg, *Darwin, Wallace and the Theory of Natural Selection*, 1959
A. Moorehead, *Darwin and the 'Beagle'*, 1971
B. Willey, *Darwin and Butler: Two Versions of Evolution*, 1960

DICKENS, CHARLES JOHN HUFFAM (1812–70): Novelist; b. Portsea, son of clerk in the Navy Pay Office; father imprisoned for debt (1824), so forced to work in blacking warehouse; articled to a Gray's Inn solicitor when family circumstances improved; later newspaper and Parliamentary reporter; became known for *Sketches* (by Boz) in the *Monthly Magazine*; *Pickwick Papers*, 1837; married Catherine Hogarth, 1836; visited America, 1842; moved to Genoa (1844) but soon returned to London; editor of *Household Words* from 1850; separated from wife, 1858; editor of *All the Year Round* from 1859; gave public readings from his works in England and America for charity from 1853, and for private profit from 1858; died suddenly, buried in Westminster Abbey.

Life by John Forster, 3 vols., 1872–4; E.L., 2 vols., 1966; G. K. Chesterton, 1906; U. Pope-Hennessy, 1945; J. Lindsay, 1950; Edgar Johnson 2 vols., 1953; rev. edn 1965; Peter Ackroyd, 1990
Collected Works, Oxford Illustrated Edition, 21 vols., 1947–58; E.L., 21 vols.;

Clarendon Critical Edition, ed. K. Tillotson, 1966–. Novels and stories in
P.C. (17 vols.) and W.C. (6 vols.)
The Letters of Charles Dickens ed. M. House and G. Storey 12 vols., 1965–
The Public Readings ed. P. Collins, 1975
For extensive list of writings see N.C.B.E.L.

See:

J. Butt and K. Tillotson, *Dickens at Work*, 1957
J. Carey, *The Violent Effigy*, 1973
R. C. Churchill, *A Bibliography of Dickensian Criticism*, 1975
P. Collins, *Dickens and Crime*, 1962
    Dickens and Education, 1963
P. Collins (ed.) *Dickens: The Critical Heritage*, 1971
K. J. Fielding, *Charles Dickens: A Critical Introduction*, 1958; rev. edn 1966
G. H. Ford, *Dickens and his Readers: Aspects of Novel Criticism since 1836*, 1955
G. H. Ford and L. Lane (eds.) *The Dickens Critics*, 1963
R. Garis, *The Dickens Theatre*, 1965
G. Gissing, *Charles Dickens: A Critical Study*, 1898
R. Golding, *Idiolects in Dickens*, 1985
J. Gross and G. Pearson (eds.) *Dickens and the Twentieth Century*, 1962
Humphry House, *The Dickens World*, 1941; new edn 1960
F. R. Leavis, *The Great Tradition*, 1950
F. R. and Q. D. Leavis, *Dickens the Novelist*, 1970
J. Lucas, *The Melancholy Man*, 1970; rev. edn 1980
J. Hillis Miller, *Charles Dickens: The World of his Novels*, 1958
J. McMaster, *Dickens the Designer*, 1986
G. Orwell, 'Charles Dickens' in *Critical Essays*, 1946
N. Peyrouton (ed.) *Dickens Studies*, 1965–70
N. Pope, *Dickens and Charity*, 1978
M. Slater, *Dickens and Women*, 1983
M. Slater (ed.) *Dickens 1970*, 1970
H. Stone, *Dickens and the Invisible World: Fairy Tales, Fantasy and Novel-Making*, 1979
D. Walder, *Dickens and Religion*, 1981
S. Wall (ed.) *Dickens: A Critical Anthology*, 1970
Edmund Wilson, 'Dickens, the Two Scrooges' in *The Wound and the Bow*, 1941

DISRAELI, BENJAMIN, EARL OF BEACONSFIELD (1804–81): Novelist,
statesman, and friend of Queen Victoria; b. London of a Jewish family but
baptized into Christian Church; educated at Higham Hall, nr. Walthamstow; articled to a London solicitor, 1821; reputation for foppery; heavily in
debt, attempted unsuccessfully to launch daily newspaper *The Representative*,
1825; *Vivian Gray* (1826) notorious for thinly disguised references to society
notables; travelled in Palestine, 1830; stood for Parliament as Radical (1832)
but twice defeated; defeated twice more as a Conservative; made political
reputation with pamphlets attacking Whig government, 1835–6; Conserva-

tive member for Maidstone, 1837; married Mrs Wyndham Lewis, 1839; 'Young England' trilogy – *Coningsby* (1844), *Sybil* (1845), and *Tancred* (1847); became leading orator in the House of Commons and acknowledged leader of splinter group in Conservative party; Chancellor of the Exchequer, 1852; Prime Minister, 1868 and 1874–80; *Lothair*, 1870; created first Earl of Beaconsfield, 1876.

Life by W. F. Monypenny and G. E. Buckle, rev. edn, 2 vols., 1929; B. R. Jerman, 1960; R. Blake, 1966
Collected Novels, 10 vols., 1870–71; 12 vols., 1926–7
Coningsby in E.L. and W.C., *Sybil* in W.C. and P.C., *Lothair* in O.E.N.
Selected Speeches with notes by T. E. Kebbel, 2 vols., 1882
Letters ed. A. Birrell, 1928; ed. J. A. W. Gunn *et al.*, 1982 – in progress
See:
E. A. Housman, *On the Side of the Angels? Disraeli and the Nineteenth-Century Novel*, 1973
V. S. Pritchett in *The Living Novel*, 1946
D. R. Schwarz, *Disraeli's Fiction*, 1979
S. M. Smith in *The Other Nation*, 1980
L. Stephen, 'Mr Disraeli's Novels' in *Hours in a Library* ser. II, 1876; repr. 1968
R. W. Stewart, *Disraeli's Novels Reviewed: 1826–1968*, 1975

DU MAURIER, GEORGE LOUIS PALMELLA BUSSON (1834–96): Novelist and illustrator; b. Paris; educated in France and at University College, London; travelled widely, painting, in France, Belgium, and the Netherlands; lost sight of one eye, 1857; returned to London (1860) and became a regular illustrator for *Punch*; novels include *Peter Ibbetson* (1892), *Trilby* (1894), and *The Martian* (1897).

Life by D. du Maurier, 1937; D. P. Whitely, 1948
Selected Letters 1860–67 ed. D. du Maurier, 1951
Trilby in E.L.
See:
J. L. and J. B. Gilder, *Trilbyana: The Rise and Progress of a Popular Novel*, 1895
T. M. Wood, *Du Maurier: The Satirist of the Victorians*, 1913

ELIOT, GEORGE – Mary Ann Evans – (1819–80): Novelist; b. Arbury, Warwickshire, where her father managed an estate; strict religious upbringing; family moved to Coventry (1841) where she met Charles Bray and Charles Hennell; under their influence became a rationalist; moved to London after death of father, 1849; assistant editor of *Westminster Review* from 1851; became acquainted with Spencer, Carlyle, Harriet Martineau, and Newman; lived with George Henry Lewes (q.v.); *Scenes from Clerical Life*, 1858; success with *Adam Bede* 1859; all her novels written between this time and Lewes's death in 1878; married J. W. Cross, 1880.

Life by her husband J. W. Cross, *George Eliot's Life, as Related in her Letters and Journals*, 3 vols., 1885–6; repr., 1 vol., n.d.; G. S. Haight, 1968; R. V. Redinger, 1975

Letters ed. G. S. Haight, 7. vols., 1954–6

Essays ed. T. C. Pinney, 1963

Selected Essays, Poems and Other Writings ed A. S. Byatt and N. Warren, 1990

Collected Works, 21 vols., 1908–11

Novels in E.L., 7 vols., and in P.C., 8 vols.; Clarendon Critical Edition, 1980– in progress

Middlemarch, Mill on the Floss and *Romola* in W.C.; *The Lifted Veil* in Virago

See:

G. Beer, *George Eliot*, 1987

J. Bennett, *George Eliot: Her Mind and her Art*, 1948

D. Carroll (ed.) *George Eliot: The Critical Heritage*, 1971

L. Emery, *George Eliot's Creative Conflict*, 1976

B. Hardy, *The Novels of George Eliot*, 1959
    (ed.) *Critical Essays on George Eliot*, 1970

B. Hardy, *The Art of George Eliot*, 1961

U. C. Knoepflmacher, *George Eliot's Early Novels*, 1968

F. R. Leavis, 'George Eliot' in *The Great Tradition*, 1948

B. J. Paris, *Experiments in Life: George Eliot's Quest for Values*, 1965

V. S. Pritchett, 'George Eliot' in *The Living Novel*, 1946

J. Purkis, *A Preface to George Eliot*, 1985

S. Shuttleworth, *George Eliot and Nineteenth-Century Science*, 1984; new edn 1987

A. Smith (ed.) *George Eliot: Centenary Essays and an Unpublished Fragment*, 1980

L. Stephen, *George Eliot*, 1902

J. Thale, *The Novels of George Eliot*, 1959

A. Welsh, *George Eliot and Blackmail*, 1985

V. Woolf in *The Common Reader*, 1925

A Century of George Eliot Criticism ed. Gordon S. Haight, 1965

FITZGERALD, EDWARD (1809–83): Poet; b. Bredfield, Suffolk; son of John Purcell, who later adopted his wife's maiden name; educated at Bury St Edmunds and Trinity College, Cambridge; contemporary and friend of W. H. Thompson and Thackeray; went to Paris (1830) but soon returned to live quietly in Woodbury, Suffolk; friendly with Tennyson and Carlyle; *Euphranor*, 1851; married Lucy Barton, 1856; translation of *The Rubá'iyát of Omar Khayyám* (1859) praised by Rossetti, Swinburne, and Monckton Milnes, soon became extremely popular; other works largely translations from Greek.

Life by T. Wright, 2 vols., 1904; A. M. Terhune, 1947

Collected Works, 2 vols., 1887

Selected Works ed. J. Richardson, 1962

Letters and Literary Remains ed. W. A. Wright, 7 vols., 1902–3

Letters ed. J. M. Cohen, 1960; ed. A. M. and A. B. Terhune, 4 vols., 1980
The Rubá'iyát and other Persian Poems in E.L.
See:
A. J. Arberry, *Omar Khayyám*, 1952
    Salaman and Absal, 1956
A. Y. Campbell, 'Edward Fitzgerald' in *Great Victorians* ed. A. J. and H.
    Massingham, 1932

GASKELL, ELIZABETH CLEGHORN (1810–65); Novelist and biographer;
b. London; brought up in Knutsford, Cheshire; married William Gaskell
(1832) and settled in Manchester; *Mary Barton* (1848) led to friendship with
Carlyle, Landor, and Dickens; Dickens invited her to contribute to *Household
Words*, where *Cranford* was serialized between 1851 and 1853; *Life of
Charlotte Brontë*, 1857; other novels include *North and South* (1855), *Sylvia's
Lovers* (1864), and unfinished novel *Wives and Daughters* published
posthumously, 1866.

Life by A. S. Whitfield, 1929; G. de W. Sanders, 1930; Y. ffrench, 1949; A.
    B. Hopkins, 1952; W. Gérin, 1976
Collected Works ed. C. K. Shorter, 11 vols., 1906–19
Works ed. A. Ward, 8 vols., 1906
Letters ed. J. A. V. Chapple and A. Pollard, 1967
*Mary Barton, North and South, Cousin Phillis, Sylvia's Lovers, Wives and
    Daughters* and *Ruth* in E.L.; *Cranford* and *North and South* in O.E.N.
Cranford and *The Life of Charlotte Brontë* in E.L. and W.C.
Cranford, Mary Barton, North and South, Wives and Daughters and *Life of
    Charlotte Brontë* in P.C.
See:
M. Allott, *Elizabeth Gaskell*, 1960
W. A. Craik, *Elizabeth Gaskell and the English Provincial Novel*, 1975
A. Easson, *Elizabeth Gaskell*, 1979
M. Granz, *Elizabeth Gaskell: The Artist in Conflict*, 1968
J. Lucas in *The Literature of Change*, 1977; new edn 1980
A. Pollard, *Mrs Gaskell*, 1965
J. G. Sharps, *Mrs Gaskell's Observation and Invention*, 1965
S. Smith in *The Other Nation*, 1980
P. Stoneman, *Elizabeth Gaskell*, 1987
E. Wright, *Mrs Gaskell*, 1965

GILBERT, SIR WILLIAM SCHWENK (1836–1911): Playwright, librettist,
humorist; b. London; son of novelist, William Gilbert; educated at Bou-
logne, Ealing, and King's College, London; civil servant, 1857–61; called to
the Bar, 1864; began publishing *Bab Ballads* in *Fun* from 1861; wrote several
plays and pantomimes with minor success, 1866–71; met Sir Arthur Sullivan
(1871) and began with him the famous twenty-year collaboration on the
Savoy Operas; knighted, 1907; drowned at Harrow Weald in 1911.

Life by S. Dark and R. Grey, 1923; H. Pearson, 1957; new edn 1975
Collected Plays, rev. edn 1920
The Savoy Operas, 1926; ed. D. Hudson, 2 vols., 1963
Complete Plays of Gilbert and Sullivan, 1936
Gilbert before Sullivan: Six Comic Plays ed. J. W. Stedman, 1967
Plays ed. G. Rowell, 1982
Bab Ballads, 1898; ed. J. Ellis, 1970
See:
D. Cecil intro. *Savoy Operas*, W.C., 2 vols., 1963
J. B. Jones (ed.) *W. S. Gilbert: A Century of Scholarship and Commentary*, 1970
M. K. Sutton, *W. S. Gilbert*, 1975
A. Williamson, *Gilbert and Sullivan Opera*, 1953

GISSING, GEORGE ROBERT (1857–1903): Novelist; b. Wakefield; educated at Alderley Edge and Owen's College, Manchester; early life spent in great poverty in London and later in America, supporting himself by private teaching: *Demos* (1886) first attracted attention, but his great realism did not make him popular; other novels include *The Nether World* (1889), *New Grub Street* (1891), *The Town Traveller* (1901), and *Private Papers of Henry Ryecroft* (1903); died at Saint-Jean-de-Luz.

Life by M. Roberts, 1912; J. Korg, 1965
Collected Works, first 10 vols., 1977
Selections from the Works with biographical and critical notes by his son, 1929
New Grub Street in W.C. and in P.C.; *The Odd Women* in Virago
Letters ed. A. and E. Gissing, 1927
Diary ed. P. Coustillas, 1978
George Gissing and H. G. Wells: A Record of their Friendship and Correspondence ed. R. A. Gettman, 1961
Collected Articles on Gissing ed. P. Coustillas, 1968
See:
P. Coustillas and C. Partridge (eds.) *Gissing: The Critical Heritage*, 1972
M. Donnelly, *Gissing, Grave Comedian*, 1954
D. Grylls, *The Paradoxes of Gissing*, 1986
J. Goode, *George Gissing: Ideology and Fiction*, 1978
Q. D. Leavis, 'Gissing and the English Novel' in *Scrutiny*, VII, 1938
A. Poole, *Gissing in Context*, 1975
F. Swinnerton, *George Gissing: A Critical Study*, 1912

GOSSE, SIR EDMUND (1849–1928): Poet and critic; b. London, son of the zoologist P. H. Gosse; educated privately; assistant in Department of Printed Books, British Museum, 1867–75; translator to the Board of Trade, 1875–1904; first volume of verse *On Viol and Flute*, 1873; lecturer in English Literature at Trinity College, Cambridge, 1884–90; librarian to the House of Lords, 1904–14; close friend of Stevenson, Swinburne, and Henry James;

critical and other works include *The Jacobean Poets* (1894), *Life and Letters of Dr John Donne* (1899), *History of Modern English Literature* (1897), *Jeremy Taylor* (1904), *Father and Son* (1907), and *Life of Swinburne* (1917); knighted, 1925.

Life by E. Charteris, 1931; by A. Thwaite, 1984
Collected Poems, 1911
Selected Essays, 2 vols., 1928
Father and Son, ed. J. Hepburn, 1974
See:
P. Braybrooke, *Considerations on Edmund Gosse*, 1925
J. Drinkwater, 'Edmund Gosse' in *Quarterly Review*, July 1931
B. I. Evans in *English Poetry in the Later Nineteenth Century*, 1933; rev. edn 1966
H. Orel in *Victorian Literary Critics*, 1984
V. Woolf, 'Edmund Gosse' in *The Moment and other Essays*, 1948

HARDY, THOMAS (1840–1928): Novelist and poet; b. Dorsetshire; educated locally; articled to an ecclesiastical architect, 1859; assistant to Sir Arthur Blomfield, R. A., 1862; won R.I.B.A medal and Architectural Association prize, 1863; undecided whether to adopt architecture or literature as his profession, was advised to write by George Meredith; *Desperate Remedies*, 1871; *Under the Greenwood Tree*, 1872; popular success with *Far from the Madding Crowd*, 1874; married Emma Lavinia Gifford, 1874; between 1874 and 1896 wrote the great Wessex novels; epic drama *The Dynasts*, 1904–8; from 1909 until his death wrote only lyric poetry; first wife died 1912; married Florence Emily Dugdale, 1914.

Life by F. E. Hardy, 2 vols., 1928–30, 1 vol., 1962; ed. M. Millgate, 1984; R. Gittings, 2 vols., 1975–8; Evelyn Hardy, 1954; J. I. M. Stewart, 1972; M. Millgate, 1982; new edn 1987
Letters ed. C. J. Weber, 1954
Collected Letters ed. R. L. Purdy and M. Millgate, 7 vols., 1978–88
Collected Works, 37 vols., 1919–20; Novels in P.C. (8 vols.)
New Wessex Edition ed. P. N. Furbank *et al.* 19 vols., 1974–7
Complete Poems ed. J. Gibson, 1976
Complete Poetical Works ed. S. Hynes, 3 vols., 1982–5
Selected Poems ed G. M. Young, 1940; ed. D. Wright, 1978; ed. T. R. M. Creighton, 1974; rev. edn 1977
Stories and Poems in E.L.; *The Distracted Preacher and other Tales* in P.C.
The Note Books of Thomas Hardy ed. E. Hardy, 1955
Literary Notebooks ed. L. Björk, 2 vols., 1985
Personal Notebooks ed. R. H. Taylor, 1979
Personal Writings ed. H. Orel, 1967
The Architectural Notebook ed. C. J. P. Beatty, 1966
See:
J. Bayley, *An Essay on Hardy*, 1978

J. B. Bullen, *The Expressive Eye. Fiction and Perception in the Work of Thomas Hardy*, 1986

D. Cecil, *Hardy the Novelist*, 1943; new edn 1954

R. G. Cox (ed.) *Hardy: The Critical Heritage*, 1970

D. Davie, *Thomas Hardy and British Poetry*, 1973; rev. edn 1979

J. Goode, *Thomas Hardy: The Offensive Truth*, 1988

I. Gregor, *The Great Web*, 1974

A. J. Guerard, *Hardy: the Novels and Stories*, 1949

J. Holloway in *The Charted Mirror*, 1960

S. Hynes, *The Pattern of Hardy's Poetry*, 1963

A. M. Jackson, *Illustration and the Novels of Thomas Hardy*, 1982

D. H. Lawrence in *Phoenix*, 1936

R. Morrell, *Thomas Hardy: The Will and the Way*, 1965

T. Paulin, *Thomas Hardy: The Poetry of Perception*, 1975

F. B. Pinion, *A Commentary on the Poems of Thomas Hardy*, 1976

J. Wain, intro. *The Dynasts*, 1965

P. Widdowson, *Hardy in History*, 1989

HENLEY, WILLIAM ERNEST (1849–1903): Poet, critic, and editor: b. Gloucester; suffered from tuberculosis as a child and was placed in Edinburgh Infirmary, 1874; sent poems from hospital to *Cornhill Magazine*; Leslie Stephen, then editor, visited him with Robert Louis Stevenson and began a long friendship; went to London, 1877; editor of *London*, 1877–82; *Book of Verse*, 1880; editor of *Magazine of Art*, 1882–6; literary editor and later editor of *National Observer* from 1888; *Views and Reviews*, 1890; *The Song of the Sword*, 1892.

Life by J. H. Buckley, 1945; J. Connell, 1949
Collected Works, 5 vols., 1921
See:
B. I. Evans in *English Poetry in the Later Nineteenth Century*, 1933; rev. edn 1966

H. Gregory, 'On Henley's Editorial Career' in *The Shield of Achilles*, 1944

S. J. Looker, *Shelley, Trelawney and Henley*, 1950

E. V. Lucas, *The Colvins and their Friends*, 1928

T. E. Welby, 'Aspects of Henley' in *Second Impressions*, 1933

HOPKINS, GERARD MANLEY (1844–89): Poet; b. London; educated at Highgate School and Balliol College, Oxford; pupil of Jowett and Pater; friendly with Bridges and Dolben and later with R. W. Dixon and Coventry Patmore; converted to the Roman Catholic Church, 1866; entered the Jesuit novitiate, 1868; ordained priest, 1877; worked as preacher and administrator in London, Oxford, Liverpool, and Glasgow; appointed Professor of Greek at University College, Dublin, 1884; his work was not published during his lifetime and thereafter only a few poems until the edition by Bridges in 1918.

Life by G. F. Lahey, 1930; E. Ruggles, 1944; B. Bergonzi, 1977; R. B.
  Martin, 1991
Poems ed. R. Bridges, rev. edn 1930; ed. W. H. Gardner, enlarged edn
  1948; ed N. H. MacKenzie, 1990
Poems and Prose ed. W. H. Gardner, 1953
Selections (The Oxford Authors series) ed. C. Phillips, 1986
Selected Prose ed. G. Roberts, 1980
Letters of Gerard Manley Hopkins to Robert Bridges ed. C. C. Abbott, 2 vols., 1935
Further Letters ed. C. C. Abbott, 1938; much enlarged, 1956
The Journals and Papers of Gerard Manley Hopkins ed. H. House, completed
  by G. Storey, 1959
The Sermons and Devotional Writings of Gerard Manley Hopkins ed. C.
  Devlin, 1959
See:
D. A. Downes, *Gerard Manley Hopkins: A Study of his Ignatian Spirit*, 1966
W. H. Gardner, *Gerard Manley Hopkins: A Study*, rev. edn, 2 vols., 1966
A. Heuser, *The Shaping Vision of Gerard Manley Hopkins*, 1958
A. Kenny, *God and Two Poets: Arthur Hugh Clough and Gerard Manley
  Hopkins*, 1988
F. R. Leavis in *The Common Pursuit*, 1952
  New Bearings in English Poetry, rev. edn 1950
N. H. MacKenzie, *Hopkins*, 1968
  A Reader's Guide to Gerard Manley Hopkins, 1981
J. Milroy, *The Language of Gerard Manley Hopkins*, 1977
P. Milward and R. Schoder, *Landscape and Inscape: Vision and Inspiration in
  Hopkins's Poetry*, 1975
W. J. Ong, *Hopkins, the Self, and God*, 1986
W. A. M. Peters, *Gerard Manley Hopkins: A Critical Essay*, 1948
J. Robinson, *In Extremity: A Study of Gerard Manley Hopkins*, 1977
G. Storey, *A Preface to Hopkins*, 1981
A. Sulloway, *Gerard Manley Hopkins and the Victorian Temper*, 1972
A. Thomas, *Hopkins the Jesuit*, 1969

HOUSMAN, ALFRED EDWARD (1859–1936): Poet and scholar; brother of
Laurence Housman; educated at Bromsgrove and St John's College,
Oxford; worked in Patents Office, 1881–92; appointed Professor of Latin at
University College, London, 1892; *A Shropshire Lad*, 1896; appointed
Professor of Latin at Cambridge, 1911; *Last Poems*, 1922; *The Name and
Nature of Poetry*, 1933.

Life by his brother Laurence Housman, *Some Poems, some Letters and a
  Personal Memoir*, 1937; I. Scott-Kilvert, 1955; A. N. Marlow, 1958; R. P.
  Graves, 1979; N. Page, 1983
Letters ed. H. Maas, 1971
Collected Poems, rev. edn 1953
Collected Poems and Selected Prose, ed. C. Ricks, 1988

Selected Prose ed. J. Carter, 1961
Classical Papers ed. J. Diggle and F. R. D. Goodyear, 3 vols., 1972
Selected Poetry and Prose ed. F. C. Horwood, 1971
See:
A. F. Allison, 'The Poetry of Housman' in R.E.S. XIX, 1943
C. O. Brink in *English Classical Scholarship*, 1986
R. W. Chambers in *Man's Unconquerable Mind*, 1939
B. J. Leggatt, *The Poetic Art of Housman*, 1978
O. Robinson, *Angry Dust: The Poetry of Housman*, 1950
C. B. Tinker, 'Housman's Poetry' in *Yale Review* XXV, 1935
C. L. Watson, *Housman: A Divided Life*, 1957
Edmund Wilson in *The Triple Thinkers*, 1938

HUTTON, RICHARD HOLT (1826–97): Editor, philosopher, and critic; educated at University College School and University College, London, and later at Heidelberg and Berlin; prepared for the Unitarian Ministry at Manchester New College; principal of University Hall, London; edited the Unitarian *The Enquirer*, 1851–3; joint-editor with Walter Bagehot of the *National Review*, 1855–64; assistant editor of *The Economist*, 1858–60; joint-editor of the *Spectator*, 1861–97; works include *Essays on Some Modern Guides of English Thought* (1887) and *Criticisms on Contemporary Thought and Thinkers* (1894).

See:
F. S. Boas, 'Critics and Criticism in the Seventies' in *The Eighteen-Seventies*, 1929
J. Hogben, *Richard Holt Hutton of the 'Spectator'*, 1899
G. C. LeRoy, 'Richard Holt Hutton' in P.M.L.A. LVI, 1941
H. Orel in *Victorian Literary Critics*, 1984
R. H. Tener and M. Woodfield (eds.) *A Victorian Spectator: Uncollected Writings of R. H. Hutton*, 1989

HUXLEY, THOMAS HENRY (1825–95): Biologist; b. Ealing, son of a schoolmaster; studied medicine at Charing Cross Hospital; surgeon on H.M.S. *Rattlesnake*, 1846–50; elected F.R.S., 1851; lecturer at the School of Mines from 1854; friend of Hooker, Tyndall, and Darwin; naturalist to the Geologist Survey, 1855; working along the same lines as Darwin, published *Man's Place in Nature*, 1863; as member of the London School Board (1870–72) did much to reform elementary education; President of the Royal Society, 1881–5; health completely broke down, 1885; died at Eastbourne.

Autobiographies of Darwin and Huxley, 1974
Collected Essays, 9 vols., 1894
See:
E. Clodd, *Thomas Huxley*, 1902
L. Huxley, *The Life and Letters of Thomas Huxley*, 2 vols., 1900
J. G. Paradis, *T. H. Huxley: Man's Place in Nature*, 1979

JEFFERIES, RICHARD (1848–87): Novelist and countryman; son of a Wiltshire farmer; first attracted notice with *The Gamekeeper at Home*, 1878; other works include *Hodge and his Master* (1880), *Wood Magic* (1881), *Bevis* (1882), and his autobiography *The Story of my Heart* (1883).

Life by Edward Thomas, 1909; S. J. Looker and C. Porteous, 1965
Collected Works ed. H. C. Warren, 1948
The Essential Jefferies ed. M. Elwin, 1948
After London in W.C., intro. J. Fowles, 1980
Bevis in E.L.
The Dewy Morn, new intro. L. Lerner, 1982
The Gamekeeper at Home and *The Amateur Poacher*, new edn 1978
Hodge and his Master, new edn 1967
See:
W. J. Keith, *Richard Jefferies*, 1966
Q. D. Leavis, 'Lives and Works of Richard Jefferies' in *Scrutiny*, VI, 1935
S. J. Looker (ed.) *The Worthing Cavalcade*, 1944
H. S. Salt, *Richard Jefferies: A Study*, 1894
A. F. Thom, *The Life Worship of Richard Jefferies*, 1933

JONES, HENRY ARTHUR (1851–1929): Dramatist; b. Grandborough, Bucks; son of a farmer; first success as a dramatist with *The Silver King* (1882), written in collaboration with Henry Herman; established reputation with *The Middleman* (1889) and *Judah* (1890); later plays include *The Tempter* (1893), *The Liars* (1897), *The Manoeuvres of Jane* (1899), *Whitewashing Julia* (1903), and *The Lie* (1914)

Life by D. A. Jones, 1930
Plays ed. R. Jackson, 1982
Representative Plays ed. C. Hamilton, 4 vols., 1926
The Liars in *Late Victorian Plays*, 1972
See:
W. Archer, *The Old Drama and the New*, 1923
R. A. Cordell, *Henry Arthur Jones and the Modern Drama*, 1932
J. B. Matthews, *A Study of the Drama*, 1910
M. Northand, 'Jones and the Development of Modern English Drama' in
    R.E.S. XVIII, 1942

KINGSLEY, CHARLES (1819–75): Poet, novelist, and clergyman; b. Devon; son of a clergyman; educated at King's College, London, and Magdalene College, Cambridge; ordained to the curacy of Eversley in Hampshire, 1842; married Fanny Grenfell, 1844; became strong supporter of Christian Socialism and sympathized with the aims of the Chartists; *Alton Locke*, 1849; *Westward Ho!*, 1855; Chaplain to Queen Victoria, 1859; Professor of Modern History at Cambridge, 1860–69; *The Water-Babies*, 1863; *Hereward the Wake*, 1866; appointed Canon of Westminster, 1873; died at Eversley.

Life by M. F. Thorp, 1937; R. B. Martin, 1960; S. Chitty, 1974
Collected Works, 28 vols., 1880–85; 1888–9
Life and Works, 19 vols., 1901–3
Alton Locke in W.C., intro. E. A. Cripps, 1983
Hereward the Wake, *The Heroes*, *Hypatia* and *Alton Locke* in E.L.
See:
S. E. Baldwin, *Charles Kingsley*, 1934
G. Egner, *Apologia for Charles Kingsley*, 1969
A. J. Hartley, *The Novels of Charles Kingsley*, 1977
G. Kendall, *Charles Kingsley and his Ideas*, 1946
S. Smith in *The Other Nation*, 1980
L. K. Uffelman, *Charles Kingsley*, 1979
N. Vance in *The Sinews of the Spirit*, 1985
Special Centenary issue of *Theology* LXXVIII, Jan. 1975

KIPLING, RUDYARD (1865–1936): Poet and story-teller; b. Bombay, son
of an artist; educated at United Services' College, Westward Ho; returned
to India (1882) and worked on the Lahore *Civil and Military Gazette*;
Departmental Ditties, 1886; *Plain Tales*, 1887; travelled through India, China,
Japan, and America to England (1887–9) to find himself already famous;
contributed to *Macmillan's Magazine*, *Lippincott's Magazine* and the *National
Observer* (then edited by W. E. Henley) from 1891; married Caroline Starr
Balestier, 1892; *The Jungle Book*, 1894; visited South Africa, 1898; *Stalky &
Co.*, 1899; *Kim*, 1901; *Just So Stories*, 1902; *Puck of Pook's Hill*, 1906;
awarded Nobel Prize for Literature, 1907.

Life by C. Carrington, 1955; A. Wilson, 1977; new edn 1979; Lord
   Birkenhead, 1978
Letters to Rider Haggard, 1965; *Letters* ed. T. Pinney, 1990– in progress
Complete Works in Prose and Verse, The Sussex Edition, 25 vols., 1937–9
Works in W.C. (8 vols.)
Stories and Poems in E.L.; *Short Stories* (selected), 2 vols., 1971
Definitive Edition of Kipling's Verse, 1940
Early Verse 1879–1889 ed. A. Rutherford, 1986
A Choice of Kipling's Verse ed. T. S. Eliot, 1941
A Choice of Kipling's Prose ed. Somerset Maugham, 1952
Something of Myself, 1977
Kipling and the Critics ed. E. L. Gilbert, 1966
For extensive list of writing see N.C.B.E.L.
See:
C. A. Bodelsen, *Aspects of Kipling's Art*, 1964
N. C. Chaudhuri in *The Continent of Circe*, 1965
L. Cornell, *Kipling in India*, 1966
B. Dobrée, *Rudyard Kipling, Realist and Fabulist*, 1967
B. Ford, 'A Case for Kipling?' in *Scrutiny*, XI, 1942
R. L. Green (ed.) *Kipling: The Critical Heritage*, 1971

J. Gross (ed.) *Rudyard Kipling: The Man, his Work and World*, 1972
C. Harvie, '"The Sons of Martha": Technology, Transport and Rudyard Kipling', *Victorian Studies*, XX, 1977
S. S. Husain, *Kipling and India*, 1965
S. Kemp, *Kipling's Hidden Narratives*, 1988
P. Mason, *Kipling: The Glass, the Shadow and the Fire*, 1975
G. Orwell, in *Critical Essays*, 1946
J. I. M. Stewart, *Rudyard Kipling*, 1976
J. M. S. Tompkins, *The Art of Rudyard Kipling*, 1959
Edmund Wilson, *The Wound and the Bow*, 1941

LANG, ANDREW (1844–1912): Historian and journalist; b. Selkirk; educated at Selkirk Grammar School, the University of St Andrew's, and Balliol College, Oxford; elected fellow of Merton; settled in London and wrote principally for the *Daily News* and *Morning Post*; greatly interested in myth and folklore; *Custom and Myth*, 1884; *Myth, Literature and Religion*, 1887; *The Making of Religion*, 1898; other works include *The Mark of Cain* (1886), *A History of Scotland from the Roman Occupation* (1900–7), *The World of Homer* (1910), and stories for children.

Life by M. Beerbohm, 1929; R. L. Green, 1946
Centenary Anthology ed. J. B. Salmond, 1944
See:
G. S. Gordon, *Andrew Lang*, 1928
R. L. Green, 'Andrew Lang and the Fairy Tale' in R.E.S. XX, 1944
G. Murray, *Andrew Lang the Poet*, 1948
H. Orel in *Victorian Literary Critics*, 1984
J. Ormerod, *The Poetry of Andrew Lang*, 1943
R. S. Rait, *Andrew Lang as Historian*, 1930
S. B. Salmond, *Andrew Lang and Journalism*, 1951

LEAR, EDWARD (1812–88): Humorist and illustrator; b. London; studied ornithology; invited by the Earl of Derby to draw the Knowsley menagerie (1832) and became a permanent friend of the Stanley family; wrote the first *Book of Nonsense* (1846) for one of their children; lived in Rome, 1837–47; returned to London, but later settled in San Remo, 1855; *Nonsense Songs*, 1871–2; *Laughable Lyrics*, 1877; travelled widely in Europe and Asia; died at San Remo.

Life by A. Davidson, 1938; new edn 1968; J. Lehmann, 1977; V. Noakes, 1968; rev. edn 1979
The Complete Nonsense ed. H. Jackson, 1947
Letters ed. Lady C. Strachey, 2 vols., 1907–11
Italian Journal, ed. R. Murphy, 1953
See:
T. Byrom, *Nonsense and Wonder: The Poems and Cartoons of Edward Lear*, 1972

J. Richardson, *Edward Lear*, 1965
E. Sewell, *The Field of Nonsense*, 1952
E. Strachey, 'Nonsense as a Fine Art', *Quarterly Review*, October 1888

LEWES, GEORGE HENRY (1817–78): Philosopher and critic; b. London; educated in Jersey, Brittany, and Greenwich; visited Germany, 1838; married a daughter of Swynfen Stevens Jervis, 1840; interested in drama and appeared several times on the stage; wrote several essays in this period later published as *Actors and Acting*, 1875; met Mary Ann Evans (George Eliot – q.v.) in 1851 and lived with her from 1854 till his death; *Life of Goethe*, 1855; wrote several popular scientific books; *The Problems of Life and Mind*, 1873–9; died very suddenly.

Literary Criticism ed. A. R. Kaminsky, 1964
The George Eliot Letters (including many by Lewes) ed. G. S. Haight, 7 vols., 1954–6
See:
M. Greenhut, 'Lewes and the Classical Tradition in English Criticism' in R.E.S. XXIV, 1948
E. W. Hirschberg, *George Henry Lewes*, 1972
A. R. Kaminsky, *George Henry Lewes as Literary Critic*, 1968
J. Kaminsky, 'The Empirical Metaphysics of Lewes' in *Journal of the History of Ideas* XIII, 1952
H. Orel in *Victorian Literary Critics*, 1984
H. G. Tjoa, *George Henry Lewes: A Victorian Mind*, 1977

LYTTON, EDWARD GEORGE EARLE LYTTON BULWER-, BARON (1803–73): Novelist, dramatist, and statesman; b. London, son of General Bulwer; educated privately and at Trinity College and Trinity Hall, Cambridge; rapidly acquired a reputation as a dandy; married Rosina Wheeler, 1827; *Pelham* (1828) immediately successful; followed by several other didactic novels; M.P. for St Ives (1831) and later for Lincoln (1832–41); *The Last Days of Pompeii*, 1843; legally separated from his wife, 1836; she continued to attack him bitterly until his death; success as a dramatist with *The Lady of Lyons*, 1838; created baronet, 1838; edited *Monthly Chronicle* from 1841; M.P. for Herts, 1852–66; Secretary for the Colonies, 1858–9; raised to the peerage, 1866; *Kenelm Chillingly*, 1873.

Life by his grandson, 2 vols., 1913; by his great-grandson, 1948; S. J. Flower, 1973
Life, Letters and Literary Remains ed. by his son, 2 vols., 1883
Novels, 30 vols., 1891–2
The Last Days of Pompeii and *Harold* in E.L.
Money in *Nineteenth Century Plays*, 1972
See:
A. C. Christensen, *Edward Bulwer-Lytton: The Fiction of New Regions*, 1976

P. J. Cooke, *Bulwer-Lytton's Plays*, 1894
J. Lindsay in *Charles Dickens*, 1950
M. W. Rosa, *The Silver Fork School: Novels of Fashion Preceding Vanity Fair*,
1936
A. T. Sheppard, *The Art and Practice of Historical Fiction*, 1930
C. N. Stewart, *Bulwer-Lytton as an Occultist*, 1927

MACAULAY, THOMAS BABINGTON (1800–59): Historian, essayist, and
statesman; b. Leicestershire; educated privately and at Trinity College,
Cambridge; contemporary and friend of Praed and Villiers; *Essay on Milton*
(1825) extraordinarily popular; called to the Bar, 1826; M.P. for Calne,
1830; established reputation as an orator; appointed Commissioner of the
Board of Control for India, 1832; M.P. for Leeds from 1833; appointed to
the Supreme Council for India, where he lived from 1834–8; returned to
Parliament as Member for Edinburgh; Secretary for War, 1839; Melbourne
ministry fell, *Lays of Ancient Rome*, 1842; *Essays*, 1843; returned to office as
Paymaster General (1846) but retired from Parliament the following year;
first two vols of the *History* (1848) enormous success in England and
America; returned to Parliament (1852), refusing a seat in the Cabinet
because of failing health; vols 3 and 4 of the *History* (1855) even more
successful; raised to the peerage, 1857.

Life by his nephew G. O. Trevelyan, 1876; A. Bryant, 1932; J. Clive, 1973
Collected Works, 9 vols., 1905–7
Letters ed. T. Pinney, 6 vols., 1974–81
Speeches ed. J. Clive and T. Pinney, 1972
Critical and Historical Essays and *Essays and Poems* in E.L. (3 vols.)
The History of England in E.L. (3 vols.)
Prose and Poetry ed. G. M. Young, 1952
See:
R. C. Beatty, 'Macaulay and Carlyle' in *Philological Quarterly* XVIII, 1939
J. W. Burrow in *A Liberal Descent*, 1981
C. Firth, *Commentary on Macaulay's History of England*, 1938
J. R. Griffin, *The Intellectual Milieu of Lord Macaulay*, 1965
J. Hamburger, *Macaulay and the Whig Tradition*, 1977
G. Levine in *The Boundaries of Fiction*, 1968
S. W. Thompson and B. J. Holm, 'Macaulay, Carlyle and Froude' in *A
History of Historical Writing* II, 1942
G. M. Trevelyan in *Clio: A Muse*, 1913

MALLOCK, WILLIAM HURRELL (1849–1923): Satirist; educated at Balliol
College, Oxford; now remembered for *The New Republic* (1877), a satire
on contemporary society and ideas, portraying eminent Victorians thinly
disguised; other works include *The New Paul and Virginia* (1878), and
Memoirs of Life and Literature (1920).

See:

A. B. Adams, *The Novels of W. H. Mallock*, 1934

J. Lucas, 'Tilting at the Moderns: W. H. Matlock's Criticisms of the Positivist Spirit' in *Renaissance and Modern Studies* X, 1966

G. Tillotson, 'Pater, Mr Rose and the "Conclusion" of *The Renaissance*' in E.&S., 1947

C. R. Woodring, 'Notes on Mallock's *The New Republic*' in *Nineteenth Century Fiction* VI, 1951

MEREDITH, GEORGE (1828–1900): Novelist and poet; b. Portsmouth; educated in Germany; articled to a solicitor (1844) but became a freelance journalist and leader of a group of young Radicals; married Mrs Nicholls, daughter of Thomas Love Peacock, 1849 (later she deserted him); early poems praised by Tennyson and Kingsley, 1851; early novels admired by George Eliot and Rossetti; *Ordeal of Richard Feverel* (1859) established him as one of the chief writers of the day, though not a popular success; wife died, 1861; married Marie Vulliamy, 1864; special correspondent for *Morning Post* during Austro-Italian war, 1866; edited *Fortnightly Review* from 1867; as literary adviser to Chapman & Hall encouraged George Gissing and Thomas Hardy; *The Egoist*, 1879; death of second wife, 1885; popular success with *Diana of the Crossways*, 1885; last complete novel *The Amazing Marriage*, 1895; after which published poetry only.

Life by S. M. Ellis, 1919; L. Stevenson, 1953, 1954; J. Lindsay, 1956; D. Williams, 1977

Letters ed. by his son, 2 vols., 1912; *Collected Letters* ed. C. L. Cline, 3 vols., 1970

Collected Works, 29 vols., 1909–12

Poetical Works ed. G. M. Trevelyan, 1912

The Ordeal of Richard Feverel in E.L. and W.C.

The Egoist in W.C.

Modern Love ed. C. Day Lewis, 1948

Selected Poems ed. G. Hough, 1962

See:

J. W. Beach, *The Comic Spirit in George Meredith*, 1911

G. Beer, *Meredith: A Change of Masks*, 1970

B. I. Evans in *English Poetry in the later Nineteenth Century*, 1933; rev. 1966

G. S. Haight, 'George Meredith and the *Westminster Review*', M.L.R. LIII, Jan. 1958

Robert Peel, *The Creed of a Victorian Pagan*, 1931

J. B. Priestley, *George Meredith*, 1926

V. S. Pritchett, *George Meredith and English Comedy*, 1970

S. Sassoon, *Meredith*, 1948

M. Shaheen, *George Meredith: A Reappraisal of his Novels*, 1981

O. Sitwell, *The Novels of Meredith and some Notes on the English Novel*, 1948

C. B. Tinker, 'Meredith's Poetry' in *Essays in Retrospect*, 1948

G. M. Trevelyan, *The Poetry and Philosophy of George Meredith*, 1906
A. White in *The Uses of Obscurity*, 1981
I. Williams (ed.) *Meredith: The Critical Heritage*, 1971
W. F. Wright, *Art and Substance in George Meredith*, 1953

MILL, JOHN STUART (1806–73): Philosopher and economist; b. London, son of James Mill; educated most intensively by his father; lived in France with Sir Samuel Bentham, 1820–21; became clerk in the Examiner's office of India House, 1822; formed Utilitarian Society, 1823; in charge of India House's relations with native states, 1836–56; *Political Economy*, 1848; married Harriet Taylor, 1851; wife died, 1858; *On Liberty*, 1859; *Thoughts on Parliamentary Reform*, 1859; *Representative Government*, 1860; *Utilitarianism*, 1861; one of the founder members of the Women's Suffrage Society; wrote *On the Subjection of Women*, 1861 (not published till 1869); Member of Parliament for Westminster, 1865; retired to Avignon (1868), where he died.

Life by M. St J. Packe, 1954
Collected Works, 20 vols., 1963 – in progress
Utilitarianism ed. J. P. Plamenatz, 1949
Autobiography in w.c.
Utilitarianism, On Liberty and *Representative Government* in E.L., 1 vol.
Utilitarianism and Other Essays, 1987
On Politics and Society (selections) ed. G. L. Williams, 1976
Letters ed. H. S. R. Elliott, 1910; ed. F. A. Hayek, 1951
See:
M. H. Abrams, *The Mirror and the Lamp*, 1953
E. Alexander, *Matthew Arnold and John Stuart Mill*, 1967
R. P. Anschutz, *The Philosophy of J. S. Mill*, 1953
G. Duncan, *Marx and Mill*, 1973
G. Himmelfarb, *On Liberty and Liberalism: The Case of John Stuart Mill*, 1974
F. R. Leavis, *Mill on Bentham and Coleridge*, 1950
A. Ryan, *John Stuart Mill*, 1975
J. F. Stephen, *Liberty, Equality, Fraternity* ed. R. J. White, 1968
Leslie Stephen, *The English Utilitarians*, 1900
W. Thomas, 'John Stuart Mill and the Uses of Autobiography', *History* LVI, 1971
W. Thomas, *Mill*, 1985
B. Willey in *Nineteenth Century Studies*, 1949

MOORE, GEORGE (1852–1933): Novelist; b. County Mayo; educated in Ireland and at art schools in Paris; on his return to England published *A Mummer's Wife* (1885) as a challenge to the accepted Victorian novel form; works of this period include *Confessions of a Young Man* (1888), *Esther Waters* (1894), *Evelyn Innes* (1898) and *Sister Teresa* (1901); returned to Ireland 1901–10; *Hail and Farewell* (3 vols, 1911–14); *The Brook Kerith*, 1916; *Héloise and Abelard*, 1921.

Life by J. H. Hone, 1936; J. C. Noël, 1966
Letters ed. R. Hart-Davis, 1957
Collected Works, 20 vols., 1937
Esther Waters in w.c.
The Brook Kerith, new edn 1971
A Drama in Muslin, new edn 1981
Hail and Farewell, new edn 1976
See:
M. J. Brown, *Moore: A Reconsideration*, 1955
R. Cave, *A Study of the Novels of George Moore*, 1978
H. E. Gerber (ed.) *George Moore in Transition*, 1968
G. Owens (ed.) *George Moore's Mind and Art*, 1968
I. A. Richards in *Complementarities*, 1977
R. P. Sechler, *George Moore: 'A Disciple of Walter Pater'*, 1932
W. B. Yeats in *Dramatis Personae*, 1935

MORRIS, WILLIAM (1834–96): Poet, painter, and typographer; b. Walthamstow; educated at Marlborough and Exeter College, Oxford; friendly with Edward Burne-Jones; entered as a pupil to an architect, 1856; met Rossetti who encouraged him to paint and write; married Jane Burden, 1859; started an interior decorating business with Rossetti and others under the title of Morris, Marshall, Faulkner & Co., 1862; published several volumes of poetry with some success; bought Kelmscott Manor House with Rossetti, 1871; declined poetry professorship at Oxford, 1877; and established Society for the Protection of Ancient Buildings; left Democratic Federation to form Socialist League (1884) and became editor of their monthly, *Commonweal*, until 1890; became interested in typography and established Kelmscott Press, 1890.

Life by J. W. Mackail, w.c., 1950; May Morris, 2 vols., 1936; E. Meynell, 1948; P. Henderson, 1967; J. Lindsay, 1975
Collected Works, 24 vols., 1910–15; repr. 1966
Selected Writings ed. G. D. H. Cole, 1934
Political Writings ed. A. L. Morton, 1973
Selected Prose ed. A. H. R. Ball, 1931
Selected Writings and Designs ed. A. Briggs, 1962
Collected Letters ed. N. Kelvin, 1984 – in progress
Letters to his Family and Friends ed. P. Henderson, 1950
See:
D. Bush in *Mythology and the Romantic Tradition in English Poetry*, 1937
B. I. Evans, *William Morris and his Poetry*, 1925
P. Faulkner, *Against the Age: An Introduction to William Morris*, 1980
(ed.) *Morris: The Critical Heritage*, 1973
A. Hodgson, *The Romances of William Morris*, 1987
G. Hough in *The Last Romantics*, 1949
Holbrook Jackson, *William Morris, Craftsman-Socialist*, 1908

P. Stansky, *Redesigning the World: William Morris, the 1880s and the Arts and Crafts*, 1985

E. P. Thompson, *Morris: Romantic to Revolutionary*, 1955; rev. edn 1977

Paul Thompson, *The Work of William Morris*, 1967

G. Tillotson, 'Morris and Machines'; 'Morris Wordspinner', both in *Essays in Criticism and Research*, 1942

J. M. S. Tompkins, *William Morris: An Approach to the Poetry*, 1988

Special Morris issue of *Victorian Poetry* XIII, 1975

NEWMAN, JOHN HENRY (1801–90): Cardinal and leader of the Oxford Movement; b. London; educated privately and at Trinity College, Oxford; became a fellow of Oriel where he met Keble, Pusey, and Froude, 1822; ordained in the Anglican ministry and became curate of St Clements, Oxford, 1824; vicar of St Mary's, 1827; inspired by Keble and Froude he helped to found what later became known as the Oxford Movement, publishing *Tracts for the Times* from 1833; editor of *The British Critic*, 1836–41; resigned the living of St Mary's, 1843; received into the Roman Catholic Church, 1845; went to Rome and was ordained priest, 1846; became an Oratorian and established Edgbaston Oratory, Birmingham, where he remained, except for a brief period as Rector of Dublin University, 1854–8; *Idea of a University*, 1852; *Apologia pro Vita Sua*, 1864; *The Dream of Gerontius*, 1866; *Grammar of Assent*, 1870; honorary fellow of Trinity College, Oxford, 1877; created Cardinal of St George in Velabro, 1879.

Life by W. Ward, 2 vols., 1927; M. Trevor, 2 vols., 1962–3; C. S. Dessain, 1968; I. Ker, 1990

Collected Works, 40 vols., 1874–1921

Apologia pro Vita Sua in E.I. and W.C.

Apologia ed. W. Ward, 1913; ed. M. J. Svaglic, 1967

Essay on the Development of Christian Doctrine ed. J. M. Cameron, 1974

Loss and Gain in W.C.

Selected Prose ed. C. F. Harrold, 1923

Theological Papers ed. J. D. Holmes, 1976

A Newman Anthology ed. W. S. Lilly, 1949

Correspondence with John Keble and Others 1839–1845, 1917

Letters and Diaries ed. C. S. Dessain and T. Gornall, 31 vols., 1961 – in progress

See:

M. Cameron, *John Henry Newman*, 1956

J. F. Cronin, *Cardinal Newman: His Theory of Knowledge*, 1935

A. D. Culler, *The Imperial Intellect: A Study of Newman's Educational Ideal*, 1955

D. J. DeLaura in *Hebrew and Hellene*, 1969

C. F. Harrold, *Newman: An Expository and Critical Study of his Mind, Thought and Art*, 1945

C. Hollis, *Newman and the Modern World*, 1968

W. E. Houghton, *The Art of Newman's Apologia*, 1945

G. Levine in *The Boundaries of Fiction*, 1968

F. McGrath, *Newman's University: Idea and Reality*, 1951

J. J. Reilly, *Newman as a Man of Letters*, 1925

W. Robbins, *The Newman Brothers*, 1966

Leslie Stephen, 'Newman's Theory of Belief' in *An Agnostic's Apology*, 1893; repr. 1931

H. L. Weatherby, *Cardinal Newman in his Age*, 1973

T. R. Wright (ed.) *John Henry Newman: A Man for our Time?*, 1983

PATER, WALTER HORATIO (1839–94): Essayist; b. Shadwell; educated King's School, Canterbury, and Queen's College, Oxford; elected fellow of Brasenose (1864) and subsequently lived mainly in Oxford; began writing for the *Westminster Review* and the *Fortnightly Review*; friendly with many of the Pre-Raphaelite Brotherhood; *Marius the Epicurean*, 1885; *Imaginary Portraits*, 1887; *Appreciations*, 1889; *Plato and Platonism*, 1893; *The Child in the House*, 1894; *Gaston de Latour* published posthumously, 1896.

Life by Thomas Wright, 2 vols., 1907; G. d'Hangest, 2 vols., 1961; M. Levey, 1978

Letters ed. L. Evans, 1970

Collected Works, 10 vols., 1910

Marius the Epicurean and *Critical Essays* in E.L.

Marius the Epicurean ed. M. Leyey, 1985

Marius the Epicurean and *The Renaissance* in W.C.

The Renaissance ed. D. L. Hill, 1980

Selected Works ed. R. Aldington, 1948

See:

A. C. Benson, *Walter Pater*, 1906

R. C. Child, *The Aesthetic of Pater*, 1940

W. Iser, *Walter Pater: The Aesthetic Movement*, trans. D. H. Wilson, 1987

D. J. DeLaura in *Hebrew and Hellene*, 1969

U. C. Knoepflmacher in *Religious Humanism and the Victorian Novel*, 1965

G. Monsman, *Walter Pater*, 1977

R. M. Seiler (ed.) *Walter Pater: The Critical Heritage*, 1980

G. Tillotson in *Criticism and the Nineteenth Century*, 1951

PATMORE, COVENTRY KERSEY DIGHTON (1823–96): Poet; b. Woodford, Essex; educated privately; *Poems* (1844) badly received but brought him friendship of Rossetti and Holman Hunt; assistant librarian in the British Museum, 1846–65; married Emily Andrews, 1847; republished earlier poems with several new ones, 1853; wife died (1862) and he joined the Roman Catholic Church; married Marianne Byles, 1865; *The Unknown Eros*, 1877; *Amelia*, 1878; after the death of his second wife (1880), married Harriet Robson and settled at Lymington.

Life by E. Gosse, 1905; D. Patmore, 1949; E. J. Oliver, 1956
Collected Poems ed. F. Page, 1949
Selected Poems ed. D. Patmore, rev. edn 1949
Memoirs and Correspondence ed. B. Champneys, 2 vols., 1901
Further Letters of Gerard Manley Hopkins (includes Patmore's letters to
   Hopkins) ed. C. C. Abbott, 1937
See:
O. Burdett, *The Idea of Coventry Patmore*, 1921
B. I. Evans in *English Poetry in the later Nineteenth Century*, 1933
S. Leslie, *Studies in Sublime Failure*, 1932
F. L. Lucas in *Ten Victorian Poets*, 1940
F. Page, *Patmore: a Study in Poetry*, 1933
J. C. Reid, *The Mind and Art of Coventry Patmore*, 1957

PATTISON, MARK (1813–84): Biographer and educationist; educated at
Oriel College, Oxford; fellow and tutor of Lincoln College, Oxford;
enthusiastic follower of Newman until the latter entered the Roman
Catholic Church; embittered by failure to become Rector of Lincoln
College, 1851; *Tendencies of Religious Thought in England 1688–1750* in *Essays
and Reviews*, 1860; elected Rector of Lincoln College, 1861; other works
include *Life of Milton* (1879) and *Memoirs* (1885).

Memoirs, 1885
See:
V. H. H. Green, *Oxford Common Room*, 1957
J. Sparrow, *Mark Pattison and the Idea of a University*, 1965

PINERO, ARTHUR WING (1855–1934): Dramatist; b. London, son of a
solicitor; started acting at the Theatre Royal, Edinburgh, 1874; joined the
Lyceum Company in London, 1876–81; success with *The Money Spinner*,
1880; wrote several successful farces, mostly produced at the Court Theatre,
notably *The Magistrate* (1885) and *Sweet Lavender* (1888); established as a
serious dramatist with *The Second Mrs Tanqueray*, 1893; later plays include
Trelawney of the Wells (1898), *The Gay Lord Quex* (1899), *His House in
Order* (1906), *The Big Drum* (1915), and *A Private Room* (1928); knighted in
1909.

Life by W. D. Dunkel, 1941
Social Plays ed. C. Hamilton, 4 vols., 1917–22
The Second Mrs Tanqueray in *Late Victorian Plays*, 1972
Collected Letters ed. J. P. Wearing, 1974
See:
F. S. Boas, *From Richardson to Pinero*, 1936
J. W. Cunliffe, *Modern Playwrights*, 1927
H. H. Fyfe, *Sir Arthur Pinero's Plays and Players*, 1930
W. Lazenby, *Arthur Wing Pinero*, 1972

READE, CHARLES (1814–84): Dramatist and novelist; b. Ipsden, Oxford-shire; educated at Magdalen College, Oxford; elected Fellow of Magdalen, 1835; called to the Bar, 1843; wrote several comedies with little success but made reputation as a dramatist with *Masks and Faces*, 1852; on the advice of Laura Seymour, this was subsequently published in novel form as *Peg Woffington*, 1853; set up house with Laura Seymour, 1854; success as a novelist with *It's Never Too Late To Mend*, 1856; *The Cloister and the Hearth*, 1861; most successful play was *Drink* (adapted from Zola's *L'Assom-moir*), 1879; after death of Laura Seymour (1879) his health failed and he wrote very little more.

Life by M. Elwin, 1931
Collected Works, 17 vols., 1895
The Cloister and the Hearth ed. C. B. Wheeler, 1915 and in E.L.
Masks and Faces in *Nineteenth Century Plays*, 1972
See:
W. Archer in *English Dramatists*, 1882
L. F. Haines, 'Reade, Mill and Zola: A Study of the Character and Intention of Reade's Realistic Method' in *Studies in Philology* XL, 1943
W. C. Phillips, *Dickens, Reade and Collins: Sensation Novelists*, 1919
E. Smith, *Charles Reade*, 1976
E. G. Sutcliffe, 'Fact, Realism and Morality in Reade's Fiction' in *Studies in Philology* XLI (1945)
W. Tolles, *Tom Taylor and the Victorian Drama*, 1940
A. M. Turner, *The Making of the Cloister and the Hearth*, 1938

ROBERTSON, THOMAS WILLIAM (1829–71): Dramatist; b. Newark; brother of the actress Madge Kendal; worked as an actor and journalist in the provinces; came to London (1860) as editor of a mining journal; minor success with *A Cantab*, 1861; established reputation with *David Garrick* (1864) and *Society* (1865); best known of his later plays is *Caste*, 1867.

Life by T. E. Pemberton, 1893
Principal Dramatic Works ed. and with a memoir by his son T. W. Robert-son, 2 vols., 1889
Plays ed. W. Tydeman, 1982
Caste in *Nineteenth Century Plays*, 1972
See:
C. F. Armstrong, *Shakespeare to Shaw: Studies in the Life's Work of Six Dramatists of the English Stage*, 1913
D. Harrison, 'Tom Robertson: a Century of Criticism' in *Contemporary Review*, April, 1929
M. Savin, *Robertson: His Plays and Stage Craft*, 1950

ROSSETTI, CHRISTINA GEORGINA (1830–94): Poet; b. London, youngest daughter of Gabriele Rossetti, Italian poet and political refugee, and sister of Dante Gabriel (q.v.); contributed several poems to Pre-Raphaelite *Germ*,

1850; sat as a model for her brother and his friends; *Goblin Market*, 1862, established her as a poet; *The Prince's Progress*, 1866; became seriously ill from 1871, and turned to religious poetry; health finally broke down completely and she died after great suffering.

Life by M. F. Sanders, 1930; L. M. Packer, 1963; G. Battiscombe, 1981; K. Jones, 1990
Poems ed. P. Porter, 1986
Collected Poems ed. by her brother W. M. Rossetti, 1904; repr. 1968
Complete Poems ed. R. Crump, 1979
Selected Poems ed. W. de la Mare, 1930
Family Letters ed. W. M. Rossetti, 1908
See:
E. Birkhead, *Christina Rossetti and her Poetry*, 1930
G. Honighausen, 'Emblematic Tendencies in the Work of Christina Rossetti', *Victorian Poetry* x, 1972
D. Rosenblum, *Christina Rossetti: The Poetry of Endurance*, 1986
S. Weintraub, *Four Rossettis*, 1978
M. Zativenska, *Christina Rossetti: A Portrait with a Background*, 1949

ROSSETTI, DANTE GABRIEL (1828–82): Poet and painter; b. London; brother of Christina Rossetti (q.v.); educated at King's College School; studied art under Ford Madox Brown and others; formed 'Pre-Raphaelite Brotherhood' with Millais and Holman Hunt (and later William Morris, Burne-Jones, and others), 1848; befriended by Ruskin; married Elizabeth Siddal to whom he had been more or less engaged for ten years, 1860; *The Early Italian Poets* (translations mostly from Dante), 1861; wife died of an overdose of laudanum (1862) and he had a number of his poems in MS buried with her; these subsequently disinterred and published, 1870; unfavourable reviews increased tendency for gloomy brooding induced by wife's probable suicide, and for a time was feared insane; under Morris's influence began to design for stained glass, and in his later years frequently stayed with him at Kelmscott.

Life by W. Sharp, 1882; O. Doughty, *A Victorian Romantic*, 1949
Collected Works ed. by his brother W. M. Rossetti, 1911
Poems 1850–70, 1913
Poems and *Pre-Raphaelite Writings* in E.L.
Pre-Raphaelite Diaries and Letters ed. W. M. Rossetti, 1900
The P. R. B. Journal ed. W. E. Fredeman, 1975
Rossetti Papers 1862–70 ed. W. M. Rossetti, 1903
Letters ed. O. Doughty and J. R. Wahl, 4 vols., 1966–7
See:
H. R. Angeli, *Rossetti, his Friends and his Enemies*, 1949
W. Holman Hunt, *Pre-Raphaelitism and the Pre-Raphaelite Brotherhood*, 2 vols., 1905
G. Hough in *The Last Romantics*, 1949

K. Preston, *Blake and Rossetti,* 1944
H. Talon, *Rossetti: The House of Life*, 1966
S. Weintraub, *Four Rossettis*, 1978

RUSKIN, JOHN (1819–1900): Critic; b. London; educated privately by his aesthetically-minded parents and travelled widely, then at Christ Church, Oxford; deeply interested in painting and architecture; *Modern Painters*, 1843–60; married Euphemia Chalmers Gray, 1848; *The Seven Lamps of Architecture*, 1849; *The Stones of Venice*, 1851–3; began lecturing publicly on painting and aroused much controversy; marriage annulled, 1854 (wife subsequently married Millais); taught classes at the new working men's colleges and became interested in social problems; *Unto this Last*, 1862; *Sesame and Lilies*, 1868; elected Slade Professor of Art at Oxford, 1869; resigned because of increasing ill health, 1884; lived quietly till his death near Coniston Water.

Life by E. T. Cook, 1911; P. Quennell, 1949; M. Lutyens, 1967; J. D. Hunt, 1981
Complete Works ed. E. T. Cook and A. D. O. Wedderburn, 39 vols., 1903–12
Selected Writings ed. M. Hodgart, 1972
Sesame and Lilies, Unto this Last and *The Seven Lamps of Architecture* in E.L.; *Unto this Last* in P.C.
Unto this Last and Other Writings ed. C. Wilmer, 1985
Letters to Bernard Quaritch 1867–88 ed. C. Q. Wrentmore, 1939
Letters from the Continent ed. J. Hayman, 1982
The Correspondence of Thomas Carlyle and John Ruskin ed. G. A. Cate, 1982
The Correspondence of John Ruskin and Charles Eliot Norton ed. J. Bradley and I. Ousby, 1987
Ruskin in Italy: Letters to his Parents, 1972
Diaries ed. J. Evans and J. H. Whitehouse, 3 vols., 1956–9
The Order of Release (correspondence between Ruskin, Effie Gray, and Millais) ed. W. James, 1947
See:
Q. Bell, *Ruskin*, 1963
P. Conner, *Savage Ruskin*, 1979
K. O. Garrigan, *Ruskin on Architecture*, 1973
H. B. Hagstotz, *The Educational Theories of Ruskin*, 1942
F. Harrison, *John Ruskin*, 1902
R. Hewison, *J. Ruskin: The Argument of the Eye*, 1976
R. Hewison (ed.) *New Approaches to Ruskin*, 1982
·G. Hough, *The Last Romantics*, 1949
G. P. Landow, *Ruskin*, 1985
N. Pevsner in *Some Architectural Writers of the Nineteenth Century*, 1972
M. Proust, *On Reading Ruskin*, trans. J. Autret *et al.*, 1987
J. D. Rosenberg (ed.) *The Genius of John Ruskin*, 1964

W. M. Rossetti, *Ruskin, Rossetti and Pre-Raphaelitism*, 1899

D. Sonstroem, 'Millett vs Ruskin: A defence of Ruskin's *Of Queens' Gardens'*, *Victorian Studies* XX, 1977

RUTHERFORD, MARK – William Hale White – (1831–1913): Novelist; b. Bedford; educated at Cheshunt and New College for the Congregational Ministry, but became a clerk in the Admiralty and later a journalist; made reputation as novelist with three books 'edited by Reuben Shapcott', *The Autobiography of Mark Rutherford* (1881), *Mark Rutherford's Deliverance* (1885), and *The Revolution in Tanner's Lane* (1887); later novels include *Catherine Furze* (1893) and *Clara Hopgood* (1896); *Pages from a Journal* (1900), and *John Bunyan* (1905).

Life by C. M. Maclean, 1955

See:

D. Davie in *A Gathered Church*, 1978

J. Lucas in *The Literature of Change*, 1977; new edn 1980

E. S. Merton, 'The Autobiographical Novels of Mark Rutherford' in *Nineteenth Century Fiction* VI, 1951

Sean O'Faolain, 'A Puritan Novelist' in *New English Review* XIII, 1946

I. Stock, *William Hale White*, 1956

B. Willey in *More Nineteenth-Century Studies*, 1956

SAINTSBURY, GEORGE EDWARD BATEMAN (1845–1933): Critic; b. Southampton; educated at King's College School, London, and Merton College, Oxford; senior classical master at Elizabeth College, Guernsey, 1868–74; headmaster of the Elgin Educational Institute, 1874–6; began reviewing for the *Academy*, 1875; joined staff of the *Saturday Review*; Professor of Rhetoric and English Literature at Edinburgh, 1895–1915; most important works include *A Short History of English Literature* (1898), *A History of Criticism* (1900–1904), *A History of English Criticism* (1911); *A History of the French Novel* (1917–19).

See:

A. Muir *et al.* (ed.) *George Saintsbury: Memorial Volume*, 1945

H. Orel in *Victorian Literary Critics*, 1984

A. B. Webster, *George Saintsbury*, 1934

SPENCER, HERBERT (1820–1903): Philosopher; b. Derby; son of a schoolmaster; little formal education; engineer on the London–Birmingham Railway, 1837–46; sub-editor on the *Economist*, 1848–53; friend of Darwin, Lewes, and Huxley; frequent contributor to the *Westminster Review*; most important works include *Social Statics* (1850), *First Principles* (1862), *Principles of Biology* (1864), *Principles of Psychology* (1870–2), *Principles of Sociology* (1877–96), *Principles of Ethics* (1891–3).

Life by D. Duncan, 1908

Works, 21 vols., 1884–1904

See:
D. Duncan, *An Introduction to the Philosophy of Spencer*, 1904
W. H. Hudson, *Herbert Spencer*, 1916
J. D. Y. Peel, *Herbert Spencer: The Evolution of a Socialist*, 1971

STANLEY, ARTHUR PENRHYN (1815–81): Historian; son of Edward Stanley, later Bishop of Norwich; educated at Rugby and Balliol College, Oxford; appointed Professor of Ecclesiastical History at Oxford, 1856; leader of the Broad Church Movement; Dean of Westminster, 1864–81; works include *Life of Dr Arnold* (1844), *Sinai and Palestine* (1856), *Essays chiefly on Questions of Church and State* (1870).

Life by R. E. Prothero and G. G. Bradley, 2 vols., 1893
See:
A. O. J. Cockshut in *Truth to Life*, 1974
F. W. H. Myers in *Essays: Modern*, 1897
F. Woodward, *The Doctor's Disciples*, 1954

STEPHEN, LESLIE (1832–1904): Critic and philosopher; b. London; educated at Eton, King's College, London, and Trinity Hall, Cambridge; became tutor at Trinity Hall after taking Orders, 1859; came to London (1864) and wrote frequently for *Saturday Review*, *Cornhill*, and the *Nation*; founded *Pall Mall Gazette* with George Smith, 1865; married Harriet, daughter of Thackeray, 1867; noted athlete and mountaineer, editor of the *Alpine Journal*, 1868–71; editor of *Cornhill Magazine*, 1871–82; friend of Stevenson, Henry James, and Gosse; inclining to scepticism, relinquished his Orders, 1875; wife died, 1875; married Julia Jackson, 1878 (a daughter of this marriage was Virginia Woolf); *History of English Thought in the Eighteenth Century*, 1876; editor of *The Dictionary of National Biography*, 1882–91; second wife died, 1891; *Studies of a Biographer*, 1899–1902; *The English Utilitarians*, 1900; *English Literature and Society in the Eighteenth Century*, 1904; knighted, 1902.

Life by F. W. Maitland, 1906
Collected Essays, 10 vols., 1907
Mausoleum Book ed. A. Bell, 1977
See:
N. G. Annan, *Leslie Stephen: His Thought and Character in Relation to his Time*, 1951
Q. D. Leavis, 'Leslie Stephen: Cambridge Critic' in *Scrutiny* VII, 1939; repr. in *A Selection from Scrutiny*, 1968
D. MacCarthy, *Leslie Stephen*, 1937
H. Orel in *Victorian Literary Critics*, 1984
F. Thompson, *Sir Leslie Stephen as a Biographer*, 1915
Virginia Woolf in *The Captain's Death Bed and Other Essays*, 1950

STEVENSON, ROBERT LOUIS (1850–94): Novelist, poet, and essayist; b. Edinburgh, son of a civil engineer; serious illness in 1858 left him permanently delicate; educated Edinburgh; became a pupil engineer, 1868; poor health made him transfer to the law; called to the Bar (1875) but did not practise; met Sydney Colvin, 1873; travelled in France, Germany, and Scotland, hoping to recover from his illness; *An Inland Voyage*, 1878; *Travels with a Donkey*, 1879; hearing that a friend, Mrs Osborne, was seriously ill in San Francisco (1879), went there at great risk to his own health; married Mrs Osborne and returned to Scotland, 1880; persistent ill health forced him to settle near Marseilles, 1882; *Treasure Island* (1883) made him a popular writer; great success with *Dr Jekyll and Mr Hyde* (1886) and *Kidnapped* (1886); moved to Adirondacks, U.S.A., 1887; began cruising in a schooner in the Pacific from 1888; settled in Samoa (1890), where he was known as Tusitala; became very interested in local politics; died suddenly, buried in Samoa.

Life by Graham Balfour, 2 vols., London, 1901; J. A. Smith, 1937; D. Daiches, 1946; J. C. Furnas, *Voyage to Windward*, 1951; J. Calder, 1980
Letters ed. S. Colvin, 4 vols., 1911
Collected Works ed. S. Colvin, 28 vols., 1894–8; ed. L. Osbourne and F. van de G. Stevenson, 26 vols., 1922–3
Novels and Stories ed. V. S. Pritchett, 1945
Short Stories introduced by I. Campbell, 1981
Complete Poems, 1913
Collected Poems ed. J. A. Smith, 1950; rev. edn 1971
Tales and Essays ed. G. B. Stern, 1950
Dr Jekyll and Mr Hyde, The Master of Ballantrae, St Ives, Treasure Island, Travels with a Donkey, etc., in E.L.; *Dr Jekyll and Mr Hyde, Kidnapped* and *Catriona, The Master of Ballantrae, Treasure Island* in W.C.
See:
D. Daiches, *Stevenson and the Art of Fiction*, 1951
E. M. Eigner, *R. L. Stevenson and Romantic Tradition*, 1967
H. W. Garrod in *The Profession of Poetry*, 1929
Henry James in *Notes on Novelists*, 1914
Henry James and Stevenson, letters ed. J. A. Smith, 1948
R. Kiely, *R. L. Stevenson and the Fiction of Adventure*, 1965
M. Lascelles in *The Story-Teller Retrieves the Past*, 1980
P. Maixner (ed.) *Robert Louis Stevenson: the Critical Heritage*, 1981
I. S. Saposnik, *Robert Louis Stevenson*, 1974
F. Swinnerton, *Robert Louis Stevenson: A Critical Study*, 1914

SWINBURNE, ALGERNON CHARLES (1837–1909): Poet and critic; b. London, but brought up in Northumberland and the Isle of Wight; educated at Eton and Balliol College, Oxford; friendly with Jowett; *The Queen Mother* and *Rosamund*, 1860; settled in London and became friendly with the Rossettis and Monckton Milnes, Meredith, and Landor; by 1867

he was established as one of the most notable of contemporary poets; health broke down under the strains of his excesses in London, 1879; retired quietly to Putney with Watts-Dunton for the rest of his life.

Life by G. Lafourcade, 2 vols., London, 1932; J. O. Fuller, 1968; P. Henderson, 1974; D. Thomas, 1979
Collected Works, 20 vols., 1925–7
New Writings ed. C. Y. Lang, 1965
Selected Poems ed. L. Binyon, W.C. 1940
Poems and Prose ed. M. R. Ridley, E.L.
Swinburne as Critic ed. C. K. Hyder, 1972
Letters ed. E. Gosse and T. J. Wise, 2 vols., 1918
Letters ed. C. Y. Lang, 6 vols., 1960–62
See:
D. Bush in *Mythology and the Romantic Tradition in English Poetry*, 1937
T. S. Eliot, 'Swinburne as Poet' in *The Sacred Wood*, 1920
C. K. Hyder (ed.) *Swinburne: The Critical Heritage*, 1970
J. McGann, *Swinburne: An Experiment in Criticism*, 1972

TENNYSON, ALFRED (1809–92): Poet; b. Somersby, Lincs.; son of a clergyman; educated at Louth Grammar School and Trinity College, Cambridge, with his brothers Charles and Frederick; friend and contemporary of Monckton Milnes, W. H. Thompson, Edward Fitzgerald, and especially A. H. Hallam, who was engaged to his sister; *Poems chiefly Lyrical*, 1830; joined Spanish Army with Hallam, 1830; returned to Somersby on the death of his father, 1831; *Poems* (1833) showed a great advance in craftsmanship; extremely affected by Hallam's sudden death (1833), published nothing for ten years; *Poems* (1842) firmly established him as the leading poet of the day and won him friendship of Carlyle, Dickens, and Elizabeth Barrett; lost all his money and became seriously ill, 1845; at Milnes's insistence the government granted him a pension; became friendly with Coventry Patmore, Browning, and Macready; *In Memoriam*, 1850; married Emily Sellwood (after a ten-year engagement), 1850; created Poet Laureate, 1850; settled in the Isle of Wight, 1853; *Idylls of the King* (1859) enormously popular; wrote several unsuccessful plays; visited Scandinavia with Gladstone (1883) and accepted a peerage from him; died at Alworth.

Life by his son Hallam, 2 vols., 1897; by his grandson Charles Tennyson, 1949; R. B. Martin, 1980
Letters ed. C. Y. Lang and E. F. Shannon, 3 vols., 1982–90
Poems ed. C. Ricks, 1968
Poems and Plays, 1953; 3rd edn 1968
Poems in E.L. (2 vols.) and W.C. (1 vol.)
See:
D. Albright, *Tennyson. The Muses' Tug-of-War*, 1986
W. H. Auden, *Tennyson: A Selection and Introduction*, 1946

A. C. Bradley, *A Commentary on Tennyson's 'In Memoriam'*, rev. edn, 1920; repr. 1966

J. H. Buckley, *Tennyson: The Growth of a Poet*, 1960

K. R. Chatterjee, *Studies in Tennyson as Poet of Science*, 1977

J. D. Jump (ed.) *Tennyson: The Critical Heritage*, 1968

J. Kilham (ed.) *Critical Essays on the Poetry of Tennyson*, 1960

F. R. Leavis in *New Bearings in English Poetry*, 1932

R. Pattison, *Tennyson and Tradition*, 1979

C. Ricks, *Tennyson*, 1972

J. D. Rosenberg, *The Fall of Camelot*, 1973

E. F. Shannon, *Tennyson and the Reviewers*, 1952; repr. 1967

A. Sinfield, *Alfred Tennyson*, 1985
    The Language of Tennyson's 'In Memoriam', 1971

H. Tennyson (ed.) *Studies in Tennyson*, 1981

P. Turner, *Tennyson*, 1976

THACKERAY, WILLIAM MAKEPEACE (1811–63): Novelist; b. Calcutta, son of a civil servant; educated at Charterhouse and Trinity College, Cambridge; contemporary and friend of Monckton Milnes, Edward Fitzgerald, and W. H. Thompson; left Cambridge without taking a degree and travelled in Germany, 1830; lost a legacy on two unsuccessful newspapers, *The National Standard* and *The Constitutional*; settled in Paris to study art, 1834; married Isabella Shawe, 1836; returned to London, 1837; became a regular contributor to *Fraser's Magazine*, where much of his early work appeared in serial form; wife became permanently insane, 1840; began contributing to *Punch*, 1845; *Vanity Fair*, 1848; *Pendennis*, 1850; lectured in America, 1852–3; *Henry Esmond*, 1852; *The Newcomes*, 1854; defeated as Parliamentary candidate for Oxford, 1857; *The Virginians*, 1859; editor of *Cornhill Magazine*, 1857–62; *Dennis Duval* left unfinished at his death.

Life by A. Trollope, 1879; Lewis Melville, 2 vols., 1910; G. N. Ray, 2 vols., 1958; C. Peters, 1987

Letters ed. J. O. Brookfield, 1887; ed. G. N. Ray, 4 vols., 1945–6

Collected Works, 17 vols., 1908; 26 vols., rev. edn, 1910–11

Vanity Fair ed. G. and K. Tillotson, 1963

Henry Esmond, Vanity Fair, The Virginians, The English Humorists, etc., in E.L. (5 vols.); *Henry Esmond* and *Vanity Fair* in P.C.; *Barry Lyndon* and *Vanity Fair* in W.C.

See:

J. Carey, *Thackeray: Prodigal Genius*, 1977

D. Flamm, *Thackeray's Critics*, 1967

J. Y. T. Greig, *Thackeray: A Reconsideration*, 1950

B. Hardy, *The Exposure of Luxury: Radical Themes in Thackeray*, 1972

J. McMaster, *Thackeray: The Major Novels*, 1971

G. Saintsbury, *A Consideration of Thackeray*, 1931

L. Stevenson, *The Showman of Vanity Fair*, 1947

J. Sutherland, *Thackeray at Work*, 1974
G. Tillotson, *Thackeray the Novelist*, 1954
G. Tillotson and D. Hawes (eds.) *Thackeray: The Critical Heritage*, 1968
D. Van Ghent, 'On *Vanity Fair*', in *The English Novel: Form and Function*, 1953

THOMPSON, FRANCIS (1859–1907): Poet; b. Preston: son of a doctor; studied for the priesthood at Ushaw College; then studied medicine at Owen's College, Manchester, but failed to qualify; removed to London (1885) and lived in great poverty; ill health made him an opium addict; sent poems to Wilfrid Meynell; the Meynells befriended him and sent him to hospital, supporting him in convalescence; lived in North Wales, 1893–7; *Sister Songs*, 1895; *New Poems*, 1897.

Life by E. Meynell, rev. edn, 1926; J. C. Reid, 1959; J. Walsh, 1968; B. M. Boardman, 1988
Collected Works ed. W. Meynell, 3 vols., 1913
Poems ed. T. L. Connolly, 1941
See:
T. L. Connolly (ed.) *Literary Criticisms of Francis Thompson*, 2 vols., 1948–59
A. de la Gorce, *Francis Thompson*, 1933
G. E. Hodgson, *A Study of Illumination*, 1914
T. H. Wright, *Francis Thompson and his Poetry*, 1927

THOMSON, JAMES – 'B.V.' – (1834–82): Poet: b. Port-Glasgow; after his mother's death educated at Caledonian Orphan Asylum and the School of the Military Asylum, Chelsea; assistant army schoolmaster at Ballincollig, near Cork; met Charles Bradlaugh (who in 1860 established *National Reformer*); most of Thomson's poetry appeared in this; dismissed from the army, 1862; settled in London as a solicitor's clerk; went to America (1872) and then to Spain as special correspondent for an American newspaper, 1873; returned to London; quarrelled with Bradlaugh, 1875; published rest of his poetry in *Cope's Tobacco Plant*; *City of Dreadful Night*, 1880.

Life by H. S. Salt, rev. edn 1914; W. D. Schaefer, 1966
Poetical Works ed. B. Dobell, 2 vols., 1895
Poems and Letters ed. A. Ridler, 1963
See:
K. H. Byron, *The Pessimism of James Thomson*, 1965
B. Dobell, *The Laureate of Pessimism*, 1910
B. I. Evans in *English Poetry in the Later Nineteenth Century*, 1933; rev. edn 1966
G. C. LeRoy, *Perplexed Prophets*, 1953
I. B. Walker, *Thomson: A Critical Study*, 1950
W. Wolff, 'Thomson B. V.: A Study in Poetic Melancholy' in *Poetry Review* XXVIII, 1937

TROLLOPE, ANTHONY (1815–82): Novelist; b. London of a literary family; educated as a day-boy at Winchester and Harrow; clerk in the London General Post Office from 1834; transferred to Ireland (1841) as a surveyor's clerk; married Rose Heseltine, 1844; published several unsuccessful novels; *The Warden* (1855) and *Barchester Towers* (1857) brought popularity and money; continued to write steadily until his death; as Inspector for Rural Postal Deliveries in S. W. Ireland, reputed to have invented the pillar-box; Post Office mission to the West Indies, 1858; settled in England (1859) but later travelled on business in America, Australia, and New Zealand; started *Fortnightly Review*, 1865; retired from the Post Office, 1867; edited *St Paul's Magazine* from 1868; lived in London, 1872–80; retired to Sussex, where he died.

Life by M. Sadleir, 1927; H. Walpole, 1928; B. C. Brown, 1950; J. Pope-Hennessy, 1971; R. Mullen, 1990

Letters ed. B. A. Booth, 1951

The Barsetshire Novels in E.L., 7 vols.; *Can You Forgive Her?* and *The Last Chronicle of Barset* in P.C.

The Palliser Novels, 6 vols., 1973

Autobiography and novels in W.C., 25 vols.

Trollope's Australia ed. H. Dow, 1966

See:

B. A. Booth, *Anthony Trollope: Aspects of his Life and Art*, 1958

R. W. Chapman, 'The Text of Trollope's Novels' in R.E.S. XVII, 1941

A. O. J. Cockshutt, *Anthony Trollope: A Critical Study*, 1955

P. D. Edwards, *Anthony Trollope: His Art and Scope*, 1978

N. J. Hall (ed.) *The Trollope Critics*, 1980

M. Hamer, *Writing by Numbers: Trollope's Serial Fiction*, 1986

J. Kincaid, *The Novels of Anthony Trollope*, 1977

J. McMaster, *Trollope's Palliser Novels: Theme and Pattern*, 1978

R. D. McMaster, *Trollope and the Law*, 1986

R. M. Polhemus, *The Changing World of Anthony Trollope*, 1968

M. Sadleir, *Trollope: A Commentary*, rev. edn 1945

D. Smalley (ed.) *Trollope: The Critical Heritage*, 1968

WARD, MARY AUGUSTA – Mrs Humphry Ward – (1851–1920): Novelist, historian, translator, social worker; b. Hobart Town, Tasmania, eldest child of Thomas Arnold the younger (scholar and school-inspector) and grand-daughter of Thomas Arnold of Rugby; educated at private boarding schools in England (where family returned 1856) and then at home in Oxford; m. Thomas Humphry Ward, scholar and journalist, 1872; secretary of Association for the Education of Women and first secretary of Somerville College, Oxford; became authority on early Spanish history and literature; tr. F. Amiel's *Journal Intime* and published *Miss Bretherton*, her first novel, both in 1884; developed non-miraculous socially-committed variant of Christianity embodied in *Robert Elsmere* (1888), her best-known novel, and

represented by her work with religious, educational and charitable Passmore Edwards Settlement; foundress of Women's National Anti-Suffrage League (1908); wrote over 20 novels on a wide range of religious, ethical, social and political themes. *Helbeck of Bannisdale* is a novel of great distinction.

Life by daughter Janet Penrose Trevelyan, 1923; Enid Huws Jones, 1973; J. Sutherland, 1990

Writings, 16 vols, 1911–12

A Writer's Recollections (autobiography), 1918

Helbeck of Bannisdale, 1983; *Robert Elsmere* in w.c.; *Marcella* in Virago

See:

V. Colby in *The Singular Anomaly*, 1970

W. E. Gladstone, '*Robert Elsmere* and the Battle of Belief', *Nineteenth Century*, XXIII, May 1888

S. Gwynn, *Mrs Humphry Ward*, 1917

W. S. Peterson, *Victorian Heretic: Mrs Humphry Ward's 'Robert Elsmere'*, 1976

E. M. G. Smith, *Mrs Humphry Ward*, 1980

J. S. Walters, *Mrs Humphry Ward: her Work and Influence*, 1912

WILDE, OSCAR FINGALL O'FLAHERTIE WILLS (1854–1900): Dramatist, poet and novelist; b. Dublin, son of a surgeon; educated at Trinity College, Dublin, and Magdalen College, Oxford; became a notorious personality as one of the leaders of the somewhat effeminate 'aesthetic' movement; *Poems*, 1881; lectured in America, 1882; married Constance Lloyd, 1884; published several books of children's stories, followed by *The Picture of Dorian Gray*, 1891; success as a dramatist with *Lady Windermere's Fan*, 1892; *A Woman of No Importance*, 1893; *Salomé* refused a licence in England and published in France, 1893; *An Ideal Husband*, 1895; *The Importance of Being Earnest*, 1895; brought a libel action against the Marquis of Queensberry (1895) as a result of which he was himself sentenced to two years' imprisonment with hard labour; left prison, bankrupt, 1897; lived in Paris until his death.

Life by F. Harris, 2 vols., 1918 (ed. G. B. Shaw, 1938); L. Lemmonier, 1931; H. Pearson, 1946; new edn 1975; H. Montgomery Hyde, 1976; R. Ellmann, 1987

Letters ed. Rupert Hart-Davis, 1962

More Letters ed. Rupert Hart-Davis, 1985

Selected Letters, 1977

Complete Works, 14 vols., 1911; 4 vols., 1936; ed. G. F. Maine, 1948

Selections, ed. I. Murray (The Oxford Authors), 1988; *Plays, Prose Writings and Poems* and *Dorian Gray* in E.L.; *De Profundis and Other Writings* in P.C.

Collected Poems, 2 vols., 1906

Selected Poems, 1951

The Picture of Dorian Gray in O.E.N. and W.C.

Essays ed. H. Pearson, 1950

Critical Writings, ed. R. Ellmann, 2 vols., 1968–9
See:
K. Beckson (ed.) *Wilde: The Critical Heritage*, 1970
E. R. Bentley in *The Playwright as Thinker*, 1946
P. Braybrooke, *Oscar Wilde: A Study*, 1930
Lord A. Douglas, *Wilde: A Summing-Up*, 1940
R. Ellmann (ed.) *Oscar Wilde: A Collection of Critical Essays*, 1969
    in *Eminent Domain*, 1970
A. Ojala, *Aestheticism and Oscar Wilde*, 2 vols., 1954–5
P. Raby, *Oscar Wilde*, 1988
R. Shewan, *Oscar Wilde: Art and Egotism*, 1977
G. Woodcock, *The Paradox of Wilde*, 1950

NOTES ON CONTRIBUTORS

SEYMOUR BETSKY Died 1988. Formerly Professor of American Literature, University of Utrecht, The Netherlands. Has published, among other places, in *Scrutiny*, *Sewanee Review*, *Essays in Criticism*, *Victorian Studies*, and the *New Universities Quarterly*.

ASA BRIGGS Provost of Worcester College, Oxford (1976–1991). Chancellor of the Open University. His books include *Victorian People* (1954), *Victorian Cities* (1963), *The Age of Improvement* (1959) and a number of other works on nineteenth-century society and culture.

R. C. CHURCHILL Died 1986. Author and journalist. Author of *Disagreements* (1950), *The English Sunday* (1954), *The Frontiers of Fiction* (1970), and *The Revised Concise History of English Literature* (1970).

R. G. COX Died 1981. Reader in English Literature, Manchester University; author of articles and reviews in *Scrutiny*, *The Times Literary Supplement*, *Sewanee Review* and other periodicals; editor of *Thomas Hardy: The Critical Heritage* (1970).

CHRISTOPHER GILLIE Formerly lecturer in English at Trinity Hall, Cambridge. Author of *Character in English Literature* (1965). *Longman Companion to English Literature* (1971), *A Preface to Jane Austen* (1974) and *Movements in English Literature, 1900–1940* (1975) and *Preface to Forster* (1983).

CHARLES HANDLEY-READ Died 1971.

JOHN D. JUMP Died 1976. Was Professor of English Literature at Manchester University. Author of *Matthew Arnold* (1955) and *Byron* (1972); general editor of *The Critical Idiom* series.

ARNOLD KETTLE Died 1987. Was Professor of Literature at The Open University. Author of *An Introduction to the English Novel* (1951); editor of *Shakespeare in a Changing World* (1964) and *The Nineteenth-Century Novel* (revised 1981).

G. D. KLINGOPULOS Formerly Senior lecturer in English, University College, Cardiff. Contributor to *Scrutiny*.

F. N. LEES Died 1981. Reader in English Literature, University of Manchester. Author of *Christopher Marlowe: Edward II* (1954), *Gerald Manley Hopkins* (1966), *English Institute Essays* (1966). Contributed articles to *Scrutiny*, the *British Journal of Aesthetics*, *Gissing Newsletter*.

LAURENCE LERNER Professor of English at Vanderbilt University, Tennessee. As well as *The Truthtellers* (1967), which discusses Jane Austen, George Eliot and D. H. Lawrence, his critical books include, more recently, *An Introduction to English Poetry* (1975), *Love & Marriage* (1979), a collection of essays, *The Literary Imagination* (1982) and *The Frontiers of Literature*, (1988).

E. D. MACKERNESS Died 1990. Formerly Reader in English Literature, Sheffield University. Author of *The Heeded Voice* (1959), editor of *The Journals of George Sturt* (1967) and Hazlitt's *The Spirit of the Age* (1969).

ROBIN MAYHEAD Reader in English Literature at the University of Stirling until his death in 1980. Author of *Understanding Literature* (1965), *John Keats* (1967), and *Walter Scott* (1968).

W. W. ROBSON Masson Professor of English Literature, Edinburgh University. Author of *Critical Essays* (1966) and *Modern English Literature* (4th impr. 1979).

ALLAN RODWAY Reader in English at Nottingham University (Retired). He is a critic, editor and minor poet. His works include *The Common Muse* (with V. de S. Pinto, 1957), *The Romantic Conflict* (1963), *The Truths of Fiction* (1970), and *English Comedy: its Role and Nature from Chaucer to the Present Day* (1975). *A Preface to Auden*, 1984, *The Craft of Criticism*, (1982).

LEO SALINGAR Formerly Fellow of Trinity College and Lecturer in English, Cambridge University; author of *Shakespeare and the Traditions of Comedy* (1974) and *Dramatic Form in Shakespeare and the Jacobeans* (1986).

DEREK TRAVERSI Professor Emeritus, Swarthmore College, Pennsylvania, USA. Successively British Council Representative in Uruguay, Chile, Iran, Spain and Italy (1948–70). Author of *An Approach to Shakespeare* (1938, 1956, 1968), *T. S. Eliot: the Longer Poems* (1976), and *The Literary Imagination: Studies in Dante, Chaucer and Shakespeare* (in press).

NORMAN VANCE Senior Lecturer in English, Sussex University. Author of *The Sinews of the Spirit* (1985) and articles on Victorian and Irish subjects.

R. K. WEBB Professor of History, University of Maryland, Baltimore County. Author of *The British Working-Class Reader, 1790–1848* (1955), *Harriet Martineau, a Radical Victorian* (1960), and *Modern England* (1968, 1980). Now completing a history of English Unitarianism.

INDEX

FOR THE BEST IN PAPERBACKS, LOOK FOR THE 🐧

In every corner of the world, on every subject under the sun, Penguin represents quality and variety – the very best in publishing today.

For complete information about books available from Penguin – including Puffins, Penguin Classics and Arkana – and how to order them, write to us at the appropriate address below. Please note that for copyright reasons the selection of books varies from country to country.

In the United Kingdom: Please write to *Dept E.P., Penguin Books Ltd, Harmondsworth, Middlesex, UB7 0DA.*

If you have any difficulty in obtaining a title, please send your order with the correct money, plus ten per cent for postage and packaging, to *PO Box No 11, West Drayton, Middlesex*

In the United States: Please write to *Dept BA, Penguin, 299 Murray Hill Parkway, East Rutherford, New Jersey 07073*

In Canada: Please write to *Penguin Books Canada Ltd, 2801 John Street, Markham, Ontario L3R 1B4*

In Australia: Please write to the *Marketing Department, Penguin Books Australia Ltd, P.O. Box 257, Ringwood, Victoria 3134*

In New Zealand: Please write to the *Marketing Department, Penguin Books (NZ) Ltd, Private Bag, Takapuna, Auckland 9*

In India: Please write to *Penguin Overseas Ltd, 706 Eros Apartments, 56 Nehru Place, New Delhi, 110019*

In the Netherlands: Please write to *Penguin Books Netherlands B.V., Postbus 195, NL-1380AD Weesp*

In West Germany: Please write to *Penguin Books Ltd, Friedrichstrasse 10–12, D–6000 Frankfurt/Main 1*

In Spain: Please write to *Alhambra Longman S.A., Fernandez de la Hoz 9, E–28010 Madrid*

In Italy: Please write to *Penguin Italia s.r.l., Via Como 4, I-20096 Pioltello (Milano)*

In France: Please write to *Penguin Books Ltd, 39 Rue de Montmorency, F-75003 Paris*

In Japan: Please write to *Longman Penguin Japan Co Ltd, Yamaguchi Building, 2–12–9 Kanda Jimbocho, Chiyoda-Ku, Tokyo 101*

Inside Alcatraz